Devil Dogs

"Devil Dogs" of the 4th Marine Brigade. Photo taken just before the Marines went into action at Verdun. The gun shown is the French 1914 Hotchkiss. (courtesy *Marine Corps Gazette*)

Devil Dogs

Fighting Marines of World War I

George B. Clark

PRESIDIO

Published by Presidio Press
505 B San Marin Drive, Suite 300
Novato, CA 94945-1340

Library of Congress Cataloging-in-Publication Data

Clark, George B. (George Bransfield)
    Devil Dogs : fighting marines of World War I / George B. Clark.
        p.   cm.
    Includes bibliographical references and index.
    ISBN 0-89141-653-6
    1. United States. Marine Corps—History—World War,
1914–1918. 2. World War, 1914–1918—Regimental histories—
United States. 3. World War, 1914–1918—Campaigns—France.
I. Title.
D570.348.C43 1999
940.4'1273—dc21   98-21853
                                             CIP

Printed in the United States of America

Contents

Brief Glossary and Description
of Abbreviations

The word which I have used most frequently is *Marine*. It can serve to identify a single Marine or a regiment of Marines. The U.S. Army has used Infantry to denote a regiment; The Corps has used Marines to denote the same thing. The latter is of more recent vintage and was not correct during the period of the First World War, but was used extensively anyway, by Marines and by army officers as well.

The Marine dictionary is somewhat different from that of the army. Actually, it is more like that of the U.S. Navy. *Skipper* is the word the Marines use to denote their company commander. *Mister* was occasionally used to denote a lieutenant. Other than those words, I have used the standard language of the American Expeditionary Force for most all others.

Abbreviations most commonly used are those to denote a company or battalion. Companies were almost always, except in official messages, identified in their numeric form rather than the AEF alpha form. When you read *1/5,* that means 1st Battalion, 5th Marines. The numerals for all the others remain consistent, even when identifying U.S. Army units. Occasionally the letters MG will appear rather than *machine gun.* Perhaps in a message you will read Bn. which of course translates to *battalion.* Rather than bore the reader with identifying all those who were awarded Distinguished Service Crosses and/or a Navy Cross I have elected, in most cases, to put a sign after their names instead. When a name appears with * following it, it means that the person named was awarded a DSC and/or a NC for an act almost as eminent as what a Medal of Honor would call for.

Preface

This story has never been completely told before. No one, to the best of my knowledge, has completed a full story of the participation of Marines in World War I. Personally, I am pleased that so many young people are becoming interested in the war in general and specifically the part played by Marines. A few, studies of very limited quality have appeared in the past thirty or so years, mainly about one battle, Belleau Wood. Some badly flawed articles have appeared in various magazines and journals, mostly, again, about Belleau Wood. Many years ago there was one nonprofessional historian who might have written a history but never did. Major Edwin N. McClellan, who later became the Corps's chief historian, composed a brief, general history and produced several articles that later appeared in the *Marine Corps Gazette*. Whereas the general history was a rendition of facts, interspered with mistakes, it was very short on descriptions of events and purposely avoided unpleasantness. In other words the complete, unvarnished facts were not published. The journal articles were adequate but every one of them left out some important material, for reasons one can now only suspect. Besides, the articles did not follow the war to its finish, the final two battles being excluded. The series ended early in the Blanc Mont period without covering that bloodbath at all. As a result the two main battles that Maj. Gen. John A. Lejeune led the division through were deleted for some unknown reason. As a serving Marine, McClellan was obviously restricted in what he could produce for general consumption.

Generally, it has been my impression that some military people prefer that command difficulties should lie dormant, never to be exposed to scrutiny. It is also my opinion that only through lessons already learned by others, can individuals perform their tasks best. I have tried to tell the "complete" story, even though several unfortunate incidents have become quite glaring under closer examination. First and foremost, the early senior leadership of the 4th Brigade was, in my candid opinion, ineffective. Some few learned while "doing." Others were dropped shortly after making blunders that cost many lives. In the chapter headed "Conclusions," I have expressed my own disdain for some individuals and the reason why, but except for the top leaders, I have decided to let the reader judge who was good and who wasn't. In general, company grade officers were reasonably good at what they did. Most had the hearts of lions. All honor to them.

A statement attributed to Col. George C. Marshall, USA, best describes what the American soldier did in France. I believe that it particularly pertains to the Marines at Belleau Wood.

> Battles are decided in favor of the troops whose bravery, fortitude, and especially, whose endurance, surpasses that of the enemy; the army with the higher breaking point wins the decision.*

To avoid the appearance of pretentiousness and clutter, notes have been kept to a minimum. Mostly what has been included are annotations. They tend not to distract the general reader; that is, the sort of person to whom this effort has been directed and who might find it of interest. The majority of the notes generated are those that add substantially to the overall story but do not need to be part of the regular text and can stand by themselves. Most of this work is based upon original material; that is, material not published before or, if so, not widely distributed. The main source is the multivolume *Records of the Second Division.*

I have tried to make this a comprehensive study and have therefore included a preponderance of detail that would not normally be found in a book aimed at general reading public. But I must warn the reader, reliable records about the 4th Brigade aren't readily available. Please use this text with discretion. I have done my best, but who knows with certainty that this is any different? I hope it is.

---

*Found in *George C. Marshall, Memoirs of My Services in the World War 1917–1918* (Boston: Houghton Mifflin, 1976), 138.

• • •

As can be expected, this writer has had help from friends and acquaintances, without which it would have been very difficult to complete this manuscript. Each contributed to the whole and, as always, some more than others. In order to show my appreciation as fully as I can I am listing their names alphabetically, including, where possible, the highlights of their contribution(s).

Colonel William Anderson at SHAPE Headquarters in Belgium, who has made the Battle of Belleau Wood his own private preserve, preserving it for future Marines, that is. Bill has helped me over the years, providing maps, photos, etc., which frequently showed locations that I would never have seen otherwise.

Jerry Beach of Canton, Ohio, has been with me nearly all the way, providing me with maps and always with encouragement. His father was a valuable member of the 23d Company, 6th Machine Gun Battalion, from the beginning of the war.

Lieutenant Colonel Ronald Brown, USMCR, of Novi, Michigan, has been extremely helpful in providing me data from his sources that has helped me to correct several errors of omission and commission. Important collaborator.

Mrs. Margaret Thomas Buchholz of Harvey Cedars, New Jersey, sent me personal material relating to her father's membership in both the 51st and 55th companies that helps to fill in some blanks, especially during the period of occupation in Germany.

Colonel Ralph D. Cail, USMC (ret), of La Jolla, California, sent me valuable information about his father-in-law, Col. Charley Dunbeck, which has filled in a load of gaps about that wonderful Marine.

Thomas and Andrew Clark, my young grandsons, presented me with suggestions that "just hit the target" every time. After all, they do take after their grandmother.

David Fisher of Indianapolis, Indiana, has provided me with information so scarce that I often wondered if he manufactured it. His support with photos has earned my eternal gratitude. You will see examples in the pages ahead.

S. Vic Glogovic, M.D., of Bridgeton, Missouri, provided me with numerous bits of information concerning individuals and the medical services.

I want to thank Douglas V. Johnson, Ph.D., of the Carlisle Barracks for reviewing my chapter on Soissons.

Daniel P. Kennedy of Gloucester, Massachusetts, has accumulated a great amount of data concerning Capt. Lester Wass, skipper of the 18th Company, and shared same with me.

Gilles Lagin of Marigny-en-Orxois, France, made my visit to the battlefield area around Belleau Wood the most productive time I've spent on this project. He knows that ground better than anyone I'm aware of, and what a magnificent collection of Marine artifacts he has accumulated from that battlefield.

Peter Meyer of Burlington, North Carolina, has provided me with a very important unpublished memoir of great interest and information—this in addition to being supportive of my efforts in writing this book. A former Marine and the grandson of a Marine.

Patricia Mullan of the Research Center, Marine Corps University, Quantico, and her "boss," Kerry Strong, provided needed photos without pain. Hallelujah! What a magnificent pleasure they are to collaborate with. Oh, that they were not alone.

Bradley Omanson of Morgantown, West Virginia, grandson of a veteran of the 6th MG Battalion, has thoughtfully collected information about him in order to pass that on for future generations. He has also helped me by making others aware of what I have been doing, thereby aiding and abetting me in my efforts.

Lieutenant Colonel Vernon Sylvester, USMC (ret), of San Diego, California, the son of a veteran of the 55th Company, has also provided me with several important pieces I had overlooked in the course of my investigations.

Bart Perkowski, art director, *Marine Corps Gazette,* for providing many excellent photos. Larry Strayer of Dayton, Ohio, for supplying many useful photos.

Colonel Charles Westcott, USMC (ret), of Provincetown, Massachusetts, a son of Major Charles T. Westcott, the man who formed the 3d Battalion, 5th Marines, in 1917 and was their original commanding officer, sent me very valuable material, some of which appears in this book. Oh, yes! His mother served with the Red Cross in France during that war. Charlie's excuse for not being there was that he hadn't yet been born. Oh, well! Everyone has an excuse for not being there. Including me.

In addition to those named above there have been many more who have supported my cause over the years—most by buying those items I have reprinted or written about Marines in the Great War and encouraging me to continue my work so as to bring this history to fruition. They are too numerous to list but they, too, aided and abetted. I know who they are. Thank you all.

Last but not least, I dedicate this book, just as I have all the previous original publications, to my long-suffering wife, Jeanne J. Clark. She has put up with me through thick (that is what she has accused me of being) and thin (that she has never had to accuse me of). To her again I say, without her this book would never have come to fruition.

Introduction

'E isn't one of the reg'lar line, nor 'e isn't one of the crew;
'E's a kind of giddy harumfrodite—soldier an' sailor too.
Rudyard Kipling.

This is the story of an anomaly: a U.S. Army division composed partly of soldiers and partly of U.S. Marines. Actually, this story is mainly about the Marines but the truth of the matter lies somewhere in between, since much of what happened during the war, and for years afterward, greatly affected the U.S. Army as well as the Marines. Therefore you will read a bit about the U.S. Army as well. Because without them we would never have had a 4th Marine Brigade.

The Marines Corps's slogan "First to Fight," according to the major general commandant George Barnett, forced the Corps to make maximum efforts to overcome the reluctance of the U.S. Army to accept them into the fray. Even in those days, the army didn't want a "second" army in existence, let alone one that performed duties that might be considered important but comparable. The general overall attitude at army headquarters was to not allow Marines in France for any reason. Since they belonged to the navy, let them find a use for the Corps. Anywhere, but not in France. But Pershing, a fine mover and doer himself, didn't reckon with the machinations of George Barnett. Barnett was well known to the leaders in government. He and his wife were well-connected and active members of that social scene. And both had positive contacts that would always stand them in good stead. The commandant just did what he believed he had to do. He went behind the scenes and within days obtained approval for acceptance of a regiment of Marines in the AEF. First from Josephus Daniels, the secretary of the navy, then from Newton Baker, the secretary of war. When Pershing learned of it, he was furious but there wasn't anything he could do about it. Fait Accompli was in command and Marines were always well versed in Latin.

Although the numbers of Marines in the AEF was minuscule—only two brigades, and only one of those entered into the fray—they made a contribution out of all proportion to their total. As part of the 2d Division, the Marines were engaged in seven distinctive engagements during the final eight months of the war. No other U.S. unit was engaged in combat practically every month. They imposed their will on the enemy and never lost ground taken. Suffering heavy losses at practically every battle they participated in, they were victors in each. One battle caused the Marine brigade more casualties than had been endured, collectively, during the entire history of that corps; another came close to exceeding that questionable goal on one day. Losses that wouldn't be equaled until Tarawa. Their turnover (read losses) was close to 150 percent and only the 3d Brigade came close to that mark or, on occasion, exceeded Marine losses.

The 4th Brigade was good. Actually, it was very good, but in the early days it was poorly led. Eventually the quality of the enlisted men and junior officers almost made up for the deficiencies of many of the senior officers. It wasn't because Marine officers were any less competent than other American officers; the U.S. Army officers, as a lot, were equally ill trained. It was because none of them were really prepared for the terrible war they were to fight. Marine officers, generally, had more actual recent field experience than did those in the army. The former led small units; a company of men, or perhaps a few more, in numerous small engagements in the Caribbean during the previous dozen or so years. It was very infrequent when the unit size was a brigade or even a regiment. Except for Vera Cruz, since the turn of the century Marines had only been engaged in conflict against defiant citizens of small island countries. Their enemy was usually an illiterate peasant with, most likely, just a machete as the weapon of choice— choice because it was the only weapon available. Infrequently, the Marines might come into conflict with "organized" bands, sometimes identified as the local militia, or even an army. That was it. As expected, the Marines always won. They were the chosen instrument of the United States State Department for a reign of terror in the Caribbean during the early years of this century. I've been told that until quite recently, Nicaraguan mothers obtained their children's obedience by threatening them with being taken by "Major Butler." Butler being Smedley Darlington Butler, the most famous leader of Marines in Nicaragua in 1912 and a man who later proclaimed that he was a "high-price muscle man" who could teach Al Capone a few tricks of the trade. That was making a real impression, one that stood, good or bad, for many years. Regardless of the lack of real opponents, somehow the Marines were better in the field than might have been expected, and their performance in France showed real promise—especially that of the younger officers, many of whom went on to high rank in the next war. Furthermore, uncommon courage, as Admiral Nimitz stated, was a common virtue. The huge number of awards and their citations speak more to the issue than my words can.

Why a book about a relatively small number of men whose impact upon the war in Europe has been irrationally denigrated by some and absurdly magnified by others? One reason is that while all American combat units contributed to the outcome of the war, the Marine brigade did have a greater overall influence on the final story than did any other single unit of Americans. Some part was caused by the naked event: their successful military exploits. Mostly it was because, over time, they were lucky enough to have caught and held the interest of the American public due to their relatively small size, to the many years the active Marine Corps brought upon themselves newsworthy successes that the army and navy found impossible to spawn. Marines were always busy: they frequently landed at trouble spots, protecting Americans from their own worst enemies—usually themselves. Missionaries were saved in China and large banking houses in New York didn't lose their investments in Haiti or Santo Domingo. Second-rate Latin American governments that had recently overthrown third-rate governments were helped out of office with assistance from U.S. Marines. Oh, yes, oftentimes that third-rate government was helped back into power again and sometimes by Marines.

If the U.S. Army had been called upon they, too, would have done all those wondrous things; but U.S. Marines were the instrument most often used by the U.S. State Department. Marines needed assistance getting there, so the U.S. Navy occasionally was cited as well. But the resounding cry so often used by the media was "The Marines have landed and the situation is well in hand." The actual facts are a bit less grandiose and actually quite simple. The Marines did land, they were always on hand, and never made major mistakes, or many minor ones either. They were the best "bang for the buck" when it came to these small encounters. But how might they be expected to perform in a real war? We'll find out.

When war against Imperial Germany was declared on 6 April 1917, the U.S. Army was notoriously short of manpower and the U.S. Navy was barely in better shape. The U.S. Marines' population had been increased slightly during the previous year and was in much better shape than ever before in its history. Marines wanted desperately to be in a "real war" and acted accordingly. They offered and the War Department accepted a Marine regiment for service in France. The Marines went over with elements of what became the 1st Division (Regulars), but their immediate melding into the army's ranks was not to be.

The army's leadership had made a decision to create divisions that would be "squared." That is, each would have two brigades of infantry (of 8,500 men each), of two regiments each, plus a machine-gun battalion. In addition the divisions would include a brigade of artillery (with two regiments of light guns and one of heavier equipment), a regiment of engineers, and assorted other service troops. The first division so structured was created and because the 5th Marine Regiment was a "fifth wheel"—four infantry regiments were available in France—it was, upon arrival, put to other, and to them, more distasteful, tasks.

When the Congress had declared war, the Marine Corps, through its commandant, Maj. Gen. George Barnett, convinced all and sundry that the Marines could provide trained troops for service with the AEF and still maintain the Corps's continuing commitment to the U.S. Navy. The Marines in general, and Barnett in particular, knew a good war when they saw it and worked overtime to see that the Corps wouldn't be left out. That was something that neither Pershing nor any of his nascent staff were willing to consider. "No Marines in France" was their cry. But Marines work in wondrous ways, and soon the secretary of war, Newton D. Baker, had been approached and had accepted the proffered 5th Marine Regiment for duty in France. Pershing, preparing for transport to the scene of war, was nearly speechless when he learned what had happened. He worked hard to reverse the intolerable situation, but he was too late. The army even tried to discourage the Marines by claiming there were no transports available to ship them. The Marines, when told that, even went so far as to obtain their own shipping. You can't keep a good man (men) down. So far, Barnett 1, Pershing 0.

Machinations aside, the truth of the matter was a bit more complicated than it seems at this long view of the telescope, eighty years later. Pershing and his crowd had enormous problems before them, and those afflicting the Marine Corps were modest by comparison. First off, a functioning staff for the AEF had to be put into formation before any other problems could be worked upon. Then a plan had to be developed for bringing trained Americans to Europe as soon as possible three thousand and more miles over waters filled with enemy submarines. When they arrived they would have to be housed and trained further in order to make them a bit more battle worthy. They would have to be fed and supplied with the modest necessities of life. Neither of these last two requirements was very successfully met during the entire period. It was a massive undertaking and the unprepared U.S. Army actually performed miracles with what it had to work with. Pershing and the AEF were superbly supported by the chief of staff, General Peyton C. March, and his "boss" Secretary of War Newton D. Baker.

As the AEF really saw it, the Marines would be hard pressed to provide enough trained men to fill more than a regiment. Later, after the Corps proved that was an incorrect impression, Pershing and his cronies asserted that one regiment did not fill anything near what was needed. They insisted that replacement of Marine casualties was also important, as were food, uniforms, minor equipment, and every service required by a modern army. Pershing couldn't guarantee space in already overcommitted ships for specific Marine requirements. Therefore the Marines even went so far as to accept that as a fact and agreed to change over to U.S. Army clothing and equipment. Whatever Headquarters, AEF came up with, Barnett and his Marines countered with reasonableness. Pershing and his people were stymied, over and over again. No matter what was tried, it didn't deter the Marines.

Meanwhile the Marine commandant managed to evoke a War Department request for a second Marine regiment, which he and his staff set about developing. In order to meet the requirement for an AEF brigade, a machine gun battalion was also necessary. That, too, was assembled. It was a time in which the Marines had manpower to spare, and they took every advantage they could to push the Marine agenda forward. Barnett was already thinking big—far beyond the brigade level. He wanted a Marine division in France. That was one thing that Pershing absolutely refused to consider. He was convinced that the Marines wouldn't be able to supply a Marine brigade or, moreover, provide sufficient replacements for anticipated casualties. He was wrong insofar as a brigade was concerned, but events would prove him right when it came to a larger formation.

For the Marine Corps, the maintenance of their navy commitment was essential. Without the normal tie to the U.S. Navy, there was little to substantiate a further need for naval infantry, which, until World War I, was what the Marines really were. Oh, they had found many ways to survive altered events for well over one hundred years, and therefore they did what they had always done: they generated a need for themselves. The new acquisitions created by our aggressive war with Spain forced a need for a stronger navy, one that could project itself across wider expanses of water, especially the wide Pacific. By 1917 we had a navy almost as powerful as that of the German high seas fleet. Consequently, Marine planners were in the process of developing what they titled an "Advanced Base Force"—a force that could take and hold islands from which to provide navy ships with fuel and other supplies. It wouldn't do much for land war on the European continent, but it was absolutely necessary to satisfy the navy's needs. The concept would expand and eventually be the primary basis for the Fleet Marine Force, which became the major thrust projected across the Pacific by the U.S. Navy in the Second Great War.

Barnett wanted to expand the Corps to be more than "naval infantry," so he used every method his fertile mind could come up with to tax Pershing and his AEF staff. Pershing held his ground for the most part and blunted nearly every Barnett attempt, until John A. Lejeune was shipped over to France. Brigadier (soon to be Major) General Lejeune was a product of the naval academy and the U.S. Army War College system. When he arrived upon the scene in July 1918, he was well known by many of the army officers already in harness and was welcomed into the "professional" ranks as few other Marines might have been. I do not know the real reason that Pershing gave Lejeune the "Marine division" after James Harbord was kicked upstairs to Services of Supply. But I suspect that the army was willing to accept one who was nearly "one of their own." With that appointment, Barnett was no longer in a position to push too hard for a division composed entirely of Marines. That problem was effectively curtailed, regardless of any further damage Barnett might accomplish in Washington, a city that he and his wife were terribly impressive in.

Although the differences between the AEF and the Marine Corps seemed to be greatly ameliorated by the appointment of Lejeune to command of the 2d Division, there was still the matter of Floyd Gibbons and the widespread tale of how the "Marines saved Paris by defending Château-Thierry against all odds." That particular claim, which the Marines were unjustly accused of having originated, served to set back the cause for amiability and perhaps semiunity between army and Marines, even to this day. Everyone moderately aware of how Gibbons managed to hoax the U.S. Army censor knows that the word spread far and wide to the effect that the Marines defended all the ground between

Château-Thierry in the south and Belleau Wood to the north. The Marines loved it, even though it wasn't true, the army hated it and the Marines for the error. The Marines did make several halfhearted attempts to stem the uproar but it wouldn't have mattered what they did, the soldiers weren't buying any excuses. To them, then and to some extent now, the Marines were "publicity-hunting SOBs" and nothing could deter that attitude.

It is nearly eighty years later and that slip at AEF Headquarters still infects the normal intercourse between two military units that need each other. The reality of the situation seems to have escaped both groups. The army was rightly offended, but ought to have their anger against the media, not against the beneficiary. At that time the Corps, unlike the U.S. Army, had no guarantee of continuance. Marines lived on borrowed time, all the time. Several presidents tried every gimmick they could conjure up to "dispose" of the Corps and each failed. The army tried every scheme they could come up with to wipe out the Corps, even until the late 1940s, and worse, the navy tried to help them, the army that is. Therefore, until the Congress enacted special laws protecting the future of the Corps, the Marines needed every ounce of help they could get, and Floyd Gibbons was the immediate instrument. Even today the average person who has heard the words *Belleau Wood* believes that the Marines won the war at that point. Not many know that there was any unit other than Marines in France. Perhaps that is a gross exaggeration, but I'm convinced it isn't far off the mark. But the die was cast on 6 June 1918, and not by a Marine. The Marines just didn't cool it rapidly, or convincingly, enough. That was their error.

One brigade of Marines was more than Pershing or the army wanted, so the 2d Division remained a hybrid unit all during the war. It probably was just as well. After a while, neither brigade could do without the other. That is why they were the best division in the AEF. During and after the war, most Marines of that division identified themselves as being "soldiers" of the AEF and when a 2d Division association was formed, Marines were in the forefront of joining. It wasn't very long ago that I saw a short list of members still alive and active in the association, and among them were six Marines. They were Marines, first, last, and always, but they had loyalties to their division just the same.

Prologue

To Pershing on the expectation of American aid:
"I hope it isn't too late."
—Pétain

The French are a broken reed
—Haig's diary entry

April 6, 1917, was a momentous day for the United States. On that day the U.S. Congress approved President Woodrow Wilson's request for a declaration of war against Imperial Germany. The United States was the last major power to enter the World War and possibly the least prepared. All in all, the U.S. military and industrial complex wasn't worth the powder to blow it to hell.

The entire U.S. military was in a sad state. The total ground forces available for war were negligible. A then-recent study had rated the United States one step below Portugal as far as standing armies were concerned. In other words, the nation was not prepared to fight a war against Portugal, let alone the finest war machine in the world at that time. The only experience the U.S. Army had recently undergone was the disconcerting campaign against Pancho Villa in northern Mexico. There had been few laurels to divide among the U.S. military forces engaged, but it did give some of the army's leaders a chance to maneuver bodies of troops larger than they had been accustomed to. The U.S. Army was not, in the usual sense, a national military force. Essentially, it was limited to foot soldiers and some cavalry, with a well-trained but ill-equipped force of artillery. There was no air force, just a few flyers and rickety planes belonging to the U.S. Army Signal Corps and those only intended for observation.

By comparison, the U.S. Navy was in pretty good shape. It was relatively modern. Money had been lavished upon it after the U.S. had, in 1898, grabbed Spanish possessions over half the globe. Since that war the navy's poor stepchild, the U.S. Marine Corps, had never been anything more than colonial infantry. Active every year, their fighting was usually against peasants armed only with machetes. Composed primarily of a small group of company-level officers, and a hard core of trained noncommissioned officers the Corps was ready for any small war. There were other officers of higher rank, but most were too senior for field service. So, in order to participate in a major war, the Corps had to rely heavily upon their more junior officers with limited abilities.

Regardless of what the U.S. Navy or Marine Corps could accomplish, the main military force was the U.S. Army. In April 1917, the army was chiefly a "police force" that had, previously, been used to restrain and contain the Amerinds on their reservations in the west, or put down rebellious Filipinos in their homeland. In addition to the Mexican failure mentioned above, the army, navy, and Marines had spent a few months annoying the Mexicans at Vera Cruz. Nothing came out of that fiasco except a bunch of ill-gotten Medals of Honor to members of the naval service.[1] I believe that the army officers involved, including Maj. Gen. Frederick Funston, had the decency not to propose any awards, or if they did, none were approved.

There was one strong element in the army, and that was the many officers who had some training at the various army schools like the War College. These men would stand the American Expeditionary Force in good stead during the war. Many of them would eventually become the staff officers whom Pershing came to rely upon so heavily in France. Fox Conner, Hugh Drum, and George C. Marshall were the most important. Others would become the few successful senior leaders: examples like Hunter Liggett, Robert L. Bullard, John L. Hines, Joseph T. Dickman, and that boor, Charles P. Summerall, are a few. At least one Marine officer, John A. Lejeune, was also a graduate, which fact would open a number of normally closed doors for him.

At the end of the Spanish war the United States, which heretofore had rejected the status of "colonial power," now definitely rated that title, but still not as much as Britain, France, and the Netherlands did. The taking and holding of the Philippines, Puerto Rico, and a bunch of other former Spanish properties, required a first-class navy to control it, and the USN could easily be accused of that status in 1917. In fact, by 1917, it was considered by the British navy to be a potential threat to its own sovereignty on the high seas. Though not as huge as the British fleet, it was close to second best, after Germany, and had been growing at an unrestrained rate. The British admiralty took note and wished they could put a stop to that nonsense, but they couldn't. At least not for the present. Maybe later?

• • •

When the United States declared war the Allies, according to British and French propaganda, were trouncing the Central Powers. It wasn't until after the declaration of war that the Allies came clean, sort of. "If you don't hurry up over here we are going to lose this war." Perhaps those weren't the actual words used, but they are a reasonable facsimile. Soon after the declaration of war, delegations of French and British officials arrived, separately, in the United States to beg for manpower and to plan for the immediate incorporation of America into the war as soon as possible. Their immediate demands were for American men to be integrated within the French and British armies as soon as possible. This was to make up for the massive losses each had suffered through their own colossal stupidity, incompetent planning, and irresponsible leadership. Each wanted American troops to train and serve with their forces in combat. Both Britain and France, with their usual noble nature, offered to take American citizens, transport them, train them, and send them into the lines as replacements under their command. Perhaps, later in the process, some American command formation (up to battalion level) might be allowed, but indisputably under their direct military control in the beginning.

Needless to state, that didn't go over well with President Wilson or his designated expeditionary force commander, Maj. Gen. John J. Pershing. Each had his reasons, dictated by personal ego for disliking the idea, but both were correct in doing so. It was quickly made quite clear to both groups that American men would not, under any circumstances, be placed in bondage to either of the two nations. They would serve only under an American command. That fact took some time to sink in, but eventually both groups were made to understand. The Allies finally, without grace, accepted the fact that a million armed men weren't waiting in the United States for immediate deployment in the lines and more importantly, when the Americans went to France they would go and remain under U.S. command.[2]

Throughout the conflict, Pershing continued to refuse their demands. Once was not enough. Clemenceau of France and Lloyd George of Britain, as well as their subordinates, continued to harass Pershing and other U.S. leaders up until the very last days of the war. Even until just a few days before the Armistice, Clemenceau was still trying to subvert Pershing, writing a highly critical letter about him to Marshal Foch, requesting Pershing's relief. The South African general Jan Smuts even had the temerity to suggest that he be given command of the AEF and

Pershing shun ed aside to handle administrative problems only. Pershing remained steadfast, refusing to permanently amalgamate American troops with French and British formations, and eventually he did create an American army, and it was that army which broke the still formidable German army in 1918.[3] Pershing continued to enjoy the complete support of his president and the secretary of war, Newton D. Baker, till the end.

The French committee, unhappy at the turn of events, then begged for an early showing of the flag in France. The morale of its people was extremely low and supposedly an American military appearance would somewhat mollify the French people. As a result, a U.S. army division was promised and by midsummer the transfer of the 1st Division (Regulars) to France began. The division wasn't complete, of course, since there were not enough trained men in the U.S. Army for a modern division of upwards of 25,000 men. The appellation *Regulars* was practically a joke. In 1917 there were very few of those in the ranks of any American military formation. The U.S. Army had little experience fighting a major war, at least not since the Civil War, more than fifty years earlier. The disgraceful showing of the American forces in the Spanish-American War was too recent and the memories too embarrassing for the more intelligent officers to summon up.[4] Many of the early arrivals in all the forces would be barely trained and definitely would require more seasoning before they could truly contribute anything substantial to the war effort. What was worse, the U.S. had little with which to provide the new recruits in the way of war supplies or equipment.

Although the United States was officially at war, the nation's military was not ready for anything like what had been going on in Europe for the previous three years. The disastrous condition of the U.S. Army, and to a lesser extent the nation's other military forces, would never be completely rectified during the period that the U.S. was engaged in that war. In addition to lacking trained manpower, the United States also lacked the tools for war. No artillery of any consequence was being cast or constructed, nor were airplanes, machine guns, or hand grenades. We were even weak in the production of rifles and ammunition. The very few automatic weapons we had were badly outdated. The exception was the venerable Lewis gun, which, because of stupidity on the part of decision makers, was not to be a part of the arsenal of our military forces.

Because initially the Americans could only supply money,[5] the nation was forced to buy most war materiel from the Allies. We had a huge manufacturing capacity but we produced almost nothing with which to make war. Many promises were made to the Allies, like planes to darken the skies of Europe, but by the end of the war we had only produced a few and their combat ability was negligible. Our major contribution along those lines was a superbly designed, but underpowered engine known as the "Liberty," used mainly for training and not combat purposes. Just a few "tanks" were produced in the U.S., exact replicas of French models, which were to be used for training purposes only. Actually, without France to supply our needs we would never have been able to field an army. They supplied machine guns, automatic rifles, grenades, aircraft, balloons, ammunition, gas masks, tanks, and just about everything else. Fortunately, France was well developed and organized insofar as production was concerned—better than any other nation in the Allied group. How unlike twenty-two years later.

We didn't even have sufficient ships to transport our forces overseas. The United States had to rely heavily upon British ships for troop transport. They had other uses for their "bottoms" and shipping U.S. soldiers to France wasn't one of them. As stated above, our navy was in pretty good shape, but the new construction was devoted primarily to swift little ships to ward off submarines. Few ships designed to carry troops or freight were coming off the ways. At the end of the war the one warlike item the U.S. was overstocked with was destroyers.

The British and French had been anxious to get the United States into the war as a belligerent, on the Allied side, ever since the war had begun in 1914. In the meantime, Germany had been just as anxious for the U.S. to remain neutral.[6] The U.S. was, when the war began in 1914, almost entirely neutral and continued so for some time thereafter.[7] Even before Wilson asked Congress to declare war upon Germany, most of the people in the country were still against going to war. The rich and influential, especially in the northeast, had large sums invested in Great Britain and naturally desired an Allied victory. British propaganda, much more extensive and intensive than that of the Central Powers, convinced many Americans that it was in their interest that Germany be defeated. As time progressed the tone became more one of demand than of invitation. Their stance finally became "We've carried you long enough, it is your war, too, when are you coming?" American newspapers, magazines, and even the relatively new medium of the movies, were hotbeds of propaganda, albeit unsophisticated, for Britain/France and against Germany. Some of it was laughable, even then, but it worked.

By late 1916, most Americans, had been brought around to a pro-British view. That happened even though the British navy had been forcing U.S. merchant ships, destined for neutral ports, into British ports for contraband examination and often the removal of their cargo. Of course there were vague promises to pay "later" for what was taken by force. In 1812, the U.S. had gone to war with Britain, and earlier with France, for that kind of unlawful procedure. Our national stance was always to maintain freedom of the seas. That was the presumed reason for going to war with Germany, but where Britain was concerned, we didn't maintain it for very long. "Our man" in England, Ambassador Walter Hines Page, worked overtime against U.S. interests. He urged the State Department not to protest too strongly against the search-and-seizure policy of Great Britain because, he claimed, the British government wouldn't hesitate to go to war "with any nation that opposed that procedure" including, as Page pointed out, the United States. Although President Wilson demanded that State press the British on this issue, Secretary Robert Lansing fell down on the job by mincing words rather than using those Wilson insisted be used in the official paper. In other words: In a pinch, our guys didn't have the necessaries.[8] When Wilson finally learned of this outrage it was far too late to change what had become fait accompli.

As stated, Page had been actively engaged in promoting Great Britain in his slanted reports to the State Department and to the president. Page's actions in Britain, too involved to be addressed here, were entirely contrary to what his post required of him. He was in fact guilty of traitorous behavior and many of today's historians are now willing to fully accept that fact. Colonel Edward House, a friend and advisor to President Wilson, also fell into line insofar as British propaganda was concerned. He, too, extolled the virtues of the Allies to Wilson at every opportunity, of which he had plenty. Wilson didn't need much prompting. He had earlier declared his personal nonalignment, but his writings and actions over the years clearly stated the opposite. It was barely weeks after his reelection in 1916 on the basis that "he kept us out of war" when he started to severely provoke the Germans. It was soon obvious to Germany that the president and his aides weren't going to be nonbelligerents for much longer. They finally realized that they must resume unrestricted submarine warfare directed toward any ships going to Allied ports. It was the only possible way that the Germans could bring an end to this most debilitating war before the Americans came in and tilted the balance irrevocably against them. The kaiser agreed and gave the necessary orders in February 1917. Soon after a ship with Americans aboard was sunk and that was all the excuse that Wilson needed.

Since 1914 the French army had been covering the greater portion of the western front. It was their strength and morale that were most important to the Allied cause. For nearly four years, their heavy man-power losses had negatively influenced army morale. Because of that enormous blood expenditure, the French army had already suffered a debilitating mutiny in 1917. Even though Gen. Henri Philippe Pétain had managed to pull the army back together, with a semblance of or-der and discipline, the war was *fini* as far as the average French soldier was concerned. It was the poilu whose family had been uprooted and dislocated from their everyday life by the occupation of their country, and for four years it was he who had borne the brunt of the war. Ac-cordingly, by the time the Americans began to arrive, the attitude of most French soldiers was only to survive the war and if, perchance, the German invaders were defeated, all would be well. In 1917–1918 most truly believed that the war would go on forever or would terminate with a German victory. Only the infusion of numerous "Yanquis," or as many called them, *les Amies ("les Sammies")*, might affect the ultimate outcome. But after a few months, because they hadn't yet arrived in the numbers anticipated, that looked more and more like a lost hope.[9]

In 1917, because of French pressure, the British high command launched a series of—to the British army—destructive assaults upon well-defended German positions. What happened to that army and to that of France is beyond the purview of this book, but suffice to state, losses for the Allies were enormous and consequently morale on the western side of the front was at an all-time low. And this was exactly what the Allies wanted to do with American servicemen if they could get their mitts on them. Because of many factors, German morale wasn't much higher—not that is, until the influx of men transferred from the east-ern front did increase the chances for victory. That fact helped to re-store Fritz's spirit considerably.

Though it has not been as widely advertised, the British Tommy was also about all done. Only the fact that Blighty, as they called Britain, was somewhat removed from the daily horrors of the war helped the British soldier to retain a slightly higher morale level than the poilu. The few "holidays" home to Britain from Flanders also allowed Tommy to get away from the daily reminder of who was suffering. Though Tommy was generally more stoic than Pierre, reports exist to indicate there was a seething mutiny lying just beneath the surface in most British formations. In fact, a number of British soldiers were executed for insubordination and other mutinous acts.

Pierre, however, never had that relief. No matter where he went in France, the war was all around him. We tend to forget that from August 1914 until November 1918, France and Belgium, bore the brunt of enemy subjugation and occupation of the most productive portions of their land. This fact naturally greatly benefited the Germans while distressing the Allies.

The French charged that Britain was not occupying as much of the line as it could and of course the British continued to cry poor, claiming that it was lacking in manpower. In late 1917 and early 1918, Great Britain had, according to official reports, as many trained troops in Britain as it had on the western front. Lloyd George, the British prime minister, had expected France to suffer a massive defeat, and, as in 1940, a decision was made not to put all its troops in one basket, Flanders. Another and possibly more important reason was that Lloyd George and some of his followers in the War Cabinet had great trepidation about providing Field Marshal Douglas Haig with any more British soldiers to squander as he had at the Somme in 1916 and at Passchendaele in 1917. Haig's colorful word for Britain's human losses was *wastage*. The word was appropriate to the situation, and Haig was the man who wasted them. And he was anxious to do the same for the Americans.

Britain and to a lesser extent France, did in fact squander nearly a half millon men in sideshow operations: Gallipoli, Salonika, Mesopotamia, and Egypt. Even though the populations of the two nations were about the same, the French continued to hold at least two thirds of the line from the Swiss to near the Belgian frontier. Britain didn't begin conscription until January 1916. Up until then she had continued to rely solely upon volunteers. The supply of volunteers dried up as the casualty rates increased. But the average Britisher immediately fell into line, accepting his fate in a stoic manner. Only the Irish fought against conscription when much later, in April, 1918, it was voted for them by the parliament in London.

Yet, all the while, Britain had been angrily demanding that American troops be sent to British formations to serve under British command, because it believed that the Americans were unable to field a modern, trained force.[10] The French believed likewise. More importantly, all they really wanted was flesh to stop the many German shells and bullets. France's supply of flesh was running out and to a certain extent, so was Britain's. After the AEF arrived in France, several attempts were made, and would continue to be made, to have General Pershing relieved of command of his forces.[11]

The reality was that France and Britain had barely managed to defend what they controlled of the western front. Most of Belgium had been occupied by the Germans since 1914, as was much of northern France. What the Germans occupied was the area in which the greater part of the French coal mines and important steel mills were located—most of the nation's wealth.

For the first three years of the war, French and British soldiers had been squandered in bloody attacks at the Verdun forts and on the Somme, among other places. Still the Germans were able to hold on to their positions. Russia had folded and gone socialist, with German assistance; Serbia and the other Balkan countries were either out of the war or very close to it. Italy was not doing well at all. Both Italy and Austria were just about finished after slamming each other for over two years. A major defeat at Caporetto was in Italy's near future (October–December 1917). German armies, relieved by the exit of the Russian armies from that bloody contest, were gathering in France as well as in Austria, with the object of destroying the Allies before the United States could bring its weight to bear against them. The near destruction of a large portion of the French army, by Gen. Robert Nivelle in the spring of 1917, caused a mutiny in which many French divisions just melted away and left unguarded large sections of the front. Finally, the incipient revolt was crushed and France was saved, at least temporarily.

Reacting to the destruction of much of the best blood of France, Pétain called a halt to all French offensives in order to preserve as much of that blood as was left to the nation. In order to maintain the numeric level of approximately three million men under arms, France extended her age limits at both ends. Men of sixty-five and sixteen were both liable for call-up in 1917, and in 1918 France was calling up its 1920 class for duty. France was in bad shape and Britain wasn't much better, notwithstanding British protestations to the contrary now that she had no volunteers coming, just men who were being drafted, and those were reluctant and consequently less reliable.

Until the U.S. joined in, the only chance the Allies had for a victory was the threat of starvation imposed upon Germany by the British and

French blockade. Even though the war had been going badly for the Allies, they had consistently refused to consider a negotiated peace with a more than-willing-Germany. The terms that Britain and France required were not realistic for either nation, each barely able to survive. But, they persisted in their demands and the war went on. Germany decided that she must win the war before starvation fully set in, and so went back to sinking ships in the eastern Atlantic. Things were going badly for all the belligerents but none had leaders who would or could face reality and bring the war to an end. The killing went on.

Germany's resumption of submarine warfare was supposedly the last straw. Wilson, who was easily convinced by the pro-Allies faction in the United States, asked the Congress for permission to declare war upon Germany. They granted him those powers. Finally, after much hemming and hawing, America was in the war—but what of it?

Wilson had recently disbanded the only substantial ground force the nation had: The one that had served on the Mexican border in the late effort against Pancho Villa. The units that had been utilized for that service had been composed mainly of federalized National Guard troops. Part of the reason for the decision to bring in the Guard had been to get them some active service in case the nation were to go to war in the near future. After a few months the guardsmen were screaming for release from federal service. They were released and in April 1917 the nation had to again start from scratch. Fortunately, several of those divisions, though permeated with politicos, were fairly well trained and most had a high morale component, especially in the 26th "YD" Division.[12]

When war was declared the nation didn't have the military-industrial capability to produce much more than rifles and their cartridges. No machine-gun design, to speak of, had heretofore been acceptable to the Ordnance Corps of the U.S. Army. There was no modern artillery, no tanks, no nothing. Yet, for some reason that only Wilson and his cronies understood, America was going to war. A real war in which the United States wouldn't be able to play a prominent part for many months, and possibly years, to come. Almost all the weapons and equipment the U.S. troops would require would have to be supplied by the Allies, mainly the French.

It would be over a year before the first organized American forces would be able to face the Germans on almost equal terms. The 2d Division, of which the Marines were a part, wouldn't really get into the war until April/May 1918 and then only to gain some experience in what was considered a relatively quiet backwater. A month later, in June 1918, they did get into it and then, as the saying goes, it was with both feet. The 2d Division was still using French guns in their artillery brigade. Some of their infantry weapons, like the Chauchat automatic rifle and the Hotchkiss machine gun, were French. Hand grenades, both American and French made, were most often unavailable when needed. They did have American bayonets mounted on Springfield rifles and would use them, but only occasionally.

The troops expected, because Pershing insisted upon it, that they would fight "American" style. That is, in open country and not in trenches. They did fight in open country, often enough, but in formations such as the British and French had been using for three years, which spelled heavy casualties for those on the attack. The use and organization of open formations was still unknown, except to the enemy. The thought, in Marine and probably U.S. Army circles, was that a commander should have complete control of his men on every field—*control* meaning that they were in close order and able to understand shouted commands. Machine guns and artillery weren't given much consideration, mainly because the American forces scarcely had any and, except for the Civil War, had never faced any before. Like the already decimated French, *l'Attaque* was the paramount configuration of the AEF in the beginning. Soon that would change slightly, but not sufficiently. Though minuscule compared to the other belligerents,' American casualty rates were much higher than the home folks expected, especially in the Meuse-Argonne campaign.

Pershing fought on several fronts, against many enemies, before the men and materials started coming to him in sufficient quantities to enable him to field a respectable army. By the end of May 1918, he only had a few divisions in France, but many more were in training in the States. Most of those lacked artillery and service units, which were not easily provided by a still unprepared United States. The British, ever mindful of replacements for their shattered forces, advised Pershing they would provide ships to transport U.S. soldiers to Britain for inclusion in their formations. He reacted to this by suggesting that if ships were available, Britain should ship American forces to him in France, since he was in need of them also. They did, sort of, but weren't happy about being caught in a trap of their own devising. Although hoisted on his own petard, Haig managed to obtain the infantry of five U.S. divisions. Pershing had finally agreed to that as a way of obtaining the transports needed. In late August 1918 Pershing reclaimed them from an infuriated Haig for his Saint-Mihiel offensive.[13]

• • •

At any rate, the Americans went to war. They shouldn't have, as they weren't prepared mentally or materially for that war, due to the faulty administration and leadership of the politicians in power before our entry. Naïveté could be the charge, but idiocy and criminality was more like it.[14]

It is now a well-known fact that Wilson, who regarded himself with somewhat higher esteem than did many of his contemporaries, desired to determine the future of the world. Therefore an army with which to settle the problems of the Old World was what was required. The instrument selected for his task was the American Expeditionary Force. They performed far beyond everyone's expectations and greatly aided in the defeat of Germany. They paid a hell of a price to do it. But after the war no one cared. The soldiers came back to a nation entirely different from what it had been when they left. Most of the veterans were in worse shape, physically, socially, and economically, than before. Few would be able to get their feet on the ground for another twenty years.

Later, many Americans were angry at the attitude of the French and British in their disparagement of what the AEF had accomplished. As Coffman stated, so well:

> In later years, when, out of ignorance or for propaganda purposes , some soldiers, politicians, and historians negated the crucial American role, they overlooked this cardinal fact which the strategists understood in 1918—*with enough Americans, the Allies would win; without, they would lose.*[15] [Emphasis added].

This same attitude, prevalent in the 1920s and 30s, was even more virulent in the 1950s regarding the American contribution in the Second Great War: the war that was caused by the failure in 1919 of French and British diplomacy and their greed. Wilson's machinations and much maligned "Fourteen Points" didn't do much to settle the Old World's problems. The treaty that came afterward was the primary cause of the unrest that led to World War II. By then America was no longer able to remain a totally honest broker and had to go over and settle the matter once again.

But we get ahead of our story.

Notes

1 The medal had not been allowed for officers of the U.S. Navy or Marines. That prohibition was rescinded. Both services worked overtime making up for that interdiction. Thirty navy officers, including an admiral, Frank Fletcher, and his son Lt. Frank J., plus numerous navy captains, were put in and awarded the medal. In addition, nine officers of Marines, including the ground commander, Lt. Col. Wendell Neville, and several other senior officers also made themselves available. Frankly it was a farce. Smedley Butler was so ashamed that he refused his but was warned that he'd better shut his mouth and accept it.

2 It might be well, here, to add the fact, which seems not to be well known, that the United States was not an ally either of France or Britain. The U.S. was an "associated power."

3 Most Anglophiles and Francophiles will dispute that statement, but this author considers it accurate.

4 If there had been a few more Spanish regulars with their smokeless Mausers, the war might have terminated sooner and with the U.S. defeated or stalemated.

5 That was a major reason we got into the war: money. Big banking firms, notably J. P. Morgan & Co., had loaned Britain and France huge sums and American bankers didn't like to lose money. To paraphrase Walter Millis in his book *Road to War,* to accuse Morgan of leading us into war is incorrect; "all they did was to facilitate it." In early 1917 anyone with a modicum of sense could see that Germany was holding many trump cards and most likely would come out the winner. On 6 April 1917, the dice came up "snake-eyes" and the American public lost. Sorry about mixing metaphors like that.

6 Never did any German official seriously consider the possibility that the U.S. might side with Germany. It was a foregone conclusion that the U.S. would only remain neutral or join Britain. Therefore our continued neutrality was of utmost importance. They went to extremes to preserve that, even for a time ceasing submarine warfare, which was stupid. It was their ace in the hole.

7 Most Americans were neutral; the major exceptions were the recent German immigrants and many of those of Irish blood, both for obvious reasons.

8 Alice M. Morrissey, *The American Defense of Neutral Rights 1914–1917.* (Cambridge: Harvard University Press 1939), 28–34.

9 *Les Amis,* or our friends, was the word used by the French people to symbolize American troops. It sounded like *"les Sammies"* to the Americans, when spoken by a native.

10 Much as the same attitude held by Alexander and other British generals in North Africa and Italy during 1942–43.

11 The French premier, Clemenceau, was, as late as November 1918, trying to have Pershing fired.

12 A regular Maj. Gen. Clarence R. Edwards, organized the Yankees and brought them to France in September 1917. They were the first complete NG division to arrive in France. He and Pershing did not get along and as a result the division was always high on the latter's "S" List. In most cases they performed at a high level, though Pershing would never acknowledge that fact.

13 See excerpts from Haig's own memoirs for interesting comments about Pershing and the Americans in general. By his own account he had no liking for or confidence in American troops, except those he would have used for "wastage" purposes.

14 Taking German possessions was, in my opinion, the main reason Britain came into the war. That and the destruction of the German naval threat and its mercantile navy. Of course, the return of Alsace-Lorraine was the most important French objective. In the George C. Marshall book cited, he makes note of discussions held at the officer's mess as the armistice was being awaited, in which the British and French army observers both argued as to which German colonial possessions would go to each of their nations. Marshall says he, in a jocular manner, told the Englishman, Major Geiger, that the only territory the U.S. was interested in claiming was Bermuda. With that he said Geiger went ballistic, yelling that something about the U.S. not having any right to those islands. Geiger never accepted Marshall's disclaimer and angrily discussed the subject for six additional days. When he left, Marshall felt that he never realized that it had simply been a joke.

15 Edward M. Coffman, *The War to End All Wars* (New York and London: Oxford University Press, 1968), 122.

1: Genesis

The Marines' best propaganda has usually been the naked event.
—*Marc Parrott,* Hazard: Marines on Mission

Major General George Barnett, the commandant of the Marine Corps, knew a good war when he saw it. After the declaration of war in April 1917, and using his most persuasive manner, he soon convinced Josephus Daniels, the secretary of the navy, to support his efforts to get his Marines into the war. As Barnett later stated in his unpublished memoir,

> When I saw that we were soon to enter the war, I went to the Secretary of the Navy and told him that in all the wars we had had, marines had served with the army, and that as far as I was concerned, I felt that it would be very largely fighting on land. I invited his attention to the fact that the law gave the president in time of war the authority to by executive order, transfer the whole or any part of the Marine Corps to the Army; and that in all previous wars, he had availed himself of that privilege. I told the Secretary that I considered it absolutely essential that such an executive order be procured, and that unless marines were to serve with the Army, we of course could not secure good recruits, and that it would *kill the Marine Corps.*[1] [Emphasis added.]

Ever mindful of appearances, Barnett added that the Marine slogan "First to Fight" would make the Corps look ridiculous if the Marines didn't get over to France with the first American troops sent. The secretary of war, Newton D. Baker, accepted their offer with alacrity. He didn't know it at the time, but the designated commander-in-chief of the AEF, Maj. Gen. John J. Pershing, was, to say the least, unwilling to accept any Marines for duty in France. The manner and method of overcoming that reluctance is a story in itself, which won't concern us here. Through the good offices of both secretaries, Daniels and Baker, the

Marines were not left behind. What some would consider "good fortune" for the Marines provides us with our story.

On 16 May 1917 Newton D. Baker officially requested of the president a regiment of Marines, organized as infantry, to accompany the expedition being sent to France to "show the flag." Eleven days later President Woodrow Wilson responded by directing an order to be issued to that effect: that a regiment of Marines was to be sent for duty with the first elements of the AEF going to France. This was all that was necessary.

A large group of Marines, recently returned from Haiti, Santo Domingo, Cuba, and off many ships of the fleet, plus some Marine reserves, were formed into the 5th Regiment of Marines. It was formally organized and established at the Philadelphia Navy Yard on 7 June 1917, with Col. Charles A. Doyen, USMC, in command. Major Harry R. Lay, USMC, another "old hand," was his adjutant. Doyen's designated second-in-command was Lt. Col. Logan Feland, who would be temporarily detached for duty with General Pershing's AEF staff in France. The regiment included three battalions of infantry, a headquarters company (1st Lt. Alphonse De Carre), and a machine-gun company, and would be heavily composed of "old-timers," at least insofar as the designated officers and noncoms were concerned. All three battalion commanders selected were long-serving regulars with adequate experience—at least for guerrilla warfare in the tropics.

Major Julius Spear Turrill, a Vermonter who'd been a Marine since 1899, was assigned to command of the 1st Battalion.[2] It was then comprised of two companies of troops from Norfolk, the 66th (Capt. George K. Shuler) and 67th (Capt. Edmund H. Morse), both formed from battleships guards. Another company, the 15th (Capt. Andrew B. Drum), arrived at the Navy Yard from Pensacola, Florida. And finally, the 49th (1st Lt. George W. Hamilton) was composed heavily of Marines recently transferred ashore from the USS *New Hampshire,* plus some of the new boot camp graduates.

On 1 June 1917, two more battalions were organized in Philadelphia, the City of Brotherly Love. The 2d Battalion, commanded by Maj. Frederick May Wise, had companies numbering the 43d (Capt. Joseph D. Murray), 51st (Capt. Lloyd W. Williams), 55th (Capt. Henry M. Butler), and the 23d Machine Gun Company (Capt. George H. Osterhout Jr.). In the meantime, Maj. Charles Tylden Westcott was busy developing the 3d Battalion, 5th Marines. The companies were the 8th (Capt. Holland

M. Smith), 16th (Capt. Edward W. Sturdevant), 45th (Capt. Benjamin S. Berry), and 47th (Capt. Frederick A. Barker) and were created from Marines recently returned from the islands.³ Turrill and 1/5 moved by train from Quantico to Philadelphia on 9 June, but both 2/5 and 3/5 had already left Philadelphia for New York that same day.

On 12 June, Turrill and 1/5 boarded the USS *DeKalb* (formerly the German ship *Prinz Eitel*) and sailed for New York Harbor, where they and the ship remained until 14 June. Both 2/5 and 3/5, plus the regimental band, boarded a ship that was to become as famous as any ship in the history of the U.S. Marine Corps, the USS *Henderson*.⁴ Meanwhile Doyen, Lay, regimental headquarters, and the supply companies boarded the USS *Hancock*. On 14 June, accompanied by the ships carrying the four regiments of the 1st U.S. Infantry Division, the 5th Marines were on their way to France. Many of these American men were regulars and were used to boarding ships and sailing off for ports of call expecting a fight. Therefore we have very little written material from them to describe that voyage. But most likely it was the same as those of the troops that would follow, and we do know that it usually wasn't terribly exciting. Seasickness was a common malady, but otherwise the trip was boring and uncomfortable. The successful transport of millions of men over a sea dominated by German submarines is one of the major triumphs of the American part in the war. I believe this was the first time in history that such great numbers of soldiers, from one nation, were transported such an immense distance to another nation by sea to fight in a foreign country. Especially since they weren't even ready for combat as yet and required extensive training before being so committed.

The first group of Marines on the *DeKalb* arrived at Saint-Nazaire, France, on 26 June 1917. The *Henderson* arrived the next day, followed by the *Hancock* on 2 July, reuniting the regiment on foreign soil. Actually, this was the first time since their formation that the regiment was together as a complete unit. But that wouldn't last very long. Pershing and his staff had been making plans for the use of the Marines.

When George Barnett became commandant of the U.S. Marine Corps in February 1914, there were about 10,000 officers and men in the Marine Corps. That number had stayed fairly steady ever since a major personnel increase following the Spanish-American War. The navy had undergone a massive reshuffling and had gained increased responsibility for the protection of all our new possessions. Therefore, an enlargement of the navy's Advanced Base Force[5] was also required. As it became quite evident, during the years that the Europeans were blowing themselves to pieces, that the United States might become involved, a rather feeble effort was made to increase the nation's defense forces. It was called "Preparedness," and it wasn't very successful. In fact it was woeful.

Therefore, by an act of Congress, on 29 August 1916, the authorized strength of the Corps went up to 597 officers and nearly 15,000 enlisted men, a fifty percent plus increase. Never before had the Corps been so large. On 26 March 1917, President Wilson, by Executive Order, increased the numbers to 693 officers and 17,400 enlisted. Less than two months later, as a result of the declaration "that a state of war exists between the United States and the Imperial German Government," an additional increase upped the Corps to 1,197 officers, 126 warrant officers, and 30,000 enlisted men. This last boost more than tripled the population of the Corps in three years.[6] Heady days ahead. More promotions; more colonels and more generals too. And even a few more privates.

Those increases caused an always-starved-for-manpower Marine Corps great elation but a less-than-prepared Marine Corps some consternation. Where would it find trained officers? Somehow, the Corps always manages to succeed. They issued a call and hundreds of qualified (and some not so qualified) men quickly answered it. Many of the earliest came from seven colleges, including, but not limited to, Princeton, the University of Minnesota, Texas A & M, and Yale. Some of those who came forward were reservists; others entered the Corps through the National Naval Volunteers, one such being 2d Lt. John W. Thomason Jr. Another was William A. Worton, a charter member of the Marine Detachment, Massachusetts Naval Militia. A third, Walter A. Powers, commanded the 1st Marine Company of the MNV but later was destined for much less acclaim than the other two men.[7]

The war's outbreak made it essential that competent men be obtained for the Marine officer corps as soon as possible. Some few came from the Naval Academy, a number of U.S. Marine Corps warrant officers were commissioned, others were graduates of military academies, civilians with prior military training, and last but not least, meritorious Marine noncommissioned officers. Corps recruiting stations were swiftly inundated with splendid men of all kinds. Many officer candidates were selected as second lieutenants in the Marine Corps Reserve and were immediately sent to Marine posts for training. Others, those who were destined for an examination to be held on 10 July 1917, were enrolled as privates in the Reserve and sent to the Recruit Depot at Paris Island, South Carolina. Their commitment was limited by the proviso that if the exam results were successful they would be commissioned as regular second lieutenants. Failing that, the men could opt to stay in the Corps as enlisted men or be discharged. Few took the latter course of action.

Men were jamming the various military/naval recruiting stations, and the Marine recruiting offices were no exception. Unfortunately, or rather fortunately, the Corps standards were maintained so high that it has been estimated that upwards of eighty percent of the applicants were rejected for various reasons. Some of the recruiters' tales of those who applied and were accepted, or even of others who were rejected, really indicates that overall American manhood was of a patriotic nature. At least that was true in 1917. In December 1941 and early 1942, volunteers would show that those patriots' sons were of the same blood.

One young man was rejected in two recruiting offices, one in New York State and the other in Pennsylvania. The reason: because of an accident he was missing his trigger finger. Undaunted, he walked from Binghamton, New York, to Washington, D.C., and as he put it on the large sign he was carrying, To Join the U.S. Marines, It is worth it. Upon arrival in Washington somehow he managed to inveigle a meeting with the commandant, George Barnett. Barnett evidently was impressed and authorized the Binghamton recruiting office to haul him in. He was duly sworn in and became a Marine. Another man got as far as removing his clothes for his preinduction physical. He didn't get any farther. His cork leg seemed to intrude upon his desire to become a Marine. Regardless of the exceptions, the recruiters worked overtime, literally and figuratively, to bring in qualified men. Many were accepted but many more weren't. The standards of the Corps were maintained throughout the war.

Because the men who were joining as enlisted Marines were of such a high caliber, it was soon decided that they would be the future source for commissioning. In short order the direct appointment of civilians as officer candidates ceased. When the going got rough, during the fighting in France, the Corps fell back on their old faithful source for officers: the better Marine enlisted men, of whom there was always a large supply. Another source found in France were those surplus U.S. Army junior officers who were a boon to the Corps in the early months of the war. Little has been written about them, possibly because they were hybrids in a hybrid organization. But they more than did their duty and deserve better of history.

Much later, after the middle of September 1918, with continuing huge losses in France of all ranks, nearly 1,500 other men were hired on as officer candidates. They were from selected colleges and universities; Harvard, Cornell, the University of Washington, and the University of Minnesota were several, as was the Virginia Military Institute, but the largest number, 190, came from the University of Wisconsin.

Officers appointed from civilian life were sent to Paris Island,[8] San Diego, or Mare Island. A few of the earliest appointments went to the U.S. Marine rifle range at Winthrop, Maryland. In each of those places, especially at Winthrop, the new officers would receive a modicum of training. Essentially, all would be transferred to the new Marine base at Quantico, when it was eventually completed. At Winthrop they mainly engaged in rifle practice. James McBrayer Sellers, a recent graduate of the University of Chicago and a newly arrived second lieutenant, described his first days in the Corps. First to Philadelphia for gear and then his adventures at Winthrop and later at Quantico . . .

> We stayed at Philadelphia . . . getting as much as we could of our supplies & left for Washington. . . . Again at Washington we continued our search for uniforms . . . without much chance of getting it for some time. We . . . arrived at Indian Head, a temporary bivouac camp at Winthrop . . . just upstream from Washington. . . . The camp was nothing but a rifle range surrounded by a few shacks and . . . tents. Most of the fellows had been there for a few days and had the good quarters cabbaged.[9]

Sellers went on to describe his joy at being on a rifle range with almost nothing else to do until the base camp at Quantico was completed. In his memoir he tells of every day being holiday routine: "baseball games, swimming, and boat riding every day. In fact we were enjoying life intensely." He was among the first directly appointed officers to be transferred there. Lieutenant Colonel George C. Reid, another old warhorse, was the base commander at Winthrop. Sellers makes us aware that "real" Marine officers were so scarce that hundreds of enlisted Marines were under the command of other enlisted Marines. He also described what had happened to a bunch of new recruits.

> I was helping coach [shooting] some new recruits . . . that were in a company which had been recruited in Minnesota. . . . About 70 were from the university. . . . They had been sent to Mare Island

in April, 1917 . . . then two weeks before arriving at Winthrop they
had been to Quantico. . . . I found out that we wouldn't have such
a picnic when we got there. They had been drilled six or seven
hours a day, until many of them were fainting. . . . The doctors had
to call a halt on the work.

An athlete himself, Sellers was greatly pleased to learn that many of
the new officers were "widely known athletes." He continued by giving
one of the most detailed accounts of qualifying on the rifle range that
I have ever seen. In painstaking detail, Sellers explained every single step
taken to qualify. There is no question but that shooting was his favorite
vocation and was what Sellers wanted to do with his life.

Meanwhile, everyone was anxiously awaiting the opening of the new
base at Quantico. Some of those officers who were transferred there
from Winthrop were selected to help with the "bull work" such as digging up bushes or other growth between the new buildings, leveling the
streets, and other such effort that would help to get the camp ready for
occupancy as soon as possible. Finally the buildings were ready. Everyone was anxious that the base open and training begin. In Sellers's eyes
the appearance of Quantico takes on a whole new perspective.

Looks like pictures of mining towns which I have seen. There is
one small street which constitutes the original town. This street
leads right up from the pier. . . . There are rows and rows of un-
painted wooden shacks. . . . The small streets between are all cut
up with rain wash, and we stumble over what is left of a former
small forest, roots and stumps, and sewer excavations. There are
always a pack of dogs and cats around Marine camps, and they always seem to be contented. Downtown there are little restaurants
where we can get an egg sandwich for 50 cents. And there is also
a dance hall where they charge 20 cents for a dance with one of
the painted ladies brought to town for the purpose. Between
nearly every two tents, there are dummies for bayonet practice,
and at all hours of the day enlisted men can be seen slaughtering
these dummy Germans.[10]

Even though the base was still only temporary, the first class of 345
officers was accepted in July 1917. Survivors of that group graduated in
October 1917. These men would join all the others and lead the 4th
Brigade in its first fights; at Verdun, Belleau Wood, and Soissons. Their

training schedule was as follows: reveille 0545, physical drill 0600, breakfast 0630, drill 0730–0930, inspection of quarters 1145, dinner 1200, drill 1300–1430, 1500–1600, supper 1800, study 1900–2100, taps 2200. Physical drill before breakfast consisted mainly of running a half mile through the company streets. The streets were still partly uncleared and that made sort of an obstacle course of the whole experience. Some of the young officers weren't in the best shape physically. A few dropped out, but inevitably those who remained settled down and eventually every one was able to do what had to be done.

The revised Marine Corps policy of utilizing only enlisted Marines for future officers was taken up in earnest. Orders were issued to commanding officers of every Marine installation to forward a list of those designated for the training camp. Each commanding officer was to convene a board of three officers to examine the qualifications of the men at each post and to send a report to Marine headquarters rating the selection. At headquarters another board convened to examine the recommendations. It was decided that 600 officer trainees could be comfortably housed and trained at any given time. With that in mind the headquarters board selected that number for the first official camp, which was established in April 1918.

After extensive training in the manly arts—infantry drill regulations, bayonet training, use of hand grenades, administration, tactics, military law, and a host of other things—the first class of former enlisted men graduated in July 1918. The second officers training school of 570 men began on 20 August 1918, and 432 were graduated on 16 December 1918. Under the same policy, 164 enlisted Marines were directly commissioned while they were members of the 4th Brigade. Chiefly, these were men who had distinguished themselves in combat. The selection and turnaround were swift. It was most important that the rapidly diminishing officer ranks be quickly infused with qualified replacements. And it was a resounding success. Another 172 were given training at the army's candidate school in France, graduating and being enrolled as temporary second lieutenants, Marine Corps Reserve. There were others, some graduating as late as July 1919, but those few were assigned to inactive status as soon as possible afterward. The army candidate school in France provided another 48 men who were enrolled as second lieutenants (provisional) in class 4, Marine Corps Reserve. Those men, except for four, were discharged or placed on inactive duty upon return to the United States. In addition, there were another 1,500 students at various colleges and universities who underwent what later would be called ROTC. But none was ever assigned to any Marine activity.

One group of officers, those who generally were recent U.S. Army recruits, provided up to fifty platoon leaders for the 4th Brigade—that is, until after Soissons, when most of the survivors were transferred to the 23d Infantry. There were a few who remained with the 4th Brigade and a few who were returned to the 4th Brigade after Blanc Mont. Those who commanded a platoon or company of Marines were generally looked upon with great favor by enlisted Marines and officer comrades. Most performed at an extremely high level of competence. Those who transferred and left a record of their service spoke highly of their Marine comrades and their time spent with the 4th Brigade. Many were morose when they learned that they were leaving the many friendships they had developed since their arrival in France. After going through some of the bloodiest battles in the war with such men, it is difficult for comrades to part company. It was an unpleasant situation for everyone involved. And it was a loss to the brigade.

There was another group of Marines, those who were of field grade and for whom there were no opening slots in the brigade because they were so senior in rank. Many of those found appropriate homes in various U.S. Army units, some earning great distinction and awards. At the time the brigade was formed and activated, there seemed to be more field grade Marine officers in France than lieutenants. In addition, there were officers already in the brigade who were senior in grade for the few slots available, or received promotions that pushed them out. Finally, there were many latecomers who wanted so badly to serve in France that they somehow managed to cross the "big pond" without any slot to fill in the brigade. And they remained. The AEF found a place and use for most of them, but not always on the fighting line.

As stated previously, in the early months of the war good material had come into the recruitment places in droves. Later, effective from 8 August 1918 onward, when by Executive Order voluntary enlistments were stopped, those enlisted men coming into the Corps would henceforth be draftees. It was the same situation as was happening to the army and navy. Regardless of what instrument supplied the men, the draftees had to choose the Corps, and the Corps only accepted those who measured up to its standards.[11] Consequently, the enlisted men continued to be Marines in desire as well as in fact. The last man inducted into the Marines for the war was sworn in on 13 December 1918.

Training for enlisted Marines continued at the various places already established; Paris Island (P.I.), Norfolk, Philadelphia, and Mare Island in California. Norfolk and Philadelphia were temporary, both only being utilized until P.I. and Mare Island were up and running at full blast. Training for all Marines was tough and thorough, just as today. The only difference was the reduction in the length of the training period. On 28 April 1917 the period went from twelve weeks to nine weeks. Then, at P.I. on 22 June 1918, it was further reduced to eight weeks. Replacements were badly needed in France. By 11 November 1918, P.I. had processed 46,202 men and another 12,000 men went through Mare Island. After "boot" training, some Marines would be sent to specialist schools at P.I., including a school to train noncommissioned officers, field musics, radio school, signal school, and, among other schools, cooks and bakers.

The coming to Paris Island was not the great delight anticipated by Pvt. Bryan Becker. In a rather lengthy early letter to his mother, Becker, from Rochester, Michigan, explained what had happened to him during the first few hours at his new home. These were his exact words, with no changes:

Well I have arrived at the much looked for and hard to get to place at last. Feel fine had my first ride on salt water after dark as it was 7.00 o'clock when the train got to Port Royal. Just got first instructions of how to make bunk for sleeping and how to leave it in the morning was told not to lose our pajamas towel and soap and also not to forget our first lesson or we would be—you know Cockey's private password sounded in the Y.M.C.A. Hut the fellows are playing the piona all popular music and singing [unknown]. Had chow which consisted of beans good hash coffee sliced onions and vinegar with prunes for dessert, not so bad. Another announcement here that the hours for chow were 7.00 A.M. 12.00 and 5.00 P.M. and if we are not there we would be out of luck. Bed time at ten eastern it is half past nine now. Got to find my bunk hide my cash and turn in got about $24.50 left it costs to travel eat and have a good time on the train. I got out pretty cheap. We get 30.00 per mo. and every once a mo. have another examination in a day or two when I get [unknown] that I get a uniform. . . . I will write then later when I get time. Goodbye Bryan.[12]

Becker's style of writing leaves a lot to be desired, but you can get a feeling for what it was like to be completely in the dark, even when the lights were on. Later, in other letters, he explained that he and his buddies were quarantined for several weeks before being allowed to move "over the line" into the regular training quarters. In subsequent letters he described how he rose at 0545 and that they had "shower baths" in "good old fashioned salt water . . . it makes your hair stiff as a board."[13] Furthermore he believed that with their new uniforms "most of us are some nifty looking sights." Other recruits must have had some similar attitudes and thoughts about the routine.

A look at the pictorial *With the United States Marines at the Paris Island Training Station: A Pictorial Souvenir*[14] shows that recruits coming to P.I. arrived aboard a boat similar to a tug with exposed passenger space. After landing and being assembled in some military order they were marched from the dock to the quarantine camp, where they were housed in wooden buildings. Martin Gus Gulberg describes his first night at Paris Island on arrival:

> I thought they had landed us on an island for the insane; but later I was told it was the old quarantine camp. The recruits that had landed the day before certainly put us on the pan. They grabbed our suit cases and greeted us something like this: "This way for your silk pajamas; right over here for your ice cream checks; white sheets, this way." They had a lot of fun at our expense and we had to like it. It was the initiation that every Marine goes through on Paris Island. The following day the fun began, helping initiate the new gang. We were marched into the mess tent for our first Army chow. We were hungry, but not for this kind of grub. Our first meal consisted of gold fish, army style (salmon salad), apple sauce, bread, and muddy coffee.[15]

Another newcomer, one who arrived in June 1917, was Warren R. Jackson of Huntsville, Texas, who described the reception he and his buddies received:

> It was quite dark when we pulled up to some sort of dock at another part of the island. . . . On short notice, we were hurried into a line, for what purpose we did not know. When I got to the head of the line, a cheap knife, fork, spoon, tin cup, and tin plate were pitched at me, with an uncerimonious [sic] caution to "hold on to 'em, if you lose 'em in four years you're out of luck!" . . . Where did he get that *four year* stuff? We enlisted for the duration of the war, we *thought*."[16]

Later on Jackson reiterates that he and the rest of his group were forced to sign enlistment papers that decreed that they were in the Marines for four years; however, the officer also told them it was just a formality and they would indeed be in only for the duration. They had already heard of what happened to other men who refused to sign, and deciding that discretion was the better part of valor, they signed. Incidentally, Jackson didn't like the meal. Not the first or the last. He complained about being served bread that was "moldy" and sausages that were "putrifying." However, "some days afterward a number of inspectors [appeared from Washington] and afterward the chow was slightly improved." Although he later says the food was really bad, so bad that several of his buddies became deathly ill. One, named Albert Ball, had a "violent attack of ptomaine. . . . Two other men were said to have died of ptomaine on the island. It was a wonder that more did not die."

After being finally accepted, sort of, the "boots" were provided with a sea bag filled with uniform clothing and necessary "782" gear.[17] They were then marched to their new quarters, which were either tents or perhaps, if they were lucky, wooden buildings. Private Rendinell describes how their first experience in a mess hall went. Their "tough sergeant" said,

> All right, boys, those of you that want chow fall in line and make it snappy. I went along with the rest. The first fellow past out bread, the next slum. It looked as though it was made of beef stew, boiled potatoes, hash, dish rags, and a few old shoes mixed together, as close as I could figure. I stepped up to the next guy, he spilt coffee. Spilt is right. I held out my cup & he poured hot coffee all over my hand & it certainly was hot. To make a long story short I did not have any supper, that dam fool burnt my hand & I dropped everything. I was sore. What I told him was plenty.[18]

Soon afterward, the quarantine men were taken to the hospital and given one final, thorough examination and "a major came in with a bible & we took the oath. We were vaccinated, & a shot in the arm. It made me terribly sick." Culp's book illustrates the process, showing men posed getting their various inoculation shots. Not much different from 1944 or perhaps 1994 either. The major difference seems to be their landing from a seagoing tug rather than over the later causeway that was constructed sometime in the 1930s.

Jackson tells us that

it is impossible for one who has not seen and experienced military discipline to understand what we were to experience. It was to be a new life and in a new world. It is no exaggeration to say that the potentates of old exacted no more severe discipline than was exacted of us. The men now over us were bent on making marines out of us or killing us.

After a few days or weeks in quarantine the new arrivals (not yet Marines) were issued their Springfield rifles and other gear and then moved to a new location, about a quarter of a mile distant. It was there they were to meet their drill instructors. In Jackson's case they were "our future sovereigns, two corporals and a black haired, dark skinned man with a deep scar on his cheek, who was to be our sergeant. His small, piercing black eyes caused us to be concerned."

The new men were put through a rigorous training period beginning at once. What would normally have been a several month "experience" was reduced to a few weeks. One of the very first things a new boot learns is his general orders, and nearly as soon he is assigned to guard duty to learn what that is all about. Usually, at that time, they were two hours on guard. No telling how many off hours, but presumably that was initially the total experience.

Next came drill. Five hours every morning of every day for ten days straight. Naturally, as every former Marine remembers, that was only a small part of the exercise. DIs (they weren't called that in 1917) would continually find fault with at least one person in the platoon. That person might catch it just once, or he might be the regular, constant sap. Everyone hoped not to be that sap. Cursing was, as later, the usual response from one of the DIs when a boot blundered; or even when he hadn't. Marines would frequently assess the "qualities" of their DI compared with the others at P.I. I remember that our DI was tougher than all the others. For some reason other former Marines have the same claim about their DIs no matter when they went through boot camp or where.

The usual punishment was to have the recalcitrant run until his tongue hung out. Then he was given another couple of rounds just for kicks. Punishment was handed out to individuals and collectively to everyone in the group, when one sap was the criminal. That villain would always dread the thought of what would happen to him if he were caught alone by his comrades. Oftentimes the cursing by the DI would resume, and when he tired of the sport the duty would be turned over to one of his assistants.

All Marine recruits of that period seem to have remembered mostly the many oyster shells lying about the island. Their recollections emphasized the picking up and removal of huge amounts of them, carrying them for upward of a mile in buckets, to pave the roadways. Brannen and others tell of the ferocious drill instructors, who, as in a later war, were barely a rung below God. He relates how Sergeant Boynton cursed a blue streak while breaking his swagger stick into several pieces, because his platoon was fouling up. He added that the treatment made him feel "that he was no earthly good to his nation. . . ."[19]

Of course, a main part of their training was the time spent on the rifle range. One recruit, Pvt. Sheldon R. Gearhart, of Wilkes-Barre, Pennsylvania, earned a Marksman medal for his efforts. . .

> We're on the rifle range now and are having life a little easier because it is quite cool here. . . . We get up every morning (Sunday included, for we shoot on Sunday too) at 4:30 A.M., have roll-call at 4:45, chow at 5, and at 5:30 we shove off for the range. It's about one and a half miles and we get there about 6 o'clock. We stay until 9 A.M., then come back to the barracks. At 11 we have chow, go back to the range at 12, and stay until 4, making a seven hour day. . . . These Springfield rifles kick just like a mule. When they go off they push you back about a foot, right straight along the ground. You shoot from three positions: prone, kneeling, and sitting. We shoot from 200, 300, 400, 500, and 600 yards. From the latter distance, those bull's-eyes look like pinheads.[20]

Gearhart continued, describing the entire experience, which included rapid fire. "You shoot ten shots in one minute. . . . The [rifle] sound like a cannon. . . . All rapid fire is done . . . at a silhouette of a man's head and shoulders, the bottom of which is 36 inches." Every Marine well remembers his time on the range. Warren Jackson remembered that he barely fired "marksman," which according to him was a score of between 202 and 238. Sharpshooter was 238 to 250, while the crème de la crème, the expert, fired higher than 250. Considering what other experiences the boot was going through, his training at the rifle range, when he wasn't on the firing line, was the only time he was allowed to relax. Marines in the making also served time in the "butts." Butts were where the men were employed when not shooting. There they moved the targets down for marking and back up again for more shooting. They were located underneath the targets, down low with a shield of built-up ground between them and the men firing. While there, a worker could have the feel and experience of the sound of bullets coming toward him, but in relative safety. After the Marine fired, the workers would run the target down and paste it with patches of paper, if there were any hits. They would then run the target back up with a flag showing the success or failure of the shooter. A waving red flag, known as "Maggie's drawers," would signify that the shooter had missed the target entirely. Oh! how each Marine dreaded that. The jeers from up and down the firing line and from the butts would cause many a man the heebie-jeebies, and most likely affected his further shooting, at least on a temporary basis. "When I was right, no one remembered. When I was wrong, nobody forgot."

Hemrick described what it was like to use the "wholly inadequate toilet facilities." As a substitute "head" the recruits had a six-foot plank with "flimsy hand railings that led out some hundred or more feet over the Atlantic Ocean." The planks were on stilts twenty feet in the air over the ocean and "at high tide, the wind and spray just didn't add one thing to one's comfort." He further explains that the trip out over that turbulent water three times or more a day "was a nerve-wracking experience."[21]

At some point during their training, certainly after the rifle-range period, some men were selected for seagoing duty. The largest and best appearing were selected and it was considered quite an honor to be so chosen; these probably had some additional schooling for the special requirements of shipboard service.[22] Many, but not all, served with the U.S. Navy in European waters. Others carried out their duties all over the world, wherever U.S. Navy ships plied their trade.

Many recruits would reflect back upon their time "in hell" but were glad that the experience they went through made them more able to face the horrors in France. Several future generals of Marines would reflect upon their time on that island and one, Melvin L. Kruelwitch, said the whole island was filthy and dirty and the beds were lousy. He believed that even the horrors of the French Foreign Legion couldn't compare to the training suffered at P.I. Perhaps his own lifestyle prior to joining the Marines was classier than the general run of recruit. One young Marine wrote home to his mother and told it best. "The first day I was at camp, I was afraid I was going to die. The next two weeks my sole fear was that I wasn't going to die. After that I knew I'd never die because I became so hard that nothing could kill me."[23]

Later, upon graduation, the enlisted men would be transferred from their boot camp and assembled at Quantico for further training with their new officers, those "veteran Marines" who had just graduated from "basic training" themselves. The blind leading the blind, so to speak. Jackson noted that when he and his fellow graduates finally left "Paris Island" they found sleeping cars waiting for them at Port Royal. When the train stopped a few hours along the line they were even served lunch in their coaches. After a trip of approximately twenty-four hours they arrived at Quantico. There the men were assigned to 250-man companies, with the numeric designation they would retain throughout their service in France.[24]

The U.S. Marine units that were slated to serve in France with the AEF had been accepted into the U.S. Army and were required to learn and follow army regulations. There were new drills, formations, and various manual exercises, so it was difficult for men who had just learned the Marine style to change again. Since most were young men, they soon adapted.

In addition to his staff, the commanding officer of a training company would have two French and four Canadian officers as advisors. The basic formation, as always, was the platoon. It became the principal training unit. The specialty schools provided the training officers and enlisted staff. There were, within the Overseas Depot,[25] various schools for machine guns, tactics, first sergeants, company clerks, armorers, and cooks. Much of their training at Quantico was based upon what foreign officers designed for them in anticipation of what the Americans would meet when they got to Europe.

Trench fighting, with all its myriad annexes, such as bayonet fighting, hand-grenade throwing, unit exercises, patrolling, and so on, was to get the Marines ready to meet the Boche, as the French had derisively named the Germans. Though ultimately the Marines would have little experience in trenches while in France, not many of them knew that at the time. Regardless of where they fought, as the Germans would later attest, their natural exuberance and desire to fight made them outstanding and tough opponents. Although it sometimes got them into severe trouble when they did, they would fight "American style." All in all, most of them believed that anything was better than what the Europeans were doing. When they did get to the killing fields and the disastrous open warfare, some of them, those who lived, preferred the protection of a hole in the ground after all. Machine guns, and especially artillery, could do that to a man. So did being in waves of aligned men moving in slow motion across wheat fields or open ground.

When four platoons had been assembled, and trained, they were then formed into a company. A company headquarters with administrative personnel was then assigned to each company to complete the unit. Consolidation of four companies brought together a battalion with its headquarters staff. Each unit was being trained in its formation by the Depot: that is, platoon, company, and battalion. When training was completed, over they went. And that was never soon enough.

But meanwhile, there was some diversion for the men. Some went into the village of Quantico, as did the officers. Some were elated to be "free" and to be able to go someplace without supervision. They even went into the "small, dirty resturants at Quantico and order[ed] what a fellow wanted without a threatening sergeant standing over [his shoulder], making one feel that his liberty, if not his very life, was at stake." Some men, those who had blouses, were able to get liberty in order to go to Washington, D.C. Blouses had been issued at Paris Island but most had been ruined when they were worn on the rifle range. So those Marines who still owned one could command fabulous fees for the loan of it to a desperate Marine, for that was what he now was, a MARINE.

But not all Marines trained at P.I. went to Quantico. Some who had been assigned to the 35th Company and later the 13th Regiment were sent to Fort Crockett near Galveston, Texas, to insure that oil from Mexico would continue to be shipped to the United States. In a letter home Bryan Becker let his mother know that

> we may get ship duty or be sent to guard oil . . . but I don't think it will be France because *we are not considered first-class men and that is all that are allowed to go to France in the M.C.* [Emphasis added.][26]

But not all men of the 13th were destined to go with that regiment. Some of the enlisted men were transferred from the 13th "into an independent casuality battlion," as Becker tells us. He being one of them.

On 19 May 1918 a unit entitled the Overseas Depot was established to bring some training and organization out of the forming of Marine units going overseas. Each replacement battalion would have a number assigned.[27] The following is a listing of the units of Marines formed by the Overseas Depot in 1918. The 3d, 4th, 5th, 6th, 9th, 10th, and 11th Separate Battalions; 2d and 3d Machine Gun Battalions; 5th Brigade Machine Gun Battalion; 2d and 3d Separate Machine Gun Battalions; 11th and 13th Regiments, all of which totaled approximately 16,000 officers and men. When the situation was really rough, two additional separate battalions, the 7th and 8th, were organized and sent to France directly from Paris Island. A lesser-known facility, the Marine Corps school of machine-gun instruction at the Lewis gun factory in Utica, New York, graduated sixty-nine officers and 2,084 enlisted Marines. Their guns had been that esteemed Lewis, but those were removed and in replacement the AEF received the French Hotchkiss machine guns as well as the Chauchat to try to stop the Boche. From May 1917 to 11 November 1918, approximately 1,000 officers and 40,000 enlisted Marines passed through Quantico.

Marines have always been stationed all over the earth, and World War I was no exception. There was one Marine each in Madrid and Samoa. Other places in which Marines were located included 608 in the Virgin Islands, which the United States had recently purchased from Denmark. The transfer took place on 31 March 1917, just a week before war was declared against Germany. Naturally there was a full company at the American embassy in Peking, and aviators and support crews were stationed in the Azores to spot and sink submarines. There were nearly 600 Marines in the Philippines, 2,400 in Cuba, 2,000 in Santo Domingo, plus many smaller groups at Guam, Haiti, and Puerto Rico. Three Marines were located at The Hague in the Netherlands, plus many more in Nicaragua, that eternal trouble spot for Marines. Of the 73,000 officers and men who comprised the Corps on 11 November 1918, only 24,555 were in France with the American Expeditionary Forces. Mustn't forget the soldiers of the sea, the over 2,200 officers and men aboard various vessels of the U.S. Navy who went wherever the navy went. Many of those were on board the U.S. Navy ships that were part of the British Grand Fleet in European waters. It was their war too. And so it was with the First Marine Aviation Force, which in the fall of 1918 was sent to support British air in northern France.

The nearly 25,000 officers and men who served in the two Marine infantry brigades lived an entirely different experience than all the others. The 4th Brigade of Marines that would make history in 1918 was composed of the 5th and 6th Regiments of Marines and the 6th Machine

Gun Battalion. As stated previously, the 5th Regiment was the first Marine unit assembled for duty with the American Expeditionary Force. Its first commander was Col. Charles Doyen, and beginning on 27 June 1917, the regiment was assigned to the 1st Division (Regular), remaining with that unit until the middle of September 1917. On 23 October 1917, Doyen, recently promoted to brigadier general, was placed in command of the newly formed 4th Marine Brigade. Three days later Brigadier General Doyen assumed command of the fledgling 2d Division (Regular), as its first commanding officer. He remained so until the arrival of Maj. Gen. Omar Bundy, USA, on 8 November 1917. Doyen even went so far as to appoint a staff. Lieutenant Colonel Logan Feland, USMC, became his and the division's first chief of staff. With Bundy's arrival, Doyen then returned to his 4th Brigade. So did Feland.

Doyen's replacement in command of the 5th Regiment had been Maj. Frederick M. Wise, who assumed temporary command until Lt. Col. Hiram I. Bearss arrived and succeeded him, on 1 November 1917. Bearss remained in command until New Year's Day, when he, too, was relieved by the newly arrived Col. Wendell C. Neville. Neville would retain command until he in turn was promoted to brigadier general and then assumed command of the 4th Brigade. Brigadier General John A. Lejeune got in there for three days late in July 1918, possibly the shortest term anyone had commanded a brigade. Neville returned to the brigade when Lejeune went to division.

At the time the 4th Marine Brigade was conceptualized, the only Marines in France to fill part of the role were the 5th Marine Regiment. On 26 October 1917 that regiment was officially transferred to the newly formed Second Division (Regulars), being the founding regiment. Until 8 August 1919, the 4th Marine Brigade was a part of the 2d Division. The other units in the division were the 3d Brigade of Infantry, the 2d Field Artillery Brigade, 2d Engineers, and an assortment of service troops. The two infantry brigades each included two infantry regiments and one machine-gun battalion. The artillery brigade had three regiments: two of field artillery and one of heavier guns.

Replacement and resupply was a major problem for the Marines, and much thought had been given to the problems and solutions. With the army units within the division it would certainly follow the usual pattern already developed. But the Marines would cause unusual problems for SOS. More important was how to replace the expected casualties of the 5th Regiment. To give Pershing and his staff their due, they had all given serious thought to what problems would lie ahead if Marines were in-

corporated into the AEF. Naturally, Barnett and his staff minimized inherent problems they wished to ignore. But, as usual, even if dropped
into a pile of manure a Marine would always come up with a gold brick
he'd found lying about. The problems were worked out and eventually
everyone seemed satisfied with the results.

Lieutenant Colonel Hiram I. Bearss, known throughout the Corps
as "Hiking Hiram," was the first commander of the Base Detachment.
This organization was formed in June 1917 at Quantico and shipped to
France on the *Henderson* in August to provide replacements for the 5th
Marines. It was built around one machine-gun company, later numbered
the 8th, and the 12th, 17th, 18th, and 30th Infantry Companies. Three
of the companies, the 8th, 17th, and 18th, were soon redeployed into
the 5th Marines. The other two became part of an aggressive AEF that
required guard units at Pershing's headquarters. These two companies
provided the needed guards.

Meanwhile, President Wilson directed, through Secretary of the
Navy Daniels, that the major general commandant organize another regiment of Marines for duty with the AEF. In July and August 1917 the 6th
Regiment of Marines was assembled at Quantico, under the command
of another long-serving Marine, Col. Albertus W. Catlin. Catlin had
been, for some months, commanding the base at Quantico. When he
assumed command of the forming regiment, he was relieved at Quantico by Brig. Gen. John A. Lejeune. If Lejeune had had his way, he would
have had the regiment instead, but brigadier generals didn't command
regiments. Lieutenant Colonel (Lighthorse) Harry Lee was appointed
Catlin's second-in-command and Maj. Frank C. Evans, a recently returned veteran of the old Marine Corps, became his regimental adjutant. Major John A. "Johnny the Hard" Hughes commanded the 1st Battalion, Major Thomas "Tommy" Holcomb the 2d, and Major Berton W.
"Bert" Sibley the 3d.

Marines needed to complete the regiment were those recent graduates of Paris Island who, upon arrival at Quantico in the latter part of
August 1917, were formed into the 95th, 96th, and 97th Companies.
Each of those companies was the fourth company assigned to each battalion; 1st, 2d, and 3d, in that sequence. The paucity of trained officers
was still the biggest problem facing the 6th Marines. The latest group
had just started their classes and the big question was should these young
men, most with little, if any, experience in leadership, be given command of an equally young group of enlisted men. Fortunately, there

were a number of noncommissioned officers in the latest class and they had sufficient knowledge of the routine to be immediately commissioned and transferred to the regiment. In addition, there were a few officer trainees who had had some college military training or who had been in the National Guard, who could also be assigned to the forming companies. Collectively, their major quality was their earnest desire to reach France as soon as possible—"before the war ended." It is probable that many young Americans who were eager for "glory" thought quite differently a few months later.

The transfer of the 6th Regiment to France was decidedly drawn out. On 16 September, the 1st Battalion, with John Hughes in command, left Quantico by train for League Island, Philadelphia. The battalion had a proper send-off by the post band even though the morning was rainy. In addition, they also got some rousing cheers (jeers?) from members of the regiment who were being left behind. Later that same evening the battalion boarded the USS *Henderson* and on the following morning they left for New York harbor where they remained for five days. On 23 September the transport left harbor at 2230 hours for France, their ultimate destination. On 5 October the convoy landed safely at St. Nazaire, with no unpleasant experiences from submarines.

Needless to say, the members of the other two battalions were unhappy at being left behind. Rumors of imminent departure were common. Everyone, including the officers, had it on authority that they would be leaving a week from now or perhaps just two days, or . . . ? One of the stories going around, according to Sellers, who was a member of the 2d Battalion, was that the battalion was being delayed because Holcomb's wife was about to have a baby, and he had enough "stuff" to stay stateside until after the event. Right or wrong, the 2d Battalion remained in the country until after Mrs. Holcomb did her duty. Shortly afterward they left, the last of the three to go.[28]

The 3d Battalion, Sibley in command, was next to leave. He received his orders on 23 October, to leave on 24 October. The 3d didn't miss their train to League Island. They, too, were honored by the disappointed 2d Battalion, who lined both sides of the train and presented arms to their comrades. The post band played them on their way with a rousing rendition of the nation's anthem, "The Star Spangled Banner." It was in this transfer that the colonel of the regiment, Catlin, left with the 73d Machine Gun Company and his Headquarters Company. Upon arrival near Philadelphia, the battalion boarded the USS *von*

Steuben at League Island, and on the morning of the 25th the ship set sail for New York. Five days later the *von Steuben* left for France, accompanied by several heavy warships of the U.S. Navy. That transfer went well until the night of 9 November, when the *von Steuben* and the *Agamemnon* collided in midocean, with the former suffering a large hole in its bow. For one full day the entire convoy scattered, not rejoining until the following day. *Von Steuben* managed to make modest repairs and then was able to maintain a speed of fifteen knots with the rest of the convoy. Later that day ten U.S. destroyers joined the convoy out at sea and the trip through the sub zone was made without further incident. At noon on 12 November the 3d Battalion landed safely in the harbor at Brest, France.

The luckless 2d Battalion remained at Quantico. Though the weather became colder, training persisted. At Christmas a generous proportion of furloughs was granted to officers and men. Finally, on 19 January 1918, it was their turn; 2/6 left Quantico for League Island, with Lt. Col. Harry Lee in command. The *Henderson* was waiting for them, and on the following day they set sail for New York. Four days later their convoy got under way. Fortunately, the trip was uneventful and 2/6 arrived at St. Nazaire on 5 February. The entire 6th Regiment was in France, as was the 5th and most of the 6th Machine Gun Battalion.

For the entire 4th Marine Brigade, this became a time of intense training during an exceedingly cold winter; the coldest in many years, according to the records. That winter was long remembered by many men in the AEF in France. It is a wonder that more men didn't get sick. There were a few without a bad cold, but very few. But most all the Marines kept up with the training no matter what their physical condition happened to be. Many of the doctors were amazed that so few men were hospitalized, considering the terrible conditions that prevailed. The entire AEF suffered the same tribulations. Back stateside the conditions weren't much better. It was the period in which the plague that came to be named the "Spanish flu" began.

By order of the major general commandant, the final Marine unit then destined for France, the 1st Machine Gun Battalion, was formally organized at Quantico on 17 August 1917.[29] Initially, it had been given that numerical designation, which later was changed to the 6th Machine Gun Battalion. The designated unit had a headquarters detachment, the 77th and 81st Companies, with two additional companies added later. Captain Edward B. Cole was named as commanding officer of the battalion, with 2d Lt. Thomas J. Curtis his adjutant and 2d Lt. John P. Harvis as quartermaster. Temporarily, each company was equipped with sixteen Lewis guns and thirty-three machine-gun carts. The battalion remained at Quantico from 27 August until 7 December 1917, all the while engaged in training and weapons nomenclature for that wonderful Lewis gun.[30] Other officers assigned to the battalion were Major L. W. T. Waller Jr., and a host of others including 1st Lieutenant Louis R. deRoode, 2d Lieutenants Clifford O. Henry and Jack S. Hart. Curtis, only recently commissioned, was promoted to temporary first lieutenant and immediately after, a temporary captain. On 8 December 1917 the battalion embarked aboard the *DeKalb* at Newport News. They were joined by the 12th and 20th Companies, and that unit became a provisional battalion.[31] Their transport sailed to New York and anchored off Staten Island until the trip to France began on 14 December 1917. Exactly two weeks later they arrived at St. Nazaire after an uneventful trip. They thereupon joined their comrades of the 4th Brigade already arrived.

Notes

1 George Barnett, *Soldier and Sailor Too* (unpublished manuscript, n.p., n.d.), Chapter XXV, 1.

2 Turrill wasn't the only Vermonter to gain fame in the Corps. One of his contemporaries, Berton William Sibley, who led the 3d Battalion, 6th Marines to fame in several clashes with the Boche, was also from the Green Mountain state. Two others of note, in a later war, were Evans Fordyce Carlson and "Red Mike" Edson. Just one more was needed to make a top poker hand.

3 Few of the officers listed would continue to command those, or any Marine units, while in France. Some went to various schools established by the AEF and others were promoted to field rank and wound up in charge of U.S. Army formations. But I haven't been able to learn why so many were moved about so widely, especially in the early months. Many just entirely disappeared from view, not to be seen until after the war. Possession of rosters might fill in some of the details, but not completely.

4 The *Hendy Maru* as she was later called, was a mainstay of the China Marine transport service and lasted in the latter service until at least November 1941, when it removed some of the 4th Marines for the dubious safety of the Philippine Islands.

5 The Advanced Base Force was a rather new idea that had been developed by Marine officers in concert with navy officers. The basic idea was to have a trained, organized force of Marines ready to take and hold coaling bases for the use of naval ships. It was to be the forerunner of the Fleet Marine Force combined with the Defense Battalion concept. The increased use of oil as a propellant soon made the coaling stations an archaic notion for defense battalions. Soon after this war terminated, the Fleet Marine Force theory replaced it.

6 A year later, on 1 July 1918, the final increase was approved so that 3,017 officers, 324 warrant officers, and 75,500 enlisted men could be Marines. But most of that hundred-percent increase never went to France.

7 Worton entered the militia at age sixteen, in 1913. Badly wounded at Belleau Wood, he later returned to active duty. He became a Chinese language specialist of note, and eventually a major general. Powers came in for some notoriety in Sellers's memoir. Also see William P. McCahill, *The Marine Corps Reserve: a History* (Washington, D.C.: Div. of Reserve, USMC, 1966), 6.

8 The official spelling was changed to Parris Island in 1919.

9 Lieutenant Colonel James McBrayer Sellers, USMC (ret). *World War I Memoirs of . . .* (original ed., Pike, NH: The Brass Hat, 1997) 19–20.

10 Ibid.

11 The Marine Corps accepted the draftees with the following proviso: The men must volunteer for the Marine Corps and the Corps insisted that they had to meet the same rigorous standards that other Marines had to meet. That way the standards were kept intact and Marines continued to be volunteers.

12 Letters of Bryan Becker, unpublished, various dates, beginning with 30 March 1918. Provided by David Fisher, Indianapolis, Indiana.

13 Eugene Alvarez, *Where It All Begins. A History of the U.S. Marine Corps Recruit Depot Parris Island, South Carolina* (Blountstown: Gayle Press, 1984), 14–15.

Alvarez tells us that everything had to be transported by boat to the island, including water. Therefore, except for drinking and cooking, salt water was used during the war. I'm not sure where the water was coming from in 1944, but it sure didn't taste as good as sea water.

14 Sergeant John W. Culp, (1918; reprint, Pike, NH: The Brass Hat, 1993).

15 Martin Gus Gulberg, *A War Diary.* (1927; reprint, Pike, NH: The Brass Hat, 1992), 2.

16 Warren R. Jackson, an unpublished memoir entitled *Experiences of a Texas Soldier, 1917–1919.* Provided to the author by Mr. Peter Meyer of Burlington, North Carolina, a former Marine.

17 "782" gear was the Marine description for all web belting and other equipment issued for field use. Examples would be ammunition belt, pack, canteen, mess kit, etc. I'm not sure that the term was ever used by the U.S. Army.

18 Corporal Joseph E. Rendinell and George Pattullo, *One Man's War: The Diary of a Leatherneck* (New York: J. H. Sears & Co., 1928), 11–12.

19 Carl Andrew Brannen, *Over There: A Marine in the Great War* (College Station: Texas A & M University Press, 1996), 5–6.

20 Kemper F. Cowing and Courtney Ryley Cooper, *"Dear Folks at Home——"* etc. (Boston: Houghton Mifflin Co., 1919), 12–13.

21 Levi E. Hemrick, *Once a Marine* (New York: Carlton Press, 1968), 16.

22 One of the most onerous and exhausting tasks for seagoing Marines and sailors was the replenishment of coal in the bunkers. Those U.S. Navy ships that served in the British Grand Fleet were supplied with British coal in two-hundred-pound bags. As one Marine remarked "It was a new game, strange coal and stranger colliers, and we did not handle it well at first, but before long we had that darned Welsh coal trained so it would roll over and play dead."

23 Cowing, *Dear Folks at Home——*, 3.

24 Marine companies, unlike those of the U.S. Army, were numeric. Shortly after its being amalgamated with the 3d Brigade in France, strenuous efforts were made by many to have the 4th Brigade conform to the AEF alpha pattern, to little avail. After a while even army officers began using the numbers when writing messages to, or telling about, the various Marine companies.

25 See description of the Overseas Depot later in the text.

26 Letter dated 8 May 1918 from Paris Island. Apparently his platoon had been told that they would never be Marines or at least were not good enough to be fighting Marines. Or something equally negative. Just like my platoon. And possibly yours too.

27 Frequently, after their arrival in France, the replacements would go into the lines with little, if any delay. They would continue being carried on the replacement battalion rolls and often the enlisted men would be killed off before they could be totally assimilated into their assigned companies.

28 In Sellers's memoir he tells of the birth of the son and the proud father holding said child up for the officers and men to see, stating something like "This is what has been holding us up." To have been able to hold up a Marine battalion from going to war intimates that Tommy Holcomb had a load of drag, even that early in his career. The son would be a Marine during WWII; serving with Colonel William A. Eddy in North Africa during the preparation stage for the famous Torch landing in November 1942.

29 Plans were afoot to send another brigade, the 5th, but it was still only provisional.

30 Those "wonderful Lewis guns" were removed from the Corps in March 1918 by AEF direction in order to make them available for aircraft. They were replaced by the heavy Hotchkiss and unreliable Chauchat, both of which the Marines hated with a passion.

31 There were two companies with the number *12th*. One, as mentioned previously, became a guard company with AEF headquarters. The other, machine gun, 12th, actually was renumbered the 15th Company and joined the 6th Machine Gun Battalion.

2: The Creation of the 4th Brigade

It isn't the size of the dog in a fight that counts;
it's the size of the fight in the dog.
—Irish proverb

The trip across was relatively quiet—"the weather was ideal and the sea continually calm." Two German submarines were sighted by the *De Kalb*, but they were driven away long before they managed to get into a firing position. Some of the men were formed into gun crews and much time was spent in target practice on the way over. Although the ships were crowded and the passengers, officers, and men, uncomfortable, the newness of being on the high seas presented a novelty to most, somewhat offsetting the minor problems. After two weeks the novelty had worn off, but by then they were nearing the coast of France. French destroyers came out to greet and protect the transports as they came close to their destination. That fact alone provided enough information for the travelers to realize their trip was nearly over.

The "old-timers" had sailed to ports on most continents, while the "boots" were making their first, and in many instances, their last voyage. Seasickness was the main cause for complaint, although the sick weren't likely to make anything but groaning sounds. Some compartments were heavy with smokers, and dense smoke added to the discomfiture of those not addicted. Some enlisted men were assigned to work details. As always, what you had to do depended upon how you got along with your first sergeant. Most details included guard or submarine watch. Some fool second lieutenants tried close-order drill, which was always soon abandoned as the ship invariably rocked and rolled to the tune of the waves. Mainly the crossings ended as they began—safely. There were occasional altercations, like a collision between ships.

On 26 June 1917, the *De Kalb* cast anchor in the harbor at St. Nazaire, and the following day the 1st Battalion of the 5th disembarked and went into camp on the western outskirts of the town. In the meantime, having insufficient stevedores for the job, the Marines alleviated the situation by turning to and unloading their own vessels. The same day, 27 June, the *Henderson* tied up alongside the *De Kalb,* but the 3d Battalion remained aboard until the arrival of the *Hancock* on 2 July 1917. The next day, 3 July, all Marines disembarked from both ships. That night the entire regiment was under canvas and together for the first time since its formation. The Americans were grandly and enthusiastically greeted by the populace. The civilians seemed, genuinely, to realize that these young men had come across the ocean to save France. All else may have made them see nothing but defeat, but this bespoke something entirely different. Les Sammies were here and France would live, after all.

Later, when the 6th Marines came across the ocean, some of their men wrote of the trip as not quite so simple as presented previously. Private Warren R. Jackson, whom we have met previously, didn't enjoy his trip one little bit. In addition to being seasick for the entire voyage he was the victim of poor placement in the bowels of the ship.

Apparently every Marine in his compartment smoked, continually. As he said,

> At hammock time the lower deck was always thick with cigarette smoke. The rocking of the boat, with that dense tobacco smoke, gave my stomach anything but a happy feeling. One whiff and I'd lose my adam's apple, to say nothing of other organs farther down. Weather permitted, a number of us . . . slept on the upper deck.[1]

Upon arrival, Colonel Doyen, commanding the 5th Regiment, reported for orders to Maj. Gen. William L. Sibert, USA, commanding the newly formed 1st Division (Regular).[2] As always the Marines were among the first to land on foreign soil, but not to be among the "First to Fight" as they always proclaimed themselves.[3] In fact, the experience of the 5th Marine Regiment during the first months they were in France was a rather unpleasant ordeal.[4] Unfortunately, the regiment was not to be accepted as a part of the division, since the army had already planned that four army regiments would compose a division and as the old saying goes, "Four's company, five is a crowd." So the Marines were assigned various tasks that insured that they wouldn't get into the fight, not if various army officers had their way. But Marines did have their way and eventually did make it to the front after all.

Marines were initially turned into stevedores, and later some detachments were assigned duties guarding the army installations then being formed. The first few days the Marines spent in close-order drill and practice marches. On 12 July 3/5 was temporarily split up. The 45th Company was detached as a deck guard and moved into town billets. The 47th was assigned as a guard to Permanent Camp No. 1 at St. Nazaire under command of Maj. Charles T. Westcott. The 47th was also assigned duty as provost guard in town and guard for the remount station. The 16th Company was sent to Nevers to provide a guard for a medical depot and as provost guard for the town. Meanwhile, on 15 July the Headquarters and Supply Companies, along with 1/5 and 2/5 plus the 8th Machine Gun Company, boarded a "40 & 8" (forty men or eight horses) train for a fast trip across half of France to their training area. Everywhere the Marines went they were accorded sincere and hearty welcomes from the local civil population. The proffered bottles of wine went far toward creating a warm climate and preparing the men for a relatively new taste treat, one that would stay with many of the survivors for years in the future.

The 1st and 2d Battalions were transferred to the Gondrecourt training area (about 50 kilometers west of Nancy). The 3d Battalion and selected officers were left behind to perform guard duty. At Menaucourt, Meuse district, on 17 July, all but 1/5 detrained. They went on to the next station, Naix-les-Forages. In both towns the citizens had erected arches of welcome and were wearing gala attire that probably hadn't been exhibited for more than three years. Colonel Doyen established his headquarters in a château located between both towns. After a couple of days' rest the training program began again with a vengeance. Troops from the famed French "Blue Devils," the Alpine Chasseurs, were assigned to train the neophytes. The 30th Battalion Alpine Chasseurs were to train 1/5 and the 115th Battalion, 2/5. The one-pounder and pioneers section plus the 8th Machine Gun Company were taken under the wing of the 70th Battalion, while the Headquarters Company Signal Detachment was the responsibility of the 8th Battalion.

Great friendships were made during that period, even though the language barriers might easily have prevented them. There were some Americans, mainly officers, with a modicum of skills in the French language, as well as others who were of French-Canadian ancestry and many who spoke Italian, a language somewhat akin to French. Frequently, while in France, the members of the AEF used Americans of Italian ancestry as translators. Essential words, like *vin blanc* or *rouge* were quickly adopted by the newcomers. Somehow, everyone managed to fumble through.

General John J. Pershing inspected both battalions on 1 August 1917. General Sibert, still in command of the 1st Division, inspected them on 15 August 1917 and again on the 19th. Generals Pershing and Pétain, the commander of the French forces, inspected the Marines as part of the 2d Division, whereupon Pétain congratulated Col. Charles Doyen on the splendid appearance of the regiment and the cleanliness of its quarters in the two towns. Pershing made several congratulatory comments, such as "[The 5th] was the finest body of men under my command."

The towns and villages the Marines, and their comrades in the U.S. Army, were transferred to were mostly a conglomerate of farm buildings, with manure piles (Frenchman's wealth) under windows and in barnyards. Cows, when not being driven through the main thoroughfares of the village, where they halted vehicular traffic, helped create the family manure piles, and were therefore the most valuable members of each family. The family was counted as successful when its manure pile grew to a size larger than was necessary to maintain vegetable growth, and the larger the pile the more important the farmer was rated by his colleagues. Wherever animals and manure piles gathered, the odors, more resplendent at the domiciles of the richest farmers, took on airs, especially where drainage flowed from a site. Frequently Marines would band together and move manure piles from under windows in their habitation, almost always in barns, to a spot as far away as they were capable of doing. So much for "home sweet home." These realignments of familys' wealth frequently brought about anguish and demands for recompense from the owners of the preserved manure piles that had been such a major resource.

The relative wealth the Sammies brought to the towns and villages soon changed attitudes toward them and their frivolous manners, especially the frequency with which they bought local *vin rouge* and *blanc*. The Americans found the local wine to be much cheaper and more available than what they usually drank in the States, therefore they used much more of it. In addition to their training the officers and men made social contact with the citizens of the various villages, which included washing and sewing, the purchase of milk and eggs, and many superbly cooked meals.

Many Marine officers and men were given the opportunity of attending specialist schools newly opened at Gondrecourt, later bringing back to their units the new phases of modern warfare not covered by the old Infantry Drill Regulations. Frequently, the officers assigned to schools were of field grade, and because only so many 4th Brigade slots were available, the graduates were often swept up for duty in other AEF organizations. Various majors, who had been engaged in the development of the 5th Marines, never returned to duty with that regiment. Many were assigned duty at Pershing's headquarters at Chaumont or with the Services of Supply. In addition, several changes occurred within the regiment that bore upon its immediate future. General Sibert, who commanded the 1st Division, of which the regiment was still a part was relieved of command. Serious efforts were made by his replacement, Maj. Gen. Robert Lee Bullard, and the staff at AEF to "dump" the 5th Marines. On 22 August the 8th Machine Gun Company was detached and transferred to St. Nazaire as permanent guard for Camp No. 1, Base Section No. 1. On 23 September, the 15th Company was detached from 1/5 and transferred to the 6th Machine Gun Battalion. That same day in September one company, the 67th, under the command of Maj. Julius S. Turrill, was detached from 1/5 and even transferred to England to aid in processing U.S. soldiers as they arrived there from the States.

One unfortunate event happened at this time. A young Marine second lieutenant named Frederick Wahlstrom, of Headquarters Company, 5th Marines, was killed in a motorcycle accident while on the way from his company's station near Menaucourt to a school of instruction at Horville. He died on 20 August 1917, certainly the first Marine officer to lose his life during this period and possibly the first American officer. There would be many more before another year had elapsed.

Marines were busily engaged in training exercises during August and September. Regardless of General Pershing's stated principles, trench training, followed by associated subjects—field fortifications, trench mortars, gas and flame throwers, and, of course, automatic rifle and machine-gun firing—continued because the French army was still convinced that open ground warfare was a thing of the past. And the French were the chief instructors of the American soldiers. More appropriate courses were given however. The French provided a demonstration of artillery fire on 1 September 1917 and two Marines were struck by fragments of bursting shells. This was followed by more extensive demonstrations of artillery support for advancing infantry, such as a rolling barrage. Even French airplanes participated in the presentation to provide more realism.

Unfortunately, while the training program was being carried on, more Marines were being sidelined from training with the regiment into duty as service troops. Although much effort went into perfecting the fighting capability of the 5th Regiment, so many units had been detached for duty elsewhere that it was extremely difficult for the regiment to function as such. As we have already seen, one company was transferred to England on 22 September 1917 and did not return to the regiment until 11 March 1918. Yet, when the time came, it performed at as high a standard as the other companies of the brigade, even without training. A member of the company, Pvt. Joseph Feingold, briefly told of the experiences during the five month period the company was directing the movement of American troops through England to France. He tells of the company being scattered in small detachments in London, Liverpool, and several smaller towns along the path. He mentions that their return to France was on 6 March and "as happy a company of Marines as ever trod foreign soil landed at Le Havre."

This was not the first alteration in the regiment's structure, nor was it to be the last. In addition, a number of senior Marine officers were assigned to army regiments[5] and many army officers were assigned to the 4th Brigade. The Corps was short on junior officers and long on those too senior to command platoons and companies. Elliott D. Cooke, a young army lieutenant, initially a platoon leader in the 18th Company, 2d Battalion, 5th Marines, wrote two of the finest articles about infantry combat it has been my pleasure to read. You will meet him in the wild ride and combat of early June 1918 and later at Soissons.

The 8th Company, the regimental machine-gun company, was directed to serve as a guard company at Chaumont, headquarters of the AEF, arriving there on 9 September 1917. Then two companies, the 15th and 23d, under Captain George H. Osterhout, left on 19 September 1917 for division specialist school at Gondrecourt. The two companies were later to be assigned permanently to the 6th Machine Gun Battalion. Many officers were assigned to special and detached duty. Captain Frederick A. Barker was transferred to Paris as assistant provost marshal. General Pershing's letter to the commandant, Maj. Gen. George Barnett, was to allay fears that Marines would be used for everything but combat.

Shortly after their arrival in August, the first designated Marine replacements, commanded by Lt. Col. Hiram I. Bearss, of the 17th, 18th, 20th, and 30th Replacement Companies, were also welcomed to France. They were soon performing guard and provost duty with elements of 3/5. Because Bordeaux was the second designated port for Services of Supply, Bearss took command of Base Section No. 2, which was established there on 8 September. Early in October three of the infantry companies and the Base Detachment Headquarters arrived at Base Section No. 2. As will be seen, each joined a battalion of the 5th Marines, which had been sent over with three company battalions and now contained four. Of two others, the 7th Company was sent instead to Chaumont, the new AEF Headquarters for guard duty and the 30th went to the Services of Supply in Paris. By September, after long, tedious marches with heavy packs on their backs, the men and their officers were ready for anything. They looked in superb physical trim and they were.

During the war, seventeen additional units of Marine replacements, most titled "battalion," were also shipped to France. The second two companies, the 12th and 26th, were disbanded upon arrival on 31 December 1917. Early on, the staff members of the AEF expressed concern that the Marines, because of their commitment to the U.S. Navy, would not be able to provide sufficient replacements for the 4th Brigade. In fact the last replacement battalion, the 12th, consisting of nine officers and 500 enlisted men, arrived in France in June 1919, and thereupon joined the AEF.

The navy provided all medical and morale services for the U.S. Marines. Sixty officers of the medical corps, twelve dental officers, 500 enlisted corpsmen, plus eleven chaplains of every faith were important members of the Marine Brigade and ancillary units. They would provide services far beyond what could normally be expected, suffering heavily in the process and receiving awards matching those of their Marine comrades.[6]

On 24 and 25 September 1917 what was left of the regiment was transferred to the Bourmont training area, about eighty kilometers south of Gondrecourt and billeted in the towns of Damblain and Breuvannes. It was at about this time that Lt. Col. Logan Feland, who was to have such a prominent part in the regiment's history, assumed command of 1/5. He succeeded Turrill and, with the two remaining companies, the 49th and 66th, entrained on 23 September for Breuvannes, Haute-Marne. They were followed the next day by 2/5 and the regiment's headquarters and supply companies, which detrained at Damblain, located about three kilometers from Breuvannes. Colonel Doyen and regimental headquarters were located at Damblain for several months, but on 3 November they, too, moved to Breuvannes.

The Marines found living conditions pretty much the same as those in the Gondrecourt area. Different manure piles, but the same odors.

The barns still had lice, or cooties, as the Americans would call them, and every soldier or Marine was home to countless of the little pests. Delousing every few days or so helped but didn't end their travail.

Colonel Albertus W. Catlin, USMC, commanding the 6th Marines, arrived, with some of his staff, in France on 1 November 1917. By 6 February 1918, the last of the 6th Regiment had arrived at St. Nazaire. The 4th Brigade was "perfected" on 10 February 1918, except for Major Turrill and the 67th Company of the 5th Marines, still on detached duty in England for another month.

In a letter dated 10 November 1917, Gen. John J. Pershing wrote to the major general commandant, George Barnett, explaining why the Marines of the 5th were being used along the lines of communication, among other onerous tasks, and complimenting him on their conduct and state of training.

Your Marines have been under my command for nearly six months, I feel that I can give you a discriminating report as to their excellent standing with their brothers of the Army and their general good conduct. I take this opportunity, also, of giving you the reason for distributing them along our Lines of Communications which, besides being a compliment to their high state of discipline and excellent soldierly appearance, was the natural thing to do as the Marine Regiment was an additional one in the Division and not provided for in the way of transportation and fighting equipment in case the Division should be pushed to the front. When, therefore, services of the rear troops and military and provost guards were needed at our base ports and in Paris it was the Marine Regiment that had to be scattered, in an endeavor to keep the rest of the organized Division intact. I have been obliged to detach a number of your officers as Assistant Provost Marshals in France and in England, all of which I take it you will agree with me was highly complimentary to both officers and men, and was so intended. I can assure you that as soon as our services of the rear troops arrive, including a large number of officers and men for the specific duties now performed by your men, the Marines will be brought back once more under your brigade commander and assigned to the duties which they so much desire in the Second Regular Division, under General Bundy. It is a great pleasure to report on your fine representatives here in France.

The 5th Marines was the first nucleus of the newly formed 2d Division. In October 1917 Doyen was promoted to brigadier general when the first elements of the 6th Regiment arrived to form the 4th Brigade of Marines. In addition to the formation of the 4th Marine Brigade, the 2d Division soon gathered together newly arrived soldiers, the 9th and 23d Infantry Regiments, plus assorted divisional troops into its assembly area. The division was slowly filling out into what was to become the anomaly of a hybrid army/marine division. Although Marines had served under army command many times over the years, the combining of the two services under one command was the first in U.S. history. Doyen, the senior field officer on hand, assumed command of the division and didn't relinquish his role until Maj. Gen. Omar Bundy, USA, who had commanded a brigade in the 1st Division, arrived and assumed command on 8 November. While Doyen commanded the division, Lt. Col. Hiram I. "Hiking Hiram" Bearss took command of the 5th Marines.

A number of organizational changes took place during this period. The 8th Company, which had been attached to 3/5, and which had received a letter of commendation from the base commander at St. Nazaire, was detached and made into the regimental machine-gun company. They and the 45th and 47th Companies entrained at Colombey-lès-Choiseul and soon were also located in the Damblain area. It was the lot of the 8th to enter into a substantial period of training in their new duties. Captain Holland M. Smith, who had been company commander of the 8th, was transferred to the Army School at Gondrecourt on 21 November 1917, and Capt. John H. Fay assumed command the same day.

During January 1918, 1/5 was reinforced by the 12th and 26th Companies, but each was dissolved and the officers and men added to the rest of the battalion's companies to bring them up to strength of 250 men each. The 17th Company, which had been part of the Base Detachment at Bordeaux, also joined 1/5 in January. The 1st Battalion now had the 17th, 49th, and 66th, but were still missing the 67th.

The 18th Company, which had also been with the Base Detachment at Bordeaux, arrived at Damblain on 16 January, and that served to complete the four companies of 2/5. They were now the 18th, 43d, 51st, and 55th Companies.

As the transfers were being accomplished, the 16th Company, which had been at Nevers, reached Damblain, as did the 20th Company, which had recently arrived in France. Now 3/5 was intact and its four companies, the 16th, 20th, 45th, and 47th, were still commanded by Maj.

Charles T. Westcott. It wouldn't be until the regiment was in the Verdun area that Westcott would be relieved by Maj. Edward W. Sturdevant, on 26 March 1918.

In 1917/1918, the Marines, like their comrades of the army, were exposed to an intensely cold winter with few comforts. Their quarters now were mainly frail wooden barracks, which were difficult to heat, and the troops had little wood to heat them with. Heavy snow added to their discomfort, especially in their intensive schedule, which included digging practice trenches. Because they were cold and had the feeling that they would never get to the front, there was a spirit of unrest that winter, particularly when it was learned that the 1st Division was at the front fighting the Germans. On 24 October, Lt. Col. Feland was detached for duty at Bourmont and Capt. George W. Hamilton assumed temporary command of 1/5. He retained command for nearly three months until Maj. Edward A. Greene's arrival on 16 January 1918. In the meantime there was much coming and going for members of the 5th. Officers and men were constantly being sent to the specialist army schools established at Gondrecourt. The regiment sent its quota of selected enlisted Marines to the Army Infantry Candidates School at Langres when it opened in December.

When the 6th Regiment started to arrive, piecemeal, they, too, were assigned duties, much as those the 5th had before them, and the entire 4th Brigade didn't make it into its final form until 10 February 1918. The brigade consisted of both infantry regiments, the 5th and 6th and the 6th Machine Gun Battalion. It was finally all together except for the 67th Company, which was still in England and would miss all the field training the other units of the division underwent that winter and spring, but not the fighting that would come soon enough after.

The 1st Battalion, 6th Marines, which had arrived on 5 October 1917, was living in rather shoddy French wooden barracks just outside St. Nazaire. Upon arrival, the battalion was assigned to ship unloading details and another two hundred Marines each day were detailed to help build a large dam near their camp. Their work was supervised by the 17th Engineers. We are told by one Marine of being practically starved at nearly every meal. Jackson tells us that breakfast, "a very scanty meal it was! The men lined up for seconds and thirds; and even when thirds were forthcoming, the whole [meal] filled a small part of the cavity. It is surprising how we could have kept healthy and strong when we finished the meals so hungry." He also complained about how overworked they were "on almost an empty stomach" with constant threats that if they didn't "do 500 percent better the Germans would kill the last of us in the first attack. . . . This kind of thing added none to the joy of living."

On 15 October Major Hughes and twelve other officers of 1/6 were sent to 1st Corps School at Gondrecourt. Captain Robert E. Adams, who assumed command of 1/6 upon Hughes's departure, shortly after received his majority. On 7 November he followed orders from the local military authorities and sent the 95th Company to do guard duty at Brest and Le Havre, two platoons to each. Jackson, who was a member of the 4th Platoon, 95th Company, adds more commentary about that duty when he states, "It is difficult to understand with such supplies already in France *why we should have had so little to eat.*" (Emphasis added.) Later he mentioned that their rations consisted of tomatoes, hardtack, and corned beef. "I am now sure that this savory combination was invented by a German spy."

It was at Le Havre that part of the 95th Company was located in a large British rest camp for a time. There the Marines became acquainted with "Limeys," Australians, Canadians, and Scotsmen "in their picturesque kilts." It appears that they all got along just fine, which must have been a phenomenal situation, to say the least. Jackson comments on the constant use, by the English, of the word *blawdy*. He mentions that one Englishman said the word four times in a very brief sentence. There are words used by Marines that also appear numerous times in any sentence, or at least that was true during World War II. Fortunately the words used are only four letters long, in most instances.

The company was reassembled on 13 December and took over the Pontanezan Barracks from the French.[7] On 17 December Adams also sent a platoon from the 76th Company and thirty men from the 74th to St. Nazaire for duty as military police and dock guards at Nantes. The balance of the battalion remained at St. Nazaire until 6 January 1918, when the three companies still available, the 74th, 75th, and 76th, entrained for Damblain to join the rest of the 4th Brigade already in residence there. Several weeks later, on 28 January, the 96th Company rejoined the battalion. The U.S. Army colonel who was in command of the Brest warehouses was very upset when "his Marines" were removed from the guard. "They were the only ones he could trust in that commissary." Not so, according to Jackson. According to his story the Marines (including himself) stole anything that wasn't tied down, especially treats like chocolates, jam, and cigarettes. Can you imagine a Marine engaged in the theft of goodies?

The headquarters of the 6th Regiment, along with the Headquarters and Supply Companies and the 73d Machine Gun Company, arrived at St. Nazaire on 1 November 1917. Two weeks later they were established at Bordeaux, followed six days later by 3/6 on 20 November. The latter was soon engaged in arduous labor, building docks near Bassens under the direction of the 18th Engineers. The battalion was soon dispersed on various work details, including provost duties, in the surrounding areas. This continued until 3/6 was relieved by the 162d Regiment, Army National Guard, and on 9 January 1918 entrained for the Damblain area, arriving three days later.

The always late 2d Battalion finally arrived at St. Nazaire on 5 February, but did not disembark until 8 February. That day the battalion entrained for Damblain, and they arrived at their destination three days later. For the first time since 1/6 entrained at Quantico on 16 September 1917, the regiment was together once again.

The story of the 1st Machine Gun Battalion, later the 6th, was only slightly different from that of the 6th Marines. The battalion disembarked from their ship, the *De Kalb,* on 31 December at St. Nazaire and immediately entrained for Damblain. Three days later they detrained at 0600 and the first thing they had to do was to turn in their beloved Lewis guns and carts to the brigade quartermaster. The next thing that happened was the detaching of the 12th and 20th Companies to be returned to the 5th Marines. The 77th Company was assigned to billets in Germainvilliers, while the 81st went to Chaumont-la-Ville. On 12 January each company was issued twelve Hotchkiss machine guns and a dozen ammunition carts to go with them. The Hotchkiss, a French gun, would remain with the Marine Brigade throughout the war, even after the long-desired Browning machine gun was standard issue in the AEF. Captain John P. Harvis, battalion quartermaster who had been detached for service with the 5th Marines was returned to his parent organization. In addition, the 15th and 23d Machine Gun Companies, which had been attached to the 5th Marines at Gondrecourt, were reassigned to the 6th Machine Gun Battalion. The latter designation was made official in General Order No. 4, which was issued on 15 January 1918.

The following officers were commanding each company at this time: Capt. Matthew H. Kingman, 15th Company; Capt. John P. McCann, 23d

Company; Capt. Louis R. deRoode, 77th Company; and lastly, Capt. Littleton W. T. Waller Jr., 81st Company. Subsequently, on 30 January 1918, Capt. Augustus Hale was assigned as second-in-command to deRoode of 77th Company. Little change to the location or training occured and the battalion settled in until their next move. That would be to enter the Verdun area for combat experience in mid-March 1918.

Until February 1918, any training of the Marines was crippled by their being shunted aside for duties previously mentioned. By mid-month, brigade training began in earnest, and it wasn't long afterward that their leadership were satisfied with the results. The usual training any Marine received prior to that time was less than adequate, at least as compared to the soldiers in the army. The average Marine received six weeks in boot camp, two more at Quantico, and practically nothing in France, whereas most soldiers received at least six months' training in the United States. Worse, the training received by the Marines was almost exclusively based on trench warfare. Their teachers after all, were French and sometimes British officers, whose total sum of knowledge about soldiering was deficient at best. Trench warfare was not what Pershing had planned as the course for his AEF, but that was the training that was received, at least by the earliest units that arrived in France. Only at the 2d Division's sojourn in the Verdun Sector would the officers and men of the division use that training. In the two months they were in that sector, they suffered few casualties—the result of trench protection from shell and machine-gun fire, no doubt. Marine rifle training excelled similar army training. Unfortunately, as we shall see, that was helpful, but no match against artillery and machine-gun fire.

Major Holland McT. Smith, Brigade Adjutant, began keeping a diary on 1 March 1918 in honor of his "baby boy." On the next day's entry, 2 March, he described what was going on as far as the fighting men were concerned.

This morning we went out in a blinding snow storm to witness the regiments manoeuvres. When we returned, the moving picture operator caught us. Our hats and overcoats were encrusted in snow and ice. We looked like we had really begun to fight. This afternoon I visited Shearer [Maj. Maurice E.] in Robécourt. We had a good time reminising. Paid my mess bill for 13 days = 110 Francs. The snow is still falling and everything is covered with slush. To-

morrow is a holiday (Sunday) for the men—they are working very
hard getting ready—for what? Poor devils—we will soon be [sic]
death in the face, but thank God, we have the courage to fight for
justice and right.[8]

The following day, Sunday, after a musicale provided by the enlisted
men, they were given tea, a "treat." Smith added: "Poor chaps! They get
few pleasures and they are the ones who pay the highest. One must respect the private soldier for he is the one who will win the war."[9] Smith
revealed that the sick list was growing: "Yesterday there were 94 men admitted to the sick list but the training went on . . . the weather counts
for nothing in France." A week later he adds, "Everyone is restless and
ready to move. How anxious we will be to get back—we hear our sector
is to be a very quiet one. I hope so." It appears, from his diary entries,
that Smith and Lt. Col. Frederick M. Wise Jr. were close comrades. Or
at least each was winning money from the other playing bridge on almost a daily basis.

General Order No. 21, 2d Division, 10 March 1918, directed, in part,
that "for convenience of designation, the rifle and machine gun companies of the—(brigade)—of this division will be lettered." Apparently,
until sometime after the termination of hostilities, the Marine units
kept their numeric designation, at least among their own records, although McClellan added alpha to his numeric designation in his history, almost as an afterthought, it seems. The remaining "lost" company,
the 67th, with 3 officers and 163 men, returned to the 5th Marines,
from Southampton, England, arriving on 11 March 1918, and now the
brigade was "perfect." Major Julius S. Turrill reassumed command from
Greene on 12 March 1918.
    It was now time for the division to enhance its heretofore minimal
training. The division was assigned to frontline duty in the Verdun Sector. The 4th Brigade remained in the Bourmont training area until 14
March 1918, when it then proceeded to Vitry-le-François, entering the
lines on the night of 16–17 March.

Notes

1 Jackson, *Experiences of a Texas Soldier.* This was in October.

2 Sibert, an exceptionally capable engineering officer, was to be relieved by General Pershing in mid-December 1917 and Major General Robert L. Bullard, USA, was selected as his replacement.

3 The 1st Division had that honor when, in October 1917, it entered a quiet area in Toul for its baptism of fire.

4 The term *Marines* didn't officially come about until the early 1930s. I use that rather than the more stilted *regiment.* Army officers would frequently refer to the "Fifth [or Sixth] Marines" in their official communiques. I also use the numbered company rather than using the alpha designation then in common use within the AEF because that is the manner used by the Marines themselves.

5 There were many major and lieutenant colonel Marines who desired to get into the fray, but there was only one Marine brigade and just so many berths open for them. The army willingly accepted the surplus and most earned enviable reputations. See a partial listing in the chapter entitled Other Marine Activities in France.

6 I haven't met every Marine there ever was, but those I know, especially those who served in combat, have the highest personal regard for navy corpsmen. They were always there when a Marine needed one. Many a Marine's life is owed to a "Doc."

7 Pontanezan became very famous throughout the AEF in later months. The conditions at what was to become the main receiving and dispersing camp for the American army were intolerable. Many men died, primarily from influenza, during the course of the year and, with but one exception, no matter who was in charge it remained a "death camp." The deviation came about when Brig. Gen. Smedley D. Butler, USMC, was assigned to clean up the mess. He did so in short order and earned the plaudits of millions of American soldiers, as well as the nickname "General Duckboard."

8 Holland M. Smith unpublished diary.

9 Ibid. This is a clear indication of what later events proved, and that is what Smith thought of the men first, last, and always.

3: Verdun

I am always glad to try anything once.
—American proverb

The 4th Marine Brigade, now consisting of 280 officers and 9,164 enlisted men,[1] remained in the Bourmont area until 14 March, when it commenced movement into sub-sectors of the Verdun front. Rumors had been flying since at least 1 March that the brigade would soon get into the front lines. To substantiate that information, trench equipment started coming in to the brigade quartermaster, such as boots, knives, and extra clothing to protect against the cold, damp trenches. As additional support for the rumors two more things happened that pretty much sealed the deal: practice billeting parties were sent out, and even more so, seabags were packed and stored. The only clothing retained was what could be carried in a man's pack. Every Marine knows what that means: "We're on our way."

On Friday, 13 March, at Damblain, 2/5 entrained, the first Marines to move toward the enemy. That date might have frightened off anybody going into action for the first time, but presumably not the Marines. On the evening of 14 March the battalion arrived at Dugny and there, at 2200 hours, detrained a very short distance from the front lines. They managed to unload all their paraphernalia, which included rolling stock and rations, and had all their gear arranged for trucks to pick it up when a German aviator spotted the train unloading and called in his artillery. In the meantime, according to reports, a very ardent YMCA worker was anxious to provide the troops with hot chocolate and insisted that they remain at the station until all were so decorated. They waited, but it wasn't long before the enemy artillery got the range and plastered the station with HE, hurting no Marines but destroying a lieutenant's trunk and nearly all the regiment's band instruments. No report on what happened to the industrious civilian. Otherwise, that was all the Boche could claim for their efforts. The balance of the brigade arrived within the following four days, and by 17 March 1918, all were in barracks or dugouts as assigned. If there were any Irish in the brigade, and most likely there were a few, some celebration must have occurred to honor the memory of the greatest saint and scholar on the calendar.

They then marched to Camp Nivolette where, on the march, for the first time the force was subjected to artillery fire. As the saying goes, that would soon separate the men from the boys. The 8th Machine Gun and Headquarters Company both left Breuvannes on 14 March and arrived at Dugny on the 15th. On their march to Somme-dieu that night shells whistled harmlessly overhead but no doubt created some anxiety among the troops. On the 15th 3/5 proceeded from Colombey to Breuvannes and entrained to travel to Lemmes. The battalion then marched to its billets at Ancemont. They were followed at Lemmes on the 17th by 1/5, which then marched to Camp Nivolette and occupied the same billets just vacated by 2/5. Their headquarters was established at Toulon. The 1st Battalion was placed in support near the center of the corps sector, Montgirmont, while 3/5 went into camp a little farther back and continued their training. The 2d Battalion's semiofficial history describes their activity in what was, in the beginning at least, a rather inactive sector.

> Here nightly patrols and wiring were carried out. There was intermittent machine-gun fire at night and an occasional bombardment, especially on rear positions and communicating trenches. Much information and experience was obtained especially in correct ways in organizing a position and patrolling in darkness. It was in this sector that we saw and felt the explosion of a tremendous land mine.[2]

The 5th Marines were relieved of their section of the line on the evening of 29 March. The next evening, having marched northward all day, but still on the Verdun front, the regiment took over the subsector Eix-Moulainville-Châtillon. On the following night, 1 April, 3/6 relieved elements of the French army just to the right of the 5th Marines. That same date, headquarters of the 4th Brigade was established at PC (Post of Command) Moscou. For the balance of the month both regiments occupied themselves with the same tasks as before and sent many officers to 1st Corps School at Gondrecourt and others to the Army General Staff College at Langres. Six Marine officers graduated from the staff college during the war: Lt. Col. Richard P. Williams and Majors Harry R. Lay, Franklin B. Garrett, Edward W. Sturdevant, Holland M. Smith, and Robert E. Adams. It was also at about this time that Marines began changing clothing. Jackson mentions that the morale wasn't at its highest because "a lot of the boys were ragged . . . by ragged I do not mean a little worn." While the 95th Company was at rest at Champigneulles they "discarded [uniforms] for new army clothes."

At this time members of the brigade engaged in the usual practices of any man in a rest camp near the front lines: buying everything one could lay his hands upon. Food, more food, and lastly, food. Chicken, eggs, fruit—mainly dried, milk, and always freshly baked French bread. The men were always hungry. Never did any, while in the vicinity of the front, ever have enough to eat or, for that matter, drink. Officers probably fared better, at least while not at the front.

Getting chow to the men in the front lines was always a spectacular event for those engaged. Usually the food (humorously called) consisted of coffee—which was always cold when it finally arrived—punk, and stew. Punk, of course, was bread, as any brig rat already knows. The "stew" was made of water, potatoes, meat, and dirt. It has been charged that the stew was probably in cold storage for lengthy periods before the mess sergeant and his fellow villains slapped it together. No flavor existed and none was expected. It appears as though the mess people used no condiments to decorate the slum, nor any other foodstuff.

Bringing the chow to the troops was the next step. The stuff was put into large metal cans and attached to long, specially made poles for carrying, with a man at each end. The trip included traversing rough ground, and the swinging cans made that voyage extremely difficult, particularly when going through a narrow trench with a base of slimy mud. Some tried traveling on the top of trenches, but a few well-placed shells soon made the bottom much more attractive. Usually, no more than six men were assigned the task of fetching the food. When they finally arrived, the amount of food was never enough to fill the stomachs of 250 men, which were continually empty. Naturally, as is always the case, some mess sergeants went through hell to get food to the troops. Others just took it easy upon themselves and stayed in safe places when the going got rough.

Possibly, the thing that adversely affected many men most was the constant availability of alcohol. The French were used to having wine, at most every meal, but not so the majority of Americans. In addition to *vin rouge* and *vin blanc* there was always the stronger cognac for those whose taste buds were already refined. Drunkenness became a common malady for many members of the AEF, including Marines and those unfortunate sailors who were associated with them. One story tells of a corpsman with a snootful—no, much more than that—who fell down in the middle of a march on a snow-swept road, going practically into a coma. No matter what the Marines around him tried, they couldn't keep him upright. He kept kicking his legs in the air, all the while muttering incoherently. He survived that experience, but who knows how many times this was repeated? Few Marines came back without some taste of the "creature," hence the fallacy of prohibition, because the rest of the AEF must also have been so afflicted.

Men were not the only creatures to suffer from the war. Mules were used for most activities requiring the carrying of supplies and rations. They frequently died at the same time their human handlers did, usually without notice. A mule train of four teams of four mules each, under command of QM Sgt. P. H. Muller, was sent out to aid the 3d battalion, 6th Marines, in their transitory movement, on the evening of 31 March. Each team was driven by a corporal; J. A. Endress, A. A. Jayko, J. J. Kozisek, and W. V. Moffett. When one team arrived at its destination, Camp Douzaine, with the property of 3/6, part of the load was dropped at Camp "A," while the other teams proceeded to Camp "C-4" where they were taken under German artillery fire. Shrapnel and high explosives bombarded the area and one shell struck directly in the center of the team handled by Endress. He was blown sky high and tossed across the road, but amazingly wasn't wounded. Three mules were killed and one was wounded, but, fortunately, the other animals and humans weren't. First Lieutenant Hugh McFarland and QM Sergeant Carlos "behaved with great coolness, remaining at their posts," as did the teamsters, who continued to unload their wagons before removing the dead and wounded animals.

Meanwhile the 6th Marines were undergoing a similar experience. Major Sibley and 3/6 relieved the French on the night of 18–19 March at Mont-sous-les-Côtes. The 82d, 83d, and 84th Companies were on line and the 97th Company in reserve. There they had another French battalion between them and 2/5 on the front line. The plan was to leave each battalion in the front line for about ten days and then relieve them. Therefore, on 28 March 2/5 and the 8th Machine Gun Company were relieved by 1/5 and 2/6 relieved 3/6. During this time the Germans launched an aggressive attack upon the British at a point near where the British and French armies joined. Major adjustments all along the line were made and the French soon were moving divisions from the Verdun front farther north to meet the threat. This resulted in a significant move by the Marines. The 5th Marines and a French regiment were assigned to hold a divisional position east of Verdun, relieving an entire French division. The arrangement was as follows: 1/5 occupied the extreme left flank and 3/5 the right. They were supported by 2/5 in reserve. The 6th Marines remained where they were but also took over the original positions of the 5th Marines in addition to their own. Warren Jackson gives a detailed description of the services of the 6th Marines and of the brigade, in and about the Verdun area—the best I've ever seen. He tells us about the relationship between the two regiments, and about being

in Sommedieue where there were also some 5th Marines, who also had our deep respect. They were older in the service than we were by several months . . . by virtue of their experience, we were hopelessly and everlastingly inferior to them. An impossible gulf lay between them and us.

Several new names replaced those administrators at brigade headquarters. Major Holland M. Smith became adjutant, with Capt. Henry L. Larsen, assistant adjutant, and 1st Lt. Benjamin S. Goodman intelligence officer and General Doyen's aide-de-camp. Captain George K. Shuler was regimental adjutant to Col. Wendell C. Neville, 5th Marines, and Maj. Edward A. Greene had command of 1/5 until Major Turrill relieved him on 13 March. Major Charles T. Westcott commanded 3/5 until relieved by Maj. Edward W. Sturdevant on 26 March. Sturdevant on 1 May 1918 was ordered to command an army battalion of the 30th Infantry, 3d Division, and was replaced by Maj. Benjamin S. Berry, who would retain command until being badly wounded at Belleau Wood. The 6th Marines remained much the same, with few changes except for the relief of Maj. Robert E. Adams at 1/6 by Maj. Maurice E. Shearer, on 25 April. Adams then joined the 38th Infantry, 3d Division, to command a battalion. Major Berton W. Sibley, who became ill, was relieved of command of 3/6 for the period between 29 March until 6 April 1918 at the tail end of the activity in the Verdun Sector.

The 5th Marines were assigned the subsector Montgirmont–Les Eparges, PC located at Ravine, and the 6th Marines at Mont-sous-les-

Côtes, PC at Boues. Special Order No. 2 assigned the 6th Machine Gun Battalion companies as follows: the 77th to 1/5; 23d to 3/5; 15th to 1/6; 81st to 2/6 with the regimental machine-gun companies taking position to support 2/5 and 3/6. The machine-gun companies participated, along with regular Marine infantry, in repelling raiding parties, in patrolling no-man's-land, and constructing gun emplacements and trenches, as well as providing indirect and harassing fire.

General Doyen toured his sector, covering about eight miles of muddy, and consequently slippery, trenches every day. On one of these inspections, on his return trip, he had a narrow escape from an explosion that occurred in an ammunition dugout which he had passed only seconds before. A private in the dugout was not as lucky; he stumbled out into the trench, covered with blood and with a severely injured left hand. Additionally, the weather was bitterly cold that winter and the men were ill prepared for its ferocity. According to a memoir, during this period, two Marines died of exposure. Possibly there were more. The falling snow, which was soon waist high and much deeper than southerners were used to, naturally affected them more than it did lads from north of the Mason-Dixon line.

Many men expired for reasons other than enemy fire. Hatred for real or imagined slights caused some casualties, as it always had when men have command over other men. One can only guess at how many commissioned or noncommissioned officers met untimely deaths or wounds from American bullets while in combat. Personal memoirs with real detail are often the outlet for men's opinions of the officers and noncoms. Many were laudatory, but some were devastatingly negative. One memoirist continually tears down every officer and noncom with whom he came in contact, in some instances calling, by name, certain officers cowards or worse. Others are more balanced and appear more reasonable in their outlook. Any war and any army will always have those who look after themselves, sometimes to the detriment of those whom they command. But most officers and noncoms of the 4th Brigade were highly courageous, and their many awards and citations are evidence of what I state. I should add that the army and navy officers who were associated with the brigade were generally of the highest type available, anywhere.

It also appears that in World War I Americans were executed for what now seem to be less than adequate reasons. Occasionally spies were found posing in American uniforms; Mackin makes that very clear in his memoir. They were disposed of without further ado. No one had the time to take them back for interrogation or trial. It was a tough life.

• • •

Upon reaching their final positions, each regiment held two battalions in reserve and one on the line. In the 5th Marines, 1/5 had the honor, and in the 6th, 3/6. 1/5 entered its position the night of 16–17 March and 3/6 on 18 March 1918. Until 13 May, all battalions had the opportunity to take their places in the front line, with patrol or raiding parties active every night. They also established listening posts and captured machine-gun positions, temporarily reducing the guns' effectiveness. They engaged in many other activities that would gain them experience. The reserve troops also kept busy digging or repairing trenches.

The Germans always seemed to be aware of a change in the occupants of sections of the line, and this operation was no different. Shortly after the 4th Brigade took up its part of the subsector, enemy artillery and aviation began to actively harass the Marines, as did the German infantry. Raiding parties and patrol encounters occurred on a regular basis, giving the new troops good training, which benefited them in later contact.

During this period several casualties occurred among the Marines. The first Marine combat casualty in France was Pvt. Emil H. Gehrke, 82d Company, 3/6, when on 1 April 1918 he received several shell fragments through his chest, killing him instantly. Privates John R. Gabriel, Anton F. Hoesli, and Harry R. Williams, all of the 82d, were also wounded, Williams dying of his wounds on the following day.

It was at this time that the 6th Machine Gun Battalion undertook to establish the field arrangement it would use for the next eight months. Each of four rifle battalions would have one machine-gun company assigned to it. The other two battalions would have their own regimental machine gun companies supporting them. In the Verdun area the 15th Company was assigned to 3/6, Sibley's group; the 23d Company went with 2/5, "Fritz" Wise's battalion; the 77th Company with 3/5, which was still commanded by Westcott but would soon change to Sturdevant; and finally, the 81st Company went with 2/6, Tommy Holcomb's lads. Because enemy air activity was so intense, no outdoor drills were held before the companies went into the trenches. Even the animals had to be protected. They weren't exercised until after dark. Other after-dark activities included, under French supervision, the digging of machine-gun emplacements and trenches. While in the Verdun sector the companies of the battalion were constantly on the move to and from their designated areas and suffered ten casualties. Five infantry second lieutenants from the U.S. Army joined the 6th Machine Gun Battalion, straight from the

II Corps School. They may have been the first to come, but it wasn't long before the Marine Brigade had upwards of fifty army officers serving as platoon leaders. Most performed at the highest possible level until the greater part of them were transferred out of the brigade after Soissons. Those who survived. Many didn't.

Private Walter A. Shanley of the 6th Marines wrote of his and his buddies' disillusionment at working harder in the ten-day rest period than while in the trenches for the other ten. He tells of using the "Italian Fountain-pen," which never got rusty like their rifles. It was a shovel he was describing. *Dig* was the war cry and dig they did. Many a Marine had thrown away the pickax or shovel he had been issued prior to reaching the sector. Most had no idea why they received them and it was just another weight to lug about. Undoubtedly, all wished they had kept them when they realized how necessary they were for survival. It was also about the same time that many were issued machetes, which were discarded along with the shovels.

Doyen, required by general orders for the physical examination that all officers of the force were obliged to take, left for General Headquarters, AEF. He was back at brigade headquarters by 11 April, unaware that because he didn't meet the physical standards established by General Pershing, he would be relieved of command of the brigade he had led since it was formed.

Joe Feingold of the 67th Company relates how the 5th Marines were marched "65 kilometers" from St. Mihiel to Camp Joffre, passing the shattered city of Verdun on the way. After arriving at Camp Joffre, the company was assigned to the "Eix Sector" and remained for "thirty days straight." He complained of scarce food consisting of only two meals a day. He described the living quarters as "dugouts forty feet below ground" and being personally dirty "as it was hard to get water." Then he comments that water was so scarce, they sometimes saved a bit of coffee to shave in.

After an artillery attack of 6 April 1918, the Germans, anxious to impress the Americans who were new on this front, attempted a raid upon the trenches occupied by the 74th Company, Capt. Adolph B. Miller commanding, in the ruined village of Trésauvaux. The raid was successfully repulsed, costing the Germans four men. One Marine was killed and three were wounded in this fracas.

On the evening of 9 April 1918, the Germans bombarded the town of Mont. When Private James E. Hatcher spotted Pvt. Clarence S.

Markham being tossed into the street by an explosion, he, without hesitating, carried the wounded Markham out of harm's way. For his bravery he was highly commended in General Order No. 35, issued on 10 May 1918. In the same orders, Sgt. Alfred G. Slyke, 77th Company, 6th Machine Gun Battalion, was also commended for bravery and self-sacrifice while continuing to command his gun in action, even though pinned under heavy timbers and debris.

It was at about this same period that the Germans delivered a heavy bombardment of gas shells on the 4th Brigade. On 12 April, all the companies of 1/6, and especially the 74th Company then in reserve at Camp Fontaine St. Robert, were heavily shelled, with the majority of the rounds gas shells. The accurate fire caught many men in their billets before they could escape. Nearly the entire 74th Company, 220 men and all of the officers, were evacuated in serious condition. Forty of them died later as a result of this bombardment. The company history says,

> 28 men died from gas wounds, and practically the entire company was evacuated to the hospitals, *where they laid between life and death for months.* On May 5 at Somme-Dieu the company was reorganized with replacements from the Second Replacement Battalion. . . . From the 11th until the 30th the new men trained at Ontrepont and Petite Serans. [Emphasis added][3]

The commanding officer of 1/6, Maj. Robert E. Adams, was relieved on 25 April by Maj. Maurice E. Shearer and assigned to detached duty.[4]

In all, the 6th Regiment had 9 officers and 305 enlisted men poisoned and evacuated to a hospital area. Two corpsman, Ph. Mate 3d Class Fred C. Schaffner and Hospital Apprentice 1st Class Carl O. Kingsbury, U.S. Navy, though suffering greatly from the mustard gas themselves, courageously ministered to the tormented Marines, seeing to their evacuation and care, until they, too, succumbed, with Schaffner dying and Kingsbury afflicted severely by the gas. These were the first corpsmen of this war to serve their patients in this fashion, but certainly not the last. Many more would join Schaffner and the nineteen Marines in the months ahead.

More action followed the gas attack on the 12th. During a four-hour bombardment of Bonchamp with gas and high-explosive shells, much damage was done to the telephone lines. It was necessary to rapidly reestablish lines of communication, so immediate repairs had to be made. A group led by Sgt. Edward La Cure, and which included Pvts.

Edmund Fons and Mac Pope, made repairs while wearing their gas masks. Much of the work took place under continuous shell fire and the effects of poisonous gas. Colonel Catlin cited them in General Order No. 35, for their gallant efforts.

A patrol of 5th Regiment Marines and French soldiers earned another commendation in General Order No. 35, for their successful attack on the night of 17 April 1918, out of Eix, near Demi-Lune. Second Lieutenant Max D. Gilfillan, backed by Sergeant Louis Cukela, were both awarded the Croix de Guerre and were both cited in General Order No. 35 for their individual actions. Corporal John L. Kuhn was killed in action, and he and Pvts. George C. Brookes and Walter Klamm were also cited. The patrol encountered a German patrol, and in the resulting firefight they suffered an additional two Marines wounded and two missing.

The 84th Company of 3/6, at 0110 hours on 21 April, repulsed a raid around the town of Villers by the "Hindenburg Circus," a group of *Sturmtruppen* that had been raising hell on the line. The Boche were equipped with flamethrowers, grenades, knives, and pistols, and assaulted just after a German box barrage terminated. From the report of the operation, the Germans used hand grenades exclusively, even after they occupied the same trench as the Marines. They also used flares to light up the night; one man in particular was seen firing flares continually from another trench. When Marines tried firing their own flares, they failed six times. They then tried two three-star flares and fared as poorly as before. "All lines of communication were cut . . . someone found two more six-star flares and they fired." A barrage from friendly artillery immediately answered the call raised by the flares, but knowing it was to cease in ten minutes, two volunteers were called for to race to the guns to request a continuance of the fire. They were Pvts. Earl H. Sleeth and Frank H. Hullinger. Both ran through an intense bombardment on the road from Villers to Mont. Hullinger fell exhausted upon reaching Mont but Sleeth made the run and returned from the artillery with new flares. Within twenty minutes from the end of the German bombardment until Sleeth returned, the enemy ceased to trouble the 84th Company. The report goes on to state that Cpl. Clarence H. Babb, while going on duty, was wounded within thirty yards of his post. He crawled to his post and was found to have eighteen wounds as he lay there exhausted. Second Lieutenant Allan C. Perkinson, Corporal Babb, and Privates Hullinger and Sleeth were all awarded the Croix de Guerre.

On the same night of 20–21 April, 1/5 was relieved by 3/5. The 45th Company of 3/5 occupied that part of the trench line through the town of Eix and connected with the 16th Company to their right flank, which was also in part of the town. They in turn connected with the 20th Company at Moulinville-la-Bas, which in turn connected with the 47th Company on the extreme right flank of the line. Between 0400 and 0500 hours on the morning of 21 April, the Germans laid down a barrage upon 45th Company followed by a raiding party that was repulsed before it got much beyond the first line of wire. Three men in the battalion were killed and eleven were wounded. The Germans seemed to have fared better, where numbers are concerned. They lost two officers, and two enlisted men killed or who later died of wounds. Reports indicate that several German ambulances were seen going to the rear, which seems to signify that many more Germans sustained losses in that raid than those previously reported. In fact, their casualties may have been quite heavy. Captain Benjamin S. Berry, then in command of the company, along with 2d Lts. E. E. Conroy and Edward B. Hope, plus nine enlisted men, were awarded the Croix de Guerre for their courageous actions during the raid.

The Supply Company of the 5th Marines was shelled on the night of 22 April with two men killed and three wounded. Losses in horses and mules were very heavy. The next night the Germans again shelled the same company killing another Marine and wounding two more. Stables were destroyed along with two more horses and thirteen mules. Two U.S. Navy men, Dental Surgeon Alexander G. Lyle and Pharmacist Mate 1st Class Tony Sommer, were cited in General Order No. 35 for acts of bravery during the incidents.

Several more Marines earned listings on General Order No. 35 for activities in this sector. Gunnery Sergeant Arthur H. Johnson of the 5th Marines "displayed conspicuous courage and leadership with his combat group while engaged with superior forces of the enemy on 24 April 1918." One Marine, Corporal Wolcott Wichenbaugh of the 18th Company, 2/5, received the following citation.

On 22 April when the patrol of which he was a member was rushed by superior numbers near the enemy's trenches, he displayed coolness and courage before and after the wounding of his leader, Second Lieutenant A. L. Sundval, whom he rescued from the hands of the enemy, and half dragged and half carried back to his own lines.

Brigadier General Charles A. Doyen issued General Order No. 1, 4th Brigade of Marines, on 25 April 1918. In it he stated that he had assumed command of the Northern Sector in "obedience to orders from the Commanding General of the 33d Infantry Division." The sector included the subsectors Moulainville and Ronvaux. General Order No. 3 of the brigade, dated 1 May, designated Maj. Edward B. Cole as brigade machine-gun officer. And on the same date, five Marine officers were detached from the brigade and ordered to the 3d Division, which had just arrived in France. The 3d was listed as a "regular" division but was short of senior officers, especially those with combat experience, and the 4th Brigade had more field officers than they could use. Major Robert L. Denig was assigned to command the 1st Battalion, 30th Infantry; Maj. Edward W. Sturdevant to the 3d Battalion, 30th Infantry; Maj. Robert E. Adams to the 3d Battalion, 38th Infantry; Maj. Harry G. Bartlett to the 2d Battalion, 7th Infantry; and Maj. Littleton W. T. Waller Jr. to the 8th Machine Gun Battalion. Within a few months most of the officers would be back with their beloved Marines, but only after Belleau Wood and Soissons were over. Waller was the only one who would return sooner to the brigade.

On the night of 28 March, 2/6 relieved 3/6 and occupied the towns of Mesnil, Bonzée, and Mont-sous-les-Côtes. The usual reliefs took place for several weeks and no real action of any kind disturbed the peace until 20–21 April. At that time two companies, the 45th of 3/5 under Maj. Benjamin Berry,[5] and the 84th Company, 3/6, were the subject of intense German attention. A platoon of the 45th, commanded by 2d Lt. Edward B. Hope, which had just finished relieving 1/5 at Eix at night, were on the extreme left of the divisional and corps sector on a commanding ridge. The Germans desired that ridge and after a severe bombardment launched a massive, well-planned raid on that section of the line. The specially trained raiding party left behind two officers and two enlisted hanging on the wire after the Marines were finished with them. Observers reported that the enemy carried a large number of Germans back with them when they retired. But Hope's losses were heavy: three Marines killed and eleven wounded. The brigade diary entry, signed by Neville, gave the date as the night of 19–20 April, but most sources agree on 20–21 as the correct night. The French recognized the implications of this success and awarded the Croix de Guerre to a number of the officers and men who had participated in the brawl. Their French liaison officer, a Lieutenant Viaud, reported to

command that "our troops behaved admirably." The 84th had a similar
experience. A raiding party, loosely identified as the "Hindenburg Circus," raided their trenches with flamethrowers and grenades that same
night. The raid was also repulsed with rifle fire and grenades. There were
no Marine casualties reported. German losses, if any, weren't noted.[6]

During these few nights there was an inordinate amount of activity
reported by Neville to division. One such bears an adequate exposure
because of the modest failures and the overall learning experience it
reflected.

1. Lieutenant Fred H. Becker, U.S.R., and 30 men of Co. E.
(18th) were ordered to place themselves in ambush in the vicinity of MANDRÉ FARM, it having been reported that two Germans
were seen making towards this place late in the afternoon of
April 19th. 2nd Lieut. August L. Sundvall, [sic][7] U.S.R., the Battalion Intelligence officer, accompanied the party. At about 1:00
A.M. six Germans were observed in the vicinity. Our party was divided, one group going with Lieut. Sundvall and the other remaining with Lieut. Becker. The object of dividing was to surround and capture these six of the enemy. The group under
Lieut. Sundvall probably got on the wrong bearing. A member
of the group, Sergeant Parks who speaks German, warned the
others that they were nearing a German working party as he
heard the language spoken and the noises made by tools. They
kept on and came upon the enemy and were challenged. All
dropped to the ground, an order was heard in German for half
the party to get their arms, they were so close that the noise of
putting on equipment could be plainly heard. Then for about
ten minutes all was quiet. At the end of this time Lieut. Sundvall
gave the order to retire by the left flank. As soon as this movement was started fire from machine guns was opened on them
and grenades were thrown. During the withdrawal Lieut. Sundvall and Private Kenneth C. Sands were wounded. Gunnery
Sergeant Elmore Butler and Private Ray Azeltine were either
killed or badly wounded, both are missing.

2. Sergeant Parks was sent to bring up Lieut. Becker and the
remainder of the party, this was unfortunate, as with the wounding of Lieut. Sundvall and disappearance of Gunnery Sergeant
Butler this group was without a leader. The group withdrew to our
lines. The group under Lieut. Becker joined with a patrol from
Co. F (43d).

3. The enemy were working on a trench east of BLANZEE, Trench de GRUSSON which had been recently destroyed by our artillery fire. They made no attempt to attack even though there were a large number of them with three machine guns or automatic rifles.

4. Private Sands, while trying to fix his pistol which had jammed, was wounded and brought in by Privates Gerald R. Cortwright and Paul Warsocki. Lieut. Sundvall was carried in by Corporal Wolcott Winchenbaugh.[8]

Holland Smith went one full month between entries, from 10 March till 11 April. On that date he noted that a German aeroplane was "driven back by shell fire. The Boche passed close over our heads and the [blank] had to hustle back." The following day he made an interesting entry that indicated that a U.S. Naval gun mounted on a train flat car were close by. "Today the large 13 inch fired on a city [Conflans] 30 kilometers away. And the other guns were firing too and we had quite a day of it. Tomorrow the reprisal will come." The reprisal, he noted, was the violent gas attack upon the 74th Company described previously. He also made a strong comment about a beating that the 9th Infantry inflicted upon the "Bosche [sic], killing, it is reported, 60 men and capturing 10 men and two machine guns."

Their time was nearly over and they had in truth learned a great deal about trench warfare and been blooded in a relatively quiet sector. It was time for the Marines to be pulled out of the lines. The brigade had spent the better part of two months in trenches on the front lines when they were withdrawn on 14 May and transferred to an area around Vitry-le-François, west of Paris, for open-warfare training. There the brigade learned many lessons of war that would assist them in the operations to come in June. Not many Marines ever got any closer than the thirty or so miles to the great city of Paris. Instead, they spent little free time in the towns and villages around them. One of the towns close by was named Marines, a fact that wasn't lost on the members of the brigade, and the name remained in many memories of those who survived the dark days ahead.

One of the most controversial actions during this period was the dismissal of Brig. Gen. Charles Doyen from command of the brigade he had formed, trained, and led. Doyen, who had failed his army physical exam, was relieved by Pershing and sent back to the States, with a modestly worded salutation. It is true that Pershing refused to keep any officers of the AEF who couldn't meet the exacting physical and mental standards set for them, and many deserved to be sent home. This action would have the most profound impact upon relations between Barnett and Pershing, and upon army and Marine Corps attitudes, one to the other, for many years to come. The Corps saw it as another attempt by Pershing and his cronies to minimize the 4th Brigade's independence and usefulness in France. It was no great secret that Pershing was not in favor of accepting any Marines in France and only took what he couldn't refuse because of the political and interservice machinations of Barnett, who worked very well behind the scenes in Washington.

There was a certain level of rancor in the brigade because Doyen was not only well liked, he was well regarded professionally. It was he who had pulled together and trained the team who would go on to such fame in the future. The official historian of the period, Edwin N. McClellan, briefly notes that

> on May 6, 1918 Brig. Gen. James G. Harbord assumed command of the brigade, relieving Brig. Gen. Doyen who had been ordered to the United States on account of his physical condition. Brig. Gen. Doyen relinquished command of the brigade *most unwillingly*, and the reasons for his relief are best set forth in the words of the citation of a Navy distinguished service medal posthumously awarded to him, reading as follows: [Emphasis added.]

> By reason of his abilities and personal efforts, he brought this brigade to the very high state of efficiency which enabled it to successfully resist the German army in the Chateau-Thierry sector and Belleau Woods. The strong efforts on his part for nearly a year undermined his health and necessitated his being invalided [sic] to the United States before having the opportunity to command the brigade in action, but his work was shown by the excellent service rendered by the brigade, not only at Belleau Woods, but during the entire campaign when they fought many battles.[9]

Pershing sent a letter to Doyen in which he said, in part, "Your service has been satisfactory and your command is considered one of the best in France. I have nothing but praise for the service which you have rendered in this command."[10] Pershing cabled home that Doyen "is an excellent officer, has rendered most valuable service and has brought his Brigade to his efficiency. I very reluctantly return him to the United States." General Omar Bundy, divisional commander, recommended that Doyen be promoted to major general with the statement that "it is a well-recognized fact that the excellent condition of this brigade is due largely to [Doyen]." Pershing, in order to quickly close whatever doors Bundy might have opened, added a postscript to Bundy's statement which expressed his regrets that Doyen's "physical condition prevents a recommendation for his promotion to major general to which he might otherwise be entitled."

One additional person made comment about Doyen's relief. Holland Smith wrote in his diary on 30 April,

> The General received notice today that he had been found phys-ically disqualified and Gen. Harbord, the Chief of Staff of Gen. Per-shing was to relieve him. We are all saddened as we feel this is the first blow. The Brigade is broken-hearted. We feel like a lost soul. May God help us in our humiliation and give us the courage to do the best we can to beat the Boche. We prophecy [sic] now that the marines will be withdrawn from France or that we may form a casual division and be under [unknown] . . .[11]

The diary continues raving about the loss of Doyen and the conse-quently lowered morale among the brigade officers. Doyen and Smith met with Neville and he, too, was "quite sad." Of course, Neville was an-ticipating a promotion to brigadier general and may have expected that he would get the brigade should that promotion happen soon. On 2 May Smith made an entry that "we expect to make a fight against the Army's decision. We have always been fortunate in our fights with them. *Tomorrow many officers are to be courtmartialed for* [blank]. It is going to be bad for the morale. General D. [oyen] is President of the Court. Puryear [Major Bennet, Jr.], Mealy [unknown, perhaps Manney?], Shearer [Maurice E.] and some of the captains are among the no. to be court-marshalled [sic]".[12]

Brigadier General James A. Harbord, USA, had been Pershing's chief of staff. He had also been a personal friend of many years and presum-ably, when it became known that Doyen was going home, Harbord had an inside track. In order for him to qualify for higher rank he had to have a field command.

Harbord got the brigade and even though the senior officers wel-comed him in an emotional statement that used the Marine oath *"Sem-per Fidelis"* to express their loyalty to him, it would not be the same as before, for anyone. Harbord led the brigade through the worst and their performance was such that later he was promoted to command the division. According to Harbord's memoir, Pershing had told him that he was getting the best brigade in the AEF and "if it fails I'll know where to place the blame." It didn't fail. They made him look very good, even though they paid a heavy price to do so.

Harbord wrote a very kind letter to Doyen, as did the commanding general of the French 33d Division, under which the brigade had served. Brigadier General Charles A. Doyen, accompanied by his aide, 1st Lt. Benjamin S. Goodman, arrived in New York on 22 May 1918, just two weeks before the brigade would be ordered into the bloodiest single day in all of Marine Corps history.

One young officer remained as aide-de-camp to the new commander of the brigade. That was 1st Lt. Fielding S. Robinson. On 7 May 1918 Harbord appointed 2d Lt. R. N. Williams II, USA, as Goodman's replacement. Major Harry R. Lay returned from Langres and replaced Maj. Holland M. Smith, who had been acting as brigade adjutant during Lay's absence. Smith was assigned as brigade liaison officer on 16 May 1918—this move probably had something to do with Smith's part in the "cabal" then brewing.

Another officer got into trouble; I can find no record of his trial, but he was "dismissed from the service of the U.S. by the Auth. of the Commander-in-Chief of the AEF. Notice of dismissal received May 30, 1918." He is listed as being a member of the 7th Company, 1st Lt. Edward L. Burwell Jr. commanding. Too bad; Capt. John C. Foster might have been of some value in the weeks ahead.

On 10 May, a runner of 66th Company, Pvt. Bernard Yoakam, was commended by General Bundy of the 2d Division for refusing medical aid for his wounded hand until Bundy's message was delivered to Major Turrill commanding 1/5. Yoakam had been wounded by a German sniper. What else would Bundy have expected?

The brigade was entirely relieved by 14 May and proceeded to Vitry-le-François for further training, opening its headquarters at Venault-les-Dames. It wasn't long before the area was deemed unsuitable for training, so the brigade moved by train and a two-day road march to Gisors–Chaumont-en-Vexin, which was just north and slightly west of Paris. Headquarters was located at Bou-des-Bois. Private Feingold tells of the refitting and reorganization of the 1st Battalion after they left the Verdun front because "we were pretty well down on clothes and food." He adds that his company, after lengthy road marches, was now billeted in "barns and farmyards" in the small village of Buerry. It was while in this relatively quiet zone that the division received its call to proceed to the Château-Thierry Sector, without delay.

The first time the German army had gotten that close to Paris was in 1914, when the French forces, riding in Paris taxicabs, rode into history. Paris was the hub of France. From it extended the spokes along which all commerce, supplies, and just about every important item necessary for a continuance of the war by France had to be conveyed. If the Germans continued their advance, Paris must fall. If Paris fell, France would fall, and if France should fall, the armies of the allies would fall too. There would be no tomorrow. The British in the north would be forced to cross the Channel should the German sweep in the south successfully reach the coast. The fledgling American army had no real base such as the French and British armies had. They would be cut off from their home base, three thousand plus miles away. No American fleet could possibly provide a Dunkirk retreat for the American soldiers in France; there were too many of them now.

At this juncture of time a division of American regulars was within calling distance. The 2d Division was an amalgamation of four of the finest infantry, and three of the best artillery, regiments, plus the pickings of the engineers and service troops in the entire U.S. military forces. The 3d Division was also nearby and would gain great glory for their defense of the bridge at Chateau-Thierry and later the Marne River line. The Rock of the Marne, they would be rightly called, for slamming that door to the all victorious German army in July 1918. Victorious until they met up with the rough and ready juvenile delinquents from across the ocean. Just as soon as they learned the ropes, they would put the kibosh on the Krauts.

Notes

1 This was the largest tactical unit ever fielded by the U.S. Marine Corps up until that date.

2 *History of the Second Battalion, 5th Regiment, U.S. Marines, Jun. 1st 1917–Jan. 1st 1919.* (n.p., n.d.; reprint, Pike, NH: The Brass Hat, (1980), 5.

3 The semiofficial company history, *74th Company, 6th Regiment, U.S.M.C., etc.* (n.p., n.d.; reprint, Pike, NH: The Brass Hat, 1993), 6. According to an entry Holland Smith made in his diary, the replacements totaled 126 men on 19 April.

4 It appears that he was being "punished" for the situation that had occurred. Adams was transferred to the command of the 3d Battalion, 38th Infantry, the famous "Rock of the Marne," regiment, 3d Division, where he performed in an exemplary manner.

5 On 25 April a message from regiment was sent to Maj. Benjamin S. Berry, CO, 3d Battalion. Perhaps he had relieved Sturdevant sometime that month without a written record being available now.

6 Like the 45th, the 84th had been the victims of an innovative tactical plan developed by the German army to attempt to overcome the stagnation of trench warfare. An interesting study, Gudmundsson, Bruce *Stormtroop Tactics: Innovation in the German Army, 1914–1918.* (New York: Praeger, 1989) is worth a look.

7 The name has been spelled in several versions, including Sundeval and Sundval, but I believe that the last shown is the correct spelling. For reasons of continuity I have spelled it as shown in the report.

8 *Records of the Second Division,* volume 7. I can find no record of either Butler or Azeltine being casualties. Both may have been captured or wounded, which records I do not have. Sundval, a U.S. Army officer, died within a few days of his being wounded. The others apparently all survived the war.

9 Edwin N. McClellan, *The United States Marine Corps in the World War* (Washington, D.C.: U.S. Government Printing Office, 1920), 39. Doyen did die several months after arriving back in the United States, not of exhaustion but of influenza, which was then raging throughout the world.

10 Ibid.

11 Smith, unpublished diary, 30 April 1918 entry. It was clear, from that entry, the Marines weren't looking forward to any grand days ahead. Actually, Harbord was soon getting their best, for at least the brigade's officers took him to their hearts. He was a good man and had leadership qualities but his tactical ability left much to be desired, as later events will show.

12 The three mentioned, if Manney was truly one of them, were all on the staff of the brigade and later the division. I have no record of the trial's outcome, but Smith indicated a few days later that the trials were probably squelched. As best I can determine, all officers were still with the division throughout the war, though Shearer had his bumps later on. The blank space should possibly have stated that those officers had raised a ruckus when they learned of the relief and replacement of Doyen. A few additional entries found Smith appreciating Harbord as a "very fair man" and later "He appears to be a good man and an efficient one too." I am convinced that two officers who were scheduled to be

among those courtmartialed were Capts. Thomas W. Quigley and James Keeley. Both are listed on muster rolls for the month of May as awaiting trial, "awaiting investigation [Quigley]" and Keeley "awaiting results of trial." Neither was
incarcerated and both were super citizens in the brigade in the months ahead.
Instead, both were charged with being "drunk in uniform." Suspicious to say
the least. Keeley paid fifty bucks for that crime.

4: Belleau Wood

The Gettysburg of the war has been fought!
—General Pershing, referring to the success at Belleau Wood

Beginning on 21 March, Germany launched a series of major offensives from the north to the south beginning in the area near the Somme River. After seriously damaging or destroying several British armies in two offensives, most notably the 5th, they then turned their attention to the French army. The massive Aisne Offensive began on 27 May, and continued until 4 June. Across the Chemin des Dames plains they came, upward of thirty-six divisions, and they quickly rolled over their weak opposition.[1] Their new power came from the many divisions that were freed up by the treaty with the Bolshevik government in 1918.

The Allied opposition was composed mainly of depleted French and a few British divisions, which had been churned up in the two most recent offensives. Ludendorff's plan was to drive to the Aisne River, with exploitation toward the Vesle River, and perhaps, if successful, on to Soissons and Reims as the major prizes. If Paris were also taken, France would have probably pulled out of the war.[2]

On the French 6th Army front, in the sector known as the Chemin des Dames, Col.-Gen. Max von Boehn commanded the German 7th Army. That was composed of three corps of seven divisions in line and two in reserve. None was considered to be of attack quality. All were either exhausted from recent offensives, or were second rate.[3] For obvious reasons, the French were not terribly troubled by their opponents in the sector. But, unknown to French intelligence, German troop concentration began about the middle of May, and by 22 May the headquarters of three new corps were located in the 7th Army area. Nevertheless, no new divisions appeared in that area, which helped maintain the French conviction that all was well.

The French commander of the 6th Army, Gen. Denis Duchêne, contrary to Pétain's specific request that he, Duchêne, establish an elastic defense in depth, instead put all his troops on the line, with no reserves or depth. That was the major cause for the ensuing disaster. He was canned, but not soon enough.

Using night marches and remaining in woods during the day, the new German divisions were able to arrive on the scene completely unknown to French intelligence. As late as 25 May, French observers had seen nothing unusual to their front. The Germans had taken special precautions against losing prisoners to their enemy, and consequently, French night raids didn't encounter any new German troops. They all just seemed to disappear. It was simple. They were all pulled back at night.

Ludendorff's attack plan succeeded far beyond what he had hoped for. Because of the earlier disasters to the British armies, the British high command had pressured Foch to commit French reserves to the north. Consequently there were few reserves before Paris, where they were now badly needed. The Germans had learned valuable lessons from their earlier successes. They were now extensively equipped with light machine guns and they had instituted training in the nearly lost art of open-field warfare. On 27 May the Boche left their positions and started their roll westward across the plateau against the Allied lines. The German armies, five corps composed of twenty-nine divisions, were on their way westward and there were more coming. The French forces, unprepared for what was coming, folded up everywhere. Only a few units managed to stand their ground until they, too, were overwhelmed. The sector was no longer tranquil.

Marshal Ferdinand Foch, commander of the Allied forces in France, had his mass of maneuver west of Compiegne, which was about thirty-five kilometers due west of Soissons. Because of their location and the relative distance between them, the best Foch could accomplish in sending reinforcements to the 6th Army would only be two divisions per day. Needless to say, the French at GHQ were extremely distressed. Even though divisions were ordered forward, it was a certainty that the line of Chemin des Dames would soon be inundated and overwhelmed by the enemy. The Germans had achieved a very rare thing in modern war: They had managed to affect complete strategic and tactical surprise.

At first Pétain hurled whatever divisions he had available into the fray, trying desperately to halt the steamrolling German formations. Later he would say it was "like dropping water on a hot stove, they would disappear." During the next few days most of those divisions were chewed up and many were completely destroyed. Pétain wasn't just sending them to the center, where the lines were crumbling, he was assigning them to each of the flanks of the German advance. In the north he sent them to the Fôret de Retz, near Soissons, where the forest would give them left flank protection. In the southeast they were sent to Reims for the same purpose. Consequently, the French hoped to bring them to a halt as they forced the Germans into an ever-narrowing wedge, a cramped area, thus creating another salient, much like the two others most recently created in the north. The battle eventually absorbed thirty-seven divisions of Foch's carefully hoarded forces. Of this group, seventeen were exhausted by 1 June, and two others were so cut to pieces that they were never reconstituted. The French were desperate. Help was badly needed and the British weren't in any condition to come to their aid. The only forces available were those few divisions of the AEF already in France.

American forces not already committed and available for immediate duty were the 2d and 3d Divisions of the American Expeditionary Force. The 2d Division and the untried but equally true 3d Division were immediately selected. Most of the other Americans in France were in training and not yet capable of serving in the lines. The 2d Division had on its rolls 1,064 officers and 25,614 men available for duty. Of this total, the 4th Marine Brigade was composed of approximately 258 officers and 8,211 enlisted men.[4]

On the 29th of May the Germans were still advancing, but just a little slower than before. In the course of their advance, they had captured 29,000 French prisoners and a major objective, Soissons. Their attack had been directed along the Aisne to its confluence with the Oise River at Berneuil and against the hills north of Château-Thierry. The German offensive was now directed at Château-Thierry and the Marne River valley. At the speed at which they were moving, in a few days the Germans would be at Château-Thierry. Although the French army was reeling backward all along the front, as Pétain had planned they were still standing well on each refused flank. Down into the funnel went the Boche. Soon he would be on an extremely narrowed front, but that would bring him to the Château-Thierry Sector.

By 31 May the German advance continued to slow down, as the exhausted troops had been on the move for nearly four days. They were now on the outskirts of Château-Thierry, and on Hill 204, a dominating position just west of Château-Thierry on the north bank of the Marne. Ordinarily they would then be able to cross the bridge southward across the Marne River. Unfortunately for them, the 7th Machine Gun Battalion (Motorized) arrived in the town of Château-Thierry on the evening of 31 May to join the French forces still there. The Americans and French slammed the door shut and the Germans were unable to cross the bridge.

In order to continue to Paris, the Germans would now have to move across the Clignon Brook and through the assorted villages to the west: Bouresches, Belleau, Torcy, and Bussiares. Their revised tactical intention was to take the Ourcq River line to where the Clignon Brook joined it. By so doing they would effectively squeeze the French into a pocket along the Marne River, forcing them to continue retreating or be captured. For the Germans everything seemed to be going better than planned. The opposite was true for the French. Nothing was going according to plan, but then they had no plans. It was at this time that the German army changed direction. It would now move westward between the Marne and the Clignon Brook. Obtaining food and water was also a necessity, the latter especially at the town of Belleau.[5]

For the members of the 2d Division, who were still in residence about Chaumont-en-Vexin, the last days of May were rather pleasant. The Marines and their doughboy comrades spent most of their time in various military exercises: forced marches, "games of cops & robbers," and other warlike training over the otherwise peaceful countryside. On 29 May the troops were made aware that many kilometers north of them, the 1st U.S. Division had scored a decisive victory at Cantigny. The men cheered wildly upon receiving that news. There were the normal competitive feelings between the two leading U.S. formations. But both were Americans and compared to the outside world, the other could do no wrong. Brigade maneuvers were also held that day, with both soldiers and Marines working out problems inherent in open warfare. American military forces reckoned that open-field warfare was their forte. They soon would get an opportunity to prove that premise, or fallacy, depending upon one's point of view.

Thursday, 30 May, Memorial Day

Decoration Day, as the holiday was then commonly known, provided the Marine Brigade with a day off from ordinary work and drill. There was some of each, of course, but basically it was a day of rest. The troops were marched to several celebrations and then returned—after which they were dismissed to engage in personal amusement, or, if they wished, in nothing whatsoever. Most wrote letters or maintained their gear, their normal routine. Many exchanged gossip. Who was doing what to whom was always a favorite Marine exercise. Eating was another, but during the coming days that was one activity they wouldn't enjoy much.

That day the division received orders from the commanding general of the French Group of Reserve Armies of the North, directing them to move into the Beauvais area, just behind Cantigny. They were under orders to relieve the somewhat mauled 1st U.S. Division. The move would begin on 31 May and would take two days. March tables were drawn up and organizational directives flowed from headquarters. Billeting parties from each organization within the division were ordered to proceed by camion into the Beauvais area to make preliminary arrangements. Though some of the billeting parties actually started on their way, they were all recalled before the day ended.

At 1700 hours that afternoon a dusty French staff officer stepped out of his open automobile and strode into 2d Division Headquarters. He brought news of the military disaster in the Marne Valley. The 6th French Army had broken. The Germans were on the Marne and the 2d Division was ordered to go to Meaux, about fifty-six miles on a straight line from Chaumont-en-Vexin. The infantry would travel by camions to be provided, but there was no word on how the artillery and other services would make the trip. The movement of the infantry would begin at 0500 on 31 May and they wouldn't travel in a straight line. The trip would take many more hours than originally surmised.

All plans or orders that would have moved the division northward went out the window. The move was to be entirely eastward, and not to relieve any American unit, but to try to save the French line before Paris, which was by now almost completely wiped out. There were no formal written orders sent, since everything had to be made to happen as soon as possible, so only telephone calls or courier service was rapid enough. To add to the mass confusion, another French staff officer arrived at division about midnight and advised the Americans that there would indeed be trains for the artillery and animal transport in the morning. This was only the first in a series of confusing and conflicting orders that were sent by the French military authorities to the 2d Division. Many more of that kind were still to come. Disorder and turmoil were the names of the game.

During the night of 30–31 May, camions driven by Tonquinese and Anamites, and some by natives of Madagascar, most wearing uniforms of khaki and crested helmets of the French style,[6] moved into the areas designated. The Marines had formed on the streets at dawn. They gulped down a quick breakfast, the last hot meal that many of those men would ever eat while on earth, and then prepared to mount up. By sunup most of the division was on its way to death and glory.

Colonel Preston Brown, 2d Division chief of staff, proceeded as rapidly as possible in his automobile to the Marne valley, through Meaux, where he found and passed the leading camions filled with the 9th Infantry. About noon, he arrived at Trilport, about six miles east of Meaux, to find the headquarters of the 6th Army to which the 2d Division had been assigned. What he found, to his dismay, was chaos. The French knew nothing of the expected arrival of American troops and, worse, had no plans for their employment. The only response Brown received was "let the 2d Division concentrate at Meaux, and we will see." He decided that the response was unacceptable, so he went over their collective French heads directly to the 6th Army commander, General Duchêne.

Duchêne explained to his visitor about the terrible conditions that existed and added, "Things are very bad." He was sorry but he could give no orders at this time. Brown explained that two brigades of infantry were coming through Meaux. Without further ado, something must be done to alleviate the terrible congestion he'd seen in that town in order to allow passage of those troops into the designated area. Maps showed that the camions could turn northward toward May-en-Multien, thereby providing a place for the Americans to form up, and perhaps, to engage the oncoming Boche. The dismounted infantry could organize in the open countryside and the anticipated defensive line, the Ourcq River, was just a short distance to the west. So that was it. The infantry of both brigades would be directed to May-en-Multien and soon, Duchêne promised, orders for the division would be forthcoming. One favorable aspect, Brown later noted, was that the enemy might come southward along the Soissons-Meaux Highway and the 2d Division would be there to greet them on their way to Paris. Preston Brown thereupon dispatched runners to meet and redirect the camions while he returned to Meaux, where the advanced elements of the division staff were already established.

For the 2d Division there was some bad news relative to the transportation of the division artillery. The trains carrying the guns could not get to where the infantry was, so the artillery would have to be detrained twenty-five kilometers west of Meaux. A relatively few French 75s were the only available support the division could immediately expect. All service units of the 2d Division, artillery, kitchen, and other service trains, would be forced to march with animal transport. This would greatly delay their arrival and availability to the troops. Eventually the division's machine-gun battalions, which had traveled by camion, would arrive. Other than that, their only other support would be the infantry's 03s with bayonet attached and Chauchats.

The camion trains, one to each battalion, had been moving southeastward on the main roads around Paris and then onto the Paris-Metz Highway to Meaux. This was the same route taken by Gallieni with his taxicabs in 1914. That ride saved Paris then. Nearly four years later it would be camions loaded with Americans on their way to save France.

In the course of the ride some Americans noted that the trip was the most thrilling they had ever taken. The drivers seemed to be attempting to see how close they could come to destroying not only themselves but everyone aboard their buses. First Lieutenant Elliott D. Cooke, USA, a platoon leader in the 18th Company, 2/5, noted that "Lieutenant [Chester H.] Fraser, also of the 18th Company, yelled, 'Lucky if we don't get killed before reaching the front,' as we won a race and at the same time missed a tree by six inches."[7]

But the fight to save France couldn't begin until the fight with the refugees had been won first. As the camions headed toward Meaux, they met those French civilians who were coming from the Boche-saturated Soissons-Reims areas. Every American of the 2d Division, whoever wrote a letter, kept a journal, wrote his memoirs, or in some manner retained a record of that day, has remembered the scene as the most pitiful sight of the entire war. Sergeant Martin Gus Gulberg, of the 75th Company, 1/6, wrote, "There were women, old men, and babies, all wandering like lost souls in a chaos of confusion. Everything and everybody seemed to be in a hurry to get away from the battle line except a few Marines."[8]

There were thousands of refugees on that road. Some were riding in horse-drawn carriages, or farm wagons loaded with household goods, or even pushing baby carriages with the few belongings they could take on this most terrible of voyages. All were visibly downcast, if not in tears. Some pushed wheelbarrows or rode on horseback, while others were on foot. One man, the mayor of a town, passed, wearing a high hat, his frock coat, and his tricolor sash of office, as he trod on the hot road in tight-fitting dress shoes. Shepherds drove their flocks of sheep and goats so as not to leave them for the Boche.

But not all were poor peasant farmers. Some were wealthy and they had poured into the few trains heading westward. Some reporters later told of their disgust at the ugly attitudes of those who demanded immediate attention to their wants, regardless of the trying circumstances going on about them. Cooke was especially vigorous in his denunciation.

Unlike those poor unfortunates trudging the highways, they were not at all resigned to the state of their affairs. No indeed. They fussed and crowded and pushed their way onto railway trains provided by the military, all the while demanding their rights and denouncing the war that had left their homes in the path of an advancing German Army. The arrival of American troops on the scene they ignored completely.[9]

Remnants of the defeated French 6th Army flowed westward through the oncoming Americans. Many had dazed looks, compounded by weariness and terror. They hurled shouts at the oncoming Americans, such as *"La guerre est finie."* There were malingerers, as always, exhausted brave men who could no longer stand and fight, walking wounded, and men whose organizations had simply disappeared. One Marine, in an effort to try to uplift the morale of the French soldiers and perhaps help to stem the rout, purportedly yelled out, "We are here." Some Frenchman responded, *"Oui,* but so is the Boche."

Despite being sidelined temporarily, all the officers and men of the division were doing the best they could to complete their journey. The 2d Division was beginning to arrive at May-en-Multien at about 1500 hours, and as each unit debused, they were given orders to go out and look for the Boche. Those weren't the exact words but that was the general idea. Though still disorganized, Duchêne and his chief of staff were beginning to formulate plans to utilize a fresh division of American regulars; numerically more than the equal of two French divisions. General Duchêne issued an order for the 2d Division, which was in pencil and not numbered. In three brief paragraphs, it noted the assignment of the division to the 6th Army; that the infantry of the division would be placed in a position in the rear of the valley of the Clignon, between Montigny d'Allier and Gandelu; that liaison would be established on the west with the French II Cavalry Corps in the region of Bois de Bourneville–Marolles, and to the east with the French 43d Division near Priez. Finally, the division was placed under the operational control of the French VII Corps, which would use it to close the break in French lines along the Rue d'Alland, and for counterattacking as soon as possible in the direction of Passy-en-Valois and Marizy-St.-Mard. French intelligence all seemed to point to a direct attack south from the direction of Soissons along the highway connecting it with Meaux. That order placed the division where the Germans were expected to come, which was just where the Americans wanted to be.

Colonel Frederick "Fritz" Wise was told by a French liaison officer that 2/5 must leave at once. The Boche had broken through and the town to which 2/5 had been assigned was behind German lines. According to him there was nothing between the battalion and the Germans who were moving rapidly in that direction. Wise retorted that he and his Marines had come thousands of miles to fight the Boche "and this place looks as good as any to start in." Besides, that Marine officer had taken about as many orders from French officers, many his junior, as he was going to. The young Marines in the ranks were delighted. That was telling 'em, all right. Just then a long, sleek automobile skidded up, showering the Marines with gravel. The car was not filled with lowly French officers. Its occupants were covered in gold braid and loads of medals. The colonel said nothing; the newcomers did all the talking. The French had learned that the German pressure was developing to the west of Château-Thierry. They told Wise that he and his battalion couldn't stop any Germans where they were, the Paris-Metz Road was now where the action was. Hop to it, move south and east where the open door to the French capital was located. It must be slammed shut.

Meanwhile, the 2d Division had been transferred from the French VII Corps to the French XXI Corps. Colonel Preston Brown got busy preparing Divisional Field Order No. 5. That order would direct the division to concentrate in Montreuil-aux-Lions, which town was located on the Paris-Metz Highway, about six miles from Crouy, where much of the division's infantry had congregated. Third Brigade was directed toward villages on the *north* side of the highway and the 4th Brigade to the *south*. That evening Brown, in an effort to relocate all elements of the division, was out and about in the May-en-Multien to Crouy-sur-Ourcq area giving the changed orders to the various unit commanders he met. While the field order was highly detailed, it served no other purpose than to bring the elements of the division into the area in which they would fight. If the plan as written had been followed, the 3d Brigade would have met the Germans around and about Lucy-le-Bocage and the 4th Brigade would have had the southern front opposite Hill 204. As we now know, that was the exact opposite of what actually happened.

The 2d Division received yet another order from the French 6th Army late in the evening of 31 May. It was ignored. In the twelve hours since noon, 31 May, the division had received four sets of conflicting orders from the French command. The latest order was for the division to march back to May-en-Multien and away from the fighting. Even down at brigade level it had become quite plain that the enemy was advancing westward, north of the Marne. That was where the division was making every effort to collect. If they were going anyplace it was toward those soldiers they had come so many miles to fight. Division, of course, informed the French what it was they were doing. Regulations required at least that formality.

Saturday, 1 June

The French were making plans to throw the American regiments into the fray piecemeal, as they had consistently done with their own troops. General Omar Bundy and Col. Preston Brown, who were both at Corps headquarters, refused to allow that to happen. They responded that the Americans would fight when their machine guns and their artillery appeared, and not before. Bundy told the French that he wasn't going to expect his forces, each man with just a rifle and a hundred rounds, to go up against the finest army in the world. Finally, after much acrimonious discussion, the French commander, General Dégoutte, gave in. Preston Brown reported that he had a final discussion with General Dégoutte concerning the quality and temper of the 2d Division. Dégoutte was still not convinced the moves being made by the division were correct. In a final question he said, "Can the Americans really hold?" Brown responded, "General, those are American regulars. In a hundred and fifty years they have never been beaten. They will hold." And, by God, Brown was right, they did hold.

The 9th Infantry, leading the rest of the division, arrived in the Meaux area first. It had embused at the most easterly point, had traveled on fairly direct roads, and had gotten an earlier start. The buses for 3/9 broke down, among other mishaps, so they were late. Otherwise, on 1 June the regiment moved east using a map that Colonel Upton had liberated from a passing, unsuspecting, French officer. On the 9th went as sounds of fighting could be heard just north of their road. It was there that small groups of French stalwarts were continuing to contest a further advance of the enemy. The two leading battalions, 1/9 and 2/9, with no stragglers, continued their march until they reached Le Thiolet, which the French command had set as the division's left flank. Fortunately, though the Germans could see what the Americans were doing from their perch on Hill 204, they had outrun their own artillery and consequently had no way to interfere with Upton and his men. At noontime, 3/9 also reached the field. The regiment was now complete and ready for anything the Germans could hurl at them, but they were out there all alone. It would be late afternoon before any more division troops would arrive in the battle zone.

Just east of May-en-Multien, both the 5th Marine Regiment and the 23d Infantry Regiment arose from their bivouac. They both had a fifteen-mile march ahead of them. The 6th Marine Regiment, which was in Montreuil, was about six miles west of the 9th Infantry. Martin Gulberg tells us that the 6th had arrived at Montreuil about 0600 and stayed until 1300. During that period they ate anything and everything that wasn't nailed down. Gulberg remarked that a French officer had told them to help themselves to anything they wanted,

> because the Germans would get everything eventually. He also said he heard one of the boys remark, "Gee, that Frog officer ain't got much confidence in us, has he?" We visited the wine cellars and helped ourselves to the choicest wines; raided rabbit and chicken coops and feasted royally. We didn't leave much for Fritz in case he should get through. He described one Marine coming down the street with a squealing pig under his arms yelling, "Pork Chops." Although many of the Marines took away much of the dressed and prepared animals, most never had the chance to actually eat their prizes.[10]

The 2d Battalion, 6th Marines, with Thomas "Tommy" Holcomb commanding, had reached Montreuil at 0400 after a day and a night in camions. Like everyone else in the division, they were bushed, but at 1430 were on the move again. After the trucks of the 2d Supply trains had dumped field rations and ammunition along the side of the road, Harbord commandeered them. With a number of vehicles in tow he rode back to where Maj. Thomas Holcomb, with his rearmost battalion of the 6th Marines, was marching toward the front. After loading the troops, Harbord then returned to where the action was developing at Le Thiolet.

Consequently, 2/6 was the first Marine unit to arrive at the scene. They jumped out of their trucks and soon deployed northward across the road from where the 9th had begun to dig in. That extended the division line along the eastern face of Bois Clérembauts, through Triangle Farm, and then to the west end of the Bois de Triangle, and finally to Lucy-le-Bocage. It was a thin line, but at 1705 Holcomb could report being in place. The regimental unit history relates that the battalion had three companies in line and one in reserve. The company that connected with the 9th Infantry, the 96th (Capt. Donald F. Duncan), had its right resting on the Paris-Metz Road at Le Thiolet. Next, to their left, was the 79th Company (Zane), which was occupying Triangle Farm. Captain Robert E. Messersmith with the 78th Company was next to the left, from the gully just northwest of the farm, to Lucy on their far left. Battalion headquarters was established at La Cense Farm. There Capt. Bailey M. Coffenberg and his 80th Company were held in reserve within a small wooded area just behind the positions held by the 96th.

While 2/6 was deploying, Maj. Edward B. Cole and the 6th Machine Gun Battalion arrived in camions and debused near Hill 201. The men dismounted from their "prisons" with genuine enthusiasm. One young Marine asked, as he and his buddies dismounted and went across the fields from the highway, "Which way is this here line?" A sergeant responded, "Line, hell! We're going to make one."[11] Turning north on the Lucy road he established headquarters at Montgivrault-le-Grande, then sent guns forward to support the line established by 2/6. These were men and guns from the 77th and 81st Companies. The entire group was commanded by Capt. Louis R. deRoode of the 77th Company with Captain Augustus B. Hale of the 81st Company as his second.

Major Maurice Shearer, temporarily in command of the 1st Battalion of the 6th Regiment while Maj. John A. Hughes was away at school, led his force northward off the highway and marched up behind the machine gunners. Continuing on the road, 1/6 reached the town of Lucy-le-Bocage, as German shells began falling in a field close by. The battalion extended its line northward on the road to Torcy, sheltering in the St. Martin Woods.

Colonel Albertus Catlin, commanding the 6th Marines, had led Sibley's battalion off the highway at Paris Farm and placed it in reserve in the woods north of Voie du Châtel. He briefly took up residence there himself. This extended the line of the 6th Marines to the west, from Lucy through both the Bois St. Martin and Bois de Champillon to Hill 142. By 1850 Catlin would report to brigade that his regiment was in position on a front of about three miles, with two battalions on line and one in support.

Meanwhile, Col. Wendell Neville, with his 5th Marines, was directed to Pyramide Farm, where the regiment bivouacked in the fields and woods opposite. Later, regimental headquarters relocated to a stone quarry at Carrières, about five hundred meters northwest of Marigny. Cooke relates what happened to 2/5:

> Colonel Wise assembled the company commanders and Captain [Lester S.] Wass, returned shortly to say that we would bivouac where we were for the night. We did it all shipshape and by the number's fall-in—right dress—stack arms—fall out. That was showing Heinie what we thought of him, but I couldn't help wondering what would happen if the German artillery spotted us.[12]

The 23d Infantry was the last regiment to arrive on the field. Shortly after dark they were in place to support the 9th Infantry. All the infantry units of the division, except the regimental machine-gun companies, were in place. They ranged from south of the Paris-Metz Highway northward to just south of the Clignon Valley, astride the most likely avenue of approach for any further German advance. French stragglers were filing back through the Americans' position as the sun started downward. One reporter later told of the

> bruised and broken remnants, with despair written on their war-weary faces ... to them perhaps the war was lost. ... One ... showed me his rifle. ... The butt had been shot away and he had been hit in the shoulder. "Beaucoup d'allemands" [Germans] . . . and he hurried away.[13]

As the division was settling in, the enemy began probing along the lines, and unknowingly came into contact with the recently arrived Americans. German troops could be clearly seen moving into the woods northwest of the Bouresches-Vaux line, opposite the 6th Marines. The Germans were aware that new, fresh troops were now occupying a line opposite them, but apparently did not realize they were not French.

Their advances continued but seemed without their usual spirit or aggressiveness. They were, after all, becoming quite tired after advancing for the previous five days, and short of both food and water. The Boche were not supermen, later claims to the contrary notwithstanding. They became even more cautious when they encountered heavy rifle and machine-gun fire, which emanated from the American lines. Some French artillery was in action but they were, unfortunately, more effective with short rounds into the 79th Company's position at Triangle Farm than against the Boche. Shortly after his arrival, Captain Zane had to report

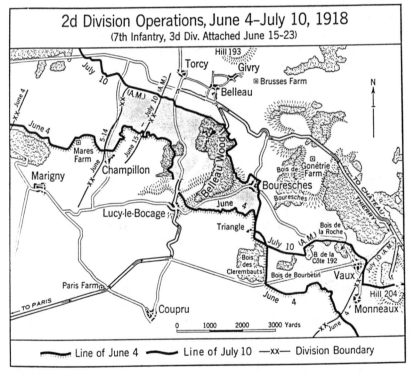

Map 1: The heavy black lines indicate the original positions of the 2d Division on 4 June 1918 and the progress made by 10 July 1918. The 5th Marines occupied the left side of the lines during most of the period, the 6th Marines to their right; the 23d Infantry next and the 9th Infantry before Vaux.

five casualties from short rounds falling into his area. Marines hoped that the painful error of the situation would soon be corrected. During the war, short rounds and inaccurate firing patterns were more common than they should have been.

Detachments of French soldiers fell back through the Marines' line, completely exhausted, and immediately fell asleep upon the ground. German artillery continued a light fire all night, which indicated they would be trying another advance soon enough. The Marines, those who hadn't disposed of their shovels, continued digging what was to be called, in a later war, foxholes.

In addition to these miseries, the day was clear and warm, so that the men in all their monumental physical activity, moving up and getting into unprepared positions, greatly suffered from the heat. Some veterans vividly recall the day as having been extremely hot, and the troops had to lie in the open all day. Soldiers and Marines were still wearing the uniform of the day, and those weren't designed for hot-weather comfort. Actually, none of them were designed for comfort at any time. Either Marine green woolen or army olive drab khaki were just as bad in warm weather as cold.

Small-arms ammunition and ration dumps had already been established in the rear of the troops, but the all-important field kitchens and regimental supply trains were absent. They were still marching on the road. There was no food except iron rations and what the individual soldier or Marine had salvaged or liberated from the vacated towns and farms they had been through on their way forward. There were few, if any, maps, and no definite information about the enemy or the French troops who were quickly putting the Americans between themselves and the Boche.

Various units were reporting up the chain to their respective senior commands. Catlin sent a message to Harbord that the 6th Marines had established liaison with the 23d Infantry. "None of the battalions were issued rations. Please send them up by truck tonight." Harbord, who had been operating his headquarters from the backseat of his automobile, had, that afternoon, finally located himself at Issonge Farm. A little bit farther north toward Marigny was the Pyramides Farm, where, later, those units going into reserve were often sent. For the time being, division headquarters was to remain back at Montreuil-aux-Lions. Neville's was by now at the Carrières quarry and Catlin's still at Voie du Châtel. Telephone lines were established by early evening. The lines were connected to most units within the brigade, even down to battalion level. But they would be destroyed during the following three weeks. Because repair was often impossible, headquarters turned to runners. Those bravest of the brave would be used to make contact between units, often under severe machine-gun and shell fire. The men were selected and then urged to volunteer because of their inherent valor and dedication to duty. For their feats of bravery, many would be awarded colorful baubles to wear on their jackets. But those couldn't stop slivers of steel or lead. Frequently during the war the runners would accomplish near miracles. Many would suffer wounds or death, which habitually accompany valor.[14]

It was the line of the Clignon that the French 43d Division had been trying to hold. The French, driven from the northern side of the Clignon, had been trying desperately to hold the southern hills and the exits from the Clignon line to the south. They had been driven back until they stood finally in the villages of Bouresches, Belleau, Torcy, Bussiares, and Gandelu, all on the southern side of the brook.

The village of Belleau was an attraction for invading armies and had been for many centuries. During 1914, when the Germans were last there, they forced women of the town to hand water to German soldiers as they passed through. One old woman of the town told of how she fainted from weariness but the Germans kept her at the task with a whip. She was known, locally, as a woman alone, but somehow or other she had managed to breed and raise nineteen children, of no stated paternity. Possibly some were German?

Just south of the town, the woods and the château of the same name were both owned by a wealthy Parisian. The château and the old church nearby had been thoroughly ruined by shell fire during the war. The gentleman had kept horses, and their stable was underground. At this time the Germans were using it as cover. It had sufficient room to house at least 150 men, and for a time in early June 1918, it was home to their regimental headquarters. A number of officers slept there in beds that had been removed from the château.[15]

The owner also had a game preserve within the woods, maintaining deer, pheasants, and hares. There also was a small stone lodge, known as the Pavillion, located near the northeastern corner. Before the war, there were many parties, with beautiful women and baskets of champagne and most likely sundry other goodies to go with the frequent festivities.[16]

The wood, known as the Bois de Belleau, was elevated above the surrounding wheat fields. On the eastern side of the wood a paved road ran between Belleau in the north and Bouresches in the south, and continued on a few miles to Vaux. Another road, along the western frontage, ran south from Torcy to Lucy-le-Bocage. South of the woods ran a dirt road westward from Bouresches to Lucy. The woods lay within the triangle formed by these three roads. The wood was approximately a mile long, a half mile across at its widest, and four hundred meters at its narrowest. During this period, the trees were in full leaf, and under the trees the ground was choked with undergrowth, through of which men could not pass easily. There was a deep ravine along the southern edge, and a narrow unimproved road within the forest. Another ravine, cutting from the western side, ran northeast to southwest in slightly angled direction, across the narrow part of the wood.[17]

On 1 June, the German order of battle had five divisions of the von Conta Corps facing the French and the 2d Division. Conta's mission was to provide a defensive flank for the thrust to the Ourcq by Winckler's XXV Corps. It wasn't to be Conta's task to aggressively attack along the line but just to keep pace with Winckler's men. But local German command kept up the probing, always looking to attain better positions on the south side of the Clignon. Consequently, the area continued to be active. While the 2d Division was taking up its positions on that first day, the Germans were doing what they were paid to do and did so well, namely to overcome resistance along the Clignon line toward its confluence with the Ourcq.[18]

The French order of battle facing the Germans was the 43d Division, under General Michel, with attached units of cavalry and elements of five or six infantry regiments. That division would take up left flank liaison with the 4th Brigade all during the coming campaign. They would continue to do their duty and do it well.

Sunday, 2 June

There had been a nearly three-mile break in the French line and troops were needed to fill it. Sometime after midnight, Col. Paul B. Malone*, USA, with his 23d Infantry, reinforced by Turrill's 1/5, plus two companies of the 5th Machine Gun Battalion and a company of engineers, were all roused out of their sound sleep. They had orders to march about six miles north and west of Lucy; to fill the gap in the French line from Bois de Veuilly westward to Gandelu. By daylight on 2 June the Americans were in position with Turrill at the Bois de Veuilly at 0625.

Unconnected elements of French troops were scattered along the line and Marines of 1/5 reported that they had found vagrant Frenchmen looting Les Mares Farm, which was located about a half mile west and north of Champillon. Lieutenant Colonel Logan Feland, assistant regimental commander of the 5th Marines, who was scouting along the line, found a French regimental commander personally serving a machine gun, while his staff and such men as could be gathered were holding back the Boche advance from the Clignon Heights. The French officer told Feland, "Looting is very bad at times like these. Everything goes. As soon as we can reorganize, we shoot a few of them, and it stops."

Meanwhile, Wise and 2/5 were assigned to fill a long gap between Hill 142, west to the Bois de Veuilly, an area about two and a half miles in length. Harbord ordered Cole to send Wise a company of guns "at once from a point where you can best spare it."

At 0300 the 2d Battalion, 2d Division Engineers arrived to begin developing fortifications for the Marines starting at Lucy-le-Bocage and working westward. For the balance of the fight before, in, and around Belleau Wood, the engineers would work and then fight. In attacks made later in the month by the decimated Marine Brigade, the engineers would advance with the Marines and fight as infantry. Each rifle company was, initially, allocated one platoon of engineers but as casualties among the engineers increased, those numbers were reduced. For many good reasons, Marines had a high regard for their buddies of the 2d Engineers.

Division issued orders that confirmed details of the deployment and reassignment of the division to General Dégoutte's French XXI Corps. The French 164th Division would be on the division's right flank down to the Marne River. The French 43d Division was posted from Lizy-sur-Ourcq, where the river meets the Marne, stretching eastward a healthy eleven miles to meet the 4th Brigade. Bundy and Brown had already determined that the 4th Brigade would fight while the 3d Brigade would stand as division reserve. They also decided that only one major unit would fight at any one time. Therefore, the main action ahead would involve Marines, in and around the Bois de Belleau.

According to German reports, they had begun to notice that opposition was stiffening everywhere along the line. Something unusual was occurring to their direct front but they weren't yet sure what. Regardless, the Germans continued their efforts to cross the Clignon in force, meeting with a minimum of resistance from the defending French. They hadn't yet run into the Americans.

German guns opened up on portions of the front at first light, concentrating on towns and farmhouses south of the Clignon. At 0900 German infantry of three divisions advanced southward. The 197th on the left moved south from the high ground between Bussiares and Torcy, but they were held up by French machine-gun fire from Hills 165 and 126. Next in line, the 237th and 10th swung southward toward Bouresches and the Bois de Belleau. They were immediately assailed by heavy French small-arms fire coming out of the north end of Belleau Wood and Bouresches. The French did their best, but they weren't strong enough to hold the overwhelming force for very long.

At midday the machine gunners of the 2d Division were kept busy by the Germans, who advanced westward, north and south of Bouresches. Division artillery was still in transit, so French artillery was in direct support of the 6th Marines' line with sixty 75mm guns and twelve 155s. Catlin was advised by Harbord that a French colonel of artillery was now located in Lucy with directions for "both your battalion commanders [2/6 and 3/6] keep in touch with him through interpreters." Unfortunately, the French batteries of 155s ran short of ammunition and it took thirteen hours, and a forty-five-mile round trip to replace the shells. But the French brought back thirty-two truckloads, which provided serious heavy-artillery fire for the next several days.

Fortunately for the defenders, both German divisions had been badly shot up and accordingly soon lost cohesion as they moved forward. Contact between the two divisions broke down, after which the left of the 237th and the right of the 10th slowed up and lost their headway. Their center just stopped its forward motion altogether. The left flank continued forward, but by noontime they, too, were stopped dead in their tracks. The 6th Marines were blocking their advance and the Germans still didn't know which organization they were facing. There was one factor that started to loom large. Accurate rifle and machine-gun fire was making a mess of their formations. Though there was a bit more activity that day, for all intents and purposes, the Germans had shot their offensive bolt. By nightfall all movement from the east had ceased.

The 15th and 23d companies of the 6th MG Battalion were assigned to provide cover for the 5th Marines on the division's northern flank. The 81st and 77th, north to south, remained in their locations just behind 2/6 and 3/6. These guns kept the "wolf from the door" during the first few days of the Aisne Defense. The '03 in the hands of trained marksmen also helped a great deal. The story has been told, many times, of the surprise inflicted upon the German attackers at finding their comrades falling in the wheat and not hearing sounds of any enemy fire, the distance being that great. So was the accuracy.[19]

The usual American method of supplying machine-gun support to the various units was to assign a machine-gun company to each battalion. The regimental machine-gun companies, the 8th in the 5th Marines and the 73d in the 6th, were usually each assigned to the first battalions of their respective regiments. Each company received a platoon of guns. Consequently, the commanding officer of the 6th Machine Gun Battalion, Major Cole, and his successors, had little direct control over the entire unit while they were engaged in combat. Fortunately the leadership down to platoons was more than satisfactory in most cases, and consequently the battalion always functioned at the top of their form.[20]

That morning, Maj. Benjamin S. Berry and 3/5 were assigned as brigade reserve and that afternoon were reassigned to corps reserve. Harbord directly passed along those orders as he did those to Maj. Julius Turrill later, when he placed 1/5 in brigade reserve. All during the action in June, it was common for Harbord to bypass his regimental commanders and send orders from his command post to nearly every lower level: to battalion and occasionally even down to company level.

Holcomb sent out a panic message to Catlin that the "enemy [was] attacking along our whole front at 8:30 A.M. They were about twelve hundred yards from our position." The operations journal for the 2d Division reports for that day: "The 6th Marines had several casualties among the officers and men—wounded only. The 6th Machine Gun Battalion stopped the German advance several times." Obviously, the attack wasn't quite as serious as it seemed to Holcomb. There were very few panic attacks like that. Perhaps being a new father had caused some of the overreaction. But based upon erroneous reports, Harbord concluded that Holcomb's 2/6 was falling back at Triangle Farm. Harbord sent Catlin an order at 1440 to "stiffen your lines." Holcomb, with a direct phone connection to Harbord, angrily replied to the admonition, "When this outfit runs it will be in the other direction. Nothing doing in the fall-back business." Later, upon learning the truth, Harbord apologized to Holcomb. Meanwhile, Harbord directed Sibley to provide "a fresh company" to Holcomb at La Cense Farm as a reserve because a German division was expected to attack the American right with two regiments. As ordered, Sibley duly sent Capt. Robert W. Voeth and his 97th Company to strengthened the junction between the 6th and 9th Regiments.

From corps headquarters came the following message:

For the Generals commanding
The 2d Div., A.E.F., 43d and 164th Inf. Divs.

Thanks to the arrival of the American 2d Division, it has been possible to stiffen the entire front of the army corps, by means of a solid line, occupied at present by the American regiments.
It should be well understood that all the French elements which are in front of that line should hold desperately against all hostile attacks. If, notwithstanding all their efforts, any French elements are driven back into the American line, the orders to be issued in advance by the division commanders will provide
  1. That the American regiments will hold in place and stop the enemy dead.
  2. That French units, if driven back, will be promptly grouped as well as practicable, and then reorganized at previously designated points, with a view to forming small, homogeneously constituted reserves.

The orders continued, specifying that the Americans would "hold in place" and let the retiring French pass through their lines and they would be reorganized "under the protection of their American comrades." Those who had retired would remain behind the American lines in support. It was obvious to everyone that the French would probably not be able to hold. But much credit should be given to those men who stood their ground against the oncoming Boche while many of their comrades folded their tents and stole away. They were exhausted, yet they continued doing their duty as best they could. All honor to their memory.

Wise's battalion, 2/5, was assigned to cover the brigade's left flank. Cooke makes note of a retrograde movement of French Chasseurs, the famous "Blue Devils," at about 1000 that day, and added, "They certainly were blue, in more ways than one. Retreating before the Boche for six days had left them utterly spent." Cooke offered one of them a cigarette, asking how things were going. The French lieutenant's face was one of despair. "My frien' . . . lose the gun and the bullet, yes, but save the shovel." Then he was gone. The battalion marched forward, having the entire battlefield to themselves, along with a few Boches, of course.

As 2/5 was moving northward, the Boche started to shell the column. Soon eleven men were down, of whom four would remain still forever. The 18th Company milled about. Captain Lester S. Wass screamed "Get going. What do you think this is, a kid's game? Move out." That did it. The skipper spoke and everyone scattered. Being a target pleases no one, especially when you can't get back at your tormentor. As Cooke later said, "All we wanted were some Germans in our sights. Just a few lousy Boches to shoot the living guts out of."

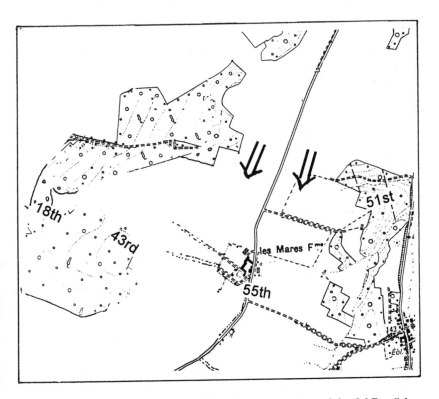

Map 2: The probable positions of the four companies of the 2d Bn, 5th Marines at Les Mares Farm during the period 3 and 4 June 1918, from which they successfully held the advancing German formations.

Les Mares Farm was located less than thirty miles from Paris and in 1918 it would be the closest that the Boche would get to that long-sought-for city. It was also to be the scene of bloody fighting on 3–4 June and forever after would be known as the "Bloody Angle of the AEF." At the farm the battalion companies split up. The 55th remained within the farm enclosures. Captain Charlie Dunbeck's 43d Company went next in line to the left. Farther left went Capt. Lester S. Wass and his 18th Company. A gap of approximately a third of a mile separated them from Turrill's 1/5, which was still stationed in the Bois de Veuilly. Captain Lloyd Williams and the 51st Company went to the extreme right flank of the battalion, into the woods, and up a hill. Shortly after, each company prepared their position for what might come. There was now a semblance of order in which to receive any attack the Boche might heave at them, day or night. The only thing they still lacked was the promised machine guns.

Meanwhile, the sharpshooters of the 43d were engaged in sniping at Germans so Lts. Fred H. Becker, USA, the 18th Company's chow hound, and Chester H. Fraser went over to see the fun. On return Becker acknowledged that though he and Fraser hadn't seen any "Dutchmen," he knew that a few had been nailed by some expert riflemen of the 43d. Williams and the 51st Company were presumed to be on Hill 142, to Wass's right, where the 51st was to connect up with Shearer and 1/6.[21] Williams and the 51st were on the nearest hill to the east, which wasn't Hill 142 although Wise and Williams both thought it was. The maps hadn't changed any, they were still obsolete and so was the map reading.

Sometime during the morning it was decided that 2/5, from Hill 142 to Bois de Vaurichart, was stretched far too thin.[22] Therefore, around noontime, the 82d Company (Capt. Dwight Smith) of 3/6 was ordered there to provide some additional strength and support. When they arrived, they moved to the right of Williams.

As the morning proceded, the Germans stepped up their artillery attacks and just after noon began to hammer the 4th Brigade positions. One/Six, still located in St. Martin's Woods, opposite Belleau Wood, were the major victims. Gulberg describes what happened to the 75th Company's first casualty. Private Warren F. Hoyle "stuck his head out and as he did so a shell took his head off." Three additional men of the 75th were wounded or shell-shocked. Captain Oscar R. Cauldwell of the 95th Company was shot through the leg, which took him out of the lines. "There were a few French soldiers in this wood walking around with rosary beads saying prayers." So Gulberg and Riley Brennan, his foxhole mate, just dug deeper. During that afternoon the Germans launched at least two attacks along the right of the brigade's line. Catlin had been informed that a German attack was in the offing, so his men were reasonably prepared. Each attack was repulsed, principally, by machine-gun fire. According to reports, "dead Germans piled the slopes."

As the afternoon developed, it soon became apparent that the situation on the left of the 2d Division was not as threatening as originally believed. The line formed by the 23d Infantry Regiment, Turrill's 1st Battalion, and the French dismounted cavalry was holding everywhere. Consequently, the Germans were making little progress in their attacks south of Clignon Brook. In midafternoon Harbord sent orders to Turrill that he and 1/5 were to withdraw from its support of the 23d Infantry. As we have seen, his battalion would now become brigade reserve. Ben Berry and 3/5 became corps reserve and were positioned just to the rear of the junction of the 6th Marines and the 9th Infantry, the weakest part of the division line.

Fourth Brigade Headquarters was beginning to shape up and settle down. Harbord advised Preston Brown that his communications "are in much better shape than yesterday" and that liaison was working regularly and that he had telephone communication with "both regimental hdqrs. and . . . HQ. of my M.G. bn., and through the latter, with the bn. nearest it, which is the bn. at the critical point on the line"—Holcomb's 2/6.

The main German effort ceased when darkness set in. All along the line they had failed to attain their objectives, and their losses in their various attacks had been unexpectedly heavy. Reorganization of their shattered units came first; then they spent the night reconnoitering and patrolling their front. All German units reported that the French had stiffened their resistance and that they had been materially reinforced. But by whom? There is no evidence that the presence of American troops had yet been noticed by the Germans. Included in their orders for the next day was the taking of Marigny, La Voie du Châtel, Lucy, and Triangle. Meanwhile, all ranks were enjoined to retain their offensive spirit, even if for a few days they had slackened off their attacks a bit. The troops had been seen skylarking, seen wearing liberated men's plug hats or women's draperies on their heads; such pranks must cease immediately. Nearly a thousand officers and men had been lost on the 1st and 2d of June, and it was noted in reports that a few men had also come down sick with influenza. The "Spanish flu" would continue to dog all the armies fighting in Europe in 1918 and Americans would be struck with extreme severity on the high seas. Many men, healthy when they started from the United States, were unloaded dead upon arrival in France.

At about midnight, 2d Division headquarters relieved 1/5 and the various other units that had accompanied the 23d Regiment to near Gandelu. After being detached, they were transferred by bus to Pyramides. The Marines' movement was interpreted, in error, by a German balloon observer's report, to be a move by the French to reinforce Gandelu. All day there had been considerable movement in the 2d Division area and the Germans were convinced that the French were sending in copious reinforcements.

Enemy artillery had been working the line, up and down, all during the night of 2–3 June, but at Les Mares Farm they seemed to lay it on more heavily than elsewhere. A coming attack became more evident to Capt. John Blanchfield and his subordinates. But it didn't come on 2 June. All five of his officers, 1st Lt. Lemuel Shepherd, 2d Lt. Hascall F. Waterhouse, 2d Lt. Lucius Q. C. L. Lyle, First Lieutenant Tillman, USA, and First Lieutenant Linehan, USA, had their men dug in around the farm, or posted inside one of the buildings. Their positions were as strong as they could be, considering their total lack of machine guns and shortage of grenades. Rations weren't getting to 2/5, so the officers and men of the 55th Company took care of their requirements in the time-honored manner. The French refugees had left a calf behind when they left the farm. Consequently, that first night the company dined on calf steak. Since there is more to a calf besides steak, I'm sure the Marines enjoyed other portions as well. There were also rabbits, fowl, and chickens. With chickens there were also eggs. The garden held vegetables, the wine cave, *vin blanc* and *vin rouge*. The 55th wouldn't go hungry the following night either. Possibly they shared with the three other companies. Possibly. Foodwise they were in far better shape than many of the other companies in either brigade.

Monday, 3 June
At midnight Shearer notified Wise that he was holding a front "line from Hill 142 to Lucy-le-Bocage. . . . Capt. [George A.] Stowell, 76th Company's left rests on Hill 142. . . ." Both Shearer and Wise had been jockeying about for hours, neither ever quite making contact where their units were supposed to meet. It would be many more hours before each

found the other.[23] Logan Feland, while out scouting the lines, had received a report from one of Wise's scouts who had found the location of both 2/5's 51st Company and 1/6's 76th Company. They were about a thousand meters apart. Because neither battalion commander decided to change the situation, that large gap was not soon corrected. Major Shearer sent a message to Wise complaining that he was not able to move any farther to his left than Hill 142. That was, according to his information, where Wise's right should be. "I cannot spare men to run line past 142. . . . The vacancy is yours." There were still some individualists among the battalion commanders. Unfortunately, Shearer didn't know he wasn't on Hill 142. Apparently Wise was suffering from the same problems, because he thought that Williams was on Hill 142 and evidently so did Williams. Fortunately, with the arrival of Smith and the 82d Company, the gap was partially filled. Later Sibley would receive orders to send more companies to the same area.

The lack of maps at practically every level, from top to bottom, became an increasingly serious problem. When French maps finally became more readily available, they were badly flawed anyway. Most had been developed in the previous century and many changes had not been recorded. With all the movement and readjustment of location, over ground they hadn't had an opportunity to reconnoiter, it is surprising that the Americans performed as well as they did.

Most everyone in the division had moved somewhere on 2 June, and consequently the men had little rest and less food. By 3 June the front was beginning to stabilize, even though there had been much lost motion and great confusion. There was some digging of trenches, especially around Triangle Farm, Lucy, and in the Bois St. Martin, but largely the men wearily dug foxholes. Rather than to meet a standard, they were dug to satisfy the individuals' own concern for protection from bursting artillery shells. According to several reports, some Marines, hungry, exhausted, and in a somewhat mutinous manner, swore they wouldn't dig another hole. Many expressed their opinion that they "were going to be bumped off anyway and if so they wouldn't have to tolerate any more shelling." Usually a shell dropping close by would terminate whatever antagonistic attitude they had toward "management" and the digging would commence again, immediately if not sooner.

After midnight the 43d Division notified Harbord that French troops would be issued an order "to retake the position they have just lost. The American troops will maintain at all costs the line of support they oc-

cupy. . . . They will not participate in the counterattack which will be
made to retake the position of the French." Their attack was to be aimed
mainly against the 197th German Division, which was located around
Hill 142 and Hill 166, but it came to nothing. They were easily stopped
and regained no lost ground. It was little more than a gallant gesture.
Shortly afterward the French XXI Corps announced the loss of
Bouresches, Bussiares, Torcy, Belleau, and the woods of Belleau. During the night of 2–3 June the French had completely withdrawn from
Belleau Woods to avoid being cut off when Bouresches was taken in their
rear. There were few if any Germans in the woods at that time. They had
the good sense not to attempt to assault a defended position when it
could easily be bypassed.

The Germans were having difficulty trying to figure out how the exhausted French could possibly have launched a counterattack. So, for
the balance of the day, they proceeded with great caution all along the
line. They were taking no chances with a foe that after taking so much
punishment still had had enough strength to attack them. Now in control of the northern heights, which was only about four miles north of
the Paris-Metz Road, the Boche were determined to push south of the
brook to utilize the excellent cover on the opposite side. All along the
line the Germans were probing for weak spots and would continue to
do so all day, especially down south where the 3d Brigade was located.[24]
It had been intended that the 2d Division would take over command
of the sector where its troops were now deployed. The counterattack to
recover the lost ground, an ego trip for the French more than any serious effort, delayed the transfer of command to General Bundy. Much
worse, the French lost more ground, which put a heavier burden on the
2d Division than before the attempt was made. If the transfer had taken
place a day earlier, the Marines could have been in the woods and the
Germans wouldn't. Imagine the possibilities of that. Meanwhile, back
to reality.
The arrival of the four regimental machine-gun companies had
been greatly delayed, since only the 5th and 6th Machine Gun Battalions had transport facilities. The 8th Company (5th Marines) and the
73d (6th Marines), along with their comrades of the 3d Brigade machine-gun companies, showed up that morning. All had been forced to
march overland with their guns and ammunition on carts from their
bases back in the Chaumont-Gisors area. This had caused real problems
for both infantry brigades. Marines had been forced to rely solely upon

the guns of the 6th Machine Gun Battalion, which was hard pressed to service all the units that needed their help all the time.

Meanwhile, Captain Wass walked over to Lieutenant Cooke and told him there was a French outfit moving in to relieve the 23d Infantry on their left,

> and those Frogs want to see a couple of Marines, they've been told our uniform is the same color as the Germans' forest green and they don't want to shoot the wrong people. Take a couple of people over to their P.C. You're wearing O.D. so they probably won't make any mistakes on you.

The French agreed that the Marines' uniform was almost the same color as the Germans'.[25] They decided that there was nothing that could be done about it, so they compromised by giving everyone a drink of *vin rouge*. Cooke, probably because he was a first lieutenant, got a slug of cognac instead. Later, when he returned to his company, that would greatly upset Colonel Wise, who could smell it on his breath. According to Cooke, there was a ruckus of some great proportion about Cooke getting drunk. At Wise's orders he skedaddled down the road and through the woods to his company, somewhat faster than a speeding bullet. Wise was always something of a martinet.

After another period of intense shelling, 2/5 was subjected to an intense machine-gun barrage, which was the signal that the Germans would soon launch an attack on their portion of the line. Some French shells fell too close and set afire the wheat field to their immediate front, providing a smoke screen for the Boche. The Marines of 2/5 might well have wondered, "Whose side are the French artillery on, anyway?"

On they came and a young Chauchat gunner next to Cooke began slamming away, letting go a full clip. "'Hey, that feels good' . . . he grinned." Cooke demanded, "Give me a try." As much as the young private, he, too, enjoyed getting even. The area was filled with lead, from a few inches off the ground and upward, and finally the Boche couldn't take any more. They removed themselves from the field, leaving it entirely to the Marines. Due to the precision of the Marines' rifle fire, the German soldiers were lying in heaps across their front. It would be another few hours before they attempted another attack across open ground in the face of something brand new to them: accurate rifle fire, something that hadn't been seen on any battlefield for several years.

• • •

By noon the 2d Division was holding twelve miles of front. As yet, the only serious enemy probing activity had been against 2/5, 1/6, and a battalion of the 9th Infantry. Otherwise the division suffered mainly from long-range artillery and machine-gun fire. There were still some Frenchmen up front making a grand effort to stem any further German advance. But, though their numbers were weak, their morale was strengthened by the knowledge that a strong line of Americans had formed up behind them, a line through which they could pass if things really got rough. In fact, that night, some of them would take advantage of that strong line. Meanwhile, on the front of the 75th Company, sometime shortly before noon,

> they [the Germans] made a few calls. . . . They came out of the wood opposite our position [Belleau Wood] in close formation. They came on as steadily as if they were on parade. We opened up on them with a slashing barrage of rifles, automatics, and machine guns. They halted, withdrew a space, then came on again. They had a good artillery barrage in front of them, but it didn't keep us down. Three times they tried to break through, but our fire was too accurate and too heavy for them. It was terrible in its effectiveness. They fell by the scores, there among the poppies and the wheat.[26]

The 8th Machine Gun Company made a rapid recovery from their long walk. Not many hours after arrival they had supplied twelve guns to support Wise's left. The 81st Company supplied four more for his right flank and the 15th Company provided another four.[27] That afternoon the field artillery regiments of 2d Field Artillery Brigade, which had marched steadily twenty-four miles overland from their railhead, arrived at their assembly point at Cocherel. The 15th FA Regiment was assigned to the 3d Brigade and the 12th FA to the 4th Brigade. Equipped with French 75s, the two regiments would support the brigades to which they were assigned, at least through the month of June. The 17th FA, with 155s, was assigned to both; a battalion behind each brigade, with the third battalion south of the highway devoted to counterbattery work. The 12th established its headquarters at La Loge Farm, which put it nearly on the Paris-Metz Road, or about three and one-half miles from the center of Belleau Wood. Now that division artillery had finally arrived through no fault of the French tranport, some of the French artillery withdrew. Although the Germans noted this arrival and the emplacement of guns, they did little to intimidate, and nothing to cause any loss to, the Americans. Perhaps they were saving up for the future.

There was better news in the afternoon. The rolling kitchens arrived, having marched overland from Chaumont. Major Henry N. Manney Jr., USMC, commanding the 4th Brigade's train, waited for many hours at division headquarters for directions and orders from the chief of staff. As late as 1650, he still hadn't even seen Brown, let alone obtained the necessary dispersal instructions. Meanwhile, Capt. Walter H. Sitz of Headquarters Company, 6th Marines, happened to be at division headquarters at the same time. Sitz had a conversation with Manney and then sent Maj. Frank E. Evans, adjutant of the 6th Marines, a message which told Evans that Manney would send a motorcycle to Sitz for Evans, but "will not give up Ford as he says that is all he has." Little possessions like a motorcar loomed large in instances where having one gave immediate prestige to whomever had it. Let Evans ride the motorcycle instead.

Because the troops had not eaten a hot meal since they had left their quarters at Chaumont-en-Vexin on 31 May, except for those scroungers who had found other ways and means, the arrival of rolling kitchens was an event of the first magnitude. The kitchens were sent as far forward as it seemed practical, with orders to keep out of sight and not to use anything but dry wood. If they didn't, the smoke would draw down a veritable hailstorm upon them. It was possible for some reserve battalions, in the back areas, to have their kitchens with them, but those on the front line would still find a hot meal an exception to a daily rule. The Marine infantry's reserve rations were mostly long gone. Many, those who hadn't found something else, had been hungry since they had arrived.[28] For many, hot food, or any food, would still not be forthcoming.

The Germans had kept up their artillery fire on Les Mares Farm most of the day. About a hundred yards in front of the Marines' position was a small knoll that offered an excellent field of fire. So, at 1700, Lem Shepherd suggested to Blanchfield that he take ten men and hold that knoll until the artillery fire became too hot for them and then they would retire. Shepherd later said he offered to do that with phony bravado, believing that his skipper wouldn't take that chance. He admitted being terribly surprised when Blanchfield promptly accepted. Out they went, dodging the still falling shells, somehow making their destination without a casualty. After posting his men, Shepherd left a sergeant in charge and returned to Blanchfield to describe what he had done. While both were talking, they noticed that the Boche had stepped up their artillery fire and that a rolling barrage was moving toward the outpost. Shepherd requested that he be allowed to return to his command out front and his skipper agreed. The barrage had already passed the knoll, and when Shepherd and his orderly moved forward they were obliged to walk through a curtain of exploding steel. By the most outrageous fortune, neither was hurt, and soon both dropped into a foxhole on the knoll, alongside the occupants.

"There come the Boche," sang out a sergeant. Looking out of their holes, the group could see the first of the German assault waves advancing toward them. Marine Pvt. Paul Bonner tells us that he saw his commanding officer, Capt. John Blanchfield, standing at the side of the road:

> "The devils are coming on," he shouted. "You have been waiting for them for a year; now go get them." He was shouting in his Irish brogue and his blood was up. He thrilled every one of us.[29]

Marines had spent much time on the rifle range learning just what they were supposed to do at a time like this. Each man did his duty; he choose his target, then squeezed them off, pulling the bolt back and throwing another round into the chamber; he continued doing the same thing over and over again. Meticulous training, steadiness, coolness, discipline, and accuracy were soon making a bloody mess of the advancing German line. The Marines were dropping many of those in the first wave and soon they were working over the second. This was a new kind of rifle fire on the western front, and the Germans recognized and appreciated it by stopping their forward motion. Down they went, in a prone position, not to fire, but simply to take cover from those terrible rifles. Even at that the Marines were still able to pick off many more.

The pause didn't last very long. In the meantime, German machine guns began firing in barrage fashion from the nearby Bois de Mares. Soon after, the Marines were also taking casualties, especially those in Shepherd's advanced position. It wasn't very long, although they were burrowed deeper into their holes, before the cries of pain from the wounded gave notice that some of the German bullets were also finding their targets. The firing of the machine guns was so intense that the Marines couldn't raise themselves to respond. Soon after dark, Lieutenant Shepherd gave the order for his detachment to fall back to the main trench line, taking their wounded with them.

Shortly after Shepherd and his men made it back to the main line, the enemy organized an even heavier assault upon the farm itself. At this time the 55th was still without machine guns. There was a gap of about five hundred yards between the left of the 55th and Veuilly Wood, with a wheat field intervening. Part of a platoon from the right wing was placed in the gap to prevent the Germans from infiltrating in that direction. As the gray waves approached again, the Marines were lining every window and doorway of the farm buildings and at the breaches created by shells in the walls surrounding the farm. Again, the Marines exhibited their marksmanship. From these positions they aimed and fired as coolly as though they were at practice, and so accurately that not one live German made it to within a hundred yards of the buildings. During this attack Gy. Sgt. Herman "Babe" Tharau exhibited his individual courage. He calmly went up and down along the defensive positions, encouraging his men while pointing out potential targets and somehow avoided the incoming fire.[30]

The first two waves of Germans made repeated efforts to penetrate the buildings, but each time, when they came within range of Marine rifles, large numbers of German casualties forced those following to turn aside and re-form outside the range of the deadly fire. The third line, apparently discouraged at the loss of numerous comrades, withdrew without attempting to make the assault. But the Germans continued to make their presence felt. Their machine guns kept up an intermittent fire until dark and occasionally their bullets found a Marine target.

During the night a detachment from Headquarters Company, with several machine guns from the 8th, 15th, and 81st, arrived and added greatly to the strength and firepower of the position. With these men and guns it was now the Marines' turn to open up on the German machine guns, which were soon forced to withdraw out of range. But the German artillery continued to make the situation nasty. The company suffered several casualties, and at least one building was set afire by the constant bombardment. That evening the division's 12th FA was emplaced. Soon after, they provided a lively fire that silenced the enemy artillery. That gave the Marines of 2/5 some much-needed rest from the nearly thirty-six hours of continuous fighting they had so far endured.

Food was very important to all of them, and it was the thing that most Marines were constantly thinking about while in France. For the next few days those Marines in 2/5 would forage and fight, and what cooking was done, often, was while the fighting was still going on. But, as always, the self-reliant Marines managed to take care of themselves, even though their army couldn't.

At 2020 Capt. Dwight F. Smith, skipper of the 82d Company, notified Major Sibley that he had not been attacked yet but "a French major on our right . . . expects attack tonight or early morning. Situation much better than I thought at first. . . . I have filled up entire gap of French troops that did withdraw. . . . Ammunition not yet received." Harbord told Catlin that he was "very glad [Smith] declined [to] retire." He also made mention that "one of Wise's companies . . . also declined." (See Harbord's note.)

But shortly after its arrival the 82d was in trouble. Four men were killed and several others were wounded by artillery fire. Sometime afterward, 3/6's Headquarters Company (1st Lt. David Bellamy), the 83d Company (1st Lt. Alfred Noble), and one platoon from the regimental 73d Machine Gun Company led by Capt. Roy W. Swink were sent to bolster the 82d Company. Since most of his battalion was now located in line there, Maj. Berton W. Sibley of 3/6 assumed command of that portion of the line running from Hill 142 in an easterly direction for about a thousand yards. Most of the line was along the edge of Belleau Wood, and at some points the Boches were also in the woods, only fifty or so yards away. It was a difficult spot for both groups to be in.

Harbord in his daily report to Bundy summarized the important happenings of the day:

> The French line has fallen back nearly to our own line, practically on our whole front. In one case, a retreating French officer gave an order in writing to an American officer to fall back from the position which we have been holding. The order was not obeyed.

This, then, was the famous order given to Capt. Lloyd W. Williams, of the 51st Company, in which his response, "Retreat, hell! We just got here," set the tone for the entire brigade. Williams, ever the professional, requested that the French "kindly not shorten their artillery range," for they might hit him.[31] That night Maj. Holland McT. Smith sent a message to both regimental COs and to Major Cole: "Gen. Harbord directs that the necessary steps be taken to hold our positions at *all costs*." (Emphasis in original.)[32] The situation was getting hairy and everyone in the brigade knew it.

Tuesday, 4 June

Major Sibley had remained with his three detached companies in the area of Hill 142. When he reconnoitered his position he found that the French had withdrawn from Belleau Wood and Bouresches, leaving a large gap uncovered on the right, as well as the territory between him and 1/6. Shortly afterward a couple of companies from 1/5, the 17th and 66th with some machine guns from the 8th Company, which were assigned to support 2/5, were sent to fill that gap between them. The distance was approximately a half mile in length and this location would continue to dog everyone who was sent to fill it. What made matters even worse was that the main road between Torcy and Lucy went right through the area. Any advance made by German forces south would naturally take this easiest pathway. The 4th Brigade's entire position would thus be in serious trouble, greatly affecting the 2d Division, the entire line, and ultimately the war.

At 0400 those French still between the brigade and the Boche were relieved and they passed through the American lines to the rear. At 0800 the French turned over command of the sector to General Bundy. Up until this time most of the dispositions of the division had been made under French direction. The major emphasis had been to support the forward French lines. Now the division and its brigade leaders were free to make their own errors. During this changeover the Americans were aided greatly by the relative inactivity of the Germans, but no thank-you notes were exchanged.

The area now controlled by the 2d Division stretched from Monneaux, at the base of Hill 204, to Le Thiolet, then to Lucy, to Hill 142, and finally to Les Mares Farm. Brigade command then issued orders that altered nearly everyone's current position. Headquarters of the brigade moved itself from Issonge Farm a half mile southward to La Loge, where it was less exposed to German observation. Ben Berry's 3/5, which had been serving as corps reserve, was returned to brigade control and now, as brigade reserve, relocated to the woods southwest of Marigny. The 5th Marines front was still held generally by Lieutenant Colonel Wise's 2/5 but they were supported by some reinforcements from 1/5 and the regimental Headquarters Company. The 6th Marines remained as they were, clustered about Triangle, with Lucy to their left and facing toward Bouresches.

The Germans suddenly became very active. Unbeknownst to the 4th Brigade they had moved into the Bois de Belleau and were organizing a defense that would stymie the Marines for the next three weeks. The 461st Infantry Regiment was now in liaison with the 10th Division at the southwest corner of Belleau Wood near Bouresches. They also established positions along the south face of the woods to the base of Hill 181 and then northward along the wood's western edge. Patrols of the 237th Regiment penetrated the Bois St. Martin just north of Lucy. Some of them operating near Lucy picked up a 6th Marine corpse, which was carried back to the intelligence section. It was the first American they had seen, but he would not be the last. There would be enough Americans to go around. More than enough to satisfy even the Germans. And, likewise.

In the afternoon, a number of soldiers from the Saxon 26th Jäger Battalion managed to creep back through the standing wheat and were heard digging in the field opposite Les Mares Farm. Because of the wheat screen, it was impossible to calculate their numbers. Therefore, it became necessary for someone to go out there and count them. Corporal Francis J. Dockx volunteered to go. He took three men with him. After crawling about fifty yards through the wheat they ran into a German patrol of thirty men and two machine guns. Regardless of the odds of ten to one against them, the Marines immediately opened up with their automatics and then charged the enemy. From the intensity of the firing, and fearing that the Marines may have gotten into a bad fix, Gy. Sgt. David L. Buford took two other men and went out to assist the small detachment. He found Dockx and his comrades fighting off the Germans and hurling back the thrown hand grenades. When Buford arrived they had already dropped several Boches. The Germans began to give way with the arrival of more firepower. Buford, an excellent shot with a clear view, took out seven of the Germans with his automatic as they tried to escape. They died, all of them. Only the machine guns remained to be dealt with. After a cautious approach, Buford*, Dockx*, and company rushed the guns. In that final rush Dockx and one other Marine were killed, but the remaining German gun-crew members were captured. Of that thirty-man raiding group only five Germans escaped to their lines in safety.

This would be the last German attempt to take Les Mares Farm and would be the closest that they would get to their ultimate objective in this war, Paris. Their spree in Paris would have to wait for another war. A large number of Marines would earn some of the highest decorations then awarded by the AEF, but many would get them posthumously. Shepherd had been wounded in the neck on the 3d of June and would earn the DSC, and later an NC, for declining medical treatment while continuing to lead his men. Tharau would get a Croix de Guerre. There were other awards, but they were too numerous to cite here. Les Mares Farm is still listed on the current, modern maps of that part of France. A recent visit indicates that it is in current use with a few modern buildings and all holes repaired.

Meanwhile, 2d Lt. William A. Eddy, intelligence officer for the 6th Marines, with two enlisted men, undertook a reconnaissance that night up the Lucy-Torcy road. They came back with information that pinpointed the location of the enemy as being south of the Clignon Brook. Eddy mentioned hearing coughing and talking in a foreign tongue. As far as we can determine, that was the only attempt, during the first week, at reconnoitering the ground over which the brigade would fight, and it wasn't much.

That evening, in his daily report to General Bundy, Harbord proudly advertised the fact that "the Brigade Headquarters were honored this afternoon by a visit from the Commander-in-Chief who expressed his satisfaction of the work of the Marine Brigade."[33] Pershing had every reason to be satisfied. His 2d Division was certainly better than any other division of the AEF, although he would have put his money on his "pets" of the great 1st Division.

As usual, the troops were fed intermittently. There was no real organization in obtaining the grub or passing it on to the front lines. Later, after the war, General Bundy would write of this time:

> Only one hot meal was served during the twenty-four-hour day, and it was frequently cold by the time it reached the men in the front line. This continued during the entire forty days in which the division held the front line. We received the French ration, a part of which was canned beef shipped from Madagascar. It had a peculiar taste which our men did not like. They called it 'monkey meat' and it soon became known by that name throughout the army.

Wednesday, 5 June

The 2d Division formed the right of the French XXI Corps d'Armée. On the division's right was the French XXXVIII Corps, which included the 10th Colonial Division with the 30th U.S. Infantry attached.[34] No systematic patrolling or reconnaissance was engaged in by members of the 4th Brigade after they took over the territory from the French. This would be a recurring problem that would only be corrected slowly. The only record of a reconnaissance was that performed by 2d Lt. William A. Eddy. The disaster that would come on the morrow was directly caused by failure to reconnoiter the ground to be taken. Harbord would be quoted later as saying something like "I thought the French had done all of that." If that was a reasonably correct quotation, brigade headquarters didn't know what was before them and consequently the regiments didn't know either. Worse, no one in charge took it upon himself to do anything about it.

Sometime during the day, Turrill sent Neville a strength report on his battalion. It reflected that there were 22 officers and 953 men, a total of 975 "present." The next morning there would be a drastic reduction in those totals.

Field Order No. 8, 2d Division, 5 June, issued at 1000, stated simply that the 4th Brigade's area of responsibility ran from Triangle to eight hundred meters north of Champillon on the Bussiares road. The 5th and 6th Marines would occupy the ground, left to right running eastward. Berry's 3/5 would relieve 1/6 on the line and 1/6 would constitute army (XXI) corps reserve.[35] Division headquarters was moving from Montreuil-aux-Lions a mile and a half southwest to Bézu-le-Guéry. Harbord issued orders to Catlin and Neville that

> on arrival of the troops of the 167th French Division to relieve that portion of your line west of but not including Champillon you will cause guides to be furnished to conduct them to their positions. . . . When they are in position you will withdraw your left battalion [2/5].

Harbord issued additional orders to both regimental officers for the following changes in the lines after dark: Berry and 3/5 would take up a position running from just east of Hill 142, southeast to a point north of Lucy-le-Bocage. In other words, facing Belleau Wood. The 23d Infantry was going to take up more ground currently occupied by Holcomb and 2/6. That regiment's left would set on, and would include, Triangle Farm. Holcomb and his lads would then be responsible for the territory running north from Triangle to Lucy. The sector of the 5th Marines would be from Lucy north and west to the village of Champillon.[36] Major changes such as these were a common occurence during the month of June. Sometimes they made sense, sometimes not. To the hole-digging enlisted Marine, they made no sense at all.

What that all boiled down to was that the area covered by the 4th Brigade would be substantially reduced. It would contract over a mile on the south and another half mile on the northwest. The 23d Infantry would move northward to fill the gap between the 9th and 6th Marines. In addition, most, but not all, of the Marines would be in position for the following day's activities.

At 2100, Frank Evans, adjutant of the 6th Marines, sent Sibley a message telling him that he and his two companies would be relieved by Turrill's 1/5 "sometime tonight," and that he should go to Ferme Blanche, on the Paris-Metz Highway, where he would find the balance of 3/6 and go into reserve. Turrill, who was slated to launch a major attack the following morning at 0345, hadn't yet received his orders at this late hour. Late receipt of orders was a common occurrence in the 4th Brigade all during the war.

Meanwhile, the German forces opposed to the 2d Division were in worse shape than was commonly known. The 47th Infantry Regiment had five rifle companies without a single officer. The second battalion of that regiment had one officer, and the remnants of the battalion had been formed into one company under his command. On 5 June, the relief of that regiment had been contemplated, but it was not carried out because of the continuing hostile attacks. Two machine-gun companies attached to the regiment were without officers. The 398th Infantry had reported, on 4 June, that its troops were no longer fit for frontline service. Its companies averaged 40 men; not enough to even man the light machine guns of the company, and certainly not enough to man the heavy guns. There was a shortage of 1,200 riflemen in the 6th Grenadier Regiment. On 4 June that regiment was reported as exhausted and incapable of further effort. A divisional artillery commander reported his command was reduced and worn out and a division commander reported that in his three regiments he was down by 3,000 rifles. That reduction in numbers would have been a disaster for any U.S. division, let alone a smaller German division. Several of the best German divisions were exhausted and behind the lines in reserve positions. Other German divisions entered the line between 31 May and 1 June and since none had as yet encountered heavy fighting, they were consequently still fairly fresh. That would change soon.

A decision, therefore, was made by the German command to attack on the morning of 6 June. On 5 June orders were issued directing them to continue their advance south of the Clignon, thereby taking as much of the ground as possible for further thrusts. The terrain was admirable for concealment and assembly. German infantry could form up for attack in those woods and depressions while his artillery immobilized the American main line of resistance.

Coincidentally, General Dégoutte was determined to order a general advance to seize several strong points and at the same time deny them to the enemy. He decided to launch an attack to regain the lost ground from Veuilly-la-Poterie to the Champillon Brook. The unit he chose to batter the Boche was the French 167th Division. In addition, an order was issued for the 2d Division to go forward with the French advance. Their assigned responsibility was to clear the long ridge of Hill 142 and to take steps to assure liaison with the new line established by the French. A second phase, to be launched later in the day, but soon after the first, would be the taking of Belleau Wood and Bouresches.

Division Chief of Staff Preston Brown, sent Harbord and Neville Field Order No. 1, which stated briefly that

> this brigade will attack on the right of the French 167th D.I. . . . from the Little Square Wood 400 meters S.E. of the Calvaire to the brook crossing [outlining Turrill's responsibility]. . . .
> The attack between the brook of Champillon, inclusive, Hill 142, and the brook which flows from 1 kilometer N.E. of Champillon, inclusive, will be made by the 1st Bn., 5th Marines, supported by the 8th and 23d Cos., machine guns.[37]

This, the first major assault launched by any unit of the 2d Division, was an unmitigated disaster from the first, as will be seen. Turrill did not receive his orders until an hour or so after midnight and he had many miles to go to get into his jump-off position. To make matters worse, two of his companies were absent. They had previously been attached to 2/5, and though orders for their relief had been issued, it was far too late for them to make an appearance in time. Neither Capt. John H. Fay and his 8th Machine Gun Company or Capt. George H. Osterhout Jr., who commanded the 23d, would be able to show up. Only ten guns from the 15th Company (Capt. Matthew H. Kingman) were there to support the attack. The 8th was delayed for several hours and additional guns from the 81st Company didn't arrive until midafternoon.[38]

Furthermore, as will be seen, an order for 3/5 to advance to its left to conform to the progress made by 1/5 was not followed. Berry's left company, the 45th under Capt. Peter Conachy, was never quite able to make liaison with the 49th Company of Capt. George W. Hamilton.[39] That deplorable situation, caused mainly by obsolete French maps, created a serious problem that hampered 1/5 most of the following day.

Finally, ravines, which flowed along the base of both sides of Hill 142, would have to be cleared, making for even greater difficulties, as would the knoll of Hill 142, held in great strength by Maxim guns and their handlers. Turrill and his two companies would have their hands full before the 6th of June was over.

Thursday, 6 June

This would be the most catastrophic day in Marine Corps history. More Marines would be killed and wounded on this single day than in all its previous existence. For the 5th Marines only 4 October 1918, at Blanc Mont, would exceed it. For all intents and purposes, the old warriors of the U.S. Marine Corps were virtually wiped out.

Early that morning Berry reported that 3/5 had relieved 1/6, and were in the positions as directed by the brigade order. Sibley and 3/6 had already been relieved by 1/5 and had moved southeast. Hughes sent a message to Catlin at 0730 that his missing two companies, the 74th and 95th, had reported in, even though the "enemy attempted to pull off small raid during relief. Driven off. Two Pvts 95th killed. Need rations." About 0300 a battalion of the 23d Infantry relieved Holcomb. He and 2/6 then proceeded to the woods near regimental headquarters, which lay just south of Lucy-le-Bocage.

(To recapitulate: Wise was relieved at Les Mares Farm and moved into Champillon Woods behind Berry. Berry was on the hillside in the St. Martin's Wood opposite Belleau Wood. Turrill with his abbreviated battalion was on Hill 176 overlooking Hill 142. Sibley had moved down to Lucy-le-Bocage. Holcomb was spread out south of Lucy to Triangle Farm and Hughes was in reserve, located near the Paris Farm on the Paris-Metz highway.)

The two available companies of 1/5, the 49th (Hamilton) and the 67th (Crowther), had spent most of 4–5 June under partial cover of the Bois de Veuilly, not far from Marigny. Because of the successive moves they had made, the two companies had not been fed during the previous few days, which created a minor morale problem that would fester among the men. In addition, on 5 June, the German artillery had been directed with fatal accuracy into those woods. Several shells caused the battalion's first extensive casualties. To make matters worse, the latest order for Turrill's moves had not arrived until 2300 on 5 June and the order designated that the companies would have to be in position within three hours of the attack scheduled at 0345 that morning.

The battalion didn't miss the bus, they went off on time, even though no one but the company commanders had maps, and not very good ones at that. First Lieutenant John W. Thomason Jr. tells us that he and the other platoon leaders had a brief look at Hamilton's: "You're here. The objective is a square patch of woods a kilometer and a half northeast, about." At this time 1/5 was located on Hill 176, slightly south and east of Champillon. The "square woods" that Hamilton mentioned were down off Hill 142 to the northeast. The woods were more rectangular than square.[40]

The terrain object before them was an elongated stretch of land rising above the valley. It was more like a large finger pointing northward with a sharp drop on each side. Along the base, on each side, ran a ravine. The entire level of Hill 142 was covered with heavy brush or small trees, becoming ever denser at the north end. The Germans had worked overtime digging in. They were well prepared.

The attack plan decided upon was for the 49th Company to take the right flank along the crest and, after eliminating the enemy, to move down into the ravine alongside. Apparently Hamilton thought he was then to go directly northeast toward Torcy, because that is what most of the 49th did. The 67th Company, 1st Lt. Orlando Crowther commanding, was to advance along the left side of the crest. They were to knock out any Germans, and then some of the company was to move down into the ravine that ran along the left side of the hill in an effort to keep pace with the French, who would also be advancing. Facing the Marines, left to right, was the Boche from the 9th, 10th, and 11th Companies who were all from the 460th Infantry Regiment and equipped with many Maxims.

At the appropriate time, 1st Sgt. Daniel "Pop" Hunter of the 67th Company, with thirty years of service already behind him, strode out before his line, checked right and left, then, with a whistle to his mouth, blew it once. Forward, over his head, and downward went his cane, pointing toward the company's objective, straight ahead. The two assaulting companies, with platoons in four waves, had advanced a short distance down the slopes into the first opening and ran head-on into a machine-gun barrage laid down by the Germans. Casualties were hor-

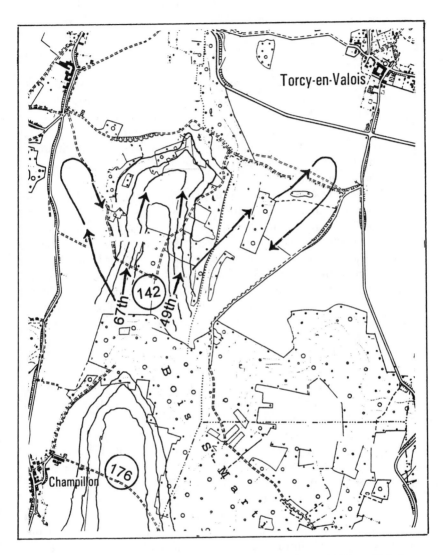

Map 3: Major Turrill led two companies, the 49th and 67th, of his 1st Bn, 5th Marines downward from Hill 176 to Hill 142, overwhelming the German defenders and driving them off the high ground. Note where both companies had to fall back after advancing beyond the original objective.

rendous. "Pop" was one of the first. Hit twice and up twice, hit the third time, he went down for good.

The 67th Company quickly overlapped and swept past the German 9th Company on the left. It then came under the fire of a heavy machine gun located on the crest of the ravine west of the hill, losing heavily in both officers and men. Private Joseph M. Baker of the 67th saw the fire from a hidden Maxim that was inflicting casualties on his comrades and exposed himself to the heavy fire in order to take up a position on the flank of the gun. He attacked and killed the gunner with rifle fire and then rushed the gun, killing the crew with his bayonet. His reward: a Distinguished Service Cross, followed later by a Navy Cross. He was one of the lucky survivors.

Marines and Germans were fighting the nastiest kind of battle—close in and with bayonets, rifle fire, and of course, worst of all, machine guns at point-blank range. Some Marines were lying just a few yards before the blazing Maxims. They were forced to keep down, not even able to look at what was troubling them. If they had, they would be minus part, or all, of their heads. Finally, able to bear no more, the Marines got off the deck and started to advance against their tormentors, taking heavy losses in so doing. One man grabbed the muzzle of a Maxim, upturned it, and lost his hand in the process. The Germans were good. The Marines were better.

When the 49th Company reached the initial objective, a very large number of its officers and noncommissioned officers were already on the casualty list. Regardless, some of the men pressed on down the northeastern slope of the hill, holding tenaciously to the additional ground they had taken, until recalled to the designated line.

The Germans had learned, or developed, many tricks in their four years at war. One that would cause a great deal of trouble for aid men, on either side, was discovered on Hill 142. Medical help was forthcoming almost as soon as the first men started to drop that morning, and no one interfered, at first. But Marines saw a German first-aid team carrying a Maxim and several boxes of ammunition on a stretcher. It had appeared, at first, like a wounded man lying with his legs drawn up, until a gust of wind flipped back the blanket covering the stretcher. "Thereafter," wrote John W. Thomason Jr., "it was hard on Red Cross men and the wounded; hard, in fact, on everybody." Naturally the Marines learned how, too, from the Boche.

A large number of men of the 49th, in their eagerness and excitement, had gone beyond the hill, down into the valley below and across some of the fields beyond. They were subjected to intense sniper fire, which caused many additional casualties. The German 12th Company, 460th Infantry, delivered a counterattack from the northeast and a Jäger battalion came from the direction of Bussiares. They killed many of the Marines and captured a few. Marines were recalled and fell back across the valley to the slopes of the north end of 142, after which they soon drove out the snipers.[41] By this time some members of the 8th Company had arrived with their weapons. They and their guns were sent down the center and along the crest of the ravine on the right to reinforce those positions. Both companies pushed their way toward the north slope, driving the enemy before them. Down the slope went the Boche, down to the flat ground and into the woods below, where they began to re-form their lines.

By late morning, even though the two original companies of 1/5 were in tough shape, the positions taken by them, and their helpers, were in moderately good order. Some of the men had dug foxholes, others had started small trenches. The remnants of the 67th and 49th Companies held their ground against many counterattacks that morning, breaking up several enemy formations.

Gunnery Sergeant Charles F. Hoffman, of the 49th, who had been trying to organize a position on the north slope of 142, saw twelve German soldiers armed with five light machine guns crawling toward his group. Hoffman grabbed a Springfield rifle, charged and bayoneted the two leaders, and forced the others to flee, leaving their guns behind. "His quick action, initiative, and courage drove the enemy from a position from which they could have swept the hill with machine gun fire and forced the withdrawal of our troops." That citation earned him a Medal of Honor, one of nine awarded to Marines during the war. Even though he was severely wounded he would survive the war.[42]

A platoon of the 66th Company under 2d Lt. Max Gilfillan arrived and Turrill established them in a line on the left side of the hill. When Capt. Roswell Winans and his 17th Company appeared, they were sent over to the right flank alongside the 49th. Several officers of the 17th would make their presence known soon enough even though they did arrive late. First Lieutenant Albert P. Baston*, though badly wounded in both legs while leading his platoon, refused treatment until he personally assured himself that all his men were under cover and in good firing positions. Another officer of the 17th, 1st Lt. Robert Blake*, volunteered to maintain liaison with the 49th Company. He continually crossed and recrossed the open ground all the while under heavy fire, returning to Winans with valuable information. Some of the enlisted men of the 1st Battalion, 5th Marines, who performed gallant acts that day were Pvt. Ernest Borah of the 17th; Sgt. John Casey* of the 49th, who refused medical attention until his men were all properly dug in; and Cpl. Arnold D. Godbey* of the 67th, later commissioned, who volunteered to rescue wounded men from a field swept by machine-gun and sniper fire.[43] Also, we must remember Capt. George W. Hamilton*, the "bravest of the brave." [44] By midmorning most of the officers of both the 49th and 67th Companies had become casualties, so Hamilton stepped in and merged the two companies, taking command of both.

This was the first major effort made by the Marine brigade since they had arrived in France, and within three hours they had successfully taken all their objectives except the "square woods," but with appalling losses. The 49th had lost five officers out of six, and the 67th, four officers of five, including First Lieutenant Crowther, the acting company commander. The losses of the men amounted to about fifty percent. Regardless of the difficulties, Captain Hamilton, who was the senior officer present, soon had the semblance of a line formed. But the battalion, even with their additional support and future replacements, was now so badly weakened that it would endure mainly on the defensive at Hill 142 for nearly the balance of the month of June.

Harbord sent Neville a message at 0900 on 6 June in which he lauded the activities of both 1/5 and 3/5 "on doing so well what we all knew they would do." The adjutant of 1/5, Capt. Keller Rockey, seemed satisfied. He told Neville that even though the 2d Battalion, 2d Engineers, had still not arrived, "all seemed to be going well." He was an optimist. Fortunately "D" Company of the Engineers soon arrived and the soldiers were immediately sent in as infantry support where they, as always, did their job superbly.

Reports going out of brigade headquarters were incredibly optimistic. Harbord saw some wounded Marines and recorded that "their bearing was cocky and that they were in fine spirits." At 0630 Maj. Harry R. Lay, brigade adjutant, sent word from the front that all was going well. It isn't apparent where he obtained his information. The count of prisoners went from 65 to 300 until, finally, 1 German officer and 15 men were actually accounted for. Extravagant accounts of success have always been a part of every war by every army. It is part of a commanding officer's justification for sending men to be slaughtered and serves mostly to elevate his military reputation for posterity.

On Turrill's right, 3/5 had been struggling to maintain an effective liaison with 1/5. Captain Peter Conachy's 45th Company was supposed to be the connecting link between the two. Just after 0600, his left platoon, commanded by Lt. Edward B. Hope, established itself at a site that was nearly a half mile from the top of Hill 142. There were consistent reports of German soldiers between the two battalions. Turrill reported at 0900 that he heard firing from Berry's group in the "woods on my right. Woods not shown on map." Hamilton requested Brigade to "push Berry up to our right." It was not to be. Conachy tried, Hope tried, everybody tried, but that gap would continue to haunt everyone involved until 25 June.

Meanwhile, 1/5, or rather what was left of the battalion, was barely able to maintain its position against continuous German counterattacks. Turrill, Hamilton, and Winans continued to beg regiment for artillery support to their front and sustenance for their troops. "Can't Headquarters Company come up and be used [to] carry water, food, ammunition, etc. Need Very Pistol or French rifle with signal rockets?" There were a great number of wounded, both Americans and Germans, and efforts to remove them to safety were on hold. The heavy fire being exchanged between Marines and Germans was too dangerous to make any movement on that fire-swept field. Until they were disposed of, German snipers and machine gunners continued to harass the Marines. Even members of the 5th Regiment's band were used to move the wounded, and many of them were shot while so engaged. Later, Harbord would issue an order that bandsmen weren't to be used in the front line for any purpose. They, unlike riflemen, were too difficult to replace. At 1310 Turrill notified regiment that the French came up on his left, somewhat easing that problem. But his right flank was still in trouble. Fortunately, the two companies of Germans who lay on that flank were not overly aggressive.[45]

First Lieutenant Elliott D. Cooke, USA, of the 18th Company, relates that his battalion was in reserve (deep in Champillon Woods) and had been waiting for news about what was going on with the 1st Battalion. They heard the sound of firing, but it wasn't until a group of Marines led by Colonel Feland came down a dirt road toward them, with a sullen bunch of Heinie prisoners, that they realized that the attack must be going well. A few minutes later, 2d Lt. Herman A. Zischke came strolling down the road with a Gladstone bag and lots of "sea stories" for the company. He had been away at school and had just now returned with several Paris newspapers. Headlines, in French but translatable, stated that the Marine Brigade had saved Paris. Zischke told his audience,

"The Frenchmen you relieved did a Paul Revere right into Paris. They warned everybody on a forty-mile front that there was nothing between Paris and the Germans but a few Americans and the whole country migrated south. So when the Germans didn't show up on the Rue de la Paix, the French decided you-all saved their capital." Our chest stuck out a little further after that.[46]

Cooke continues, "If it was that easy to save Paris maybe they should just go on and take Berlin by themselves." The conversation then degenerated into exchanges of opinions on Rhine wine and frauleins, just as though any members of the group had tried either one.

Turrill's battalion would continue to fight off German attacks for most of the balance of that day, but by noon 1/5's active attack operation was definitely over. They had won, but at what cost. Their total casualties, dead, wounded, and missing, numbered 8 officers and 325 men, of whom most were in the 49th and 67th Companies. The 8th Machine Gun Company lost 10 men and the 51st Company 1 officer and 45 men. Conachy's company, the 45th, suffered casualties of 2 officers and 71 men.[47] Although, not all the designated objectives were reached, the Marines were tactically on them all. Because of losses sustained, the 67th Company had not been able to go to the Little Woods just at the northwest tip of Hill 142, but their final position made the woods untenable for the Germans. The unimproved road on the right at the brook crossing was also under the command of the Marines' rifles and machine guns. The French were on the left and the battalion's right flank was refused southward along the ravine to the Bois St. Martin. There was still a break, but Conachy's company was closer now. The 10th and 11th German companies were still lying low at X-line 263.0.

The operational report on what happened at Hill 142 and its surrounding environs was sent to Neville by Turrill at 2100 and it is the best single overall description I've found as to what happened that day. Therefore, I've taken the liberty of reproducing it nearly in its entirety:

I arrived on the first line trenches at 3:45 a.m. Went down the front line and found some of the men over the top and about 25 yards out—so I gave the word to advance to the whole line—which consisted of the 49th Company Capt. Hamilton on the right and the 67th Company Lt. Crowther on the left. The other two companies

were not relieved in time to get them up to support the advance;
neither could the 8th M.G. Company get relieved in time, the 23d
M.G. Company which was supposed to report never appeared—
so we made the attack with two inf. Cos. instead of with 4 inf. Cos.
and 2 M.G. Cos. There was a barrage from some M.G. Cos. under
Major Cole. I remained in the jumping off trench 100 yds north
of the figure "2" in 142 until the fourth wave of the 2 Cos. disappeared in the woods 1/2 kilometer north of "142." About that time
a platoon of the 66th Company under Lt. [Max D.] Gilfillan arrived abreast of me & I advanced it to the north edge of the above
mentioned woods, where I established my P.C. on the wood-road
(wagon trail). There were quite a few wounded in the grass in the
field up in front. About 4:30 a.m. the 66th Company (rest of it),
came up and I built up a line east & west of me. The 8th M.G. Company then came up and braced the line. The 17th Company, Capt.
Winans arrived and was put on the right of Capt. Hamilton.
Winans worked down the ravine and woods on our right to get in
position. By 8:00 A.M. we had reached our objective and started entrenching. In the excitement and eagerness in chasing the Boche
the men went very fast. The French were at least a kilometer behind us on our left and the situation was the same on our right.
There were snipers in our immediate front in the grass or else in
the trees who caused many casualties. These were finally driven
out. Capt. Williams Company (51st) 2d Bn. came up with 3 platoons and I put him advancing down the left ravine to build up
the front line on the left of our objective. Machine guns were sent
by Capt. Fay to crawl through the grass to our front to build up
the center. During the afternoon the French pushed forward on
our left—in the morning they were apparently made to retire by
artillery falling short in their own lines. Lt. [Walter T. H.] Galliford[48] returned during the afternoon and reported the left of
Berry's Bn. rested on the point from which we started in the morning. One platoon [Hope's] had been advanced a few hundred
yards. The large woods between our right ravine and the road to
Torcy, which woods are not shown on the map, had not been penetrated. In view of the fact that it was less than a 100 yards from
our ravine (incomplete message).[49]

Late that night Hamilton received a message from Captain Rockey,
Turrill's adjutant, which notified him, "The rations sent you tonight are
for all companies. . . . Our ration truck was struck by a shell and rations

scattered all over the country. This is the best we can do tonight." Winans was also in direct contact with Rockey, sending him a message sometime after he had moved into line next to Hamilton.

I am on the right of Hamilton. There is nothing on his left. Just now the Germans are attacking Hamilton's left working around on him. I sent 10 then 20 men to help and protect his flank. Get something in to plug up the hole on our left. We are on the edge of the ravine facing north and northeast. Send up two machine guns for the ravine on the left. Get some help on our left. We don't know whether there are Marines on our right. Can't establish liaison to right or left yet. Get us some artillery on our front. We have a good position but we can't extend anymore. We can hold our own front, I think, with a single line at 5–10 paces interval but we need more reinforcements, food, ammunition. Hamilton is o.k. signed R. Winans, Capt. Comdg. 17th Company.[50]

Later in the month, George Hamilton took a few minutes from his duties to write a letter to a close personal friend, back in his hometown of Washington, D.C. He described things as he saw them:

I was supposed to guide left and keep in liaison with the French.[51] I couldn't see them and knew that at 3:45 they had not started. At 3:50 I started things myself, and we were off. Hadn't moved fifty yards when they cut loose at us from the woods ahead—more machine guns than I had ever heard before. Our men had been trained on a special method of getting out machine guns, and, according to their training, all immediately lay down flat—some *fell*.

I realized that we were up against something unusual and had to run along the whole line and get each man (almost individually) on his feet to rush that wood. Once inside, things got better, but from here on I don't remember clearly what happened. I have vague recollections of urging the whole line on, faster, perhaps, than they should have gone—of grouping prisoners and sending them to the rear under *one* man instead of several—and of snatching an iron cross ribbon off the first officer I got—and of shooting wildly at several rapidly retreating Boches. (I carried a rifle on the whole trip and used it to good advantage.) Farther on, we came to an open field—a wheat-field full of red poppies—and here we caught hell. Again it was a case of rushing across the open and getting into the woods. Afterwards we found why it was they made it so hot for us—three *machine-gun companies* were holding down these woods and the infantry were farther back. Besides several of the heavy Maxims we later found several empty belts and a dead gunner sitting on the seat or lying nearby. It was only because we rushed the positions that we were able to take them, as there were too many guns to take in any other way.

After going through this second wood we were really at our objective, but I was looking for an unimproved road which showed up on the map. We now had the Germans pretty well on the run except a few machine gun nests. I was anxious to get to that road, so pushed forward with the men I had with me—one platoon (I knew the rest were coming, but thought they were closer). We went right down over the nose of a hill [142] and on across an open field between two hills. What saved me from getting hit I don't know—the Maxims on both sides cut loose at us unmercifully—but although I lost [men] heavily here I came out unscratched. I was pushing ahead with an automatic rifle team and didn't notice that most of the platoon had swerved off to the left to rout out the machine guns. All I knew was that there was a road ahead and that the bank gave good protection *to the front*. It happened, however, that there was a town [Torcy] just a few hundred yards to the left, and while most of the Germans had left, about one company was forming for a counter-attack. I realized that I had gone too far—that the nose of the hill I had come over was our objective, and that it was up to me to get back, reorganize, and dig in. It was a case of every man for himself. I crawled back through a drainage ditch filled with cold water and shiny reeds. Machine gun bullets were just grazing my back and our own artillery was dropping close (I was six hundred yards too far to the front). Finally I got back, and started getting the two companies together, and I sent out parties to the right and left to try to hook up with our French and American friends, but it wasn't until the next day that we got a satisfactory liaison.

And now came the counter-attacks—five nasty ones that came near driving us back off our hill—but—we hung on. One especially came near getting me. There were heavy bushes all over the hill, and the first thing I knew hand grenades began dropping near. One grenade threw a rock which caught me behind the ear and made me dizzy for a few minutes. But I quickly recovered my senses when I saw one of my gunnery sergeants [Hoffman] jump toward the bushes with a yell and start shooting to beat the devil. Not twenty feet from us, was a line of about fifteen German helmets and five light machine guns just coming into action. It was hand-to-hand work for several strenuous minutes, and then all was over. We hauled the guns in later and buried most of the Germans.

After the counter-attacks we settled down to the work of digging in. Gee, but it was a long day! The night proved to be worse, and on account of my flanks I was more worried than I cared to admit. The Boches went up the valleys to our right and left and from their flares I thought we were all but surrounded. Two more companies had come up [17th & 66th], however, and the fire from the rifles and auto-rifles of several hundred men must have made the Germans nervous, too, for about dawn they went back and only left several machine guns to worry us during the next day [7 June].

I'm tired of telling about the fighting and am going to knock off. We held the positions; the lines came up on our right and left, and we now have satisfied the Germans that they haven't a chance as long as they are up against Marines. [All emphases in the original.][52]

At 0550 that morning, more than two hours after Turrill started forward, the French had launched an attack toward their front against the 273d German Infantry. They did begin pushing that regiment back and slightly eased the pressure on Turrill's left. Seeing both its flanks being pushed back, but its center holding, the 273d called for artillery support against its former position. At 0610, German shells started raking Hill 142. At 0715 the Germans reported that they had been assailed by a brigade of American troops. That wasn't the only extravagant statement of the day; the infantry brigade of the 197th Division alleged that they were being assaulted by American, French, and English troops. All at once, I presume. The 273d Regiment was ordered to retake all the ground they had lost, up to the top of Hill 142. None was retaken, although strenuous efforts were made all during the forenoon. By the end of the day the 273d Regiment was so badly mauled that its frontage had to be substantially reduced. The Germans were becoming worried about their entire Clignon front. The Americans weren't the only people being hurt that day.

A few days later a Marine took an unmailed letter from the body of a German corporal which had been addressed to his father. In it he said,

"The Americans are savages. They kill everything that moves." The Marines might have written the same sentiments about the Boche snipers and machine gunners. It was a brutal war, and on Hill 142 there was no quarter given. The Germans called the Marines *Teufelhünden,* or "Devil Dogs," and that name sticks to this day. The Marines had a different selection of names that they used for the Boche and used them frequently. Most aren't provided here in deference to polite company.

Field Order No. 2, dated 6 June 1918 and issued from headquarters, 4th Brigade, at 1405, covered the second attack of the day. It outlined in detail just what was expected from the attacking force. On its surface it appears like a reasonably good example of staff work, but the outcome was such a disaster that salient points bear repeating.

The attack will be in two phases
To take the BOIS DE BELLEAU.
To take R.R. station BOURESCHES. . . .

Harbord's orders were very complex, but essentially they boiled down to several maneuvers that in themselves would place four battalions of Marines in jeopardy. First, the taking of Belleau Wood would require that Berry's battalion, in full view, move down a hill and cross an open wheat field, over ground that hadn't been trod by Americans before and which no one had reconnoitered. Then move into woods that were known to be occupied by Germans in force. Originally, Berry was to leave a company behind, Conachy's 45th. Additionally, a right flank advance would be made by Sibley's battalion down the Lucy-Bouresches road and then into the same unreconnoitered woods, the southern edge of which was also teeming with the enemy. Holcomb's 2d Battalion, 6th Marines, would conform to the movements of 3/6, keeping pace with the advance. In addition, 3/6 was also to take Hill 181 in the woods and Hill 138 west of Bouresches. The three battalions would be controlled and coordinated by Col. Albertus Catlin, commander of the 6th Marines. It appears that Berry was informed of this, but not clearly enough.

In the second phase, Berry's battalion, after they had taken the woods, would then join Sibley in taking the town of Bouresches and the railroad station north and east of the town. Turrill's badly beaten 1/5 was to join the victorious movement along with one company from Wise's 2/5 (51st) and Conachy's 45th, to take the hills north of Belleau

Wood to secure the northern flank. This plan was finalized sometime in midafternoon. This was after Turrill and his men had been badly chewed up and that fact was, or should have been, well known to brigade headquarters by that time. Logan Feland would control the left (1/5) of the second phase and Catlin would continue to control the center and right.

> The artillery preparation will be made in accordance with the orders from the C.G. 2d F.A. Brig. The attack on BOIS DE BELLEAU will begin at 5 P.M. The second phase will begin as soon as the first phase has attained its objective. Wise's 2/5 (less 1 Company, the 43d) will constitute the Brigade Reserves in the woods northwest of LUCY-le-BOCAGE.[53]

Even though he was responsible to Colonel Catlin for the operation, at 1345 Berry dutifully sent Neville his order of battle for his forthcoming effort. For some reason the alteration in command structure never seemed to have been made clear to everyone on the field. On the far right was Capt. Philip T. Case's 47th Company, in the center Capt. Richard N. Platt and the 20th Company, while on the left flank, stood Capt. Robert Yowell of the 16th. Conachy and the 45th were the reserves. But, while Conachy was away at Turrill's PC, Berry took it upon himself, unbeknownst to Conachy, to take most of the 45th Company with him into Belleau Wood.[54] Changes had been made and confusion reigned. For a time, Capt. Robert Yowell and the 16th Company would constitute the battalion reserve. But no one told Conachy. Shortly afterward Berry sent a modest change: "Each Company has a platoon in reserve. One platoon of the 16th Company is on line with 20th Company."[55]

Orders were passed on to Fritz Wise to make preparations to move 2/5 into positions vacated by Berry. First Lieutenant William R. Mathews, 2/5's intelligence officer, related the difficulties his battalion experienced while moving through the woods northwest of Lucy:

> Enemy balloon observers spotted our movement and we were hardly in the woods before their artillery was inflicting casualties. Just after we got there Wise met Berry . . . at the southeast corner of this woods, and I saw them talking earnestly with Wise shaking his head and Berry looking quite worried. *At 4:45 he [Berry] had received orders for his battalion to attack at 5:00. It was of course impossible for him to get word to all of his units in time.*[56] [Emphasis added.]

• • •

In his memoir, Catlin states that he was unaware of his forthcoming responsibilities until quite late in the day and was justifiably critical of what he had seen so far. He received a copy of his orders from Harbord at 1545, for an attack that was to begin just a little more than an hour later. "I was supposed to direct Berry's movements, though he had also received the orders from his own Regimental Headquarters." Catlin tried but was unable to communicate with Berry by telephone because 3/5 was beyond his reach. "I must confess that this situation caused me considerable anxiety. I don't know whose fault it was, but the communications were *far from perfect*." [Emphasis added.]

> It looked as though we would have to attack without proper co-ordination, and as a matter of fact, that is what we did. I was fully aware of the difficulties of the situation, especially for Berry. He had 400 yards [much more than that] of open wheat field to cross in the face of galling fire, and I did not believe he could ever reach the woods. It looked as though Sibley's battalion would have to bear the brunt of the action.

Catlin wasn't alone in his realization that the scheme was ill advised and ill planned. Unfortunately, the man giving the orders didn't seem to know. Catlin also divulged the fact that nearly everyone was already aware that the enemy was occupying the woods; in fact they would have been fools if they hadn't known. "It had been impossible to get patrols into the woods, but we knew they were full of machine guns." In his memorable history of the AEF, Harbord let it be known that at the time it would have come as a big surprise to him if the woods had been occupied. The French had implied that the wood was probably not held at all but if it was, it would be weakly held. Harbord believed that. Even if they had been, he believed at the time that to hit it with artillery before the jump-off would have put the Germans on notice of what was coming.[57] If the Germans, after the experiences of the morning, with the loss of the heights on the south side of the Clignon, weren't aware of what they could expect elsewhere along the line, they would have been fools. How Harbord could have imagined that after the bloody events of the morning the Germans could still be surprised, is difficult to fathom at this late date. They were far from being unaware of what was coming. The Germans reinforced the 461st Infantry with two additional battalions from their corps reserve. The movements of the 4th

Brigade had been duly noted and, in fact, their artillery had fired upon Marine units (2/5 and 3/5) while they were moving up. Surprise, indeed.

At 1700 five hundred Marines of the 3d Battalion, 5th Marines, jumped off with, an observer commented, "an almost perfect skirmish line." Another blunder made that day. On the left was the 45th Company,[58] in the center the 16th and 20th, and on the extreme right flank was the 47th Company. Three platoons of each. What was still not known officially, mainly because no American reconnaissance had been undertaken beforehand, was that the woods were full of Germans and the approaches were thoroughly covered by their artillery. In addition, and more immediately devastating to the Marines, were the many heavy Maxim guns that had been placed in advantageous and interlocking positions within the wood. Sibley and Berry's opponents, the 461st German Infantry Regiment, which consisted of 28 officers and 1,141 men, held strong positions in Belleau Wood. The Germans' numbers far exceeded the totals that 3/5 and 3/6 could put against them. To make matters even worse, they were well dug in. Three to one, attackers' favor, would have been very poor odds under the circumstances, but one to one was a prelude to disaster. Especially since the two Marine battalions would be operating independently, though presumably commanded by a central authority, Colonel Catlin.

As soon as 3/5 left its wooded place of safety to move downward and then across the open wheat fields lying before them, deadly machine-gun fire was encountered long before they could enter the edge of the dark, foreboding wood. Losses to Berry's battalion, while crossing the open ground to their immediate front, were terrific. Berry's battalion was supported by machine guns of the 77th [deRoode] and the 81st [Sumner]. Unfortunately, those guns were unable to penetrate the deep woods with their barrage and when the fragments of 3/5 disappeared into the woods, their assistance ended. German Maxims worked the line over and Marines of 3/5 went down in droves. Most were wounded, but many were dead. In just a few short minutes the 3d Battalion, 5th Marines, was just a memory. The wounded who could crawl back did, but if they did, they, too, became dead shortly after. The Maxims never let up.

In his memoir, Lt. George V. Gordon, USA, a platoon leader of the 16th, tells of standing with a friend and while they talked shells began dropping along the edge of the woods and across the wheat field. Both

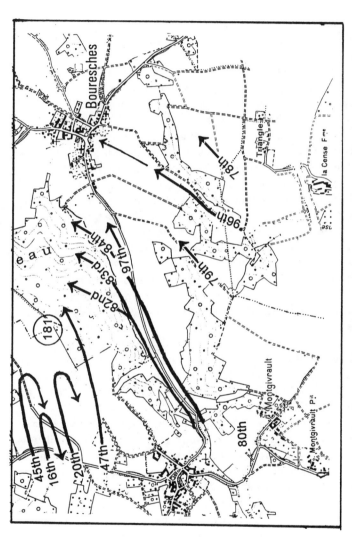

Map 4: This map shows the attacks of both 3d Battalion, 5th Marines and 3d Battalion, 6th Marines, on the afternoon of 6 June 1918. The 3d Bn, 5th, led by Major Berry was badly damaged and most were forced to retire. The 3d Bn., 6th, led by Major Sibley, although badly handled, made their way into the southern face of the woods, where they managed to hang on for several days.

men were mystified until a few minutes later when "Captain Larsen came running over and yelled, 'Get your platoons ready immediately, you should have started across with the barrage.'" Gordon states that this was the first he'd heard of an attack. No objective had been given, no maps were seen; the only thing they were sure of was the direction. Just as he was getting ready to go, new orders came from Larsen to remain in position, "we had the extreme left of the sector." He and his unnamed friend watched as the three other platoon leaders blew their whistles, pointed their canes toward the very dark woods, and shouted the usual Marine officer's challenge, "Follow me," as they charged into hell. The enemy wasn't slow in their response.

Within one hour Berry would report to Harbord, "What is left of the battalion is in woods close by. Do not know whether will be able to stand or not. Increase artillery range." A short time before, Berry had notified Neville that two platoons of the 47th Company had reformed and were attempting to "protect the left flank of adjoining organization on right [3/6]. 20th reforming on similar mission. Nine men only reported of three platoons of the 45th that went over the top." His adjutant, Captain Larsen, began sending messages to Neville from battalion headquarters, and the reports were a continuance of Berry's gloom and doom. "Three of my companies average about two platoons each and not over 25 men present with the 47th Company. Am getting them rounded up as best I can." In another report to Neville, Larsen stated that "three platoons of the 45th went over. Only a few returned." The objective had not been reached, let alone taken, and Larsen was sure the battalion hadn't gone much beyond the edge of the woods. Without further support, he maintained, "they must withdraw what few of them there are out there." And Larsen still hadn't heard anything directly from the 47th Company.

Nothing had been seen of Berry for several hours. He and four of his runners had gone into the Hellwood looking for his line. It was learned, later that evening, that Berry had suffered severe damage to his left arm. Even though he was attempting to remain in control, it was obvious to him, and those about him, that he would soon have to relinquish his command, what there was left of it. Floyd Gibbons, a reporter who went with 3/5, best described what happened:

Major Berry had advanced well beyond the center of the field when I saw him turn toward me and heard him shout, "Get down everybody." We all fell on our faces . . . withering volleys of lead

swept the tops of the oats just over us . . . coming from a new direction—from the left. . . . Then I heard a shout in front of
me . . . from Berry . . . making an effort to get to his feet. With his
right hand he was savagely grasping his left wrist. 'My hand's gone.'
A ball had entered his left arm at the elbow, had traveled down
the side of the bone, tearing away muscles and nerves of the fore-
arm and lodging itself in the palm of his hand.[59]

A few 3/5 men were awarded decorations, but there were so many
casualties that honors were largely forgotten. Corporal Oliver D. Bernier
of the 16th Company exposed himself to a very heavy concentration of
Maxim fire by rushing forward alone to break down some wire obstacles he knew would delay his men and cause them undue casualties. For
his bravery he received a DSC, NC, and four Silver Star citations as well
as a commission to second lieutenant. Ben Berry received the same
awards and the Legion of Honor for his valor and leadership, even after he had been badly wounded. Private James L. Clarke of the 47th, although badly wounded, crossed enemy territory over one mile to deliver a message, then collapsed from loss of blood. His reward was the
DSC, NC, and Silver Star, and he survived the war. First Sergeant John
Grant of the 20th got the same decorations for being killed while trying to deliver an important message to his company commander across
a fire-swept field. Many other noncoms were awarded the DSC and NC
for being killed in action, "[giving] the supreme proof of extraordinary
heroism which will serve as an example for hitherto untried troops."
Harbord soon put a stop to that citation, of which there were many.

According to its semiofficial history, at 1700 3/6 jumped off in two
columns from their positions just east of Lucy down both sides of the
Lucy-Bouresches road. On the north side was the 82d Company (Dwight
Smith) in the lead with the 83d (Noble) in support. On the south side
of the road was the 84th Company (Mark Smith), supported by the 97th
Company (Robert W. Voeth).[60] It also says that there was no time to reconnoiter the area and no maps, and that the company commanders
were taken forward to have a quick look at what terrain they would be
going over and through. When they looked they saw a road that was
more of a ravine.

The enemy was not holding the western portion of the wood that 3/6
would enter as they left the environs of Lucy-le-Bocage. When the 82d
Company reached approximate coordinates 175.5–260.7 they slowed

down appreciably. In fact, in very short order they ran into another wall of Maxims as 3/5 had, only 3/6 did have some cover on their way to that point. At about the same time the 84th and 97th Companies crossed the road to the north side, continuing their advance toward Bouresches.

The official report states that the "battalion advanced according to schedule until about 8:30 P.M., when enemy artillery and machine-gun fire became so heavy that further advance was impracticable." At that time the 83d Company had jumped past the stalled 82d to take the lead. The 82d had been held up by terrific enemy machine-gun fire and the 83d, led by 1st Lt. Alfred H. Noble, who "was conspicuous for his judgment and personal courage," had fought their way past and moved close to the eastern edge of the woods. "Our casualties had been heavy. . . ."

Both companies soon captured several *minnenwerfers*—heavy mortars—and much ammunition. Those guns would later be turned around and used against their former owners. The 23d Machine Gun Company, in support, laid down two barrages. One was a covering barrage over 3/6 just before zero hour; the other was laid upon the enemy lines before the advancing Marines. After the minor objectives were taken, the machine guns were moved forward to consolidate and strengthen the positions occupied by 3/6. Losses to machine-gun companies, although not as heavy as those to the infantry, were constant.

Second Lieutenant Louis F. Timmerman Jr.*, a platoon leader in the 83d Company, led three of his men in a bayonet charge against superior numbers of the enemy. They captured two machine guns and seventeen prisoners. Timmerman was wounded in the face, but continued to perform his duty for twenty-four hours more before giving up and going back for aid.[61] Corporals Benjamin A. Tilghman*, Joseph A. Dargis*, and Howard J. Child* were the other three men who followed Timmerman into the face of death.

There were many other courageous acts by members of all companies on 6 June 1918. Both the 84th and 97th advanced through open wheat fields under constant observation and direct artillery and machine-gun fire. Their task was to take Bouresches. The battalion history says, "The capture of Bouresches was not to begin until the Bois de Belleau had been freed from the enemy. . . . Consequently it was impracticable for the two right companies [84th and 97th] to advance beyond the line occupied by the two left companies." But before that decision was made Captain Voeth yelled, "Ninety-seventh Company, take that town!" and almost immediately Major Sibley responded from his position in the woods, "Ninety-seventh Company, stand fast!"[62] So they stayed put where they were, as did the 84th. All the companies of 3/6 had taken a load of punishment and their losses were staggering, though not yet of the magnitude of 3/5.

"Just about the time that Sibley's men struck the woods a sniper's bullet hit me in the chest." Catlin, describing what happened to him, goes on to write, "It felt exactly as though someone had struck me heavily with a sledge. It swung me clear around and toppled me over on the ground. When I tried to get up, I found that my right side was paralyzed." Along with so many other Marines, out went the commander of the first phase. Catlin describes how his French liaison officer, Captain Tribot-Laspierre, rushed over to his side and began to drag him toward safety. He headed for a trench, out of the line of fire, located about twenty-five feet away. Even though Catlin was huge and the Frenchman was small, he successfully completed his mission. "My life has been spared and I owe a lot to that Frenchman."[63] Lieutenant Colonel Harry Lee, upon learning of Catlin's having become a casualty, assumed command of the 6th Marines.

It was becoming obvious to Harbord that much help was going to be needed if a portion of the attack order was to be a success. It was decided that the 84th and 97th Companies should remain where they were and protect Sibley's rear and for someone else to break through and take Bouresches. The 96th Company (Duncan) of Holcomb's battalion was selected. The orders to jump off at 1730 were received by Holcomb at 1630. Soon after, a modification was issued: The three remaining platoons of the 79th (Zane) were to support the 96th. Second Lieutenant John West of the 79th Company mentioned in his memoir that his 3d Platoon had been assigned to follow 3/6 into the woods. The other two companies of 2/6, the 78th (Messersmith) and 80th (Coffenberg), were to remain in place and provide flank protection as well as fire support. First Lieutenant Jack Hart, skipper 81st Machine Gun Company, went forward with the assault upon Bouresches accompanied by two guns from his company, four guns from the 77th, and four more from the regiment's own 73d Company (Swink).

At 1730 the 96th went forward and Duncan* was wounded almost as soon as he stepped off. First Lieutenant James F. Robertson* assumed command and without a breather continued going forward toward Bouresches. Proceeding through the wheat field, against emplaced heavy machine guns and terrible shell fire, the losses of the 96th were horrendous. Meanwhile, as Duncan was being helped to a place of safety by 1st Sgt. Joseph A. Sissler and the regimental dentist, Lt. Weedon E.

Osborne*, USN, a shell landed directly upon them. It killed all, including Duncan's two stretcher bearers, at the same moment.[64]

Robertson, in an effort to put together a command, called out for 1st Lt. John D. Bowling Jr., his 3d Platoon leader, "Where is Johnny?" and then he saw Bowling get up, face white with pain and go stumbling ahead with a bullet in his shoulder.[65] Bowling was just one of many. The advance of the 96th was made over six hundred yards in an open wheat field, under intense artillery and machine-gun fire, with no Marine units on either flank. The 2d, 3d, and 4th platoons went forward in a skirmish line, keeping up a running fire as they approached Bouresches. When the 2d platoon was within three hundred yards of the town, they went prone, in an effort to secure superiority of fire. When the German fire got too hot to bear, the 2d and 3d platoons took refuge in the ravine to their right, but the advance continued. Robertson and platoon leader 2d Lt. Clifton B. Cates*, with the remnants of one platoon, some twenty-four enlisted men, raced forward.

Within two hundred yards of the town, Cates was knocked temporarily unconscious by a machine-gun bullet that whacked his helmet. Gunnery Sergeant Aloysius P. Sheridan, known as "Jack" in the company, poured a bottle of champagne (that he'd been carrying for a long time) over Cates, who soon responded. Then both quickly joined Robertson, who was leading a platoon into the western part of Bouresches. After a very difficult struggle they took the town from the Germans occupying it.[66] Private Herbert D. Dunlavy*, Robertson's orderly, single-handedly captured a German machine gun and turned it upon the Boche. This action helped greatly to blunt the presence of the enemy in Bouresches. Two days later, Dunlavy would be killed in action while helping to repulse one more German attempt to recapture the town.

The casualties of the company had been extremely heavy. Most of the 96th was still lying on the open ground between Lucy and Bouresches. Shortly after his arrival at the town, Robertson recognized that if the Germans made a serious attempt to recapture Bouresches, his slim detachment couldn't hold on very long. He left Cates in charge in the town and retired to bring more Marines up as fast as possible. That is, if he could find any who were still alive.

Cates proceeded to organize his few Marines and they began cleaning up the Germans. A Maxim located in a church tower covering the center of the town proved to be a serious problem for the new inhabitants so they took it out straightaway. As the Marines advanced farther into the town, another Maxim killed or wounded six more Marines. Now down to a mere handful of Marines, Cates decided to ignore the Germans for a while as he proceeded to establish four posts in advantageous positions around the town. Within twenty minutes the 2d and 3d platoons had wended their way through the ravine and into the town. That provided approximately sixty officers and men for Cates to hold on to the most important objective in the entire area.

Although the Marines held Bouresches, they still didn't have the railroad station, which was located just a bit farther north on the road to Belleau. The Germans would continue to hold that position for the balance of the engagement. Fortunately, that was not as important as retention of the town itself. As there weren't any trains moving, it was a moot point.

Across from the town, in Belleau Wood, Sibley and 3/6 were still in desperate trouble. At 2045 he sent the following message to Lee:

Unable to advance infantry further because of strong machine gun positions and artillery fire. Have given orders to hold present position at far edge of woods. Losses already heavy. Await instructions.

Lee passed along the same information to Harbord and advised him that the "47th Company 3d Bn. [was] reorganizing to go forward at this point." Lee must have had some knowledge of the numbers of men left in Phil Case's 47th Company, and there couldn't have been very many. The company had been in "it" as deeply as any other company of 3/5. No one knew for sure what their numbers were because there was a lack of substantial contact with the company since they had gone into the woods earlier. Their location would continue to be a hot spot for days to come. It was along the western edge of Hill 181, which was still controlled by the enemy.

Shortly afterward, evidently quite angry, Harbord assailed Lee for what Harbord perceived as an abundance of all kinds of feasance, mis-, mal-, and non-, since he had taken over command from Catlin. "I am not satisfied with the way you have conducted your engagement this afternoon." He was especially hard on Lee for not assuming control of 3/5. "Major Berry, over whom you should have asserted your authority, is reporting to his own Regimental Commander."

At this late date it isn't possible to know what was going through Harbord's mind at that moment. He was demanding that Lee push Berry, who was personally out of action. That fact alone should have been known to brigade headquarters, in addition to the terrible losses that 3/5 had sustained in trying to take the wood. He was, at this time, sending rather peculiar messages to Lee. One ordered him "south along the BOURESCHES-TORCY Road [it is the Belleau-Torcy Road] and send Sibley to take BOURESCHES." At this time it appears that Harbord didn't know that 3/5, and to a certain extent 3/6, were washed up, as was part of Holcomb's battalion.[67] Lee was hard pressed to control what was left of the 6th Regiment following the afternoon's disastrous attack, which he had not planned or had much part in initiating.[68]

Before they continued their advance and still out in the open, the remnants of the 79th had closed up with some members of the 96th Company. All just tried to stay alive during the terrible pounding they received that afternoon. As soon as the heaviest part of the shelling slowed down a bit, they made efforts to cover the ground between them and Bouresches. Several members of the 79th remembered later that there may have been some artillery support, but not enough. Private Charles Vanek said "none" but 1st Lt. Graves B. Erskine said it was "ten minutes of very light artillery." First Lieutenant Wallace M. Leonard, USA, temporarily in command of Erskine's 2d Platoon, who was described as "unpopular with some of the Marines," fired his .45 caliber automatic in the air and yelled, "Come on, men, for God's sake, don't fail me now!" Perhaps that reproach may have been part of the reason he was disliked. First Lieutenant William A. Worton was another of the 79th's casualties on the way over.[69] He would recover and become a most valued officer of the Corps, especially during a later war.

Reinforcements from Zane's 79th Company were soon in and around the town and began to consolidate their holdings. Cates turned over command of the town defenses to Zane, the senior Marine officer present. Shortly after, the battalion PC was established in a ravine about eight hundred yards southwest of Bouresches.[70] Holcomb, in a message to Catlin at 2127 (he didn't know that Catlin was hors de combat, hours after the fact, and that Zane and some of his men were already at Bouresches) telling him that Zane's 79th had

one effective platoon left and cannot advance. Will ask 23d Infantry to hold Messersmith's line [78th Company] and if they will do so, will send him into town. Our line of resistance from Lucy to Messersmith should be reinforced at once.

It just goes to show that not even a battalion CO was on top of it every time. Later that evening Holcomb reassigned 2d Lt. West and his 3d Platoon from 3/6 back to the 79th Company "to reinforce Robertson." Meanwhile, Messersmith of the 78th had been trying to communicate with Holcomb to advise him that 1st Lt. James McB. Sellers*, one of his platoon leaders, had been badly wounded.[71] Shortly afterward, the 78th was heavily gassed, particularly Sellers's and 1st Lt. James P. Adams's platoons. The gas attack would effectively eliminate Messersmith's company from any offensive activity for some time to come.

Near midnight Lee received a message from Harbord authorizing Sibley to "use reorganized 82d and 83d Companies" to move to Bouresches in support of the few Marines of the 96th and 79th Companies who were there. I presume that was an error; evidently he wanted to send the 84th (Mark Smith) and 97th (Voeth) into Bouresches in support. Sibley remained with his two badly damaged companies, the 82d and 83d, while they dug in for the night at their tenuous positions on the south edge of Belleau Wood. Sometime during the night Maj. Milo P. Fox of the 2d Engineers arrived with two companies and was assigned to an infantry support position in the rear of the 82d Company. Sibley received orders from brigade to end his offensive, dig in, and wait for morning before making any further efforts at trying to throw the Boche out of the woods. Ending his offensive was probably very high on Sibley's agenda. In fact he wasn't in any condition to attack anyone, let alone throw the Boche out of the woods.

For the balance of the evening, Sibley was at his PC, which was located in a slight ravine to the east of the woods. He was having great difficulty communicating with brigade and regiment. His telephone line was shot out and his runners found it difficult getting by the gas in the area between the PC and Lucy. Few rations made it to the two companies in the woods and only a trifle more water, which had to be carried in canteens from Lucy. During the night German artillery kept up a harassing barrage of high explosives and gas, and the latter was the most distressing. Wearing a mask for hours was preferable to gasping for breath, but that would happen with or without the ineffective masks anyway.

Many Marines suffered from the gas in the woods. It lay down at the same level at which the Marines were lying and remained there for days. The only way to get a breath of relatively fresh air was to climb something, a hill, a boulder, or any height if it was available, or get out of the woods, where the air could blow freely. Neither the latter, nor any of the former, were available to 3/6, so they just suffered. Sibley was a long-serving Marine who was described later by Catlin as one of

> the most picturesque characters in the Marine Corps. . . . He is a short, swarthy man, wiry and of great endurance. . . . He was born in Vermont on March 28, 1877, and was appointed a Second Lieutenant of Marines on July 23, 1900. Thus far he seems to have borne a charmed life and I hope his luck will not desert him. . . . A man who has never been known to get rattled. His men love him and would follow him anywhere.[72]

In the meantime, Conachy and what he had managed to gather together of the 45th Company were waiting to begin the second phase of the day's work, but it was not to happen. The situation faced by the several battalions already worked over, especially 3/5, was that there were very few Marines to carry out that second phase. Harbord gave up on the "second phase" portion of his grandiose scheme for the day. Perhaps he finally realized that he had virtually destroyed four battalions of Marines that day and didn't have many left to squander. His messages at 2210 ordered overall entrenchment on what had been gained at Bouresches. He also wanted Sibley to attempt to make contact with the right flank of the 47th Company.

Among the Marines of 3/6 who were decorated with the DSC for that day's work was Pvt. Andrew K. Axton, 83d Company, who was killed while attacking an enemy machine-gun nest with his automatic; Cpl. Charles Brooks of the 83d, later commissioned a second lieutenant, whose citation for "repeatedly going through heavy machine gun fire with messages" earned him a DSC as well. Private Elbert E. Brooks of the 83d was another DSC awardee for "placing his body in front of his platoon leader while under heavy machine-gun fire." There were many other awards to Marines from 3/6. Members of the 96th Company were also decorated for their extreme bravery in the capture of Bouresches. Second Lieutenant Clifton B. Cates was awarded his first DSC for his work that day, as was Pvt. James W. Carter. Captain Donald F. Duncan got his for giving "the supreme proof of heroism." There were so many other awards on 6 June in both 3/6 and 2/6, but too many to list here.

At 2335 Lee notified Harbord that he was "holding the reorganized 47th and 20th Companies [3/5] to care for hostile M.G. position located to far north in west edge of Bois de Belleau. [He meant around Hill

181.] Need grenades and 37 m/m guns." (One pounders.) Lee was now in charge and letting Harbord know it.

The capture of Bouresches from the 7th and 8th Companies, 398th German Infantry, was only the second successful action of the day, but it would earn the 4th Brigade a French unit Croix de Guerre. It was a costly success, but the town was the most important position in the entire area in which the 4th Brigade was involved. In the engagement the 96th lost their one and only Marine prisoner of the war, Pvt. Alexander T. Cunningham, who was in an ambulance that was driving into the enemy lines.[73]

The Marines in Bouresches were, for a period, isolated from the main body and were subjected to artillery and machine-gun fire for most of the night. The situation was bad enough for Sibley to send them reinforcements. They did receive rations and ammunition, which were delivered via truck over the rough track humorously identified as the "road" between Lucy and Bouresches.[74] First Lieutenant Thomas T. McEvoy placed twenty-five men of his 1st Platoon, 97th Company, at positions near the northeast part of the town under Cpl. William T. "Nap" (short for Napoleon) Scanlon with orders to defend this part of the town until further notice. This was just a few hundred yards south of the railroad station and nearby bridge, which were strongly held by the enemy. That night the Boche launched an attack against this point as well as the eastern edges of the town. Flares were followed by shells, and then a powerful formation of German infantry shattered themselves against the defending Marines. An hour later, when the attack finally ceased, upward of fifty dead and wounded enemy were lying before their positions.

One casualty, not a Marine but a war correspondent named Floyd Gibbons, was to have a greater impact on the Marine Corps, the AEF, and the folks at home than any other individual for some time to come. Gibbons joined the assault with Berry's 3/5 and subsequently was badly wounded, losing his left eye. He had taken the trouble to send a news story to the censors in Paris, before the assault even took place, clearly intending to fill in a few colorful words after the fight was over. His being wounded that same afternoon was duly reported widely and word reached the censor who had the story in Paris. Since Gibbons hadn't shown up at any aid station, the reaction was that he must have been killed. Therefore, the censor, a longtime former newsman and friend, allowed the story to go through uncut. That wouldn't have made much difference in most cases, but in this one its impact clouded relations between Marines and the U.S. Army for the next half century. For Gibbons had, contrary to AEF regulations, mentioned that he was with the Marines, and the 4th Brigade were the only Marines in France with the AEF. And his bloodcurdling embellishment made it seem as though the Marines were the only American troops fighting in France. When Gibbons's "information" became known in the United States, along with the news of the desperate fighting at or near Château-Thierry, the public easily put two and two together and got the U.S. Marines for an answer. It would be the Marines that were fighting the Germans for the next month or so, as far as the American newspaper-reading public was concerned, and the army howled. The use of the word *Château-Thierry,* the name of a sector as well as a town, would infuriate the 3d U.S. Infantry Division, which was, and would continue, doing their collective damnedest to hurt the Germans right at that spot. The 3d Brigade was equally in an uproar. "Those publicity hungry gyrenes . . . etc." The Marines were entirely blameless for the blunder, but soldiers of all ranks never accepted their excuses or forgave them.[75]

It was later that Gibbons wrote of the "old Gunnery Sergeant who commanded the platoon in the absence of the lieutenant, who had been shot and was out of the fight." He told of the sergeant's longtime service, with service bars showing he had fought in China, Haiti, Santo Domingo, and Vera Cruz, and his wind- and sun-bronzed skin. When the order for the advance came the sergeant ran out to the center of his platoon. Swinging his bayoneted rifle over his head with a forward sweep, he said to the men of his platoon, his mates, the men he loved, "Come on, you sons-o'-bitches. Do you want to live forever?" That did it! With a yell the Marines came up from the ground and stormed across the bullet-swept field—to hell.[76]

The 6th of June 1918 was finally over, and presumably it might also be called "The Longest Day," at least for the 4th Marine Brigade. The losses for the day, 31 officers and 1,056 men, would exceed, collectively, the total of all previous casualties of the Marine Corps in its entire history. The largest proportion were suffered in the afternoon among the three battalions engaged, 3/5, 3/6, and 2/6. Turrill's 1/5 lost heavily in two companies, the 49th and the 67th; the other two, the 17th and 66th, not being involved in the initial assault, were hurt less. Of the 4,598 casualties in the Marine Brigade during the period 1 June through 9 July

1918, nearly twenty-five percent were inflicted on this day alone. And they would provide a hefty proportion of the total losses for all deaths, 2,764, suffered by the 4th Brigade from 15 March 1918 until 11 November 1918. Moreover, there were still several more major attacks to be launched before the brigade had finally paid its dues at Belleau Wood.

Friday, 7 June

The 7th, although not entirely quiet, was a time to live. Few Marines died and likewise few Germans opposite them. But Sibley and his battalion had a bad night. Little sleep, if any, and no food or water. After making a thorough reconnaissance of his "holdings," he moved Capt. Egbert T. Lloyd's 80th Company, which had been assigned to him in support, to the southwestern portion of the woods. After moving his own PC back a few hundred yards, Berton Sibley sent his popular adjutant, 1st Lt. David Bellamy, to report on what 3/6 had been doing. As Bellamy tells us in his charming and illuminating memoir, "I was sent back to brigade headquarters to explain the situation to the General [Harbord]. Incidentally I got the first cup of coffee and even hot meal in many, many days." He was lucky. Hot meals were very uncommon for Marines in the front lines and would continue to be for many days to come.

The officers and men hadn't had a hot meal in eight days, and most had not been able to sleep during the previous night. Some of the Marines in Bouresches managed to locate some vegetables in the many gardens within the town and soon were devouring potatoes and greens, including asparagus, which one man found tough and spat out before swallowing. Even Captain Voeth relished the liberated potatoes, having his "dog robber" gather up as many as he could find. Voeth was even seen chasing a rabbit—without success, I might add.

In addition to the common distress, the enemy held a dangerous, harassing position around Hill 181 that had greatly contributed to the overall misery of 3/6. Still in the nearby vicinity, neither Case of the 47th nor Platt of the 20th had been able, in their weakened state, to drive the Germans off that hill. So Sibley hoped that Lloyd might be able to deliver the coup de grâce and alter that situation. At 0215 Captain Walter H. Sitz, regimental adjutant, 6th Marines, received the following message from Sibley, which described the positions, as he knew them:

Three (3) platoons 96th Company, all 97th and 79th hold BOURESCHES.

84th Company on right flank.
78th Company on right of 84th.
82d Company on left flank.
83d Company on left of 82d.
No communication with 3d Bn. of 5th Regiment.

Turrill and 1/5 were still entrenched upon Hill 142. Several times during the morning the enemy made attempts against them but all failed. That morning several companies from the 6th Machine Gun Battalion supplied Turrill with some badly needed rapid-fire support. German soldiers were assembling in and around Torcy, but fire from the 23d Machine Gun Company succeeded in breaking them up and repelling an attack. Meanwhile, Jack Hart of the 81st brought together some guns from a variety of sources and helped to break up an ineffectual attack around and about Bouresches. It was the edges of the brigade that were being probed. But there were no substanial changes in the lines that day.

In his daily operations report Holcomb wrote that at 0830 the Germans held the railroad station and were entrenching behind the tracks. He also charged his companies' losses the previous day to machine guns. "79th Company loss very heavy & 96th Company loss very heavy. In one platoon of 79th it was reported that there was only one man left." That was heavy. But direct advances in open fields, against entrenched machine guns, will bring heavy casualties every time.

Lee was able to advise Harbord that "the situation looks better this morning." He said the 79th Company had "one effective platoon left [which didn't sound too promising]. The 78th . . . about eight casualties. . . . The 80th have few if any." One German prisoner told Holcomb that his company had but 80 men left and his battalion had 154. The Marines had been taking some hard knocks, but the enemy wasn't doing all that well either.

Harbord came to see Feland at 5th Marine headquarters to obtain an update on what was happening up around Hill 142. Feland always knew what was going on in the regiment. Harbord had to bring a map, so evidently the second-in-command of the 5th Marines didn't have a map even at this late date.

Turrill had "arranged with Father [John J.] Brady* about burying the dead" and had requested that Sgt. Maj. Carl J. Norstrand* send him supplies.[77] Norstrand answered, "Plenty of rations. . . . No arrangements . . . for carrying forward. . . . Am trying to get men from headquarters." It was the usual problem that every Marine ran into during the war, trying to obtain the "goods" so that they could carry on the war. Another message about 1/5 that day which deserves repeating:

> The 1st Bn. 5th Marines were hardly in [a] position to make an attack owing to heavy losses yesterday morning. 67 Company loss Lt. Crowther*, [Francis S.] Kieren, [Aaron J.] Ferch, and one other [2d Lt. Thomas W. Ashley].[78] 49 Company Lieut. Simons [sic] and all other officers except Capt. Hamilton.[79]

Roswell Winans advised Turrill that he was having two companies of engineers digging positions for the 17th. Then he coyly asked, "Have I the authority to keep them here until we get reinforcements? We have lost fifty percent and cannot do our own digging." He also asked for a doctor and Chauchat ammo.[80] At this time, and later, doctors were at a premium and possibly so was Chauchat ammunition. Certainly fighting men were, and that's why Winans wanted to keep those engineers.

Harbord directed Neville to send the fragments of 3/5 to Mont Blanche, wooded high ground on the main Paris-Metz Highway, a little more than a half mile east of Paris Farm. But it was his reasoning that doesn't quite add up. Because it would be easier to supply and "more accessible if needed again." What more Harbord expected of 3/5 is not possible to discern at this late date.

Wise and his battalion were ordered to take up a position on the left of 3/5, which Harbord "presumed to be near Hill 133, and *the north end of the Bois de Belleau.*" (Emphasis added.) Two/Five was to be in a position to assist in the planned "2d phase" of the day's operations. For some reason Harbord didn't know, at this late hour, that Berry's battalion was nowhere near the north end. Only two companies were still in the woods, the 20th and 45th, both of which were in the southern leg. Wise started out at 0200 to carry out the order "numbered 83," which Wise had received from Harbord. The battalion moved from just west of the Bois St. Martin, eastward around Hill 200 to the Lucy-Torcy road, and then proceeded southward along the road.[81] It was near daylight and 2/5 found themselves alongside the Lucy-Torcy road. They were right between 3/5's old positions and the Germans who were still located in Belleau Wood. The 55th was leading off, with Charley Dunbeck's 43d in the center and the 18th bringing up the rear. Williams and the 51st was still with 1/5 on Hill 142. The moon was shining and the Germans had a clear view of them marching along the road. As they were forging their way into the Bois St. Martin they spotted some recently dug trenches to their left, where the battalion came to a halt. They had obviously been left by 3/5.

Wise had Capt. John Blanchfield send a platoon from the 55th forward, which group almost immediately drew fire, both from the Germans in the woods and from Marines of 3/5, each side sure that they were being attacked. Blanchfield* and his second, Lem Shepherd*, were both hit. Soon more Marines were casualties and the platoon was withdrawn. Private Paul Bonner describes what happened next:

> Blanchfield led the column down the Torcy road. We did not know the Germans were there. They let us pass, and they opened up from the flanks. I saw Blanchfield fall, right on the road. Everybody scattered. I started to run, then I thought of Blanchfield, and I started back. I rushed across the road, machine gun bullets whipping the air everywhere, and I made the Captain's side. He was still alive. He was twice my size, but I picked him up and carried him back. I got him into the woods to a doctor and left him to look for the company.[82]

All of a sudden the woods burst into flames as the Boche artillery found their easy target. "To the rear!" someone shouted, and then again, "To the rear!" Cooke looked at 1st Lt. Gilder D. Jackson; Jackson looked at him. According to Cooke "there was no such thing as going to the rear because of shells." Quickly it was passed on by Captain Wass that Wise had ordered the retrograde movement. "That was different. We wouldn't run from the Boche, but if Fritz Wise . . . said to run it was time to get going." Back the column went, back toward where they had come from. Within a few minutes, however, the battalion was ordered to return—but into the woods, not along the road. When they got back there the two officers inquired, of a sergeant leaning up against a tree, where the front line was, and he told them. "You're standing on it." At this point they were wandering down a steep hill into no-man's-land, into a wheat field, where everyone lay down and most went to sleep. Cooke narrates what he saw happen, as daylight came up:

> Up ahead I heard some talking, then shouts and the chug-chug of a heavy machine gun . . . the air was full of bullets. Down! I yelled at the men. Keep down! Then from the woods to our left rear, more

guns opened up. Our own guns—firing into our column. . . . It was bad enough to be shot at by the Boche but there was no sense in being killed by friendly troops.

At that point something happened that Cooke relates with relish. Captain Wass yelled,

Jackson! "Yes, captain," Gilder responded. Where are you? "Right here, across the road," was the answer. Stand up so I can see you. "Captain," Jackson shouted above the crackling roar of machine-gun bullets, "if you want to see me, you stand up."

According to Cooke that last part of the verbal exchange brought forth laughter from up and down the line. It was learned shortly after that a gun-shy 3d Battalion, 5th Marines, gunner had been firing at 2/5. The firing was soon quelled and 2/5 was saved for destruction on another day.

The battalion extended north- and southward and took over the positions of the remnants of 3/5. Whereupon 3/5 was finally pulled out of the lines and sent back for rest and reorganization. Since Lieutenant Shepherd had also been wounded, Wise selected Cooke to command Blanchfield's 55th. Wise then ordered Cooke to proceed to the extreme left of the line, to relieve "Captain Carnegie of the 1st Battalion" at the "little square wood" east of Hill 142. There was no Carnegie, instead it was Conachy, skipper of the 45th Company, and it was actually 3/5 not 1/5.[83] Wise and 2/5 would remain in 3/5's old positions for three days. Then it would be their turn.

The balance of the day passed rather quietly for all Marine units, at least as compared to the previous day. Major Hughes was vexed as usual, this time with his French liaison officer, Lieutenant Merou, who, according to "Johnny the Hard," was "utterly useless to me and a decided nuisance. Spends all his time with the French and could not establish proper liaison with them." So much for wartime alliances. In the afternoon 3/6 was greatly harassed by artillery fire placed upon those positions they still held. First Lieutenant Hugh McFarland, platoon commander in the 84th Company and three of his men were severely wounded on the Lucy-Bouresches road while carrying rations to Bouresches. Rations were scarce and anytime they didn't arrive was a gurantee of more hours, or even days, between meals.

In the afternoon Harbord sent for Sibley to give him specific orders for an attack on the following day. His battalion was to be in position at 0300. The 82d Company was on the right, with its right resting on the southeast corner of the woods. The 83d was to the 82d's left. Both were to attack in four waves. Two platoons of the 80th Company were in support with instructions to protect the left flank. A detail of the 2d Engineers was to support the 82d Company along the eastern edge of the woods. The remaining two platoons of the 80th and the balance of the engineers were placed in reserve. The 83d, being somewhat in advance of the line, was withdrawn a bit in order to be in liaison with the others. Sibley returned to his PC and immediately made the necessary arrangements to comply with Harbord's directive.

In his daily report to Bundy, Harbord described what his lines looked like at 1500 hours, and delineated his plan for the balance of that date. One comment he made, which I'm at a loss to understand, was that "we hold the town of Bouresches with a few more men than I consider necessary. I will endeavor, when night comes, to withdraw a company or two to enable me to get a little echelon. . . ." The remnants of the 79th and 97th Companies were in the town at that point, with the very few survivors of the 96th. Not exactly an overwhelming proponderance of numbers to defend what cost so much to take. In his daily report to Bundy, Harbord also explained that he wanted to straighten out his line southward, from Hill 142 eastward. "There is on 174.1–262.6 a small rectangular wood which is occupied by the Germans . . . about 200 yards in depth . . . 400 yards long. Artillery playing on it now. . . . [Later a] feasible attempt will be made to straighten the line. . . ."

Saturday, 8 June

At midnight Bouresches was under heavy attack, in the town and on their right flank, but an hour later the firing had died down considerably. "Bill" Moore of the 97th Company could relate at 0200 that machine guns had arrived in the town just before the attack commenced and the "line held beautifully. No Germans advanced. Captain Zane and Robertson had everything well organized." Evans immediately passed that information on to Harbord. A half hour later Moore advised brigade that a new type of gas was being used, "not mustard. Headache, burned throat. High explosive. Heavy and tickled nose."

The attack of 3/6 upon the southern edges of Belleau Wood was preceded by a short bombardment by Stokes mortars, which had been brought up and emplaced during the night. On account of the density of the forest it was not very effective, but the attack began as scheduled. At 0520 Sibley reported that "action has commenced."

A half hour later he was sending messages to regiment advising that some machine guns were out of action. But he added, "Mowing our men down pretty fast. 83d Company reports many machine guns delaying advance. Good progress in some points. This information from wounded."

The battalion history mentions that the German guns were "well fortified in the rocks and held an exceedingly strong position. The fire from these machine guns was terrific." In addition to the facts as stated, the Germans were well supplied with hand grenades, which they used resourcefully from their protected advantage. Regardless of how good the German defenses were, the battalion managed to capture four machine guns and kill many of the defenders. Because the Marines lacked most everything needed to fight a "modern" war, they met the opposition with rifle fire and, of course, bayonets, both of which contributed to the demise of many Germans. But not enough.

The 97th Company, which had been relieved from duty in Bouresches and was not far out of Lucy, now attempted to provide 3/6 with muscle. They arrived and got caught in a barrage that caused them to immediately dig in the stony soil as best they could. During one ferocious artillery barrage, many Marines of 3/6 fell back and into those places where the 97th had dug in. There was some fighting among the Marines as to who would occupy the few shallow holes. A few were even killed during their encounter. One Marine was bayoneted by another Marine, who was then immediately torn to pieces by a German shell. Panic among Marines wasn't completely unknown at that time. Times like that sometimes make number one more important than a comrade or anyone else.

A little after 0600 the messages going back to brigade headquarters were no longer mildly positive. In fact, they rapidly became quite negative. Lee told them that "Sibley's advance has been checked at points and they are finding many more M.G.'s than expected and [it] may be necessary to employ part of or all of one of the support companies." Captain Dwight Smith reported himself in wounded. The 83d and 84th Companies had become mixed up and the 82d requested replacements. Captain Zane, who was in Bouresches, reported hearing a Marine yelling in the woods, "Get that son of a bitch." He also told brigade that he no longer had liaison with anyone in the woods "but thinks it O.K." Lieutenant Bill Moore related that enemy reserves were coming in through the north end of the woods and he asked for artillery on that portion to slow them down. "Losses heavy."

According to the history of 3/6, hard fighting continued until about 0830. The battalion had identified four strong points, and had surrounded two. But Sibley recognized that further loss of life was all that would be accomplished if his shattered battalion continued with what was obviously becoming a lost cause. He directed Noble and the 83d Company to hold its ground while the other companies fell back to positions where they could dig in with some cover. After ten A.M. Sibley let it be known that

> they [the Germans] are too strong for us. Soon as we take one M.G. the losses are so heavy that I am reforming on the ground held by the 82d last night. All of the officers of the 82d Co wounded or missing and it is necessary to reform before we can advance. . . . These M. guns are too strong for our infantry. We can attack again if it is desired.[84]

Obviously Sibley's heart hadn't been with it. By 1130 these movements were completed and a reconnaissance was taken of the immediate area with a report of their findings submitted to Harbord. The latter even sent a staff officer over to look at the mess. At 1230 Harbord, possibly influenced by the staff officer's report, responded with an order for 3/6 to retire out of the woods "in the ravine (gully) at south edge of woods. I will have artillery play on the wood. Any further orders will be given you later for other movement by you." (In other words, Harbord had finally smelled the smoke.) During the afternoon, Sibley's battalion was again subjected to a heavy period of enemy shelling, but the biggest losses occurred within the 80th Company. At the time of the shelling, the 80th lost three officers killed and three wounded; huge losses for any company, especially in such a short period. Those down for good were 2d Lts. Clarence A. Dennis*, James S. Timothy*, USA, and Charles H. Ulmer, who died of his wounds the following day.[85] The three wounded were 1st Lts. Julius L. Cogswell*, Harold D. Shannon, and Thomas S. Whiting. The company lost Pvts. Raymond A. Behan, John F. Corbet, Medford O. McClanahan, Cpl. Elmer A. Reese. Sergeant Charles H. Meyer would die on 9 June of wounds received on the 8th.[86]

Finally, at 2030, Sibley received word from Lee that his battalion would be relieved by 1/6. Later, it was learned that there was not to be a relief but 3/6 was to vacate the territory they had fought so hard for and suffered so much to take, what little they had. The official reason given was that the artillery was to have a clear wood in order to pulverize it. That evening after dark, 3/6 moved out, all except for the 84th Company. The battalion would be reassembled on the morning of the ninth, a little over a mile south of Marigny at the Bois de Platière. Another day would elapse before the 84th would be relieved.

Going out of the line was welcome, but the officers and men were exhausted and hungry. Not having eaten a regular hot meal since 31 May made even a retrograde movement a terrible physical effort. Lieutenant Timmerman later said, "I had only 19 people left out of my platoon and we were just about on our feet." Regardless of the additional pain, they gladly went. Marine replacements for the brigade began to arrive from St. Aignan, and by the following day six officers and 128 men were received into the 3d Battalion. Not enough to fill the badly depleted ranks but still very much appreciated by everyone.[87]

At 1820 hours Harbord sent Hughes a message notifying him that his battalion had been relieved from duty as corps reserve and that he and his men should proceed that night to a point southeast of Lucy to relieve Sibley and his battalion,

> The regimental commander has arranged to have guides meet you at the bridge crossing over Gobert Brook. It is desired that you start at such an hour that your march will not be apparent to balloon observation of the enemy . . . etc.

The *etc.* meant that 1/6 was to take itself into the woods. Hughes assumed it was so that 1/6 would be in a position to move into Belleau Wood and relieve Sibley. As seen, Sibley and his men had been pulled out before any relief could commence. Evidently, Harbord finally realized what tough shape 3/6 was in and that there should be no delay in relief. The removal of 3/6 meant that the enemy could move back into their positions at the southern edge of the woods. For some reason, they didn't. The few Marines of the 20th and 47th Companies, plus the 84th, still in the southwestern portion of the woods were all that were left occupying Belleau Wood.

Returning from Harbord's PC that afternoon, Hughes sent Sgt. Gerald Thomas, of his battalion intelligence section, to locate a gully, or sunken road, beginning at about the Paris Farm and continuing northeastward toward Lucy, from which 1/6 could make its way to the designated woods under partial cover the entire way. Thomas, finding the mouth of the gully, quickly returned to report to Capt. George Stowell, the officer Hughes had left in charge while he was away at the brigade PC. Thus would begin a series of events that would cause the time delay in effecting the capture of Belleau Wood, nearly as much as the badly planned offensives of the 6th and 8th of June.

Major Maurice Shearer relieved Capt. Henry Larsen, who had been in temporary command of 3/5 since Berry's incapacitating wound made that necessary. One of the first instructions the new battalion commander received was not from his regimental commander, but directly from Harbord, who advised him to go over to Bouresches "early tomorrow morning" and "familiarize yourself with the line he [Holcomb] is holding." He continued, "It is the present intention that your battalion will relieve his tomorrow night." Three/Five had received reinforcements but they were, as was always the case, very green. Since Bouresches was still a hot spot and the key to the 2d Division's entire position, the decision to send the recently mutilated battalion to hold that most important objective seems, at this later date, highly questionable. In fact, a few days later, a major German attack came close to retaking the town.

Sunday, 9 June

Stowell, the skipper of the 76th Company and a competent officer of many years' service, took off on his trip to the woods near Lucy at 2100 on 8 June. It was midnight before the battalion reached the sunken road, and at a crucial junction in the dark the rear half of the column took a left turn, marching off to the northwest, the wrong direction. When asked by Sergeant Thomas where they were going, 1st Lt. Charles A. Etheridge, the recently appointed battalion IO, replied that he had not reconnoitered the trail "because Hughes had not told him to."[88] It took three hours to collect the stragglers and correct the error. Adding to Stowell's dilemma, the French guides promised by Harbord at Gobert Bridge weren't there. As dawn broke, German observation balloons spotted the battalion in open country. German shells started to drop in their area and Stowell ran the battalion into a nearby small wood, where, contrary to Hughes's desires, it would necessarily remain all day. Hughes returned to 1/6 outraged to find that his orders had not been obeyed to the letter. He immediately relieved Stowell of command of the 76th Company, appointing 1st Lt. Macon Overton in his place. As will be seen, following, this decision probably added greatly to the failure of the forthcoming attack by 2/5 on 11 June.

Hughes received orders from Harbord late in the day to resume his march after dark to the designated woods south of Lucy and to be in position on 10 June to enter Belleau Wood after a smashing artillery barrage. Harbord set the limit for the penetration of 1/6 as "X line 261.7," which was nearly halfway up the dreaded Hellwood.[89] After dark 1/6 set off again, down to the designated jump-off position, the woods south of Lucy. There was now but one company from 3/6 between it and the German forces in Belleau Wood.[90]

In the early afternoon, Shearer received orders directly from Harbord to send a company to the wood southeast of Lucy "as soon as it is dark tonight" as regimental support for the 6th Marines. Additionally he was to relieve the three companies of 2/6 in Bouresches with his remaining three. No directions as to the route he should take, but presumably it would be across the wheat field south of Belleau Wood because the southern portions of the wood were not occupied by the Boche. That route would be reasonably safe in the dark.

That day Frank Evans wrote a letter to the commandant about the Marine replacements that the brigade had received. It was very flattering.

> . . . remarkable conduct of raw replacement troops . . . which joined organization on the night of 8 June. . . . The 213 included among it a large majority who enlisted two months before reporting to this organization. . . . It was necessary to detail the five officers . . . to the 3d Battalion for the purposes of reorganizing that battalion . . . the green men obeyed the orders of the regimental sergeant major . . . without a word, moved in splendid order and across terrain which was shelled by the enemy. . . . Their arrival in the lines of the 2d Battalion relieved a pressing need for men at a vital point.

A few more point-making remarks like that would insure that Barnett knew he and the home staff were doing something right with their training methods.[91] Harbord added his comments to the forwarded letter. "To say that these men [the replacements] showed themselves of the same fine material as that already composing the 4th Brigade is extremely high praise, but in this case is deserved."[92] The replacements, relatively untrained as they were, did perform miracles when they were put into action. No one could ask for better men than that, but they were still raw recruits.

Monday, 10 June

The Marines in Bouresches were subjected to "heavy gun fire . . . all night . . . and [it] is still falling there." Shortly afterward someone in the

6th Marines determined that it wasn't American or French artillery that was doing the firing, which, presumably, made it all right. By 0200 the reports from the 6th Marines had changed to "Everything quiet." *Leutnant* Tillmanng, a German officer, wrote that the 10th of June was "the worst night of my life. I am lying in thick woods . . . in little holes behind rocks . . . heavy artillery fire, until six o'clock in the morning. It is a wonder that the fellows were all at their posts when the Americans attacked. The attack, thank God, was repulsed. God has mercifully preserved me. They fight like devils."[93]

At 0245 Lee received a confirmation message from Hughes that 1/6 was "in position." Regiment responded with the reply "If the leaves start dropping near you from 3.30 to 4.10 withdraw a bit to protect your men from [shell] splinters." Field Order No. 3, for an attack on 10 June by 1/6, specified that the attack would be launched at 0430. The report to Bundy late in the day stated that "at 3:30 A.M. the 1st Bn., 6th Marines . . . took the southern half of the Bois de Belleau." Obviously they were an hour or more off and the proportions were dead wrong. They barely occupied the southern fringes of the woods. Gulberg writes that he and his buddies of the 75th Company were advised that the battalion was "going over the top" that morning to

> capture the woods, which lay about five hundred yards in front of us. Just what we had been waiting for. A week ago we had lain in a wheat field and had been forced to take all the Germans had to offer and now at last it was our turn to give. We owed them plenty for the buddies they had taken from us.[94]

Thomason wrote that "Major Hughes attacked at daylight on the 10th and *reoccupied the positions reached by Major Sibley.*"[95] (Emphasis added.) Which meant that Hughes had not gotten anywhere near the middle of the woods, which, much later, Harbord was to learn to his anguish. But for the moment, Hughes was apparently unaware of that fact. Hughes's report to Harbord at 0451 briefly stated, "Artillery barrage working beautifully. Three or four casualties in the 74th Company coming in. Otherwise, all O.K. Kindly have artillery fire on machine guns firing down the line we have to cross." At 0520 Lieutenant Moore sent a message to brigade to advise that "Action in woods deemed finished." A half hour later 2d Lt. Bradford Perin, with the 6th Marines as liaison officer for the brigade, sent a message in Lee's name to Harbord. "The Bn. advanced *obtaining objective without opposition.* At present engaged in consolidating position." (Emphasis added.) As yet, no one seemed to question the reports coming in. It was common knowledge that 3/6 had been badly handled for several days in the same area, yet 1/6 was evidently having an easy time of it. What had happened to the Germans? Had they retired? Not likely. They were still located where Sibley and his crowd had pushed them.

At 0712 Hughes sent Harbord a message in which he brightly said, "Everything going nicely. No losses coming across. Have received no word from companies, but there is practically no firing. Artillery has blown the Bois de Belleau to mince meat." In his näiveté, Major Evans duly reported the final statement to Colonel Malone of the 23d Infantry, perhaps to others as well.[96] It may have looked like mincemeat where Hughes was standing, but there would be plenty of woods for two additional weeks. In his dash forward Hughes had support from the 77th and 23d Machine Gun Companies.

Meanwhile, on Hughes's left, Fuller and his 75th Company were having a devil of a time with some Boche machine guns, those directly before them and those around and about Hill 181. Major Edward B. Cole*, commander of the 6th Machine Gun Battalion, was up forward with the 75th Company, trying to get his guns in the proper positions to support Fuller's efforts. His guns in Bouresches were valiantly trying to suppress the Boche guns on Hughes's right flank, within the southeastern end of the woods. Nothing seemed to be working well, regardless of Hughes's sanguine messages to Lee and Harbord. About 0800 Hughes had the rather unpleasant task of reporting that Major Cole had been badly wounded. Cole would die a week later and earned his well-deserved DSC, NC, Legion of Honor, and several lesser decorations for his actions during the period. Captain Harlan Major, his second-in-command, immediately assumed command of the 6th Machine Gun Battalion. Meanwhile, Gulberg, of the 75th, relates how he and his buddies were hard pressed to cut through the obstacles and swarm over the terrain because

> machine guns were everywhere, in the ravines, behind rocks, and sometimes in the trees. . . . We had to rush each gun crew in turn, in the face of their deadly fire. It was a furious dash from one nest to another.[97]

Harbord was excited that one of his battalions was finally in position in the woods and just might bring a rapid conclusion to what was becoming a very embarrassing situation for him. At a few minutes after 1000 he sent a motorcyclist with the following message:

> Very important that you give me your judgement on what is north of you in the BOIS DE BELLEAU. Push your reconnaissance and let me know at the earliest possible moment whether you think it possible to take wood north of your present position.[98]
>
> Let me know 1st: Whether you think it will be practicable to take the part of BOIS DE BELLEAU north of your present position with your force as it now stands.
>
> 2d: How much further artillery preparation should there be on that part of the wood.
>
> 3d: If you think your forces are not equal to it with artillery preparation, give me your opinion on the forces necessary. All this on the assumption that machine-gun fire along the railroad will be kept down by our artillery and that Wise can advance on the left of the BOIS DE BELLEAU.[99]

Shortly after noon Shearer and 3/5 had completed their relief of 2/6 in Bouresches. Holcomb and 2/6 headed for the woods situated just southwest of Lucy for a well-earned rest period. As a battalion, 2/6 still hadn't launched an attack, but as will be seen, they were and would continue taking an inordinate number of casualties at Belleau Wood until the end.

At 1745 brigade issued Field Order No. 4, which, based upon the still uncorrected impression that most of the southern end of the woods was held by 1/6, ordered Wise and 2/5 to attack the northwestern side of the woods the following morning. They were to turn left with 1/6 on his right flank, and then both battalions were to take the entire woods including Hill 133 at the far northwest tip. The salient points in Field Order No. 4 are as follows:

> The attack would be made by 2/5 and would include the entire northern portion of the woods as its objective, plus Hill 133. When objective was obtained, liaison would be established on the right with 1/6. Hughes would advance his left to conform to the progress made by 2/5.[100]

The balance of the order established 2/6 as brigade reserve in the woods southwest of Lucy. Machine-gun support would be provided by twelve guns of the 6th Machine Gun Battalion. The guns at Bouresches would lay a barrage along the Belleau-Bouresches road for thirty minutes after the attack began. There would be artillery support as ordered by Brig. Gen. William Chamberlaine*, division artillery commander. Finally, the attack would begin at 0430. Of course, this order was doomed to failure, since 1/6 was unable to carry out its designated part no matter what other successes, failures, or errors occurred.[101]

In his memoir, Wise tells us that he had Harbord's permission to plan his attack on 12 June without interference from brigade. His story contradicts everything we've learned elsewhere except for one important record. (See following.) In it he quotes a private conversation with Harbord as follows. . .

Wise, the Sixth Marines have made two attacks on the Bois de Belleau. The first one [3/6] failed. The second *made little headway on the southern edge of the woods.* You're on the ground, there. You know the conditions. It's up to you to clean it up. Go ahead and *make your own plans* and do the job. [Emphasis added.][102]

After that conversation, Wise went to Neville and asked for the return of Williams and the 51st Company, which was approved. A short time later, the 51st Company arrived back into the fold from where it had helped defend Hill 142 for the previous three days. They would have been better off if they'd stayed with 1/5 for a while longer. Wise describes his own plans which appear to be excellent, if only they had been followed:

I didn't see any use following the same line of attack which had failed with the Sixth Marines. . . . It was common sense to hit them where they weren't looking for it . . . so I determined to risk everything on the unexpected and attack them from their rear . . . thus I would get between them and their lines of support, which were along the railroad in front of the northern edge of the Bois de Belleau.[103]

Wise, at that point relates that he sent for his four company commanders, Wass, Williams, Dunbeck, and Cooke. "They were red-eyed, dirty, unshaven. We sat down under a tree." He then explained his plan and they all agreed that it seemed most feasible. He then states that he established 0400 as zero hour. "After we got to the northern edge of the woods, any German shelling would hit among the Germans as well as us." So far, so good. Harbord's Field Order No. 4 was not far apart from Wise's plan. There were a few differences, but overall either would have been acceptable under the existent circumstances. Wise then went over to speak with Hughes in his PC and came away, according to Wise, with the feeling that Hughes agreed with his plan wholeheartedly.

From here on Wise's story varies with just about everyone else's. Cooke tells us that "two plans for our attack were under consideration: an encircling maneuver by two columns, mopping up afterwards; the other, a straight frontal attack with a rolling barrage. *We held out for the frontal attack.*" (Emphasis added.)[104]

In his history, Thomason covers some of the confusion in his note number 1, page 152, in which he mentions that he agreed with Wise's planned assault upon the northern edge of the wood.

> His description is vague (in his memoir), but north of Hill 169 lay the only sheltered approach . . . that the Brigade Commander, in the afternoon of 10 June, approved his plan; that he had made all arrangements for it; that about midnight he received a written order from Harbord, directing him to attack across the open ground opposite the southern half of the Bois de Belleau, a frontal attack which he desired to avoid . . . and that he made the attack as ordered by the Brigade Commander in his written order.

Thomason explained that if Wise had followed Field Order 4 exactly, 2/5 would have encountered few Germans. German records indicate that only one company was around and about Hill 169. Further German records indicate that few of them were in the northern half—most all were instead concentrated in the south, where 1/6 Marines had already actually struck.[105]

This, then, was the beginning of what was yet another disaster for the 4th Brigade. The entire following story is extremely confusing and still hasn't been cleared up, nor probably will it ever be. It is sufficient to state that regardless of the disorder, the Marines did their collective best, as always.

Tuesday, 11 June

Wise wrote that he received a message sometime during the night of 10–11 June that he couldn't believe.

It was an attack order. . . . My battalion was ordered to attack the Bois de Belleau FROM THE SOUTHERN EDGE at four o'clock that morning, behind a rolling barrage. . . . It was signed "Harbord." [He adds that he was] dumfounded, all my plans were up in the air. I knew that piece of paper . . . meant needless death of most of my battalion. . . . Now, instead of hitting the Germans from the rear, I had to take that battalion to a frontal attack against a prepared position.[106]

He added that he notified his four company commanders and Hughes of the changes. Although the "order" specified that Hughes would support 2/5, Wise clearly states that Hughes "never got any such order."[107] Yet, order received or not, Hughes did tell Overton to move on 2/5's right flank, maintaining liaison with them, which movement was a complete failure. Lots of stories, few records.

At 0430 the whistles blew and the sticks went up and over their leaders' heads and 2/5 went across the open ground just as 3/5 had. Their route of attack did not conform to Harbord's plan, or to that of Lieutenant Colonel Wise either. According to reports, the weather was not helpful, even though at the time it appeared to be so. There was a heavy mist and that, plus some darkness, didn't allow much visibility. Temporarily, the impaired view helped to save Marines from those terrible German machine guns emplaced near the edges of the woods; but for such a short period of time. The leading waves soon were brought under that fire and were soon shot to pieces. The major volume of lead coming at them was from the right front in the angle of the woods near where Overton and the 76th Company were located. The battalion was in what was then called an "artillery formation." The formation consisted of two companies in front and two behind, both in platoon half columns. The 43d Company (Dunbeck) was on the left in two platoon waves, followed by Wass's 18th Company, also in two waves. The right was headed by Williams's 51st in two waves, and they were followed by Cooke's 55th Company.

The orders required the Marines to move in a northeasterly direction, a direct attack against the northern edge of the wood, as the coordinates in Field Order No. 4 specified. Instead, the two columns aimed in a modified southeasterly direction. It appears possible that Williams lost his direction in the mist. Dunbeck followed the right guide, as would be expected, and also headed in the same direction.[108] Wise began following the battalion shortly after they went across the open ground. After both lead companies were badly handled by the Germans (from the front, the right, and the left), the remnants entered the woods considerably south of where their directions should have led them. All of Wise's responses and reports that followed, except his memoir, lead one to believe that he truly believed, for some hours, that he was going according to Field Order No. 4.

The semiofficial history of the 2d Battalion, 5th Marines, is rather vague but does elaborate on what it ran into that morning.

The attack swept across wheat fields over rough hilly ground and on into the Bois de Belleau over a front of about one kilometer. The enemy was profusely equipped with machine guns, to which their crews stuck in many cases until killed, inflicting heavy losses on the attacking lines. Strongest resistance was met on the right, making it necessary to use more men in that half of the line. The enemy made good use of cover, sometimes hiding machine guns until a line had passed, and again firing machine guns from tree tops. . . . [That night] about 150 replacement men arrived.[109]

Cooke relates how Wise, in a conversation with his officers the day before, while telling them of the planned attack, said he didn't think they would have any trouble because there probably weren't any Germans in the woods anyway. He then asked Cooke, "Have you seen any Germans in those woods, Cooke?" Whereupon Cooke, very uncomfortable at being put on the spot by his CO, admitted that he'd not seen any Germans in those woods, which were a mile away. Wise replied, "Of course not. There probably aren't any Boche in those woods at all. That means we will simply have to walk over and take the place." Wishful thinking that Cooke thought of again shortly after the attack began, because for a very short period they weren't being fired upon. "'The Old Man must have been right after all,' I said to [2d] Lieutenant [John H.] Parker, commanding my reserve platoon. 'There don't seem to be any more Dutchmen around.'" Minutes later he had cause to regret his hasty conclusion. They went into an angle, where the arm of the forest went westward out of the body, and all hell broke loose.

Both support companies quickly merged with the two assaulting companies and forced their way into the woods. Soon after entering the

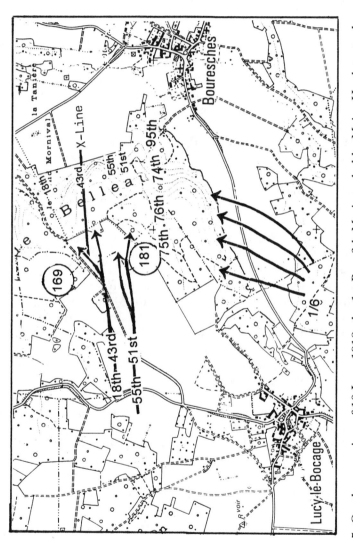

Map 5: On the morning of 10 June 1918, the 1st Bn., 6th Marines, led by Major Hughes, took over the space previously occupied by 3/6, but falling far short of his objective. The following day, Lieutenant Colonel Wise led his 2d Bn, 5th toward where 3/5 had fallen apart on 6 June. The individual companies' final position is based on official records.

woods, Wass and the 18th moved in a northeasterly direction to the 43d's left. When Cooke arrived, he moved to Williams's left with all four companies now in line. Left to right: 18th, 43d, 55th, and 51st in line. The trip over was well described later by 1st Lt. Samuel C. Cumming, a platoon leader of the 51st Company:

> Line after line moved off toward a wood six hundred meters away, across an open and level field covered with grass six inches high. The ground became covered with a sheet of machine gun bullets from a Prussian Guard machine gun battalion and their supporting infantry. . . . We moved forward at a slow pace, keeping perfect lines. Men were mowed down like wheat. A "whizz-bang"* hit on my right, and an automatic [rifle] team which was there a moment ago disappeared, while men on the right and left were armless, legless, or tearing at their faces.[110] *whizz-bang is what soldiers called a small high speed shell that arrived at about the same instant as the explosion.

Cumming said he was hit at about fifty yards from the woods. It was at this point that he crawled toward Cooke, who later quoted Cumming, when he asked him where the 51st was, as saying, "The machine guns got 'em. As far as I know I'm the only one left of ten officers and two hundred fifty men." Cooke then realized that if the 51st had been wiped out, the 43d, to their left, was badly exposed.[111] Cumming agreed with that premise, "Yes. If there is any Forty-third left." Cooke responded, "By God, they can't all be dead." Just then someone hailed him from the woods. It was an officer asking if Cooke was with the 51st Company. Cooke responded that he was with the 55th.

> The officer looked dismayed and embarrassed. "I was supposed to go forward with the Fifty-first," he said apologetically. Then I understood. He commanded the company of the 6th Marines that was to have assisted our attack. Because of the heavy mist he had failed to see our assaulting waves go by. No wonder the 51st had been cut to pieces by flanking machine gun fire.[112]

By this time Cooke "shucked off fear" and now it was rage that "took command of my thoughts." He adds,

> Those damn Boche couldn't go shooting up our whole outfit and get away with it like that. . . . He then stood up and blew his whis-

tle whereupon . . . faces looked up. . . . I pointed to the woods to our right front. Parker, Brown, and I walked forward.[113]

After Cooke and Parker made an easy capture of a Boche machine gun they were startled by a sound to their rear. It was two men from the 6th Marines who "had come forward to join us." (Members of the 76th Company?) He also adds that they had a Chauchat, which greatly contributed to his firepower. Brown and two other men picked up the Maxim they had captured and all started forward. Soon they were being fired upon, but in short order the Marines were able to squelch that. Lieutenant Parker "squatted over our captured machine gun and rattled off a whole belt in that direction." The Germans asked to surrender but mistook Cooke's movements and fired upon him when he raised his automatic toward them. He hit the deck after taking one bullet in his side. The Germans were soon begging to surrender after the Marines turned on them with a vengeance; the German request was presently accepted. Apparently his men thought he was down for good, but Cooke soon determined it was a minor scratch and he was on his feet in a few minutes.

Wise describes what he saw that morning, and his account varies slightly with what appears to have really happened. His memoir depicts his battalion going across in a line, which no one else but Cumming affirms. He does add that "the Germans couldn't have had better targets if they had ordered the attack themselves. . . . The barrage kept crawling on . . . men dropping, men dropping, men dropping. . . ." Then he tells how when the battalion finally reached the woods and entered, the firing slackened by a great amount. He emphasizes that there were "heavy casualties."

The 18th Company's history vaguely relates their impression of what happened to them, but significantly states that "our casualties were very heavy, the fourth platoon being almost completely wiped out when it was sent out on the left flank after some machine guns that were holding us up."[114]

Instead of finding 1/6, 2/5 found, and overran, the German 40th Infantry on its flank. The 40th were between 1/6 and 2/5 and were torn to pieces. More importantly, their machine-gun defenses were broken up. The Marines destroyed the German 1st and 4th Companies. Most of the German commanders were killed or wounded, or led away as captives. The enemy 8th Company, the liaison unit, together with the 3d Company, was driven back eastward into the woods. The German line, from Hill 181 to X-line 261.7, was swept out of existence. Finally, a Marine battalion landed on the X-line, and it was 2/5, not 1/6. Hughes and his battalion were still farther south.

The 461st German Infantry, which received 2/5, fared badly at first, but they had an energetic commanding officer who had a strong reserve line preserving their overall cohesion in the woods. They continued to mutilate 2/5 for hours to come. One additional fact that was of some importance: the German units opposed to 2/5 were then in the process of being relieved. The 40th Regiment was relieving the 462d Regiment, and as a result, the Germans were less well disposed than they might have been. That was one of the few breaks 2/5 received that day.[115]

In a report to Harbord at 0705 Hughes told him that "Lieutenant Overton reports that Wise is held up by constant machine gun fire. 3 platoons 76th Company in connection with them." According to the report, Overton had finally made the connection. At 1015 Evans sent Lee a message in which he said, "Message just received from Brigade. Tell Col. Lee to get word to Hughes that Wise passed 2 or 3 M.G.'s. on his (Wise) right and *leave no gap for M.G's. to work into rear.'*" (Emphasis added.) Five minutes later Evans duly sent a same worded message to Hughes. By this time Hughes must have been aware that 1/6 wasn't supporting Wise as he had been ordered to. Lee's message to brigade at 1348 said that "Overton just beat off Boche counter-attack" and added, "Just sent two platoons to Wise as he said enemy were on his left." That had only one explanation: To Wise's left was the northern end of the woods, which meant that as late in the day as nearly 1400 hours the Germans were attacking 2/5 on their left, right, front, and rear. According to Hughes's messages, 1/6 still hadn't moved forward from their original positions. Meanwhile, George Osterhout relieved Harlan in command of the 6th Machine Gun Battalion.

In the morning, upon his return from the western edges of the wood, Lt. Bill Mathews, Wise's IO, gave him some warning of the trouble he was getting into based upon a piece of intelligence that he'd gathered. In his travels Mathews had come across Capt. Alphonse De Carre*, "skipper" of Headquarters Company, 5th Marines, who had been the only commanding officer to lead his men in the correct direction during the advance. De Carre told Mathews that he had just returned from a wooded area around Hill 169 where he and his men were able to surprise a German company, and captured approximately 180 officers and men.[116] He gave Mathews specific information as to where the Germans were located, emphasizing that the entire left (the north end) of Belleau Wood was occupied by Germans. Mathews hurried back to Wise with the information, which Wise unwisely refused to even consider. It was received just a few moments before Dunbeck heralded that he and the 43d were on their objective, and Wise was convinced that his officers knew where they were.[117] Wise told Neville the news and Neville notified Harbord, and from there, right on up the line the "good" news spread like the bubonic plague.

At 0545 Colonel Lee reported an advance by the Germans upon Bouresches. A few minutes later, Shearer, holding the town with a rejuvenated 3/5, called for an artillery barrage to break up a Boche attack of infantry and machine guns that was advancing along the railroad tracks toward the town. Ultimately it was learned that the advance was not on Bouresches itself. Instead, the Germans were attempting to reinforce their men in the woods. That they failed was fortunate for 2/5, who already had enough Boches in the woods to keep them busy for some time to come.

Cooke tells of turning his part of the woods over to the 6th Marines and taking his men to join up with Capt. Joseph D. Murray, Wise's assistant battalion commander. Wass was also there with what remained of the 18th. The latter still had Lts. Gilder D. Jackson, Chester H. Fraser, "and about a third of his men. It turned out that Lieutenant Luffburro (sic) and sixteen men were all that was left of the 51st Company."[118] By now Dunbeck had been wounded and Murray had taken his place in command of the 43d. But Murray would soon be recalled by Wise to his position as battalion executive officer and 2d Lt. "Drink" Milner, the minister's son, would replace him. Cooke still had Parker and 1st Lt. Lucius Q. C. L. Lyle plus eighty men. Wass and Cooke were the only "old-timers" now. The two other companies were being commanded by second lieutenants. Cooke added,

> A bitter price to pay for a piece of woods that stank of high explosives, crushed shrubbery, and scattered human flesh. Dead men littered the ground and lay hidden in every thicket and rocky cleft. Even the living walked about in a sort of shell-shocked daze.[119]

At 0633 the 6th Regiment reported that 2/5 had taken all its objectives; that the "attack" on Bouresches had been broken up; and that machine guns with 3/5 had slaughtered Germans retiring from the east edge of Belleau Wood. The first point was entirely incorrect, but the rest were, to a certain extent, exaggerations. I'm not sure where Lee obtained his information, but it was all wrong.

Because of the heavy fire coming from his right, at 0858 Wise requested that Neville provide artillery support on the "northeast end of the woods. . . . The Germans are massing in front." The coordinates given were about halfway between the town of Belleau and Bouresches.[120] The fire, if the coordinates had been followed, and there is no reason to believe they wouldn't have been, would have fallen on open ground. What was seen, probably, were the same Germans Shearer had seen and who would have already been on the list to be blasted, but in a different location. At the same time Wise reported "Captain Williams wounded."[121] Many years later Charley Dunbeck, skipper of the 43d, described what happened to Williams:

> I went to look for my next door neighbor [Williams] and found him sitting on a stone writing a message to Colonel Wise. It was 5:30 in the morning, when a German machine gun opened up to our front and I remarked to Williams that we were in a dangerous place and should move: he said 'Yes, Dunbeck, I agree with you.' So we started to change our position, to take shelter behind the rocks, when Williams was wounded. His wound was in his right side and right shoulder. It was not very serious. Two of his men made a stretcher of a woolen blanket and I had four German prisoners carry him to the dressing station at Lucy.[122]

Obviously this took place before Dunbeck himself was wounded. Wise reported that his losses were very heavy and that there was no contact with Hughes yet. He repeated the same message at 0925, nearly five hours after his jump-off. Quite unknown to him, 2/5 was still surrounded by Germans.[123] Meanwhile, Neville requested two companies of engineers to assist in "consolidation" work; meaning that the Marines were shot to hell and desperately needed live bodies to fill the blank spots. As usual, the engineers would work miracles in preparing defensive positions and when they had finished them, they would fight like hell.

Harbord wrote to Bundy at the same time, complaining of the poor phone service and adding, "In my judgement, the capture of Bois de Belleau is the most important event that has taken place for the Allied holding in this vicinity." He also said that there would not be any successful advance made by the enemy in the region, "without first an attempt to dislodge us from the Bois de Belleau." Naturally Bundy was also convinced that the wood had been taken, so he sent Pershing a telegram, advising him of the great success. On the following day the *New York Times* headlines stated, OUR MEN TAKE BELLEAU WOOD, 300 CAPTIVES. And in column, "American troops this morning [1 June] brilliantly captured Belleau Wood." There would be many red faces on the morrow.[124]

By the middle of the morning, prisoners were wending their way back to the American lines and by 1040 the two German officers and 169 men, captured by Headquarters Company, 5th Marines, were at division. Wise was able to report that he and Hughes had finally made contact, and at 1100 Neville reported to brigade that the "situation was satisfactory in the Bois de Belleau."[125] At 1045 Wass sent the following message to brigade:

> Have obtained our objective. The enemy are preparing a *counterattack on our left flank. We need barrage immediately along Bouresches-Belleau Road, the northwest [?] along our front.* [Emphasis added.][126]

An hour later, with obvious joy, the following message from Harbord was sent to Lt. Col. "Fritz" Wise, the hero of the hour.

> The Division Commander is at Brigade headquarters and sends hearty congratulations to you and your gallant men. He says the task could not have been performed any better. The objectives of the Brigade have been attained everywhere, after days of fighting which the Division Commander has never known to have been excelled. To this I add my warm personal greetings and congratulations.[127]

But all wasn't well. Wise sent a message to brigade in which he let it be known that the "positions are now well organized; in perfect touch with the 6th [Marines]. . . . I will inspect and can then give an idea of losses. . . . We have lost quite a few officers." And he could have added, "and men." Even though Wise hadn't believed De Carre's assertion of what his true location was, he sent Mathews out to reconnoiter the ground to his left. Mathews later reported the following in his official summary:

> When we came near the woods we ran on to scores of wounded who were lying unattended calling for help. We started giving first

aid as best we could. . . . Mike Wordarzeck [sic] came marching
out of the woods with a large group of prisoners. . . . We could find
no one in the north [?] part of the woods. . . . I asked Mike what
was over there and he said nothing. I went back into the woods
with Mike. . . . I found Dunbeck, Wass, and Lt. Cooke standing together. . . . I said to them "are you sure you have reached your objectives?" All of them spoke up and said yes, and . . . Dunbeck said
"we are at the north end of the woods, because there is Torcy
(pointing to Belleau) and there is Belleau (pointing to
Bouresches)." When I told them that a great mass of woods to the
left was still unoccupied, they insisted that it was all behind them
and therefore safe.[128]

Mathews was convinced that he was right and that all of the others
were wrong. Accordingly, he went to his left and formed a small observation point with a few of his men and then returned with his report to
Wise's PC. He "emphasized that the whole left flank of the woods was
absolutely unprotected." Mathews tells us that Wise replied, "You goddamn young bonehead, you don't know what you're talking about. I
have messages from my company commanders saying they are at the
north end of the woods." But Mathews's bullheaded insistence forced
Wise to reconsider his own intransigence. At 1125 he sent Harbord a
message: "I think my left flank is weak." That didn't faze Harbord as he
was still content with and satisfied by the early reports of success. There
wouldn't be any gloom and doom for him. Neville, being nowhere near
the action, sent a message to Harbord that declined further help for 2/5.
"Do not need anymore companies now. Everything O.K. Believe our casualties light." Naturally that message was exactly what Harbord wanted
to receive. It served to strengthen his own impression and desire.[129]

In his memoir Wise makes it plain that because of the hectic conditions he didn't really get around to his companies until shortly after
noon. Leaving his adjutant, 1st Lt. James H. Legendre* at the PC, and
starting on the right of his line with the 51st, Wise and a runner made
a circuit of his companies. He arrived to find that Williams had been
wounded and now with

some junior . . . in command [Loughborough] who told Wise of
the terrific fighting they'd had. Foot by foot they had pushed their
way through the underbrush in the face of continuous machine-
gun and rifle fire. Snipers had shot them from brush piles on the

ground; from perches high in the trees. Germans they had left
sprawled on the ground for dead as they went on, had risen and
shot them in the back.[130]

He went farther down the line, where he came upon Cooke, "who
had lost several of his juniors and a lot of his men." There he got the
same story as from Loughborough, and more. . . .

Whenever we took a machine-gun nest, another one opened up
on their flank. . . .The second one would never fire a shot until we
had taken the first. Then they opened up on us.[131]

Farther down the line Wise found Dunbeck and what was left of his
company. He told Wise

how Lieutenant Heiser had died. Leading an attack on a German
machine-gun nest, Heiser had been literally decapitated. His head
had been cut clean from his body by a stream of machine-gun bullets that caught him in the throat. . . . Down on the left flank I
found Wass. Most of his juniors were gone, and half his men. What
was left of his company had dug in too. . . . Every one of those four
companies had fought its way clear through those woods, from one
side to the other.[132]

When Wise returned to his PC he found Major Hughes waiting for
him there. "'Can you lend me a company to clean out the northeast
point of the woods?' . . . He said he would."[133] Meanwhile Mathews and
his men were busy at the observation post. Mathews drew a small map
on which he outlined the woods as he viewed them, which he then sent
to Wise. Wise responded that it didn't look anything like his map, which
had been supplied by the French. Bill Mathews then went back to Wise
to further argue his case. At that moment a Marine chaser came through
the PC with a German prisoner, a medical orderly. The prisoner told
the group that if they, 2/5, had acted sooner, all the Germans in the
north would have surrendered to them, but now they were being reinforced. To his chagrin, Wise now realized that Mathews had probably
been correct. Mathews again urged Wise to fill the gap and Wise responded, "Where in the hell am I going to get them [the men]?" Mathews suggested using men from the uncommitted 74th Company, which
had been assigned by Hughes as Wise's support. Wise agreed, so Math-

ews went back and found Lt. Edgar Allan Poe Jr., and his platoon from the 74th. They were the first of the three platoons to have arrived. Mathews sent them in to support his observation group in the northwest. By this time Wise had begun to wonder where he was and what he was going to do about it. But as Mathews said, "[he] was about six hours too late."[134] Wise then pulled Cooke and the 55th from the right and shifted them to the left. Hughes extended his line northward to maintain contact but basically remained pretty much where he'd been since his arrival in the woods. There was still no evidence of what he was thinking about, or why he hadn't gone farther into the woods as ordered. There never would be any explanation.

Soon upon reaching their new location, Cooke and his company reconnoitered their flank and drew heavy fire in response. The Germans, who were in force in the north, began wending their way past the left flank of the Marines. Major Hartlieb had collected his shattered German formations and with his reserves began moving down the west face of the woods to a point just north of Hill 181. Also a battalion of the German 110th Regiment, from the 28th Division, was sent in to replace the destroyed 40th. After dark they would work their way eastward to come within fifty feet of the Marines, thereby making life very uncomfortable for everyone concerned. At this time 2/5 was truly surrounded.

At 1340 Capt. George K. Shuler, adjutant of the 5th Marines, sent the following information to brigade, which sums up what he thought had happened to 2/5 in the nine hours since the attack began: "Companies 43d, 51st and 18th have about 30 men each lost and 55th about 83. I hardly believe the latter." The following day would provide a clearer picture of what had truly happened. Wise still hadn't the faintest idea what losses his battalion had sustained and as a result his reports were still relatively optimistic.

A few minutes later Harbord sent Wise a message telling him to "refuse your left flank slightly, along ravine or higher up along edge of woods." There is a ravine running out of the woods from north to south about a quarter mile from the northwestern face. So evidently Harbord was still accepting, without question, the messages received from 2/5. He added that a thousand replacements were arriving "for the Brigade today." Unfortunately, Wise didn't receive that message until late that evening. But at once he attempted to follow the order. He took Mathews with him and went forward to "refuse his left flank." They arrived to find Lieutenant Poe and his platoon in a very brisk firefight with the Germans to their left. At Wise's orders, Mathews successfully pulled them back to where Wise believed "the ravine" was located. But instead of the ravine being in the middle of the northern end, they found another ravine—one that was just a small trail and about eight hundred yards farther south, near the wood's waistline. Brigade and division headquarters were still ecstatic about the "capture of Belleau Wood" and hadn't noticed anything wrong with the messages being received. At least, not yet.

Wise was now aware that his left line on the east was at about X-line 261.7, a far cry from where he had initially supposed he was. Runners were now being picked off and some being captured in the supposed "captured areas." Those who weren't were reporting to battalion headquarters that Germans were in the rear. German-speaking Marines were calling on the enemy, to the left flank, to surrender and for their pains were driven in by heavy rifle and machine-gun fire. Wise even considered moving his flank to form a front and push northward, but dropped that idea as impractical.[135]

Cooke mentions that Lieutenant Poe[136] had wandered off to the left earlier, looking for members of his company, the 74th. He found a "hell of a lot of woods over on our left. . . . I think there are some Germans over there too." Cooke and Poe, under orders, went over again for a look-see. They found more Germans than they had bargained for. When they tried to entice the Boche to surrender, the response was less than friendly. Cooke sent for Parker and his platoon but soon learned that they faced a company of Germans. The Marines were now facing northward, at right angles to the 18th Company, and "as far as I could see, the nearest friendly troops on our left were in the Bois de Champillon [aka Bois St. Martin]—a gap of over a thousand yards." He said he told Poe that "if these Dutchmen attack they'll cut off our battalion and roll up the Sixth Marines."[137] At that point he was assigned a welcomed addition of seventy-five replacements for his company. He must have suffered at least 100 casualties by this time, to earn seventy-five replacements. Cooke was ordered to fall back because, he was told, division was going to "steamroll this place." Meaning, of course, the same old tired bit about what the artillery was going to do, but never quite seemed to accomplish.

Major Frank Evans notified brigade that there was heavy shelling by "150's and 210's" on Lucy and on Colonel Lee's PC. Most of the seventy casualties were German prisoners who had been working there. He also indicated that the prisoners complained that they hadn't been fed for three days. "German officer complained that they had been up against

Canadians and British but that they had found us a bit worse." Most likely that comment gained him better food and treatment. A German soldier, Private Hebel of the 461st Infantry, 237th Division, wrote a letter on 11 June in which he described his situation and his opponents:

> We are having very heavy days with death before us hourly. Here we have no hope ever to come out. My company has been reduced from 120 to 30 men. . . . We have Americans opposite us who are terribly reckless fellows. In the last eight days I have not slept twenty hours.[138]

As the day drew to a close it was determined that the losses of 2/5 that day had been 6 officers and 176 men killed and wounded. The numbers far exceeded Shuler's optimistic statement earlier in the day. Additionally, the entire battalion, which had been under fire since 2 June, was now completely exhausted. There had been no issuance of hot food since just before they left Chaumont-en-Vixen on the 31 of May. Water was only available in Lucy and the weather was very hot. Harbord, a decent, humane man, had recognized what his brigade had been going through, and at 0800 that morning, in his report to General Bundy, had specifically addressed the issue. It is worthy of complete inclusion here.

> I desire to call the attention of the Division Commander. . . . This Brigade has been in the line since June 1st and has been almost continuously fighting. *Its line has receded nowhere and has everywhere advanced.* Officers and men are at a state scarcely less than complete physical exhaustion. Men fall asleep under bombardment and the physical exhaustion and heavy losses are a combination calculated to damage morale, which should be met by immediate arrangements for the relief of this Brigade. . . . [The French army believes] that fighting 5 or 6 days by them excused them for falling back before the enemy. This Brigade has more than doubled the time. . . . I strongly urge that immediate arrangements be made for its relief to enable us to rest and reorganize. [Emphasis added.][139]

Captain Lester S. Wass*, "skipper" of the 18th Company, was cited for "extraordinary heroism in action in Bois de Belleau, 11 June 1918. When all the officers of his company became casualties, he displayed marked heroism in leading his men forward in the face of heavy machine-gun fire, assisting in the capture of many machine guns." Several of the enlisted men of the company were cited: one for assisting the wounded under fire; another, a runner, for carrying messages under heavy artillery fire. After all the other members of his group had been killed or wounded by enemy machine-guns, Private Jean Mathias* of the 43d Company charged a machine-gun position alone, killing three of the crew and capturing the gun. First Lieutenant Drinkard B. Milner, the only officer remaining in the 43d, carried forth the attack vigorously and managed to preserve close liaison in spite of the fact that all his runners were either killed or wounded. According to his citation for the Silver Star, "he protected his left which was the left flank of our whole position."[140]

There were many other heroes, some from the 51st, like Sgt. James Fallon, Cpl. Ira J. Gothard, Pvts. Ronald Fisher, John R. Lawrence, Frank Morrison, Walter V. Norton, John F. Russell, Jr., Merwyn C. Shawe, and 2d Lt. Tolbert Wagoner, all of whom were decorated for their undeniable courage during that hectic day. First Lieutenant Samuel C. Cumming received a Silver Star citation for his bravery. Second Lieutenant Hascall F. Waterhouse, of the 55th, although wounded, continued to lead his platoon all that day. He was killed in action on 13 June. Private Paul Bonner was awarded two Silver Star citations for carrying his wounded company commander, Elliott D. Cooke, to a place of safety.[141] Another private of the 55th, Dilmus Brown*, "after all the other members of his squad had become casualties . . . single-handed[ly] charged and captured a hostile machine gun." Privates Jerry M. Davin and Hal L. Hartzog each received Silver Star citations for their courage and Sgt. William J. Vierbuchen* earned a commission. Though wounded, he made a reconnaissance of the machine-gun nest that got him and that information was largely responsible "in the successful capture of this nest a few hours later." Naturally, this is not a complete listing of all the brave Marines and the U.S. Army officers of 2/5 who fought and died that day while giving that last extra bit. What manner of men were these?

No members of the 1st Battalion, 6th Marines, were cited specifically that day. Three officers, Hughes included, received awards for their heroics for the period from 10 to 13 June 1918. Hughes received a Navy Cross plus a Silver Star for leading his men "superbly under most trying conditions against the most distinguished elements of the German army, administering . . . their first defeat." His battalion adjutant, Captain Arthur H. Turner, was awarded a Silver Star and the Legion of Honor, for being at all times "in the forefront of operations against the enemy." Finally, 1st Lt. Charles A. Etheridge earned two Silver Star citations for his reconnaissance and for finding a gap in the enemy lines on the night of 12 June. I cannot find that any enlisted men of 1/6 were recognized during the month of June. Perhaps it was an oversight?

At day's end Harbord was satisfied that 1/6 had cleared the southern portion of Belleau Wood and that 2/5 was well situated in the north end near Hill 133. Calculations brought the total number of prisoners to about 400, with some fifty of them working under the command of Colonel Wise, helping to clear Marine wounded out of the woods. In addition, the reports indicated that three or more *minnenwerfers* plus at least thirty machine guns had also been captured.

Bundy released 3/6 from corps reserve, and they were replaced by 2/6. Sibley and his men received orders to take up residence in the woods northwest of Lucy. All in all, according to the information received, it had been a very successful day for the Americans. At least that was the supposition at brigade headquarters.

Meanwhile the commanders of the two German divisions, the 237th (461st Regiment, Major Bischoff in line) in the north and the 28th (40th Fusilier Regiment, Major von Hartlieb) to the south, each blamed the other for the loss of the Belleau Wood positions. Major von Hartlieb faced 1/6 during most of the action. On 10–11 June, his companies were nearly destroyed by attacks from both flanks. It wasn't until 2/5 moved northward that Bischoff became involved, but not with Hughes and 1/6.

Wednesday, 12 June

During the night of 11–12 June, the woods were relatively quiet. Marines and Germans were each attempting to reorganize quietly without bringing the wrath of the other upon them. Wise welcomed Maj. William A. Snow* and his two companies of engineers, which he sent to the "far edge of the woods as infantry." He also received 150 Marine replacements that were immediately distributed throughout the companies as needed. And were they needed! Mackin mentions several times in his classic memoir that he and his buddies were considered "damn replacements." But usually that "accolade" was thrown at them after the fighting was over. The 18th Company history describes what they and their comrades were facing that first night:

That night we got replacements of new men who never before had heard the whistle of a shell. No one except the men who joined us in the woods that night can realize the sensation of coming from a peaceful world directly into a hell hole like Belleau Woods was at that time. The scent of the unburied dead was something fierce, and there was always a rank odor of mustard gas in the low places. The lines were never connected, you seldom knew who was on your right or left, liaison being next to impossible. In our rear in the thick woods or underbrush there were a few enemy snipers and machine gunners who had been passed up unseen by the ever-thinning lines during the first attack.

The story went on to mention how difficult it was to obtain food that night. Some Marines discovered cans of monkey meat, others loaves of bread, but water had become a thing of the past. But that history insisted that their morale was still high.[142]

All reports emanating from 2/5 were giving brigade the impression that all was well; meaning that 2/5 was holding the northern end of the woods with a refused left flank. And that they could easily overcome what was believed to be the few Germans still in the woods. Early that morning Wise was present at a conference of the regimental commanders at which he expressed his belief that, with some artillery preparation, he could dislodge the Germans by the afternoon. Orders were issued accordingly, with the 12th Artillery being directed to shell the supposed positions of the enemy, after which, at 1700, 2/5 would jump off again.

After making the world aware that the woods had been taken, Harbord and Bundy now realized they hadn't been and now had to be. All was well and good at either headquarters, where shells and machine-gun bullets infrequently fell. On the line the Marines were still exhausted, and worse, badly depleted. To add to their misery, during the previous night the woods caught hell from the Boche artillery, which sent over many HE and gas shells. Wise sent a message to Harbord at 1000 that should have made some impact upon the recipient. . . .

Men in fine shape and line is holding but getting thinner. Heavy shelling and some gas. About out of officers. Request barrage immediately. Are getting hell shelled out of us.[143]

Cooke wasn't quite as sanguine in his reports to Wise, as the latter to brigade. He made it very clear that his men and he were used up, their will beginning to falter from the constant strain. They had a few replacements but their experienced officers and men were often dead or wounded. "Reaction from the attack of the day before had left us low in morale and courage."

Colonel Malone, commanding the 23d Infantry, sent Harbord a congratulatory message at 1430 that lauded the 4th Brigade.

Hearty congratulations of the splendid work of your Brigade. It will inspire all Americans. I got a little slice myself but only a little. Am in hopes that the opportunity will soon come again. We rejoice in your victory.[144]

Harbord, still unaware of the actual situation in the woods, responded a half hour later in a benevolent manner.

My Dear Malone—Many thanks for your much appreciated message. The Marine Brigade is certainly a splendid lot of officers and men. As for yourself and the 23d, all you need is the opportunity which I hope you may get soon.[145]

The plan for the afternoon's attack was that three companies (more likely in platoon strength by now) were in line from left to right, 55th, 43d, and the 18th on the right. All that remained of the 51st was Loughborough and what has been described as a "handful of men," who would provide a pitiful reserve. When Hughes moved forward he would attempt to keep up with the advance of 2/5. The artillery began its shelling on time but gave an indifferent performance, at least as far as Wise and his artillery officer were concerned. At 1630 Neville received a message from Wise complaining about the indifferent effects of the so-called bombardment, and requesting additional shelling and a delay in the attack. Both were approved but by 1730 it was time for 2/5 to meet its challenge.

The Marines crawled out of their mock shelters at the sound of the whistles from their few remaining officers, and off they went. They would always go: no matter how bad things had been or would be, they'd go— Springfields at the ready and with bayonets fixed, the weapon the Boche seemed to dread most. As Cooke later made clear, everything the Boche had was used against them. "Light machine guns . . . in trees, heavy guns on the ground, grenades, rifles, pistols . . . everything at once."

Within fifty feet of the jump-off line the Marines met the Germans, who at once offered a stubborn resistance. Soon the enemy frontline positions were overrun and the line of Maxims right behind them was also broken. The Germans continued to savagely resist the onslaught where they stood. The Boche were brave men and suffered heavy

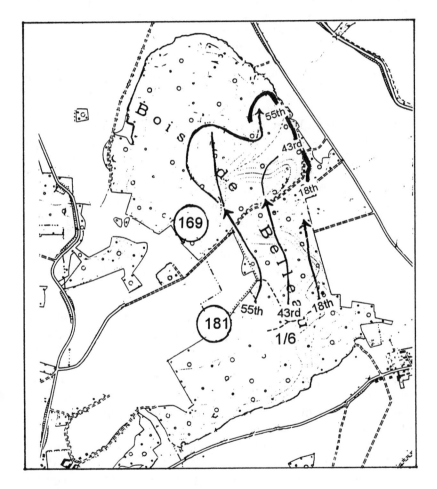

Map 6: After regrouping, 2/5 followed orders from brigade to advance on 12 June and take all of the woods. By the end of the day, the battalion managed to hold on in high, rocky ground in the northeast but failed to take the entire woods.

losses, but they extracted an even heavier loss upon the Marines of 2/5. The Marines' formation became thinner and thinner by the minute. Gilder Jackson of the 18th went down. "Drink" Milner, the "too nice" minister's son, was in command of the 43d, and he fought like hell. As the officers fell, sergeants took over, then corporals, then privates, but they still went forward. It took the battalion about half an hour to get where the heavy machine guns were, which were protected on each flank by German infantry. But arrive they did and they continued their forward motion, wiping out those tormenting Maxims and the men with them.

One of Cooke's men, Private Gascovitch, potted a German officer hiding in a tree, and as the man fell, Gascovitch was on him, taking his wallet and watch before his buddies could get to him first. Marines have always been souvenir hunters. One of Cooke's officers had been badly hit in the face and was "writhing and clawing at his face, begging to be gotten out of there." Cooke said,

> Then in the field on our left, from where they had been working around our flank, a group of gray-clad figures got up like a covey of frightened quail. Big, husky Huns, running over the ploughed ground with stilted awkwardness in their heavy boots . . . clawing out my automatic, I let go an entire clip at their retreating backs. The whole company discharged a scattered volley—and we never hit a damn one![146]

Cooke adds that he could see Wass chasing a frightened Heinie and Gy. Sgt. David P. Colvin* of his 18th Company was going up a rocky cliff after a machine gun, and he got it. All the young Marines, prodigiously supplied with fear and loathing, were hoping to get their bayonets into a Boche belly to partly get even for what they had been going through these past few days. The Germans crowded into the underbrush, and soon after the Marines were in there with them. The scattered remnants of 2/5 followed them in "hot pursuit."

No reasonable marks of company organizations remained. As they chased the Germans, Marines from every company were blended into other companies. Milner and the 43d somehow managed to cross the lines of the 55th and made their way toward the shell-damaged hunting lodge, portions of which still remained in the northern part of Belleau Wood. Milner climbed to its top and could see the remains of the town of Belleau not far off and Germans running through the streets apparently looking for cover. Moments later he was confronted by a German officer and his ponderous unit. Milner offered the officer a cigarette and inquired as to who was whose prisoner. The German asked Milner to guide them back to surrender and Milner had to decline since he wasn't exactly sure of his own nor his battalion's location. But the German knew precisely; he proceeded to orient the Americans and warned of an impending German attack. Dropping their weapons, the German soldiers followed their leader back to the American lines.[147] It was that kind of battle.

The 18th Company came out on the northeastern edge of the woods. Thomason later wrote that he was confident that for a short while all, or certainly most, of the organized German troops had indeed been driven from the forest. It wouldn't be long before they straggled back in as officers collected the "sick, lame and lazy" from the surrounding area. Two/Five's high casualty rate greatly interfered with their ability to form a continuous line. This resulted in eased pressure on the Germans just when they were finally on the run. The losses in Marine company commanders was really starting to impact on the battalion as a whole. Wass was the only captain still functioning in the entire battalion.

For some reason, the order was still to guide right, so that is where the main body headed. In effect 2/5 was "locking in" any Germans to their left. But then the opposite might also be considered; the Boche could be charged with surrounding 2/5 because technically 2/5 was in truth now behind German lines. The 43d and 55th moved right, looking for Wass. Wass had dropped back in order to have his right flank connect with 1/6, which had slowly moved northward in the rear of the stampeding 2d Battalion, 5th Marines. Wise believed and reported stories told by the walking wounded that things were really going very well up front. But he later relates his reaction when a young private told him that things were really bad up front. Wise asked what source had told him that and the lad said "the wounded." Wise says he told the youngster that the wounded are the worst possible observers. That depends upon which ear is listening.

Meanwhile, the organization of the 461st Regiment was in complete disarray and the battalion of the 110th Regiment that had relieved the 40th Fusiliers had been torn to pieces. It wasn't only Marines who were taking it on the chin that day. But Hartlieb, the commander of the 461st, saw that the American pressure upon his troops was beginning to flounder and he immediately took advantage of the situation. As soon as the

Marine units filed off to their right, remnants of the 461st, who were still holding out, were ordered to keep in contact with the retiring Marines. At 1815 Wise notified brigade that all objectives had been reached. They had learned from prisoners that at least 500 Germans had been opposite them. Also that they had been heavily bombarded and "still think the line rather thin as our losses are heavy. . . . Dunbeck and Jackson [Gilder] wounded." Along with Wise's report he also included that report from Wass to him: "No connection on left yet. Am trying to connect with 51st and machine guns on right. Need guns and men. . . ."[148] During the same period, Wass notified Wise that he had half of a platoon from the 55th and about two squads of his 18th left. "Line is thin." He also wanted, in addition to more troops and Chauchat ammunition, a barrage. "Am getting hell shelled out of us now." Milner, acting skipper of the 43d, sent his message to Wise at 1930 in which he described where he was and with whom.

We reached our objective and returned from the crossroads to the left. . . . We are in touch with the 55th Company on our left but have not gotten in touch with the 18th Company. Captain Dunbeck wounded at the start but [not] serious. Losses were heavy.[149]

A little later Wise warned Neville that he wasn't sure if they could hold, since they were so weak.

Lost a great many men. We are getting a devil of a shelling, and quite accurate. . . . Men in fine shape, but as I put in my report I am afraid of the reaction. P.S. *This is a different outfit from the one of yesterday.* [Emphasis added.][150]

Cooke described his own condition, remembered after nearly twenty years, in a pithy manner:

We lost the sense of emotion. Dull eyed, resigned, lacking the courage to go forward or back, yet we clung desperately to that rocky edge of woods. It seemed to be all we had left in the world and we would not give it up. Not for Heinie, Kaiser Bill, nor the devil himself.[151]

He was drawn back as far as battalion headquarters, where Colonel Wise told him,

You need a rest. He said a mouthful. My nerves were completely shot. I cowered in a foxhole at the sound of every shell and cringed at any unexpected noise. If a man had suddenly yelled in my ear, I'd have probably shot him dead. Jackson came through on his way to the hospital and I thought him lucky.[152]

At 2000 hours, Hughes wrote Colonel Lee that he had relieved the 51st Company and had taken its place in reserve.[153] Wise, putting on a good face, told Neville that they had taken all their objectives (still not quite correct) and many guns and prisoners. What Neville should have learned for himself was that 2/5 didn't have enough men to hold what they'd taken. Logan Feland made attempts to assess the situation on a fairly regular basis. Even Harbord seemed to move around a bit. But not Neville. As far as I can determine, he never moved out of his PC to go to the front lines during the entire campaign.

About dusk, Harbord sent Neville a message in which he advised that 3/6 would pass under his command. They would then relieve Turrill and 1/5 in their positions around Hill 142, which would have them take over the line defending the northern section of the brigade front. After that 1/5 would become brigade reserve "in the same woods now occupied by 3/6." He also directed that before they were relieved and before the enemy could, 1/5 was to take the ravine that lay about half a mile south of Torcy. Harbord continued, "Sibley's line would then hold from the Champillon brook [to east of the town of Belleau]. What would have happened if followed as directed, is that 3/6 would flank the northern approaches to Belleau Wood. But the process was altered upon receipt of information from the captured German officer.

Hughes informed Lee that he was being shelled and that he was attempting to relieve "Wise's 51st Company, on the line, as he needs men." (See above.) At 2000 he sent a message to Wise that told of his relieving "that company on the right" but that he only had one company in support and that Lee had instructed him to keep that. At 2020 Lee sent a message to Captain Richard Platt of the 20th Company, 3/5, that he was being returned to Neville for further orders. Platt and his company were going in "to close the gap" and support 2/5.[154]

Meanwhile, Hughes was still grumbling to Lee. He wanted "strong, hot coffee" and good hot food, for his battalion. Evans responded early the following morning with words something like "forget it." The diary report of 12 June states that at 2100

[a] captured German officer stated that a German attack was to be expected [tonight]. This information reached these headquarters from several different sources. Orders had been given for the relief of the 1st Bn. 5th in the line south of Torcy by the 3d Bn. 6th Marines and the latter battalion started out at dark when the news of an expected attack was received and artillery preparation begun by the enemy, the authority of the Division Commander was used to order the 2d Bn. 6th Marines, which was Corps Reserve in woods N.W. of these headquarters, to the woods N.W. of Lucy, to arrive by 3:30 a.m. The 1st Bn. 6th, which had been under orders on relief to go into position as Brigade Reserve in the wood N.W. of Lucy was directed to position along the Torcy-Lucy road in position to flank an attack on the N.W. part of the Bois de Belleau.[155]

In a German report for 12 June, the IV Reserve Corps advised the 7th German Army, "This day the wildly-fought-for Bois de Belleau remained in the hands of the enemy." Corps ordered a counterattack to retake the Woods. As darkness approached, the German pressure on the Marines' left became extremely serious. The left was severely refused along the steep contours of a rocky knoll, forming what became known as the "Hook." The line began very near the northern tip of the woods and moved downward in a southwesterly direction. Since both sides were in very close proximity and exhausted, no serious trouble was generated that night by either side.

At 2300 brigade received what appears to be a justifiable complaint from Wise. Hughes had promised Wise that he would take over the rear areas at 2000. Upon a reconnaissance of the area by an officer of engineers, Wise learned that Hughes had failed to do so. Shortly afterward Wise sent another message in which he warned of an attack by "a fresh division," according to a dying German officer. He also added, "Have not 350 old men left and seven officers. They are shelling very heavy."

Late that evening, a wounded German officer and 42 men of the 461st Regiment surrendered under a white flag. The officer informed the Marines that a counterattack was anticipated the next morning by elements of the 237th and 28th Divisions, to recover the woods. That intelligence was forwarded to Neville and then on to brigade. The information was strengthened when a massive enemy artillery fire was laid upon the woods, which members of the battalion reckoned was the heaviest they had ever suffered or remembered. It continued unabated, all

along the front, throughout the night. The American guns, in retalia-
tion, harassed the German rear and approach areas. Neither the exhausted German soldiers nor their equally exhausted Marine opponents
were able to focus on much sleep that night.

Thursday, 13 June

As we know, Sibley and 3/6 relieved 1/5 during the night, taking over
its positions northeast of Hill 142. A little earlier, two officers and 125
replacements had been assigned to 3/6, but Sibley was unable to accept
them at the time. He was moving to Hill 142 and did not have time to
consolidate them. Later, during the 13th, Sibley did manage finally to
obtain and integrate his badly needed replacements. They were welcome additions.

This was the first relief that Turrill and his men had had since taking
the Hill on 6 June. The battalion had been under constant artillery harassment, and under periodic infantry attack, ever since taking the position a week before. But their relief didn't last very long. Within a few
hours 1/5 took up a position in St. Martin's Wood along the Lucy-Torcy
road. Their job would be to outflank any attempted German advance
or flanking movements down the west side of the wood.[156]

Early that morning Capt. Roswell Winans and his 17th Company were
sent into the northwest portion of Belleau Wood. It was their job to establish contact between 1/5 now in St. Martin's Wood and the western
flank of Lieutenant Colonel Wise's battalion. Details of Wise's position
were still vague, so Winans sent a small patrol led by 1st Lt. Robert Blake
to make a reconnaissance. The patrol crossed the road near the fork
where a road branched off toward Belleau, noting many dead men on
the open ground to their right. Undoubtedly, most were Marines from
3/5 and 2/5. They continued through the scattered trees around Hill
169, where they found a corporal of 2/5 with a few Marines. They had
been left there by Mathews on 11 June to cover the battalion's left when
he went back to confront Wise with his findings. There had been no
communication between them and 2/5 since. It must have been a wonderful time for the strandees. Continuing on, the patrol entered a small
ravine that led to the west face of the wood just north of X-line 262. It
was there that they found the wreckage of a machine-gun nest with dead
Germans and Marines surrounding it. The patrol continued north of
the ravine and found a road running eastward across the wood. A little
farther on they also found Germans. The only Marines the patrol found
around anywhere were dead. But there still were more than enough

Boche to satisfy all of the live Marines. Blake and his patrol then returned to Winans with the report of their findings. Winans asked for reinforcements, and at 0700 Turrill sent him one platoon of the 49th and one from the 66th Company.

Meanwhile, Winans decided to put his company in motion. The leading platoons, in an advance guard formation, worked their way across Hill 169 into Belleau Wood. They then followed the general route taken by Blake and his group. At the ravine Winans sent out several scouting parties to locate the live Germans. When an enemy plane flew over their position at treetop level, the skipper expected shell fire to follow very soon after. Deciding that discretion was the better part of valor, Winans had his party withdraw, back to where they had come from. Almost immediately there occurred an intense bombardment of that portion of the wood they had so recently visited.

From the two patrols Winans deduced that the northern end of the wood was saturated with Boche and few Marines. After his reconnaissance in force, he had no better idea where 2/5's northern position was located than he'd had before. Winans then sent two enlisted Marines to find Wise, at his supposed PC in the area of Hill 181 and also notified Turrill of what had been learned.[157]

The Germans started early that morning. At 0130 they attacked the northwest portion of Belleau Wood and, as the division diary simply states, "were repulsed." An hour earlier, Harbord had directed Holcomb to move his battalion to the "wood northwest of Lucy to arrive by 0350. Hold it in reserve there pending further orders." At 0323 the enemy artillery began another massive shelling of the wood which lasted until 0350. After this, Lieutenant Moore, IO of 3/6, was able to send a message to brigade, "German artillery quiet."

What was to be one of the strangest incidents in the entire battle then began—a headache that would trouble the brigade and the division for several hours. At 0410 Captain Jackson, Adjutant of 3/5, sent the following message to Neville, asking that it be delivered by phone:

Maj. Shearer just reported by runner that enemy had taken the town of Bouresches this A.M. and requests barrage laid on town immediately. Runner reports enemy still advancing.[158]

Harbord passed along the information to division at 0448. Twenty minutes later Division responded with its own report.

Lieutenant Villmuth who is with 1st Bn. 23d Infantry reported Germans have taken Bouresches. Immediately after transmitting that message to me the 3rd Brgade repeated pressing message from 1st Bn. 23d asking that the request for artillery fire be canceled as Bouresches was still in our hands.[159]

At 0510 Harbord had sent "two companies of the reserve [2/6] to go over to the valley southwest of Lucy and be prepared to counter attack [Bouresches]." He also heard from the regimental dressing station that "Captain McConahy [sic] came in wounded . . . and that Germans were in town . . . between 2:30 and 3:00 A.M. He was wounded in ten minutes and got out . . . nothing from Bouresches for hours after that."[160] Harbord notified division at 0530 that Bouresches was still held by 3/5. "A lieutenant of the replacements, who joined yesterday, got stampeded in the town and ran up to ———— and stated the town was taken." One skittish replacement officer, who had only arrived on 12 June, had managed to stampede a division. Wonder whatever happened to Lieutenant Villmuth? And who was the more senior officer recipient of that news, who also should have been named for so easily accepting and passing on that story from a young, inexperienced lad? Was it Shearer or Jackson?[161]

At 0827 Holcomb reported his arrival at his assigned location, with the 78th and 96th Companies. He was now at the southern edge of the St. Martin Wood, northwest of Lucy. The order to retake Bouresches was soon rescinded, but the 79th and 80th Companies remained where they were. The "crisis" was over.

Later it was found that two companies of the 109th Grenadier Regiment had penetrated the defenses of Bouresches. The Marines hurled them out almost as fast as they came in. Fifteen dead Germans littered the streets and another forty were found lying in the nearby fields. The survivors did manage to capture one Marine as they retired. A German officer who was captured during the attack related that his men came from the east and another group was to come down from the northern approaches to make contact in the center of town. They never made it.

After the ensuing repulse of the Boche the entire front of the 4th Brigade settled down, although the German artillery continued to plague them and the shelling would be called "the most violent so far experienced." During the late morning, officers of the 3d Battalion, 23d Infantry, reported to Major Shearer. They were there to reconnoiter Bouresches, preparatory to taking it over from the 4th Brigade. The official orders for the transfer of responsibility had been developed by both brigades and division and would be issued later in the afternoon by the 4th Brigade. The monstrous losses suffered by the Marines were making it impossible for them to continue holding as long a line as they had been doing. Bundy's original plan of having just one active brigade at a time was starting to come apart at the seams. Certainly the leaders of the 23d were anxious to get into "it," as evidenced by the messages exchanged between Malone and Harbord. The same could most certainly be said for the 9th Infantry. But Bundy and Brown had other plans for a major relief.

Hughes was still impatient to get coffee and food to his men. At 0505 he was asking Lee to send him German prisoners to carry hot coffee. He also described what 1/6 had gone through that night. "Trenches mostly obliterated by shell fire. Estimate casualties at under 20%. . . . Capt. Fuller killed and Burns [sic] wounded." Again at 0745 he guaranteed Evans that he was "assured a constant stream of coffee from the cook. . . . Can't you even give me Boche prisoners to carry it?" And a few hours later he sent Lee his casualty figures for the previous day. "Killed 16, wounded 74, missing 12, that includes officers." There can be no question that Hughes looked out for his men as best he could. Unfortunately, the supply system throughout the AEF, especially food delivery, at every level, was, and would continue to be, terribly archaic until the war ended.

Wise sent a report to Neville that morning which described what was going on in his small portion of the world.

> Things quiet at present. Getting supplies up to the front line. Have one replacement officer per company left and about 300 men not including replacements. Engineers are getting well dug in. As all these woods are ranged to the yard they are absolutely torn to pieces. When this is going on it is absolutely impossible to get men or supplies up to the front. Captain [Joseph D.] Murray has been out for some time making reconnaissance of the whole line and then can give a more full report. Not having officers makes it hard getting detailed information promptly. My idea is that attack will come from the N.W. All company commanders request men.[162]

Shortly after, Shearer reported that all was quiet in Bouresches. "Dead Germans in town and wheatfields," a message Harbord called into division within fifteen minutes. He was always very versatile at making good news widely available. After all, for twelve days it had been mostly bad and much of it erroneous. Sibley reported to Neville that the night before, he had started patrols toward the ravine near the crossroads, but had withdrawn them in the face of the massive artillery shelling during the night. His men did ascertain, though, that the ravine was already occupied by German infantry. Noble's report said,

> Patrol returned and reported a number of the enemy were heard in the right end of the ravine. Seemed to be digging. Could hear them talking. My patrol was not discovered by the enemy. We now have listening posts out in front but cannot occupy the ravine as intended. Believe the artillery should be notified to be prepared to drop barrage in ravine when called for.[163]

If perchance the Germans decided to attack him from that position, Sibley asked that the artillery be prepared to support his subsequent defense. He did outline plans to do a more thorough examination of the ravine that evening. During the day orders were issued to 2/6, directing Holcomb to relieve 2/5 in Belleau Wood. In the afternoon the German artillery increased the volume of their shelling. Later that evening they began using mustard gas shells to add to the discomfort of the Americans. Mostly it was directed toward where the 78th and 96th Companies was located, and to 1/6 in the southern part of Belleau Wood.

But before this happened, late in the day, Hughes sent a lengthy memo to Lee in which he complained about Wise.

> 1. According to Brigade Commander's orders yesterday I had a conference with Lieut.Col. Wise taking my Intelligence Officer with me. I showed him exactly where the machine gun nests were. The conference as usual resulted in nothing.
>
> B. I went over my whole line taking with me [2d] Lieut. [R. H.] Loughberry [Loughborough, USA], 51st Company [commanding], [who] agreed with me that his right and my left were almost exactly where they showed on the map. We went back to see Col. Wise and found everybody shooting. I stayed there 15 minutes but Col. Wise wouldn't notice me. There was great confusion and a heavy bombardment going on.
>
> 2. Between 7:00 and 8:00 P.M. last night, I got a message from Col. Wise who wanted to know whether I ever intended to relieve his right company [51st]. I sent two platoons of the 95th Com-

pany under [1st] Lieut. [Morgan R.] Mills [Jr.] to relieve the 51st Company which was only half strength and to tell Lieut. Loughberry [sic] to report to Col. Wise. Lieut. Mills sent back word that Loughberry refused to be relieved, claiming that he had no orders. Lieut. Mills stayed there entrenching himself on the left of the 76th Company, where he had been ordered to go and he is still there. At 8:00 I got another note from Col. Wise stating that Lieut. Loughberry reported that he had not been relieved. I wrote back that I had relieved him at 9:00 P.M. and that he had refused to go.[164]

In his memoir Wise described his ongoing difficulties with Hughes in a summary of what his thoughts had been regarding a unified command in Belleau Wood. He said he had been trying to convince brigade of that and after Holcomb's arrival he made the case even more strongly. Concerning his relationship with Hughes he added,

I was in one regiment; he was in another. I couldn't give him an order. Every time I told Hughes that I wanted to do something and he ought to do certain things to back me up, he would tell me it was against Lieutenant Colonel Lee's orders.[165]

Lieutenant Colonel Logan Feland, assistant regimental commander, arrived at Wise's PC and, according to Wise, took him to task. "General Harbord is sore as hell because you didn't clean out the woods." Wise responded that the battalion had done the best they could but

on the original attack the men got a great deal of punishment from the right. They naturally drifted toward it to take the machine guns in that sector. We simply didn't have enough men to cover the whole front.[166]

At 1630 Field Order No. 5 was issued. Its major provisions were that the brigade's front would be reduced, effective midnight 13 June, and that the 3d Brigade would take over command of "Bouresches—Triangle inclusive." The 4th Brigade's new responsibility was "Bouresches, exclusive to the east front of Bois de Belleau, along northwest to the Champillon brook inclusive." The 5th Marines would hold the right of the line and the 6th Marines the left. This was a complete change from their previous locations. Besides that, Lt. Col. Hiram Bearss was assigned as Lee's second-in-command. Bearss had been a sort of utility man for weeks, filling in here and there, but too senior for any role less than a battalion or regimental command. According to various reports Bearss and Wise did not get along, making his presence in the 5th Marines less than pleasant.[167]

Friday, 14 June

This was the day of the gas. It was the worst time for the men on the line, those forced to wear their masks for many hours, if perchance they'd been able to put them on in time. The number of gas casualties was immense. Whole units suffered greater losses than they often had if they had been involved in frontal attacks. The greatest number of gas casualties was in 2/6, Holcomb's unit. The semiofficial history of the 78th Company tells us,

> At 12:30 A.M., June 14, just as we started out of our positions in the woods to make the relief, we were caught in a box barrage of gas shells and shrapnel. This lasted for two hours, and *all but twelve men of 78th Company* were killed, wounded, or gassed. [Emphasis added.]

That same history adds that the 4th Replacement Battalion was rushed to the front to reinforce 2/6 and of that group, 160 men were assigned to the 78th Company. Beginning shortly after midnight, reports going into the 4th Brigade notified them that the whole brigade front was receiving heavy incoming, mostly gas. Holcomb told Lee that the expected relief of Wise would be delayed. "Gas in the Bois de Belleau." An hour later Holcomb advised Neville that his battalion had "been gassed and shelled with H.E. Pretty well shot up." Hughes added to the clamor at 0325 when his message to Lee stated, "Fairly heavy gas shell fire on all my companies." A short while later, 1st Lt. Henry E. Chandler, the gas officer of the 6th Marines, sent Lee a message describing what had been taking place on the regiment's front.

> Gas attack on woods East of Lucy entire ravine east of Lucy and sector of front line entering BOURESCHES and Triangle Farm *very serious.* Men have had on respirators 5 ½ hrs. Suggest men be moved from infected areas. Mustard Gas is being used. Request Division Gas Officer. [Emphasis in original.][168]

The gas shelling attack would continue for hours. As late as 0900 messages would reverberate between the 3d and 4th Brigades about what to do with gassed Marines and soldiers who somehow had managed to lose their units. (See following extract.)

At 0140 1st Lt. James F. Moriarty, a platoon leader in the 15th Company, called Capt. George H. Osterhout Jr., by phone, telling him that the "Germans are massing 100 yds in front of our first line." The coordinates placed the assembly to the east of Hill 142, which was now defended by Sibley's battalion. Most likely Sibley would also have seen what the enemy was doing and was busy preparing for what could be expected.

Sometime before dawn Shearer's 3/5 was relieved at Bouresches and ordered to report to the woods northwest of Lucy. There they would remain for the next few days, resting, relaxing, and eating, although still close to the fighting lines.

Around three that morning Holcomb made an attempt to get through the wood in order to relieve 2/5 with his two remaining companies. But the 79th and 80th lost a number of their men to gas and shells in the process. When Holcomb did arrive, Wise refused to be relieved by such a paltry number of men. He later related why.

> Holcomb told me that Colonel Neville had said that I could pull out with what was left of my outfit and turn over the place to him. I didn't do it. It would have been lunacy to have turned over that part of the line to 325 men who had never seen it. . . . I stayed.[169]

And in a message to brigade:

> Holcomb arrived with 1¾ companies at 3:00 A.M. and other two companies badly broken up, from shells and gas. About 150 of those have showed up. My men physically unable to make another attack. Have just made another reconnaissance of the line and consider my present line unsafe unless whole woods are in our possession and not enough troops on hand and if those woods are taken there must be enough troops to hold them, or it will be the same story again; that is they will filter in. *The woods are larger than shown.* Request permission to withdraw slightly to make the line safer and that Holcomb be given more men as many of them have had gas. Some gas here. [Emphasis added.][170]

Lloyd's 80th Company, which to date had suffered the lightest casualties of Holcomb's battalion, was sent to occupy the left end of the Wise line, which pushed the refused left farther southward. Other Marines, those from depleted units already on the scene or those from the 79th Company, helped to strengthen 2/5's sparse companies. But the continued weakness of the entire Marine position in Belleau Wood would continue to dog Wise for a few more days.

According to a report from Lieutenant Colonel Bearss, who had been sent to the scene by Lieutenant Colonel Lee, most of Holcomb's losses to the gas attack occurred in the 78th Company. Their losses numbered 110 officers and men, which Frank Evans reported as "125 men." An additional fifty members of the 96th Company also suffered the same fate. First Lieutenant Chandler, regimental gas officer, sent Lee a request for "600 Complete suits of clothing for gas cases." Part of Bearss's report covered the disaster that had afflicted a company of the 9th Infantry, which was badly shot up while attempting a relief. A later report from Colonel Malone advised Lieutenant Colonel Lee,

> . . . 157 Marines belonging to 78th Company are with him, reporting that they were gassed while attempting to relieve another unit. No officer with them. About 20 are being evacuated. Information requested as to where the others should go.[171]

Lee responded by telling Malone that three officers were at Hill 201 and that arrangements were under way to move those men not evacuated by the medical officer. Navy doctor Lt. George L. White advised the regimental surgeon that "75 to 150 men evacuated since arrival this morning. Practically entire battalion physically unfit due to gas."[172]

Major Ralph S. Keyser, temporarily commanding 3/5, sent the following message to brigade that morning:

> Officers and men are exhausted. They are doing good work but on their nerve only; physically they are all in. Major Shearer is in care of the 6th Regiment Surgeon suffering from temporary exhaustion.[173]

Shortly before noon orders were issued by the 5th Marines for Hughes to have barbed wire installed before his position. Hughes complained to Lee and the latter replied, soothingly,

> I should like to do all you ask and am as ever much interested in you and the 1st, but you are now under the 5th Regt. And should

ask these things of the 5th Hdqs. Am sure that they will comply. We wish and will *do anything* permitted by the 5th. Congratulations on your fine work.[174]

Hughes did not easily accept the answer or situation. Although Lee had made him aware that his battalion was now under the orders of the 5th Marines, Hughes, looking for direction, continued communicating with Lee. At 1440 he sent a message to the latter in which he questioned the lack of guidance in his orders to wire his frontage. His queries asked when he should plan to begin construction. "Do not believe it will be possible to begin wiring until after dark as slightest movement in the front line draws heavy shelling." Shortly after, Frank Evans sent Hughes a notice that he was sending two officers to replace those that 1/6 had lost to enemy action.

Am sending Lt. C.[lyde] P. Matteson, Hdqs Co., Comdg 1-pds Plat. & 2d Lt. F.[rederick] J. Scheld, Inf. USR to you. Matteson is a bearcat, strong, fearless & made good at BOURESCHES with Holcomb. [And with] Sibley in Bois de Belleau. You can have absolute confidence in him. Scheld is Infy. Officer by training, was formerly in 82d Co before being detached as instructor in 32d Div. So far as I know he's good.[175]

Harbord, no doubt fed up with the seeming inability of Hughes and Wise to work out their differences, put Lt. Col. Logan Feland entirely in charge of all the Marines and their future operations in Belleau Wood. (Long overdue, I might add.) The various units in the wood included 2/5, 1/6, and the remnants of 2/6. Into the woods went Feland with Maj. Ralph Keyser as the new second-in-command of 2/5. They found Wise at his PC, near Hill 181 at 1500 hours. Keyser immediately undertook a reconnaissance of the lines in the woods and quickly came to the conclusion that the Germans were still in force in the northern end of the wood. It wasn't realized at the time that the Germans had extended their line south along the western edge of the woods. The aggressive new Marine leaders immediately planned an assault by a worn-out 2/5. Fortunately it quickly came to their attention that an assault upon the rocky knoll above the flank of 2/5 would be extremely costly. As a result, new methods were considered instead. Somewhat earlier that afternoon Winans was ready to go back into the wood to try to link up with 2/5. After discussions with Turrill and Feland, it was decided that

Feland and Winans would make a thorough reconnaissance of the wood together and decide upon the details of what the 5th Marines were going to do next.

At 1410 Holcomb received an apologetic message from Harbord.

Regret the necessity of having to put your fine battalion in again with so little rest, and when so many have been gassed, but do it with perfect confidence that you and they can be depended upon under adverse circumstances.[176]

That afternoon the chief surgeon of the 6th evacuated two "skippers," Capt. Robert E. Messersmith of the 78th and 1st Lt. James F. Robertson of the 96th, who were suffering from the effects of gas. Additional gas casualties included 1st Lt. George B. Lockhart, and 2d Lt. Donald D. Page, USA, plus 150 men, all of the 96th. Hughes and 1/6 were also having their trouble with gas lying about on the ground. Much of the gas was being blown toward Hughes's PC and he was obviously suffering greatly from it. The regimental gas officer urged Hughes to move out of the positions he occupied in the woods to higher ground, but Hughes countered with "My orders are to stick." The gas officer insisted that evacuation to higher ground for him and his men was the only solution. Hughes still refused to go. By that time Hughes had already had 185 Marines evacuated and it would not get any better. Harbord sent a detailed message to Neville at 1700 in which he insisted that no more than one company of 1/6 should remain in the woods because of the mustard gas.

These men with care can get far enough into the open to strike sunlight and be out of the gas which remains in the woods. Withdraw the rest of the command to the neighborhood of [Hill] 181 and [Hill] 169 sheltering them as best you can. The enemy is not liable to attack within several days a wood which he has filled with Yperite gas.[177]

Harbord explained that most of the area in the southwest portion of Belleau Wood was saturated with gas. An hour or so later, he received a message from Evans telling him that Hughes's position, as far as the gas saturation was concerned, was still a serious problem. "Long exposure. Men have worn masks about six hours, and some of them have taken them off. . . . Hughes showing effects." Hughes himself was finally evacuated and was replaced in command of 1/6 by Maj. Franklin B. Garrett.[178] Garrett was a long-serving Marine officer with little combat command experience. He was safe, because he could be counted upon not to do anything foolish with his newly acquired battalion.

At some time that morning, Neville apparently realized that Harbord was in a modest depression and sought to bring him out of it if he could. In Harbord's own memoir of this period he tells of going to Neville's headquarters and what took place there.

> Here, we think it is about time you put these on, Neville told me as he handed me a set of Marine collar devices. You, knowing . . . Neville's gruff manner, can realize just how he said it, and it is needless to say that I was as much thrilled by his brusque remark and his subsequent pining them on my collar . . . as I have ever been by any decoration. . . . I wore those Marine Corps Devices until after I became a Major General, and I still cherish them as among my most valued possessions. I think that no officer can fail to understand what that little recognition meant to me, an Army officer commanding troops of a sister service in battle. It seemed to me to set the seal of approval by my comrades of the Marine Corps, and knowing the circumstances, it meant everything to me.[179]

Late that afternoon Evans sent a message to Capt. Fred C. Patchen, the commanding officer of Headquarters Company, 6th Marines, in which he outlined some ongoing problems related to food delivery to the troops.

> 3d Bn.'s coffee cold when delivered last night. Trouble due to containers cooling off on long haul. Col. Lee urges the great importance of solidified alcohol so that the coffee can be heated by the troops. Also the tobacco ration is short and the men need it and ask for it. Do everything possible to get both. Gen. Harbord deeply interested.[180]

Later, the brigade adjutant, Major Henry Lay, called Harbord and related the following interesting tale:

> 5th Marines has sent down a Russian prisoner to us. He speaks neither French nor German. He was found loafing near their Hq.

They think their lines have been tapped and that this prisoner had something to do with it. The prisoner is being sent to Division Hdqs.[181]

Saturday, 15 June

It was on this day that the relief of the 4th Brigade began. There had been a certain level of confrontation between the commander of the French XXI Corps and General Bundy relative to the units involved in the relief. General Naulin, who had replaced General Dégoutte, argued that the 3d Brigade was the likely unit to replace the Marines. But Bundy and Preston Brown refused to dissipate the strength of the 3d on the Bouresches-Vaux line. Both officers refused to have one brigade used up while the other was fighting, with no brigade to provide support should that become necessary. Harbord had been asking, nay, demanding relief, since 10 June. By this date the 4th Brigade had no more than fifty-percent effectives in both officers and men. The losses had to a certain extent been made up by replacements, many of whom had been in France barely a few weeks and with little advanced training. They were usually incorporated into their companies while the unit was under fire, or at best, waiting for an encounter with the enemy, certainly not a solid base upon which to build a stable unit reorganization.

The question of what to do to solve the problem was decided by General Bundy. He and Brown suggested to Naulin that the 7th Infantry, which was in the rear along the Marne and unemployed, should be the unit to relieve the Marines. After a heated argument, Bundy threatened to exercise his seniority as ranking American officer present in both the 2d and 3d U.S. Divisions by assuming command of all American troops for such purposes as he saw fit. Naulin finally gave in and issued the orders for the 7th Infantry to move up to the relief of the 4th Brigade. On the same day at 1430, Harbord issued Field Order No. 6, which announced the temporary detailing of the 7th Infantry to the 4th Brigade. He also announced the coming relief of 3/6 from their positions along the ridge running north of Hill 142, by the 167th French Infantry Division. After nearly fifteen days of constant action the battered but unbowed 4th Marine Brigade was finally going to get some rest.

Major Berton W. Sibley notified Lee at 0255 that his phone lines were out, artillery fire was going over their heads, and "no enemy infantry reported as yet. . . . Some sniping by the enemy." Five hours later Sibley wrote to Lee,

A French officer appeared here this A.M. and stated that a French battalion will relieve us tonight, and Bat [French] officers would be here to reconnoiter at 9 A.M. Have you any information about it? Please send Everett or Macarde or both to me as soon as practicable. Runner can show way.[182]

He also suggested that the phones not be used, since they were so very close to the enemy, their voices could be heard easily. At 1040 he received a message from headquarters of the 6th to be ready to be relieved that night. There was no information as to where and when, but Evans did mention that "you are in for a good rest & you and your fine outfit certainly deserve the best." Lee sent a message a few minutes later that requested a total of replacements required and "place and time rations needed and any other things you need for health and comfort of your command. . . ." Late that evening, Sibley finally received directions for his relief. They were to be relieved by the 167th French Division. When relieved they would take up residence in the woods about a mile south of Marigny. They were not entirely clear of German artillery but far enough away to make that seem okay.

At daylight the 17th Company had entered Belleau Wood, supported by the fire of four machine guns from the 8th Machine Gun Company. Although a sharp resistance developed immediately, the German defenders south of the rocky knoll were soon driven in and forced aside. Fighting their way across the wood, the 17th met leading elements of 2/5 about 0730. Those Marines in the wood were mainly fragments of 2/6 and 2/5 working in unison. A line was established soon after, with units from left to right straight across the wood. During this operation Captain Winans was wounded in the foot and Capt. Thomas Quigley, who had been with the 49th, was sent over to assume command of the company. He brought reinforcements with him.

The 17th Company in the BOIS de BELLEAU was attacked by a force of the enemy with 4 heavy and several light machine guns and have withdrawn to their former position. Winans shot through the foot. Quigley in command of the 17th Company.[183]

The left platoon of the 17th attempted to drive northward along the western face of the wood but was stopped in its tracks by a group of argumentive Boche. They did make contact with the right of Case's 20th

Company in the near corner of the St. Martin Wood. Case was effectively tying in the entire line for the first time since the 2d Division had taken over from the French. Total casualties of the 17th Company for the three-day period was one officer and forty men killed and wounded, of which twenty-two occurred on this one day. The left flank of 2/5 had been in the air for five days and if the Germans had been more aggressive, the already badly used battalion would likely have experienced a disaster. Although the Germans had patrolled the northern area at will and 2/5 didn't have the strength to defend even the small area they covered, the Germans never tried a serious assault upon their lines. Either those Boche opposing 2/5 in Belleau Wood were also near physical collapse, or their nerve was gone. Probably both.

One bright moment in an otherwise dark day: Just after noon Hughes could report that 1/6 still had fifteen officers and 633 men, a considerable difference between it and the other three battalions that had also been exposed to the dreaded "Hellwood," as the bois was quickly becoming known.

Although Colonel Anderson, regimental commander of the 7th Infantry, arrived on the scene, Colonel Neville retained full command of all operations in the Belleau Wood sector and Feland commanded in the woods. Accordingly, Lt. Col. John P. Adams, commanding 1/7, reported to Neville and then made a reconnaissance of the positions held by 2/5 and 2/6 in the northeastern portion of the wood. Harbord had already indoctrinated him and his party before they started by telling them of the terrible losses the Marines had suffered and that they must hold the woods at all costs. By 2000 the reconnaissance was completed. Soon after dark, 1/7 entered the wood to begin the relief, which was completed by daylight with minimum losses. At the same time the Germans were relieving one of their units in the woods. There were several small patrol clashes between the 7th and the Boche, which were reported by 1/7 as a major attack that had been repulsed. They would soon enough find out what a major attack was really like. Adams placed his four companies in line, from right to left, A, C, D, and B. A connected with 1/6 at X-line 262.0, C prolonged the line to the north, D was around the angle known as the hook, and B Company extended the left southwesterly across the wood toward its western face, the position established by Winans that morning. A Company lost a platoon for battalion support while each of the other companies provided a platoon in support of the main line. There was no second line to provide depth.

The general plan, accepted by Adams, was that the Germans in the wood would be encircled gradually and captured or dislodged, without an assault.

Later, Wise described his relief.

As fast as a company of infantry took over their part of the front, what was left of one of my companies came out. In single file that handful of men marched out of the woods they had won and held, and headed back toward the rear. Two miles back was our rendezvous. Two weeks' growth of beard bristled on their faces. Deep lines showed, even beneath beard and dirt. Their eyes were red around the rims, bloodshot, burnt out. They were grimed with earth. Their cartridge belts were almost empty. They were damned near exhausted. Past physical limits. Travelling on their naked nerve. But every one of them was cocky—full of fight.[184]

Cooke of the 55th, as always, poignantly described what happened to him and his company.

On the night of June 15th, our whole outfit was relieved. Another battalion was to finish what we were too few to accomplish. My company, with some of the 43d attached, filed silently back through the spectral forest and the ruins that had once been Lucy. . . . We kept no formation. Each man simply followed the one in front. No one was going to allow himself to be left behind. We wanted to hurry but our legs acted as though gripped by an undertow. Weak, starved, and apprehensive we bent forward, painfully propelling ourselves up the hill from Lucy, pathetically eager for escape. . . . Shells dropped along the road. The battle . . . diabolically determined not to let us go. A man came running up. . . . I'm going for a doctor . . . that last shell got my buddy and you goddamn bastards would go off and leave him.[185]

Cooke admitted that he didn't make an issue of the Marine's lack of courtesy because, just then, he would also have enjoyed telling off a superior too.

The relieved Marine battalions withdrew to their assigned places of rest. Wise and the few members of 2/5, after finding their packs had been looted, went to Mery-sur-Marne, which was located in the narrow tongue formed by the bend in the river, between Luzancy and Saay-sur-Marne. Holcomb and 2/6 went west to Bois Gros Jean, just to the west of La Loge Farm, while 3/6 had already been sent to woods south of Marigny. Needless to say, each would finally realize some rest and food before the slaughter would begin again. The only battalion not relieved was 3/5, which was still in St. Martin's Woods.

Sunday, 16 June

This day was generally quiet, as a Sunday should be. Mainly it was concerned with the relief of 1/6 by the balance of the 7th Infantry. In the afternoon, at 1630 to be precise, Harbord sent Neville the following orders:

> On the arrival of the 2d Bn., 7th Infantry please relieve with it the 1st Bn., 6th Marines in the south half of the BOIS de BELLEAU. The 1st Bn., 6th Marines, when relieved, will proceed by marching to the vicinity of MONTREUIL where it will take trucks and proceed to near MERY to the station vacated by the 2d Bn., 7th Infantry. The battalions will exchange temporarily their transportation, rolling kitchens, ration and water carts, etc. Details of this temporary change will be arranged by battalion commanders. Command passed when relief is complete.[186]

At 1255 Lt. Col. Harry Lee sent a message to Harbord, asking what he should do since his battalions had already been relieved in the "6th Marine Sector." He added, "If my responsibility in the sector has ceased, I shall move my PC back." It appears that Lee was also tired. He had assiduously taken command of his regiment since Catlin's demise, proving that he was the right man at the right time. A few hours later he received confirmation of his relief directly from Harbord. He also told him that he wanted Lee to spend much of his time and energy during the following period in the "reorganization of your two battalions that are now in rest and the one which will go tomorrow."

Captain P. J. Hurley, USA, and some of his officers made a reconnaissance of the land held by 1/6. After dark, the soldiers began their relief of the last Marine infantry remaining in the wood. The army lads set to work continuing the wiring job in which 1/6 had been engaged at the time of relief. They also worked at burying the dead Marines and Germans and collecting scattered war matériel from both sides. Some of the dead must have been there for at least a week, so the stench was horrible. In a week, the bodies would have begun to decompose and handling them would have been most difficult. Burial parties commonly used gas masks to protect at least one of their senses.

Monday, 17 June

Gulberg described how at 0400 in a little patch of woods they had their first meal in twelve days. "Our mess sergeant made up for a lot of his bum meals by putting milk in our coffee and fixing up some extra good slum." Other Marines were anxious to remove their cootie-laden clothing and bathe for the first time in weeks. Lucky ones were issued new uniforms—army, not Marine. There wasn't a Marine uniform in France then, except on the backs of the newcomers. Mainly, the men all wanted sleep, sleep, blessed sleep, with no interruptions. For many, no matter how hungry they were, sleep was number one on their list of things to do. Besides, the food, if Gulberg had it right, wasn't all that great anyhow. But there was plenty of hot coffee to wash down their mediocre meals. They did begin to receive special items, like cigarettes and other tobacco products, jam, and mail from home. Some hadn't seen any since long before the trip from Chaumont. Many letters and packages would remain unopened and unanswered forever.

As late as 1800 that day, the 73d Machine Gun Company had four guns in the line. Not finding any reply or order to the contrary, it is presumed that by now they have been relieved. That night Marine 1/5 was replaced without incident by Army 3/7, Maj. Jesse Gaston commanding. The 7th was now all on the line, but there was nothing much for Colonel Anderson to do but watch. The only members of the 4th Marine Brigade still active were those of the supply train and the 6th Machine Gun Battalion plus 3/5, now brigade reserve. The 6th Machine Gun Battalion would also be relieved, in incremental units, over a long period. I'm not sure if Feland or Neville ever received any relief during the period. Certainly Feland needed some, since he had been so active.

According to Harbord's daily report to General Bundy, other than some artillery shelling of the woods north of the Paris Farm, the 5th Regiment's dressing station and PC at La Voie du Châtel, "Nothing else of importance to report." Oh, yes! Harbord also directed that no bandsmen were to be used as stretcher-bearers, and they were to be kept with the rear echelon. Too difficult to replace.

Tuesday, 18 June

The Harbord report had this to say about the day: "Quiet." He also added, "Enemy artillery about as usual. Several 150 caliber dropped to-day in and in the vicinity of Montreuil. Enemy aviation active as usual. Allied aviation passive or nonexistent." What Harbord didn't mention in his report was a contentious meeting he had with Lt. Col. Frederick "Fritz" Wise.

> He [Harbord] was sore because I hadn't cleaned out those Germans in the woods. . . . I was sore at that last-minute change of orders . . . after Harbord himself had given me a free hand. It wasn't a pleasant interview. "Twice you reported to me that those woods were clear of Germans when they weren't." I did, but the minute I found out my error . . . you were notified about it. Then I learned what was irking him. He himself had reported the woods clear, and had had to back-fire on it! [Wise describes his loss of temper.] If you had so much doubt about those woods being clear, why the hell didn't somebody from Brigade [Harbord?] come out and take a look? I asked him. I don't remember exactly what I did say after that. It must have been plenty. . . . Harbord wasn't pleased. He departed. I knew my goose was cooked. . . .[187]

At 1135 the liaison officer of the 23d Infantry sent Colonel Malone a message that described what was going on to their left. The colonel was notified that 2/7 was the connecting unit to 3/23, and added, "Nothing new to report."

Wednesday, 19 June

The 1st Battalion, 7th Infantry, tried to obtain identification from German soldiers lying dead or alive in a ravine about a kilometer south of Torcy but were defeated in their attempt. They did report that they killed about a dozen German soldiers during their excursion. Additional orders were issued to try again that night. Later, 3/7 advanced three platoons of L Company northward to the ravine near the crossroads, one kilometer south of Torcy, which 3/6 had hesitated attacking on 13 June. They quickly organized a defensive position from the ravine to the main Lucy-Torcy road. Records of the 237th German Division, which had held this position in force a few days before, seem to indicate that its relief division (87th) thought much less of this advanced position, hence the ease in taking it.[188] That night Gaston would supply two platoons from I Company with which the line was extended from the road toward the western edge of Belleau Wood.

Thursday, 20 June

The 23d Machine Gun Company was relieved at 0430 by Company A, 4th Machine Gun Battalion. The 23d went to its relief station in the Bois Gros Jean at 0835. It would not be until 22 June that another company from the battalion would also be relieved.

Early on this cool and cloudy morning, 1/7 launched the first of two attacks upon the German machine-gun positions before them in Belleau Wood. Two platoons from D and one platoon each from A and C advanced into the northern end of the wood but were beaten back, losing eleven killed, forty-five wounded, and seven missing. Neither of the two platoons from D Company was in its position when the attack was launched, and they may not have even been involved in the fighting. Harbord's report for the day:

> Companies of the 7th fell back when a few casualties occurred. One company commander, Captain Russel, 7th Infantry, relieved by battalion commander for inefficiency and sent to report to regimental commander [Anderson].[189]

At 0950 Harbord sent a message of congratulations to Major Gaston on his successful occupation of "the ravine to the crossroads without loss." He also gave him instructions as to a reconnaissance to the left to try and locate the French troops expected to be there. If no French were there, Gaston was to take a company "through the woods and take it as you did the ravine." But if he found it occupied by the enemy, he was cautioned to report to Neville first "before attempting to send a company in there." Major Shearer, who had reclaimed his command, received a message from Harbord that was lengthy and highly detailed.

> 1. It is believed that by the judicious use of sharpshooter snipers you can reduce the German positions without much expenditure of men. These men should be provided with canteens of water, with some rations and crawl out toward the German positions exerting every effort, exercising the patience of Indians and waiting for shots without exposing themselves. Pairs to be sent in on all sides. Additional pairs to be sent in at night along the west side of the BOIS from both north and south. These will stop any further infiltration if any has taken place. Some should be sent in where the tree bordered road which runs from LUCY toward CHATEAU-THIERRY touches the BOIS de BELLEAU [175.2-262.3] to scout up the road watching for a chance to snipe.

2. The wiring up on the east and north of the BOIS must proceed. Just as soon as it is completed the line can be held with comparatively few men and remainder dug in support and out of shell fire.

3. It is not practicable to withdraw again and give further artillery preparation. With the sniping which should worry the enemy you should be endeavoring to get the machine gun nests surrounded so you can rush them when ready and put an end to them.

4. The 3d Bn. 7th Infantry holds the ravine from 174.0–263.4 to crossroads 174.8–263.0 and tonight will extend that line to the east to vicinity of 175.3–262.5. That will enable you to control any approach of Germans down that road from LUCY toward CHATEAU-BELLEAU.[190]

The next message Harbord sent to Lieutenant Colonel Adams that day said, insultingly,

Your battalion will be relieved tomorrow [21 June] night. Tomorrow morning is its only chance to redeem the failure made this morning. If you clear the northern half of the BOIS de BELLEAU the credit will belong to the 1st Battalion, 7th Infantry and will be freely given. The Battalion cannot afford to fail again.[191]

Lieutenant Colonel Adams had given some serious thought to what he and his men were to do the following morning, so he sent Harbord a reasonable declaration that asked for removal back while artillery worked the forest over. Then he said, "I can assure you that the orders to attack will stand as given, but it cannot succeed." Stallings believes he meant just that; it would fail in any case. At any rate, Harbord sent another message to Adams, which briefly described what support Harbord could offer and what he expected from 1/7 early the following morning. Simply put, it told him to withdraw to X-line 262, beginning at 2345, "carrying out the movement with utmost secrecy. From 2:00 to 3:15 A.M. the artillery would make a thorough preparation of the part . . . vacated by your troops. . . . Your troops will attack at 3:15 and capture or destroy the enemy."

Adams dictated the orders to his company commanders and they assembled in formations of two waves each. A and B Companies were to be in the lead with C in support and D as battalion reserve. Later reports indicate that the artillery went off on time, but the preparatory fire and barrage upon the objective was light and ineffective.[192]

Friday, 21 June

Companies A and C went forward at 0315, and when A reached the German positions they attacked; B Company, following instructions, moved toward the left, to the western edge of Belleau Wood. They failed to participate in the fight. A Company had gone in alone. Company C, supporting A, about 150 yards to the rear, moved up into line and they, too, became engaged but there was no penetration of the German lines. A Company was repulsed with a loss estimated at 140 to 150 killed and wounded. The losses to C amounted to about thirty. Company D did not participate at all. German artillery fire dispersed the battalion somewhat, but at 0730 all but B were in their original positions, on X-line 262. Adams's only message to Harbord simply said, "Everything is not going well." One officer "fatality" was the commander of A Company, Lieutenant Helm. He, somehow, managed to get separated from his company and wandered into Gaston's PC, "without his men, stating that A Company was shot to pieces."

When Harbord received this message, he ordered the officer to the 5th Regiment PC, immediately. Shortly afterward Gaston sent another message to Harbord in which he described the arrival of B Company at the rear of M, his far right company. The officer in charge reported that "the Germans have broken through." M Company was located on the Lucy-Torcy road and just northwest of Hill 169. The soldiers reported firing to their right rear, which meant that the Germans had moved south again, behind the American lines.

Shearer's 3/5, which was nearby as brigade reserve, sent 47th Company south to Hill 169 to investigate. Upon arrival, the Marines sent back word that they could find no Germans thereabouts. Later, when 3/5 went in to relieve 1/7, they found that the soldiers had fallen back, leaving empty much of what the Marines had conquered in the north. Fortunately, the Germans seemed not to have learned that. A story told by Stallings clarifies why the 7th wasn't yet ready for combat. He tells of a doughboy guide leading 3/5 in to 1/7's positions that evening and how rapidly the lad was moving—so fast that he often had to stop so the Marines could catch up. The leading officer said harshly,

Do I have to shoot you in the ass to slow you down? The doughboy was anguished. He cried, "Officer, don't shoot me, officer! I got no business here. I only been in the United States Army five weeks."[193]

In a lengthy and elaborate report sent by Harbord to Bundy, he cited all the difficulties the 7th encountered but finalized it with a brief statement that

> this whole situation arises in my opinion from the inefficiency of officers of the 7th Inf. And the lack of instruction of the men. The 1st Bn. is untrustworthy for first line work at this time. The 2d Bn. has given satisfaction in the south end of the Bois de Belleau where there has been nothing but watching required of it, suffering some casualties from shell fire. [He was somewhat more conciliatory toward Gaston's 3d Battalion.] Except that it has shown no enterprise in carrying out orders for outpost patrols. [Then he elaborated a bit more, lauding a patrol carried out by Lieutenant White, USR on the night of 20–21 June.][194]

It isn't necessary to go into further details about the hapless 7th Infantry and its officers, but suffice to say that Harbord was also critical of the regiment's commanding officer. Harbord ordered Shearer and his company commanders to go into the wood that morning on a reconnaissance, since that evening they were to be sent in to relieve 1/7.

Another Marine, this one bearing a famous name, Maj. Littleton W. T. Waller, arrived on that day and relieved Capt. George J. Osterhout Jr., who had been temporarily in command of the 6th Machine Gun Battalion since the 11th of June. Until his services had been especially requested by the 2d Division, Waller had been in command of the 8th Machine Gun Battalion, 3d Division. Osterhout returned to command the 23d Company. The rest of the 6th Machine Gun Battalion would remain pretty much in place. It would be much later in the month before most of that battalion would find relief, rest, and food.

That night a German deserter from the 3d Reserve Ersatz Regiment of the 87th Division came into the lines and gave information regarding enemy dispositions. Lieutenant Colonel Feland made a personal reconnaissance and found the report was true. The 4th Brigade, for the first time since 10–13 June, learned that the German line was solid and that they continued to own the northern end of Belleau Wood. All previous plans to envelop the enemy in the woods were based upon erroneous information and were naturally doomed to failure. Harbord informed Shearer that it would be his task to clear the area with the forces under his command, with no artillery preparation. Nothing but hand grenades and trench mortars were to be used before the attack. Marine snipers were sent out in pairs and for a day, through 22 June, they produced good results. German Major Hartlieb's troops were the victims, suffering severe losses to the "deadeyes."

Other operations of the brigade included orders as follows: Sibley and 3/6 to the wood just northeast of Lucy on the night of 21–22 June; Wise and 2/5 to Bois Gros Jean as division reserve the night of 21–22 June and to the wood occupied by 3/6, as brigade reserve on the following night; Sibley and 3/6 to relieve 2/7 on the night of 22–23 June; and Keyser and 2/5 to relieve 3/7 on the night of 23–24 June. On the night of 23–24 June, Holcomb and 2/6 were to go to the wood northwest of Lucy as brigade reserve. Hughes and 1/6 were ordered to Bois Gros Jean as division reserve on the night of 23–24 June, followed in the same location and same night by Turrill's 1/5.

Harbord outlined the regimental sectors with the 5th located, "exclusive to west of 2d Div." The 6th Marines sector would be "Y-line" 174. The 6th would now be in the northwest and the 5th the southeast, a complete change from their original positions. But Neville and the 5th Marines still retained the troublesome Belleau Wood. Their total casualties for the period, which were nearly twice that of the 6th, would reflect that "honor."[195]

In his daily report, Harbord notified division that most of the men of his brigade required clothing, and that the supply of seventeen hundred pairs of shoes ordered since 20 May had never been delivered. "One battalion reported as having no underclothing except those worn; probably others the same condition."

On that day the 96th Company received a welcome 140 enlisted Marines and two officers as replacements. Captain Wethered Woodworth assumed command of the company and the other officer, 1st Lt. Robert L. Duane, of a platoon. These were the men who replaced those 150 enlisted and three officers who were removed on 14 June from the effects of a gas attack.

Saturday, 22 June

Major Shearer prepared and submitted his plan for the attack ordered by Harbord, which was rapidly approved. His right flank began where the "rocky knoll" was located. The line then moved in a southerly direction to about the middle of the woods, then moved northward toward the northwest face. At this point the Germans were nearly squeezed out of the wood. Just a little push might do it. The companies of 3/5 were located as follows, left to right: the 45th, 16th, 20th, and 47th, with a reserve, composed of one platoon from each company, posted in the rear of the right center.

Harbord also pushed 3/6 to complete the wiring that Hughes had started, way back when. Sibley also received orders to make connection with the 23d Infantry in the environs of Bouresches. As usual, Sibley satisfactorily followed directions on both counts, no questions asked.

Sunday, 23 June

Sometime near noon, Maj. Ralph Keyser relieved Frederick M. Wise in command of 2/5. Harbord believed that old Fritz was ill, or perhaps he needed more education, or something. At 1340 Keyser had Joe Murray, who was still adjutant of the battalion, send a message to all platoon leaders, tightening up his command.

> The battalion commander insists on immediate attention to the following: (1) Camouflaging worst openings in the woods which would permit enemy observation; (2) Collection of arms, equipment, etc., scattered through the sector which will be turned in at Batt. Hdqtrs. each time any carrying parties make a trip; (3) string of low trip wires in front of each platoon; and (4) absolute prohibition of use of paths for trails which are not completely concealed both overhead and toward the front. Cans, paper, and all other material which cannot be used or salvaged will be buried at once. Tools, ammunition, and fireworks are available and are being distributed. Put in for what you really need and will try to get it for you.[196]

The above order was in preparation for taking over the ground held by 3/7 that night.

At 1900 sharp, the attack began. Captain Yowell and his 16th Company, plus a platoon from the 47th, was on the left. The 20th Company, led by Capt. Richard Platt, plus fifty men from the 45th, were on the right. Small groups of Marines went first with hand and rifle grenades. These men quickly encountered enemy resistance, especially from the numerous machine guns, which they assaulted with grenades and rifle fire. Both of the second-line companies extended their lines, the 45th to the right and the 47th on the left, to close the line behind the leading two companies. Up front, the advance party was running into the usual stubborn resistance and well-placed machine-gun nests. The German machine-gun crews would, when the Marines got too close, retire, removing their guns. As each nest was taken out, German flanking fire was opened up at once upon the former position. The fire did not slacken and the Marine casualty rate soared, soon becoming too high in proportion to the ground gained. It wasn't long before contact was lost in the center between the leading 20th and the 16th Companies. Shearer was aware of the difficulties his Marines were encountering, for he sent Harbord a message an hour after the assault began that simply stated, "Making progress slowly."

Closest to the enemy line, 20th Company was barely able to move forward up the rocky knoll, just north of the hook, about twenty yards in all. Within minutes, machine guns made that position untenable. Although the 20th wiped out three nests, the enemy got away with their guns and wounded.

The 16th moved farther forward but was unable to dig in or organize new positions, suffering heavy casualties. Two trumpeters, David Ruff and James C. Toner, received multiple Silver Star citations for running messages through heavy artillery fire, the former four, the latter three. Gunnery Sergeant Harry Burns, also of the 16th, gathered up the wounded, removing them from the front line, at the grave risk of his own life. He, too, was awarded four Silver Star citations. Private William L. Barron*, another member of the company, delivered an important message even though he was badly wounded. Afterward, he fell unconcious from the loss of blood. Sergeant Joe Bell* got separated from his own platoon in the confusion and joined another. When he learned that the platoon's runners were all out of action he assumed that role and made several trips across an open area subjected to continuous and intense artillery and machine-gun barrages.

Both advancing companies had to reverse their forward motion, being compelled to fall back to their original positions. The 16th lost an officer and 75 men; and the 20th lost 26 men. Both the 45th and 47th suffered 2 casualties from the artillery concentration upon their areas. One private from the 45th, George F. Brautigan*, helped to carry a wounded officer to safety after spending most of the night carrying messages across a field swept by intense artillery fire. First Lieutenant George H. Yarborough*, also of the 45th, moved from one foxhole to another, calming and encouraging his men. Four times he was wounded by shrapnel but refused all aid until his wounded were treated and taken to a place of safety. Yarborough died of his wounds on 26 June 1918.

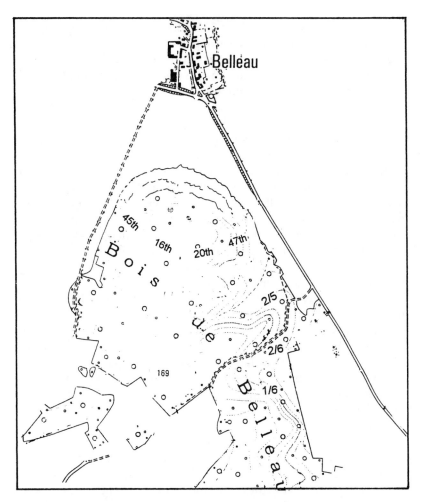

Map 7: This shows the approximate positions of 3d Bn., 5th Marines, led by Major Shearer, from after they relieved the 7th Infantry until the close of day, 24 June 1918. The following day they drove the last living German out of those woods. It shows the approximate location of 2/5, 2/6, and 1/6, at about the same time.

Sergeant Clarence W. Kelly, of the 47th, was another hero that day. He earned three Silver Star citations for his gallantry in charging and capturing a German machine gun. All in all it was a good day for courage but a bad day for survival.

Neville received a report from 3/5, which he forwarded to brigade. It explained that the attack was stopped and that the battalion would dig in and proceed in the morning. The attack was a complete failure. No ground gained, no prisoners and no machine guns taken. It was still the same Belleau Wood. Nothing had changed. Just different victims.

Monday, 24 June

During the night two platoons from the 83d Company, 3/6, were sent forward to reinforce Yowell, and I'll bet they were thrilled about it. At 0105 Neville sent Harbord a message indicating that 3/5 had been in serious trouble the night before. "Things are rather bad. One company almost wiped out." A half hour later Shuler reported that "Platt's losses were light. He was held where he was but would take another crack in the morning." A few minutes later, 2/5 reported that they were in position. Turrill sent in his report that he was okay, "in place in woods at Bois Gros Jean," which was more than four miles in the rear. Some things were working well for some people.

At 1100 Shearer submitted his report of how the attack failed. Nothing new; he maintained that his company commanders had done what they could but he was satisfied that they were unable to crack the German line. "Men and officers showed good discipline and advance and withdrawals were made without confusion." He explained why the attack was unable to proceed: those Marines carrying grenades were "getting lost in the woods." If they had been where they were supposed to be earlier they "could have been used to advantage." The rest of the report is illuminating.

> The enemy seemed to have unlimited alternate gun positions and many guns. Each gun position covered by others. I know of no other way of attacking these positions with chance of success than one attempted and am of opinion that infantry alone cannot dislodge enemy guns. Water is difficult to obtain and scarce. Men and officers very tired but retain their spirit.[196A]

About forty-five minutes later Shearer sent in another report, which identified four men killed and three wounded by enemy one-pounders at short range. "My officers and men are showing the effects of being constantly on the alert and under frequent shell fire. Lieut. [Jacob H.] Heckman is slightly shell-shocked but I think he will be all right in a little while."[197] Captain Gaines Moseley, who had replaced Phil Case as skipper of the 47th Company, sent Shearer a report, in which he described what was happening to the platoons of the 47th:

> The positions held by the 4th Platoon (Heckman) and 3d Platoon (Stallings) are catching hell from whiz-bang firing, which in many cases caves in the parapet of the trenches owing to the nature of the soil in which they are constructed. In many cases the enemy seems to be able to enfilade the previously mentioned positions with his whiz-bangs.[198]

Second Lieutenant James H. Legendre, Keyser's adjutant, notified Colonel Lee, to whom 2/5 was reporting, that the Germans seemed to be moving from northwest of the wood in a westerly direction. "Some shelling at 173.7–262.6." The coordinates signify that poor old Hill 142 was being whacked again. Replying to a report from Keyser, Harbord ordered him to place two of his companies back at his, Harbord's, PC to be used as needed. Two companies being considered adequate for the line he was to hold. Harbord also found cause to complain that 2/5 wasn't holding the same exact lines that 3/7 had held before them. He wanted Keyser to move and stretch his line to the left a half kilometer; "this will greatly facilitate operations in the Bois." Later that evening Harbord issued orders for Lee and Neville to exchange their own PCs "for the greater conveniences of handling the sectors of which you are in charge."

At a meeting, Generals Bundy, Harbord, Chamberlaine, plus assorted regimental and battalion commanders, discussed what they could each do to make the next assault upon Belleau Wood the last one necessary. Their final decision was to withdraw the infantry behind the front lines and let all divisional artillery shell the hell out of the northern end. More orders from Harbord to Shearer. This time he commanded Shearer and 3/5 to fall back to the oft-used

> X-line 262 before 0300 tomorrow morning, June 25th. The artillery will be free to fire from that hour anywhere north of the line 262 as far east as the railroad and as far west as the road with the double row of trees which runs just west of the BOIS de BELLEAU. It is desired that the fire be intense enough from 3 o'clock on to prevent the entrance of any Germans and that for a period of about an hour before 5 P.M., June 25th, it be made of maximum intensity. It will be the intention to follow the artillery preparation

by an attack with the 3d Bn. at 5 P.M. on the 25th. The rate of advance of the infantry will not exceed 100 meters each three minutes. The objective of the advance is the north edge of the BOIS de BELLEAU.[199]

Tuesday, 25 June

At 0145 Harbord responded to a message received from Keyser late the previous evening, indicating displeasure with its content. This message cannot be found in any volume of *The Records,* but the reply suggests that Harbord seemed to be having problems with the new battalion commander. He mentions that the "clump of trees . . . containing machine guns was occupied by the 7th Infantry night before last and visited yesterday." Then he goes on to explain that if Keyser and his battalion had been on the job they would have observed any German takeover.

> Send out a patrol. I want your patrols to dominate the whole region, day and night. . . . It ought not be necessary to specify. . . . Let me reiterate that your occupation includes necessary patrolling etc.

He was obviously angry and had every right to be so. He also ordered that 2/5 advance

> his line tonight and bring the right of the line on the double tree road just west of Bois de Belleau. This will begin just after dark. Please notify [Shearer] . . . so in the dark he will not confuse it with a possible counterattack.

At 1700 3/5 went "over the top" as planned. Within the hour Shearer sent a message about the progress of the attack to Captain Shuler at brigade headquarters. It was received two hours later.

> Attack started at 5 P.M. Heavy firing on us just before we jumped off. Several casualties. Very little machine gun fire. Telephone line out. Runner reported 7 prisoners and one captain also prisoner, carrying back wounded. The two left platoons 16th Company reported grenades and sniper working on them. No report from companies yet. Will go through if humanly possible.[200]

Meanwhile, 2d Lt. Jacob H. Heckman*, of the 47th and two men of his platoon, all of whom displayed extraordinary courage and coolness under fire, rushed a German position. They did this under heavy machine-gun and shell fire with total disregard for their own safety. Heckman showed outstanding ability and command presence in capturing and controlling one officer and ninety German soldiers through the same firestorm. I cannot find the names of the two enlisted men who went with him. A large number of men from the 47th were cited for awards. Sergeant Christie Collopy wiped out a machine-gun nest with hand grenades. Corporal Victor M. Landreth was a runner for the four final days, he captured a machine gun that had been pouring heavy fire on the flanks of his company. Corporal Edward J. Melcher*, although wounded in his head and thigh, continued to lead his men through heavy fire to their objective. Corporal Jacob S. Laul led his Chauchat crew to victory over a machine gun and its crew. He fell unconcious from shell concussion. But in short order he was up, resumed command, and again led his men forward. Sergeant Charles P. McFarland attacked and captured an enemy machine gun alone, while Cpl. Allison M. Page was cited for gallantry in action but received his SS posthumously[201] as did Cpl. David K. Peers. Another hero who died that day was Sgt. Henry B. West*, who unselfishly exposed himself in order to bring down an enemy sniper who had wounded several members of his group. The 47th Company wasn't the only organization with its heroes. The outstanding exploits of Gy. Sgt. Walter Sweet* of the 16th began on this day. He took command when his company commander, Capt. Robert Yowell, was severely wounded. Re-forming the badly shot-up company, Sweet led them forward, smashing two machine guns and capturing their crews. After he consolidated a defensive position it was soon harassed by enemy trench mortar fire, causing his company heavy losses. Sergeant Sweet took a handful of grenades and went out after the guns and their crews. He wiped them out and took five more Germans prisoner. He rightfully received a commission and went on to more heroic deeds at Blanc Mont and the Meuse-Argonne. There were other heroes in all four companies, many who were cited for their actions over several days.

At 1900 hours Shearer sent another detailed message to the 4th Brigade headquarters about the progress of the attack.

47th Co. gained objective—20th and 47th digging in. 45th still in reserve but will occupy positions just as soon as things settle. 16th still working into position. Estimated 150 prisoners, by 20th and 47th companies. No report of 16th as to prisoners. More prisoners coming in too numerous to count. I am making prisoners dig and carry wounded. Every one doing fine work. Yowell, 16th, meeting resistance. Will send him help. Will need all my company to hold new line. Can't Keyser send me two platoons. Just reported counter-attack on 47th. Am sending two platoons 45th to help. Report capture of some of the 47th Co. Our casualties will make help necessary. Please keep artillery and machine guns going to stop reinforcements of enemy.[202]

A little later, Shearer was a bit more emphatic. *"We have taken practically all of the woods but do need help to clean it up and hold it.* Do we get it?"(Emphasis in original.)

Harbord sent Keyser a message at 2310 that said,

In moving your line forward it is important that you send a platoon to clean up in the edge of the Bois, parallel to the double tree road. The 16th Co. in trying to come out to position on that side of the road is meeting some resistance. Send your platoon by your right rear to come up on the left and help clean it out. I do not believe the remainder of your line will meet much resistance.[203]

Ten minutes later Harbord wrote to Neville with a soothing message.

Your Shearer battalion has done splendid work. I have no fear of a counter-attack by the Germans tonight. You are in charge of the BOIS de BELLEAU and can divert such part of Major Sibley's battalion as you think best.[204]

Facing Shearer in the woods was the 1st Battalion, 347th German Infantry. And it was their four companies being pushed back. The Marines penetrated the line at the point where the 3d and 4th Companies joined and rolled them up. Continuing their success they went after the 2d on the left and the 5th from the Reserve Ersatz Regiment on the right. Marines who had been captured the night before were still in that area and were rescued by their buddies of 3/5. Brigade Sergeant Major William J. Geary, who had begged Harbord to be allowed to participate in the fighting, was killed in action while leading a platoon that night. He was awarded a DSC and two Silver Star citations. His replacement at headquarters, Sgt. Maj. Hobart A. Segrist, won a citation for a Navy Cross "for assuming the duties of [office] during one of the most bitter attacks of the brigade. . . ." A young Marine who served meals to the officers at brigade asked Harbord to allow him to go out and get himself at least one German. He added that his replacement was there and ready to fill his role at the next meal. Harbord reluctantly let him go also. He, too, was killed that evening.

Several detachments of Germans were still holding out in the wood and there was a movement in the north, toward the Torcy-Belleau road, where 1/347 was making attempts to re-form. All the while the 2d Division artillery, aided by that of the French 333d, laid their heavy stuff on the rear of the Germans. There were reports that many Germans were trying to surrender, but because the Marines' blood was up they kept popping at them anyway. Additionally, one of their own machine guns would let go on them if any German tried to run toward the American lines. The gunner was probably a future Nazi. Shearer decided that he held most of the wood and that a further attempt to attack would have been fatal to his men. So far his losses on this day alone were four officers and 119 men and in three days his total loss was five officers and 260 men, more than twenty-five percent of his total force. Old 3/5 had to pay the bill once again.

There was also the distinct possibility that 3/5 had passed Germans in the woods, but Shearer decided he had no men to patrol the rear. Besides, heavy enemy artillery began shelling his line, causing more casualties. His plea to Lee for help brought about a release of Sibley and 3/6, located in the southern portion of the wood. It also caused Keyser to move toward the east to make that connection on the northwestern edge of the wood. Some of Sibley's men moved northward and connected up with 3/5, but a few were left behind their completed wire defenses to correct any potential suicide attempts against the Bouresches–Belleau Wood line.

With these alterations, Sibley's men were now covering the northeastern edge, while 3/5 moved to their left to connect with 2/5 on the western edge. The design of 3/5's line now looked like a shepherd's crook. They formed on the entire northern edge with 3/6 continuing down the eastern edge. Keyser sent in a platoon to back up the rear of the weakened 16th Company. Fighting between small units continued for the balance of the night, but there was no German counterattack.

They had finally gotten the message the Marines had been sending them for nearly the entire month: No Heinies allowed in Belleau Wood.

Wednesday, 26 June

Though the Germans continued their activity on the Torcy-Belleau road, they slowed down appreciably in the wood. At dawn, 3/5 held all the edges of Belleau Wood that faced the enemy. At 1050, 216 German prisoners, including four officers, had passed through brigade headquarters while numerous wounded prisoners were sent through the dressing stations. The losses for the Marines were high, as usual: 3/5 alone had 250 wounded processed through the dressing stations.

There was even one lot of seventy-eight German prisoners captured by a lone Marine private named Henry P. Lenert. Lenert, a runner for Shearer, was captured on the 25th when he stumbled into a German position. During his brief interrogation, the senior German officer in charge said that he knew exactly which units, down to the numbers of companies, made up his enemies, and told Lenert the facts. When he asked what was behind the 16th and 20th Companies, the young Marine altered the situation somewhat and told him the 6th Regiment of Marines. That was good enough. The officer asked if Lenert would take them as prisoners, to which the young Marine agreed, probably with some enthusiasm. Discarding their arms, at Lenert's instructions, the Germans followed him back to brigade headquarters. Upon arrival, the lad asked a very surprised staff officer, "Hey, bud! What will I do with these prisoners I've just captured?"[205]

At a final tally, German prisoner losses totaled seven officers and 302 men. The 16th Company reported capturing ten heavy and eight light machine guns while the 20th took one heavy and five light. German losses in the 347th Regiment totaled five officers and 369 men killed and missing with another two officers and sixty-four men wounded, a total of seven officers and 433 men out of action. While the Boche were taking a beating, when it came to manpower losses, the Marines were taking extreme punishment.

As far as things went in the Belleau Wood battles, 3/5 had been more roughly handled than any other Marine battalion: June 6 was the worst of all, when in their first attack they lost their battalion commander and were repulsed with tremendous losses. It was kind fate that gave the remnants of 3/5, through their battalion CO, the right to scream, "BELLEAU WOODS NOW U.S. MARINE CORPS ENTIRELY."

Now, finally, changes could be decreed. At 0815 Harbord issued an order for Holcomb and 2/6, "as soon as possible tonight, June 26–27, will relieve the Third Battalion, Fifth Regiment Marines in the north end of Bois de Belleau." Fifteen minutes later he ordered 1/6 to go into the woods northwest of Lucy as brigade reserve. In addition, they would provide work details for construction of trenches in the sector. Most likely there weren't many engineers left to do that job. They had been up to their ears in fighting all during the month of June and not many were still "healthy." Keyser and 2/5 weren't left out. Harbord ordered that he "swing [his] line forward so that it will run . . . straight from the crossroad south of Torcy to the double-tree road," as soon after dark as possible.

Following this, Harbord then sent out some administrative directives. One in effect stated that now all was quiet, so the number of troops on the front line could be minimized. This meant that more men would remain in reserve as support troops. It was long overdue. Everyone was exhausted and barely able to continue doing anything, let alone fighting. The fact is, the Marines outlasted the Krauts. But barely.

Thursday, 27 June, to Friday, 5 July

The ensuing period was a time of minor action for the 4th Marine Brigade. There was some moving about of various battalions and of course consolidation of the area controlled. There was even some shooting. But for the most part it was "quiet time." Brigade began the necessary reorganization of each unit. Shearer and his battalion were relieved by Sibley and went to the Bois Gros Jean for rest and relaxation. The following day, 28 June, is mentioned as being "without incident." On 29 June the commander of I Corps, AEF, Maj. Gen. Hunter Liggett, visited brigade headquarters. General Harbord visited the wood and in his daily report noted, "No one who has not visited that wood can comprehend the heroism of the troops which finally cleared it of Germans." That night 1/6 moved into the woods to relieve 3/6, which also went to Bois Gros Jean for the same treatment accorded to 3/5. On 27 June, Turrill and 1/5 replaced 1/6 in St. Martin's Wood as brigade reserve. They remained there until 30 June, when they relieved 2/5, which then took its place in the wood as brigade reserve, not quite musical chairs but nearly so.

That evening, orders were issued for all frontline units to relax. On this day, the 3d Brigade finalized its plans to attack Vaux. Both 3/5 and 3/6 were made available to division in case they should be needed in the attack. That same night all but two battalions were removed from the front lines. It was now 1/5, from the French right at Hill 142, to Belleau Wood, while 1/6 was in the wood itself. Both 2/6 and 2/5 were in the St. Martin Wood as reserve. Sibley and Shearer were still in Bois Gros Jean, but on alert if needed. Guns of the 6th Machine Gun Battalion, supplemented by the division's 4th Machine Gun Battalion, remained in place to support the 4th Brigade, with two companies on line and two out.

On the 2d of July orders were received by brigade to dispatch two companies to Paris for the Fourth of July Parade, one from the 5th Regiment and the other from the 6th as brigade representatives. Each regiment selected twenty men per company; one sergeant, two corporals, and seventeen privates, and ten privates from Headquarters Company. Captain Voeth, Lieutenants Mason, J. W. Overton, M. C. Overton, Church, Maack, and Timmerman were the officers selected from the 6th, plus Surgeon Farwell and three hospital apprentices. I cannot locate an additional detailed list of officers from the 5th. Major General Hunter Liggett summoned Colonel Neville to meet with him at La Ferte. That may have been the first time Neville had a relief during the entire Belleau Wood period. Shortly after, he was evacuated and sent to a hospital because of exhaustion.

On the night of 4/5 July, Lt. Col. "Hiking Hiram" Bearss with one officer and twenty-five men of the 67th Company, made a raid on the German positions south of Torcy. In the process they killed 2 Germans and captured two more. That morning the two companies of Marine officers and men selected, paraded in Paris in honor of Independence Day. Private Richard K. Kennedy of the 84th Company wrote a letter to his sister in which we have a description of what that day seemed like for one young man.

> For the second time in my life I drew a winning number. July 3d our platoon commander came around and selected nine men and five of these nine were to go. . . . Was lucky enough [to get the short straw]. . . . A short time and we were on our way. [That] evening found us in Paris, a big band and a vast crowd to meet us. Morn found us up bright and early . . . for the big parade. . . . It was wonderful the way the people treated us. Cheers and flowers from everywhere. Most everyone wore an American flag . . . and plenty of smiles. Treated royal[ly] one American soldier and ten fair

misses to a table. Dancing . . . sight-seeing. . . . I missed out on a meal . . . so I could see more of the place. Bright lights . . . cease to shine after 9:30. . . .[206]

Also on this day, officers of the 52d Infantry Brigade, 26th Division, reconnoitered the brigade front, and the following day, the 5th of July, saw the beginning of the relief of the 4th Brigade.[207] The "YD" did what they were supposed to do. They held and then later they attacked, pushing the Germans back even farther eastward.

There were many laudatory messages, telegrams, and personal congratulations received at division. The greatest, as far as the 4th Brigade was concerned, was General Dégoutte's order issued on 30 June which read,

> In view of the brilliant conduct of the 4th Brigade of the 2d U.S. Division, which in a spirited fight took BOURESCHES and the important strong point of BOIS DE BELLEAU, stubbornly defended by a large enemy force, the General Commanding the VI Army orders that henceforth, in all official papers, the BOIS DE BELLEAU shall be named Bois de la Brigade de Marine.

In addition, all three Marine units received citations, which, with another awarded later for Soissons, would entitle the Marines to wear a unit fourragère, in the colors of the Croix de Guerre. There were so many personal decorations awarded to officers and men during this period that I have intentionally avoided mentioning very many. See "Editorial Comment" at the end of this chapter..

A number of units of the French army added their thoughts, which were all acclamatory. The French mayor of Meaux sent a letter of congratulations, and with thanks, for the 4th Brigade's share in stopping the Germans so close to Meaux. He didn't say that but that was what he meant. Pershing sent a message, as did Malin Craig, the chief of staff for Hunter Liggett's I Corps. Major General Clarence R. Edwards, USA, the beloved commander of the 26th Division, added his and added, "We are all proud of you." Indeed, the major general, adjutant, Royal Marines, sent a nice telegram for his corps. The "Tiger of France," Premier Clemenceau, added his good words and unstinted praise for the

4th Brigade, even though he was not allowed by Headquarters, AEF, to visit with the brigade.[208] The article in the *Marine Corps Gazette* describing Clemenceau's visit diplomatically concludes with "[He] was invited to visit the Brigade Commander which the shortness of his stay prevented." Even the German army added their congratulations. A report liberated from a German officer in July 1918 read:

> The 2d American Division may be classified as a very good division, perhaps even assault troops. [What did they believe had been going on for a month?] The various attacks of both regiments on Belleau Wood were carried out with dash and recklessness. The moral effect of our firearms did not materially check the advance of the infantry. The nerves of the Americans are still unshaken.[209]

In a letter to Brig. Gen. Neville, dated August 1918, the commandant, Maj. Gen. Barnett, had this to say about the men of his Corps in France:

> Your Marines are too close to what an unprecedented thing they have done [Belleau Wood]. To them it is just fighting, in good, hard, Marine style. But to all America it is not only a series of glorious battles, but also the cause of new hope, new determination, and new confidence. Please tell your Marines that their commandant and their brother officers and men are thinking of them constantly and that they are, by reason of such example, even prouder than ever before of being Marines.

The French consul general, Gaston Libert, added his praise.

> The beginning and the end of the war from the Germans were the battles of the Marne—and with the name of the Marne will always be associated that of the glorious American Marines.

There were a large number of other laudatory messages, some coming several months later, but there were two that were exceptionally important. Both came from recognized military figures who came to their conclusions from disparate points and at a much later time: one, a noted military authority, the other a senior U.S. Army officer during the war in France. An Englishman, Basil Liddell Hart, wrote the acclaimed general history of the war, *The Real War, 1914 to 1918,* published by Little Brown, Boston, 1930. On page 417 he wrote:

The appearance and fierce counter-attack of the 2d American Division at the vital joint of Château-Thierry was not only a material cement, but an inestimable moral tonic to their weary Allies.

The other person being quoted here, Lt. Gen. Robert Lee Bullard, who commanded the 2d Army, AEF, was no friend of the Marine Corps. In fact, in the book being cited he castigated the Marines for the publicity they received while in the Château-Thierry sector. The book is *American Soldiers Also Fought* (New York: Maurice H. Louis, 1939).

"With the help of God and a few marines," was a phrase descriptive of the halt of the march on Paris, which was not fair to other units. The marines 'didn't win the war' here. *But they saved the Allies from defeat.* Had they arrived a few hours later I think that would have been the begining of the end: France could not have stood the loss of Paris. So today at Belleau Wood stands perhaps America's finest battle monument. [Emphasis in original.]

Well, it was all over but the shouting. The total losses of the 4th Brigade will be listed in Appendix A, but it isn't too early to say that the losses were horrendous. When, shortly after Belleau Wood, Mrs. Frederick Wise asked "Fritz" "How are the Marines?" He replied, "There aren't any more Marines."

Editorial Comment

Unlike any descriptions of other battles and campaigns, I have purposely avoided indicating most of those men who were awarded serious decorations for their courage and fearlessness while in this campaign. There were so many that the accounts would have been cluttered with description and extended far beyond what it now is. Needless to state, there were many, literally hundreds because, essentially, all the men were brave and all who were not cited, should have been. Valor was as common as was the apparent contempt for death. None of those men disregarded death, of course, they just did what had to be done, regardless of the outcome.

Notes

1 Other writers have listed the number as large as fifty divisions. Thirty-six appears to be the most accurate total.

2 Most historians now agree, if Paris had been taken, the will of the French people and army to continue fighting would most likely have ceased. The British army, which was close to the northern ports, probably would have been able to extricate most of their troops. That would have left only the few divisions of the AEF as a cohesive force to oppose the victorious, multitudinous German army. Then what?

3 Meaning *Landwehr* or "Fortress troops." *Landwehr* were "old-timers" brought back in for limited duty. The latter were better suited to defend a fortress.

4 At the end of the month of June there would be 4,677 fewer, of which 1,062 were battle deaths. The other elements of the division would lose an equal number, which would drop the divisional strength by more than a third; in a single, inconsequential battle the division lost nearly nine thousand men.

5 Located in that town was what many travelers considered to be the finest water supply in all of France, and perhaps Europe. Its name is derived from "good water."

6 The French colonial infantry wore an anchor on the front of their helmets. That was to distinguish them as colonial but reporting to the French navy rather than to the army. Consequently, they considered themselves Marines rather than regular infantry. In actual fact there were French Marines who wore a uniform similar to that of the French navy and who were landed from ships at trouble spots.

7 Elliott D. Cooke, USA, *We Can Take It!* and *We Attack!* (1937; reprint, in one volume, Pike, NH: The Brass Hat, 1990). His name was often erroneously spelled "Cook" in messages and official reports.

8 Martin Gus Gulberg, *A War Diary*, 22.

9 Cooke, op. cit., 3.

10 Gulberg, *A War Diary*, 22–23.

11 John W. Thomason, *The 2d Division Northwest of Château-Thierry: 1 June–10 July, 1918,* (unpublished manuscript).

12 Cooke, *We Can Take It!*, 4

13 Gulberg, *A War Diary*, 24

14 For the best description of a runner's existence read Elton Mackin's *Suddenly We Didn't Want to Die* (Novato, CA: Presidio, 1993). He was a runner for 1/5, and earned the DSC and NC plus Silver Star citations, etc.

15 In 1927 workmen at the château discovered the cadaver of an American soldier from the 26th YD Division, who evidently had crawled in and died sometime during the division's July occupation of the area.

16 I've seen the lodge and it is only big enough for two persons. It's sort of round with no corners to hide in. It could also hold a basket of champagne and perhaps one bed.

17 Most of this physical description, based upon period description, is still correct. The entire area is little changed except for that the main roads were paved.

18 German divisions were normally about half the size of an American division and this group was in bad shape. Therefore the force facing the 2d Division was probably no more than 40,000–50,000 total.

19 During the war artillery and machine guns were the major weapons that were man-killers. Rifle accuracy was really an academic exercise, fine for small wars and defense against exposed troops but not all that important in World War I.

20 Because the guns and gunners of the 6th Machine Gun Battalion were intermingled with the infantry companies, it was not deemed practical to make frequent reference to their individual participation in the battle, which was always extensive. The same can be added for those engineers, corpsmen, and doctors who also contributed so much to the 4th Brigade during the entire war.

21 As will be shown, the linking up of the two battalions became a long, tedious process.

22 When Turrill and his battalion retired from their position in the north, a portion of Wise's 2/5 filled the mile-long gap. Wise was now covering over two miles and would have been in serious trouble if he had been hit all along his line during that period. He still wasn't on Hill 142, at least a half-mile distance north.

23 It appears that Williams believed he was astride Hill 142 when in fact he was on another piece of high ground, just west of the Bussiares–La Voie du Châtel road. Later it would come out that Shearer did not stretch all the way to Hill 142 either. For some hours there was a hole big enough for the Germans to have driven a battalion between them. They were nice. They didn't.

24 Just because this book is concentrating on the Marine Brigade, we mustn't forget that the infantry of the 3d Brigade were also taking it on the chin. The 23d Infantry was especially badly hit during this entire period.

25 This makes it seem that the majority of the members of the 4th Brigade had not yet changed over to the army's OD uniforms, even though Doyen, when he still commanded the brigade, had sent around an official order, sometime in late April, that every Marine was to begin making the change as "soon as possible."

26 Gulberg, *A War Diary*, 26. In a few days the situation, at this point, would be reversed.

27 *Records of the Second Division*, vol. 5.

28 The failure of the American army to feed its troops in France was a major flaw that was never corrected. France, though shattered by nearly four years of war was different; their army insured that its troops were well fed. If they hadn't, Pierre and his pals would have gone home for something to eat.

29 Craig Hamilton and Louise Corbin, eds., *Echoes from Over There* (New York: Soldier's Publishing Company, 1919), 69–70.

30 Unfortunately he wouldn't last the war out. He was killed later in the Marbache Sector, but not before being decorated for additional heroics at Soissons.

31 Several other individuals laid claim to having made that statement, but most everyone now agrees that it was Williams. Wise claimed the phrase as did McCloskey of the 12th Field Artillery. Perhaps more than one person uttered those or similar words at one time or another. But several people, who were nearby, agreed that they remembered hearing Williams say it.

32 On 15 February 1918, Major Smith was detached from the 5th Marines

for duty with 4th Brigade Headquarters as [adjutant vice major]. On 16 May he was appointed brigade liaison officer. He would remain in an administrative role during the entire period the brigade was in Europe. The Japanese wouldn't be as lucky as the Germans were.

33 *Operation Reports, 4th Brigade,* vol. 6.

34 Attached to the 2d Division were five groups of French artillery and assorted aeronautics, such as the 27th Escadrille and Balloon 21 of that service. The Field Hospitals, 1, 15, 16, and 23, were distributed between Bézu-le-Guéry, Château La Rue, and Meaux. Ambulance companies were in Sablonnières, Coupru, and Bézu-le-Guéry. Part of the U.S. 3d Division, the 30th Infantry, led by Col. E. L. Butt, was at the time defending the south bank of the Marne River in the Château-Thierry area. They, along with their sister regiment the 38th U.S. Infantry, would render outstanding service by withstanding and checking the main German assault across the river on 15 July 1918.

35 Major John Hughes had just returned from school at Chaumont and relieved Shearer, who returned to, and remained with, the 6th Marines, but only for a few days.

36 *Records of the Second Division,* vol. 5.

37 *Records of the Second Division,* vol. 2.

38 Thomas J. Curtis, *History of the Sixth Machine Gun Battalion* (1919; reprint, Pike, NH: The Brass Hat, 1990), 15

39 That connection around Hill 142 was still causing problems for the 5th Marines. It wouldn't be solved easily, even at this point.

40 Thomason was mistaken. The woods he was referring to were just below Hill 142's northeastern tip. That would be taken by 1/5 the following day. The wood he had mentioned in the message was far to the right front, before the front of 3/5, and wouldn't be taken until 25 June. Besides, he didn't show up until 7 June as a replacement, so the description of this attack was based upon other men's memory rather than his own.

41 Three Marines from the 49th Company actually entered the town of Torcy and occupied a building. A corporal sent back word with one wounded private that he taken the place and wanted reinforcements and ammunition. The two remaining Marines never came out. In 1927, the French farmer who owned the building and land was clearing away brush and weeds that had grown up around the hole and found the corpses of two Marines and two Germans down in there. Semper Fidelis.

42 His real name was Ernest August Janson but he served under the name of "Hoffman." He certainly wasn't the only man in the military services using a nom-de-guerre at that time.

43 In the first few days at Belleau Wood, many officers and men were cited and awarded a DSC. Harbord, after receiving many citations of a similar nature, sent a message to the brigade that his officers should show more selectivity in whom they would recommend for a high award, and not just for being killed. After all, that was expected of Marines. After the war, in 1919, the navy usually, but not always, approved an award of the newly created Navy Cross for the same citation.

44 Hamilton would be awarded two DSCs and an NC plus four Silver Star citations and two Croix de Guerre during the war. What a Marine. It is my opinion that an MoH would have been much more appropriate.

45 *Records of the Second Division,* vol. 5.

46 Elliott D. Cooke, *We Can Take It!* and *We Attack!* Cooke was one of nearly fifty U.S. Army officers assigned to the 4th Brigade. Most of the few survivors were reassigned, mainly to the 23d Infantry, after the mess at Soissons. Cooke, though wounded at Soissons, was one of the few who returned and remained with the 4th Brigade throughout the war.

47 Those losses also include those of the ill-fated attack made by 3/5 in the late afternoon.

48 Galliford was brigade intelligence officer. He earned the Navy Cross and a Silver Star citation later at the Meuse-Argonne.

49 *Records of Operations, Second Division,* vol. 5

50 *Records of Operations, Second Division,* vol. 5.

51 I believe he meant with the 67th Company.

52 Cowing, *"Dear Folks at Home———,"* 126–129.

53 *Records of the Second Division,* vol. 2. Incidentally, the second phase was never implemented because the first phase failed to attain its objectives. That was the only break the Marines received that whole day.

54 When Conachy returned to his company only 2d Lt. Edward E. Conroy's (USA) platoon remained behind. In his absence Capt. Henry Larsen, Berry's adjutant, had shifted the other three platoons to form Berry's left flank. Obviously, though Conachy was to form Turrill's right flank in the proposed "second phase," he wouldn't be able to do anything like taking Hill 133 with one platoon. The blunder had to have been caused by a misunderstanding on Berry's part (or perhaps it was Larsen's error?) of what his orders directed him to do in the "first phase." Confusion reigned. As Asprey stated, and I thoroughly concur, "It was quite proper for men to die—that was one reason they were there—but for God's sake why slaughter them?"

55 What actually happened, it appears, is that instead a decision was made to leave one platoon per company behind rather than an entire company. Consequently three platoons in each company went over.

56 Quoted in Robert B. Asprey, *At Belleau Wood* (New York: G. P. Putman's Sons, 1965), 169. The official records give a much earlier time of arrival for the order.

57 James G. Harbord, *The American Army in France, 1917–1919* (Boston: Little Brown, 1936), 289–290. "It is now established that the Germans had three lines of trenches in the Wood." Harbord blames the lack of reconnaissance as "due to inexperience." Whose inexperience?

58 As mentioned previously, when Conachy returned to his company he found but 50 Marines. He managed to accumulate two platoons of engineers and a little later 30 men from the 16th Company, who had fallen back with the rest of 3/5, who were also impressed into service with the 45th, as were scattered survivors of other units. Conachy's remaining few were lucky. Only 9 men were left of the three platoons that went over with Berry.

59 Floyd Gibbons, *And They Thought We Wouldn't Fight* (New York: George Doran,1918), 311.

60 Asprey says the skipper of the 97th Company was Capt. Thomas McEvoy. See page 171. But it was still Capt. Robert Voeth and would be until Soissons when he was wounded.

61 David Bellamy, and others, tell us that Timmerman became a successful

lawyer between the two wars and, like Bill Eddy, would join the OSS and add more laurels to those each won in WWI.

62 William T. Scanlon, *God Have Mercy On Us!* (Boston: Houghton Mifflin, 1929), 18. The author was there, from corporal to gunnery sergeant, until 11 November 1918.

63 Albertus W. Catlin, *With the Help of God and a Few Marines* (Garden City, NY: Doubleday, Page & Co., 1919), 118.

64 Osborne was awarded the Navy Medal of Honor and a DSC in addition to two Silver Star citations for assisting the wounded during the period, including Duncan.

65 This incident was described by Maj. Frank Evans, regimental adjutant of the 6th, in a letter to the Marine commandant later in the month of June.

66 Sheridan, a neighbor and close friend of Duncan's in their hometown of St. Joseph, Missouri, had enlisted to be with his buddy and wound up in Duncan's company. Sheridan remained with the company and later, at Blanc Mont, after his leader was wounded, took command of his platoon, leading it until the brigade was relieved, seven days later. Two Silver Stars and a Croix de Guerre were his awards.

67 Between 1 and 19 June, Holcomb's 2/6 had the highest number of casualties of any battalion at Belleau Wood, 21 officers and 836 men, and yet they had never delivered a formal attack. Many, if not most, were caused by heavy gas attacks. From Thomason, *Second Division*, 260.

68 In his fine biography of "Jerry" Thomas, Allan R. Millett said "Perhaps stung by his own *shortcomings as a commander,* Harbord lashed out at the new commander of the 6th Marines, Lt. Col. Harry Lee, and demanded that the attack be renewed." [Emphasis added.]

69 Peter F. Owen, "Courage Amid the Chaos: The 79th Company of Marines, June 1918." *Over There! An Illustrated Journal of the First World War.* 6, no. 1 (Spring 1993), 9. and Robert B. Asprey, *At Belleau Wood,* 182.

70 L. H. Vandoren, *A Brief History of the 2nd Battalion, Sixth Regiment, etc.* (reprint, Pike, NH: The Brass Hat, 1994), 3, and Willard I. Morrey, *The History of the 96th Company, Sixth Regiment, in World War I* (Quantico: The U.S. Marine Corps, 1967), 51. Cates is frequently incorrectly credited with authorship.

71 Sellers, who was badly wounded, would return to take command of the 78th Company late in September, just in time for the debacle at Blanc Mont.

72 There seems to be no question that Sibley was adored by his men. The semiofficial history of 3/6 was dedicated to him. He was awarded the Navy Cross for his courage and devotion to his duty and his men. The citation "for exceptionally meritorious and distinguished service and unexcelled gallantry as battalion commander. . . . When all the officers of the 82d Company had been wounded he advanced with that company and displayed fine courage and dash throughout the action. He retired, officially, on 28 March 1941. That the war took its toll of Sibley is evident in reading a Holcomb response to a letter from Mrs. Sibley, which the commandant wrote in October 1939, telling her to advise her husband that he wouldn't be recalled, "that he did enough for the nation in the previous war." Gibson B. Smith, *Thomas Holcomb 1879–1965, Register of His Personal Papers* (Washington D.C.: History and Museums Division, Hdqs., USMC, 1988), 104.

73 Morrey, *96th Company, Sixth Regiment*, 51.

74 A Ford truck, driven by 2d Lt. Moore with an old hand, Sgt. Maj. John Quick, sitting in the passenger's seat, made the trip over the terrible path toward Bouresches under terrific German shelling and machine-gun barrages. They were a "team," the "college boy" and the long-serving Marine NCO who, incidentally, had been awarded the MoH for his bravery at Guantánamo Bay in 1898. Years later Moore testified to a friend that it was all a figment of Marine Corps publicity. Moore claims he made the trip, accompanied by a falling-down drunk Quick who wasn't even able to stay awake, let alone drive or help the twenty enlisted Marines, who did all the loading and unloading.

75 In 1942, Douglas MacArthur, after he was urged to recommend units in the Philippines for a Presidential Unit Citation, was questioned by President Roosevelt as to why he hadn't included the 4th Marines in his listing. He responded, "The Marines received enough credit during the last war."

76 Floyd Gibbons, *And They Thought We Wouldn't Fight*, 304. Later 1st Sgt. Daniel Daly insisted that what he really yelled was "For Christ sake, men—COME ON! Do you want to live forever?" No matter what Daly really said, everyone believes Gibbons's much better version.

What is less commonly known is that Daly, already with two MoH's, was awarded a DSC, and later a Navy Cross, and a few other trinkets, for various courageous acts while in France. He was in line for another MoH but it was downgraded to a DSC because, according to the story "no one should have three." In Jack Janual's fine article "Devil Dog Dan" in *Over There!* Vol. 8, No. 4, we are told that a young Marine replacement, upon being told that Daly was his First Sergeant responded "My God! Do you mean he's real? I thought he was somebody the Marines made up—like Paul Bunyan." Smedley D. Butler, no mean fighting man himself, has been quoted as saying that Daly was "the fightin'est Marine I ever knew."

77 Chaplain Brady was a "regular" who had enlisted in the U.S. Navy in 1914. Norstrand was promoted to 2d lieutenant and awarded a DSC and NC for rescuing the wounded the day before.

78 Crowther and Ashley were both killed in action. Kieren and Ferch were both wounded but returned to duty, Kieren within a month. Ferch was killed in action on 1 November 1918 at the Meuse-Argonne. Crowther, all by himself, took one machine gun and crew, then attempted another, at which time he met his maker.

79 *Records of the Second Division*, vol. 5. "Simons" was 2d Lt. Vernon L. Somers, who was killed in action as was 2d Lt. Walter D. Frazier, who had been killed in action the previous day, 5 June. Others wounded were Capt. Fred C. Eastin Jr., 1st Lt. Jonas Platt, who had only joined the 49th on 5 June, and 2d Lt. Murl Corbett. But the latter returned to the 49th on the 7th of June. Somers, Frazier, Platt, and Corbett were all awarded the DSC and NC.

80 *Records of the Second Division*, vol. 5.

81 Wise stated in his memoir, and in his battalion report for 2–18 June, *Records of the Second Division*, vol. 7, that the Brigade Order he received was 83. No record of that order exists in the official divisional records. My copy of *Northwest of Château-Thierry*, which belonged to Thomason's aide in the preparation of the semiofficial history of the division, 1st Lt. William R. Mathews, Intelligence Of-

ficer for 2/5, has on p. 149 a handwritten note signed by Mathews that states, emphatically, that he saw the order. "I held the flashlight while Col. Wise read it. *Harbord omits all reference to it in his brigade war diary. Why?*" Harbord answered Mathews's query, on the same page, in his own handwritten note, which clearly states that there was no number 83, that it was "Field Order #3 issued on June 9th referring to a third attack on Bois de Belleau. Field Order no. 4 was of June 10th." I believe that Harbord is correct.

82 Hamilton, *Echoes from Over There,* 70–71. On 8 June, Blanchfield died of his wounds.

83 It was definitely Conachy. Failure to recollect names after so many years is understandable.

84 *Records of the Second Division,* vol. 5.

85 Ulmer received a Silver Star. Timothy's citation tells us he was killed by a high explosive shell on 15 June 1918, but the semi-official unit history of the company, based upon Lt. Lucien H. Vandoren's writings, *A History of the 80th Company,* states he was killed on 8 June.

86 The personnel information was derived from *A History of the 80th Company.* . . . See above note. Information about enlisted Marines isn't as readily available as data about officers.

87 The Marine Corps formed replacement battalions at Quantico, which were sent to France and were retained and trained at St. Aignan, in the Loire valley. At the time of Belleau Wood, there were four replacement battalions in France. Shattered battalions, like 3/5 and 3/6, weren't withdrawn from active service, but received their replacements, some while still fighting the enemy. Many of the replacements were recent recruits, some with but two months in the Corps. Within a very few hours the replacements were nearly as good as the veterans they joined. Within days they were doing the same incredible things.

88 In a private meeting, Thomas told Asprey that Etheridge asked him, "For God sake, don't you know where we're supposed to go?" Thomas responded that he "had no idea. Major Hughes said you would know the way." Etheridge's reply was "Hell! I don't know anything about it."

89 Field Order No. 3 set as the objective "the southern edge of Bois de Belleau with X line at 261.7. Limits of Sector: Eastern: 176.5–261.0 to the Bouresches-Torcy road connecting with the Marines now holding Bouresches. Western: 175.6." The attack would begin at 0430, 10 June.

90 For some reason the Germans clearly didn't realize that the Americans had withdrawn from the southern edge of the woods, or if they knew they felt it impracticable to expose their men to artillery fire at the woods' edge needlessly. This fact would make Hughes's forthcoming attack much easier.

91 *Records of the Second Division,* vol. 5.

92 Ibid.

93 Cowing, *Dear Folks at Home———,* 192.

94 Gulberg, *A War Diary,* 27.

95 Thomason, *2d Division Northwest of Château-Thierry,* 150.

96 It is very difficult to understand how a capable officer of the experience and stature of Hughes could tell brigade what an easy experience 1/6 had "coming over," and why he didn't realize that he was nearly a half mile south of his objective. The history of the battalion and its leader, at this time, is quite strange.

97 Gulberg, *A War Diary,* 28.

98 Harbord, with nothing but Hughes's reports at hand, was still convinced that 1/6 was at 261.7.

99 *Records of the Second Division*, vol. 5. This mentions Wise's attack and emphasizes his attack on the left of Belleau Wood. This point becomes important later on.

100 *Records of the Second Division*, vol. 2.

101 I can find no report from Hughes in the official records that might have addressed why he didn't go to the "X-line." Asprey also noted the lack of a reply from Hughes, and added that with the faulty maps available, Hughes probably assumed he was on the X-line. Years later McClellan relates the incorrect report to Bundy at 2000 hours, which states that the "1st. Bn., 6th Marines . . . took the southern half of the Bois de Belleau . . . [to] 261.7 with liaison to Marines on right and left." McClellan should have known better.

102 Frederic M. Wise and Meigs O. Frost, *A Marine Tells It to You* (New York: J. H. Sears & Co., 1929), 214–215. Which statement, according to Wise, would have meant that Harbord knew of Hughes's failure. At this point in time all other records reviewed seem to prove otherwise.

103 Ibid., 215.

104 If Cooke remembers correctly, Wise was right, they were wrong. Thomason describes, based upon Mathews's notes, that the general plan was to drive through to the east edge of the woods, then turn north and roll up the Germans in the west face, and it was to be a frontal assault. It appears as though the attack was delivered much as Mathews said it was planned.

105 Probably the company captured by Capt. Alphonse De Carre and company. Thomason speculates on the missing "written order" but never comes to a conclusion about its location. He does relate a story regarding the French officer attached to 2/5 who was told by Wise that 2/5 wouldn't need any interpreters where they were going, and he might as well report to regimental headquarters. The Frenchman, in high dudgeon, told Wise he'd been with 2/5 since they arrived in France and he thought that this would be a strange time to be leaving it. He stayed and provided fine service.

106 The *War Diary, 4th Brigade, Second Battalion, 5th Regiment Report* says it was 2200 hours, 11 June, and was based upon Harbord's Field Order No. 4, and no different from what Harbord supposedly sent to Wise at 1745 hours. But the notes of Lt. William R. Mathews, IO, 2/5, state it was midnight, and that the barrage started at the same hour. His records concerning the artillery appear to be incorrect. Those of the 12th Artillery Regiment specify 0330 as the time the barrage really began. Who knows?

107 It appears that ten years after the fact Wise must have been suffering from severe memory loss. He has stated in his memoir that he did plan an encircling movement, which was somewhat contradicted by Harbord's Field Order No. 4, but Cooke remembers the company commanders decided against any fancy moves. He tells of the other order, which both Mathews and Cooke verified having seen. Wonder where that order is now? It is not a part of any of the *Records* that I can find, but Wise's own report for that date explicitly states that it was FO No. 4. In fairness, I've found other discrepancies in the official reports, including items deleted or changed, after the fact, by someone in the "works." Or was it simply the original order that showed up late, or as a duplicate of the first [?] or . . . ?

108 Wise, *A Marine Tells It,* 235. Explaining to Feland later, Wise told him "on the original attack the men got a great deal of punishment from the right. They naturally drifted toward it to take the machine guns in that sector."

109 *History of the Second Battalion, 5th Regiment of U.S. Marines,* 9.

110 Cowing, *Dear Folks at Home————,* 89–90. Marines of the time were anxious to add luster to their cause by including "Prussian Guards" in all their stories of Belleau Wood. There weren't many PGs facing them at that time.

111 This is a strange entry, unless Cooke was completely unaware that Wass and the 18th had moved to the 43d's left flank.

112 Cooke, *We Can Take It!,* 13. The officer was Macon Overton, who had replaced the "disgraced" Captain George A. Stowell in command of the 76th Company a few days earlier. There are many variations of this story. One told by Millett, op cit., pg. 40, was that Sgt. Jerry Thomas was ordered by Hughes to make sure Overton supported Wise's right. When Wise questioned where the 76th was, we are told that Overton was "indeed in action and successfully so. Under Overton's inspired and intelligent direction, the 76th had destroyed the last German positions around Hill 181 and opened Belleau Wood for Wise's battalion." Thomas indicated that Overton was "mildly amused" at Wise's concern and Thomas is quoted in Asprey as having heard Overton comment "I've done what I was supposed to do. If Wise had brought his outfit into the woods instead of deploying them out there in the wheatfield, he wouldn't have lost all those men." Thomas accepted Overton's contention that he had everything under control. Nevertheless, when needed, the 51st Company did not receive support on its right flank, otherwise the Germans behind them and on their right flank wouldn't have killed and wounded so many Marines. I believe Cooke's story. In the seventeen or so years after the fact he may have had an occasional lapse of memory, but as a professional U.S. Army officer he had no reason to misrepresent the situation for any possible gain. It appears that Overton blundered, and worse, if Thomas was correct, he was callous too.

113 Cooke calls him "Sgt. Brown," but most likely it was Pvt. Dilmus Brown that he was including in the story.

114 H. B. Field and H. G. James, *Over the Top with the 18th Company, 5th Regt., U.S. Marines, a History* (n.p., n.d., c. 1919), 19.

115 *Records of the Second Division,* vol. 4.

116 The official citation states that De Carre went ahead of his company, captured two machine guns and crews, and then went forward with his 60 Marines and captured the balance of the German machine-gun company, 3 officers and 169 men. Those Germans must have played havoc on the 43d and 18th Companies as they went through the wheat.

117 Of course this was all wrong. They were at the eastern edge, not the northern edge. This helped to create the illusion under which Wise was to suffer for a bad call. Later, in his memoir he completely changes the events to suit what he learned later. See Wise, op cit., p. 220–226.

118 Cooke was only close to the name. It was 2d Lt. R. H. Loughborough, USA (pronounced "Luffborro"), who would assume command of the 51st since he was the only officer of the company still on his feet. He earned three Silver Star citations and a Croix de Guerre at Belleau Wood.

119 Cooke, *We Can Take It!*, 15.

120 Assuming that Wise still believed himself to be on the north face of the woods, rather than east, those coordinates would have placed the fire to his right flank outside the woods; southwest of Bouresches.

121 Williams, of the famous retort "Retreat, Hell, etc." died of his wounds that same day. See George B. Clark, *Retreat, Hell. We Just Got Here!* (Pike,NH: The Brass Hat, 1989).

122 Clark, op. cit., 14–15. We have to assume that this was before the 55th Company came into the woods between the 43d and the 51st. Incidentally, Dunbeck went from gunnery sergeant on 4 June 1917 to marine gunner on 5 June 1917, to second lieutenant on 14 June, first lieutenant on 15 June, and captain on 16 June 1917. Those were days of rapid promotions. From his son-in-law, Colonel R. D. Cail, USMC (ret).

123 For some reason, possibly because the Germans were also in a state of turmoil during their unit relief, they never took full advantage of the open ground between 2/5 and 1/6.

124 *Records of the Second Division,* vol. 6.

125 *Records of the Second Division,* vol. 4.

126 What this means, it appears, is that the officers of 2/5 were well aware, at this point in time, of what they were looking at. If they truly believed that they were at the north end, the Germans would have been on the Torcy-Lucy road, which area they couldn't possibly have seen from their location. Yet Wass used "Bouresches-Belleau," and his last few words specify *"the northwest along our front"*—which, for the road mentioned, is all wrong anyway. Very strange indeed. Perhaps someone tinkered with the message? Or no one gave an in-depth look at it before sending or after receiving.

127 *Records of the Second Division,* vol. 5.

128 William R. Mathews, *Official Report to Headquarters, U.S.M.C.* Incidentally, Mathews spelled the name wrong. It was Wodarezyk.

129 Neville only occasionally shows up in the official records during the month, and he's always back at the regimental headquarters when he does. His assistant, Feland, was all over the place, making decisions, scouting the front, and other things one would expect from the CO of a regiment.

130 Wise, *A Marine Tells It to You,* 221.

131 Ibid.

132 Ibid., 220–222. The dead man, Lt. Robert S. Heizer, USA, was from Osage City, Kansas.

133 Ibid,. 223–224.

134 Mathews in a personal letter, as reported in Asprey, op. cit., 255. According to Thomason, op. cit., pg. 160 note 3, Mathews reported, in his notes, that by noon Wise was aware that his flank was in the air. Mathews must have provoked Wise beyond repair, because he was soon after relieved as IO and returned to his company as a platoon commander, which office he performed equally well.

135 In his memoir, Wise referred to the confusion among the survivors of his battalion at about this time, as to their location. He added, "If you turned around twice you lost all sense of direction and *only your compass could straighten*

you out. " [Emphasis added.] If he had a compass, how come the confusion? He also admitted that he finally realized that 2/5 didn't hold the left flank: "Their presence put me in a devil of a fix. . . . I reported to Col. Neville that those woods were cleaned out . . . and [he] had reported that back to Brigade." Op. cit., 223. Wise now knew that the fat was in the fire.

136 Poe was the nephew of the great author and father of a friend of mine of forty years ago in Baltimore, Maryland.

137 Cooke explains that he left Poe in charge and went back to Wise to ask for help with this "new war." According to him Wise refused, telling him it was his job to force the Germans to surrender. Cooke, *We Can Take It!,* 15.

138 Cowing, *Dear Folks at Home———,* 191.

139 *Records of the Second Division,* vol. 6. Laurence Stallings, *The Doughboys,* (New York: Harpers, 1963), 100, sh ɔw Fox Conner, Pershing's G-3, as not being in agreement with the condition of the 4th Brigade. He is quoted as saying, "Do not insist on relief. The reports we have show that conditions are not very bad." Conner was back at Chaumont, many miles from the sector, and I'm sure eating and sleeping very well.

140 Wass got the DSC and NC both for this action and for his later courage at Soissons, where he was KiA. An amusing entry in Wise's memoir tells how he was concerned with Milner, a minister's son: Was he strong enough to lead men? Wise concluded that he was that and more.

141 Cooke was down, temporarily, but certainly not out; not yet anyway. A few days before, Bonner had done the same for Blanchfield.

142 Field, *Over the Top,* 20.

143 *Records of the Second Division,* vol. 5.

144 *Records of the Second Division,* vol. 4. Malone was writing about the unfortunate and ill-timed statement that the wood had been taken.

145 Ibid.

146 Cooke, *We Can Take It!* 17.

147 Thomason, *2d Division Northwest of Château-Thierry,* 173–174.

148 Both messages, *Records of the Second Division,* vol. 5. Wass was wrong. They were to the west, not the northeast.

149 Ibid.

150 Ibid.

151 Cooke, op. cit., 20.

152 Ibid.

153 For a description of what transpired during this relief, see Hughes's memo to Lee on the following day.

154 On 9 June Harbord had ordered Shearer to send one company to support the 6th Marines. The 20th was selected and forthwith assembled in the wood southeast of Lucy that night. Since that date they had continued as a reserve unit for the 6th Marines.

155 *Records of the Second Division,* vol. 6. Entry for 13 June 1918.

156 Fourth Brigade headquarters was still convinced the Marines held the northern end of Belleau Wood.

157 Thomason, *2d Division Northwest of Château-Thierry* based upon several reports, from Winans and Blake to 2d Div. Hist. Section File, p. 186–187.

158 *Records of the Second Division*, vol. 5. I haven't been able to find anything from Shearer, then or after, that would indicate that he actually sent that message. Although it is possible that he was the unnamed recipient mentioned in later messages. See following. Captain David T. Jackson was adjutant of 3/5.

159 *Records of the Second Division*, vol. 4.

160 Ibid. The officer was Captain Conachy.

161 See what happened to David Jackson at Blanc Mont on 4 October.

162 *Records of the Second Division*, vol. 4.

163 *Records of the Second Division*, vol. 5.

164 *Records of the Second Division*, vol. 5. After reading the memo one can easily read into it almost any scenario. Were Wise and Hughes "getting even" at the expense of their battalions? Or did they, under the strain of active combat, misunderstand what the other was saying and doing? Editorial comment: How childish can grown men get?

165 *Records of the Second Division*, vol. 5.

166 Wise, *A Marine Tells It to You*, 235.

167 Mentioned in Sellers's memoir.

168 *Records of the Second Division*, vol. 5.

169 Wise, op. cit., 231.

170 *Records of the Second Division*, vol. 5. Wise complained about his map. That may have contributed to everyone's problems in the original attack.

171 Ibid.

172 Ibid. Probably referring to Holcomb's battalion.

173 Ibid.

174 Ibid.

175 Ibid.

176 *Records of the Second Division*, vol. 4.

177 *Records of the Second Division*, vol. 5.

178 Severe gas poisoning would ultimately end Hughes's Marine career. Just after the war he would be disabled out of the Corps and join his father in the export-import business in New York City. He and that company would become directly involved in the machinations of "Pete" Ellis during the early 1920s.

179 E. N. McClellan, Capture of Hill 142, Battle of Belleau Wood, and Capture of Bouresches. *Marine Corps Gazette* (September–December, 1920).

180 *Records of the Second Division*, vol. 5.

181 *Records of the Second Division*, vol. 4.

182 *Records of the Second Division*, vol. 5. Neither of the two names used by Sibley can be identified absolutely. Possibly both were runners.

183 Ibid. Quigley was a "troubleshooter." He was also, apparently, one of the officers who were nearly court-martialed in May 1918 because of involvement with the cabal that resulted over the appointment of Harbord to replace Doyen.

184 Wise, *A Marine Tells It to You*, 237–238.

185 Cooke, op. cit., 20.

186 *Records of the Second Division*, vol. 5.

187 Wise, *A Marine Tells It to You*, 240–241. The author has a copy of the memoir that is inscribed to someone named "Willie Moreno, a friend of my youth, who came to the front & wore a brand after I had cussed a general out. Fred-

erick May Wise. 1931." Wise was correct when he said his goose was cooked. He was relieved on 23 June 1918, ostensibly to attend the School of the Line at Langres. He would be back right after Soissons but lost his battalion shortly after he returned when he was promoted to full colonel. He was then assigned to the successful command of the 59th Infantry and then the 8th Brigade, both of the 4th Division.

188 There is a bit of confusion concerning the date shown for this attack by 1/7. Lieutenant Colonel Adams and Major Gaston of 3/7 both give the date as the 19th. Second Division records show the 20th.

189 *Records of the Second Division*, vol. 6.

190 *Records of the Second Division*, vol. 5.

191 Ibid. Harbord apparently expected an ill-trained battalion, with limited resources, to be successful where three blooded Marine battalions had failed. In Adams, though, he found a feisty individual who told him off in no uncertain terms. Adams only asked for items to fight the battle with and they were not forthcoming any more than they had been for the Marines before him.

192 Thomason, *2d Division Northwest of Château-Thierry*, 201, explains that 1/7 was supported by the 12th and 17th Artillery Regiments but according to their own records they show nothing for Belleau Wood that night at all; and nothing much beyond harassing fire elsewhere.

193 Laurence Stallings, *The Doughboys*, 103.

194 *Records of the Second Division*, vol. 6.

195 E. N. McClellan, The Battle of Belleau Wood, *Marine Corps Gazette*, 5 (December 1920), 378.

196 *Records of the Second Division*, vol. 5.

196A *Records of the Second Division*, vol. 7.

197 Ibid.

198 Ibid.

199 *Records of the Second Division*, vol. 5.

200 Ibid.

201 Page was the nephew of Walter Hines Page, the ambassador to Great Britain who was very instrumental in getting the United States into the war.

202 *Records of the Second Division*, vol. 5.

203 Ibid.

204 Ibid.

205 *Records of the Second Division*, vol. 6. Thomason, *2d Division Northwest of Château-Thierry*, 214. Asprey, *At Belleau Wood*, 306. Private Henry P. Lenert [aka Leonard] received a Silver Star and Croix de Guerre. Lenert was better on the firing line than in the rear. Later he went to Paris and was charged with being AWOL while with the famous parade detachment. But he remained in the combat ranks until after 11 November 1918, when subsequently, he was tried for his indiscretion.

206 Cowing, *Dear Folks at Home*——— 227–228.

207 The author heard about that day, many years later, when a favorite uncle, a sergeant in the 103d Machine Gun Battalion, asked why the Marines jeered at them when they came in to relieve them. He mentioned catcalls such as "Don't call us back when you lose this ground, like you did before," etc.

When he heard what the 7th hadn't done, the wonderment ceased and he laughed, finally realizing after thirty years what had happened to him and his buddies and why.

208 The story told is that no one from the 4th Brigade, including Harbord, was invited to attend the affair. Perhaps some staff officer worried about what Marines might say to the old fellow.

209 *Marine Corps Gazette,* op. cit., 399.

5: Soissons

We really took a shellacking.
—Sgt. Gerald Thomas, 75th Company

The entire affair known collectively as "Belleau Wood" had been finally brought to a close. On the 10th of July the U.S. 26th "YD" division officially relieved the 2d Division. After losses of nearly 10,000 Americans, the fighting men of the division were finally going to get some long-needed rest. Effective the 4th of July, the 2d Division had been returned to the control of the AEF and had been incorporated into the I Army Corps under Maj. Gen. Hunter Liggett. That corps, which had been created in January, 1918, included the 1st, 2d, 26th, and 42d Divisions.

On 15 July, the Germans launched their final attack of the war. It ranged from the Argonne to the Marne, and five U.S. divisions were affected. The 42d was located farthest east around Suippes in the Champagne; and the 3d about twenty-five miles farther west, near Château-Thierry and south of the Marne. The 28th was in the process of moving up in support and the 26th was northwest of the Château-Thierry area. The 4th Division was a bit north of the 26th and split into two parts. When the Germans hit the lines, each served the cause extremely well, but the major honors had to go to the 3d Division for the defense of the river line, with special mention for its 38th Infantry, forever after known as "The Rock of the Marne."

Coincidentally, Marshal Foch, the French general who had been selected to "unite" the Allied and American armies, had developed a plan for an attack to begin on 18 July, just three days later. Several American divisions would be required for him to have the barest chance of success. Most of those mentioned previously were already part of the French 6th Army, formed about the Château-Thierry Sector. But he needed more for Mangin's 10th Army in the Soissons area.

Those selected for Mangin were the 1st and 2d Divisions. Neither was close to Soissons, the assigned attack zone. As we know, the 2d was down

222

near the Marne River, resting up a bit from their month-long exertions. The 1st was in the Froissy-Beauvais region. They and the 2d had already become the basis for a newly formed III U.S. Corps, which was to be commanded by Maj. Gen. Robert Lee Bullard, one of the stars of the AEF. In a memo to his corps he advised them of the singular honor that had been bestowed upon them at having the 1st Moroccan Division as their companions in the big fight looming ahead.[1] The North Africans' reputation was well deserved. The Germans hated them. Hated especially their very long and very disabling sharp knives with which they disemboweled the Krauts. Part of the division was composed mainly of Moslems. Their religious philosophy was that to kill a nonbeliever would get you into heaven. They were extremely religious and most probably all went to heaven.

Foch's plan was for the 10th Army to rupture the enemy lines between the Aisne and the Ourcq rivers, pushing forward in the direction of Père-en-Tardenois, which lay approximately fifteen miles southeast of Soissons. The French 6th Army's left wing would conform with this advance. If successfully completed, this would punch a strong salient into the enemy lines, forcing him to pull way back in order to avoid a disaster along the Marne. The two American divisions selected, plus the 1st Moroccan, were formed into XX French Corps under General Berdoulat. A feeble attempt was made by Pershing to keep the American divisions separate and under Bullard's command, but time wouldn't allow for that to happen.[2] As additional support, both American divisions would each have one French 75mm regiment and French tanks.

Since the relief of the Marine Brigade at Belleau Wood, Lt. Col. Harry Lee had been the officer in command. Neville, the senior Marine officer, was absent, having been evacuated to a base hospital at the time of the relief. Harbord, having received notice of his promotion to major general on 11 July, had taken five days leave. Both officers would return in time to participate in the next offensive, with Harbord now in command of the division and Brig. Gen. Neville the brigade. Other senior Marine officers during the period included Logan Feland, now commanding the 5th Regiment, and Harry Lee the 6th. With one exception, there was no change in the battalion commanders of either regiment.[3]

Meanwhile, the 2d Division, still in relatively safe quarters, had a declared holiday on Sunday, 14 July, the famous Bastille Day.[4] The 4th Brigade was quartered between Montreuil-aux-Lions and the Marne River, mainly about the town of Crouttes. The 3d Brigade was north of the town with the balance of the division scattered about in the same area. That night all the troops were disturbed by the shelling of long range German guns, caused by the all-out German attack mentioned previously. On 16 July the 2d Division headquarters received Field Order No. 8, issued at 0830 by I Corps. The order partly read:

1. The 2d Division stands relieved from duty with the First Corps, July 16, 1918, movements to be executed in accordance with instructions already communicated from the VIth Army. Infantry of 2d Division will embuss beginning at 4 P.M. Point of embussment to be notified later. First destination MARCILLY where officer of Tenth Army will give final destination.

Following instructions within 2d Division Field Order No. 14, same date, the infantry were directed to mount up at 1600 hours that day. Thomason tells us that lunch was an hour early and consisted of beans. "Boys, we're going somewhere. We always get beans to make a hike on. . . . What's that sergeant yellin' about—fill your canteens? Gonna get ving blonk in mine!" Others added their wisdom to the collective knowledge. "Camions! They rode us to Chatto-Terry in them buses—" "Yeah! an' it was a one-way trip for a hell of a lot of us too!"

Other plans were designed for the machine guns and motorized units. That evening the 4th Brigade infantry moved in camions from Nanteuil-sur-Marne northward toward Soissons. They arrived the next morning and afternoon of 17 July in and around the Forest of Retz. Brigade headquarters was established at Vivières, a village about three miles north of Villers-Cotterêts. The 6th Machine Gun Battalion arrived the next morning at about 0300, but without their guns. The ride was, as usual and as expected, painfully uncomfortable. No one could ever sleep in a camion. They were designed with no springs and, as Thomason said, to find every hole in every road they traveled upon. This trip was no different.

Harbord later complained in his book *Leaves from a War Diary* that control of the division had been effectively taken completely away from him. Part of his criticism was that the 2d was moved without his agreement, without his observation, and without his input.

I complained of the utter confused and unregulated condition of traffic on the one forest highway as tending to make the arrival uncertain. The answer to that was more shrugs and the statement that it was the affair of the Army [10th] to arrange that.[5]

Wednesday, 17 July

The 5th Regiment's history[6] briefly describes the movement of the regiment, by battalions. With Maj. Ralph Keyser now commanding,[7] 2/5 embused at Crouttes at 1900 on 16 July and arrived at Brassaire at 1100 on 17 July and debused. The other two battalions left several hours later and all wound up in the Fôret de Retz near Keyser's positions. The members of the 8th Machine Gun Company mounted their camions at midnight and arrived the following afternoon at 1300, disembarking at Retheuil. Their guns and carts were shipped with the regimental train, commanded by Maj. Bennett Puryear Jr. They wouldn't be able to offer any support on the morrow because their guns didn't show up in time.

The 6th Regiment's history[8] is unusually brief insofar as Soissons is concerned. The only definite statement made is that the regiment, after arrival and debusing at Brassaire, hiked to positions in the Villers-Cotterêts forest.[9] Hardly any mention of 17 July other than the fact that they had a twenty-kilometer march "in a heavy rainstorm, over crowded roads, [and] finally went into bivouac in the Bois de Retz." The regiment was selected as corps reserve. But their time for glory would come.

Positions of the three divisions selected to launch the attack were as follows: the 1st Division, USA, to the left/north; the very capable and well-used-up French 1st Moroccan Division in the middle; and finally the fighting 2d Division on the south.[10] Undoubtedly, for a successful breakup of the major salient the Germans had thrust into the French lines, these three were the finest divisions available to Foch. The 2d would have a division from the French XXX Army Corps as its right flank. The French general Mangin, a successful fighter of great reputation, commanded the 10th Army of which the three divisions were a part. If anyone could make a success of this operation, Mangin was the man.

Thursday, 18 July

At five minutes after midnight Logan Feland received a message from Col. Preston Brown, the division chief of staff, in which he was directed to "march with all possible speed to your attacking position—send an officer to report your status." The 5th Marines, by obeying that order, suffered extreme agony getting to their appointed positions. All manner of excuses or conjecture have been summoned up to explain why the notice of movement forward was so very late. Simple truth is that Foch intended to keep his attack a surprise and the lack of movement seen would help greatly. What price the troops had to pay for that surprise was terrible, but evidently not important. The night of 17/18 July was an almost indescribable horror for the various regiments that had to march through the Fôrest de Retz to their jump-off point and in a rain that may have been best described as a continuous cloudburst. According to the semiofficial history of the 5th Marines,

the men were exhausted at the outset [from their camion ride]. The night was pitch dark and the pouring rain made the road bed a mass of slippery clay. But the greatest difficulty of all was due to the fact that the highway was filled with and indescribable [?] of infantry, cavalry, tanks and wagons of all descriptions. These continually cut through our ranks and so dark was the night that when once the single file of men on each side of the road was broken, it was only with the greatest difficulty and the best good fortune that the line joined again and moved forward. Each man held on to the coat tail of the man in front and with grim determination pushed forward eight kilometers to the jump off line. No sooner had the designated position been reached that our barrage started and the companies had to deploy at once without being given the opportunity to rest.[11]

De Chambrun, a French colonel, notes the difficulties in his history:

On the torn-up roadway three files of wagons, caissons, ammunition trucks, lorries, and tanks moved slowly and heavily forward. The American infantrymen [Marines] in their yellowish tunics, *much darker in color when the troops belonged to the marine brigade*, clambered in Indian file along the embanked ditches which border the roadway or pushed through the undergrowth of the adjacent forest.[12] [Emphasis added.]

The entire 5th Regiment was in trouble. The events noted were just the beginning of their torment. No machine guns were available because the guns didn't arrive until late that afternoon. There being no time or opportunity to supply the individual Marine with auxiliary weapons, the attack was to be made with only the rifle, bayonet, and Chauchat. Divisional order of battle called for three regiments to attack, with the 6th Marines, 2d Engineers, and 4th Machine Gun Battalion as Corps reserve. The 5th Marines constituted the left flank boundary of the division, with the Moroccans on their left. The 9th Infantry was to

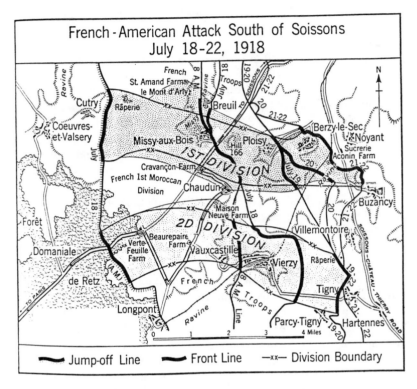

Map 8: A general map of the area over which two American divisions, the 1st in the north and 2d in the south, with the French 1st Moroccan Division between them, launched a major assault on the enemy, one which has been acclaimed to be the turning point of the war. The important city of Soissons lies just north of this map. Note how much farther the 2d Division advanced on the first day than did all other troops.

be in the center and the 23d Infantry, the right flank. The 6th Marines were a mile and a half behind, following the front lines.[13]

Warren Jackson tells about the reaction of those men of the 6th Marines, who were not in the attacking wave but in support. They were rudely awakened out of a sound sleep by the volumes of noise emitted by the artillery bombardment. But the 6th had an opportunity to savor something different from the usual. Usually they had "asbestos-flavored

French bread." This morning they had fresh "American bread and molasses." What a treat that must have been.

The 1st and 2d Battalions of the 5th were selected to lead, with 3/5 to remain in support. The position of each company of 1/5 was: left to right, 49th Company (Hamilton), 17th Company (LeRoy Hunt), 66th Company (William La. Crabbe), with the 67th (Frank Whitehead) in support. The companies of 2/5 were left to right: 55th (Cooke), liaison with the 66th, 43d (Joseph D. Murray), 18th (Wass), and the 51st (William O. Corbin) as liaison with the 9th Infantry. The 5th Marines were aided by a group of approximately thirty, some say fifty-four, French, *St.-Chamond* heavy tanks.

First Lt. Elliott D. Cooke, USA, commanding the 55th Company, tells of his difficulty in seeing the one map that the battalion adjutant, Legendre, had carried from French headquarters. Keyser, the battalion commander, gathered his officers in a circle on the ground and described what each company was to do. Lastly he said, "The Fifty-fifth Company will maintain contact with the First Battalion." Keyser also said, "One officer and twenty men from each company will be left behind." Cooke then asked, "I only have a hundred sixty men now, Major. Why leave any behind?" The answer curdled his blood. "They will be needed as a nucleus to build new companies on, after the attack." Keyser, Cooke noted, didn't look up from the map when he answered the question. Probably he was too distressed to let his juniors know what he expected was coming. "Well, I got what I asked for and I wished I'd kept my mouth shut. So did everybody else."[14]

In order to arrive at their jump-off point on time, the 5th Marines were forced to double-time for a considerable distance. Consequently, even those not already exhausted from sleep deprivation and near starvation, barely made it. The French guides who were supposed to lead in the advancing battalions, weren't at their designated posts when 1/5 and 2/5 arrived. Those for 1/5 never showed up. Only enough guides showed up for two companies in 2/5, the 43d and 55th and according to the official histories, they led those companies far to the north, placing them in a position north of the Paris-Maubeuge Highway. Somehow, the 43d discovered the error in time and managed to relocate themselves to almost cover their designated sector. Though lost during the move to the jump-off line, the 55th finally managed to get together with 2/5 before they were even missed, according to Cooke. Other records say otherwise. There is no question but that Cooke and his lads were up to their hip boots in Heinies all day, but mostly they were in Moroccan territory while so engaged.[15]

In a questionable history entitled "A Short Account of the 2d Division in the Great War, 1917–19" the time given for the attack was 0435 and only the 9th Infantry was in position. According to it the 23d Infantry also had to double-time in order to reach the jump-off point, arriving at exactly 0430 when the rolling barrage began. The 1st and 2d Battalions, 5th Marines, came up on the run and continued, without stopping, going from column into attack formation.[16] Confusion reigned.

Elton E. Mackin[17] describes the beginning of 1/5's ordeal and what followed that morning of 18 July. He was by now a battalion runner and with Major Turrill most of the time. Turrill explained to his officers that "we are in two waves: 67th and 49th will lead.[18] A barrage will lay for five minutes on Heinie's firing line, then roll on to the first objective. Tell the captains to follow the barrage." Certain runners were directed to go forward with the attack and to report back to him when the "companies have cleared the woods."

Keyser's 2/5 wasn't having it any easier moving toward the attack positions than was 1/5. Cooke mentioned that his company was last in line. The group they were following, possibly the 51st, stopped the line. One Marine was putting on his leggings and the entire line had stopped behind him until he was finished. By the time Cooke and the 55th were on the move again they were distracted by the new skipper of the 51st, Capt. William Corbin, Williams's replacement.[19] Corbin just had his men sit by the side of the road while Murray and Wass continued somewhere up ahead. In the darkness Cooke couldn't tell where they had gone. Since he hadn't heard all of Keyser's instructions, or gotten a look at the map, he was quickly getting into trouble. His major concern was to be to the right of Crabbe's 66th Company of 1/5 and to the left of Murray. After catching up with Keyser, he explained his problem to him; Keyser then provided a French soldier to guide them forward to find the two officers. Cooke knew he had to be where they were when the attack started, so he started to run. He and his runner ran forward while his company followed. All the while the Frenchman protested, "*Mon Dieu,* the front line, she is approached with caution! *N'est-ce pas?*"

Then the big bang exploded. The 10th Army's artillery opened up and all hell seemed to break loose. Cooke's company followed as rapidly as possible and soon, to everyone's great surprise, they found themselves swarming over the Heinies' front lines. After exchanging some grenade tosses and rifle fire, the Germans realized what a predicament they were in. *Kamerad!* was their common reaction. They were anxious to surrender and get to the rear out of range of everything. So much so that when they were told off under guard they began running for cover. The Marines sent to propel them back for collection were forced to fire over their heads in order to make them slow down.

The firing started at 0435[20] and "the world went mad in a smashing burst of sound." In the midst of utter confusion, the attack began in the forest where many Germans still resided. The trees were quickly being torn to pieces by the great volume of gunfire blasting it. Many heavy branches fell to earth, taking men's lives as surely as though they had received a round in their bodies. Every two minutes the artillery gunfire kept to a steady, rolling, increase of one hundred meters in advance of the troops. The Marines and doughboys went forward, as did the French tanks. German soldiers were trying to crawl out of their holes in which they had crouched to make the semblance of a stand against the storm of Americans, or more often to surrender. Though *Kamerad!* was routine, a few Germans tried to make a fight of it. Most died while so doing. Many trees had Boche snipers with light machine guns. Soon the Americans were firing into practically every clump of leaves overhead. Many rounds were wasted but so were many snipers. Private Albert A. Taulbert* raced far out ahead of his company, the 66th, into the hail of lead coming from the many Maxims and quickly captured one really troublesome gun and its crew, thereby saving many of his comrades.[21] The Boche machine guns did wicked work, as always, but they, too, soon fell silent as the Marines and their bayonets reached them. Some took prisoners back, but not all were able to satisfactorily complete their task. Thomason tells about a lieutenant, obviously himself, who directed a freckled-faced Marine to take prisoners back to the rear but had to warn him when it was obvious that the Marine wanted to use his bayonet on them, "No! No! Take 'em back. They've quit. Take 'em to the rear, I tell you!" Not long afterward the freckle-faced one, with red stains on his bayonet, came back with a "them damn Heinies tried to run, and I jest natcherly shot 'em up a few." The lieutenant didn't believe him but then, what could he do?

Sergeant Louis Cukela of the 66th also raced out into the woods, showing unusual heroism, resourcefulness, and utter disregard for his own personal danger, as his Medal of Honor citation stated. He charged, single-handed, an enemy strong point that was holding up his company. He came in from the rear, using his bayonet, and must have surprised the Heinies no end as they were being killed by this seeming madman. Then, with no sense of propriety, he used their potato-mashers to eliminate the rest of the occupants. During this moment of glory, Cukela took four prisoners and two undamaged Maxims which were, as soon as practical, turned upon their former masters. Louie Cukela was promoted to second lieutenant for his outstanding action and leadership example. While Cukela was so engaged, a fellow countryman, of the "old" country, that is—Sgt. Matej Kocak, duplicated his compatriot's feat by also capturing a nest and crew with his bayonet and grenades. He too, was made a recipient of the Medal of Honor and several other decorations for his trouble.[22]

McClellan's article about the battle attests "the battalion's advance was, however, unimpeded, and at sun-up the unit had reached the edge of the forest, while the enemy scurried over the sky-line, leaving in his wake only machine gun nests which held out in considerable numbers to the last." Unimpeded? Who sez?

With the forest mostly cleared of Germans, some of the leading Marine units rested while their buddies took up the quest. With the tanks leading,[23] Marines chased the fleeing Germans across the mildly rolling fields covered in full-grown wheat. Meanwhile, French cavalry waited in the rear so as to be able to effect a German rout when, and if, the time ever came for them to charge forward. The ground was well broken, the wheat fields too dense, and the German machine guns too wildly scattered about for the cavalry to ever come forward. As usual in the war, cavalrymen could just dream about that fantastic last charge to glory.

Both the Translon and Verte Feuille Farms were soon taken, but since the Moroccans had not kept pace the 5th Marines took horrendous flanking German machine-gun fire. Translon Farm was just within the 2d Division's boundary but already the Marines were edging beyond in that direction. That gap between the two divisions forced some of the Marines to bear too far to the left and soon they were advancing almost entirely in the Moroccans' sector. The Marines were trying to knock out that element of the enemy which was doing so much damage. This caused some additional difficulties for the 17th Company, which "finding its left flank exposed, *boldly swerved to the left*," going far north and out of its own sector. This would have a major impact upon the entire affair, as you will see in the following.

The 23d Infantry had the shortest route to the jump-off line: as a result they were on their first objective at 0450. The 9th, with a longer distance to go and with their left flank in the air, the 5th Marines not being up yet, advanced a half mile to near the Verte Feuille Farm, where they began taking enemy fire. By that point the 9th was already out of their bounds. Some of 2/5 came up and both regiments put the kibosh on those Krauts holding the farm. The actual seizure was accomplished by the 18th and 43d Companies. Near this point in place and time, both the 5th and the 9th had "an awkward change of direction to make." It was planned for them to make a partial right turn. The 5th Marines had a large front to cover and as 1/5 moved forward and spread in a northward direction, it became even larger. This change was to create extensive problems for both regiments, the 9th and 5th.

Corbin's 51st Company was last to reach its post and had some difficulty making contact with the 9th Infantry, which was moving forward quite rapidly. Nevertheless, the 51st had Pvt. James H. Roberts*, who more than made up for the company's delay in getting into action. Armed with a Chauchat, Roberts crawled through a barbed wire entanglement and disabled one machine gun with a hand grenade and forced the crew of a second gun to surrender. This action made his company's advance nearly casualty free.[24]

Back where the 51st was sitting by the roadside, the 55th, as the division history states, "diverged to the north." As the 5th Marines came past the Translon Farm, instead of taking a turn toward the right they continued straight forward for some considerable distance, taking them well into the Moroccans' territory.

The Moroccans had the responsibility to take the Bois du Quesnoy, just outside the 5th Marines' northern boundary. They planned a flank movement against it, but they were slower than the Americans. That resulted in the Germans' still firing on the flanks of the 5th Marines. Responding to this fire, the 55th Company, which was way out of sync with where it was supposed to be, attacked them in a northerly direction. After that, never changing direction, they remained in the Moroccans' sector most of the day.

But the Marines weren't the only ones going wrong. At the point where the division's boundaries made a gradual turn and, shortly afterward, a sharp turn southward, some units followed one turn, and some didn't. Those who didn't, continued onward and partially covered the Moroccans' zone for some distance. In fact, elements of the 1st Battalion, 9th Infantry, also continued in the same direction. It wasn't very long afterward that the units became entangled, with each other, Marines and soldiers. Captain Charles E. Speer*, leading 1/9,[25] continued onward northeast and came upon Maison Neuve Farm, which they took with the assistance of Cooke's 55th Company.[26] The lucky Moroccan Division had some of the best American infantrymen fighting their battle for them. It was a good thing, because the Moroccans were having a difficult time keeping apace with the Americans anyway.

Back within the division boundaries, the first wave advanced at least two and one-half miles in the first two hours and was well out of the cover of the woods by then. Fifteen minutes later the 75s were moving forward and by 1010 the 2d Battalion, 15th Field Artillery, was in advanced positions east of Verte Feuille Farm, which lay a half mile east of the division's jump-off point. The 3d Brigade was moving as rapidly as the 4th. Both colonels, Malone of the 23d and Upton of the 9th Infantry, were soon calling for water, food, and ammunition for their "Tigers." As always, the infantry of the 3d Brigade was maintaining its reputation as a worthy match for the 4th Brigade. At Soissons, the 3d Brigade would suffer more casualties than would the 4th Brigade. The same thing happened at St. Mihiel. (What a way to earn a reputation.)

By 0900 Turrill's Battalion post of command was established about a half mile north and east of Translon Farm on the division boundary with the Moroccans. Twenty minutes later, Turrill tells us in his official report, he moved his PC to the right and forward to where he met the national Paris-Maubeuge road. He had sustained sufficient losses by 0800 to move the 67th Company on line in order to close a gap that had developed between 1/5 and 2/5. The 17th was still far to the north. At this point two companies from 3/5, the 16th (Yowell) and 20th (Richard Platt), came up to the 1/5 PC to be utilized as support.

The organizational arrangement of 1/5's companies was by now quite convoluted. The battalion was supported by two companies from 3/5 and a portion of the 49th. The balance of the 49th was still maintaining liaison with the Moroccans, who had finally made it up to where the Marines were located. Another DSC man from back at Belleau Wood, 2d Lt. Murl Corbett of the 49th, commanded the platoon assigned to maintain liaison with the Senegalese. He soon found them and they stayed together that day. One of his men, Sergeant Joe Carter*, somehow got separated from the 49th and shortly after was following a tank with two soldiers from the Moroccan Division. In spite of intense enemy fire he and the two French soldiers, captured sixty-three Germans, including one officer. Another notable 49th Company First Lieutenant was John W. Thomason Jr.*, who, with his company "gunny" and six additional men, went out and destroyed a machine-gun nest that had been impeding the advance of the 49th. They killed thirteen Boche and captured two guns. He was also a victim that day, receiving, instead of sending, lead. But he would survive that as well as several future bloodbaths during this war.

The balance of 1/5 had pushed ahead with 2/5 on its right. Resistance increased as the Marines went forward and ordinary liaison between their own units became more difficult to maintain. Shortly after the advance resumed, Capt. Joseph Murray was wounded. His company joined the 18th and passed under the command of Capt. Lester Wass. Most of the other officers of the 43d were also down. Gunnery Sergeant Herman "Babe" Tharau* of the 55th, whom we've already met at Les Mares Farm, went out ahead, reconnoitering with some members of his company to establish liaison with the company on his right. Then he found a machine gun and captured same while killing its crew. That Buffalo, New York, native didn't last out the war. He was killed in action in the relatively soft Marbache Sector in August.

Meanwhile, the Germans were attempting to pull together some of their forces in the area. They had been completely surprised by the attack. Unfortunately for them, their reserves from front-line divisions were unable to stem the tide or even to establish a line. The 219th German Infantry made a brief, vain attempt to stop the Americans at Beaurepaire Farm, but like their artillery, they, too, were quickly overwhelmed. Beaurepaire was the "First Intermediate Objective" of the division and was now bypassed. The German commander, General von Watter, had better success when he pulled together reserves and formed a line from southeast of Chaudun through Vierzy. Artillery was rushed forward and their effort succeeded. The enemy finally was able to stop the Marines and infantry of the 2d Division. The 1/5 semiofficial history states that

> Enemy aeroplanes rendered the advance from this point on, a considerable problem. Sweeping low over our lines, the Hun aviators operated their machine guns upon the infantry with considerable effect.[27]

Keyser, in a later report, told regiment what had happened to 2/5. He indicated that what he was writing was based upon reports from the company lieutenants, not the skippers, since all of them except Corbin were down. He wrote that Corbin and the 51st were the only company that did not reach the first objective. He explained about Cooke and his company—where they had split, some "going northeast toward Maison Neuve Farm and the remainder going to southeast." It had been at the point where the division's boundary had changed direction.

In his memoir, Cooke described in word and diagram where he and his company had gone, although it isn't always that clear. They had been traveling north of the division's left boundary, having been unintentionally led astray by their one French guide. Cooke, still lost, had aided the 9th Infantry at Maison Neuve and then gone to a point just west of Chaudun. Seeing a village being occupied by Marines and without a verification of any kind, he reported back that Vierzy had been captured. Instead, he learned shortly after, it was Hunt and the 17th at Chaudun. Hunt was also lost. Cooke's erroneous report, combined with the overall ignorance of what was going on up front, confused the division, both brigades, and all regiments. The 4th Brigade lines were in a terribly agitated state though they maintained reasonable liaison with the 3d's right flank and continued fighting the Germans. Marines and soldiers of every stripe and shape were mixed up and spread northward well into the sector of the Moroccans, who, for all their vaunted reputation, were still not keeping up with the Americans.

Maurice Shearer and 3/5 had a relatively easy time of it compared with 1/5 and 2/5. Yet, the men and officers of 3/5 had been severely taxed by their movement forward and about daybreak had rested at the location of the divisional ration dump. After a rest of about ten minutes, Capt. Thomas Quigley, skipper of the 45th Company, received word that the line was broken and that 3/5 had moved forward. In fact only a few men had. The others were so tired and sleepy from their great exertions that morning they hadn't heard the orders when the word was passed and consequently didn't fall in. Quigley sent runners back to the 16th and 47th Companies, both of which were in the rear of the 45th, to get their companies in motion. Quigley led the battalion forward and they were just a few minutes late arriving at their allotted place in line. At 1000 Major Shearer sent Quigley's second, 1st Lt. Raymond E. Knapp, with the 45th Company to reinforce the 55th Company in a front line position west of Vierzy. Knapp, with apparent utter disregard for his own safety, inspired his men to greater efforts, and through a withering machine-gun and heavy artillery fire they went for a distance of at least a mile and a half. So the 45th Company was rendering support to 2/5 and as already seen the 16th and 20th Companies were aiding Turrill and

1/5.[28] As Shearer later reported, 3/5 mostly just followed the other two battalions that first day, adding support where needed. That report wasn't completely accurate. Several officers of the 47th were out, as the company had been knocked around a bit, so Sgt. Frank Sockel was cited for his "brilliant leadership of his platoon" as well as his own gallantry in action. Poor man would only survive this final day, being killed in action on 19 July 1918.

The advance of 1/5 was continued between the Maison Neuve Farm on the right and the village of Chaudun on the left. As we have seen, the 17th Company, under Captain LeRoy Hunt, in a bold attack had captured it. As Thomason so vividly put it, "The 17th Company went in and stamped the Maxims flat." The 17th then halted and soon the Moroccans passed over to their right. Corbett's small liaison patrol from the 49th Company, finding liaison satisfactorily established, returned to Turrill's PC. Keyser's battalion proceeded forward and entered the ravine known as Vallée de Clancy. Clancy ran between Chaudun and Vauxcastille, a distance of about one and one-half miles west of Vierzy. There they encountered heavy machine-gun fire and a halt had to be made until those could be cleared out by tanks. Lessons learned at Belleau Wood would greatly help many of the 5th Marines to survive Soissons. Don't assault a machine-gun nest in a frontal attack! Unfortunately that lesson had to be relearned time and again during the war.

Heinies held the eastern side of Clancy and kept up a constant artillery and machine-gun barrage upon the western edge. At this point it was almost impossible for 2/5 to scale the opposite slope, it being that steep. Therefore Keyser sat for a spell, trying to decide how best to continue forward without losing his entire command. The decision was soon made for him by the staff of the 3d Brigade.

Cooke and the 55th finally came back within the division's boundaries. He was to have been at the left flank of 2/5, with liaison to the 66th Company led by William Crabbe. "Gunny" Herman "Babe" Tharau*, out scouting for that elusive right flank company personally captured a machine gun and killed its crew. According to Cooke, he moved in a southward direction until he and Crabbe made contact. Crabbe didn't know where he was, so the two skippers readjusted their formations to adapt to the fouled up situation. Cooke continues his narrative, telling us that neither Crabbe nor he had any idea where they were nor where anyone else was. Cooke suggested they both maintain liaison, as ordered but change direction and move forward. As Cooke said,

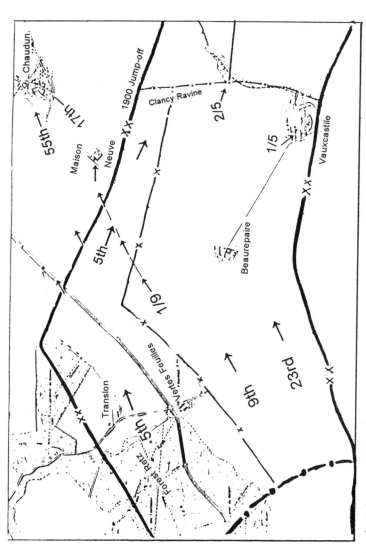

Map 9: Advance of the 2d Division on 18 July 1918 at Soissons showing diversion of several companies of the 5th Marines and of 1/9 out of division boundaries, including the line reached by the 5th, 9th, and 23d Infantry regiments.

Bill, I tried to grin, it looks as if we've got to take on the whole German army by ourselves. "Fair enough," Crabb [sic] hitched up his
belt, "you knock 'em down and I'll count them." Taking out my
notes on the attack order, I suggested that we make a change in
direction before going any farther. Bill agreed with a shrug. He
wasn't any brass hat. Whether we fought Germans at eighty degrees
or at a hundred and sixty was all the same to Captain Bill Crabb.[29]

Both skippers blew their whistles, waved their arms, and ran up and
down to change the men's direction from right to forward. Then they
all went forward. Several men from the 9th Infantry, without arms, were
tagging along with the 55th. Cooke learned that they had been captured
by the Germans and when the Marines came along and ran over them
the soldiers naturally joined them. He had noticed that they were
scrounging through some material the enemy had left lying and when
he inquired he learned that they were looking for their Springfields that
the Heinies had taken from them. As Cooke said, they learned that "we
were not alone on the battlefield. Other people were present—if we
could only find them." Crabbe almost walked into a battery of German
artillery hidden in a shallow ravine just to their front. Though the Germans were caught by surprise, they recovered quickly and began sending big rounds toward the Marines. The heavy artillery fire soon began
to fall upon the 55th and that company scattered. As Cooke said "It certainly seemed as if our god of Luck had paid his lodge dues and was in
good standing." In other words, the Marine casualties were relatively
light. The two companies quickly overran the guns and their gunners,
and some Marines stopped long enough to collect souvenirs from the
deceased foe. As the two companies came out of the ravine they saw both
the 18th and 43d Companies just coming over the rise. From which direction Cooke doesn't tell us. It was also about this time that the Moroccans, dilatory all day, were finally seen advancing on the left. About
this same time Corbin's 51st, which had been hugging the left flank of
the 9th Infantry most of the day, had joined the 18th and 43d Companies in the ravine northwest of Vierzy. Cooke and his lads joined the support line of 2/5, in a ravine, just about northwest of Vierzy. Shortly afterward Cooke, the last of the "old-timers" of 2/5, got nailed. His
wound was serious and it took him out of the battle.[30]

At 1330, in conformity with Corps plan for exploitation, the 3d
Brigade took over the lead. Since early morning the front had been

three regiments abreast but now it would be reduced to two. The 9th and 23d Infantry Regiments were to advance and the 5th Marines plus the 6th Machine Gun Battalion (their guns had finally arrived) in support. Harbord gave Brig. Gen. Hanson E. Ely, the 3d Brigadier commander, control of the 5th Marines. Third Brigade issued orders at 1630 that the attack would be made at 1730 by, right to left, the 23d Infantry, with 2/5 on their right, and the 9th Infantry with 1/5 on their left. Three/Five would continue to constitute division reserve. Unfortunately, as was so often the case, orders were issued late. As a result, the regimental commanders weren't able to issue commands or assemble and organize their units to advance at the designated hour. The original plan was modified: Two/Five, located in the ravine northwest of Vierzy, would now advance with the 9th Infantry and help take that town. Keyser hurried to the proper location with the 18th, 43d, and 51st Companies. He immediately sent a runner to the 55th to notify them of the proposed attack. The message was delivered but the 55th, having just lost the "skipper" and still being way off in the distance, could not arrive in time. Therefore only the three companies would advance in two waves with a five-hundred-meter front to cover.

Finally, after nearly a two-hour delay, the attack jumped off at 1900. The left was 2/9 with 1/9 and 3/9 in support and 2/5 on their left flank. Although Upton and his men were initially held up by severe machine-gun fire, they still were able to make five hundred meters progress in relatively short order. But because the Moroccans still weren't keeping pace with the Americans, the left flank was again wide open. The 9th Infantry and 2/5 soon cleaned up the obstacles before them and continued onward. Corbin and the 51st Company encountered heavy resistance from machine guns but made an advance of a half mile. While the 51st and 18th Companies were busy cleaning up, the 9th Infantry continued their advance, taking a part of the 18th with them. Meanwhile six French tanks were just then returning from a previous attack and were moving through the advancing infantry units. German guns had been concentrating upon the metal monsters as they retired, resulting in intense casualties to the advancing infantry. It was at this time that Capt. Lester E. Wass, skipper of the 18th, was mortally wounded. To add insult to injury, four of the six tanks were also destroyed. It was also at this time that 2d Lt. Fred H. Becker*, USA, the renowned "Chowhound" of the 18th, earned his award and a few other "trinkets" the hard way. Going forward in advance of his platoon, Becker destroyed a machine-gun nest. This prevented many more deaths or serious injuries being inflicted upon his men, allowing them to go forward with a greater chance of surviving. Unfortunately, as he completed his job he was killed that same moment.

At 1900 the 23d Infantry had formed up for the attack with their 1st and 2d Battalions in line and with 3/23 in support. At the same time 1/5 had pulled themselves together and marched forward to Vaux-castille. The castle is perched on the western height above Vierzy. It lies at the southern end of the Vallée de Clancy. Turrill, with his battalion staff, clerks, and runners, was holding a position overlooking the village of Vierzy at 1900. An army lieutenant colonel came rushing up in an automobile and upon descending demanded to know why the major and his unit hadn't gone forward to take the village. Before this had happened Turrill had sent for a platoon or two from the nearby companies to assist in the planned assault upon the village. But the soldier was out for bear. He demanded of Turrill, "Major, just where in hell are you or where in hell do you think you are?" "Here colonel, see," Turrill explained pointing to his map. "We've been held up and—" That did it. "Held up, hell, you were supposed to have that town by four o'clock, and here it is six-thirty and the sun is going down! Go get that—" More of the same was exchanged when finally the army colonel let Turrill and all Marines present, have both barrels.

At that moment the colonel made a silken purr, loud enough for all to hear; you could feel his satisfaction. One could easily picture some-place where we gyrenes had stolen glory and a fair share of the news from this old soldier's own good army outfit. The grimace was, I guess, a smile. He glowed, and was so human that he took the time to catch the eyes of men who listened, softly saying, "They are Marines, aren't they major?"

"But sir, you see—"

"See, hell! I don't give a damn if you only got twenty of them, they are Marines, my dear major, and I'm ordering you to take that goddamn town!"

"Aye, aye, sir. . ." We then took the town.[31]

The 5th Marines were scattered about, somewhat. They were now the division's far right and far left boundary. Shearer and 3/5 were supposed to be in support, but some of his companies were mingled in with both 1/5 and 2/5. On the road to Vierzy from Vauxcastille, Turrill had met Capt. John H. Fay and his 8th Machine Gun Company. Their guns had

finally arrived only two hours before and they were looking for somebody to use them on. The 8th immediately joined 1/5, adding a lot of
strength when and where it was badly needed. The little group pushed
forward in the dusk toward the strongly held town.

As late as 1715 hours, while still up north, Turrill had not received
his orders to attack, which were so late as to prohibit his getting his entire battalion assembled in time. The next morning he sent the following message to Logan Feland:

> Five-fifteen P.M. yesterday, rec'd order to support 3d Brig. for an
> attack at that hour. Took my support consisting of parts of 49th,
> 16th & 20th cos. to Vierzy [about 150 men]. Arrived before 23d
> Inf. and with 8th M.G. Co. attacked thro' town. When half-way
> thro' town 23d came up and continued the attack. Now in support
> to 23d Inf. Need rations. Also would like packs of 30 men of 49th
> Co. Have here Capt. Platt with 40 men, Capt. Yowell—4 off. 70
> men. Hdqtrs. 7 off., 35 men, 30 men of 49th Co.—total 187.[32]

Overcoming much resistance, the 3d Brigade pushed on toward
Vierzy, where the Germans were forming a new line. Turrill's men moved
forward from Vauxcastille and entered the west end of the ravine leading into Vierzy town at 2000. Moments later Ely[33] ordered 1/5 and 1/23
to clean up the town and the various ravines leading to it. Turrill
brought 1/5 toward the town from the west while the commander of
1/23 led his men from the northwest.

The town itself was set in part of the ravine running north to south.
It provided German machine gunners and riflemen with fine positions
from which they could sweep the town. In the Marines went. By the
time they had taken "four-5ths of the town" the 23d Infantry entered
the town from the northwest, and passed through the Marines' lines
to take over the assault. Marines remained behind 1/23 just east of the
cemetery located southwest of the town as the soldiers raced through.
Not long after, the Germans were cleaned out of the town. In fact 1/23
managed to advance far ahead of the rest of the division by about a
half mile.

The 6th Marines were keeping their half mile or so distance from the
advancing regiments, but they, too, were not going entirely without pain.
A German plane swooped down upon Hughes's 1/6, the lowest level that
many Marines ever remembered seeing one. Barely clearing the de-

nuded trees he was in on the troops and then gone in seconds. Only the black crosses on his wings gave evidence of whose side he was on. Firing his machine guns into the columns, this pilot surprisingly only managed to drop one man in the 95th Company. A little after sunset the 6th Marines continued forward through the stretch of open country that lay before them. Columns of many German prisoners were being escorted back to the rear with usually only two Marines in charge of them, one in front and one in the rear. Obviously those prisoners were glad to be out of the war; otherwise the two men could easily have been overwhelmed. At dark the regiment stopped their forward movement and dug in on a slope just west of Vierzy. Tomorrow would be their big day.

Keyser and his battalion were, or appeared to be, surrounded by machine guns in the tall and dense wheat. He and his runner were temporarily separated from his command and they had to crawl in a ditch so as to avoid exposure, eventually making it back to the battalion. The location of the 9th Infantry wasn't apparent, so he saw no profit in trying to go forward since both his flanks were in the air and it was now dark—or as he later said, "I deemed it advisable to attempt to clear the ground." He then ordered his command to retire to their original position—the position where they had been located at 1900—which they managed to reach by dusk. In Keyser's report he stated (see following) that he had no grenades to attack the machine guns hidden in the wheat fields, so he stayed where he was for the night. Independently, without consulting his commanding officer, Ely of the 3d Brigade, he made the decision that to try to go forward in the dark would just inflict additional unnecessary casualties upon his already decimated battalion.[34]

In his later report Keyser added some detail about Wass's company. "As all of the officers of this company [the 18th] are casualties, the information regarding it is meager." The single-page description for the 18th Company in its semiofficial history declares, "It seemed impossible for us to go through another attack that day, but that's what we did just before dusk that evening—advanced five more kilometers over the wheat fields and ravines to the left of Vierzy." The history also added that "this company had the center of the attack. The advance was made in the face of frontal and flank machine-gun fire and heavy artillery fire; men dropped like flies. . . . Finally the tanks came up and helped us through the last few hundred meters of the push. What was left of our outfit dug in and held overnight [in a ravine] and through the next day and night." During this period, 2d Lt. Joseph B. Carhart* was cited for "extraordinary heroism." Taking a small detachment of men from the 18th they charged German machine guns, killing the crews and capturing the three guns, which they immediately turned on their enemies with great delight. This opened a path for the company's advance, which had been held up by the enemy's fire. The advance made little real progress and contributed little of importance to the overall situation of the 18th Company. But they did try.

Later that evening, at 2200, Keyser sent a message to Feland explaining what he and 2/5 had accomplished and where they were.

> Will you please communicate C.G. 3d Brigade, under whom I am operating that I am occupying old trench line with about 120 men who were my battalion support in operation of this afternoon. We are delayed in going forward with advanced companies by heavy shelling controlled from aeroplane and . . . by M.G.'s . . . forward companies failed to locate . . . I have just received word from my left company [55th] that it was unable to proceed further than a few hundred yards beyond my position so I've ordered them to retire here. My right company [51st] I have news of.[35]

Keyser adds that he had no grenades or tank support and he believed it impractical to attempt to eliminate the many machine guns before him without both. "I shall remain here holding line until further orders. My whole battalion is utterly exhausted, having had no hot food or drink for sixty hours." Nothing ever seemed to change. No food, no rest, nothing.

Sometime during the night the 55th Company, being in proximity to the Boche, had some close contacts with the enemy. Corporal Joseph L. Hopta* ran out in front of the company and took a machine gun and its crew single-handedly, under a heavy concentration of machine-gun fire. Private Frank J. Barczykowski* displayed extraordinary heroism in charging three machine-gun nests with the aid of a few of his comrades, those listed following, killing the crews and capturing all the guns. They thereupon turned the guns upon the Germans, freeing up his company, which had been held up because of them. Among his comrades who were also awarded both decorations were 2d Lt. Joseph B. Carhart*, Cpl. John Doody*, Pvt. William A. Justensen*, Pvt. Albert Barrows*, Pvt. Paul T. Hurley*. Meanwhile four more Marines of the 55th, Pvt. William McIntyre*, Pvt. Elias J. Messinger* and Pvt. Dolph

Wood*, all led by Cpl. Bernard W. Montag*, fearlessly exposed themselves to the accurate fire from a machine gun. Even though all four were wounded in the encounter, down went the gun and down went its crew. All in all, this listing constitutes a bevy of American names from a variety of origins.[36]

Both the 9th Infantry and the 23d Infantry had made their way forward and ultimately, near midnight, the 23d finally cleared Vierzy of the remaining Boche. That was the final action of the division for 18 July. Three regiments were used up and exhausted. Having suffered severe casualties they could make no further effort then or, as we shall see, later. Now it was up to the 6th Marines to carry the standard forward.

The 5th Marines were finished with 18 July. So were the 9th and 23d Infantry. Tomorrow would put their buddies of the 6th Marines in the forefront. Meanwhile the 2d Division had advanced over three miles and held a final line a half mile east of Vierzy. In so doing they collected several thousand prisoners, hundreds of machine guns, and practically all the enemy artillery of two German divisions. Still, the entire organization of the 10th Army was in disarray for most of the day. Orders were consistently delayed in origin and late in arrival. Liaison between units, very necessary at all times, was poorly maintained, if at all. Maps were practically nonexistent. Men were not receiving sufficient food, water, or ammunition, at least those of the 2d Division. The men were exhausted in getting to their area and pushed into an advance without being able to even catch their breath, let alone to orient themselves. So far, the Aisne-Marne Offensive was far less a success than it was later touted to be. Foch was rated a genius by the Allies and Americans, but if he was, then, based upon this his first major effort, he appeared to be served by fools or incompetents, or both.

On 18 July three tough regiments were on line and advanced against a surprised enemy. Their losses, for all of them, were substantial. So far only one infantry regiment of the division remained relatively unscathed, the 6th Marines. Even the 2d Engineers were in no position to aid the 6th, though that possibility had been seriously considered. On the morrow, that one regiment would attempt to accomplish what three regiments couldn't with almost the same frontage. As one recent author proclaimed, "[18 July was] an American victory, but the 5th Marines, 9th Infantry, and the 23d Infantry were no longer combat effective."[37]

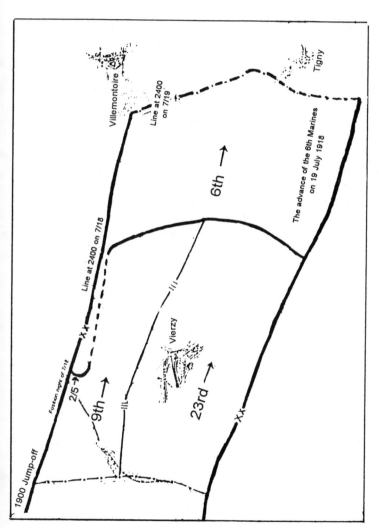

Map 10: The advance of the 6th Marines on 19 July 1918, was decidedly brief and bloody. The dot dash line was as far as they went. The regiment managed to hang on until a French unit replaced them early the following morning.

Friday, 19 July

At 0300, 2d Division Field Order No. 16 ordered an attack on the morning of 19 July. Selectively extracted, we find that item III (b) stated, "The infantry attack will be made by the 6th Marines and the 6th Machine Gun Battalion, Lieutenant Colonel Lee, USMC commanding." Item III (c) added, "The First Battalion, 2d Engineers, and the Fourth Machine Gun Battalion will constitute the reserve, Lieutenant Colonel Brown, 2d Engineers, commanding." That was it. It appears that the 5th Marines and both the 9th and 23d Infantry regiments were all washed up. Otherwise, I would assume, they, too, would have been supporting the front-rank attack force. One regiment was to go up against the Germans who had devastated most of the 2d Division the day before. Further instructions mentioned that the 6th Marines would "effect a passage of our present lines at 7.00 A.M." Then orders would be given for the disposition of those "holding the line." They would continue doing so until the 6th Marines had attained their objectives. Those were given as the "line Hartennes-Eteaux" which was from Bois d'Hartennes to the Bois de Cornois, located on the road between Château-Thierry and Soissons. This line was approximately two and one-half miles ahead. In addition, the regiment was to consolidate the position attained, "with as little delay as possible." Liaison on the left was "assured." It would be by the 6th Brigade of Dragoons (French). The 38th French Division would be on their right. The dragoons were not to be used until there was a collapse of the German lines. In actual fact they did participate and their losses, especially of horses, was tremendous. Machine guns can do terrible things to cavalry, but the French still seemed not to have learned that fact so late in the war.

Meanwhile, the Germans, who weren't dummies, could see that the 18th of July was a precursor of things to come. They began to strengthen their front and by daylight on 19 July batteries of 77s were clearly seen in the near distance. Maxims had also been brought forward, as had been fresh infantry. Tough times ahead.

The attack lineup of the 6th was as follows: One/Six on the right; 2/6 on the left with 3/6 in the support line. Hughes still commanded 1/6; Thomas Holcomb, recently promoted to lieutenant colonel and assistant to Lee, had at his own request, within hours resumed command of 2/6 from Maj. Robert L. Denig, and Sibley still had 3/6. All were capable but, under the circumstances, could do nothing to abort what was going to happen to them and their battalions that day. At 0730 the regiment moved forward from their place of repose. Two battalions went into their first line at Vierzy. Hughes battalion, 1/6, moved to the right flank and Holcomb's 2/6 the left flank. Sibley's 3/6 would support the first line. Hughes had gone forward and settled his men in an open wheat field, somewhat exposed to artillery and Maxims. Most of Holcomb's men were inside a walled cemetery that initially provided some protection. Several hours before the 6th Marines were to jump off, the artillery had already fired their rolling barrage. Hence, when the 6th took off from their positions at 0830, in and about Vierzy, there was no rolling barrage for them. Worse, the Boche were ready for them. The only artillery fire they witnessed was incoming and dropping on them. The regiment had to cross over two miles to their target. Most wouldn't make it.

Denig, who went along as an observer, describes in a lengthy letter home what he saw in the first few minutes on that first day, 18 July 1918.[38] He had been in the 5th Marines for a spell, so many of the officers mentioned were friends of his, like Wass and Murray. Denig also described what his first day, 19 July, was like.

At 8.30 we jumped off with a line of tanks in the lead. For two "kilos" the four lines of Marines were straight as a die, and their advance over the open plain in the bright sunlight was a picture I shall never forget. The fire got hotter and hotter, men fell, bullets sung, shells whizzed-banged and the dust of battle got thick. Overton [John] was hit by a big piece of shell and fell. Afterwards I heard he was hit in the heart, so his death was without pain. He was buried that night and the pin found.

A man near me was cut in two. Others when hit would stand, it seemed, an hour, then fall into a heap. I yelled to [Pere] Wilmer that each gun in the barrage worked from right to left . . . looked for Hughes way over to the right; told Wilmer I had a hundred dollars and be sure to get it. You think of all kinds of things.[39]

Some sixty Germans tried to surrender but their machine guns opened up on 2/6 and the Marines returned the fire. The machine gunners retreated and a company from 2/6 chased them, leaving a gap in the line. At that point Sibley advanced one of his companies to fill the gap. He also dispatched one platoon each from the 73d Machine Gun

Company, the 81st Machine Gun Company, both the Stokes mortar and one-pounder platoons, and the 83d (Noble) and 84th (Mark Smith) Companies to back them up.

The advance to the front line, a bit more than half a mile ahead, was across perfectly wide open but rolling wheat fields. Because the tanks in front were slow, the line of Marines was forced to move at a snail's pace. That made them a perfect target for the Boche artillery, which laid down an extremely heavy barrage. One of Noble's runners, Pvt. Orr V. Lotspiech*, displayed the kind of stoic courage and bravery that ordinary men have to admire. While passing through an unusual barrage of artillery and machine guns he wound up with a bullet that broke his leg. Undaunted, Lotspiech dragged himself to his skipper's PC and reported that his mission was completed, thereby saving the dispatch of another runner over that terrible ground. Gulberg of the 75th Company, describes what happened to him and his buddies:

> The whistle blew and we were off behind a platoon of whippet tanks. These tanks were a great help to the infantry in cleaning out machine gun nests, but I would rather take my chances without them rather than follow them, because they draw artillery fire. But we had to advance right behind them and if a shell missed the tank, there was a good chance of us getting them.[40]

As the Marines advanced the 77s ate them up and the 105s tore up the ground, Marines, and tanks. Then the machine guns finished what the artillery hadn't accomplished. The 6th was forced to go to ground early on. The fire of the machine guns, especially at their legs, allowed them few chances to avoid being struck, unless they hit the deck, although still not guaranteed. Lying out in the fields gave the Boche artillery even better odds against them. Gulberg tells of a big shell landing near Pvt. Roy L. Daniels and the latter getting the full blast although Gulberg himself was thrown six feet from its concussion. A few hundred yards farther on Gulberg got his. Two machine-gun bullets pierced his right leg and he, too, was out of action. He'd be back, but Daniels wouldn't.[41]

The worst fire seemed directed toward 1/6. They took plenty as they approached Tigny. Many of the German gunners were on their left and right flanks. That devastating fire, across the nearly straight formation of Marines, couldn't miss. There were so many officer casualties in 1/6 and especially the 75th Company, that Sgt. Jerry Thomas took command of the company.[42] The 95th Company was positioned on the extreme right of the regiment, and because the Algerians didn't keep up with the Americans the Boche guns were aimed at them instead. Sergeant Oliver C. Farrant's* platoon leader was down, so he assumed command of his platoon and led it with "remarkable coolness" as they advanced against the terrible fire coming toward them. Even though he, too, was wounded in the holocaust he managed to remain in place and by his inspiring example his platoon routed the Boche before them. He had taken more than he was able to stand, and on 22 July expired because of his wounds. Although the enemy continued to fall back they would resume firing every five hundred yards or so. Their artillery was quite close and as a result their aim was even better. The fire was nearly point blank at this stage of the advance. The loss of buddies was barely noted under the impact of the shell fire. Everyone was suffering from concussion; it couldn't be escaped no matter where a man was. Even the horrifying sights of men being torn to pieces by direct hits was not as important as the safety of number one. Still the heroes continued. Private Royal H. C. Shepherd* of the 95th started out with a badly burned foot, which fact he concealed from his platoon leader and managed to stay in line. He continued forward with his buddies for a few minutes when he received a wound in his shoulder. Now unable to keep up with the rest of his company he fell behind but almost immediately began carrying other wounded men to shelter; he continued thus for six hours. He only yielded to treatment when he became exhausted and near collapse. Second Lieutenant Scott M. Johnston* of the 76th led a small detachment forward and succeeded in knocking out a machine-gun nest that was inflicting terrible losses on the 6th. Although he was seriously wounded, he refused to be relieved and stayed with his men until ordered to a dressing station by the skipper. Those wounds were fatal and he died on 15 August.

From the semiofficial history of 78th Company, 2/6, we find that they were in the front wave.

> For the time it lasted, this was one of the bloodiest battles the . . . company was ever in. Our losses were heavy. . . . There were fifty-three men left in the company . . . and the 2d Battalion was about the size of a regulation war strength company.

From the semiofficial history of the 6th Marines:

> When the front lines were passed the enemy machine guns proved most troublesome. A halt was made after a gain of about one kilometer for the reason that *the casualties had so reduced the*

regiment that further advance was practically impossible. [43] [Emphasis added.]

Again, the history, sans emotion, adds:

What remained of the regiment took shelter in a line of semi-complete entrenchments constructed by the Germans, where from 10:30 A.M. until dark the regiment was subjected to the enemy's artillery, one-pounder and machine gun fire.[44]

The 6th had managed, somehow, to attain positions just outside the western side of Tigny, barely a mile or so east of where they had started. Denig reports that at 1030 "the attack just died out." He adds that Holcomb was next to him in his not-very-deep hole:

Wilmer some way off. We then tried to get reports. Two companies we never could get in touch with. Lloyd [Captain Egbert T. skipper of the 80th Co.] came in and reported he was holding some trenches near a mill with six men. Cates, with his trousers blown off, said he had sixteen men of various companies; another officer on the right reported he had and could see forty men, all told. That, with the headquarters, was all we could find out about the battalion of nearly eight hundred.[45]

At some point, according to his citation, Maj. Pere Wilmer* assumed command of 2/6 from Holcomb and led it with great courage and utter disregard of personal danger. In so doing they crossed exposed terrain, under intense artillery and machine-gun fire, toward the town of Vierzy. It was during this time that he earned a Navy Cross for courage and leadership. There were many others, especially among the runners, who continued crossing the open ground to deliver their messages under the most appalling conditions. "Johnny" Overton*, the famous runner from Yale, caught a bad one and collapsed from his wound, which would be fatal that same day.

Lieutenant Cates was the only officer still able to function in the 96th Company. He'd been wounded, as had the skipper, Capt. Wethered Woodworth, 1st Lts. Robert L. Duane and James Robertson, and 2d Lt. Bernard L. Fritz. Cliff Cates took command and continued the attack with what was left of the 6th Marines. Cates later wrote a message, which he sent to Holcomb. It has been repeated many times but is worthy of another glance.

I have only two men out of my company and 20 out of some other company. We need support, but it is almost suicide to try to get it here as we are swept by machine gun fire and a constant barrage is on us. I have no one on my left and only a few on my right. I will hold.[46]

Cates was in pretty bad shape himself. His leg had been scraped by shell fragments a second time and worse, his trousers had been blown off. In order to protect his extreme modesty he had wrapped a blanket around his waist. I wonder what the Boche thought of that? Probably they were too busy to even notice.

Corporal William K. Skaggs* of the 76th was cited for multiple acts of bravery; one of which was for carrying a wounded comrade over three and a half miles to an aid station, even though wounded himself. Then he resumed his duties by bringing important messages to his platoon commander under the same trying conditions.

One of the bravest men on that battlefield was a corpsman, Pharmacist Mate 3d Alvin W. Pilkerton*, who was cited for caring for the wounded out in the open fields where there were so many lying about. Later, at St. Mihiel, he was awarded a DSC for continuing to give treatment to the wounded even though badly wounded himself. Another champion was Pvt. Walter E. Furr* of the 84th Company, who crawled forward of his unit's line, entered an underground tunnel where he found and captured five German soldiers, and then brought them back through the murderous fire on the field.

At 1545 Colonel Lee sent to the COs of the 1st, 2d, 3d Battalions, Headquarters Company and 1st Battalion, 2d Engineers, the following message . . .

The division commander directs us to dig in and hold our present line at all costs. No further advance will be made for the present. *He congratulates the command on its gallant conduct in the face of severe casualties.*[47] [Emphasis added.]

The history of the 6th adds that "conditions were bad throughout the regiment. It was practically impossible to send out water details and canteens were empty." The Boche continue their relentless artillery fire causing many additional casualties. The enemy had the range of the 6th Marines to a T, and they made it hot. Additionally, the weather was also hot—as a furnace, some said. A very brave corporal of the 76th Company, William H. Faga*, who was already a hero from Belleau Wood, added an oak leaf cluster to his first DSC. Angry at the telling machine-gun fire working his section over, Faga charged out and attacked one gun that was doing the most damage, capturing it and the crew and then bringing them all back to his company.

Many of the wounded were brought back to Beaurepaire Farm, which was serving as an advanced aid station. But many men were still lying out in the wheat fields calling for help. Their cries got weaker as the afternoon passed. Then most cries just seemed to die out completely. That evening many Marines and corpsmen made efforts to locate those still alive and one, Cpl. Raymond W. Hanson* of the 75th, along with a corpsman named Earl S. Grauer, at the risk of their own lives went out to help Pvt. William A. Weaver, who was lying out in front close to the German lines. Stopping the flow of blood from Weaver's wound by binding it, they carried him to a position of shelter from the fire of the enemy, thereby saving his life.[48]

The men tried digging but most were unable to make any appreciable impression in the ground. In addition to the oppressive heat, the effort expended while trying to dig while under fire soon exhausted those so engaged. Losses continued throughout the day and into the night. Many Marines were missing. During the advance some men just dropped where they were, not hit, just assuring their own well-being. No sergeants or officers could closely supervise their platoons under these frightful conditions, so control was practically nonexistent. It was that kind of trial and tribulation where even the best of men occasionally considered the alternatives.

Late that evening, at 2100 hours, the remnants of 2/5 under Major Keyser were ordered forward to occupy the left flank liaison with the French and on their right the remnants of the 6th Marines. Finally their relief, the Algerians came and the remaining members of the 6th Marines started back through the town. Vierzy was a gas trap; to add more misery, the troops had to put on their masks, which exhausted them even more. Back toward the forest they continued, and upon arrival near Translon Farm, most fell down and embraced Morpheus. They slept during most of the twentieth as well.

Saturday, 20 July

It was after 0400 when 2/5 was relieved and as the history states, "the Battalion was shifted to a position running about parallel with the main road to Soissons." Probably that was the road between Longpont on the south and Chaudun to the north.

Although the machine gunners were unable to contribute much to the attack on the 18th they were way up front on the 19th. The 81st Company, with two platoons from the 77th Company, were just west of and facing Tigny while the 15th protected the northern side of Vierzy, facing Charantigny. The balance of the 77th and headquarters of the 6th Machine Gun Battalion took up positions in Vierzy and the 23d Company was posted to their front. The 81st had one officer killed in action, Capt. Allen M. Sumner; so was 2d Lt. Herbert K. Jones, USA of the 23d. The battalion's total enlisted casualties numbered eight killed and forty-three wounded.

The unlucky 6th had more difficulties in their supposed place of repose. During the night the regiment was subjected to long-range shelling by Austrian 130s. Because of the continuous shelling, there was extensive damage to the huge trees, broken limbs and trunks partly severed, with many Marines killed by falling trees or branches. "All of this added greatly to the mental and physical exhaustion of the troops." The 5th, according to their history, were in the Fôret de Retz near Carrefour de Fourneaux, about a mile west of the Verte Feuille Farm.

Officer casualties in both regiments were exceptionally high. Many company commanders of the 6th fell that day, most wounded; some would return. Many wouldn't. Those killed in Hughes's 1/6 included Capt. John Kearns, 95th Company, 1st Lt. David A. Redford, 75th Company, and 2d Lts. Carleton Burr, 74th Company, Donald S. Gordon, 95th Company and Scott M. Johnston, 76th Company. Captain Arthur H. Turner, battalion adjutant, was wounded, as were seven other officers. Eventually, Turner lost a leg.

The losses for 2/6 included Lts. Charles H. Roy and John W. Overton, both of the 80th Company. Only three company-grade officers remained: Capt. Egbert T. Lloyd of the 80th Company and 1st Lts. Amos R. Shinkle of the 78th and Clifton B. Cates of the 96th. When relieved, sometime after midnight, 800 effectives marched out. The losses for the two leading battalions of the 6th were calculated at seventy percent for the day.

Sibley's 3/6 was in support for that few hundred yards the regiment traveled but they, too, suffered severe casualties. According to a message Major Sibley sent to Colonel Lee, their numbers before the attack were thirty-six officers and 850 men. The best total of survivors that 1st Lt. Ralph W. Marshall, the battalion intelligence officer, could come up with, after a visit to each company, was twenty officers and 421 men. Four hundred twenty-nine enlisted casualties and twenty officers. They rated it thirty-nine percent for officers and it appears as though fifty percent of the enlisted were also out of action.

The 6th Marines marched into battle with 2,450 Marines and a dozen hours later went out with a total of 1,150. Losses totaled 1,300 officers and men in that few hours. In 1921 McClellan provided figures of 305 killed in action or died of wounds. Another success like that and the 6th Marines would have been nothing but a memory.

The 5th Marines had also suffered intense casualties on the 18th, though certainly not to the same extent as the 6th. Their losses in killed included Capt. Lester S. Wass and 2d. Lts. David P. Colvin of the 18th Company, William H. Mack of the 20th, and John M. McClellan, Headquarters Company. Major Edwin N. McClellan's figures were seventy-nine killed or died of wounds. The wounded numbered eighteen officers and 360 men with another thirty-four missing.

Both regiments spent the 20th of July remaining pretty much in place. The following day, 21 July, the entire brigade moved to the woods south of Taillefontaine, where they remained until 25 July, putting up with nearly constant rain to add to their discomfiture. On 21 July, Harbord of the 2d Division issued General Order No. 46, which proclaimed to all that the division had received the "affectionate personal greetings" of General Pershing and his praise. After describing the horrors that the division had to put up with because their leaders weren't able to provide better, Harbord told what they had accomplished. "Three thousand prisoners, eleven batteries of artillery, over a hundred machine guns, etc. . . . The story of your achievements will be told in millions of homes in Allied lands tonight."

In addition the division received countless other messages of praise from Bullard, Secretary of the Navy Daniels, Mangin, and others of that ilk, but most importantly they were again cited in French Orders. That was sufficient for the brigade units to be awarded the Croix de Guerre and consequently to be allowed to wear the coveted fourragère.[49]

The third Medal of Honor awarded to the brigade at Soissons was to Pharmacist Mate 1st John M. Balch, USN, of the 6th Marines, who tended the wounded in Vierzy all during that fateful 19 July. "The risk of life that he took was beyond that of his comrades, and the services rendered were greater than could be expected of one man." There was more to his citation for which he was awarded the Navy Medal of Honor and the U.S. Army's Distinguished Service Cross. He would take another DSC at Blanc Mont plus two foreign awards, which included a Portuguese War Cross and an Italian War Cross.

Notes

1 The division was composed of two brigades of infantry. One was of three battalions of black Senegalese and one of the Foreign Legion. The other brigade was composed of Algerian Zouaves and Tunisian Tirailleurs. All, except the Legion and possibly the French Colonists of Algeria, were Moslems and all were ferocious. *Savage* might be a better term to use. The individuals were collectors of note: ears, noses, and anything else that would confirm that a German soldier had died at their hands. They hung these newly acquired items on their belts for all to see. The Americans were suitably impressed.

2 I'm sure there was some collusion in this matter. Third Corps and Bullard didn't learn of the offensive until 1400 on 15 July. Even though he and his staff could have arrived on the scene on 16 July, it was deemed insufficient time for successfully carrying out Foch's plan. Bullard, in his memoir, put the best face possible on the entire matter by stating that he decided "my two divisions should go into battle . . . in a French corps. . . ."

3 The exception was Maj. Robert L. Denig, in for Holcomb at 2/6. Holcomb became Lee's second but during the advance on 19 July, Holcomb would resume command of 2/6 for that day. The gas-afflicted Hughes returned to command 1/6 on 16 July.

4 Thomason, *Fix Bayonets!* (New York: Scribners, 1925), 74. "July 14 came. 'Sort o' Frog Fourth of July,' explained a learned corporal, standing in line for morning chow."

5 Harbord, *Leaves from a War Diary* (New York: Dodd, Mead & Co., 1925), 319. My own impression is that Harbord, seven years after the fact, was covering his butt for the slaughter that ensued.

6 George B. Clark, ed., *History of the 5th Regiment Marines (May 1917–December 31, 1918)* n.p. (Pike), (n.d., n.p.; reprint, Pike, NH: The Brass Hat, 1994), 20.

7 Lieutenant Colonel F. M. Wise, formerly the battalion's commander, was now variously sick or in training at the army school at Langres and wouldn't return until after the battle had terminated.

8 George B. Clark, ed., *A Brief History of the 6th Regiment United States Marine Corps from its organization, July, 1917, to dat. . . . at its present station . . . Leutesdorf, Germany, etc.* (n.d., n.p.; reprints Pike, NH: The Brass Hat, 1993).

9 The Bois de Retz is frequently referred to as the "Villers-Cotterêts Forest" because that town is wrapped in its folds.

10 General Pershing, when he learned of the French decision to form the 1st and 2d into a French corps, had made great exertions to have the two American divisions remain in the III Corps or at least to remain side by side in the upcoming fight. It was not to be.

11 *History of the 5th Regiment*, 21.

12 De Chambrun, *The American Army in the European Conflict* (New York: Macmillan, 1919), 174. What he noticed, of course, was that the Marines were now wearing army uniforms, not their greens.

13 E. N. McClellan's *MCG* article, "The Aisne-Marne Offensive", *Marine Corps Gazette* 6 (March 1921), erroneously states that the 9th was on the right, the 23d in the center, and the 5th on the left. Other records show the 5th, 9th, and 23d, left to right. The other records are correct.

14 Cooke, op. cit., 22. He was referring to a system that the AEF adopted from the British. That is, the leaving of ten percent of the men behind with one officer so as not to lose everyone in any attack. This, hopefully, would maintain a semblance of trained men with which to rebuild upon. Cooke selected Lt. Lyle and 20 men who had been through the most and worst action, so far.

15 There are many stories about what happened on 18 July. Some are quite unusual and, to a certain extent, unbelievable. Read on.

16 *Report of the 2d Division,* vol. 7. In Turrill's official report he states that 1/5 waited twenty minutes after the barrage began to advance. I've discovered that some of the reports placing the regiments in their respective jump-off positions are wrong. The semiofficial *The Ninth Infantry in the World War* said the 9th was definitely in the center, the 5th left, and the 23d right. See following for correct placement.

17 Mackin, *Suddenly We Didn't Want to Die,* 91–92

18 That statement of Mackin's was obviously incorrect. The real order of attack was with the 67th supporting the other three companies.

19 Corbin, a Marine Gunner promoted when the war came, reverted to his former rank when the war terminated. Like any old soldier he didn't intend to push too hard. I'm not sure what happened to him after Soissons. He just sort of disappeared from sight.

20 One/Five semiofficial history states that it was 0345. The 5th Regiment semiofficial history states, clearly, *"The attack started at 6:00 A.M."* (Emphasis in the original.) Another time given is 0445 and another at 0435. The latter time was correct according to General Order No. 227, Headquarters, 10th Army. The official U.S. government publication, *2d Division: Summary of Operations* clearly states, "No artillery preparation was ordered, but there was a rolling barrage . . . without support from machine-gun companies. . . . The tanks were likewise late in arriving."

21 In addition he was awarded a Silver Star, Médaille Militaire, Croix de Guerre, and the Italian War Cross for his courage.

22 As was the case in all but one award of the MoH, Cukela received the army award and later also the navy issue. In addition, he was the recipient of three Silver Star citations, plus the Legion of Honor, Médaille Militaire, and two Croix de Guerre from the French. He was quite a guy. So was Matej. In addition to the MoH he received two SSs, the Legion of Honor, and a CdG from the French while also receiving an Italian War Cross. Later in the day, separated from his own men, he managed to gather together a platoon-size body of French African troops, which he successfully led for the balance of that day. The Corps lost another great man when he was killed in action at Blanc Mont, like so many others, on 4 October 1918.

23 Contrary to the 2d Division summary, the French tanks must have arrived shortly after the attack was launched.

24 Roberts paid for his courage with his life on the night of 10 November while crossing the Meuse.

25 The 3d Brigade, or at least the 9th Infantry, must have been catching hell. For a captain to lead a battalion indicated extreme losses of majors. Fourth Brigade battalions were still being led by majors up until Blanc Mont.

26 Remember, no one had been given much direction or complete orders

or had maps, so the lack of cohesion can well be understood. One regiment, the 5th, was rushed forward to make jump-off on time, barely making it and then not entirely on time. The 2d Division's part in this offensive was badly planned and implemented. Later, Harbord admitted that fact.

27 *History of the First Battalion*, op.cit., 14.

28 The division commander, Maj. Gen. James Harbord, ordered that one company, the 47th [Case], provide a provost guard of two officers and thirty men at Cré-de-Montgobert. The balance of that company was used to escort prisoners to the rear and to bring ammunition forward.

29 Cooke, op. cit., 27. The officer's name was really Crabbe. Cooke made a number of spelling errors like that but after twenty years, who cares. I have a strange feeling that he was really floating back and forth over the boundary lines, for most of the day. I've had to assume that the 66th Company was also lost, at least at that moment. Read on.

30 He had been the only U.S. Army officer who had served as a commanding officer of a Marine company throughout most of both major conflicts. Cooke retained command even though he never rose above the rank of first lieutenant, and there were many Marine captains in the brigade during the period who could have replaced him. Probably because he was well liked and generally did an excellent job.

31 Mackin, *Suddenly We Didn't Want to Die*, 109–110. This came about after the division CG, Harbord, directed 1/5 and 3/5 to come under the orders of Brigadier General Ely. Orders from Ely to both at 1650 gave his command for them to support the 3d Brigade at "H hour 5.15 P.M., 18th July. Separate orders have been given to the 2d Battalion, 5th Marines." See the account for the second attack for the day which will, perhaps, clear up some of the confused situation.

32 *Records of the 2d Division*, vol. 5.

33 Ely earned a DSC, DSM, two SSs at Soissons. He was later promoted to major general and to the command of the 5th Division (Regulars) in October 1918.

34 The 3d Brigade was left with a huge gap, about a half mile, on its left rear. After F. M. Wise returned from detached duty, on or about, 21 July 1918, Keyser was relieved of a combat command. He thereupon became Assistant Chief of Staff of the division. I find no complaint registered, though Upton's report leaves no doubt that he didn't know where 2/5 was and that his left was in the air that night.

35 *Records of the 2d Division*, vol. 5.

36 Barczykowski received an Oak Leaf Cluster in place of a second DSC for his heroics at Belleau Wood on 11 June 1918.

37 Alan R. Millett, *Semper Fidelis: The History of the United States Marine Corps* (New York: Macmillan, 1980), 51.

38 Denig certainly had one of the most varied careers of any Marine officer in France. In early May 1918 he was in command of the 1st Battalion, 30th Infantry, 3d U.S. Division. He appeared with the 5th Marines in early June 1918 at Belleau Wood, duties unknown. At Soissons he had been briefly in command of 2/6 until Holcomb decided to resume command of the battalion, for some reason. On 30 July 1918 Denig was again assigned to the 9th Infantry but now in command of the 3d Battalion. With the latter unit he served until Blanc Mont,

where he was badly wounded and awarded the DSC and an NC, plus the Legion of Honor and a Croix de Guerre.

39 Cowing and Cooper, op. cit., 253. The pin mentioned was one that Johnny Overton asked his friends to send to his mother if he didn't make it. Overton was awarded both a DSC and NC for his extraordinary heroism while leading his platoon through the intense artillery and machine-gun fire.

40 Gulberg, *A War Diary*, 36

41 Ibid. Daniels, from Booth Point, Tennessee, also of the 75th Company, died of his wounds that day.

42 Gerald Thomas was soon commissioned and stayed in the Corps following the war. He eventually rose to the rank of general.

43 *A Brief History of the 6th Regiment* , op. cit., 14.

44 *A Brief History of the 6th Regiment,* ibid.

45 Cowing, Dear Folks at Home———, 254. For some reason, which I haven't been able to determine, Wilmer, a reserve major, rather than Denig, replaced Holcomb on 19 July.

46 *Records of the 2d Division,* vol. 5.

47 *A Brief History of the 6th Regiment,* op cit. That morning Harbord had told XX Corps that he only had the one regiment for the attack "—a force considered by me to be inadequate—"

48 I cannot locate any corpsman named Grauer. I have found the likely replacement. Edwin P. Groh, Hospital Apprentice 3d Class, who received a Silver Star citation for that day.

49 The author remembers being annoyed at several "boots" wearing the fourragère because they were members of the World War II 5th Marines. Boy, did they flaunt it.

Lieutenant Colonel Hiram I. Bearss, sometime CO, 5th Marines, later CO, 102d Infantry. Holder of Medal of Honor, DSC, and Legion of Honor for his acts at Marcheville, September 1918.

Brigadier General Wendell C. Neville, 4th Brigade CO. He received the Army and Navy DSM, the Legion of Honor, and two Croix de Guerre.

Colonel Logan Feland, CO, 5th Marines. Feland received the DSC, Army and Navy DSM, and five Silver Star citations.

Colonel Albertus Catlin, CO of the 6th Marines. He was made a member of the Legion of Honor and received two Croix de Guerre.

Lieutenant Colonel Julius S. Turrill, CO, 1st Bn., 5th Marines. Turrill was awarded the DSC and the Navy Cross.

Lieutenant Colonel Frederick M. Wise, CO, 2d Bn., 5th Marines. He became CO of the 59th Infantry, then the 8th Brigade, 4th Division. He was awarded both the Army and Navy DSM.

Lieutenant Colonel Charles T. Westcott, CO, 3d Bn., 5th Marines.

Captain LeRoy P. Hunt, CO, 17th Co., 1st Bn., 5th Marines. Later CO of 1st Bn. He was awarded the DSC, Navy Cross, and four Silver Stars.

Captain Charley Dunbeck, CO, 43d Co., 2d Bn. 5th Marines. Dunbeck received the DSC, Navy Cross, and four Silver Stars.

Major Henry L. Larsen, commanding the 3d Battalion, 5th Marines, from just before Blanc Mont through Bois to the Meuse River campaign. He earned a Navy Cross and three Silver Star citations plus a Croix de Guerre.

Major John A. Hughes, CO, 1st Bn., 6th Marines. Hughes was awarded the Navy Cross and three Silver Stars.

Major Thomas Holcomb, CO, 2d Bn., 6th Marines. Holcomb received the Navy Cross, Legion of Honor, and four Silver Stars.

Colonel Harry Lee, CO, 6th Marines. Lee was awarded the Army and Navy DSM and the Legion of Honor.

Lieutenant Colonel Berton W. Sibley, CO, 3d Bn., 6th Marines. Holder of the Navy Cross and three Silver Stars.

Major Frederick L. Barker, commanding the 1st Battalion, 6th Marines after Soissons. Remained through the Meuse River campaign. He earned a Navy Cross and at least four Silver Star citations plus the Croix de Guerre.

Ernest C. Williams, CO, 2d Bn., 6th Marines. Recipient of the Medal of Honor, the Navy Cross, and three Silver Stars.

Major George K. Shular, CO, 3d Bn., 6th Marines. Holder of the Army and Navy DSM and Legion of Honor.

Private Elton E. Mackin, author of remarkable memoir *Suddenly We Didn't Want to Die*. Photo taken in Germany, 1919. (courtesy Wallace Mackin)

Officers of the 2d Battalion, 6th Marines, leaving Belleau Wood after being relieved. From left, lieutenants Gordon Grimland, and George L. White, USN, Capt. Graves B. Erskine, 79th Co., Capt. Egbert T. Lloyd, 80th Co. Capt. Randolph T. Zane, 79th Co., unknown, 2d Lt. E. J. Stockwell, USA, 79th Co., Maj. Thomas Holcomb, 2d Bn.; 1st Lt. Cliffton B. Cates, 96th Co.; 2d Lt. John G. Schneider, 80th Co.; 1st Lt. Amos R. Shinkle, 78th Co. (courtesy Larry Strayer)

Three privates of the 16th Co., 5th Marines. Sitting from left, Paul Lubawski; J. E. Mason; standing, Henry P. Lenert, (recipient of Silver Star and Croix de Guerre for taking 78 German prisoners at Belleau Wood on 25 June 1918). (courtesy David Fisher)

From left, Pvt. Joseph A. Keller, 95th Co.; Pvt. Arthur G. Marsh (with BAR), 79th Co.; 6th Marines. Marsh, along with another man, carried a wounded officer back to safety through terrific machine-gun fire. (courtesy David Fisher)

Belleau Wood after the German, French, and American artillery had made it look this way. The view is what the Marines saw as they tried to take what was left of it. (courtesy USMC University archives)

Private Edwin T. Beach, 23d Machine Gun Co., 6th Machine Gun Bn. Photo taken before he went to France, when his uniform was still clean and new. (courtesy Jerry Beach)

Unidentified group of soldiers from the Headquarters Co., 2d Engineer Regiment. Possibly taken in Germany after the war because they appear to be reasonably well dressed. (courtesy David Fisher)

Battery F, 15th Field Artillery, 2d Artillery Brigade, 2d Division, in support of the 4th Marine Brigade at Belleau Wood on 5 June 1918. The 15th was usually the 4th Brigade's artillery support throughout the war. (courtesy USMC University archives)

Official portrait of 2d Division CO, Maj. Gen. John A. Lejeune, showing his various decorations, including the French Legion of Honor. Most likely this photo was taken shortly after his return to the United States. (courtesy USMC University archives)

General Pershing frequently awarded decorations for heroic acts among troops of the AEF. Photo taken shortly after Belleau Wood because officer on extreme left (wearing a French helmet) is Brig. Gen. James G. Harbord who commanded the 4th Brigade. The officer holding his right hand to his face appears to be Maj. Gen. Omar Bundy, CO of the 2d Division. The others are unidentified. (courtesy *Marine Corps Gazette*)

Group of senior Marine officers in the trenches, Verdun sector. From left, Maj. Holland McT. Smith, 4th Brigade Liaison officer; Brig. Gen. Charles A. Doyen, CO, 4th Brigade; Lt. Col. Frederick M. Wise, CO, 2d Bn., 5th Marines. (courtesy USMC University Archives)

Marines resting on a roadside in France. They are probably just returning from the Verdun Sector, May 1918. (courtesy USMC University archives)

Marines digging graves for dead German soldiers at their command post in the Verdun sector. (courtesy USMC University archives)

Major General Bundy, 2d Division CO, talking with Col. Albertus Catlin, 6th Marine's CO, in the Verdun sector.

Marines in the Belleau Wood area, preparing to resume their forward movement toward the front. Note the horse drawn, wheeled vehicles. (courtesy USMC University archives)

Group photo of the officers and men of the 23d Co., 5th Marines in Waldbreitbach, Germany, 4 April 1919. This was just after the 23d Co. of the 6th Machine Gun Battalion had been transferred as an infantry company to the 5th Marines which had suffered immense losses during the war and from the men who had been discharged early from the regiment. (courtesy Jerry Beach)

Marines mounting camions for a ride, to or from Belleau Wood. Probably before, because their uniforms appear to be in good shape—that wasn't the case after the June fighting. (courtesy USMC University archives)

The 6th Marines parading in Washington, D.C., 12 August 1919. (Signal Corps photo, courtesy Larry Strayer)

Fifth Marines headquarters group, taken just after the end of the Belleau Wood campaign. Seated from left, Col. Wendell C. Neville, CO, and Lt. Col. Logan Feland, assistant CO. Neville was awarded the Army and Navy Distinguished Service Medals and the Legion of Honor. Feland was awarded the DSC and both the Army and Navy DSMs, plus five Silver Star citations and six Croix de Guerre. (courtesy *Marine Corps Gazette*)

The last parade of the wartime 6th Marines, showing their colors as they marched in downtown Washington, D.C., on 12 August, 1919. (Signal Corps photo, courtesy Larry Strayer)

Major General John A. Lejeune, 2d Division CO, pinning Croix de Guerre on Pvt. E. E. McCormack, 83d Co., at Leutesdorf, Germany, on 4 January 1919. (USMC University archives)

Two German strong points on Blanc Mont. (USMC University Archives)

Brigadier General Wendell C. Neville, 4th Brigade CO, pinning Croix de Guerre on Maj. Gen. John A. Lejeune at Leutesdorf, Germany, on 4 January 1919. Neither man was tall, but Neville was obviously the taller one. (Signal Corps photo, courtesy Larry Strayer)

Group of Marine enlisted men of the 79th Co. 6th Marines, in heavy marching order. Probably on a regular route march while stationed in Germany. (courtesy David Fisher)

Headquarters of the 6th Marines while in the Verdun sector. The buildings were probably left over from the previous occupants who would have been from the French army. (courtesy *Marine Corps Gazette*)

Each of the Rhine River patrol boats mounted machine guns as "heavy" weapons for the watch. These guns are German Spandaus. Effective and accurate, they were more popular than were the French Hotchkiss the men were used to. (courtesy *Marine Corps Gazette*)

6: Marbache Sector

The good and the wise lead quiet lives.
—Euripides

The 6th Regiment of the 4th Brigade was relieved of front line duty near Tigny, at midnight on 19 July. They were retained in a reserve position until 22 July, when they were reassigned to a reserve position farther in the rear. Headquarters was established at Taillefontaine, about fifteen miles west of Soissons. Two days later the brigade was finally relieved from this active sector and ordered to billets in the area of Nanteuil-le-Haudouin, about thirty miles equidistant from Paris and Soissons. Brigade Headquarters were at Nanteuil, the 5th Marine's headquarters were at Silly-le-Longue, the 6th at Versigny, and the 6th Machine Gun Battalion at Brégy. They remained in that area until 31 July, resting, re-fitting, and working in their replacements. It was time for the entire 2d Division, and especially its active infantry brigades, the 3d and 4th, to be given a relatively quiet sector, if for no other reason than the preservation of the division as a viable unit. The 4th Brigade's losses at Soissons, especially for the 6th Marines, were, in proportion to time engaged, as great as those at the Aisne-Marne defensive. Nearly 1300 officers and men of that regiment were casualties, most of them on 19 July. The 3d Brigade was badly battered as were the 5th Marines on 18 July. The 2d Division needed a rest.

Brigadier General John A. Lejeune assumed command of the 4th Brigade on 26 July, and issued General Order No. 16, which stated:

I have this day assumed command of the Fourth Brigade, U.S. Marines. To command this brigade is the highest honor that could come to any man. Its renown is imperishable and the skill, endurance, and valor of the officers and men have immortalized its name and that of the Marine Corps.

259

But just three days later Lejeune succeeded Maj. Gen. James G. Harbord as commanding general of the 2d Division, certainly becoming a candidate for the shortest term of any brigade commander during the war. Therefore, Lejeune never had the opportunity to lead the brigade in combat; but, alternately, he was only the second Marine officer ever to command a division, and an army division at that. He had previously commanded an army brigade.[1]

On 7 August 1918, official word was received that Lejeune had been promoted to major general and his friend, Wendell C. Neville, who was now in command of the brigade, to brigadier general. Lieutenant Colonel Earl H. Ellis, who had traveled to France with Lejeune at the latter's request, assumed Lt. Col. Harry R. Lay's position as brigade adjutant when Lay was appointed division inspector on 10 August 1918. Lieutenant Colonel Hugh Matthews was division G-1, with Maj. Bennet Puryear as his assistant; Maj. Ralph S. Keyser was now G-2; Maj. Franklin B. Garrett became provost marshal; and finally 1st Lts. Robert L. Nelson and Fielding S. Robinson, both USMC, were aides to General Lejeune.

Second Lieutenants Clagett Wilson and Carl R. Dietrich were Neville's aides. Neville's staff included: 2d Lt. William A. Eddy, who served as aide for the period 11 August to 31 August 1918, but before and after that he had distinguished himself as the regimental intelligence officer of the 6th Marines.

Colonel Logan Feland now commanded the 5th Marines with Capt. George K. Shuler (until 8 August), followed by Captain John H. Fay as adjutant; Lt. Col. Julius S. Turrill still had the 1st Battalion; Lt. Col. Frederick M. Wise, the 2d Battalion;[2] and Maj. Maurice E. Shearer, the 3d Battalion.

Colonel Harry Lee commanded the 6th Marines with Lt. Col. Frank E. Evans, adjutant (until 9 August) followed by his replacement, Capt. Walter H. Sitz; Maj. Frederick A. Barker had the 1st Battalion; Lt. Col. Thomas H. Holcomb the 2d Battalion; and Maj. Berton W. Sibley, the 3d Battalion.

On 29 July, the day following Neville's reassumption of command, the brigade entrained for a twenty-four-hour journey that took them to an area around Nancy, about a dozen miles east of Toul. Brigade and 5th Marines' headquarters were both established at Villers-le-Nancy, with the 6th Marines' headquarters at Chaligny and headquarters of the 6th Machine Gun Battalion at Houdémont. Upon arrival in Nancy, considered one of France's most beautiful ancient cities, the soldiers and Marines of the 2d Division had a limited chance for leave. Though now thoroughly exhausted after their trying time at Soissons, they grabbed at any chance for civility. But only for a few short days were they to enjoy their first opportunity for a diversion since arriving in France; for some it had been as long as one year. They had been in small villages and towns, but nothing along the lines of a city the size and beauty of Nancy. Some of the officers and men enjoyed a day's liberty in Nancy while in the immediate area, but not all, unfortunately. I hope it was the "old-timers" who were given first shot to explore the "bon secteur" as the French poilu would say.

On 8 August 1918 both regimental commanders, Feland and Lee, assumed responsibility for territory then occupied by the 64th French Division in the relatively quiet Marbache Sector. The following day brigade and division assumed like responsibilities. Division headquarters closed their books at Nancy on the 9th, and reopened them the same day and hour at Marbache, a small village north of Nancy but south of Pont-à-Mousson. The main town in the sector was Pont-à-Mousson, along the Moselle River, a short distance south of the front lines. During this period of rest, the Marine brigade welcomed into its ranks 2,000 much-needed replacements.

On 5 August the assistant secretary of the navy, Franklin D. Roosevelt, inspected the 3d Battalion, 5th Marines, a few days before they entered the front lines in the Marbache Sector. Roosevelt asked Neville what he might do for the 4th Brigade[3] and Buck's reply was that it would be a "splendid thing to authorize Marines to wear the Corps device (Globe, Eagle, and Anchor) on their collars, left and right, just like the officers, only smaller." Roosevelt did authorize the emblems, but the Marine paymaster in Paris, Maj. Davis B. Wills, even though directed to secure the emblems Neville had in mind, instead ordered flat round buttons with the Marine Corps device stamped on them. These devices did not materially distinguish Marines from men in other services, since by this time they were outfitted in army uniforms and not their easily distinguishable forest green. Although this wasn't what Neville wanted, the Marines of the AEF did wear the emblem with pride.[4] While in France, Marines used every means possible to wear the emblem, even mounting it on their helmets to distinguish themselves from army troops. On 25 February 1920, all enlisted men in the Corps were authorized to wear the collar device originally conceived by General Neville. Better late than never.

The command of the western subsector passed to 4th Brigade control on 9 August. The 4th Brigade was in position as follows: 2/5 in the first line supported by 1/5 followed by 3/5, in depth. The 6th Marines had 2/6 in the first line followed by 1/6 then 3/6 in the final position. The 6th Machine Gun Battalion companies were allocated as usual, in addition to the two regimental machine-gun companies, which made an allocation of one Machine Gun company to each infantry battalion.

The sector, although a relatively quiet one, was astride the Moselle River, and the highways and railways, leading to Metz and Nancy. That is, leading to Metz if one could get through the German lines. The left flank of the 2d Division was a half mile north, and the same distance west, of Pont-à-Mousson and extended five miles eastward, then dropping southward at the bend of the Seille River another two miles. Several points of conjecture made the rounds as to why the 2d Division was assigned to this particular area. One was that it was a bluff to make the Germans think a major attack would be made here rather than in the St. Mihiel Sector. Second Division officers did whatever they could to lead the Germans along that primrose path, frequently enhancing their obvious presence with patrols designed to impress the Boche that an attack was developing here, and very soon.[5]

As early as 6 August, shortly after the Marines took over their section of the line, a patrol from 2/5, the 18th Company, under 2d Lt. Marshall E. Simmons, saw a large German force coming in their direction. What happened next is rather vague but seems to have been as follows: A huge explosion occurred among the German raiding party, followed by artillery shells falling in their midst with heavy machine-gun and rifle fire from the Marine companies on line, all of which caused the Boche to run. The artillery shells landing among the Germans seem to have been caused by a barrage called down by the Germans themselves, but falling among them rather than on the Marines. The accuracy of the artillery improved as the fire shifted toward Pont-à-Mousson, which was held by the 18th and 55th Companies, of 2/5, and by sheer coincidence, the only ammunition dump in the area was hit, blowing it sky high, and causing several casualties in so doing. Lieutenant Colonel F. M. Wise reported to Feland that eight men were killed and wounded from the shell fire.[6] Later, the Marines learned from German prisoners what had caused the explosion. It was a badly handled "long pipe" being carried to open a path through the American barbed wire, obviously a bangalore torpedo, but not recognized as such by the reporting observers. The brigade suffered two casualties during the raid.

A Marine patrol in the west subsector was fired upon by a German patrol, but two Boche from that patrol were captured, one being severely wounded. On the same evening, 8 August, the 79th Company, 2/6, suffered heavily from a box barrage laid down by the German artillery. French officers told the Americans that a German school in Metz specialized in training young officers as Sturmtruppen and it appeared as though they were then, as a sort of commencement exercise, assigned to the Marbache Sector to raid the enemy trenches opposite them. So far, according to the French, the Germans had shown spectacular success in their graduation "parties"; a large number of French soldiers had been taken prisoner in various recent raids.[7]

The 23d Company of the 6th Machine Gun Battalion, which arrived at Pont-à-Mousson at 2120 hours on 6 August, went into the line to support 2/5. The 81st Company arrived a day later and was assigned to support 2/6. They were in turn followed by the other companies, two of which went into reserve. The 77th Company joined 3/5 in reserve, whereas the 15th Company joined 3/6 in reserve at Liverdun at 2000 hours on August 8th. The 23d Company supported the 18th Company in repulsing the Boche, during the raid of August 7th, mentioned previously. Again on August 8th, when the enemy attempted another raid, the 81st Company supported the 2d Battalion, 6th Marines.

During the next few days German artillery was quite active. First Lt. Walter A. Powers reported via phone, on the early morning of the 9th, to the regiment's assistant commander, Lt. Col. Thomas Holcomb, that he and the 79th Company were being bombarded. Holcomb, quite disgustedly, reported to Lee that he had called the 2d Artillery Brigade for a barrage, got an okay from someone, but nothing happened. An hour later the division artillery began and continued for just over thirty minutes. A platoon leader of the 79th, 2d Lt. Gardiner Hawkins, who commanded the left platoon on the line, sent a message to Powers that was duly passed on to Holcomb, that although the German artillery had been caressing his platoons they hadn't responded. The 79th suffered two casualties that night. The main activity of both Marine regiments was to patrol their front. This they did on a daily basis until the brigade finally left the sector.

On 9 August, Ellis went right to work. He was soon sending brief, daily messages to Neville. Most covered a few lines but enough detail to explain what Neville's brigade was up to.

On 10 August the chief of staff of the 2d Division received a letter from Headquarters, AEF, in Chaumont, advising that General Pershing had approved the French recommendation that 204 officers and men of the brigade be awarded the Croix-de-Guerre. Pershing also agreed that Brig. Gens. Wendell C. Neville and Albertus W. Catlin together with Maj. Edward B. Cole, deceased, could be made Chevaliers of the Légion d'Honneur. All proposed foreign awards to American units had to be first approved by AEF, GHQ. The reason for the rather severe restriction was because of something that had happened back in April 1918. The French had directly awarded medals to officers and men of the 26th Division, following the victory (or debacle, depending upon your viewpoint) at Seicheprey. In point of fact, General Pershing had been planning court-martial procedures for several of that division's officers when he learned that the French had made copious awards to many of the officers and men for valor during that German raid. Naturally that put a stop to any courts-martial and outraged Pershing.

The actual awards for the 2d Division, American and French, were presented to the awardees in a parade ceremony held on Sunday, 25 August. The ceremony was attended by French and British officers of high rank and Maj. Gen. Hunter Liggett, commanding I Corps, was on hand as Pershing's representative. Many of the awards were for activities during June, at Belleau Wood. The others were for bravery at Soissons. Thirty-eight Distinguished Service Crosses were awarded to officers and men of the 4th Marine Brigade. They included both the 5th and 6th Marines and several to members of the 6th Machine Gun Battalion, as well as one to Hospital Apprentice Carl O. Kingsbury. First Sergeant Daniel Daly was a notable awardee. A recipient and Chevalier of the Légion d'Honneur was erroneously reported as "Captain E. A.[sic] Cook[sic], 5th Marines." It was, of course, 1st Lt. Elliott D. Cooke, an army officer who served with great distinction in the 5th Marines through most of the early battles in 1918 until wounded, and after being "repaired" would return to the brigade.

On 14 August 1918, the Brigade received a delegation from the Committee on Naval Affairs, which made an inspection tour of the sector. Though the Marines may have been wondering, they were still part of the navy, as reaffirmed by this visit. The following day the brigade was relieved by the 82d U.S. Division from the sector, and on that and the following day marched toward the Colombey-les-Belles area, with division headquarters closing on 19 August at Marbache and reopening at Colombey-les-Belles the same hour, about twenty-five miles south of Pont-à-Mousson. It is remembered by most Marine reporters as a quiet sector in which, for the most part, the 2d Division was able to relax and rest up after their escapades of the previous two months. One benefit did accrue to many Marines—they were taught to swim in the Moselle and twenty-five percent of the reserve companies were granted liberty in Nancy.

An amusing feature of this "quiet" period was the famous change in the steady diet of the Marines. The standard, reliable "Irish spud" was temporarily replaced by "love apples." There appeared to be an over-abundance of tomatoes growing in the area and Marines were encour-aged to eat them, as many as possible, in place of the potato that was their steady diet. They gorged themselves the first day, but by the sec-ond they were begining to long for the old standby. Some of the Marines, probably those with Irish blood, were praying for the return of the potato and within a week the tomatoes were gone and "King Spud" was welcomed back with some rejoicing among the gourmands.

During this period, several changes in officer personnel were made: Lt. Col. Julius S. Turrill, who had commanded 1/5 since its inception, left the battalion to be assistant to Feland at regiment. He was followed in succession by Capt. Raymond F. Dirksen for the next eight days and from 29 August through 19 September, by Lt. Col. James O'Leary.[8] Ma-jor George W. Hamilton, the hero of Hill 142, replaced O'Leary as com-mander of 1/5 and retained command until the end of the war. Lieu-tenant Colonel Frederick M. Wise had recently returned to 2/5 after a brief illness had caused his relief.[9] Major George Shuler, regimental ad-jutant of the 5th Marines was transferred to the 6th Marines. Captain John H. Fay, formerly in command of the 8th Machine Gun Company, was reassigned to Shuler's post, and Lt. James A. Nelms replaced him in command of 8th Company. The 5th Marine headquarters eventually wound up at Camp Bois l'Évèque, a training ground, as did most every-one else in the 4th Brigade.

Headquarters of the 6th Marines was now at Harmonville with its bat-talions scattered close about. Though in different locations, the two reg-iments and the 6th Machine Gun Battalion had much the same expe-riences. The regimental history stated,

> Effective work at reconnaissance was carried out and patrolling was successful, but the ambuscades of this regiment met with no suc-cess. Apparently the enemy was content to rest within his own wire.

Lieutenant Colonel Thomas Holcomb moved to second-in-com-mand of the regiment and was replaced by Maj. Ernest C. "Bull" Williams in command of 2/6. Upon its being relieved on 17 August, the following dispersement of the regiment occurred: First Battalion was billeted at Harmonville, 2/6 at Bois de l'Évêque, and 3/6 at Autreville.

The 6th Machine Gun Battalion, upon being relieved, marched to their new billets at Camp Bois de l'Évêque in easy stages, arriving about 17/18 August. Captain John P. McCann, recently released from the hospital, arrived and assumed command of the 23d Company, relieving 1st Lt. William B. Croka.

While in the rest area both infantry regiments and the machine-gun battalion received their replacements and merged them into the training routine for the next fight. All units received orders, on or about 22 August, to prepare for a series of marches to take the brigade into the St. Mihiel sector for the first almost wholly American offensive. The 5th Marines were now billeted at or near Sélancourt. and the 6th Marines at or near Gollivers, for a short period after their relief. They were also later assigned to Sélancourt.

The casualties while in the Marbache Sector were entirely among the enlisted men and were very light, compared to what had happened in June and July and what was to occur in October. Two men were killed, one from 17th Company and the other from 55th Company. The number of wounded were limited to nine, of which three were from the 55th Company, overall a hard-luck unit. Five of the others were also from the 5th Marines and there was but one from the 6th Marines, although an early history of that regiment states that two men were "slightly wounded" on or about the 8th of August.

Not much can be said about the Marbache Sector except that it was relatively quiet. But that certainly didn't hurt the feelings of the fighting men of the brigade. After two bloody battles, one lasting an entire month, a quiet sector was just what the entire division needed.

Notes

1 Brigadier General Charles Doyen was the first Marine to command a division. He was in command of the 2d Division for a period of time during the fall of 1917 until Major General Bundy arrived and relieved him .

2 "Fritz" Wise was soon to be transferred to the 4th Division (Regular) to command the 59th Infantry of the 8th Brigade. He was later promoted to full colonel and later acquired the 8th Brigade command.

3 Roosevelt, had "responsibility" for the U.S. Marine Corps as part of his duties. His reason for making the offer was an effort to improve the morale of the men after their devastating losses at Belleau Wood and Soissons within just over a month.

4 I have recently been advised that even those flat discs didn't appear until after the armistice.

5 The German leadership had been anticipating an attack by the American forces, which made it easier to keep them on edge. Several "phony" efforts were being made, the most notable being the one aimed at Belfort along the border with the former French province of Alsace. See the book by James Hallas, *Squandered Victory: The American First Army at St. Mihiel* (Westport, CT: Praeger, 1995) for a valuable, detailed description of that entire period.

6 *Records of the Second Division*, vol. 7.

7 For an excellent overview of the splendid training and consequent expertise of the German army in that specialty, see Bruce I. Gudmundsson's *Stormtroop Tactics: Innovation in the German Army, 1914–1918* (New York: Praeger, 1989). The author was a Marine officer and is presently historian for the Corps.

8 O'Leary was just "passing through," or so it seems. He briefly commanded 1/5 at St. Mihiel.

9 His "illness" was brought on by Brig. Gen. Harbord shortly after Wise had chewed him out in front of several officers and enlisted men following a Harbord harangue against Wise in June. Wise was sent back, ostensibly to go to an army school but also to be examined for "stress and overwork." Wise got an unwanted several weeks' rest, then returned to his battalion, somewhat subdued. Soon, he would receive his colonelcy and be transferred to the 4th Division as a regimental commander. Later he commanded an army brigade as well.

7: The Saint-Mihiel Offensive

Nothing except a battle lost can be half so melancholy as a battle won.
—Wellington

After leaving the Marbache Sector, the brigade moved about twenty-five miles south of the Pont-à-Mousson line to Favières, where it established headquarters in late August 1918. The 5th Marines were at Choloy and the 6th Marines at Harmonville. The 6th Machine Gun Battalion took up quarters at Camp Bois de l'Évèque. The very first item on the agenda was (what else?) training, of course. Training to keep the old-timers sharp but also, and most importantly, to bring the replacements up to brigade standards.

The training program was under the guidance of Lt. Col. Julius S. Turrill, late commander of 1/5, now second in command to Col. Logan Feland of the 5th Marines. Under his tutelage, each battalion spent a few days at Camp Bois de l'Évèque, in rifle firing, one-pounder and Stokes mortar exercises, grenade throwing, machine-gun and automatic-rifle firing, and terrain exercises to round out their combat training. The 6th Machine Gun Battalion was assembled with the regimental machine-gun companies. Together with the entire divisional machine-gun units, they were engaged in a special training exercise at the same camp. Likewise, each of the regimental pioneer platoons was assigned to the 2d Engineers for a special training course. Then, on 30–31 August 1918, the entire division held maneuvers.

In the meantime 1/5's new commanding officer was Lt. Col. Arthur J. O'Leary. Major Robert E. Messersmith, who formerly commanded the 78th Company, would soon command 2/5, while Maj. Maurice E. Shearer was still in command of 3/5. Lieutenant Colonel Thomas H. Holcomb had finally relinquished 2/6 to Maj. Ernest C. Williams and was now Col. Harry Lee's assistant in the 6th Marines. Major Frederick A. Barker had 1/6 and Maj. Berton W. Sibley was still in command of 3/6. Major Littleton W. T. Waller Jr. continued to command the 6th Machine Gun Battalion during these operations.

On 2 September a schedule of march orders was issued to move the division. A special note was included directing each of the commanding officers to see to the concealment of the move. The 4th Brigade issued Field Order No. 3 on the same day, which specified that the brigade headquarters would close at Favières and reopen the same day at Bainville, which was on the Madon River, about one kilometer south of where it flowed free of the Moselle River. Each of the regiments issued its own orders, which were substantially the same. The 5th Marines did not allow any halts in any towns, whereas the 6th only insisted upon compliance with march discipline. Each stressed concealment but varied on distances between units on the march. Individuality was still allowed in the Corps.

This was the beginning of the move to the area of the St. Mihiel Salient. In the same general area was Verdun to the north and Nancy on its southern flank. The salient had been there since the early days of the war, and though the French army had attempted to eliminate it several times, it was still there in September 1918. It was so apparent on maps that General Pershing saw its potential as a raison d'être, or objective for the fledgling American army, almost immediately upon arrival in France. He and some of his senior planners had envisioned that portion of the front-line area as a perfect place for the Americans to call their own. And deleting the salient was paramount in their planning. The British were in the north and the French protected the approaches to Paris. That left only the south for an independent American army. The seaports that France had allocated to Pershing for the AEF made that section of the line most convenient for transportation of supplies and people.

Even though most of Pershing's hours, since July 1917, were devoted to building an army, he had several officers working on a plan for the salient, notably Capt. George C. Marshall after his transfer from the 1st Division to the 1st Army as chief of operations. Beginning in July 1918, Marshall went through a number of revisions as the numbers of potential divisions increased. By September, his plan, with many revisions and assistance from other top-flight staff officers, was now complete and ready to be enacted. And what would a battle be without the 2d Division? So naturally the new commanding general, Lejeune, and his men were selected to be part of the whole.

The division had already spent some time in the area. In the early fall of 1917, it had trained near and about Gondrecourt, twenty-five miles southwest of Toul. Their first actions around Toul were in the Verdun Sector close to the right shoulder of the salient. Lately the division had been in the Marbache Sector around Pont-à-Mousson, farther north and east into the same shoulder of the St. Mihiel Salient.

After a series of night marches on 8 September the brigade arrived at an area around Manonville. Manonville was three rough miles south of Limey with no regular roads evident but with several brooks crossing the pathway. Limey, which was located a mile south of the division section of the lines, was the entryway to the division's section of the line. Field Order No. 26, issued on 8 September, directed the division to take over the Limey Sector one-half kilometer east of Remenauville, thereby relieving elements of the 89th and 90th divisions of the American IV Corps. Both divisions had been strung out farther than was practical for an offensive. The final positions for the 2d Division on the southeast would place it fourth in line from the shoulder on the right. To their immediate right would be the 5th Division (Regulars) and to their immediate right flank the 90th and 82d in that order. General Hunter Liggett's I Corps, which included the aforementioned divisions, had the 2d Division as its left flank. Fourth Corps was to their left and included the 89th, 42d, and 1st Divisions, right to left, in that order. From that point onward, along the line, until the other shoulder was reached, it was composed of French divisions in the lineup. The 26th "YD" Division was just about opposite the 1st Division across the salient with the 4th Division (Regulars) at their left and at the shoulder. Essentially, it was to be an American offensive with French support.

This salient had been an endless insult to the French army, but one that they had so far been unable to reduce. All told, Pershing had managed to allocate nearly a half million American soldiers to this operation. But Foch had made several attempts to reduce the American participation in order to obtain American divisions for a planned assault up near the Argonne forest. Foch had planned the massive operation to begin soon, but Pershing, ever inflexible, refused to make any reduction in his forces, making Foch angry. He and Pershing were not exactly "buddies" and had in fact clashed a number of times before. It appeared to Foch to be another effort to belittle the commander-in-chief of the combined Allied armies. If not that, then Pershing was clearly showing his disdain for the man selected to lead the Allies and the United States to eventual victory. Pershing and Foch never seemed to bury their differences and always appeared to find different courses to follow. Foch wanted American forces split up and divided according to French plans and Pershing insisted that American forces would fight as an American army, only. To make matters worse for Pershing, Haig agreed with Foch.[1] Meanwhile, entirely unknown to Foch or Pershing, Maj. Robert Messersmith, formerly of the 78th Company, 2/6, relieved Maj. Harold L. Parsons in command of 2/5, on 11 September.

Private Cedric D. Southern,[2] who along with several other Marine replacements had just joined the 20th Company, described what he and

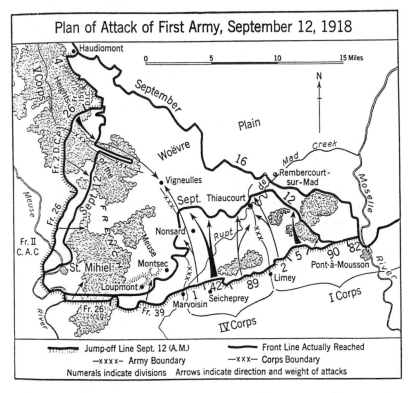

Map 11: The overall attack plan of the American 1st Army for the closing off of the Saint Mihiel Salient. Note that I Corps, and especially the 2d Division, nearly attained the ultimate objective line on their first day. Also note the pattern of advance of the 102d Infantry, 26th Division, commanded by Col. Hiram I. Bearss, USMC.

some of the other replacements did when they arrived. "The first thing we had to do was turn in some of our clothing and equipment and draw new."[3] He and his buddy had a few hours to themselves and decided to give away personal belongings that "we did not absolutely need, and of course a few letters and other things that we determined to hold on to." He further described the afternoon and the assembly in preparation to moving up to the lines. "The muddy roads were congested with autos, trucks, guns, ration carts and rolling kitchens, mules horses, and thousands of men going in both directions." At 0100 hours they arrived at a town from which they entered a communications trench just as "the famous 'million dollar barrage' opened up . . . and, believe me, it was 'some' barrage." Of course he reduces the impact of that statement somewhat, when he adds that it was the very first barrage he'd ever heard up close. Southern's picture of the trek through the communications trench "always ankle deep in mud" and with a pack that was "growing heavier every minute" must have been a common complaint of most front-line soldiers no matter which army they were part of. This was happening on the evening of 11–12 September. They were just in time for the "Big Push" that was scheduled for a few hours in the future. Sergeant Karl McCune of the 55th Company, noted in his diary that the barrage lasted until about 0500, "raising tremendous havoc in the Boche position." And he noted that the machine-gun barrage started an hour earlier: "Machine guns were so thick that bullets fairly rained into the hostile lines." Then started the creeping barrage, following which the infantry attacked.

Division's task was to advance and take two towns, Thiaucourt and Jaulny, to their northeast front, and continue moving until the line was straightened out, a distance of approximately six miles. The entire army advance was scheduled for 0500 hours on 12 September. Unfortunately, the Germans had gotten wind of the planned attack by the allied forces and they in turn had planned a retirement.[4] They expected an attack along the southern face of the salient, which is where it was to be. The French army was to sit in place until the Americans had forced the German forces to their front to retire. The French forces would then move forward and pinch out the "nose." There was one exception to the general rule and that was to be performed by the 1st and 26th Divisions. Orders for the 26th were for it to punch down from the north to meet the 1st Division at the town of Vigneulles, closing off whatever German troops remained in the pocket. It is important to our story here, because the leader of the 102d Infantry of the 26th "YD" was none other than Colonel "Hiking Hiram" Bearss, a fighting Marine whose story will be picked up in its logical place.[5] As always, he was right up front where the action was.

On the first day, the 23d Infantry was to advance in a column of battalions on the left of the division sector, while the 9th Infantry would be on the division right.[6] The Marines were to support the infantry. Two companies from the 6th Machine Gun Battalion, the 15th on the left and the 23d on the right, were to lay down a barrage for the infantry's advance. The 4th Brigade split its regiments in the following manner: on the right flank behind the 9th Infantry, the first line was to be 3/5 (Shearer) and the 77th Machine Gun Company (Hale), followed by 1/5 (O'Leary); then 2/5 (Messersmith) and the 23d Machine Gun Company (McCann) would bring up the rear. Behind the 23d Infantry, Barker with 1/6 and the 73d Machine Gun Company of the 6th Regiment were on the left flank and slightly forward, as liaison on the left with the 89th U.S. Division.[7] They were charged with protecting the left rear flank of the 23d and as a result were put under the control of the 23d for that exercise. Consequently, Lee of the 6th Marines had but two battalions under his control that day. Thus 3/6 (Sibley) led off the 6th Regiment, supported by the 15th Machine Gun Company (Major) and in their second line was 2/6 (Williams) with the 81st Machine Gun Company (Hart). The Marine Brigade's reserve was made up of Companies B, C, E, and F of the 2d Engineers along with one company of light tanks and the division's "own" 4th Machine Gun Battalion.

Thursday, 12 September

The attack order, dated 11 September 1918, set the parameters of the division. Field Order No. 9 issued by the 4th Brigade defined and described the plan, stating that the brigade would "form the 2d line (reserve) and support the 3d Brigade in executing the division's mission. It will be prepared to pass through the 3d Brigade and continue the advance to the Army Objective." The army objective for the first day was to be the high ground between Jaulny and Xammes, the last named a mile or so west of Jaulny and partially in the zone of the 89th Division.

A bombardment was laid down beginning at 0100 and lasted for four hours. At 0500 division artillery began a rolling barrage. The 3d Brigade took off a few minutes later at approximately 0500, and the Marines were to begin their advance about an hour after the infantry took off, leaving one-half miles between battalions. It was too late. At 1000 Feland was having difficulties bringing his battalions up in order to close with the 9th Infantry. According to Feland's reports, it was difficult trying "to get word from one Bn. to another." As late as 1135 that morning Neville was urging Feland forward to close with the 3d Brigade, which had "advanced from 1st phase as per schedule." Neville also reported that the 5th U.S. Division had already reached the army objective. Obviously angry at being pressured, Feland lectured Shearer about not using the French tanks assigned to him properly, and asking that he send in location reports every half hour.

The light tanks were having considerable difficulty with the terrain. In addition, the speed of the infantry was such that the tanks were unable to keep up. According to reports, the tanks were constantly out of position and consequently were almost ignored by the battalion commanders, hence Shearer's reluctance to utilize them, even after being ordered to. The machine-gun companies assigned to the barrage, the 15th on the left and the 23d on the right, advanced when the 3d Brigade infantry took off, and did not cease their advance until about 0545, after they had fired off fifteen hundred rounds each. The 15th picked up with 3/6 as it passed their positions and the 23d did the same when 2/5 arrived in their zone.

At noon Feland was able to report to Brigade that 3/5 was within two thousand meters of the intermediate objective. Barker with 1/6, which had been the advance unit of the regiment on the far left flank, was close to being within a thousand meters of the same target. A few minutes later Feland was haranguing all three battalion commanders to "close up on 3d Bgd." The 3d had just completed its first phase and had advanced beyond it. The army infantry was doing its job that day, and the 5th Marines were apparently having a devil of a time keeping up.

It also appears that Lee's 6th was doing much better than the 5th. They were able to follow the 23d Infantry at the assigned thousand yards. What must later have been embarrassing was that Williams, commanding 2/6, was a day off in his reports for the morning of 12 September, which he continued to date "11 September," and that fine Marine, Sibley, 3/6, had mistaken day for night, recording "9:25 P.M." when it should have been 0925. But they were all moving forward, doing their jobs well as support for the 23d Infantry. The 23d was doing well enough through their own efforts so it was nearly a moot point anyway. Lieutenant Colonel Richard Derby, USA, on the division medical staff, voluntarily went up front to help his friend, Surgeon Joel Boone of the 6th Marines, to set up forward dressing stations. Derby brought twenty-three stretcher bearers from his staff along with him and set up in a culvert under a road running north out of Xammes. He also moved his ambulances to those centers, directing them through a continuous and severe shell bombardment and the ever-present Maxim fire. In addition, Derby also assisted Boone and his staff to evacuate the wounded, all at his own great risk.[8]

At 1340 Major Shearer, 3/5, sent Feland a report explaining what had really happened between him and the French tank officer earlier. He told the Frenchman that he didn't have anything for him to do "at present" and to send his liaison officer to Shearer for possible later use. His next query and request were interesting. He asked that if his 45th and 47th Companies could be located, "please send them up." Records indicate that both companies were "lost" and for some reason never received orders to advance with their battalion. More communication problems.[9]

The first line of infantry passed through Thiaucourt at 1700, and were practically at the army objective. In Shearer's report he indicated that his battalion, or rather the two companies, were within six hundred yards of the 9th Infantry at 1800 hours that evening and bivouacked in a ravine on the south edge of the Bois du Fey. This forest was located just east of Thiaucourt, one of the two towns listed as the objective for the division that day. At 2015 Col. George W. Stuart (9th Infantry, commander) requested both of Shearer's available companies be sent up to support him. Shearer was frantic and requested details from Feland about the 45th and 47th Companies if known. He related that, as requested, he had sent the 16th and 20th plus part of the 77th Machine Gun Company forward to help defend the left flank of the 9th Infantry. That didn't leave him with many troops to defend his own position. What he didn't know was that his two missing companies, the 45th and 47th, were in front of his other two companies, the 16th and 20th (I cannot determine why). The 45th was on the right side of the river[10] with support from the 16th Company, the 47th on the left side supported by the 20th Company.

Private Southern mentions, among other things that an American plane, accidentally hit by American artillery fire, crashed to earth in flames only a few hundred yards away from where he and his company were located. He tells of digging in early that evening after the division had gained its objective "very rapidly." He also tells of a Marine who captured a German horse, mounted it, and was having a devil of a time getting the animal to move. "Someone yelled, '*Raus mit ihm!*' and you should have seen that horse run . . . to see that fellow bouncing up and down on that horse's back. . . . the valley echoed with the peals of laughter." Later that evening the rolling kitchens came up and served a meal "which tasted better than Thanksgiving . . . even though it was only corned willie." Elton Mackin relates the tale of the wounded soldier who was passing through the 5th Marine lines headed back for "repairs" when an earnest young Marine replacement yelled, "Hey, buddy, how's things goin' up there?" His response sent a laugh through the Marines who heard: "Aw, hell, son, goin' fine. We're goin' through them like a dose of salts through a tall, thin woman."[11]

Another plane, this one German, also fell to earth that day, and if the reports from the 55th Company are to be believed, their rifle fire brought it down. Later, in the afternoon, Mackin was ordered into Thiaucourt to locate the battalion water wagon and to bring it up to 1/5. Major Hamilton added that he wanted to find it full of water when it arrived. Mackin describes what was taking place in that town already occupied by American forces, and it was total disaster. Traffic was tied up in every direction and soon the Germans had the range and whanged away with their artillery. That cleared the town out quickly. Even the wounded in stretchers were dropped so that the bearers could escape that much faster. The joke bruited about, weeks later, was that so-and-so was still wandering lost around the fields at Thiaucourt, looking for a battle. The higher the rank, the grosser and juicier the tale.

Well, the story has often been told that everyone in the 2d Division had a walkover that first day, but the young intelligence officer of 1/9, 2d Lt. J. C. Murphy, in a report, estimated their casualties to be fifty percent on 12 September. If the rest of the 3d Brigade fared as badly, they had a bad day, overall. No wonder they needed two companies of Marines for flank defense that night.

Friday, 13 September

The Germans, by now well aware that a serious attack was in progress, removed ammunition dumps, evacuated hospitals, and moved three divisions forward as a reserve for defense against the offensive they knew was coming soon. The situation for the next few days wouldn't be quite as easy for the Americans and their French comrades.

The 4th Brigade was to form a column of battalions with the 5th Regiment on the right flank, and the 6th Regiment to their left. One battalion of the 6th plus the 73d Machine Gun Company, was assigned to the 3d Brigade "to maintain combat liaison with our 4th Corps on the left of our Division." The 6th Machine Gun Battalion and the 4th Machine Gun Battalion were assigned to "barrage positions north of the Flirey–Pont-à-Mousson road to support the attack of the division." The 5th Marines were to advance with three battalions in column and the 6th in a column of two battalions. Each battalion was to form with two companies in the first line and two companies in support. The 3d Battalion, 5th Marines, was to lead with 1st Lt. James A. Nelms and his 8th Machine Gun Company supporting them.

On the afternoon of 13 September Lejeune issued orders for the relief of the 3d Brigade by the 4th Brigade. Two companies of the 5th Marines, plus 1/6 and 2/6 that had supported the 3d Brigade, rejoined their parent units. The relief was made without any unusual incident that afternoon and evening. It was finally completed at 0400 on 14 September. The relief followed Field Order No. 10, which stated,

3. (a) The 5th Regiment will relieve the 9th Regiment and the 6th Regiment will relieve the 23d Regiment, battalion for battalion.

(b) The 1st and 2nd Battalions of the 6th Regiment now stand assigned to that regiment.

When relieved, the 3d Brigade occupied the positions vacated by the 4th. O'Leary, in his first combat with 1/5, remained with it at its assigned position just north of Jaulny for the next three days. Messersmith, in his first combat with his new battalion, was assigned a support position in a ravine on the southern edge of the Bois de Fey where they also remained for the next two days, advancing to the north of Jaulny on 15 September to repel an attack that never came off. Lucky them. Shearer and 3/5 had a more visible existence. They were in the middle of all the shooting during the brigade's maneuvers.

Saturday, 14 September

Early on the morning of 14 September, the 6th Marines sent out patrols to the "Army Objective Line." The reconnaissance teams went out about two kilometers and established an outpost line and a system of advanced posts. They then patrolled "as far as they could," to the "Line of Exploitation," approximately to the line Rembercourt-Charey, which was within the limits of the 4th Brigade. Charey, incidentally, was the location of advanced positions of the famed Hindenburg Line.

Meanwhile, the enemy was firing its artillery upon the Marines' lines but inflicting few casualties. During this time the rear battalions ad-

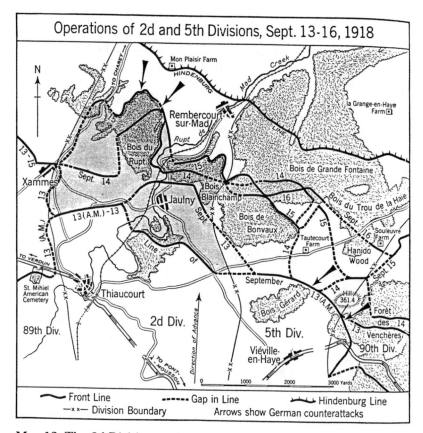

Map 12: The 2d Division again moved rapidly ahead of most other divisions. This map indicates that the division was far ahead of most other divisions, almost to the Hindenburg Line, by 15 September 1918. Marine patrols actually ventured to close contact with the Germans at the Michael Line, the German Main Line of Resistance.

vanced to support the strong patrol action. Consolidation was begun on the outpost line and effective combat liaison established with both the 89th Division on their left and the 5th Division on their right. For some reason, the 89th had not advanced, which necessitated the detailing of a flank guard on the left flank of the 6th Marines.

Lejeune wasn't satisfied with the limited information he had to work with, so Field Order No. 28 was issued at 1630, which described what was desired. In essence it directed Neville to send out

> strong patrols, [at 1700 hours], of two companies from each regiment to reconnoiter the division sector in front of the "Army Objective Line" to a distance of about two kilometres . . . [to] make the line more secure and determine the enemy position and strength.

The order further directed Neville to send the patrols "as far as they can [go]," to at least the "Line of Exploitation" (i.e., line Rembercourt-Charey). Lejeune specifically wanted knowledge of how far the enemy had fallen back. Further, the units were to keep aware of enemy artillery and especially "fire from the division on our right."

Unfortunately, as was so often the case, the orders were delayed, so the patrols didn't receive the message soon enough, preventing their departure until 1830 hours. Their trip through the woods, mainly at night, was extremely difficult and liaison with their flank units was practically impossible.

Sibley was leading the 6th Regiment. His orders were to occupy positions on the high ground to his front, northwest of Jaulny to the north of Xammes. While the going through the woods was extremely difficult, soon after dark 3/6 made their objectives. The 97th and 84th Companies were in the forward positions, while the 82d and 83d were ordered to remain in their positions because of the difficulty in moving in the dark. Two platoons from the 15th Machine Gun Company were supporting them. The patrols met no enemy resistance during the night.

Sunday, 15 September

It was early on the 15th when "Bull" Williams and 2/6, now leading the regiment, encountered numerous enemy machine-gun nests in a ravine between Xammes and Charey, south of the Bois de la Montagne. Though the walls of the ravine were extremely steep, it didn't take 2/6 long to overwhelm these guns, and they soon advanced to the north ends of both the Bois de Hailbat and Montagne. There they took heavy shelling from German artillery. At this time 2/6 was divided into two components, one led by Williams and the other by Capt. George W. Martin of the 79th Company. Liaison between companies broke down and it was several hours before they made a connection. One/Six had the same trouble in the Bois de la Montagne. The 84th and 97th Companies of 3/6 sent out patrols to locate them.

Williams's battalion was in close proximity with the German lines and consequently suffered heavy machine-gun fire for hours. For an unknown reason Barker's 1/6 was divided and advanced to both the left and the right flanks of 2/6. The 76th was on the right flank, supported by the 74th Company while the 75th Company, supported by the 95th, was on the left. Williams and his lads were taking heavy punishment, so at 1030 Sibley was also ordered to reinforce 2/6. He sent in two platoons from the 83d Company. The official history states that "casualties were light," but why the need for so much support? As was very common, bad news was taken lightly, later.[12]

But the enemy was taking his licks, too, and when attacking German soldiers turned and fled from the scene, Gunnery Sergeant William Ulrich* of the 80th Company followed them yelling in German for them to surrender. Most of them stopped and appeared to be responding to his direction. Just then, unfortunately, a nervous young Marine private opened up on them. This caused panic among those with their hands up and again they ran. Catching up with them Ulrich, again using his native German tongue, soon convinced the remaining group, all fifty one of them, to surrender to him. They did and he brought them back through the jittery Marines without further incident.[13]

Williams again leading 2/6 forward soon found himself faced with a strong enemy force in the woods ahead. After taking a few more interlocking enemy Maxim positions the battalion was stalled by a strong point along a ridge a few hundred yards ahead. Williams's response was a call for artillery as his men took cover.

Private John Joseph Kelly, a runner in the 78th Company, frequently appeared in the front lines, but not always running. As he would do at Blanc Mont three weeks later, on 15 September, he aided in the capture of an enemy machine gun and four prisoners. As he had at Verdun and would again later at Blanc Mont, "Johnnie" earned three Silver Star citations this day for his courage.

About this time his skipper, 1st Lt. John A. Connor, USA, went down with two wounds. "Johnnie" tried to locate someone to take command, but could find no one. All the company officers were down, as were numerous enlisted men. The battalion was taking it quite hard along with the regiment. Kelly, using utmost persuasion, impressed that fact upon Sgt. Henry S. Bogan*, urging him to do something to prevent further destruction of the leaderless company. Bogan, no mean fighting man himself, gathered together a small detachment and led them in taking the Maxim that was causing such fatalities. After that feat he continued his advance, entered the enemy's trenches, and cleared them for another 150 yards. He remained exposed to enemy fire for the balance of that day.[14]

At the same time, Kelly rounded up a few more Marines but his crowd was soon caught in a crossfire and forced to hide behind some boulders. That group of sixteen Marines was then attacked by a platoon of German soldiers. The Marines fought like mad with rifles, grenades, and Chauchats, but took significant casualties. Still, the Boche were temporarily scattered, so Kelly and his followers gained some room. When only eight men remained of Kelly's detachment, they had to go to ground to avoid complete annihilation. Again the enemy came. The lone Chauchat gunner fell wounded, so Kelly took over the gun, keeping up a smashing fire that again drove the enemy back. He then turned the gun over to another Marine and started to pull the wounded gunner to the rear. Just then a shell landed close to his replacement, putting him out of action and, as Kelly soon learned, wounding him badly. Fortunately, other Marines were working their way forward thus saving the remaining few men of Kelly's dedicated band.

The 78th Company was not the only outfit fighting that morning. First Lieutenant Graves Erskine, a platoon leader of the 79th Company, bravely placed himself at the head of a conglomerate of headquarters and intelligence men, leading them forward against German machine guns until he was so badly wounded he could not move forward. One of his men, Pvt. Archie M. Vale of the 96th, heaved Erskine onto his shoulder and lugged him off the field covered by a friendly machine-gun barrage and shell fire. Another platoon leader of the 79th, 2d Lt. Gardiner Hawkins, continued his reconnaissance of enemy machine-gun positions, while subjected to continual heavy fire from German artillery and Maxims. Private Albert Meyer*, also of the 79th, while engaged in carrying wounded Marines to the rear, saw a buddy about to be captured by a large force of advancing enemy; he rushed out to kill two of the Boche and then brought his pal back to safety.

The 80th Company added to the day's tally when Pvt. Florian L. Frillman hurled grenades at two machine-gun nests putting both out of action. Two company lieutenants, Henley Goode and David Kilduff, both were cited for performing at the highest level, fearlessly exposing themselves to enemy fire while attending to their duties. Kilduff was mortally wounded. Corporal Donald M. Parker* joined a company officer in attacking and silencing a machine gun on the left flank that was causing numerous casualties. Unfortunately, although he was holding his position under intense enemy fire, a sniper finished his life and career.[15]

The 73d Machine Gun Company was another unit that earned awards. If, as I presume, they were servicing their usual battalion, 1/6, they were at the heart of the position held by the Marines near the Bois de la Montagne. Sergeant Hildor B. Ellison earned a couple of Silver Star citations and a Croix de Guerre for maneuvering his gun to a more advantageous position, even though he was under heavy fire while doing so. Sergeant Lyle C. Houchins*, fearlessly exposing himself to enemy fire, moved his gun forward from his sheltered position and with utter disdain for his own safety opened up enfilade fire on the advancing Germans. Corporal Casey V. Loomis*, at the opposite end of the line, duplicated Houchins's act. These two men broke up that counterattack within one hundred yards of the American line.

The 1st Battalion companies of the 6th Marines also served. Second Lieutenant Julian P. Brown of the 74th, throwing caution to the winds, constantly placed himself in an exposed position so as to spot machine-gun nests. In the same company, Pharmacist Mate 3d John R. Litchfield*, USN, did what corpsmen do so well and so often, rendering first aid to the wounded. He attempted to remove a wounded Marine from a trench and move him to the rear. Unfortunately, he and the wounded Marine were killed in action while he was so engaged.

First Lieutenant Henry E. Chandler* of the 75th Company constantly and fearlessly exposed himself while locating enemy machine-gun nests and then led his platoon forward in the face of fearsome fire to knock out those German weapons. Private Grover M. Chatman* of the 75th took exception to three snipers who were giving the members of his platoon hell in front of the lines. Over fire-swept terrain he swiftly moved until he reached the enemy and finished them off.[16]

First Lieutenant Clive E. Murray, of the 76th Company, added to the day's total by not only encouraging his men while subjected to intense artillery and machine-gun fire but also by refusing to leave his post when wounded until his skipper ordered him to. Sergeant Kenneth D. Lockwood got a couple of Silver Stars for assuming leadership of his platoon when his platoon leader was wounded.

A few good men of the 95th were also cited for outstanding service and bravery. Private Howard C. Cook*, who regularly carried messages for Major Barker, exposed himself to heavy fire for several hours, while spotting machine-gun nests and enemy snipers for his buddies to nail. Private Curtis H. Freiman refused to retire despite being wounded. He remained with his company until they were relieved. Pharmacist Mate 1st Class Raymond Kaga* was cited for "exceptionally meritorious and distinguished service . . . in action against the enemy." We are told in Strott's history of the medical personnel of the 6th that Kaga's citation also said "[he] disregarded all personal danger and was indefatigable in rendering assistance to the wounded under heavy constant shell fire."[17]

Silbey's 3/6 had its share of heroes that day. A former enlisted man, 2d Lt. Joseph C. Grayson of the 96th Company, though wounded in the knee as the advance began, refused to pull back and continued forward in the absence of his wounded company commander (Capt. Wethered Woodworth), assisting in holding a strong point captured from the enemy. Trumpeter Maurice S. Hardin did his company proud by sniping and killing four Germans in a machine-gun nest, then advancing and taking two guns and destroying two others. Corporals Norman Jelly and Thomas E. Mack and Pvt. Roy J. Schafer went out together and knocked over two more nests. Private Lester H. Nutting* moved two hundred yards behind the enemy lines to spot and signal back the locations of enemy positions. But, as was too often the case, he was killed in action while returning to his lines. There were many more heroes in all companies; these are just a few of the eighty or so officers and men of the 6th Marines who were cited that day.

On the morning of 15 September, 2d Division Field Order No. 29 informed the 4th Brigade that the 5th Division had taken Rembercourt at 0100 and was digging in. The 89th had started to move forward and so would the 4th Brigade to protect the left flank of the 5th Division. In the afternoon, Field Order No. 30 from division alerted the 4th Brigade to a pending relief of the division by the 78th Division on the night of 15–16 September. Almost as though they knew of the pending relief, the Germans attacked again. Perhaps they did know, as security wasn't very secure in that war. That evening at approximately 2000 hours the enemy put down a heavy bombardment on the front line of the 6th Marines and launched an attack on their left front with infantry and machine guns. It was repulsed by sustained rifle and machine-gun fire augmented by American artillery that fell upon their ranks and lines. The enemy finally had had enough and withdrew without making a substantial gain of any kind.

The night of 15–16 September saw the relief of the 4th Brigade, satisfactorily completed with little loss during the movement of lines. All were retired except for Waller's 6th Machine Gun Battalion, which stayed put for another twenty-four hours. Late on the morning of the 16th, Neville passed the command of the sector over to the commanding general of the 155th Brigade, Brig. Gen. Mark L. Hersey. The 5th Marines' own machine company, the 8th, was retained in line by request of the commanding officer of the 309th Infantry.[18] Otherwise all other Marines proceeded to a new area on 17 September.

This was also a time of the great influenza offensive. The long time that the members of the brigade had spent in severe exposure to the continual rain and mud and the constant strain of battle was bad, not only for morale but for their health. Several hundred were evacuated due to sickness, mostly the flu. First moves for the brigade had been to an area about four miles south of Limey. The town in which brigade established its headquarters was Manonville, while the men were located in the Bois de Minorville, another mile and a half farther southwest. A few days later, 20 September, the 4th Brigade was moved farther south of Toul, which town was within a five-mile southern radius of each of the locations both regiments would occupy. The 5th was assigned to the following towns: Chaudenay, Pierre-la-Treiche, Moutrot, Blénod-lès-Toul, and Mont-le-Vignoble. The total manpower of the 6th was recorded as 4,202 men and 114 officers. They were assigned to Foug, Lay-Saint-Rémy, Meuillot, Choloy, Domgermain, and Charmes-la-Côte. The 5th Marines reported an enlisted strength of 4,004 with 104 officers. The 6th Machine Gun Battalion occupied Bicqueley with twenty-one officers and 595 enlisted men. The totals quoted were close to the numbers before the event of late May 1918.

After the few days on active combat duty the normal Marine routine resumed. On Sunday, 22 September, Marine diarist Cpl. John E. Aasland of the 55th Company noted that the men had to open their shirts so the officers could "see how dirty it was," both shirts and, I suppose, the necks over which the shirts were worn. Daily showers were in the future, not 1918.

The brigade remained in the newly assigned area until 25 September, when in accordance with Field Order No. 32, 2d Division, they were ordered south, by rail, to an area south of Châlons-sur-Marne with 4th Brigade Headquarters to be located at Sarry. Châlons was some fifteen miles south of Suippes. This was located about seventy-five crow-miles west of their last location. The rail journey at the time would of necessity be convoluted and not crowlike. Most likely they traveled through Vitry-le-François and perhaps Neufchâteau as well; better than walking. There was no chance of that, because the needs were great and the time short. The 2d Division would be wanted as soon as possible and in the best shape possible. Corporal Aasland indicated in his 29 September entry, "No money in sight yet, but we signed the payroll today, *so those who live through the next battle should get some money in about a month.*" (Emphasis added.)

The officer casualties at St. Mihiel were numerous. Three were killed in action while another seventeen were wounded. Those killed were Capt. William B. Black, skipper of the 95th Company and Capt. David R. Kilduff and 1st Lt. Albert C. Simonds, both platoon leaders of the 80th Company. Those wounded included Capts. Bailey M. Coffenberg, skipper of the 80th Company; Graves B. Erskine, platoon leader of 79th Company; Jack S. Hart, skipper 81st Machine Gun Company; John F. Horn, 75th; Clive E. Murray, 76th; John N. Popham Jr., 95th; and Wethered Woodworth, skipper of the 96th. Also wounded were 1st. Lts. James A. Conner, of the 95th,[19] and Archie W. French, both of the 78th, and 2d Lts. George Bower, 81st Machine Gun Company; Fitzhugh L. Buchanan, 77th Machine Gun; Charles F. Dalton, 75th; Herbert G. Joerger, 77th Machine Gun; Samuel W. Meek Jr., 82d; Thomas R. Wert, 80th; and Albyn A. Wilcox, 73d Machine Gun Company.

From this it is evident that the dead and wounded were mainly from the 6th Marines and the 6th Machine Gun Battalion. Among the 129 enlisted dead were twenty-eight from the 5th Marines and 101 from the 6th. The total wounded were also heavily from the 6th Marines. Those casualties were 416 to 143 for the 5th Marines. The 6th Machine Gun Battalion had an additional forty-one wounded. So all in all it was a busy few days for the Marine Brigade. Although the 4th Brigade later generally referred to St. Mihiel as a "piece of cake," no one ever needs a second helping of that kind of dessert. With 132 dead and over 600 wounded, they found it easy to gloat at how well they had had it, compared to their comrades of the 3d Brigade. The total losses for the division amounted to 1,041. Too many pyrrhic victories such as St. Mihiel would finish off both the 3d and 4th Brigades. The next "victory" would nearly do so, and it really did make this one seem like a "piece of cake." It was called "Blanc Mont," and the 5th Marines would really pay for taking their ease at St. Mihiel. But so would the 6th Marines and the rest of the division too.

Notes

1 It appears, according to Haig's own journal, that he and Foch wanted American support to relieve pressure on the British. The only way to obtain that was by reducing the proposed assault and reduction of the St. Mihiel salient and moving the Americans farther west.

2 *NYLIC, War Stories, etc.* (New York: New York Life Insurance Co., 1920), 198–208.

3 Ibid., 200, the replacements probably drew U.S. Army uniforms to replace their forest-green Marine uniforms.

4 It appears, then and now, that the attempts to keep information about the coming attack from the Germans were just that; attempts. They had spies everywhere, newspapers had been less than careful in their pronouncements than they should have; many of the French civilians in the area were well aware of what was coming, etc.

5 There is a special section that includes many of "Hiking Hiram's" special deeds while so engaged with the 102d Infantry. Chapter entitled "Other Marine Activities in France."

6 The infantry would move forward in a column of battalions. Major Robert Denig, USMC, and his 3/9 led the procession on the right.

7 It seems evident that the 2d Division command was not all that confident of the untried 89th Division being able to "keep up" with the big boys during an advance against an entrenched German force. They did, mostly, and they performed quite well on the Meuse in November.

8 Derby, the son-in-law of former president Theodore Roosevelt, wrote a marvelous memoir entitled *"Wade in, Sanitary!" The Story of a Division Surgeon in France* (New York; Putnam, 1919). One of his brothers-in-law, Quentin Roosevelt, lost his life while flying over Château-Thierry.

9 This would eventually become a serious problem for Shearer and Feland. According to the history of the 5th, the two companies had been ordered forward to the Bois de Hailbat, late on 14 September. But as it continues the explanation "the two companies *finally* took position on a height which dominated the town of Rembercourt and the valley of the Mad River." They were miles ahead of where they were ordered to be. No wonder Shearer hadn't the faintest idea what happened to them.

10 The maps indicate that the name of that river is/was "le Rupt de Mad Rau." I had to give up on the translation, could not locate any of those words in my extensive dictionary, although the history of the 5th Marines identifies it as the "Mad River," which makes sense.

11 Mackin, Elton E. *Suddenly We Didn't Want to Die,* 141.

12 Originally, Williams's position was on the high ground, level with the enemy. He evidently soon realized that he was exposed and fell back to the ravine for a small amount of cover.

13 Ulrich remained in the Corps and sometime prior to WWII retired a major.

14 In addition to a DSC Bogan was also awarded a navy DSM, then he duplicated the former at Blanc Mont; was promoted to 2d Lieutenant and con-

tinued to distinguish himself for the balance of the war. He was one of only two enlisted Marines of the 4th Brigade who received the NDSM during the war. It was a medal that was usually reserved for senior officers, although a few Marine aviators were also recipients.

15 Parker was posthumously awarded a DSC and NC. The others all received Silver Star citations.

16 Chatman, also received two French awards, the Médaille Militaire and a Croix de Guerre.

17 Like most corpsmen, Kaga continued doing his duty and sometimes exceeded what would normally be required of him. He earned two more Silver Stars at Blanc Mont.

18 Evidently that officer had requested of Neville that the 8th remain.

19 Connor is not listed in any of my USMC records so he most likely was a U.S. Army officer. I have deduced, from my available information, that Connor was at least the acting skipper of the 78th Company at St. Mihiel.

8: Blanc Mont

The taking of Blanc Mont is the single greatest achievement of the 1918 campaign—the Battle of Liberation.
—Marshal Pétain

Both the 4th French Army in the Champagne region and the U.S. 1st Army in the Argonne began their offensive operations at the same time. The French attack was located in an area about twenty-three miles to the east of the city of Reims; Blanc Mont was in that sector. For nearly four years the French had been trying to retake that very important ridge. Unfortunately for the French, possession of that high ground had given the Germans unlimited observation of the ground that any attack must come across. Every attempt by French forces to take that all-but-impregnable height had ended in complete failure. In their attack, beginning on 26 September, the French XXI Corps gained limited objective against the strongly entrenched German forces in the area. The French had advanced about three miles along the front and had successfully taken several German positions on the lower ground. But eventually the Boche moved their well-prepared positions just north of the town of Somme-Py and there, on 30 September, stopped the limited French advance. After four days of attack, the French forces were exhausted. Needless to say the French were frustrated at their losses and lack of accomplishment. Some new muscle and some new plan was required if the bloodbath was to cease and the French were to be successful.

Earlier in September the French high command, anticipating great difficulties in their coming Champagne offensive, had requested the loan of American troops from General Pershing. He gave them the trustworthy 2d Division and the brand-spanking newly arrived 36th National Guard Division, to be used in whatever manner Marshal Foch saw fit. With a simple phone call, later put in writing, the 2d Division was officially transferred to French control on 23 September.

• • •

The 2d Division commander, Maj. Gen. John A. Lejeune, USMC, had already been orally apprised of the transfer of his division to the French High Command. Subsequently, when General Gouraud summoned him to the headquarters of his 4th French Army, Lejeune assumed, without having any written confirmation, that his division had been already been assigned to Gouraud. When Lejeune arrived at Marie-sur-Marne, he was informed that Gouraud requested his presence at his headquarters in Châlons-sur-Marne as soon as possible. Lejeune tells us that he was "greeted most cordially." It was during the following lengthy discussion that Gouraud told Lejeune "that he, too, was a Marine, as indicated by the khaki-colored uniform which he wore."[1] The Marine general was impressed by Gouraud and sensed that "he was a man of power with a will of iron, but kindly withal. I acquired confidence in his judgment and . . . justness."

On the following day, 27 September, Lejeune was greeted with a disquieting rumor that upset him greatly. Colonel James C. Rhea, USA, his chief of staff, told him that plans were being considered by 4h Army Headquarters to break up the 2d Division and assign each infantry brigade to a French division. Without further confirmation and assuming that the report was true and taking no chances, Lejeune took the first opportunity to interrogate Gouraud concerning the rumor.

The American stood with the Frenchman in his private office while the latter outlined what was happening to a major French army attack then trying to overcome the strong defensive position held by the Germans since 1914. The French forces had been stopped but were now holding Somme-Py westward to Ste. Marie à Py, a distance of about two miles, and then south to the Suippe River. The enemy was strongly entrenched in a fortified range of hills known locally as "Les Monts." About two and a half miles north of Somme-Py lay another and more difficult target. A high ridge in the center of the position, "le Massif du Blanc Mont," dominated the entire area; even its sloping offshoots, those near Médéah Farm and the village of Orfeuil. The ridge had been, and would continue to be, dangerous to any attacking force. Gouraud further advised Lejeune that

> If I could take this position by assault, advance beyond it to the vicinity of St. Étienne à Arnes, and hold the ground gained against the counter-attacks which would be hurled against my

troops, the enemy would be compelled to evacuate 'Notre Dame des Champs and Les Monts,' thereby freeing Rheims which he has been strangling for four years, and fall back to the Aisne, a distance of nearly 30 kilometers . . . my divisions, however, are worn out from the long strain of continuous fighting and from the effects of the heavy casualties they have suffered, and it is doubtful if they are now equal to accomplishing this difficult task unless they are heavily re-enforced.[2]

Lejeune immediately caught Gouraud's broad hint and offered to accomplish the "impossible" by taking "Blanc Mont Ridge, advancing beyond it, and hold a position there," if Gouraud would promise not to break up the 2d Division.[3] Lejeune admitted to being caught somewhat off guard when Gouraud told him he had no intention of breaking up the division and that in fact it wasn't a part of his army anyway, but belonged to Foch and Pétain. "I will, however, bring to Marshal Pétain's attention what you have just said."[4] Lejeune's hasty reaction and ill-conceived promise was to cause serious repercussions for the division in the days ahead. Lejeune's miscalculation was apparently what the French were hoping for, and they instantly took full advantage of it. The American had made a commitment and therefore it had to be honored.

Later that day Lejeune was advised that at Gouraud's request Pétain had assigned the division to Gouraud's army. Orders were then being prepared for a move to a forward position in the Souain-Suippes area, which was located about three miles south of Somme-Py. Until 25 September the 4th Brigade had been near Toul, in the Verdun Sector, before moving by rail to Châlons-sur-Marne. The order that Gouraud issued on 28 September put the division on the move again, this time by camion, to an area just south of Somme-Py.

The 4th Brigade received a field order, dated 29 September, specifying that the two infantry regiments would move by camion, but, as frequently happened, the division and regimental machine-gun companies would march with the assistance of animal transportation. The Marine Brigade was positioned in the advance as lead unit of the division. When they arrived, the brigade would be located a single night's march from Somme-Py.[5]

Orders from the 4th French Army, dated 1 October, formally assigned the 2d Division to the XXI French Corps. Headquarters, XXI Corps, directed the division to relieve the exhausted 61st French Division in the

front lines on the night of October 1st and 2d. The assigned position
in the trenches for the division took up approximately two miles. Each
brigade would occupy one mile, the 3d on the right, the 4th on the left.[6]
The French 21st Division occupied the territory left of the 2d Division,
and the French 170th Division was on the 3d Brigade's right flank. When
orders were received to advance, each French division was to advance
in unison on either flank of the 2d U.S. Division.

On that same day, General Lejeune sent an "inspiring order"[7] to his
division, about which he later exclaimed, "The order had an excellent
effect." It gave few details as to what the division would do in the forthcoming days but was heavy with vague historical references in the first
part and terribly mawkish in the second. The message in effect called
upon the division to fall upon the enemy "and once more gloriously defeat" him.[8]

Early that afternoon Operations Memo No. 9, 4th Brigade, spelled
out the brigade's responsibility, which was to move forward that night
and be in readiness to attack on the morning of 2 October. From the
very beginning there was great confusion at corps headquarters. Division attack orders for the morning of October 2d were not issued until
2350 hours the previous night. Those orders stated that the 21st French
Infantry Division, with the 2d Division on their right, "will attack at 1150
hours after an artillery preparation, the duration of which will be fixed
later." The next morning Lejeune was at corps headquarters "presumably for orders." The exact sector to be occupied was, "of course, unknown." For some good sane reason the attack on 2 October did not
come off as scheduled. But there was some activity by members of the
6th Marines. A newly commissioned second lieutenant of the 78th Company, Hugh Kidder, on the morning of 2 October led a small patrol into
the enemy's trenches and captured two guns and crews that were threatening his platoon. He would again hurl his gauntlet in the Boche face
on the morrow. At 1600 hours, Memo No. 10 called for the brigade unit
commanders to send officers out to reconnoiter the areas to their front
and obtain whatever information they could from the French troops
then holding the line. During the war, reconnaissance was not a strong
point of the Marine Brigade, however.[9]

Brigade field orders issued at 1820 hours on 2 October gave a brief
description of where heavy weapons should be placed in the forthcoming fight and stated that General Lejeune's headquarters would remain at Suippes. It was from near that town that Lejeune would direct

his division. His PC would be about eight miles from the division's objective. Those were the days before radio, and telephone communication was almost nonexistent. Eight miles from the action was obviously not conducive to good management but there he was and there he stayed.

Brigadier General Wendell C. "Buck" Neville commanded the 4th Brigade; Col. Logan Feland the 5th Marine Regiment with Lt. Col. Julius S. Turrill as his second in command. The battalions were commanded by the following officers: Maj. George W. Hamilton, 1/5; Maj. Robert E. Messersmith, 2/5; and Maj. Henry L. Larsen, 3/5. Colonel Harry Lee commanded the 6th Marines with Lt. Col. Thomas H. Holcomb as his second in command. Battalion commanders were; Maj. Frederick A. Barker, 1/6; Maj. Ernest C. Williams, 2/6; and Maj. George K. Shuler, 3/6. Major Littleton W. T. Waller Jr. commanded the 6th Machine Gun Battalion.

The formation of the 4th Brigade as assigned for the attack to be made on 3 October in a column of battalions was as follows:

Left:

2d Battalion, 6th Marines, and 81st Machine Gun Company
Twelve light French tanks.
1st Battalion, 6th Marines, and 73rd Machine Gun Company
Twelve light French tanks.
3d Battalion, 6th Marines, and 15th Machine Gun Company

Right:

2d Battalion, 5th Marines, and 23d Machine Gun Company
3d Battalion, 5th Marines, and 77th Machine Gun Company
1st Battalion, 5th Marines, and 8th Machine Gun Company

Lejeune tells us that the task on 2 October for both the 2d Division and the French 21st Division was to clear out the Essen and Elbe trenches at their front. On that day the Americans were successful with their section but the French were not, a situation that did not bode well for the next day's attack. The German trenches were located about a mile north and a mile west of Somme-Py.

The 6th Marines lost fifteen men from fire emanating from the Essen Hook to their left front, but the 5th Marines had a relatively easy time taking the German trenches before them. Colonel Harry Lee of the 6th Marines reported to division that a reconnaissance of the Elbe and Essen trenches, directly to his regiment's front, had found them to be unoccupied, but that the strong points northwest, notably the Essen Hook (i.e., the 21st French Division sector) were able to completely control any ground that the regiment would advance over. He added that for his troops to attempt to overcome these strong points before the advance scheduled for the following day would do irreparable damage to his lead battalion. He suggested that the position be neutralized by artillery fire when his troops were in their jump-off positions. Edward C. Fowler, a second lieutenant in the 78th Company, led his men into an enemy trench, cleared it without a casualty, and later that night went out alone and attacked the crew of a machine-gun nest with grenades, killing them all. He would perform some real work on the morrow when he got up to the top of the hill.

General Lejeune was instructed to report to 21st Corps Headquarters that morning. He brought along with him both of his brigade generals: Ely, of the 3d and Neville, of the 4th. When they arrived, they learned of plans that the corps commander, General Naulin, and his staff, had developed. Naulin pointed out that the attack on the right made by the 170th French Division on the previous day had created a bulge in the lines that he thought would provide the 3d Brigade with added advantages during the 3 October attack. He expressed his fear that the frontal attack against the enemy's formidable positions on the high ground would not succeed. To which Lejeune responded "that I felt no doubt whatever as to the ability of the 2d Division to overcome that resistance," but he added that he agreed with Naulin, that the ground taken by the French in the next sector would greatly enhance their efforts to attain the objectives.[10] After reading General Naulin's plan for the attack, Lejeune proclaimed it impracticable, so he and his officers discussed the situation privately for a few minutes and then proposed their own plan. They wanted to split the division by brigades with a large area in between to be bypassed by both. The 4th Brigade would advance on the left and the 3d Brigade on the right, in an oblique attack. The plan "avoided an attack on the Bois de la Vipère and several other strong points."[11] Both brigades were to arrive at the ridge at the same time and turn on the enemy still located in the bypassed Bois de la Vipère. After discussion, Naulin approved Lejeune's new plan.

Thursday, 3 October

Field Order No. 35, which described the division's attack plan for 3 October, was not issued until 2300 hours on 2 October and did not arrive at 4th Brigade headquarters until 0440 hours that morning. Yet as early as 0130 on the morning of 3 October it was known at Lee's headquarters that it had been issued. A message from H. (Holcomb?) to Capt. David Bellamy indicated that the actual orders for that day's attack were "not yet received. I hear brigade has them." Were they received as early as "H" indicated, or was the officially recorded time "0440" correct? Perhaps division headquarters held them for a long time. Was it because there may have been some trepidation among the designers of the attack? Why Neville and company held them so long, if indeed brigade had them, has never been explained.

The term *objective* is found in many official orders and documents but not the specific objective itself except in the map coordinates. The following terminology is used in U.S. Army Monograph No. 9, which does not give a definitive objective, but intimates that the Massif was indeed the intended objective for that day. "The troops advanced at 5:30 A.M. and at 8:30 A.M. were on their objective, *but Blanc Mont itself was still controlled by the Germans . . .*" (Emphasis added.)

The commanding officer of the lead battalion of the 6th Marines, Maj. Ernest C. "Bull" Williams,[12] had not received his copy of Field Order No. 35 until H hour. He read it after his battalion attained what he thought was their objective,[13] the road running between Médéah Farm and Blanc Mont.[14]

Meanwhile, the 3d Brigade was having difficulty meeting its obligations. French guides were to have led the brigade from their positions near Navarin Farm, somewhat south of Somme-Py, on a four-mile night march to its jump-off position. They never showed up, but the 9th and 23d Infantry regiments did their best to make the line on time anyway, even though they had to find their way through strange country in the dark. The 9th Infantry was to lead off in their subsector and then to converge with the 6th Marines at the apex of the triangle, some two miles ahead. When the two brigades joined, they were then to turn on the bypassed Germans in the triangle and mop them up.

Several serious problems occurred that made the division's advance even more difficult. The orders from division directed the 3d Brigade to a certain jump-off position, which was back in the enemy's hands. At about 1800 hours the previous evening the Germans had launched a successful counterattack against the French forces holding that point of the line, pushing them back a quarter of a mile. No one bothered to advise Brig. Gen. Hanson E. Ely or any other member of his 3d Brigade staff about what had happened. When H hour arrived, the brigade was positioned about a quarter of a mile short of where their orders had placed them. Therefore, in addition to having a bad night behind them and a full day's work before them, the 3d Brigade had to first fight the Germans who were occupying their starting line, just so they could jump off.

Essen Hook, which was still controlled by the Germans, became an extremely vexing problem for the 4th Brigade. The French 21st Division had as a first task the capture of that venerable position. Unless that defensive system was taken by the 21st Division, before the advance of the Marine Brigade, there would be hell to pay. The "Hook" had been declared by military experts to be the strongest natural and artificially fortified position protecting the approach to the Blanc Mont ridge. In addition, following their initial headaches, both brigades had to advance over almost two miles of rising ground. At the end they would have to broach the next main line of Boche trenches, which the Germans had had almost four years to develop. Moreover, they would have to fight the various other machine-gun and light artillery emplacements that would harass them along their way. Their plates were full.

H hour was to be at 0550 hours on 3 October. A five-minute artillery barrage by the 2d Artillery Brigade, assisted by the guns of the 61st French Division, was to precede the advance of both brigades. That would be followed by a rolling barrage as the battalions climbed toward their objective. It would continue for three hundred meters beyond the goal, and then, after the arrival of both brigades at their objectives, there would be a standing barrage of a half hour duration on that line. After that another rolling barrage would be laid down to a line about thirteen hundred meters beyond that point to support patrols and other activity. The barrages went well, considering the various problems inherent in the peculiar attack arrangement.

So the advance would be: 2/6 in the lead, followed at a thousand meters by 1/6 and then by 3/6, also at a thousand meters. The 5th Marines, which up to this point had been to the right of its sister regiment, were to fall in behind the 6th and follow its path upward toward Blanc Mont ridge—with 2/5 leading, 3/5 next in line, and finally 1/5. The last had a special task to perform before following its sister battalions onward and upward. Careful instructions were given to guard the left flank for the entire advance to Blanc Mont ridge and to maintain liaison with the 3d Brigade on the right. At 0920 on 2 October, Col. Harry Lee, CO of the 6th Marines, sent a message to his three battalion commanders giving special instructions for the following day. He excused the fact that grenades would probably be in short supply and suggested that the Marines should look within their own sector for their supply, meaning Boche potato mashers, I suppose. The message ended with the following sentence:

> Impress all men with the fact that musketry is still *KING* and they have but to sit tight and shoot straight, insuring superiority of fire and guaranteeing success.[15]

Such rhetoric was probably received contemptuously by the lower ranks. They were a bit more intelligent than they were usually given credit for. Troops destined to advance up a steep incline, against some of the best defended and nearly impregnable positions on the western front, were told that they should be "sitting tight." But being Marines they went forward anyway, and probably grumbled, or more likely just had a laugh.

The 4th Brigade jumped off and 2/6 immediately came under flanking fire from the "Hook." The two leading companies, the 80th (Powers)[16] and the 79th (Zane), were positioned left and right in line, with the 80th taking the most heat from the German flanking fire. If Sellers's memoir is to be accepted as written, the 80th was practically leaderless and didn't keep its place during the advance, making even more difficulties for the other three companies. The 80th and 79th Companys were followed by the 78th (Sellers) and the 96th (Cates) Companies in support. The 6th Marines were soon heavily engaged in "sorting out" the Germans who were pouring in rifle and machine-gun fire from the left flank and front of the brigade. One of the most active of the men was Cpl. Oscar Moreland of the 96th. Moreland was wounded but would retain his place in the line. Tomorrow he would give the Boche hell. French forces were not yet advancing and the German guns and gunners were taking great advantage of that situation. One observer recalled in his memoir what the scene looked like to him.

> The section [of Marines] was attacking a Boche machine gun, deployed in a long thin line; first a few men on one flank would rush forward a short distance, then, as the fire was directed at their attack, those on the other end would make a quick advance . . . five men lay still on the ground. . . . One, two, four men dropped. . . .

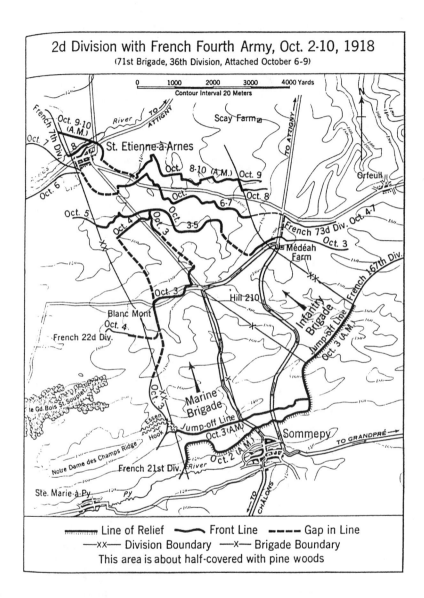

2d Division with French Fourth Army, Oct. 2-10, 1918
(71st Brigade, 36th Division, Attached October 6-9)

0   1000   2000   3000   4000 Yards
Contour Interval 20 Meters

TO ATTIGNY
River
Oct. 9-10 (A.M.)
French 7th Div.
Oct. 7
Oct. 8
St. Etienne-à-Arnes
Scay Farm
Orfeuil
Oct. 6
Oct. 8-10 (A.M.)
Oct. 9
Oct. 6-7
Oct. 8
Oct. 5
Oct. 4
Oct. 3
Oct. 3-5
French 73d Div.
Oct. 4-1
Oct. 3
French 167th Div.
Médéah Farm
Oct. 3
Hill 210
Infantry Brigade
Jump-off Line
Oct. 3 (A.M.)
Blanc Mont
Oct. 4
French 22d Div.
Marine Brigade
le Gd. Bois St. Souplet
Essen
Hook
Jump-off Line
Oct. 3 (A.M.)
Sommepy
TO GRANDPRÉ
Notre Dame des Champs Ridge
French 21st Div.
River
Oct. 3 (A.M.)
Oct. 2 (A.M.)
Ste. Marie-à-Py
Py
TO CHALONS

Line of Relief ━━▸ Front Line ━ ━ ━ Gap in Line
━xx━ Division Boundary ━x━ Brigade Boundary
This area is about half-covered with pine woods

Map 13: The 2d Division pattern of attack as approved by Lejeune and the French. Note the triangle in between both the 3d and 4th Brigades, which were bypassed, and the daily advance of the division as shown in the heavy lines on the map.

They were close now, but where there had been thirty men a few moments before, only nine were still able to move.[17]

At 0620 Pvt. John Joseph Kelly, a runner of the 78th Company, dashed forward through the division's rolling barrage at least one hun-

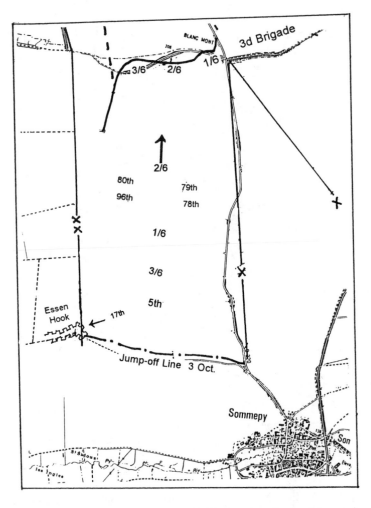

Map 14: The main attack of 3 October 1918, showing the positions taken by each battalion of the 6th Marines as they advanced up the hill against extensive German emplacements.

dred yards in advance of his own battalion. Kelly attacked an enemy machine-gun nest, killing the gunner with a grenade and then shooting another member of the crew with his pistol. He reappeared through the barrage with eight prisoners. At that point, Kelly yelled to his comrades, "Just what I told you I'd do." That action earned him the Medal of Honor. Interestingly, both MoH's for Marines at Blanc Mont were earned by enlisted men in the 78th Company.

Facing the Marine Brigade were the remnants of the 51st Division and, in support, the 200th Division, both of the Imperial German Army. In addition, elements of another German regiment and a Jäger infantry battalion were holding several strong points on the left of the Marines, pouring in heavy machine-gun and rifle fire during Williams's advance. By 0830 the leading elements of Williams's battalion were about seventy-five yards north of the Blanc Mont–Médéah Farm road. Williams had attained what he thought was his initial objective and began forming a line to the left. Additionally, 2/6 had made contact with the 3d Infantry Brigade on their right, which had also successfully completed this segment of the advance. During the advance of 2/6, Cpl. John Henry Pruitt of the 78th Company personally attacked two machine guns, killing two of the gunners and captured forty prisoners in a nearby dugout. Pruitt earned the Medal of Honor this day for his courage. Unfortunately, he was killed by artillery fire soon afterward.

The 96th Company of 2/6 formed left to protect the exposed left flank. One corporal of the company, Roy R. Reeves*, and five other men were in a protected spot along the path going upward when a potato masher landed in their place of repose. Reeves, without a second thought, picked up the grenade and hurled it out. It exploded several yards away but he was struck in his face and head, putting him out of action for the balance of the battle. Voluntarily leading four Marines through a heavy barrage, 2d Lt. James P. Adams*, of the 78th, and his men killed a machine-gun crew that had been enfilading their front line. This cracked the whole German defensive system at this point and made it possible for the cleaning out of many other guns that had stymied his company's advance. While Adams was so engaged, four privates from his company, Julian W. Alsup* plus three others, made a flank attack upon another gun that had been enfilading the 78th. With hand grenades and their rifles they killed the three crew members and captured twenty-five others. Bruce H. Mills*, Roy H. Beird*, and Richard O. Jordan* were the other men. Another private, Lambert Bos*, with two other volunteers from the 78th, flanked a nest, capturing fourteen men and two guns even though one of the Marines had been wounded. Further up the hill he also aided in the capture of forty prisoners in a dugout. Privates Samuel Simmons* and Joe Viera* joined Bos in that last endeavor. Before that Simmons and two other Marines had knocked out a machine gun in front of the company lines, killing all the crew. Meanwhile Pvt. Carter L. Anderson* went forward with his Chauchat and cleaned out several enemy positions that were also troublesome to the 78th. Hugh Kidder*, whom we met on 2 October, with his platoon was again after the enemy. They captured four machine-gun nests and many prisoners. Then he went to the aid of two of his men who had been wounded. The Corps lost a good man later that day when he was killed while arranging his men into better defensive positions in the face of intense artillery and machine-gun fire. First Lieutenant John McHenry*, who had just been released from the hospital, traveled two days and nights to get back to his company on time for the "Big Push." When he arrived, Sellers offered him a "soft job" so that he could recuperate, which he indignantly refused and instead took his platoon into the line with the rest of the 78th. While engaged in leading his men, he was killed by a machine gun that they were attacking. This sad event aside, it was a busy and successful day for the men of the 78th Company.[18]

While this was happening, the first serious distress signal made its appearance at brigade headquarters. Barker, whose 1/6 had moved past 2/6 to the right of the line, notified them that the battalion on his left (2/6) "has passed over second ridge. *They are encountering heavy machine gun fire on their left.*" (Emphasis added.)[19] The men of the battalion soon put out as many of those guns as they could find. First Lieutenant Macon Overton, a man with an insatiable desire to kill as many of the enemy as he could manage, was, as always during this war, all over the place. Leading his company, the 76th, in the second line, he found many Boche still living after 2/6 had worked the lines over before them. Although they were temporarily halted, Overton got his troops moving again and within minutes the 76th had decimated a machine-gun nest and an artillery piece that had been firing point-blank into their ranks. He and they would continue their grudge during the entire period the 6th Marines would be in action on that hill.

Barker was now connected with the 23d Infantry, after it had passed through the leading 9th Infantry. His two leading companies, the 75th (Chandler)[20] and 76th (Macon Overton*)[21] were still in the same positions in line, left to right, and both were still supported by the 74th and 95th Companies. In Overton's report he described the advantage his company had while advancing over the "first 2 1/2 kilometers . . . over rolling terrain during which we were subjected to artillery and indirect machine gun fire from the front and left flank. . . . By taking advantage of the slight cover the ground afforded, few casualties were experienced." He also mentioned the assistance given by the French tanks. They had been called in to provide weaponry in order to overcome the many machine guns and artillery the Marines would run into on their route upward. Tanks were finally coming into their own, but they were too slow and still drew artillery fire whenever they appeared on a battlefield. That was often fatal to the men accompanying them. Shuler's 3/6 followed 1/6 in order and was shortly afterward in a support line, located to the rear of both 2/6 and 1/6. Shortly after they would move down "south" a little to add to the left-flank protection of 2/6. That entire left-flank area was still controlled by the Germans, as the French still had not advanced to keep abreast of the 4th Brigade.

Another morning message concerning problems on the left was received in a phone call from a Major Roberts, liaison officer from division to 4th Brigade.

Still encountering heavy machine gun fire on the left, but saw a body of troops on the left which [was thought to be] 5th Marine flank guards. Know nothing of French operations on the west.

A half hour later this message, "Williams advancing half way up hill Mont Blanc [sic], easily without trouble. Tanks operating with him. . . ."[22]

In his memoir, Sellers described his feelings about his "heroes":

The heroism of Kelly and Pruitt was not isolated. Time after time the courage of our men shone through. These men were trained and disciplined for any circumstances. When the fighting was thick and communications broke down, they had the intelligence and the intestinal fortitude to act on their own and continue to our objective, not needing their officers behind them, goading them on. They were Marines, and I considered them to be among the finest men the country had to offer. My proudest moment in France occurred that Thursday morning in October at Blanc Mont Ridge, where I had the privilege of leading these men of the 78th Company over the top.[23]

Messersmith, with 2/5, was leading the 5th Regiment of Marines with the 18th (David T. Jackson) and 51st (Keeley) Companies, left to right, and the 43d (Dunbeck) and the 55th (Peck) in support. Captain James Keeley, skipper of the 51st, "won" the Silver Star the hard way. Just as the 51st was going into position, he got it. The regiment's semiofficial history states that they moved "over trenches and ground strewn with French and enemy dead" on their way up. "Soon machine gun fire and an increasing artillery fire from the left showed that the French on our left were not advancing and *that flank was exposed.*" (Emphasis added.) Further on, it also goes on to state that the battalion moved to "the gap on their left" and alludes to the successful taking of the ridge at dusk. Of course that was not correct, and it would be several days more before it was true. The history also mentions that they joined with the 6th Regiment to their right and the "10th Battalion of French Chasseurs on the left." Unfortunately, regardless of what the history states, the real objective, Blanc Mont (aka Hill 210), was still controlled by the enemy. Most likely the Marines were on the slopes and even perhaps near the top, but the fact of the matter is that the Germans continued to control the top until 5 October. They not only controlled the top, they also owned the entire western flank from which they could pour more fire down upon the Marines and later the French, when they finally showed up.

The hill was shaped something like a snub-nosed revolver so that its "barrel" ran west to east but its handle ran from north to south. Although the enemy didn't control the barrel, they were on the "cylinder" portion, the highest and best-entrenched portion, and most of the handle. Another factor that enabled the Germans to conceal themselves so well during the entire period was that the hill was heavily wooded, especially at the top, and loaded with tunnels and dugouts. The attacking force of Marines, who could not see the Boche positions, were greatly hindered in trying to locate the enemy during the first few days. Many would die trying.

Since 0745 that morning the French 21st Division had been vainly attempting to take the German trenches that lay before the Essen Hook. On the right and slightly north of those trenches was Essen Hook, which lay upon a hill that was about twenty meters higher than most of the ground around it. When 1/5, the rear element in the Marine Brigade's attack pattern, started forward, the 17th Company, assisted by a platoon from the 8th Machine Gun Company, commanded by 2d Lt.

Arthur Wilkinson,[24] a one-pounder (37mm gun) and several French tanks, moved westward and launched an attack against it. According to a report made by 1st Lt. Carl J. Norstrand to the division chief of staff in July 1919, Capt. Leroy P. Hunt, "skipper" of the 17th Company, selected targets and within a few minutes four German machine guns had been wiped out by the one-pounder and the American machine guns.

> At the distance of about 300 meters from the enemy I [Norstrand] was ordered to proceed with my platoon around the enemy's right flank and to attack from there.

He also relates, writing of the other three second lieutenants of his company, how Edward C. Lindgren* with his 4th Platoon swung around to the left flank and both Gillis Johnson with the 1st Platoon and Jacob Lienhard* with the 2d made a frontal assault. Norstrand also added that he was held up on "arriving at the crest of the hill by terrific machine gun fire," whereupon he requested one of Wilkinson's guns which, because they were at only two hundred yards distance, was able to overwhelm the German gun. The platoon continued its assault, but before much more could happen, "the Boche surrendered, more than 100 . . . being taken prisoner."[25] Both Lindgren and Lienhard were cited for leading their men in the attack upon exceptionally strong defensive positions and taking them, after both had been severely wounded.

The prisoners were turned over to the French infantry on the left of the Marines. The 17th Company completed the capture of the position by 1030 hours and then handed it over to the French 21st Division, which in turn lost the Essen Hook that afternoon when the Germans launched a counterattack to regain it.[26] Norstrand also mentions that between 1100 and 1130 the 17th Company rejoined 1/5, which was farther up the hill. At this hour the French forces were still where they had been when the attack began.

Meanwhile, the 6th Regiment was well on its collective way toward obtaining control of the ground below the Blanc Mont Massif and its eastern slopes. At 0940 Lieutenant Noble reported to Shuler that 1/6 had passed through 2/6 to the right and had reached the objective on Blanc Mont Ridge.[27] While the men of the 6th were fighting hard to take the ground on the massif, unknown to them were the huge numbers of Heinies all over that hill. Many were dug in to caves or dugouts and wouldn't be found for several days to come. But another private, Samuel

Glucksman*, found some that day. He took one German captive and then forced him to lead the way toward more. The dugout they entered had another twenty who immediately surrendered to him. About this time Lt. Ed Fowler*, whom we met yesterday, came up with a little help from his platoon found some Germans just waiting to be taken. He and his men managed to capture eighty prisoners and fifteen machine guns. The 78th Company had been very busy making heroes that day. "Mac" Sellers, the skipper, probably got writer's cramp from all the citations he wrote for his "boys," as he called them.[28]

Shuler's 3d Battalion had advanced with the 97th Company (McEvoy) on the left and the 83d (Noble)[29] to its right. They were followed by the 84th Company (Mark A. Smith) behind the 97th and the 82d (James H. Johnston) behind the 83d. When Shuler received that message from Noble, he ordered 3/6 to halt in a reserve position eight hundred meters behind 2/6. Meanwhile, Barker was sending messages to Shuler that indicated that his battalion had "reached our objective" and was consolidating the line. He had made contact with the 23d Infantry on his right and 2/6 on his left, but made it known that his left flank was exposed and that he would be very happy should that be corrected as soon as possible. Barker also indicated that he was expecting a counterattack and added, "Have you seen 5th Marines?" Barker sent Shuler his coordinates to which Shuler replied that his farther most unit was "800 metres in your rear," and how can I help you? Barker's response was that everyone in his battalion was on the front line and that he was "in need of a support line. Can you help us out?" Williams was also complaining to Shuler that "we need support on our left flank. The French have not come up and our left is in the air." He also said that the Germans, 700–800 strong, were moving around to "our left and threaten an encircling movement. Can you give us any help?" Shortly afterward Shuler reported to brigade that he was digging in to support both the 1st and 2d Battalions, both of which were still at least eight hundred meters to his front. It soon became evident that the 6th Marines were near the objective but still not on it and had, along with the 5th Marines, a mile and a half of exposed left flank that had to be filled as soon as possible in order to ensure safety for the brigade and to consolidate and preserve the gains made thus far.

Not realizing that Messersmith's orders were to find the French right flank and tie into it, Williams complained to Lee that 2/5 had moved, leaving his left flank open. There was no French right flank anywhere near 2/5, and as Messersmith moved southwestward, the gap between him and Williams expanded. The Germans took advantage of that situation and their patrols moved to get in between the two Marine battalions. Shuler advised Colonel Lee that he would now begin moving his battalion to the left to extend the regimental line. It was at about this same time that elements of the Marine Brigade, assisted by two companies of the 3d Brigade, finally turned on the Wood of Vipers and cleaned out the Germans who still remained within.

Major Robert Messersmith was still trying to "fill in the gap" that existed between the left of the 6th Regiment and the phantom French, a spectral force that not even the Germans on the hill had as yet seen. Messersmith extended his flank so that it was now so far to the left that his battalion had a front that was facing due west. His companies began to "disappear" as they moved southward. Meanwhile Shuler and 3/6 moved in a westerly direction and filled in the gap between 2/5 and 2/6, thereby preventing the further incursion of Boche on that flank.

Larsen's 3/5 maintained its second position in the 5th Regiment's advance up the hill, receiving the usual harassment by machine guns and artillery fire from the left flank. As the battalion later reported, "Enemy was entirely cleared from territory in our advance as supporting battalion, and there was no mopping up necessary."[30] Hamilton, with 1/5, which had maneuvered in a northwesterly direction as it fought its way up the hill, now moved in a westerly direction, extending the line of 2/5 farther to the left, and, while still expecting the French to show up on the left flank, were instead facing hordes of Germans. What had occurred, because of these extensions to the west, was that the division's approach zone had been exceeded by approximately a third of a mile. As if the Marines weren't having enough trouble with the Germans who faced them to their front, they also took on those who would have been facing the 21st French Division, had it been there. Private Carl H. Stensson*, a stretcher bearer with the 18th Company, continued his laborious task all that morning, displaying great courage while so engaged. When he discovered that his helper had been wounded, he immediately went across a road swept by machine-gun fire to his aid. In his attempt to rescue his buddy he was killed.

The men of the 6th Machine Gun Battalion were every bit as busy as the infantry. Corporal Edward Bald* led his squad independent of his platoon, making great strides through heavy enemy fire until they were finally behind the German positions. There he opened a flanking fire causing untold damage. Another corporal, Olin J. Butterfield*, of the 77th Company, refused to withdraw when the infantry fell back. Instead his crew kept their places until most of them were wounded by a German "potato masher." Working as rapidly as possible he and his men got their gun up, reset it, and opened up on the Boche, who were a scant twenty feet from them, causing the enemy to break and run. Privates Fred Haefliger* and Grannis L. Sylverson* supported Butterfield.

Meanwhile, on the division's right flank, the 3d Infantry Brigade, after a disastrous initial approach that morning, was on its objective, with the leading regiment, the 9th Infantry, taking the Médéah Farm by 0840 hours. Their losses had been substantial, but that was not unusual. The 3d Brigade casualties during the war nearly equaled or often exceeded those of the 4th Brigade—amounting to some 150 percent. The 23d Infantry passed through and to the west of the 9th Infantry moving nearly another mile before it, too, found both its flanks exposed to enemy fire. The 9th Infantry sent two battalions forward to tie in on the right flank of the 23d and then refused their right flank back to where the French 67th Division lay just north of Médéah Farm. By this time 1/6 had regained contact with the 23d Regiment.

Because the French 21st Division still wasn't doing very well, the corps commander ordered the 170th French Division to move in to the rear of the 2d Division and proceed to support their left flank. The 170th made contact with 2/5 and 3/6, both of which now formed left flank protection for the 2d Division. Colonel Rhea, chief of staff to Lejeune, sent the following message to Col. Harry Lay at division headquarters:

Say to the general [Naulin] that General Lejeune appreciates the way he has backed us up; that his order [sending in the 170th Division] has just been received and *we admire his soldierly qualities and the way in which he has backed us up.* [Emphasis added.][31]

Lay responded to advise that the

whole corps line is now intact. In other words, the two divisions on our right [French liaison with the 3d Brigade] are up to the objective. The right division has progressed past Orfeuil. Our line extended through Orfeuil as the Corps Line.

Lay was saying incorrectly that the French were maintaining contact with both flanks of the 2d Division; but, not so. The Marines' left was still in the air and would continue to be so for two more days.

Otherwise, it was only 1240 hours and although the objective had not yet been reached and their flanks were still exposed, the 4th Brigade was in relatively good shape. Neither it nor the 3d Brigade, however, which also had been very busy during the morning, was in any condition to continue the attack that day. Someone at brigade headquarters, possibly Ellis, decided differently.

At 1300 hours Lt. Col. Earl Ellis, adjutant for the 4th Brigade, sent Feland an order that the 5th Marines were to form up behind the 6th Marines, pass through them, and advance up the St. Étienne–Somme-Py road to trenches that were just about six hundred yards southeast of St. Étienne. Operations Memorandum No. 12 marked "Secret" pointed out that

> in the event that the progress of the French along our left flank makes it desirable [if they had moved into perfect liaison with the 4th Brigade] the advance of the 2d Division will be continued later in the day in the direction of St. Etienne, etc.[32]

The memo continues by directing the 5th Marines to pass through the 6th and continue the day's attack. The 5th Regiment would move in a column of battalions. The 6th would follow and be charged with the protection of the left flank. Feland designated 2/5 to lead the regiment, but Messersmith was having difficulties in the Bois de Somme-Py and on the left flank of the division. His position at 1500 was at the division boundary, and at that time he wasn't in any condition to advance against anything, let alone a fighting German army. His plaintive message "Have again lost track of 51 [Keeley] & 55 [Peck] Cos." revealed that he had no idea where two of his companies were located. Meanwhile at about 1700, the always "Johnny-on-the-spot" Hamilton found Peck and had him close up with his battalion.

At 1545 an order was sent out of Lee's PC instructing the 6th Marines in what they were going to do.

> The 5th Regiment will pass through the 6th Regiment . . . and will advance to the new objective. When the 5th has passed through, the Bns. of this regiment . . . will reform and be prepared to follow . . . at a distance of 1 kilometer . . . should their advance make that necessary . . . in a column of Bns. in order—Barker [1/6], Williams [2/6], Shuler [3/6], and will assure the protection of the left flank of the 5th.[33]

Colonel Logan Feland reported to Neville that his 5th Regiment, led by 3/5, would start forward at 1915 hours and would pass through the

6th Marines by 1930 hours. Messersmith and 2/5 were to lead off. But by this hour the 5th Regiment was in a state of complete confusion. Most battalion commanders couldn't find some of their companies and company commanders were having difficulties locating their platoons. Captain Frank Whitehead, skipper of the 67th Company, and nearly everyone's favorite officer,[34] couldn't locate his battalion PC or any of the other companies of 1/5 either. It would be about 0300 before Major Hamilton and Whitehead made contact. Hamilton had only two halves of two other companies at that time, so Whitehead wasn't alone in his dilemma. Some of the company commanders had been wandering around looking for their battalion PC for hours.

The entire attack had to be canceled because of the 5th Marines' confusion. For most of that day they had to spread around on the left flank to cover the left rear for the advance made by the 6th Marines. They just couldn't pull the whole thing together by the time directed on 3 October, so the advance did not happen that day. But by 0600 hours on 4 October 1918 all the regiment would be available and assembled for what they were about to receive that day.

Meanwhile back on the Blanc Mont Massif, the German occupiers, mainly elements of the 200th Division, were in dugouts shielded from American and French artillery and machine-gun fire. Consequently they were as safe as anyone could be at that time. One German observer was able to keep the more distant commander apprised of what was happening about the hill. At 0815 he reported that the Americans were on the hill because he could hear them talking. He also advised that the 2d Jäger Brigade in the front lines were holding their own with the Marines. But it wasn't long after that the headquarters of the Jäger Brigade abandoned Blanc Mont and fell back to the rear. The observer, Lieutenant Reichert, and the artillery headquarters remained. A few hours later the Marines located those dugouts and either captured the occupants or demanded their surrender. The entire headquarters group was captured. That effectively put the artillery out of business as far as shelling the hill was concerned. But there was still a heavy concentration of machine guns on and about Blanc Mont. It would be a long time before they were put out of action.

The lack of French support on the left was becoming a very serious problem for the division. Someone at division, possibly Rhea, had a phone message exchange at 2145 with Colonel Harry Lay, USMC, liaison officer with the French corps. Some of it follows:

The left [French] didn't get an inch. They were where they were yesterday. Ours [position] is right where we expected to be. *They are about 200 yards from where they started.* They didn't go forward, why? . . . We don't want to go too far on the right, [3d Brigade] because we will have them both up in the air . . . if we have both of our flanks up in the air you are liable to land on your tail . . . they [French] are still in the trenches. We cleared the trenches for them and they are [still] in the trenches about 100 yards to the extreme right.[35]

On the night of 3/4 the 22d French Division had relieved the dilatory 21st Division, which was still located well south of Blanc Mont. Although the 22d had advanced northward, the advance was in a northwesterly direction, leaving a large area still under enemy control, and consequently did little or nothing to relieve the pressure upon the 2d Division.[36] Meanwhile, the 67th French Division, which was in contact on the right flank of the 3d Brigade, was also having serious difficulty. They had been stopped before noon near Médéah Farm, where the 9th Infantry was holding, but neither unit was as far forward as the 1st Battalion of the 23d Infantry. Already far in advance of any other unit of the division, and now located a few hundred yards southeast of St. Étienne, they had proceeded forward toward the ridge which lay just northeast of that village. The 1st Battalion soldiers made their usual valiant effort. But their attacking waves soon came under heavy artillery and machine-gun fire, causing them enormous casualties, including their battalion commander, who was killed by shell fire. After advancing about three hundred yards the attack stalled and the battalion then retired to their former position, in captured German trenches, but still well out in front of everyone else in the division.

Their opponents were a pitiful few members of the 15th Bavarian Division, which only the day before had been pulled out of the line because they were exhausted. Exhausted or not, back in they went on 3 October and gave 1/23 a rough time. The 31st Bavarian Regiment of that division was down to about two hundred men. German strength was slim and they, too, were desperate for fresh troops; worse, they didn't have any reserves that they could count upon.

Friday, 4 October

As Colonel Logan Feland stated for the official record, "Owing to the difficulty in organizing the battalions, this regiment did not pass through the positions occupied by the 6th Marines, until 6:00 A.M." For the October 4th morning assault, 3/5 was to lead off, and proceed up the road toward St. Étienne, to be followed by 1/5 and, finally 2/5 in a column of battalions. This was all without benefit of artillery preparation, just like the 6th of June at Belleau Wood. Division Field Order No. 37, issued at 0600 (always late, it seems), directed a resumption of the advance that had stalled the previous evening. The designation of H hour was postponed until aircraft could detect the position of the delinquent French units, presuming the planes had sufficient fuel for that lengthy flight.[37]

In two columns of companies Larsen led off shortly after 0600, with the 47th Company (Moseley) leading on the left and Yowell's 16th Company on the right. The second line was composed of the 45th Company (Quigley) behind the 47th and Platt with the 20th behind Yowell. Hamilton's 1/5 in second spot and Messersmith with 2/5 was in support bringing up the rear as regimental reserve. They were heading for their objective, a line of trenches about six hundred yards southeast of St. Étienne on the left side of the main road. Each was advancing with approximately five hundred yards distance between battalions. The heights just south of the town, named by the Germans "Ludwig's Rucken (Crest)," was where most of the enemy artillery bombardment was coming from. Almost as soon as the 5th emerged from cover, it immediately ran into strong machine-gun fire coming from the northwestern side of Blanc Mont Ridge, as well as from their front and each flank. As they continued to move forward, the three battalions were exposed to terrible artillery and machine-gun fire that lasted for the entire advance. Three/Five was the heaviest hit, since they were in the lead. Fortunately it was over broken ground, which at times provided minimal shields. The regiment kept going, advancing about a mile before they were stopped. They received orders to dig in where they were, which they instantly obeyed.

At about 1100 hours, 3/5 was located up to a line about a half mile north and west of the Blanc Mont–Médéah Farm road. Larsen had advanced until he made contact with the 1st Battalion of the 23d Infantry on his right; this battalion was located about six hundred yards west of where they should have been and well into the 5th Marines' sector. After the 16th Company tied in to the left flank of 1/23, and the balance of the battalion spread westward, Larsen personally visited the infantry commander, who said that he believed he had reached his objective and that he wasn't going to move unless and until he received orders from his superiors to do so.[38] Meanwhile, the 77th Machine Gun Company had advanced forward to where 3/5 was now located and soon set up its guns to provide as much support to each of its companies as possible. The left flank of 3/5 was tied into a road leading north from Blanc Mont Massif toward St. Étienne. This meant the battalion was covering nearly a mile frontage. Neither 2/5 nor 1/5 had come that far forward, but regardless they were taking Boche fire.

Larsen's battalion was suffering heavy casualties from another German strong point located nearby. He requested that the other two battalion commanders help him since "heavy reserves [enemy] moving into wood to our left." Just after 1100 the skipper of the 55th Company (Peck) reported that both his company and the 17th Company (Hunt of 1/5) would head for what appeared to be a trouble spot, "where" he added "considerable resistance has been encountered." The map coordinates given put that location just south of St. Étienne, and if they made a slight turn to the left they would be between Ludwig's Rucken and Blanc Mont and facing another hill the Germans named "Petersberg."[39]

Reduced to pleading, Larsen sent messages to Hamilton and Messersmith that the 1st or 2d must come up to take over or assist. "I cannot hold front line [much] longer." At the same time he wrote much the same to Feland, adding, "Having hard time to hold men together . . . am being shelled heavily and m.g. fire from 270° of compass. . . . Situation is critical." He told Feland of his lack of contact and control over his companies with the dismal statement, "My companies seem to have lost liaison with one another." Each of the companies was taking hell from incoming fire, but there remained a few machine gunners to provide some semblance of firepower emanating from 3/5. The 77th Co.'s 1st Sgt. John McNulty*, though severely wounded himself, remained with and continued operating a gun on the firing line, the crew of which had been knocked out. Needless to state, McNulty's actions provided stimulus to other Marines who observed his stalwart behavior under severe conditions.[40]

But not long afterward the situation appeared to have improved. Both 2/5 and 1/5 moved up to the line as rapidly as possible with 2/5 immediately relieving the left flank of 3/5, and Larsen was soon once again in control of his battalion. First Lieutenant Fred Thomas*, Quigley's second, displayed extraordinary heroism during this very trying period. The left platoon had somehow lost contact with the balance of the 47th. Thomas went out and found them. Though he was wounded seriously, he, through skillful maneuvering, formed a strong defensive position, thereby breaking up a major German attack. He then brought the men back although they had suffered severe casualties. Gunnery Sergeant Martin S. Rodgers*, also of the 47th, though wounded, led a small patrol out before the lines to successfully bring in several wounded men. His platoon leader was down and he assumed command, leading his men through "the most trying and difficult conditions," until he was wounded a second time and forced out. "Top" Sergeant George Markley* volunteered to ascertain the exact position of several machine guns enfilading his 47th Company. Out he went under terrible shell and machine-gun fire, exploring the enemy lines, and brought back invaluable information to his company commander. He was killed later that day while scouting ahead as his company was making an attack on the enemy lines. The men of the 43d were also giving a good account of themselves. Corporals Guy H. Clark* and David Bernstein*, seeing many men of their company lying wounded out in no-man's-land, volunteered to rescue them, and rescue them they did. Making several trips across ground literally impassable because of artillery and machine-gun fire, each corporal brought in several men so that they might live. Second Lieutenant Merwin H. Silverthorn*, recently commissioned and now with 20th Company, at a critical time, carried several important messages over fire-swept ground to Major Larsen. He was wounded but refused to go to the rear and resumed command of his platoon, staying with the company the balance of the day.[41]

Messersmith's 2/5 formed left of Larsen. But soon after he notified Feland that he was taking hits from artillery located directly to his left flank. He added, "Have seen a number of casualties. Our left flank is exposed. Plenty of Hun planes, no allied." That was a cry heard frequently among troops of the AEF throughout the war. Colonel Logan Feland sent a directive to his battalion commanders to take up good positions and "get up stragglers and straggling units."

The Marines' left flank continued to be completely in the air, with no French troops there to protect them. Larsen asked for the 6th Marines to come up and protect their left rear since he had a fear he would be cut off by the Germans, who seemed to have had free and easy access on the flanks of both 2d Division brigades. Both Larsen and Messersmith reported an estimated sixty percent casualties during the period. We know from records that eventually Hamilton's 1st Battalion was in even worse shape, but for now, he came up into line on Messersmith's left flank, putting the entire regiment on line, with no reserves.

According to the reports prepared by each battalion after the Blanc Mont affair terminated, at about 1430 hours the 2d and 3d Battalions formed a line, extending across the St. Étienne road and with the 1st Battalion on their left flank, they all dug in under heavy fire. Reports of all three battalion commanders in the official *Records* cease at about this point and resume on the following day, 5 October. Little of what they reported was completely accurate, however, according to the other official or unofficial records. It is evident that each was "instructed" in what the report should state. Fortunately, a later report produced by LeRoy Hunt, by then commanding the 1st Battalion, gave a more accurate portrayal of what really transpired than what was "sanitized" for official consumption. One can only surmise the identities of the sanitizers.[42] There were a number of men engaged in heroics that day, before and after the debacle as described. First Lieutenant Thurston Davies* of the 45th had assumed command of the company after Thomas Quigley was wounded. Continuing the advance through the heavy artillery fire, he showed remarkable ability and courage and carried his company forward, stabilized his lines, and repelled an enemy counterattack on the still open left flank. Captain Charley Dunbeck* of the 43d, back after suffering a severe wound at Belleau Wood, was nailed again, this time in the head. He refused to be evacuated until he fully briefed his second, Capt. Nathaniel H. Massie. Charley would be back in time for the last go, along the Meuse River. When his platoon leader was felled, Sgt. Leon W. Inman*, also of the 43d, led the platoon by example, keeping several yards in front of his men. While helping dress wounds under heavy fire, he, too, was wounded and refused to leave until so ordered by a medical officer. Corporal Gerald V. Regan* was cited for extraordinary heroism while acting as section leader in the 18th Company. Rendering great assistance to his platoon leader and company during an attack, he led in advance of the section and received a mortal wound that afternoon.[43]

What happened that afternoon to 1/5 deserves some detailed description. Hamilton formed his battalion for an advance from the St. Étienne road, in a westerly direction, to hook up with the other two battalions on their left flank. He planned to continue along another unpaved road northward and, if at all possible, take the ridge (Ludwig's Rucken) just in front of the town. As another 1st Battalion Marine related much later, the second-in-command asked his skipper, "We're swinging half left. This will take us right to St. Étienne, won't it?" And the skipper is supposed to have replied, "The Boche have come out of St. Étienne—two full regiments . . . and a bunch of Maxim guns . . . and hit the 2d and 3d in the flank. Must be pretty bad."[44] While 1/5 was maneuvering behind 2/5, something happened that hasn't seen the light of day for eighty years. Later that evening, after the furious engagements of the day, Hamilton sent a message describing the conduct of the 5th Marines on 4 October 1918:

> From: C.O. 1st Bn.
> At: P.C. 266.5-281.8.
> To: C.O. 5th Regt.Oct. 4, 1918.

At about 1:30 P.M. the regt. started to advance with 1st Bn. in support of 3d Bn. and the 2d Bn. in reserve. Immediately a heavy machine gun fire was laid down from the left flank. The woods which the companies had entered was heavily shelled and about 2 P.M. there were numbers of men seen running to the rear. In some instances officers were leading in what appeared to be a grand rout. Among those whom I noticed particularly was Capt. [DeWitt] Peck,[45] Capt. [David T.] Jackson [2d Bn.], and Major Messersmith. There were also several lieutenants whom I did not recognize. Major Messersmith explained that he had lost all his officers, but didn't show any initiative or leadership. Capt. Jackson was hopeless. When it became evident that the retirement had become a rout, Lieut. [James A.] Nelms ran out and endeavored to turn the men back. His task was a hard one and attempted at great personal exposure to machine gun fire and a violent artillery bombardment. *We then were forced to draw pistols, and it was only by this method that we were able to stop the retreat.* [Emphasis added.] Then, as best we could we disposed the men along the edge of the woods and made them dig in. The position is a bad one and the machine gun fire from both flanks & from our left rear is causing much damage. I don't believe the French have advanced on our left and this leaves our whole flank exposed. The ground that the 3d Brigade passed over has not been cleaned of machine guns. I suggest that the 6th Regt. be requested to put out a strong flank guard. From the number of wounded seen I estimate the regiment's casualties at between 35 and 45 percent. Will report later. Hunt [Captain LeRoy P.] sends word that the Germans were seen massing an hour or so ago on the left flank. He gives our left front as shown on attached sketch. Do not know where leading elements are on right. [sgd] Hamilton.[46]

Meanwhile, Hamilton and his lads were taking too much heat from the Boche. He then did what he was noted for: rapid advancement against those hurting him. Off went Hamilton and 1/5 across the flat ground toward the slope of Ludwig's Rucken, directly ahead of them. To their left rose another slope (Petersberg), which, as they advanced, was soon directly behind them. The other two battalions advanced in a line, keeping pace with 1/5. It wasn't very long before all the Marines of the 5th became aware that the enemy was in force on the three hills by which they were encompassed, and all dreaded what they foresaw as their future. The first shell broke over the 49th Company and it was poison gas. It was followed by many others as the Marines kept moving forward, under high explosive, shrapnel, and gas. Machine guns and Mausers also helped mow them down. Marine Gunner William E. Nice took over the 2d Platoon of the 49th when its leader was a casualty. Many other platoon leaders and some "skippers" went down, wounded or worse. By this time the casualties were so heavy that even the support platoons were now in line and the front was very narrow. Mackin tells us,

The men were stunned; lashed down to earth by flailing whips of shrapnel, gas and heavy stuff that came as drumfire, killing them. There was no place in all our little world for us to go. The fellows bunched against the fancied shelter of the larger trees in little close-packed knots, like storm-swept sheep, and died that way, in groups . . . It was a deadly place. With reason were the hundred odd survivors who came out of there to name it in their memory, "The Box."[47]

But up the slope they went; the Prussians, amazed that such men just wouldn't die, fought with their accustomed zeal and courage. Soon the bayonets on both sides were being fully engaged. Corporal Robert Slover* brought his rifle, bayonet attached, up from the ground and as he plunged it into the Boche's neck the trigger was pulled, blowing the German's head off. There were many other frightful scenes remembered by 4th Brigade veterans of 4 October 1918. Captain Frank Whitehead* of the 67th was wounded once again during the assault, this time severely. But before he was knocked out of action he fulfilled his duty

by leading and directing the company with his usual bravery and coolness. Captain Francis S. Kieren, Whitehead's second, immediately assumed command until he too was wounded. Whereupon 1st Lt. Felix
Beauchamp*, now the senior officer of the 67th, took command, even
though he, too, had been wounded by the same shell blast that had
taken Kieren out. Continuing to move forward, Beauchamp, even
though in great pain, was finally stopped when he was wounded in the
groin. The officers of the 5th Marines were taking the heat as much as
anyone and few of them survived this day intact. LeRoy Hunt* of the
17th, after doing a fabulous job on the Essen Trench the day before, was
repeating his heroics on this day.[48]

It didn't take long for the remaining Germans to take off running.
The Marines, quickly adjusting to the change of circumstances, began
taking prone positions and getting off aimed rounds, something
Marines naturally did well, killing many Boche as they ran. An unlucky
group of enemy artillerymen, manning "77s," at the bottom of the slope,
also were caught in the general massacre. At this moment the battalion
was down to just more than 100 men, and as they continued sniping they
saw the Germans near St. Étienne preparing for a counterattack. Soon
German artillery and machine-gun fire opened up again in earnest. The
two remaining machine guns in 8th Company were manhandled to the
crest of the hill so that they, too, could extract revenge for the loss of
the rest of their company. Enemy shell-fire soon blasted them, and then
there was one gun left. Corporal Jack Jordan* and Pvt. Peter Funk*, both
of the 8th Machine Gun Company, hauled their lone gun forward, setting it up under a hail of lead, then opening up on their tormentors
with great effect. Both remained firing until their ammunition was exhausted. Second Lt. Vern Coverdell*, also hit, dressed his wound and
those of three enlisted Marines nearby, then reorganized his platoon
before writing a full report on what had transpired. Only then did he
allow himself to be evacuated.

First Lieutenant Francis J. Kelly Jr.*, finding himself the lone survivor
of seven company officers, assumed command of the 66th just as the
enemy began a counterattack. Although outnumbered three to one and
just having been ordered by Hamilton to retire to a better position, Kelly
did what any Marine would do in the same situation; he ordered his company to advance. The advance broke up the German attack and completely routed them, with their remnants captured. One of Kelly's
sergeants, Arthur E. Lyng*, managed to upset an aggressive party of Germans trying to impose their collective will upon the 66th Company.

"Gunny" Lyng, out scouting in front of his company's position, spotted a large formation of Germans with their Maxims approaching in the 66th's direction where it was poorly defended. Running back to the lines, he managed to accumulate a small force, later named "Lyng's Co-manches," and led them forward, screaming like Indians, smack into the enemy formation. Whether it was the "Comanche" yells or the ferocity of the attack or both that vanquished the Boche, I'm not sure, but break up the advance they did. In so doing they captured ten of the raiding party plus six of their guns.

Captain Percy Cornell, skipper of the 49th Company, holding the extreme left flank of 1/5, had led his company courageously through a hail of fire, as they attacked the hill. They managed to hold their ground against repeated enemy counterattacks. Later in the early evening he and the 49th skillfully covered the balance of the battalion as they left their forward positions.

A telephone message from Ellis to division, at 1830 hours, reported that the 17th Company had two officers still on their feet: LeRoy P. Hunt, the skipper, and 2d Lt. Carl Norstrand, as well as thirty-five enlisted survivors. First Lieutenant Francis J. Kelly Jr. was the only officer left in 66th Company and he had about the same number of enlisted men as the 17th. The 66th was a considerable distance forward of the other companies and liaison was not good.[49] While Kieren was still in command, he, along with his second-in-command, Beauchamp, had "about" forty men altogether. The count couldn't be more specific because the two men and their immediate commands were separated. Nordstrand estimated that their casualties were about seventy-five percent. Hamilton, who had sent Ellis the original message, also indicated that they didn't have enough men in the 1st Battalion to send for rations and asked, "Can rations carts come down?" He also mentioned that the 8th Machine Gun Company was "practically wiped out, all platoon sergeants and commanders killed."[50]

The few officers remaining in the battalion, or rather what was left of the 1st Battalion, decided that they could no longer hold the exposed position. The regiment had run into a hornet's nest of Maxims and 77s and would go no farther forward that night. Hamilton and his men could not possibly hold their ground; they were so far forward without any chance of support. So back down the hill they went to join the remnants of the regiment dug in around the road to St. Étienne. That night, under partial cover of darkness, the battalion, all 100 plus of them, made its move, the 66th Company leading; they were heavily shelled and machine gunned during the entire movement. One/Five, after taking more casualties, was finally able to take up a position alongside and to the left of the 2d Battalion. The 5th Marines were well out by themselves. To their right rear lay a badly shot up battalion from the 23d Regiment whose commander was not sure he belonged where he was. Lee's 6th Marines were behind the 5th down the road a bit and they, too, were exposed to fire from various machine-gun nests.

Although no time is mentioned, it appears that the following message was sent to regiment by Hamilton sometime during the next morning [5 October]:

> . . . advance held up by machine gun and artillery fire. I have the entire 67th and 17th Companies and parts of the 49th and 66th Cos. Capt. [Raymond F.] Dirksen has been gassed & evacuated. Casualties . . . believed to be heavy . . . yet within a kilometer of objective. . . . Large portion of left not cleaned of machine guns . . . which are working hard and fast at all times from both flanks and rear. We are in a precarious position . . . and unless we can make our last night's objective pretty quick,[51] it is very probable that no advance can be made as *last night's advance was a fiasco.* [Emphasis added.] We need artillery and we need it badly. Also food and water. [Sgd] Hamilton

Late on the evening of 4 October, Brigadier General Hanson E. Ely, 3d Brigade, advised Neville that he had to withdraw that part of the 23d Infantry (1/23) which was out in front and on the right flank of the 4th Brigade. Ely was concerned that Feland might withdraw back to Blanc Mont Ridge and leave his left flank in the air. Evidently the reverse situation was okay. Ellis sent a message to 5th Regiment describing what Ely was up to and added, "The General [Neville] *insists that Feland hold his position.*" (Emphasis added.)

The regiment held on all night despite heavy, concentrated artillery and machine-gun fire. Sometime during that night the 5th broke up two enemy counterattacks and two companies of 1/6 were ordered forward to protect the 5th's left flank, which was uncovered. Although they were in a bad spot because of their exposed position and unable to do much communicating with either the 6th Marines or with brigade, the 5th held on. Enemy pressure placed on the 3d Brigade had forced them to retire earlier, but they later resumed their position in line on the right of the Marine Brigade before any serious damage to the integrity of the division occurred.[52]

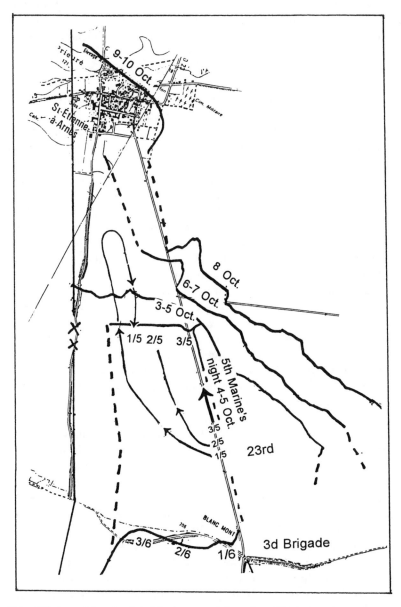

Map 15: Attack by the 5th Marines on 4 October 1918, showing advance of 1/5 toward St. Étienne and subsequent positions of the 6th Marines and portions of the 23d Infantry during the following six days.

The story is told of Lejeune's being awakened by his chief of staff, Colonel Rhea, to tell him that his troops were in trouble and that his 5th Marine Regiment was entirely surrounded by the Germans. Lejeune is supposed to have responded, "I am sorry for those Germans,"[53] then went back to sleep.

That morning of 4 October, the 6th Marines had what appeared to be a relatively sweet day ahead of them, at least as compared to the day before. Their main job was to support the 5th Marines, if required. But instead, they, too, were to be very busy. Several attempts were made by the 6th Marines to drive the Boche off the Blanc Mont Ridge during the early hours of 4 October, before the 5th advanced, but the regiment did not meet with success, instead taking heavy losses. The Germans continued to control the massif, and because the French still hadn't come up to the 4th Brigade line, a critically exposed flank continued. What was seriously needed at this point was control of the western slopes of Blanc Mont in order to force those Germans still on the hill to retreat or face being cut off from their own units.[54]

Barker, who was still on the left flank, complained to Shuler that "our left flank is badly exposed," but there wasn't anyone available to fill that gap. The 6th Marines were still waiting for the French to connect up with them. Consequently they were spread thinly across the ridge. Just after noon, Colonel Lee sent a message through Shuler to notify Barker to move forward to relieve the 5th from the fire they were taking at their rear and left flank. The other two battalions were to remain in place until 1430 that afternoon, which was to be H hour. At 1355 hours Williams sent Lee a report on the condition of his battalion. He had lost forty percent of his officers and had barely 300 enlisted still available for duty. One officer was badly shaken, but continued in line. He was 2d Lt. George W. Hopke, a former enlisted man. A shell burst completely buried him, and although terribly weakened when dug out, he refused to be sent to the rear. He not only continued his duties, he also volunteered to hold a position of great importance, where he resisted a strong enemy attack. His enlisted men continue to make a grand show of it. Several men of the 78th volunteered to make a flank attack on the Boche when their battalion was held up by enfilading machine-gun fire.

The Boche still held much of Blanc Mont. The entire massif was honeycombed with tunnels and dugouts, most of which weren't apparent to those on the surface. Several attempts to take the hill during the morning were unsuccessful, so the slaughter of Marines continued.

Williams and Barker were to move forward at H hour in support of the 5th. An artillery barrage was planned to tear up the woods on top of Blanc Mont and hopefully dislodge the enemy. Shuler was to wait until 1520, later changed to 1535, and then go up and clean out the top of Blanc Mont. An hour after H, under severe machine-gun and artillery fire, Shuler's 3/6 still hadn't been able to move out of their positions, let alone take the hill. At 1550 Barker told Shuler he was taking "severe machine gun fire from our left rear." A few minutes later Shuler asked for more artillery fire on the hilltop.

At 1625 Feland asked Barker and Williams, as directed by brigade, to come up and support his cut-up battalions. It was midafternoon and the 6th Marines were still bogged down about Blanc Mont, unable to help the 5th. After the artillery preparation an unsuccessful attempt was again made by Shuler to take the hill. The Boche position was still so strongly held that "special preparations would be required if undue loss in manpower was to be avoided."[55]

Shuler complained to Lee at 1635 that

no real heavy artillery fire [was] put in woods [on Blanc Mont] up to the present time. They [2d Division artillery] are now firing an occasional seventy-five which is not effective. Machine guns are firing from there all the time. It is strongly held.

Lee responded by asking that Shuler stay where he was and to forward any messages from 2/6 or 1/6 and "lose no time in getting the information here." As if the Marines weren't having enough trouble, brigade also received a message from Marine 2d Lt. Arthur Pelander, liaison officer with the French, who were complaining that the 4th Brigade hadn't maintained liaison with them. Pelander said that the French had already widened their right front *"more than their sector calls for."*[56]

At 1715, in a phone call to regiment, Shuler explained to the assistant regimental commander, Thomas Holcomb, that he was not able to take the hill because the artillery had not reduced the machine guns. Holcomb promised heavy artillery fire from 1800 to 1830. But at 1800 Neville canceled the attack orders for the 6th. They were to dig in and instead support the 5th. A little later Shuler was still telling Lee about the strength of the enemy in the woods on the hill. He said that a German prisoner had told him there were three German battalions, with twelve machine guns per battalion, in the woods on the hill. Lee responded with his warning that "most of them [prisoners] lie like hell" so be "on the alert." At 1900 hours Lee reiterated the previous order, Williams and Barker were to dig in and support the 5th Marines. "There will be no further advance tonight."

A recent biography of Lejeune suggests that the last remaining unoccupied section of Blanc Mont was taken by the 6th Marines, along with 204 prisoners and seventy-five machine guns and trench mortars, by 1700.[57] That was not so. At 0735 on 5 October the information was passed on to Shuler that his 82d, 83d, and 97th Companies had taken, that morning, "that portion of Blanc Mont which had not already been taken . . . and they were digging in."[58]

In July 1919—at the request of the division chief of staff—LeRoy Hunt, then a major and commanding officer of the 1st Battalion, 5th Marines, prepared a statement that clarified the situation on 4 October 1918, as a then company commander of that same battalion saw it. He indicated that the situation for the 2d and 3d Battalions was critical and what was needed was "immediate and bold action." The enemy were closing in on the left flank, endeavoring to cut off the salient caused by the Marines' advance. In his report Hunt gave Hamilton credit for his "wonderful initiative and power of quick decision." He states that the most important thing was to relieve the stress on the left flank and to extend the line in that direction. He adds that "Hamilton gave orders to form the battalion to attack in a westerly direction and hook up with the other two battalions on their left. . . ."

With all four companies on line facing westward, 1/5 started forward at about noon. As soon as they started forward the enemy machine guns opened up and continued firing during the entire period, with no let up even when the Germans launched a counterattack, which was broken up. When the left flank finally reached the road those two companies swung to the right with both then facing northwest; parallel to the road. The ridge before St. Étienne lay directly before them and as they started forward and upward the enemy infiltrated around to their rear opening fire from that direction as well as to their front. Their left rear was also enveloped by the enemy, leaving them practically surrounded. They were now taking firing from three directions.

There was but one course of action open to 1/5 on 4 October and Hamilton took it, an advance straight up the hill in order to stem the galling fire from that direction. As Hunt said, "No one but those present will ever know or fully appreciate what the battalion went through during the charge up this hill. The rate of casualties was far above anything we had experienced, but the men kept on." The crest of the ridge was taken by storm, the Marines taking about 100 prisoners and many machine guns. But their travail was not yet over. Hunt explains that though they had taken that ridge, there was another just to the north of the town that was running parallel and on which German artillery was well placed; it was higher with great lines of sight. In less than fifteen minutes of relative security, the Boche guns began laying direct fire upon 1/5 which was so effective that Hunt feared the battalion would be wiped out in short order. Hamilton did something characteristic. With no support on either flank and receiving terrible fire from many directions, he elected to advance toward the town. They started forward, getting away from the fire they were taking from the rear and left rear, but when they had gone about two hundred yards they started receiving direct artillery and machine-gun fire from in front of the town. Hunt says, "This fire was so intense and casualties were occurring at such a rate that it meant annihilation to continue the advance with no support and no liaison on either flank. We were absolutely alone and at this point receiving fire *from all four sides*." (Emphasis added.]

Hunt avoided mentioning the potential rout anywhere in his report. At this point he simply states that it was "imperative to connect up with the regiment," so they gathered their wounded and withdrew to the woods on the crest of the ridge. Finding no solace there, they continued through the woods eastward, taking casualties the entire way, until they managed to connect up with the other two battalions at about 1630 hours,[59] at the point where they started nearly five hours before. Hunt does give a bit of detailed information about individual acts of heroism that brighten an otherwise disastrous afternoon. The group led by Kelly had managed to get to a point about eight hundred yards before the town and remained there until dark, when they then rejoined the battalion. The regiment dug in with both flanks refused and during the night of 4–5 October was practically surrounded and under terrific artillery and machine-gun bombardment. A heavy counterattack from the left flank was repulsed and many German prisoners were taken. The following day the 6th Marines cleared the enemy from the rear of the 5th Marines and communication in the brigade was reestablished.

Hunt gives a detailed breakdown of the condition of each of the companies of the battalion at 1800 hours on 4 October 1918. It is indicative of what happened in that short period of time that has been called "the worst single day's casualties for the Marines during the war."[60] Those remaining in 1/5 totaled 168 according to Hunt's figures. They are broken down by him as follows:

17th Company	2 officers	35 men
49th Company	2 officers	29 men
66th Company	1 officer	22 men
67th Company	2 officers	40 men
Bn. Hdqs. Group	5 officers	30 men
Total	**12 officers**	**156 men**

Saturday, 5 October

A few minutes after midnight, Messersmith reported to Feland that his right flank was in the air: "23d Infantry withdrew without any warning being given until time of withdrawal." He continued, "Tonight our own artillery fired upon us." Five minutes later Larsen also reported to Feland that the 3d Brigade was moving its lines and he was trying to accommodate the changes on his right flank. He added, "They [the Boche] have been giving us hell with artillery all day as well as the worst M.G. I have ever seen." All that night of 4–5 October the 5th Regiment was anxious about its right flank. It wouldn't be until early morning when the 23d Infantry returned and later the 6th Marines would pass through their lines.

The 5th Regiment, though badly mauled, managed to survive that frightful night. Early on the morning of 5 October, Lee sent all American units, and the French, a memo that cautioned all units to back away from Blanc Mont during an early morning bombardment, which was scheduled for 0515 through 0615. There was no need to caution the French units, since they were still some distance away from the site.[61]

Hamilton responded to a message from Feland indicating that the 5th was to advance when the "French attack on right and left." In his response Hamilton clearly states that he does not have enough men to expand his front to connect up with the French. His further thoughts are expressed rather eloquently.

This battalion will go, or attempt to go, where you order it. You should understand though that your regiment is now much depleted, very disorganized, and not in condition to advance as a front line regiment even though the enemy forces in front are found to be small. It is hard to say "can't," but the Division Commander *should thoroughly understand the situation and realize that this regiment "can't" advance as an attacking force. Such advance would sacrifice the regiment.* Hamilton. [Italics added, but underlining in the original.][62]

So that was the end of the fighting at Blanc Mont for the 5th Marines. They were finished for this campaign. That wasn't an official declaration, but it was the truth. Nothing was ever put in writing, but no one had the gall to commit the 5th to any more engagements on Blanc Mont.

At 0920 Lejeune sent Feland a message that began, "Fine work out there. That was a hard job." He rambles on a bit about how everyone was doing his duty, both the front and rear formations, and how he had almost convinced Gouraud that there was no need to advance farther toward St. Étienne. Gouraud thought differently.[63] He equated the retreat of the enemy on the Reims front with the splendid showing of the 2d Division, because the Germans feared the advance at St. Étienne. Lejeune continued, "They stopped us all right; but the taking of that ridge is what pushed them off the line." The ridge he was writing of was the one the Marines and doughboys, through their own superlative courage, went up and took even though they had suffered terrible losses in order to do so.[64]

Lejeune adds his let's go get 'em routine and justifies his order for the 5th to stand where they were by saying, "If you had fallen back before the Boche he would have thought he got your goat, and if you stick your heels in the ground you got his goat. He is not shooting us up, is he? I think he has gone. I think he just beat it." "He" wasn't gone, not quite yet. The 6th Marines and after them, the 36th (Texas-Oklahoma) Division, would share many remaining Germans among themselves during the next few days, and understandably all would be fully satisfied with their portion. Lejeune's message to Feland continued by telling him about how great Shuler and 3/6 was with help from the French 170th Division and that he, Lejeune, didn't believe that the casualties [to the 5th Marines] were quite as heavy as reported.[65]

At 0615 the final attack on Blanc Mont began. This time 3/6 was successful in its bloody task, capturing more than 200 German prisoners and at least 65 machine guns. Those guns wouldn't destroy any more Marines, but there were still many others that would. Larsen, in a message to Feland at 1020, advised that the French were advancing on the left with "apparently little opposition." What could have been added was that the Marine Brigade made that possible! Midmorning Williams reported to Lee about the condition of his battalion. There were seventeen officers and 325 men "in line." He was also covering about a mile of frontage with that badly depleted battalion. Lieutenant Ralph W. Marshall, Intelligence Officer for 3/6, reported at noon to Colonel Lee that he and two enlisted men had reconnoitered to within five hundred yards of St. Étienne and found that the French were west of the town but that the Germans were in trenches all around the town. Five minutes later, Lee sent orders to his battalion commanders to advance to conform with the French who were on the left flank but not to move faster than the 3d Brigade, whose progress would be predicated upon the progress the French forces on their right would make. But under no circumstances was the 6th Regiment to go beyond St. Étienne without further orders.

At 1715 1st Lt. Clifton B. Cates, skipper of the 96th Company, reported to Colonel Lee that a major of the 23d Infantry had given him orders to halt where he was but

will hold here until further orders, as it is a needless sacrifice of men to try and take this nest. . . . Company hung up by barbed wire and terrific machine gun fire. Lt. [John A.] West[66] was killed and losses were heavy. It will take a good heavy barrage to get the guns out—at least eight in the nest.

He also mentioned to Lee that he had forty-five men of his company and forty from the 79th Company. One of his men, Corporal Moreland,* already mentioned from the day before, was all over the place. He was busy organizing his company's flank and all the while hurling grenades at the enemy to keep them off balance and away from his position. He continued holding his ground, throwing back three enemy counterattacks and killing or capturing all the members of a Boche patrol. A few minutes after Cates's message, Shuler reported that a gap existed between Williams on the left of his battalion because of enemy machine guns on the hill to the right front, "apparently in the sector of the third [sic] Brigade." Williams sent Lee a message at 1740 detailing the situation to his front as he saw it. According to him, the German machine guns were scattered before St. Étienne and additional troops with heavy machine guns were filing out of the town southward toward the 6th Marines. He told regiment that he was taking fire on his front and both flanks and requested artillery to reduce some of the nests so that he could move forward. At 1800 Cates sent a message to Williams that West was still alive and lying wounded in the woods with many other Marines.

Should we shell the woods under those circumstances? We can hold them here, but it will take an extra heavy barrage to get them [Germans] out *and more men*. [Emphasis in original.]

The "new" skipper of the 79th Company, 2d Lt. John A. West*, continued in command even though he had been severely wounded and refused to be evacuated until a proper replacement became available. West had, for the past three days, since the first excursion into the enemy's trenches on 2 October, consistently been leading his men in a heroic manner. He was properly cited.

The 2d Battalion was taking its licks. Williams and his lads had been up front since the initial advance on 3 October and were exhausted. Colonel Lee decided to make some changes and sent orders forward to his battalion COs at 1820. They were for the 3d to relieve the 2d in the front line and the 1st to relieve Shuler in second spot. Shuler suggested to Lee that it would make more sense to wait until morning for the 3d Battalion to relieve the 2d. "It would be especially difficult to locate Williams positions in the dark. We do not know where Williams or his companies are." Lee agreed and notified both of the other battalion commanders that the relief would take place during the darkness, before dawn on the following morning, 6 October.

Sellers, in his memoir, suggested strongly that the advance over open ground without artillery support was idiotic and what happened to his friend Messersmith wasn't fair . . .[67]

He [Messersmith] asked for a hearing but never got one, because from then on until the armistice we were continually moving. The poor fellow was in a motorcycle sidecar with a corporal driving him and no command or responsibilities. He had looked after his men, and the messages he sent back [complaining about the advance on 4 October] were correct, since this later advance was ridiculous. I know. I advanced there.[68]

Hospital Apprentice Second Class Hal E. Martin, USN, spotted a wounded 1/6 man lying in no-man's-land where he had been dropped when his bearers had all been wounded by an exploding shell. Out Martin went, in the best traditions of that service, and rescued the Marine as has happened since time immemorial. For his heroism, then and until 10 October, even though he fell ill with a high fever, he was decorated with a Navy Cross and two Silver Star citations.

Lejeune later wrote that he recognized that the 2d Division was rapidly falling apart and it was time to see that they were relieved. Both the 23d Infantry and the 5th Marines were already finished and the 9th Infantry and 6th Marines were close to it.

Sunday, 6 October

Near midnight, Lieutenant Cates sent an urgent message to brigade telling them, "Our artillery shelling 23d Inf. they are dropping back & we are also." For a while Williams had been wondering what had happened to his 79th and 80th Companies. Later that evening he learned that they were in the 3d Brigade sector and would rejoin 2/6 after it had taken up its reserve position. Williams told Lee that he had 253 officers and men and 1/6 had a total of 589.

The only other momentous news was that the 2d Division was ordered to reset their timepieces at 0100, back to midnight. At last, Standard Time. Things had to get better now.

At 0130 Lee set the time for the 6 October morning attack at 0630. It was to be preceded by a one-hour artillery preparation. At attack time, the barrage would move forward to a preset line where it would remain until 0700. Soon after 0530, when the division artillery opened up, red rocket signals caused the 5th Marines to send a message saying that the shells were falling short and that the 6th Marines were falling back; the 3d Brigade reported, however, that the fire was coming from the Boche. The commander of the 2d Artillery Brigade angrily responded to the charges by stating that if "any Marines were running back from the front line it was because they didn't withdraw to required five hundred yards distance from barrage line." Everyone's nerves were a bit frayed by now.

At 0653, 2/5 was reporting that about half the shells were again falling to their right rear. A few minutes later the 18th Company sent green rockets up, which message meant that heavy artillery was still falling short. They couldn't all have been seeing things. It wasn't the first, nor would it be the last time during the war, that artillery inadvertently found targets among its own men.

Shuler reported that Boche machine guns began holding him up as soon as he jumped off. Two of his officers, Capt. James H. Johnston of the 82d and 1st Lt. Charles D. Roberts of the 83d Company, had been hurt almost immediately and the 97th Company, led by 1st Lt. Alfred H. Noble, was being "held up by our own [artillery] fire." Shuler was soon complaining about a "hell of a nest in the woods" and was told to "use a Stokes on it." According to interrogated prisoners, there were loads of machine guns on the hill 3/6 was trying to take. Possibly those prisoners were lying, too, as Lee had charged earlier, but somebody, in addition to the 2d Division artillery, was beating hell out of the 6th Marines.

Almost an hour later, Holcomb passed information along to division that the Germans were advancing behind a smoke screen and that Shuler had bypassed a machine-gun nest to his front that was beginning to become troublesome for his unit. Shortly afterward a special barrage, dropped behind 3/6, dealt with that annoying spot. Holcomb responded that "everything looks rosey." Maybe it was where Holcomb sat, but at 0824 Shuler was calling to ask what had happened to the Stokes and one-pounders he had requested earlier. About an hour later, Holcomb was telling division that the French were in the western part of St. Étienne and the Germans in the eastern, and that Shuler was doing fine; his battalion was well organized and he, Shuler, reported being "very confident."

At 0930 Shuler reported that 3/6, and the 23d Infantry to their right, had both attained their objectives and that the two units were in "perfect liaison." He also reported that his casualties were now about thirty percent and added that the division's artillery barrage had broken up a counterattack planned by the enemy. Within a half hour Lee advised Neville that the French 22d Division had arrived on Shuler's left and the three units, the 22d, 3/6, and the 23d Infantry, were in liaison. Lee, always quick to praise, said that 3/6 had performed at the highest level for two days in succession by efficiently "dealing with machine gun nests." At 1030 the French notified Shuler that no Germans were left in St. Étienne and that they held the town. That report was not true. The Germans were still in St. Étienne and would continue to cause trouble for both the French and Americans for some time.

Some really good news came soon afterward, however. The 141st Infantry, 36th Division, had arrived and were ready to move into the lines to relieve the 23d Infantry. The Texas/Oklahoma "cowboy" infantry, as the Marines and 3d Brigade Infantry soon called them, now teamed up with the 9th Infantry, which was to remain in line. Each of the 9th's battalions were placed alongside a rookie 141st battalion. Then the 142d Infantry moved in with the 6th Marines, part of which now removed themselves back to Blanc Mont. The 5th Marines still remained in a support position, farther back.

Shortly afterward brigade sent Lee an order to provide men to search for stragglers in the rear areas. Lee's return memo very strongly suggested that his regiment was not in any condition to do anything "in the rear" and that the "twenty percent" left behind as a reserve should be used for that purpose.[69] Apparently Lee, like Feland, had just about had his fill of the nonsense that continued to emanate from Neville's headquarters.

The 36th had "officially" relieved the 2d Division during the night of 6–7 October, with its 71st Brigade taking over from both the 3d and 4th Brigades. Each of the relieved brigades was to leave one battalion in line so as to provide some continuity and experience for the 36th Division.[70] Barker's 1/6 was the lucky Marine battalion selected for the dubious honor. Sellers mentions that as soon as the doughboys moved in,

> the battle-weary Marines scared them to death with the gory tales of our experiences. When the order came for the 36th to advance, their lieutenant colonel, a West Pointer, had a very difficult time trying to rout these inexperienced men out of their trenches and dugouts.[71]

Monday and Tuesday, 7–8 October

Since the 36th Division were without heavy weapons, the 2d Field Artillery Brigade, with attached French field artillery units, was to stay in position and support them.[72] Two battalions of French tanks were assigned to them as well. The balance of both the Marines and infantry were to remain in support positions unless and until called upon. For most of the day the "rookies" were getting used to their new home and were even credited with bringing in some German prisoners. Now Cpl. Warren Jackson, whom we have met before, described what he saw happen to his fellow Texans.

> I think it was October 7 that a regiment of the 36th Division came up and leap-frogged us. It was one of these men, or some that passed us a day or two afterward, that two stories were told which were not flattering. . . . This was their first trip to the front and they had just passed through our lines. A lieutenant of that division became so excited that he committed the most unparalleled blunder of advancing his men under fire in a column of squads, or some other close formation. As they advanced "Pop" Ansel, a 95th man who was a private by choice, hollowed [sic] out to the looie:
> "What the hell you pulling off there?" he demanded.

The men who witnessed this swore that the lieutenant begged Ansel to come out and get the men in proper formation for making the attack, which request Pop ignored. It was thought that a great many of the 36th were killed because of their lack of training and due to the incompetence of many of their officers.

Jackson's second story is humorous . . .

Along with one of the advancing organizations . . . was a Frenchman. . . . A falling shell brought the cry of "Gas! Gas!" . . . the men were putting their masks on when the [Frenchman] attempting to correct the mistake, shouted "Pas Gas, pas gas" [no gas]. [The] 36th officer came to a better appreciation of his grave responsibility . . . and took up the cry in frenzied tones: "Put on your masks, men, put on your masks. That's the WORST gas there is."

The balance of that day seemed to be solely a time of readjustment for the remaining 6th Marines with various reports of German advances and retrogrades, to and from St. Étienne. Now that the French had finally arrived where they should have been during the previous four days, the Marines were no longer taking severe artillery and machine-gun fire on their left flank. Later that day the French conceded that they had lost the town of St. Étienne, and then later reported that they had retaken it. In fact the Germans were still jockeying with the French for its possession and it appeared likely, despite their protestations, that the French barely had a toehold in the town. While it wasn't entirely a day of rest for the Marine Brigade, it was as close to it as they had experienced during the hectic previous week.

At 0200, 8 October, Colonel Lee received Operations Memorandum No. 17, which advised him that the brigade (which meant the remnants of the 6th Marines) would move forward at 0515 that morning toward the town of Machault, which was about three miles directly north beyond St. Étienne. The second part of the memo was phrased rather peculiarly. "The Commanding Officer, 6th Regiment, will detail an officer to command the *inter-regiment combat liaison group*" [emphasis added] and continued by explaining that one battalion of the 6th would serve as flank protection and liaison with the French forces.[73]

For obvious reasons no members of the 5th Marines would be involved, especially since the regiment had pulled back on the evening of

6 October to a position about directly east of Blanc Mont, and would remain there until early evening of 9 October. Private Elton E. Mackin, in his memoir, said, "The Battalion had come back from Blanc Mont Ridge. No," he corrected himself, "the Battalion was still up there."[74] Later in the month a recapitulation for the 5th Marines indicated that they had suffered 1,120 total casualties, of which sixty-one were officers and 1,059 were enlisted men.

The attack began at 0515 on the morning of 8 October, but a great deal of confusion reigned in the headquarters of both the 36th Division and its 71st Brigade. Eventually orders directing the attack reached the troops that were to launch it. The 6th Marines had the post of honor, the left flank. Within an hour Barker was able to report that there was little opposition on his right. Another hour passed and Barker phoned in a message that the 76th Company (Overton), on the extreme left of the American line, was held up by machine-gun fire. Where were the French? Lee responded with caution and concern, asking for written messages since the phone connection was not very good. Captain Gardiner Hawkins of the 79th reported "satisfactory progress along the whole line," but added that fighting around St. Étienne was still going on. At 0750 the 75th Company (Chandler) was held up by "heavy machine gun fire" northeast of St. Étienne. Barker added that "Chandler, [2d Lt. Edward F. Dunk] Durk [sic], and [2d Lt. Jeremiah J.] Dalton are wounded."[75] Literally within minutes the company lost two commanders. Chandler was wounded after trying to obtain support from French tanks and 2d Lieutenant Palmer Ketner Jr. took command. In less time than it takes to tell he was also wounded, later dying of the wounds on 2 November 1918. Whereupon, with all the other officers severely wounded, Sgt. Aralzaman C. Marsh took command of the badly depleted company. Under Marsh's leadership the men's rifle fire kept the enemy from using their machine guns. So successful was this small group that soon after, the German machine guns were surrounded and captured. At Marsh's request Major Barker soon sent Major George A. Stowell to assume command of the approximately fifteen men who remained. Marsh received a Silver Star.

A half hour later Barker was still reporting heavy machine-gun fire on both the 74th and 76th Companies and that they were also receiving artillery fire and were therefore unable to advance. "Request artillery action immediately." Lee responded at 0910, telling Barker to sit tight and try sniping the machine-gun nests. Meanwhile he would request artillery fire, and where did Barker want it? It is evident that the French had not wiped out German resistance in, around, and before St. Étienne. Some members of the 76th Company were getting into St. Étienne; in fact, at least two platoons, superbly directed by 1st Lt. Charles Z. Lesher, made it. Second Lieutenants Walter S. Gaspar and Walter S. Fant Jr., each leading one platoon, somehow managed to enter without a casualty to either platoon, although it was still a German strong point. After getting into the town they routed the Boche, capturing a great number of prisoners. Even though the Marines had to shake the enemy out of the houses and off the roofs, the cemetery, and the streets, the command only suffered two men wounded. One other platoon, led by 1st Lt. Frederick W. Wagoner, USA, withstood the brunt of the main body of the enemy attack hurled against them. But Wagoner, in displaying outstanding ability and personal fearlessness, had his men hold their fire until he gave them the command. That sheet of fire caused such destruction that the enemy turned and ran. The 76th remained in the town against several further counterattacks. They were supported by a platoon of the 15th Machine Gun Company led by 1st Lt. Victor Bleasdale*, who ordered his men to become regular infantry. They then overwhelmed two enemy Maxim positions, capturing the crews and the guns.[76]

All morning, Germans from a variety of regiments and divisions were being sent to the rear as prisoners. Regardless of what was happening to the Boche, Shuler reported to Lee that his battalion, which was in the second spot, was "getting in very bad shape physically." He added that their spirit was good and admitted he had heard no complaints, but his battalion had been taking hell and was still under constant shell fire. He was able to advise that the troublesome machine-gun nests, which had been bothering them for so many days, had finally been wiped out. Even Neville, who didn't often seem to consider what effect constant punishment might be having on his brigade, replied to Lee's suggestion that he would recommend withdrawal of Shuler, but not until he knew what shape the 141st Regiment was in.

At 1410 Stowell, who was still with the remnants of the 75th Company, relayed back the condition that company was in; it was very bad. The message implied that he was CO but as far as can be determined he was trying to put the 75th back together again after the beating they had been taking all morning. He reported that he hadn't seen any of the officers because they were all wounded, and worse, he could only find one sergeant, two corporals, and ten privates from the 75th. Stowell suggested that the remnants be relieved but that a standing barrage should be laid down first in order to safely effect it.

At 1535 Earl Ellis sent a message to Col. Harry Lee advising him that Shuler's message asking to be relieved "is thoroughly realized." Ellis goes on to add that Neville had gone to division "where he will take this matter up." All brigade needed was more information about the 141st Infantry so that a decision regarding Shuler could be made. The day was not a good one for the 141st and 142d Infantry, nor was it any better for the 6th Marines. At 1900 1st Lt. Macon C. Overton, 76th Company, notified Barker that his company was under heavy attack, which had been repelled on his *right*. (Emphasis added.) Although he was in liaison with the French on his left he was dubious about his contacts with the 142d Infantry on his right. He felt that the right was not strongly held and requested that fault be corrected forthwith. Barker added that he and Shuler had been "picking up stragglers from 142 Inf. and am placing them in line to connect with Shuler's position on the right." From all additional reports the 141st Infantry had taken a shellacking, as had both 1/6 and 3/6, and as we have seen, the 142d on the right of the Marines hadn't fared much better. Late afternoon, after German guns had laid down a terrific barrage on the town, the Boche had tried to come back to St. Étienne in overwhelming numbers. They weren't finished yet, but they weren't very successful either. The French and Americans continued to keep them at bay.

During the late afternoon Lee responded to the message Earl Ellis had sent him. In the first part Lee stated, "I am very much afraid that the situation is not thoroughly understood by *many in authority*.[Emphasis added.]"[77] He added, the casualties in each of his battalions had reduced the force to about 250 men in each with the officers' losses "equally as large." Lee then added his comments about the request that he supply data and general information about the 142d "and the other organization on its flank," making it quite plain that he didn't know anything about them other than that they were in a complete state of disorganization. He did comment that both had managed to keep the 6th Marines aware of what the enemy was doing and had protected themselves from counterattacks. Lee ends by stating that at the moment (1705 hours) the enemy had laid down a tremendous barrage that was forcing Marines in front of the town to retire into it.

A soldier of Company K, 142d Infantry, in a memoir written many years later, describes what he saw at exactly 2000 hours that evening:

Emerging from the wood, in full view of the Germans, we fanned out immediately, six or eight paces between men, and started across, a *small* detachment of Marines accompanying us on our left. The Marines are mentioned by the Colonel as a "detachment"; the attack order reads "one battalion of Marines will maintain combat liaison on the left and will occupy St. Etienne. Their number was *no where near a battalion.*" [Emphasis added.]

He goes on a paragraph later to describe what happened next.

[The Germans opened up with artillery and machine guns from behind their barbed wire and] the veteran Marines, too experienced to walk into such a trap, turned and sprinted back to the wood just as Lieut. Porter happened to be looking. In the excitement, and seeing the greenish gray field uniforms, he pulled his Colt .45. "They're Marines. Don't shoot!"[78]

Later that same day, the 6th Regiment sent brigade a report on its battalions which indicated that 861 officers and men of the regiment still survived but with reservations about the correct figures for both the 1st and 3d Battalions. Sometime during the evening hours, Lieutenant Overton of the 76th Company reported that he was connected on his left with the 62d French Infantry but had no liaison with any unit on his right. Private Ernest K. Aselton* helped make those connections. He volunteered to establish liaison for his company through heavy shell and machine-gun fire and brought reinforcements back to the line at an extremely critical time. Those men made the difference. An enemy attack was repelled but Aselton lost his life.

Wednesday, 9 October

At 0305 Lee asked Overton to send a small reconnaissance party out to "the works" on his left front to ascertain whether they were occupied by the enemy. He emphasized that it wasn't to be a forceful investigation, "therefore, it must be light." Lee told him division wanted this information as soon as possible so that they could "pulverize it" if the Germans were there. Overton responded (no time given) that yes indeed, the Boche were there and in fact a French major had requested that the entire front be plastered with artillery, since he knew that the enemy was massed in large numbers in the woods and on the right front.

October 9th was somewhat brighter for the Marines than had been the case for some days past. The infantry were reporting that they and scattered companies of Marines were holding stronger positions despite various enemy activities, and they were dug in on the north side of town and would hold. Lee was able at 1305 to advise his battalion commanders they would be relieved that night, although machine-gun units on line would remain for twenty-four hours after relief. An interesting footnote was that Lee sent a message to 1st and 3d Battalions to turn in "all Browning guns and equipment . . . at regimental dump." Second Battalion was told to turn theirs over to the ordnance officer of the 142d Infantry.[79] Both of the 2d Division machine-gun battalions were retained by the 36th Division longer than had been anticipated but they, too, were finally relieved during the afternoon and evening of the 10th of October and then they were sent to rejoin the survivors of the division.[80]

Barker reported that his battalion, 1/6, suffered a total of 280 casualties, including thirty-nine evacuated sick, as well as lauding the 73d Machine Gun Company and Overton's 76th and Chandler's 75th Company. That morning Chandler lead his platoon out toward St. Étienne in the final attack made by Marines at Blanc Mont. One private from Chandler's company, Dean F. Smiley*, was certainly active that day. In fact he went all the way. Going out alone, he rushed a machine-gun nest single-handed, killing three of the crew and capturing the remainder. While taking his prisoners to the rear he was killed by enemy shell fire.[81]

The 2d Battalion Report of Operations for 10 October tells us,

> The relief was completed early on the morning of October 10 and the battalion proceeded, by companies, to NAVARIN FME., where a good breakfast did much to put new life into a tired but confident battalion.[82]

Williams, who signed the report, also gave credit to the 81st Company, 6th Machine Gun Battalion, "which has always operated most efficiently with the 2d Battalion." During the entire Blanc Mont affair all the various companies of the 6th Machine Gun Battalion deserved the accolades bestowed by Williams. They were always up front with the attacking groups, suffering accordingly. The same must be added for the heroics of the navy men, corpsmen, and doctors who saved many legs, arms, and lives. Numbers of them were awarded various decorations for their courage and ministrations of mercy on an unemotional battlefield.

Harry Lee's report for the regiment attempted to absolve the division artillery from the previous charges of dropping shells on their own troops. "I think it more than probable that the enemy fire from the flank . . . gave that impression upon those whom fire was directed that it was our own artillery." He was only partially correct.

The battle for Blanc Mont was finally over for the 2d Division. Both brigades had suffered heavy casualties, as had the other attached machine-gun and engineer units. It was a relatively short period, compared to the Belleau Wood campaign, but it was as intense and as bloody and, according to the veterans of both, worse. As Thomason, one of the few survivor officers of 1/5, said in his famous book *Fix Bayonets!*,

They [the 2d Division] had hurled the Boche from Blanc Mont and freed the sacred city of Rheims. They had paid a price hideous even for this war.

He added in his other great book, *Salt Winds and Gobi Dust,*

We were shot to pieces in the Champagne—I never enjoyed the war afterward.

Both brigades would need reorganizing and refitting as well as many replacements. They would also require a long period of rest in order to regain their sanity. Unfortunately, their relaxation and respite would last less than three weeks, when they would once again be called upon to "put out another fire" at the Meuse-Argonne.

Notes

1 John A. Lejeune, *Reminiscences of a Marine* (Philadelphia: Dorrance, 1930), 337. Gouraud pointed to his anchor collar insignia, which indicated that it was for colonial infantry, of which he had been a part in his early service years. The French navy also had/have Marines operating from warships. Confusing.

2 Ibid., 342

3 Ibid.

4 Ibid., 343.

5 Edwin N. "McClellan", The Battle of Blanc Mont Ridge. *Marine Corps Gazette,* VII, no. 1 (March 1922), 6–7.

6 The luck of the draw. Just as at Belleau Wood, the Marine Brigade drew what was to be the most difficult assignment: the Blanc Mont Massif.

7 *Marine Corps Gazette,* op.cit., 8.

8 Lejeune, *Reminiscences,* 346–347.

9 What happened at Bois de Belleau on 6 June 1918, because of the lack thereof, is a case in point.

10 Lejeune, *Reminiscences,* 349. The Germans retook the lost ground and the 3d Brigade had more difficulties because of it.

11 Lejeune, Ibid., 350. This was certainly one of the strangest plans of attack ever seen. Earl Ellis has frequently been cited as its author. The triangle in the center, which at its base extended one mile, effectively split the division before the enemy as did no other. It was successful, which must have surprised everyone, including Lejeune, Naulin, and possibly Gouraud too. It also appears that the development of "Lejeune's" plan was rather late in taking final shape, just hours before the advance was to begin.

12 Williams's nickname was of a good-natured variety, as was he. He was well known to "like to leave everything up to his adjutant while he would try to get up to the front line with an automatic rifle."

13 Field Order No. 35, dated 2 October 1918 at 2300 hours, just concerning the 4th Brigade, directed that the 6th Marines take a certain set of coordinates that do not conform to any I have been able to locate on any map seen. Basically it was for 2/6 to take the Massif. He didn't know then and for some time that the Germans were dug in all over that hill, mainly in hidden "caves." Williams just scratched the surface and no one at brigade seemed to know the difference.

The 1st Battalion, 6th, established themselves to the road junction on the right and spread left, toward Williams. Third Battalion took a position in the rear of 2/6 as support. The 5th Marines took positions extending south and to the west to protect that flank from any substantial German attack from that direction.

14 The French 21st Division, on the left flank of the 2d Division (i.e., the 4th Brigade), had as its objective Elbe and Essen trenches, about a mile and a half in the rear of the 4th Brigade's objective. That completely exposed the left flank of the Marine Brigade to the German forces for several days.

15 This comment brought back to mind an article that Lee had written for the *Marine Corps Gazette,* December 1916, in which he espoused the merits of close battlefield control and the dominance of the rifle. This was a common

nineteenth-century attitude and approach among many regular officers, army and Marines. They literally ignored artillery and machine guns, which aided in the destruction of the Marine Brigade.

16 Lieutenant Colonel James McB. Sellers's memoir "The 78th Company at Blanc Mont". *Marine Corps Gazette*, (November 1993), 47, claims that Capt. Walter A. Powers, who was commanding the 80th Company, was guilty of not confiding in his platoon leaders or keeping up with the other companies in the advance. He also accuses Powers of not being with his company during the initial stages of the advance, in other words of "cowardice." Sellers believed that Ernest "Bull" Williams, battalion commander, should have court-martialed Powers but only relieved him of command of the company. The company history does not even mention anyone by that name, or add much about the company's activities at Blanc Mont. Powers had a varied career in the 4th Brigade. He also served briefly in the 75th Company (twice) and the 79th Company. Sellers also stated that the company first sergeant was a cashiered British officer, but nothing additional by way of a name.

17 Captain Wendell Westover, 4th Machine Gun Battalion, *Suicide Battalions* (New York: GP Putnam's Sons, 1929), 209.

18 Even though a number of Marines from other companies were cited that day, it appears that only Captain Sellers worked overtime sending headquarters the better "written," higher-award recommendations.

19 What was happening was simply that the Germans still held the high ground to the left of 2/6. There was, as was later learned, a heavy concentration of machine-gun nests all over that ridge and many dugouts that weren't always obvious. The Germans had controlled this area for a number of years.

20 Captain Henry E. Chandler was killed in action on 9 October 1918.

21 Captain Macon C. Overton, two DSC, NC, three Silver Star citations, three Croix de Guerre; with most awards at Blanc Mont (NC and DSC) but some at Belleau Wood also. He would be killed in action on 1 November 1918 in the Meuse-Argonne. Former enlisted Marine promoted when war began. One of the outstanding fighting Marines of the war.

22 Both messages from *Records of the Second Division*, vol. 4.

23 William McB. Sellers, unpublished memoir, 64.

24 Wilkinson was to die of wounds on 5 October 1918. He received two Silver Star citations for his work at Blanc Mont.

25 *Records of the Second Division*, vol. 5.

26 Lieutenant Colonel Ernst Otto, *The Battle at Blanc Mont (October 2 to October 10, 1918).* (Annapolis: United States Naval Institute, 1930.)

27 This was an error. What Noble was reporting was that 1/6 had moved to the road junction to meet the 23d Infantry. I don't believe that 1/6 was ever really on the Hill.

28 Glucksman had been Sellers's "bat boy" upon arrival in France. Sellers complained, sort of, that Glucksman washed everything he owned that wasn't nailed down and frequently washed it again even though it hadn't yet been worn.

29 Captain Alfred H. Noble, already with a DSC, NC, and a Silver Star citation at Belleau Wood, would also receive two additional SSs at Blanc Mont and another SS plus a Croix de Guerre in the Meuse-Argonne.

30 *Records of the Second Division*, vol. 7, Report of Major Henry L. Larsen, 12 October 1918.

31 *Records of the Second Division,* vol. 4. Message dated 3 October 1918 at 1050 hours. Phew! That was some message.

32 *Records of the Second Division,* vol. 2. Notice how they were hedging their bets?

33 *A Brief History of the Sixth Regiment U.S. Marine Corps July, 1917–December 1918,* (n.p.,n.d.; reprint, Pike NH: The Brass Hat, 1993), 23.

34 Frank Whitehead, another enlisted Marine commissioned at the beginning of the war, was a likable man, exceptionally proficient in his task of leading a company of Marines. He was wounded several times and would also be again at Blanc Mont. But later, just after the Meuse-Argonne fracas began, he returned to his beloved company again. Made brigadier general in WWII.

35 *Records of the Second Division,* vol. 4.

36 Otto made a bald, unadorned statement on page 66 of his book in which he simply stated that the 22d had replaced the 21st but "one can safely say that this fresh French division accomplished little."

37 *Records of the Second Division,* vol. 6. This day's attack by the 5th Marines is conveniently ignored completely in the operations report for the 4th Brigade. No mention of the day at all except to state "This attack, however, was not carried out until the next day [meaning 5 October]," a blatant lie.

38 He probably was the only sane man on the entire field. (Editorial comment.)

39 Otto, *Battle at Blanc Mont.* See map on p. 58.

40 McNulty was promoted to Marine gunner for his actions this day.

41 Thomas was also awarded a Navy Distinguished Service Medal. A very large number of enlisted Marine runners received both the DSC and NC during this entire period, but especially on 4 October. One can only imagine what crossing those fire lanes must have been.

42 During this troublesome period, the records of the 4th Brigade are vague, incomplete, distorted, or downright incorrect.

43 Massie and Quigley both received a Silver Star and Croix de Guerre.

44 Thomason, *Fix Bayonets!,* 175. I believe that Thomason was the "second-in-command" of the 49th Company at that time.

45 Originally dashes were included in the message at some point in time by a person or persons unknown now. The actual names might have been excised by practically anyone who was out to preserve the status quo. The reason is quite obvious. Captain Peter Owen, USMC, found the original document in the National Archives, and kindly sent a copy to me.

The Sellers memoir in the November 1993 issue of the *Marines Corps Gazette* clarifies the name of Major Robert E. Messersmith, CO of 2/5 and formerly CO of the 78th Company, 6th Marines. Messersmith was relieved. He was later assigned to the Paymaster's Department in 1919.

DeWitt Peck was wounded at Blanc Mont. He continued to serve until at least 1945, when he was made a major general. He served during the war years mainly in staff positions for various admirals. Later he became assistant to the commandant, A. A. Vandegrift. One of my correspondents suggested that his wound "saved him." Jackson left the service following the war. Even the bravest of men can take just so much.

46 *Records of the Second Division,* vol. 5.

47 Mackin, *Suddenly We Didn't Want to Die,* 188. I've seen that ground and it is wide open. Then the enemy occupied hills on three sides.

48 Kieren received two Silver Star citations.

49 Kelly actually had but twenty-two men on their feet at that time.

50 *Records of the Second Division,* vol. 4, dated 4 October 1918, 1830 hours.

51 "Last night's objective" was a section of trenches that lay just before the town of St. Étienne, and which the 5th Marines only got close to. Hamilton, an astute observer and non–mincer of words, obviously thought little of the rapidly developed plan for 4 October.

52 *Records of the Second Division,* vol. 6.

53 Thomason, *Fix Bayonets!* 191.

54 The operational report for the 4th Brigade explained that the Marines didn't follow the attack order No. 37 on 3 October because "it was considered inadvisable to advance leaving the machine-gun nests on the western slopes of Blanc Mont intact." Efforts continued to be made, mainly by the 6th Marines, against the guns during the afternoon of 4 October and into the evening, all without success.

55 *Records of the Second Division,* vol. 6.

56 Yes, the French complaint that the Marines' front was narrowed beyond the acceptable was all too true. It had been narrowed because of their inordinate losses caused by the lack of left flank support.

57 Merrill L. Bartlett, *Lejeune: A Marine's Life, 1867–1942* (Columbia University of South Carolina Press, 1991), 88. According to *Blanc Mont, Monograph Nine,* and the 2d Division diaries, the actual taking and clearing of Blanc Mont took place as described: the morning of 5 October 1918.

58 *Sixth Regiment,* 25.

59 This time must be incorrect. All other reports indicate an evening retrograde, which makes much more sense.

60 Allan R. Millett, *Semper Fidelis, The History of the United States Marine Corps* (New York: Macmillan, 1980), 314. He also gives a total casualty figure of over 1,100 Marines at Blanc Mont, of which most came from the 5th Marines, and the majority of those in 1/5.

61 *Records of the Second Division,* vol 5. Major Messersmith, CO 2/5, sent Feland a message at 0745 and the first words were "No signs as yet of the French on right or left."

62 *Records of the Second Division,* vol. 5.

63 After the expenditure of thousands of American lives to take that ground it seems, now and I would presume then, foolish to even consider not finishing the task assigned when the enemy was also in bad shape.

64 A French officer witnessing the advance of 1/5 on 4 October was quoted as saying, "But this is inhuman valor—the good God Himself could not stop those men."

65 There is no apparent reason for the commanding general to question the reports he received from his officers relative to the number of casualties in a regiment unless he knew, or surmised, that the company and battalion officers were deliberately falsifying records for reasons now unknown.

66 Cates was in error; West was severely wounded but survived the war. Indeed, he earned the Navy Cross and Distinguished Service Cross along with sev-

eral other minor awards for his actions at Blanc Mont between 2–5 October 1918.

67 Messersmith was relieved of command of 2/5 shortly after the 5th was withdrawn.

68 Sellers, op. cit., 66.

69 After the slaughter at Belleau Wood the brigade, intending to preserve enough Marines from each company upon which to build a new unit, set a quota to always retain twenty percent of the total of a unit, including an officer, before each battle for that purpose. This is the group that Lee, in very strong terms, was suggesting be used by brigade for the work at hand.

70 *Blanc Mont: Monograph No. 9* (Washington, D.C.: U.S. Government Printing Office, 1922), 19. Additional information indicates that both brigades were to leave the Stokes mortar and 37mm gun detachments and both the 5th and 6th Machine Gun Battalions to support 36th Division.

71 Sellers, op. cit., 66.

72 The 36th was one of the U.S. divisions brought over without anything except infantry. Pershing had to promise infantry and machine guns only, if he wanted ships to cart them to France. The British and French insisted that was what they wanted. Pershing felt forced to agree.

73 I could find nothing further in the official records that might clear up the meaning of the phrase or that would suggest that anything happened along those lines. It appears as though the 6th Marines were to "shepherd" the soldiers of the 36th toward the enemy and direct them while so engaged.

74 Mackin, *Suddenly We Didn't Want to Die,* 206.

75 Only Dunk survived. Chandler is listed as "Killed in Action" 9 October and Dalton died of wounds on 21 October 1918. Possibly because of the rapid turnover in personnel his CO didn't get a chance to even meet Dunk.

76 Wagoner was awarded two Silver Star citations and two Croix de Guerre, as were Gaspar, Fant, and Lesher.

77 Wendell Neville or John A. Lejeune? I'll bet on Neville.

78 Archibald Hart, *Company K of Yesterday* (New York: Vantage Press, 1969), 69–70.

79 "Browning guns" meant, of course, the BAR, which had just become available to U.S. troops and replaced the despised Chauchat. Mackin relates in his memoir about how his best buddy "Baldy" reacted when he got his BAR; just like a kid with a new toy. The "BAR" was a popular toy in WWII also. Sellers, in his memoir, explains that the Marines had "liberated" the soldiers of the 36th Division of their "BARs" and trench knives, both of which were just then becoming available to American soldiers. All those guns were rounded up and returned to the doughboys.

80 Curtis, *History of the Sixth Machine Gun Battalion 44,* Sellers says it was 9 October. But he also stated that "Blanc Mont was the most skillful operation in which we participated, despite Powers' unforgivable actions as a commander." Then he adds that he "only had 83 men . . . left in the company out of 250." Skillful?

81 Smiley received a Navy Distinguished Service Medal, plus a Silver Star and the inevitable Croix de Guerre in addition to the DSC.

82 *Records of the Second Division,* vol. 7.

9: The Meuse River Campaign

The Paths of Glory lead but to the grave.
—Thomas Gray

The 2d Division was pulled out of the Blanc Mont lines on 10 October 1918. They then took up station in the Suippes-Somme region and were assigned as 4th French Army Reserve. The division spent four days resting and refitting. Then, on 14 October, they marched to the Bouy-la-Veuve–Dampierre area, establishing headquarters at Bouy, north of the Châlons-sur-Marne area. There the badly depleted infantry of both brigades was filled with replacements. Those of the 4th were from the 1st Marine Training Regiment. According to Colonel Feland's report on his 5th Regiment, dated 26 November, the 1st Battalion and the Headquarters detachment were in residence at Dampierre-au-Temple, the 2d Battalion at Camp Carrières, while the 3d Battalion resided at Camp Tombeau-des-Sarazins for three days, 17 to 19 October. On the 20th everyone marched to Camps Montpelier and des Souches. The 2d Division, still an entity of the 4th French Army, received orders to send one infantry brigade back into the lines in order to relieve a French division. The 4th Brigade was selected and assigned to the IX French Corps where they were provisionally ordered to take up a sector in the Attigny-Voncq-Aisne River region. On 21 October the brigade was on its way to the Suippes-Nantivet-Somme-Suippes area with their headquarters to be at Suippes. This was, of course, not far from where the brigade had taken such a walloping in early October. Leffincourt, where brigade headquarters was established, was just a few miles northeast of St. Étienne. Just as the brigade was in the process of assuming the responsibility for a sector from the French army, they received orders to rejoin the 2d Division. The following day they marched back to Châlons. Then the division was ordered to join the 1st U.S. Army in the Argonne. The Marine Brigade moved to Les Islettes, where it rejoined the rest of the 2d Division. From there the division marched to Exermont and began serious preparations for what was to be the last battle of the war.

General Neville sent an Operations report to division for the period 11–23 October, which ended with the following interesting statement:

> Nothing much of interest occurred during the movements just noted [see above]. A very good idea was obtained as to the marching endurance of the Brigade. The units composing it marched from 80 to 110 kilometers in four days with one day of rest included, the march being made under bad weather conditions except on the last day. Remarkably few men (reported, not over 50) were evacuated with foot trouble but on the last day about 20 percent of the command marched with difficulty and conditions were beginning to grow serious. The trouble was mainly due to English shoes which had been issued just before leaving the BOUY area on the 20th October. The replacements (about 1,500) recently joined, stood the marches very well considering conditions.[1]

Meanwhile, General Lejeune spent most of the time entertaining a visitor, Adm. Henry T. Mayo, commander of the U.S. Atlantic Fleet, and his staff. He later wandered about the Champagne region visiting churches and especially the city of Reims, which his division had saved while expending their life's blood at Blanc Mont. On the morning of 24 October Lejeune and Col. James C. Rhea, USA,[2] his very efficient chief of staff, went to 1st Army Headquarters at Souilly to obtain the release of the division artillery, engineers, and trains, which were still under the control of the 36th Division and to "obtain a sufficient number of replacements to bring the division up to full strength."[3] Brigadier General Hugh Drum, Pershing's chief of staff, offered the artillery brigade from the U.S. 1st Division and a regiment of engineers but Lejeune objected. He responded that the 2d Division artillery and engineers and the two infantry brigades of the 2d Division were very comfortable with each other and that he wanted his own division intact. Drum suggested that Lejeune go in to see Maj. Gen. Hunter Liggett, the new commander of the 1st Army, which Lejeune did at once. Liggett was, as always, supportive and he immediately contacted the French General Gouraud and obtained the release of the assorted 2d Division units still under Gouraud's command. By 1 November, the division was all together again. That was the date that the division was to participate in the "great attack of November 1st."[4] It was cutting it close, but somehow it all came together on time.

In the meantime, since 26 September the 1st U.S. Army had been very busy in the Argonne. So far their attack had gone through two phases. Initially they had succeeded in driving the Germans back about six miles. Then the enemy stiffened their lines and throughout the month of October, short advances had been limited to specific objectives. The eastern portion of the famed Hindenburg Line (or Kriemhild Stellung) had been taken but the western end was still in German hands. Directed against fortified positions, all of this activity had already cost the AEF heavily in manpower.

When the 2d Division arrived, it was assigned to V Corps, which was located in the center of the American army's position. They were assigned a frontage of approximately a mile. Their neighbors were the 80th Division on the left and the 89th Division on its right. This time artillery was heavily allocated to the division: three brigades and much corps and army artillery—three hundred guns in all. It would be the "veteran 2d Division's" responsibility to drive a wedge deep into the enemy's position. In addition to the 2d, the 89th Division was also part of the main thrust for the whole U.S. Army. The advance in the direction of, and the capture of, Sedan were the ultimate objectives. Hopefully, that advance would allow for exploitation and further successes. But for a few days, the division had some rest from their exertions. This was the first time since June that they hadn't been propelled into an assault immediately upon arrival. This fact had a great effect upon their overall success in the next dozen or more days.

Saturday, 26 October–Thursday, 31 October

The departures and arrivals of the Marine regiments were scattered over several days. On 25 October the 5th Regiment left the vicinity of Semide by camions and that same day Headquarters Company, plus 1/5 and 2/5, debused at Les Islettes while 3/5 arrived at Camp La Nouse. From there 2/5 made a night march through the Argonne Forest, arriving near Exermont, camping there four days undercover. On the night of the 30th they were again marched, this time to woods near their jump-off position. The next night they moved into position along the road running east of Sommerance, where the next morning they would jump off. Three/Five also had moved several times in several days—from just northeast of Apremont to woods a mile northeast of Exermont, then the next night into the ravine north of the Sommerance Road. After sev-

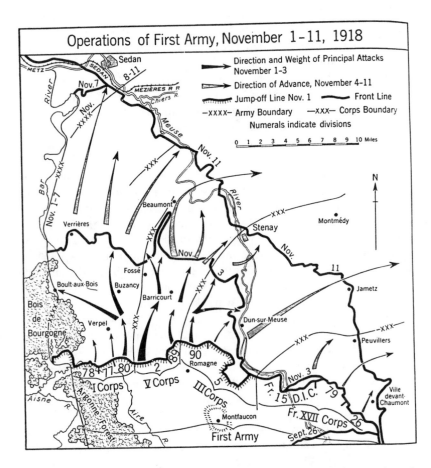

Map 16: Operations of the American 1st Army. Note the central positions occupied by the 2d Division on 1 November 1918. The division was especially placed in its position by 1st Army so as to help some of the newer divisions to maintain their pace. Note especially the long advance of the 9th Infantry, leaving its right flank almost entirely unguarded as they galloped northward on 3 November 1918.

eral moves, the 1st Battalion arrived in position on 31 October. The 18th Company (Gilder Jackson) was assigned liaison duty with the 89th Division on the right.

On the afternoon of 26 October, the 6th Marines marched through the Argonne Forest, arriving in an area south of Exermont early the following morning. The regimental history states they remained in that

area four days, during which time the men were given a much needed rest. The nights and mornings were cold, but the days were bright and comfortably warm, and the men had their full equipment—blankets and overcoats.[5]

They also add an interesting tidbit: "On the 29th of October the regiment was issued twenty-five Browning Automatic Rifles." Presumably the 5th also was a recipient of this largess, just twelve days before the war ended.

On the night of 30–31 October the 6th moved into the forward areas. Three/Six relieved "the support battalion of the 166th Infantry, in a position on the southern slope on a high hill a kilometer and a half south-southeast of Sommerance."[6] The 166th reserve battalion was relieved on a hill just north of Exermont by 2/6, while 1/6 took up a position in the vicinity of Sommerance. At 2200 the battalions of the 6th moved up into preparatory positions for the next morning's jump-off. In the meantime, a large detachment, composed of the 95th Company, a company of the 80th Division (the 319th Infantry), plus a platoon of the 73d Machine Gun Company, all under the command of Maj. George A. Stowell, was detached for liaison service with the 80th Division to the left of 1/6. This was an extremely important and difficult assignment because, in addition to being between two divisions, it was also liaison between two different corps, I and V. Stowell was always a superior officer, Hughes notwithstanding.[7]

Friday, 1 November

Early on the morning of 1 November the division relieved the 42d Division just south of Landres–et–St. Georges. The 23d Infantry was to occupy the right wing of the division's front with two battalions forward and one in support. The 9th Infantry and 4th Machine Gun Battalion constituted division reserve. For the 4th Brigade, the 6th Marines were on the division's left at St. Georges and the 5th in the middle at Landres, both in three-column formations. Each of the two small villages was located in a ravine and the ground before them to be taken was quite steep. After a heavy artillery barrage the Marine Brigade and the 23d jumped off. With the division went eighteen tanks. According to George

Marshall five hundred tanks had been scheduled to go but the former number was all they could pull together in time. The division had been selected and placed in the battle line so that

> its known ability might be used to overcome the critical part of the enemy's defense. The salient feature of the plan of attack was to drive a wedge through Landres–et–St. Georges to the vicinity of Fosse. It was realized that if the foregoing could be accomplished the backbone of the hostile resistance west of the Meuse could be broken and the enemy would have to retreat east of the Meuse. Success in this plan would immediately loosen the flanks of the First Army. The Second Division was selected to carry out this main blow.[8]

A report of observations filed by 2d Lt. George R. Grant (evidently serving with the 2d Division Artillery Brigade) noted that both General Neville and his adjutant, Col. Earl "Pete" Ellis, were critical of the plan proposed by Field Order No. 21, which outlined the division artillery's proposed support of the coming attack. Each declared that he would have been more confident and was sure that the troops would agree with him, that a rolling barrage was just the thing to instill confidence in the officers and men who would be closely following, and very importantly, improve chances for success. Both also condemned the use of smoke shells, saying "they would rather advance without." No reason was given for that statement. And also no information as to whether the plan was altered to suit the Marines or not.

The Order of Battle formation for the attack was in a column of battalions and as follows:

Left	Right
6th Marines (Lee)	**5th Marines (Feland)**
1st Battalion & 73d MG Co. (Barker)	1st Battalion & 8th MG Co. (Hamilton)
3d Battalion & 15th MG Co. (Shuler)	2d Battalion & 23d MG Co. [Dunbeck]
2nd Battalion & 81st MG Co. (Williams)	3d Battalion & 77th MG Co. [Larsen]

The attacking battalions each would average 850 officers and men, considerably less than the 1,000 that four companies would be expected to have in the "best of times." The brigade also had supporting troops in the beginning. One officer and ninety-six men of the 2d Engineers (wire cutters), the 1st Provisional Tank Company (French tanks, American tankers), and last but not least, Company "D," 2d Battalion, 1st Gas (and flame) Regiment. The attack was also going to receive aerial, as well as strong artillery, support and a heavy machine-gun barrage within range. Their final objective: the Freya Stellung, part of the Hindenburg Line.[9]

The formation for 1/5 around and about Landres was, from left, the 49th Company (Fisk) and 66th (Blake) in assault with the 17th (Hunt) and 67th (Whitehead) following.[10] The formation for 1/6 was from left to right, the 76th Company (Macon C. Overton), the 74th (Hermle); the second line, Stowell's small battalion, which included the 95th Company, on the line behind Overton and the 75th (Shannon) supporting Hermle.[11]

Allied artillery batteries began their two-hour preparation barrage at 0330. All of the machine-gun companies of the 6th Machine Gun fired heavy barrages forward of the assaulting battalions. At H hour, 0530, the 1st Battalions of each regiment led off the attack. The first-line companies each deployed two platoons in front in the first wave followed by two platoons in support. The second line of companies formed into a line of groups. Although there was some confusion and a mixing of the various units, they eventually straightened out after daylight arrived. Meanwhile, 1/6, while forming up, lost approximately 100 men, killed and wounded, due to enemy artillery fire. Within a few hours a number of officers of that battalion, including company commanders, fell dead and wounded, greatly affecting the attacking line. One of the first down was that paragon of the 6th Regiment, Macon Overton. He and his men wiped out five machine-gun nests and their crews, partly with the help of tanks that he helped to direct. Some of these positions were taken from the rear, and that must have surprised the enemy. Screaming young Marines thrusting their bayonets forward would be inducement enough for anyone to yell, *Kamerad!* One of those screaming Marines was Pvt. David T. Depue* of the 76th. When his company was held up by the wire, Depue, even though he was only thirty yards from the Maxim that was making life very unpleasant, grabbed a Chauchat from a dead gunner and off he went. Firing from the hip as he ran, he

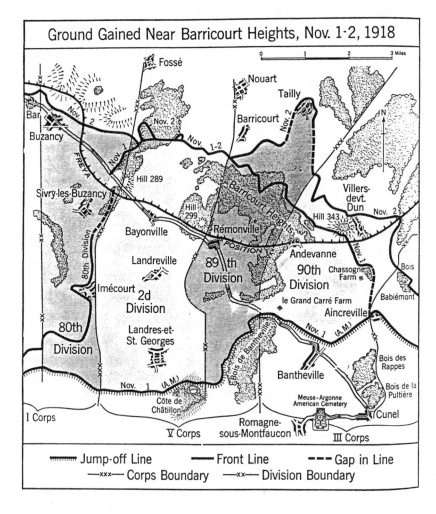

Map 17: A detailed examination of the ground over which the 2d Division advanced on 1/2 November 1918.

charged through a hole in the wire. Hit twice and down twice, up he got and again went after the Boche. When he finally reached the enemy position, his ammo was gone so he used the gun as a club. Swinging it over and down, *clunk* it went on the enemy in their holes. When his platoon reached him he was lying mortally wounded with battered Germans all about him.

The Allied artillery fire was so intense that little ground was left unscathed in the enemy's front lines. Both Marine regiments followed the barrage closely in a north-northeasterly direction and soon were upon the first line of German machine guns. The terrain was rolling, broken with small patches of woods and stunted trees. The enemy had placed their artillery and machine guns in many of the small ravines that passed through the area. Grenades and automatic-rifle fire in the hands of these veteran Marines soon took care of that problem. With their customary dash and bravery the troops soon were on a hill just south of Landres–et–St. Georges.[12] That was part of the enemy's main line of resistance, but it, too, was soon overcome. Second Lieutenant Wilbur Summerlin of the 74th showed great promise during this period of the attack. He led his platoon with distinction, holding them together even though raked with shell and bullets. When he discovered that the regiment's right flank was exposed, he quickly moved to fill in and cover it. During this time they managed to capture 155 German soldiers along with one officer and seventeen machine guns. Another officer new to the "game," 1st Lt. Leo D. Hermle*, added his platoon's weight to Summerlin's, aiding in the capture described previously. Shortly after he proceeded to the village of St. Georges, taking it and many more machine guns. Hermle was wounded his first time out, but he'd be back. This assault upon the village was greatly aided by a fifteen-man detachment led by Capt. Robert M. Montague*, Headquarters, 6th Machine Gun Battalion. Montague and his men entered the village through the rear under immense artillery and machine-gun fire both within and without and managed to eliminate a number of nests that were contributing to the Marine casualty list. Meanwhile, 2d Lt. Edwin J. Davenport promptly took over from Hermle and continued the fight, displaying remarkable skill and courage, as he had at Blanc Mont. And though his men were plastered with heavy artillery fire, they continued forward in their proper place in line under his command. Sergeant Fred Marlowe's* platoon leader went down and shortly after, his lead sergeant was also a casualty, so Marlowe took over command. Taking two other men with him, Marlowe rushed a Boche machine-gun nest and put it out of action. That gun held the key to the entire front at this point, and it forced the rest of the enemy gunners to surrender. Eighty prisoners and nine machine guns was the take. Best of all, the line was able to move forward once again.[13]

Marines found the town of Landres–et–St. Georges completely reduced by the artillery barrage. The enemy was either dead, wounded, or had retreated, as the Marines encountered little or no resistance. Summerlin led his men into the village of St. Georges, which had also been ruined, and captured that also. Landres was soon outflanked by Hamilton, and his battalion was well able to keep up with the barrage. The gas and flame troops gave great support during the outset and aided considerably in smothering enemy machine-gun fire that the barrage had missed. The one serious point of resistance was the usually well-placed German artillery, which effectively covered the front until they, too, were overrun. At 0800 Hamilton reported losing five officers but only a few enlisted men. He only mentions that "Captain Cochran was wounded & Lieutenant Ferch killed."[14] It was only 0800 but the brigade was already at the first objective and had captured over 500 German prisoners in the process. Hamilton's men reported capturing a battery of German 77s even before reaching their first objective. Both 3/6 and 2/6 passed through the lines of 1/6, taking the lead. At that time Shuler sent the following message to Lee:

> My two leading companies are on first objective. Following companies on ridge in position to advance at proper time. Few casualties. Barker [1/6] is near me. Have met two companies of Williams' [2/6] back of St. Georges. Made good time since last message.[15]

Barker ran into considerable difficulty in a small wooded area just south of St. Georges. For some reason the artillery hadn't managed to penetrate it sufficiently to do any damage to the Boche. Captain Macon C. Overton of the 76th, a real pusher and doer, met his end while pushing the enemy out of those woods. Five hours after the jump-off, Barker reported his battalion had suffered one officer killed (Overton), five officers wounded, and 143 enlisted men wounded. One loyal corporal, Cortez L. Thompson, stayed behind with Overton under a heavy concentration of fire, until he was sure that his skipper was dead. He then buried him unaided, still under that dreadful artillery fire. Overton and some of his officers were down, but this was when a great noncom proved his mettle. Sergeant Frank Simon*, with two of his men, advanced alongside a tank they were guiding forward in front of the 76th and encountered terrific enemy fire. Cutting their way through barbed wire, they continued. But the occupants of the tank and the two men following Simon were killed and he was wounded. Undaunted by his wound, he continued forward and captured six enemy gunners hiding in a dugout.[16] Another sergeant of the 76th, Lloyd J. Roy, assumed command of his platoon when his leader was killed and led it through the balance of the campaign. And a corporal, William H. Faga* of the same company, had just been hit badly, but as he was being evacuated he realized that his platoon was now leaderless. Both his lieutenant and "gunny" were down and he was the only noncom left. Returning to the lines he immediately assumed command, led the platoon forward, and remained at the head for the remainder of the attack.[17]

Barbed wire was extremely thick at this point and the Marine efforts to get through it generated numerous casualties inflicted by the Boche artillery and machine guns. There were some tanks in the procession, and these did help a great deal to crush the wire and make egress a little easier. But all in all the 5th and 6th Marines did what they were paid to do. Namely, they reached their first objective, roughly two miles from the jump-off line to the stream line running east from Imécourt. The 23d Infantry reached its first objective at about 0900 and reorganized. They had been taking heavy fire and were subsequently ordered to retire into a support position behind the 5th Marines. At that point the 4th Brigade constituted the front for the entire division.

Shuler and 3/6 took the regimental lead and it wasn't long after that that Cpl. George W. Schreech and four privates, Charles S. Gibson, William A. Kruezman, DeMarr E. Myers, and Clarence D. Troup of the 82d volunteered (you, you, and you), to move forward and reconnoiter a ravine to their immediate front. When they arrived they found an infestation of artillery and machine-gun positions. They returned with four prisoners and left behind an unknown number of enemy casualties.[18] Leading his platoon, way out front, was Sgt. Otto Gullion, all the while exposing himself to intense enemy fire. Into a ravine he went and moments later had captured four men and an officer, single-handedly. The platoon officers of the company were being knocked down, and the sergeants were taking their places. Sergeant Anthony A. Kryzaniak picked up two Silver Star citations and a Croix de Guerre for assuming command after his "mister" was wounded. Their new skipper, Capt. Pink H. Stone, in his first battle, showed what a good Marine could do even when he bore such a fight-provoking first name. Stone was always with them and took special care of his wounded, during and after the battle. That is what a good leader always does.

Stone wasn't the only "new" officer in 3/6. He had a companion in Capt. Arnold W. Jacobsen of the 84th. Jacobsen displayed unusual courage and resourcefulness in leading his company forward to their objective. When he reached Bayonville he established a first aid station for his wounded by using the services of a captured German doctor and his assistant and then set about having the wounded in the town brought in for care. Another good Marine was Sgt. Frank F. Geiger* of the 97th Company. Geiger, with utter disregard for his own safety, led his section against several machine-gun positions and was badly wounded while rushing one of them unaided. His skipper, Capt. Thomas T. McEvoy, kept his company well in hand all the way, and had since he'd relieved a wounded Capt. Robert Voeth at Soissons. Personally supervising the establishment and organization of a new line, he himself was wounded late in the day. That was the end of the war for McEvoy. One of the young Marines of the 77th Machine Gun Company, which was "servicing" 3/6, was cited for remaining with his gun crew during a Boche counterattack. His name was Melvin N. Johnson.[19]

Meanwhile, the center division of V Corps, the 77th, failed to attack. Consequently that slowed down a goodly portion of the 80th Division as well. Stowell quickly came into action to protect the left flank of the Marines. He and his semibattalion attacked Imécourt, which was in the 80th's boundary, and after a brief skirmish took out its 150-man garrison. Thereafter he kept apace with the 6th Marines while doing service within the 80th Division's sector.

Supporting the 1st Battalion, 5th Marines, about five hundred meters in the rear, the 2d Battalion, led by the 51st (Cumming) and 55th Companies (C. D. Baylis, USA), which were followed by the 43d (Massie) and 18th (Foster), at 0830 leapfrogged the 1st about a half mile south of Landreville, located slightly northeast of Imécourt in the 5th Marines' sector. The 2d almost immediately ran into heavy resistance, especially from the right flank, and spent much of its effort reducing Landreville, where "the enemy had machine guns placed in windows throughout the village."[20] Next in line was Bayonville, almost directly north of Landreville. About thirteen hundred yards before Bayonville the battalion found it necessary to detach the 55th Company to execute a flanking movement and surround Hill 299, from which the enemy was impeding further advance. At 1150 3/5 moved forward through 2/5, which had attained its objective, taking its place as the forward element of the regiment. Hamilton and 1/5 now occupied the rear at eight hundred meters behind Dunbeck and 2/5. The companies of Larsen's 3/5 were arranged with the 20th and 45th Companies in the lead position followed by the 16th and 47th in staggered group formation.

The 6th Marines were having an easier time of it than the 5th, but both were doing extraordinarily well during the early phases of the day. Both regiments abreast had the same third objective: Farm des Parades on the left and Farm Magenta on the right. It was also the Corps's objective as well. By 0900 Shuler had "leapfrogged 1/6." McEvoy and his 97th Company, on the left flank, were being held up, with the 83d Company (Noble) on its right flank. The 82d (Stone) was in the rear of the 97th and the 84th (Jackson) in Bayonville. Second Lieutenant Claude B. Taugher* of the 84th, with great dash, led his platoon in surrounding Boche dugouts in the village before the occupants had a chance to escape or organize effective resistance. Even though he had been wounded in the ankle he managed to capture sixty-one of the enemy. Soon afterward, Shuler was advising Lee that the 97th had had to fall back three hundred meters "to avoid our own barrage"—but added, "as soon as barrage lifted they took up position on objective." They, too, were continuing on their way forward, as was most of the division. All battalions were passing back plenty of prisoners. At 1100 Shuler reported,

> We are in Chennery and Bayonville and pressing up to second objective. Took about 100 prisoners here by using tanks assisted by riflemen. Have taken six 88s. Enemy are shelling woods north of Bayonville.[21]

Messages like that were pouring in to both regimental PCs as the Marines kept moving forward. So far it appeared that it was going to be a fairly easy one, except for 1/6 whose losses were quite severe, at least as compared to what the regiment ran into on 3 October as it went up the hill toward Blanc Mont Massif. Williams, with 2/6, reported that they were 250 yards behind the leading 3/6, which, he said, was 250 meters in front of his position. But Williams had a complaint that he sent to Shuler just after noon. "I am ready to pass through and continue but am held up by own artillery falling short." That wasn't anything new for the Marines. The division artillery had been firing "short" ever since Belleau Wood. Both brigades complained, but while not a constant occurence, it was a frequent one and the infantrymen were usually the victims. All kinds and types of excuses about the shortfalls emanated from the 2d Artillery Brigade but it never stopped. The situation on the left was anything but smooth because of the short-ranged divisional artillery and the not-so-rapid 80th U.S. Division. In fact, Colonel Lee warned the 9th Infantry to watch their left very carefully because of that delay.

News from Williams at 1515 to Lee proclaimed, "We are on our objective. Have liaison with Major Stowell (one company) on our left and with 5th Regt. on our right." He continued, "Some MG encountered from that part of Bois de la Folie which we have not yet taken. Casualties among men not so heavy. Officers about fifty percent."[22] By 1720 Shuler reported that both regiments were "connected." Williams, on the line, sent exploitation parties forward to keep the Boche off balance and not allow them to organize. But they wouldn't get beyond that forest for another two days no matter what else they did.

The 18th Company, 2/5, was connected with the 23d Infantry on their right at 0900 and nearly a half hour later, after the 23d fell back in support, were also in liaison with the 89th U.S. Division on the same flank. It appears that the 89th hadn't been able to keep up, so the 23d filled the zone until they could. The 3d Brigade was advancing behind the 4th and when the 80th wasn't with the 6th Marines, the 9th Infantry, like their sister regiment the 23d, did its duty. This is one of the main reasons that the 2d Division was the best division in the AEF. They had the best of both worlds, best soldiers, best Marines. While this maneuvering was taking place, Cpl. Henry J. Worth, Pfc. Harry D. Crarey, and two privates, Joseph J. Courchane and Walter Peltoniemi, of the 18th, must have gotten tired of sitting around doing nothing, so off they went out front. They went through the usual hail of fire until they came upon a nest of three Maxims, which they immediately took out, capturing thirty German gunners. All four were awarded Silver Star citations for this deed, which often earned other folks a DSC. That kind of discrepancy has happened more often than not in every war.

Larsen almost yelled with excitement when he sent the following message to Colonel Feland at 1430 hours: "*Gained Objective* (3d) am pushing strong patrols to front to Exploitation Line—meeting no opposition, except our own artillery falling short. Captured six pieces of artillery and about 100 prisoners." Second Lieutenant Bruce G. Lubers, a platoon leader of the 45th Company, displayed unusual resourcefulness and courage when he assisted in flanking and capturing ten machine guns and ninety prisoners. These must have added greatly to the 100 prisoners that Larsen had been "bragging" about.[23]

Hamilton was also elated. His men were on Hill 300 at 1600 and just short, by one and a half kilometers, of the third objective. He asked for artillery to be dumped just forward of the objective line to silence machine guns firing from Bois de la Folie. He also requested rockets (flares—to notify artillery) "for artillery falling short." He added, "Lieut. [Robert C.] Babcock [20th Company] killed, reported."

All during the advance that day, reports continually stated that losses were exceptionally light and that prisoners were being scooped up everywhere, not huge numbers, but continuously. About noon, 5th Marines reported that a battery of 77s was captured, although a later report told of artillery firing from "Côte 300." They probably meant Hill 299, which was well screened by trees, and consequently the guns weren't easily discernible. Feland told Barker that "if everything goes well will establish my P.C. in the woods 200 yds southeast of Hill 300."

At 1140 the 5th Marines could report that they were entering the "Arbre de Remonville." An hour later Feland told Brigade he had attained second objective and losses were still light. A "Lt. Lane," of the 354th Infantry, 89th Division, liaison officer with the 5th Marines, reported to Logan Feland that "our patrols [354th Infantry?] have entered Bois de Barricourt and now hold it." This meant that the 89th Division was nearly keeping pace with the 2d Division. Sergeant Theodore Keller*, with a detachment from the 47th, had established liaison with the 89th Division and maintained it through three desperate counterattacks by the Boche.

The brigade had made a six or more miles advance and the time was only 1320 hours when they reported. Thirty minutes later, Hamilton reported that "the 3d Bn. is apparently on the 3d obj. with 2d Bn. in close support." He mentioned that he was going to establish his PC in the ravine he was in and dispose his troops so that they could cover the entire sector. Côte 313 was in the middle of the division's third objective. The left was in the southern part of the Bois de la Folie and the west just south of the town of Barricourt. Only the Bois de la Folie would remain unconquered and a forthcoming problem for the 6th Marines, especially Williams's battalion.

Larsen confirmed that his battalion was indeed on and over the third objective for the day and was now pushing the Exploitation Line and, best, not meeting much resistance. He also crowed that they had taken six artillery pieces and about 100 prisoners. At 1520 Hamilton told Feland that his battalion was doing well, still in and around the ravine. "Men in good spirits but physically weak on acct of diarrhoea [sic]. When can we have some chow." A few minutes later Dunbeck of 2/5 reported "1 officer and 12 men" wounded. They had also taken another 130 Germans prisoner.

Later that afternoon much of the activity by the 6th Marines involved the attempted exploitation of the Bois de la Folie, which lay directly before them. At least one platoon of the 80th Company wasn't having an easy time of it. That platoon, led by 1st Lt. John G. Schneider*, had been taking plenty of incoming fire, so much so that Schneider, though badly wounded himself, refused to be evacuated and remained on duty with his company. He continued the advance until he was wounded a second time. This one kept him down, and in two days, on 3 November, he would die of the wounds. Williams was notified at 2135, by 6th Marines' Headquarters, to either push forward into the forest or "if you consider it impossible to carry this work out in darkness, you will proceed with it at daybreak." Needless to say, Williams wasn't stupid. He took the opportunity for his battalion to just sit and recover from the day's exertions.[24]

Late that evening, just before midnight, Logan Feland found it necessary to harass his number-one battalion's leader, Maj. George Hamilton, for failing to keep his headquarters informed of what they were doing that day.

> Have received only one report from you dated 9:00 a.m. Col. Turrill and Captain Winans have gone forward to establish P.C. in the area to the Northwest of Landreville (sic) et St. Georges. Locate them and send in to them *frequent* reports.[25]

Late that evening or perhaps continuing into the next morning, Gy. Sgt. Arthur High, leading two corporals, Rufus B. Page and Raymond C. Pierce, and ten privates, Kenneth Benrud, Frank R. Nolley, Nicholas Marunich, Archibald D. Miller, Harold L. Moldestad, William R. Brock, Joseph T. Bromell, Walter E. Cooney, Laurence V. Johnson, and Joseph G. Saunders, all of the 77th Machine Gun Company, must have upset the Boche a lot. Acting as infantry, they went out to a ravine near Magenta Farm, which was far in front of the division's objective, located a battery of enemy artillery, which the Germans were in the process of removing, and captured the entire unit.[26]

An example of what can happen to a company in a few days is well expressed through the experiences of the 73d Machine Gun Company at the Meuse-Argonne. On 1 November the 73d, commanded by 1st Lt. George R. Jackson, was assigned, as usual, to 1/6, commanded by Maj. Frederick Barker. As we know, 1/6 led off for the 6th Regiment. The 1st Platoon leader, 2d Lt. John L. Hunt, accompanied the 74th Company on the right flank, while the 3d Platoon leader, 2d Lt. Charleton Lee, accompanied the 76th on the left flank. Sergeant Hildor B. Ellison commanded the 2d Platoon, attached to the 95th Company, which was part of Stowell's minibattalion, on the far left of the division boundary. First Lieutenant Hamlet C. Sharp was in charge of the company train in the rear echelon.

Within five minutes of the attack's start, Lee's platoon suffered heavy casualties from German shell fire, losing three of its four guns and most of their crews, killed or wounded. Later that day Lee was wounded and shortly after had to be evacuated because of utter exhaustion. Sergeant John L. Fogle assumed command of what remained of the 3d Platoon. Meanwhile Hunt's 2d Platoon was vital in the capture of Imécourt, where about 350 Germans and twenty of their machine guns were taken.[27]

The following day, 2 November, Jackson was also evacuated from exhaustion caused by the flu. John Hunt, the only officer remaining with the company, took command. Later that day Maj. Louis E. Fagan Jr. was detached from 3/6 and ordered to command the 73d, with which company he remained until after the armistice.[28]

The company spent from 3 to 5 November encamped in woods with the new commander of 3/6, Maj. Maurice S. Berry, who replaced Maj. Frederick Barker, who had been evacuated with the flu. In fact, many officers and men of the division were sick and dying, not from Boche attacks, but from the flu. Sergeant Ellison and the 2d Platoon rejoined the company that night. On the afternoon of 5 November, the new CO of 3/6, Maj. George Stowell, having replaced Berry, now moved his battalion and the 73d to a new wood where they again encamped for the night. Stowell would continue in command until 21 November. The 6th of November found the company again encamped in woods, this time nearer the Meuse River. That evening Lieutenant Hunt was also evacuated from exhaustion, while 2d Lt. David Duncan, who had been away at school, reappeared on 7 November and rejoined the company.

The last action of the 73d Company was on the evening of 10–11 November. The 6th Marines and their units were to attempt to cross the river. The company had but four guns at this time. Fortunately for the entire regiment, they were pulled out and only the 5th Marines went forward. Incidentally, Hunt went AWOL and apparently stayed in France, because he was still so listed as late as 1920.

Saturday, 2–Tuesday, 5 November
The only serious exercise the 4th Brigade was involved in on Saturday was the struggle between 2/6 against the entrenched German forces in the Bois de la Folie. Williams and his men pushed forward

until they reached the enemy outpost lines, where they were stopped. An exception to the relative repose of the balance of the 6th Marines, 1st Lt. Neil F. Dougherty* of the 83d, found a way to exercise. Dougherty led his platoon against an enemy artillery battery in action and through skillful maneuvering gathered in forty-two prisoners, ten pieces of artillery, and five machine guns. The balance of the brigade took a respite after having made their mad dash through the countryside on the previous day.

Feland sent Larsen a message saying that the 18th Company (John R. Foster) would occupy a position north and east of the regiment to liaison with the 89th Division. Larsen advised Feland that his patrols had seen the enemy on the skyline of "Hill 315," or "Côte 313," in the middle of the objective line already reached on 1 November. In the morning, Larsen's battalion moved forward a small distance, and that height became his soon after. He also asked, if the 23d Infantry were going forward with an artillery barrage he be advised so that he could pull his patrols back in time. "Everything is O.K. Would appreciate blanket rolls and chow." The wind in France is just as bad as it is in New England in November. Two hours later Feland ordered all patrols to pull back, the 23d was running a little late. Torkelson, intelligence officer of 3/5, reported as late as 1315 that the regiment hadn't shown up yet. Nearly six hours later Feland relayed the message that the 3d Brigade would pass through the regiment and that the 5th were to "stand pat." The Marines would now be division reserve in the vicinity of Bayonville-et-Chénnery. During the night of 2–3 November the enemy continued its retreat. The 3d Brigade leapfrogged the 4th and took the lead for the division, and off they went.[29]

The 3d Brigade made another seven-mile advance their first day in the lead, one mile farther than their comrades of the 4th had on the first day. The 4th Brigade followed the 3d closely as support. Even the 80th and 89th Divisions on each flank were keeping pace during this advance. That night the 3d Brigade, the 9th Infantry in the lead, advanced along a single road, making no serious effort to control either immediate flank, as it wasn't necessary. The enemy were still falling back and making little attempt to forestall the American advance. The 3d arrived at La Tuilerie Farm and stopped. They had made an absolutely marvelous march deep into enemy territory up a single road. The advance team was composed of soldiers who spoke German. Their job was to further confuse the enemy and talk them into surrendering. They were a very accomplished team. At the request of Col. James C. Rhea*, USA, commanding 3d Brigade, the 5th Marines maintained a close support contact with his unit, all the way up. Midday on 3 November, Major Stowell advised Col. Harry Lee that his minibattalion was now just the size of one company of Marines. The 80th Division had sent orders that its participating company return to the fold. He also urged some support for his 95th Company. "Would like to have a map north of Fosse with division sector marked on it." That would have been of great help to the liaison manager, to know where he was headed. Such was the kind of war the officers and men were trying to fight. Another fascinating feature of this latter part of the war was the use of nicknames for various units. Neville was frequently "Sister" while Feland was "Slap" and Lee was "Site," most of the time. More often than not, in a message, one or the other would use his nickname and common name within the same message. Oh, yes! Third Brigade was "Sink," which wasn't too auspicious, for them or their buddies.

The next day, 4 November, at the request of Col. Robert O. Van Horn (DSM), USA, commanding, 9th Infantry, the troops of 2/5 moved east and were engaged in cleaning up that part of the sector. The 5th also advanced forward a short distance, about a mile, more or less, until they arrived at a road about a mile and a half southeast of Beaumont. That town was at the 2d and 80th Division's boundary and would lend its name to the forthcoming battles. At this point 2/5 went into line with the 3d Brigade. Later the entire 5th Marines moved up to make a line with the 89th Division, which was on the right and helped them clean up their sector as well. Turrill sent Feland a message at 1055 in which he described the conditions under which the regiment was functioning. "Advise getting kitchens & rations up *soon*. 1st Bn. has had practically nothing, since day before yesterday. Rations are being held up on the roads. Men very weak." Dunbeck, in a message to Logan Feland near midnight, was looking for "my galleys" and added that he had sent out strong patrols. One of his patrol leaders, 2d Lt Vincent A. Brady of the 55th, was brought in badly wounded from machine-gun fire; he would expire on 14 November. Dunbeck's message also advised Feland that his battalion had undergone "heavy bombardment (gas and artillery) all afternoon. . . . Casualties up to 20%. Men forced to wear gas masks for four hours." Earlier that evening, Feland wondered if Dunbeck had advanced too far. As a result he ordered Dunbeck to hold on where he was.

The 6th Marines remained in reserve south of the Bois de Belval, some four miles in the rear. One sergeant of the 77th Machine Gun Company, Alfred G. Slyke*, performed an outstanding act of courage this day. He was cited for his extraordinary heroism in rushing out before his position and grabbing badly needed ammunition for his guns. He had to move through a heavy grenade bombarding that the Boche had opened upon his line. Returning, he immediately turned his gun and routed the enemy, who had already injured three of his crew.[30]

The following day, 5 November, was spent mainly, by the 5th Marines, in helping their neighbors of the 89th Division to clean out their portion of the Jaulny Forest, which lay mostly within that division's boundaries. Neville advised Feland that "division directs us to make all haste to send a patrol to the bridge at Pouilly and of course cross if you can." He added, "3d Brigade is now getting very weak and they are now willing to allow the *2d Division* [4th Brigade?] the honor of crossing the Meuse if they can't. Push things along." (Emphasis added.) Dr. ("Major") Robert J. Lawler*, USN, was having trouble and requested the officer in charge of the ambulance company to "pick up four cases who have been waiting here since early last evening. Ambulances refuse to stop here." Meanwhile, the 5th Marines gained a good position on the Meuse River, preparatory to forcing a river crossing against an entrenched enemy. Early that afternoon, an embarrassed Larsen apprised Feland that

> 356 Regt. beat me to it. Their first wave went over at 10:00 A.M. and had M. guns covering bridge before we arrived in place. This Bn. of 89th covers exact same section as assigned to us and has same mission. I have taken up positions as per sketch. We have reconnoitering parties to front and will keep connected up O.K. Sorry they beat us to it. Enemy positions freshly dug cover front lines on northern slope. . . . Am in close support.[31]

That night and the early hours of 6 November saw the enemy falling back from positions at Beaumont and across the river to the east bank. Their 236th Division crossed the Meuse at Villemontry and at Mouzon, farther north. The 9th Infantry followed them up to the river extending its line south to Villemontry and north to the 23d Infantry around Mouzon.

Neville advised Lee that if it were possible for the 5th to cross at Pouilly, he and the 6th were to "follow in close support." As we have seen, they didn't.

Wednesday, 6 November
On this day Lejeune requested that each brigade ascertain the reliability of reports that the Germans had vacated the immediate banks on the east side of the river. The consequences of an empty bank was to push "bridge heads and seize a portion on the other side of the river." There were other messages, like one from 2d. Lt. Joseph D. Broderick, regimental intelligence officer, who requested a "small quantity of paper for the making of reports." Another advised that "the Colorado Code goes into effect at 3:00 A.M. November 7th, 1918."

A serious report from Lt. Preston A. McClendon*, USN, of 1/6 advised Maj. Maurice Berry that "the physical condition of this battalion becomes increasingly worse. Diarrhoea, exhaustion and influenza are rampant, numerous cases of subnormal temperatures, showing an exhaustive condition of the men. . . ."

The 5th Marines, except for 3/5, remained in a position overlooking the town of Pouilly, located on the northeastern side of the river. They found that two battalions of the 89th had moved to their left and had pushed patrols across the river into that town but had found few Germans. So, the honor of being first across the Meuse in this area, at least temporarily, belonged to the 89th Division.[32] At 1400 Capt. Robert Blake and his 66th Company probed the right flank to establish liaison with the 89th Division, this was unnecessary, as the 89th was already into the area of the 5th Marines, and the Americans overlapped each other at many places. About an hour later, under regimental order, 2d Lts. Carl J. Norstrand (17th Company) and Leonard E. Rea (66th Company), both of 1/5, took out a patrol of forty men with the twofold purpose of finding what they could about the enemy and if the river was fordable in their vicinity. They returned at 2200 with information that the enemy was so well placed on the opposite bank, that their artillery and machine guns could easily sweep the entire frontage of the west bank should any attempt be made to cross.

That evening 1/5 received conflicting orders, finally setting their course. This moved the regiment westward to the Bois du Grand Dieulet, two miles west of Beaumont. In the meantime the 6th Marines were relocated to the Bois du Fond de Limon, about a mile west of the Bois de l'Hospice, almost opposite Villemontry on the west bank of the river. Each regiment would be moved about some, during the next two days.

Thursday, 7 November

Another, equally serious report, this from Lee to brigade, indicated that his regiment, which should have had at least 3,000 officers and men, was down to seventy-two officers and 1,728 enlisted men. This was the regiment that was scheduled to make the major assault across the Meuse River in four days.

During this night, 6–7 November, began what later became known as the "Sedan Incident," one of the strangest movements of the war. While not of intense interest or concern to the 4th Brigade, it was of sufficient importance to the entire division to be described here.

The 1st U.S. Division moved up and relieved the 80th Division on the left flank of the 2d Division. There were several American generals involved in what took place. Pershing had somehow managed to obtain the agreement of the French army group commander, Gen. Paul Maistre, to allow the Americans to take Sedan.[33] Pershing told General Dickman, commanding the I Corps, he wished Sedan taken and his corps had the honor of doing it. Dickman was thrilled.

Meanwhile, Pershing had Brig. Gen. Fox Conner, at AEF Headquarters, draft a message to Dickman and General Charles P. Summerall, who commanded the American V Corps. First Army Commander Hunter Liggett's chief of staff, Brig. Gen. Hugh Drum, returned and found the message. He and Col. George C. Marshall redrafted it and sent it on to both corps commanders. No one took the time to notify Liggett, although they issued the order under his name. The most important part of the message stated, "Boundaries will not be considered binding." The idea, of course, was that Dickman would take Sedan and that Summerall, the corps commander on his right, would know what was going on.

Summerall, never one to shy away from making himself the center of attention, decided to take the initiative. He went to the 1st Division's headquarters and ordered its division commander, Brig. Gen. Frank Parker, to take Sedan. That relatively new division commander didn't hesitate to obey the orders, having no knowledge that any other units might be making an effort to do the same thing. In addition, and much more serious, Parker and his division would have to march across practically the entire front of 1st U.S. Army, through the boundaries of many divisions. Parker didn't even bother to notify any division commanders of what he was doing. After all, he commanded the illustrious 1st Division, (Regulars), Pershings "own."

Soon the 1st was encountering soldiers of the 77th Division, exchanging fire with them, and shortly after they ran into the 42d Division, which was also closing on Sedan. Menoher, CO of the 42d, was irate, and Dickman flew into a rage. The latter told Menoher to take command of all troops in his area, including the 1st Division. He also told Brig. Gen. Henry Reilly, commanding a brigade of the 42d, to stop Parker and tell him to get his men out of the area.

No American troops took Sedan. On 8 November boundaries were altered so that French troops could take the city, which was appropriate. Liggett ordered Summerall and Parker to make reports explaining whatever it was they had been trying to accomplish. Neither report was satisfactory to Liggett, but Summerall's was the less credible. Yet, when Liggett and Pershing discussed the atrocity, they both decided, since the Germans were beaten, to drop the entire issue.

The real outcome of the situation was that several cliques were formed and the U.S. Army was not the beneficiary because of them. Dickman and Summerall became intense enemies; Drum and Marshall, who had both failed their commander, Liggett, grew closer together. The matter was not settled for many years and was carried forward among the lower ranks even into the next great war.[34]

Friday, 8–Saturday, 9 November

The crossing of the river was greatly delayed by lack of bridging equipment. In addition, the Americans had outrun their feeble supply lines and the congestion in the rear precluded an early resolution to their problems. Traffic was jammed on every road into the area, so much so that even the wounded and sick could not be taken to hospitals in the rear. Even the easily agitated French premier, Clemenceau, who was then in an auto headed toward the front, was unable to continue. Needless to add, he was highly upset. The lack of bridging forced the division to call off the planned crossing of the Meuse several times during the next few days.

Meanwhile, in the I and V Corps areas, the Germans were fighting to the death to retain the various river crossing points so as to protect retreating German troops leaving the west side of the Meuse. The enemy was short of everything except guts and artillery shells. These they rained down upon the Allies as they pushed forward. Half a dozen depleted German battalions were opposing the 2d Division. Their main

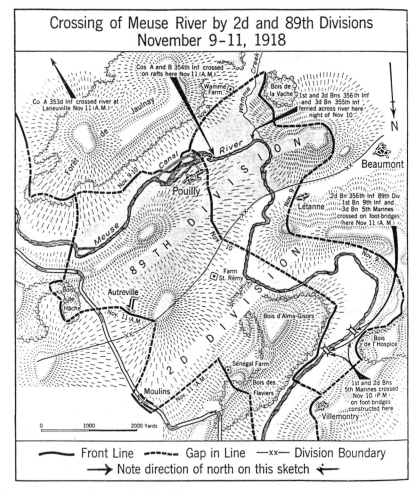

Crossing of Meuse River by 2d and 89th Divisions November 9–11, 1918

Cos A and B 354th Inf crossed on rafts here Nov 11 (A.M.)

Co A 353d Inf crossed river at Laneuville Nov 11 (A.M.)

Wamme Farm

Bois de la Vache

1st and 3d Bns 356th Inf and 3d Bn 355th Inf ferried across river here night of Nov 10

N

Forêt de Jaulnay

Canal

River

Beaumont

Nov 9·10

Meuse

Pouilly

89TH DIVISION

Létanne

2d Bn 356th Inf 89th Div 1st Bn 9th Inf and 3d Bn 5th Marines crossed on foot-bridges here Nov 11 (A. M.)

Nov. 9

Nov. 10

Farm St. Rémy

Bois de Hache

Autreville

Nov. 11 (A.M.)

2 D DIVISION

Bois d'Alma-Gisors

Bois de l' Hospice

Sénégal Farm

Bois des Flaviers

Moulins

Nov. 11 A.M.

1st and 2d Bns 5th Marines crossed Nov 10 (P.M.) on foot-bridges constructed here

Villemontry

0   1000   2000 Yards

━━━ Front Line   ┄┄┄ Gap in Line   ━xx━ Division Boundary

⟶ Note direction of north on this sketch ⟵

Map 18: Map is askew. The left bottom is northwest. Bridge positions on map place the one on the left before the 9th Infantry's line. The 89th Division was one of the few that could almost keep up with the 2d Division; that is why they were placed where they are.

line of resistance was on a rise to the northeast and across the river opposite Mouzon. That hill exceeded 336 meters in height and was exceedingly steep. It was going to be difficult for the 6th Marines to cross
the Meuse. The enemy was badly demoralized and exhausted but determined to hold back the Americans as long as possible. They were a
tough bunch and would remain so.

The crossing of the river was planned as a joint effort by the 89th and
the 2d Divisions. The ridge mentioned previously was the proposed target. For days, reports to both divisions mentioned that all approaches
from the western bank were covered by Maxims and artillery. If they did
not take the ridge, the Allies would be subject to direct fire and suffer
enormous casualties. The 4th Brigade was selected to make the supreme
effort for the 2d Division. Both the 6th and 5th Marines would cross the
river and seize the ridge, taking it all if possible. The troops didn't know
then that an armistice was being negotiated between the combatants.
If they had, it is unlikely that many would have continued forward, suffering wounds and death, as they did for the last several days, just to gain
a few more yards of ground.

Artillery support for the crossing was to be from the 2d Division Artillery and more from Corps. It was decided that the main effort was to
cross at a point about a mile northwest of Mouzon. A smaller, diver-
sionary crossing would be made slightly south of that point, between the
towns of Villemontry and Létanne. The latter crossing is continually referred to in official reports as being "near Létanne." For that crossing
there would be one battalion from the 89th Division and 2/5. It was
planned that the entire 6th Marines and 3/5 would make the main crossing farther north at Mouzon and seize the ridge. Captain LeRoy Hunt,
now commanding 1/5, would support Dunbeck's 2/5 but remain in the
woods on the west side of the river until called upon. Major George
Hamilton would command both battalions.[35]

Sunday, 10–Monday, 11 November

Early in the morning Maj. Ernest Williams sent a personal message to
Colonel Lee that said, "Evacuated last night. If I can get into better
condition here will not go to the rear but will rejoin the battalion." He
didn't because a newcomer, Maj. Clyde H. Metcalf, took over 2/6.[36] It appears that "Bull" was sick, probably with the Spanish flu, like so many other
men in the AEF, so he was finished insofar as the war was concerned. He'd
be back, just after the division began its move into Germany.

During the day several things of import happened. Sergeant William
M. Feigle* of Headquarters Company, 5th Marines, did something that

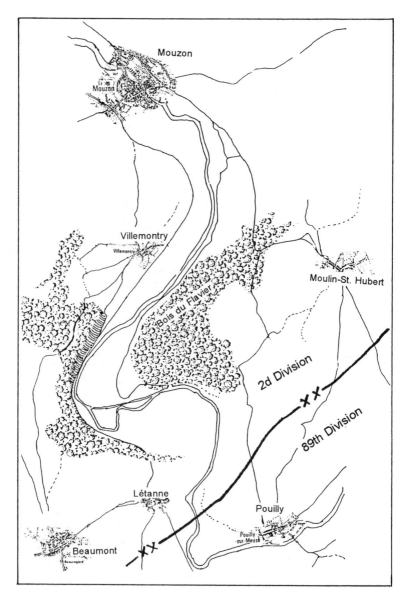

Map 19: The final area occupied by the 2d Division before and after the crossing of the Meuse River on the night of 10–11 November 1918. Moulin–St. Hubert was the farthest point reached by the 2d Division on 11 November. It was attained by the 66th Company, 1st Bn., 5th Marines.

could only be described as extraordinary heroism. While an ammunition train was passing through the town of Beaumont, one of the trucks was hit by a shell and set a fire. The driver abandoned the blazing truck, as any sane man would. Feigle, knowing that it would soon explode, leapt aboard and drove it to the outskirts of town, only then disembarking. It blew, but Feigle's quick thinking and actions saved at least thirty-five people.[37]

The planning for this operation—which, unknown to the troops, would be the last—had been in the works for several days. Orders were issued by Ellis at 1400, but as was usual, they were not received by the battalion commanders until after 1730, 10 November. The actual start time wasn't nailed down even at that late an hour. It remained vague until shortly before time to go. Presumably, the vagueness had to do with the hour the 6th would cross to the north.

When it came time, the 6th Marines were to march northward more than three miles to Mouzon in the dark, keeping well away from the river so as not to allow the Germans a view of their forward motion. At an appointed time they were to cross over on two footbridges and take the two dominant heights before them: Hill 336 and, about a mile farther northwest, Hill 345. The time was finally nailed down to 2130 for the 6th Marines, that being the earliest hour that troops could be expected to be in position. Major George Shuler, CO of 3/6, was in overall command of the operation.

Within a half hour of receiving their orders, the three battalions were on their way. The Germans had obviously realized that the Americans were going to cross at this point, so they laid artillery fire upon the whole area and forced the 6th to take a divergent track to the river. It was 2230 before they reached the rail yards opposite where they were to cross. There they learned that only one footbridge had been constructed, the fire being too heavy for the engineers to do the second.[38] A Marine work detail was ordered forward by Shuler to support the engineers and further attempts were made to complete the second bridge, under heavy fire.

In a report Shuler sent just after midnight, he explained his projected course of action to Lee.

[Engineer Officer Slade] suggests that he put one bridge over and start one battalion and then put the second one over. I have told him that we want both to go over at the same time. This is the only way to do now that we know that the enemy are opposite and on the alert. As soon as Stowell [1/6] and Larsen [3/5] come up with

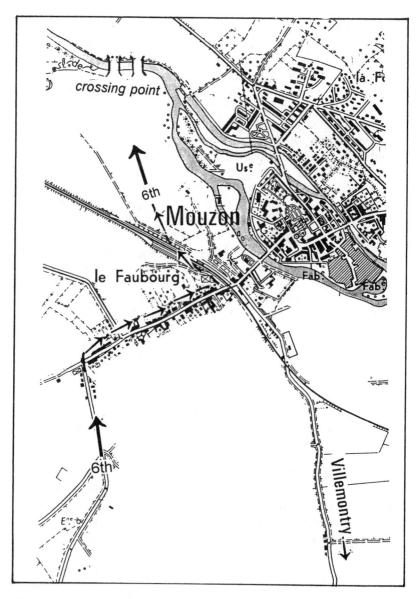

Map 20: An enlarged view of the path taken on the evening of 10 November by the 6th Marines supported by 3/5 to cross just north of the city of Mouzon. The crossing point is approximate, based upon a survey of the ground and official records. The crossing did not take place.

their battalions and Slade gets his report that they are ready we
will go across and do our best. I will let Slade have 40 men to carry
the second pontoon to river.[39]

About an hour later Larsen erroneously reported that Stowell had
taken his own battalion, 3/5, across the river. Confusion reigned. As late
as 0300 the next morning, Shuler reported that if they weren't able to
cross before 0400 he would have to call off the operation because daylight would make it impossible for them to cross against a defended
riverbank. But by 0400 on 11 November it still wasn't ready and the crossing by the 6th Marines was called off. From the 2d Division history the
following statement explains what happened:

> The Mouzon crossing failed. All night long the engineers, assisted
> by details from the [9th] infantry, labored to throw the bridges.
> But the Germans promptly discovered the attempt, located the
> crossing point, and brought so heavy machine gun and artillery
> fire to bear that all efforts were fruitless.

Now it was going to have to be the 5th Marines farther south to make
the serious crossing instead of just being support for the 6th. One battalion from the 89th, 2/356 under Maj. Mark Hanna*, was allocated to
the crossing along with 2/5 (Dunbeck), but the former never made it.
As a result, 1/5 under Hunt would replace it. Hunt would lead and Dunbeck would follow.

Following an artillery barrage of one hour, 1/5 and 2/5 were to cross
two pontoon bridges already partially established for that purpose in
time to follow up a rolling barrage beginning at 2130.[40] Their first target was the height within the extended wood of Bois d'Alma-Gisors and
Bois des Flaviers. As soon as the American barrage began, the Germans
countered with an even heavier barrage of their own, causing numerous casualties on the approach to the bridges. Gas shells and steel flayed
the area, but 1/5 kept going toward the river.
   Elton Mackin, a Pfc. of the 67th Company and runner for Maj.
George Hamilton, recalls what going to the bridge and crossing it under fire was like, especially what they thought, since most of the men
had heard the rumor about an armistice that following morning.

> German gunfire came to meet us. Most of it was high explosive
> stuff. . . . It opened gaps in files of men too closely bunched. . . .We

entered a ravine and scrambled down. . . . Lower toward the river, we walked into a fog. . . . There was a tendency for the men to linger in the shelter of the gully slopes. The movement slowed. . . . Noncoms cursed and raved . . . trying to keep the men in motion . . . death lashed . . . at the mouth of the ravine . . . men took deep breaths to fortify themselves before walking into hell.[41]

Men were running the wrong way, purposely. Captain George R. Coxe, adjutant of 1/5, caught one man and pistol-whipped him as he fought back, still trying to run away. Coxe demanded, "Where is the bridge? Come on, guide us." With a .45 stuck in his ribs he went back as directed. Unfortunately, Coxe stumbled and the man ran and got away that time. Most of the Marines went, as they always did although they were being senselessly destroyed for a few yards of ground. A few surviving engineers from the venerable 2d Engineer Regiment stood their ground and guided the 5th Marines toward the bridge. "This way, come on, Marines!" Many of the men fell when the searching Maxims found them, but enough made it across to harass and kill the Boche on the east bank.

Due to the shelling and machine-gun fire pointed at the bridges, plus the darkness, it was 2230 before what was left of 1/5 finally managed to clear the pontoon bridge. The upper bridge was nearly wrecked, and Hunt was even further delayed. But it didn't really matter anymore. When they finally got across, only about 100 officers and men remained in what had once been a Marine battalion. Those survivors were re-formed into a very light company. Two of them, Cpl. William J. Ferguson* and Private Hans M. Naegle* from the 17th Company, raced ahead and eliminated a machine gun that was just opposite the bridge on the eastern side. Both, somehow, survived. An exceedingly brave corpsman, Pharmacist Mate 2d Class Alvin L. Bowman*, USN, was one of the earliest "docs" across and immediately set to work. Under withering machine-gun and shell fire, Bowman dressed Marines' wounds, with no apparent thought of personal danger. Unaided he carried three men back across the Meuse so that stretcher bearers could haul them to the first-aid station. Gunnery Sergeant Samuel Clarkston* of the 8th Machine Gun Company led the one remaining gun crew across the river and, under extremely trying conditions, established a stronghold from which he and his men inflicted severe losses on the enemy. One of the corporals of that same company, Guy F. Heryford*, helped to man that lone gun and provided the "cement" necessary to maintain the morale of the badly hit unit.

The east bank was an even greater morass of barrage fire, both artillery and machine guns, causing many additional casualties. Various sources are clear that a few guns were located just opposite the footbridges. Possibly coincidental, because most of the guns were set farther back on firmer ground. By that hour, the few Marines of 1/5 had pushed the Boche guns backward or had eliminated many of them, so that a line could be formed, a single line, a very thin single line. There weren't enough Marines left to provide any support. All night the weakly held positions were covered by enemy fire. It doesn't seem, now, that anyone could have survived that crossing and the subsequent abuse, but somehow they held on. Some of the heroics by those Marines of Hunt's battalion are almost unbelievable.

It was another hour before 2/5 also managed to land on the east bank. Dunbeck's orders were to "march across the foot bridge . . . screen the bridge while other units pass over." Whoever wrote the orders hadn't the faintest idea of what the Marines would be facing going across that river. After getting across, 2/5 was to move northeastward toward the national highway. The 43d Company was to "capture the Stone Quarry, Senegal Farm and mop up Bois des Flaviers." The 51st would follow the 43d and pass through their line moving forward to capture Moulins–St. Hubert. Orders to the 18th Company were even more extensive. They were to cross the river and then move south of the Bellefontaine Farm, eastward "toward the National Highway, thence toward Vaux-les-Mouzon, occupying Hill 341 and Folie Farm, thence push forward and capture Vaux and connect with the 6th Marines operating in that vicinity . . . etc." The national highway runs along the east bank north to south. These orders had absolutely no basis in common sense. There were at least the remnants of two German regiments on high forested ground with many machine guns and much artillery just waiting for that crossing. Of course there was no way that Dunbeck's already badly depleted battalion could do much more than get across the river. The 6th Marines had not crossed, so that part of the order wasn't feasible. Although Dunbeck later stated that most objectives were taken, neither Vaux nor Moulin was included in his report.

Lots of Marines from 2/5 showed what they could do under those fearful conditions but the 55th Company shone especially brightly that dark night. Corporal Walter S. Hiller*, under direct fire from seven Boche machine guns, led his detachment directly across and took out a machine gun facing the exit of his bridge. Private John Haney* voluntarily moved forward toward a machine gun that was firing directly on the 55th and demolished it by himself. Another private, Wilbert W.

Sinclair*, went Haney one better. He went out alone and reconnoitered the positions of several machine guns holding up the advance of his company and, after locating them, knocked two of them out, as did Sgt. Tony W. Kane*.[42] Many of the platoons in all companies were now being commanded by noncommissioned officers, since the officers were being wounded, just like the privates. Gunnery Sergeant Irving G. Hamilton* led his 55th Company platoon against numerous machine-gun nests that early morning, destroying all they met, despite the terrific enemy fire directed toward them.

First Lieutenant Ralph M. Wilcox*, with Headquarters, 1/5, was assigned as liaison between Hunt and Dunbeck, compelling him to expose himself to heavy fire from all sources. Following orders he moved forward through the enemy lines, routed one German outpost, and established liaison between 1/5 and 2/5, defeating a Boche attempt to isolate both units. The 23d Machine Gun Company, led by 2d Lt. James P. Schwerin, his skipper having been killed, was assigned to cross with the 5th Marines, but only one gun and crew survived. After arrival on the eastern bank they set up and defended the bridge, so that if the Marines were forced to retire they could use the badly shattered link with the western side. If they couldn't cross that flimsy wreck of a bridge, they could swim. That's what John V. Bridgford*, a private of the 51st Company, did. In order to deliver an important message to regimental headquarters, Bridgford had to swim the river, at night in November, all the while exposed to intense fire from the Boche, who could readily see him. He did his duty; the message arrived safely.

Finally, at 0400, 2d Battalion, 356th Infantry, of the 89th Division, made a crossing and went into support of 1/5, followed later by 1/9. Two hours later another infantry battalion from the 356th passed through the lines of the 5th Marines on the eastern side and attacked the defending Germans. But the Marines received little rest. Hunt's survivors went forward to support 2/356 as best they could, arriving behind their line at 1100 hours on 11 November. The following description is what the division combat liaison officer, Maj. George W. Hamilton, reported to Neville:

> 1st and 2d Bns. of the 5th Marines did not complete crossing of Meuse until 11:30 P.M. last night due to heavy shelling, a break in upper bridge and confusion of moving in dark. The Bn. of 89th got lost at the start and at 6:00 A.M. this date [11/11] had only gathered together some 300 men. Major Hanna was here but has

disappeared now.[43] Crossing made under heavy artillery and machine gun fire. The 1st Bn. on the right, ran into a machine gun nest immediately after crossing and had great trouble keeping the men together. The entire Bn., numbering approximately 100 men, is now combined as a company and under command of Captain Hunt. The 2d Bn. advanced to the north through the Bois des Flaviers but had to hold up movement until daybreak on account of machine gun nests and heavy underbrush. This morning at 6:30 A.M. the 2d Bn. on the left and the Bn. of the 89th on right advanced toward the objective. Sniping and machine guns overcome and advance going smoothly at present. Enemy artillery fire heavy. On account of the very small number of men it is going to be difficult to organize this position in depth. Urge that another battalion be sent across the river to reinforce us. Message just received from Captain Dunbeck states that advance progressing satisfactory and that he is taking many machine guns. . .[44]

At 1145, a messenger came forward to notify all troops to remain on the ground that they had seized by 1000 hours. The 67th and 49th Companies of 1/5 reached the ridge near Senegal Farm and the 66th Company advanced as far as the outskirts of Moulin. The latter learned of the armistice and withdrew to the ridge. It appears as though the 66th had penetrated farthest eastward.[45] Several patrols from 2/5 went forward and one was to have entered the town of Moulin, but apparently didn't. Sergeant Ernest R. Love, who wasn't showing the Boche much love that morning, led his patrol from the 55th Company near Mouzon, the target of the 6th Marines the night before. Love's patrol cleared the wheat fields and woods of enemy snipers and machine guns. All the while he kept his men intact, making the advance of the 55th that much easier. No other Marines, except those of the 66th at Moulin, seem to have gotten that far before the "witching hour."

There was scattered shooting for a few hours afterward in several areas. Orders had to be issued to some of the units that were up front because some apparently had not gotten "the word" and continued fighting well past 1100 hours. Captain (later Major General) Samuel C. Cumming, skipper of the 51st Company, later described to his grandson what his experiences were like that final day of the war. Possibly there were others much like it.

Whenever we saw any Germans we fired on them and this continued until about 2:15 in the afternoon of November 11th. I noticed the Germans were not returning our fire and suddenly all along the main highway fronting us, there appeared above the embankment German rifles with bayonets with flags and white handkerchiefs waving. I ordered my men not to fire and we waited to see what they were going to do.[46]

The war was over. Mostly, the German soldiers just lay still. As later reports stated, they were overjoyed to be alive and aware that they wouldn't have to face another bloody day of war. The Americans made some noise, but generally were also quiet, still unable to grasp the immediate effect. Although the troops were warned against fraternization, there were some open exchanges between the former enemies. The Germans came over and met the Americans, some carrying brandy and cigars, and they were met with friendship and cigarettes. Fighting men are like that. When it's over it is over, and respect for their courageous opponents is contagious. But it wasn't long before the headquarters bureaucrats arrived at the fighting front and demanded a cessation of kindly acts of any kind by the Americans. Possibly it was the first time any of them had been that far forward, but it was safe now.

Otherwise the troops all remained where they were for at least another day. Sleep, precious sleep, was something the Americans, and no doubt the Germans, had done without. On 11 November 1918 that was the order of the day. On the following day the Americans fired off some of their pyrotechnics and built bonfires, around which many sat and sang songs. But generally it was the civilians in the United States and the Allied countries that made the most noise. Germany and its civilians were notably quiet. For more than four years they had bled, and for what? In a dozen years a few leaders would come forward and remind them of their disaster. They would know how to make things right.

Shortly after the guns all stopped, Lejeune noted that he visited a 2d Division field hospital and among the wounded he questioned one sergeant whose leg had been amputated.

I then said, what induced you to cross the bridge in the face of terrible machine gun and artillery fire when you expected that the war would end in a few hours? The sergeant responded . . .

Just before we began to cross . . . Dunbeck [spoke]. 'Men; I am going across that river, and I expect you to go with me.' What could we do but go across too?

Lejeune added. . .

[that exchange] gives one a better understanding of the practice of leadership than do all the books that have been written, and all the speeches made . . . on the subject.

Editorial Comment

There seems not to be any question, in the official records, that the Marines went from the Bois de l'Hospice down a very steep embankment, then across a railroad track to a bridge constructed over the Meuse River. The records do make the statement that the 5th Marines formed up at La Sartelle Farm, which lies on the high ground south of the Bois de l'Hospice, and from there they approached the bridges. If they had used the modest but very steep ravine flowing downward from that farm the effort, in the dark, would have proved very strenuous, possibly dangerous, noisy and have caused pain to the troops; as well as being quite exposed to the Germans across the river. The ground on the eastern side of the river at that spot is/was soft until reaching a road just before the woods. That would have proven to be a very poor spot for troops to cross during daylight, let alone in the dark. I can't believe that any officer of the 2d Engineers was so incompetent as to select that particular position for his bridges.

I have gone over the ground thoroughly and am convinced that the map, numbered VII in the 6th Machine Gun Battalion's history, shows the wrong crossing point. I have found other maps in such publications as the ABMC American Armies and Battlefields in Europe, especially page 304, which places the bridges in a different location but in my opinion also incorrectly. The latter shows it being further north, closer to Villemontry. Remember, a battalion of the 89th, which division was located some distance farther south, was also to have crossed on the night of 10–11 November with 2/5. Besides, the 9th Infantry occupied that space before Villemontry.

I believe I found the ravine down which 1/5 and 2/5 went to the riverbank and the obvious point at which both pontoon bridges must have been located. That ravine would have provided more cover for troops and a much easier flow toward the river, which is also narrower at that point. And the entrance is only a half mile south of the farm. To further strengthen my contention I later found that the French topographical map of that area shows, at my point, the following text: "Ravin du Fond de la Bataille"—emptying out exactly at the bend of the river.

My translation of the name is "at the bottom of the ravine where there was a battle." My further reasoning would suggest that no other battle in French history would have been fought at that same place anytime to have caused that name to be given to that particular ravine. My map indicates both possible crossing sites, theirs and mine.

Possibly the actual location of the crossing isn't all that important in the scheme of things but that is how larger errors get continued in history books—because no one dares to question "officialdom." I question!

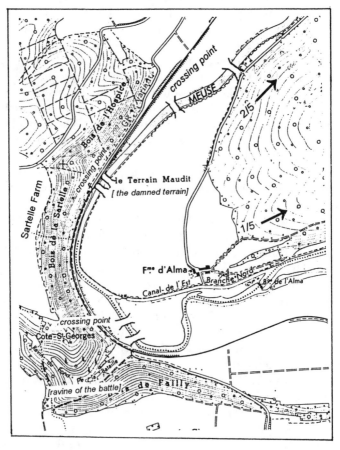

Map 21: Crossing the Meuse (three possible points shown; top, offical records; middle, possibly from Sartelle Farm; bottom is my own impression of where they crossed).

Notes

1 *Records of the Second Division,* vol. 6. They had little or no trouble possibly because they were wearing American shoes.

2 Rhea earned the DSC and DSM, plus a large assortment of lesser awards, while doing a superlative job as chief of staff for Lejeune while the division was at Blanc Mont.

3 Lejeune, *Reminiscences,* 371.

4 Ibid., 372.

5 *A Brief History of the Sixth Regiment, etc.,* 28.

6 Ibid., 29. The 166th was mainly composed of Iowa National Guardsmen; part of the 42d U.S. Division.

7 See the affair at Belleau Wood when Major Hughes, then commanding 1/6, sacked Stowell for no rational reason.

8 Part 4 of a citation for the 2d Division from Maj. Gen. Hunter Liggett, commanding the 1st Army, to General Headquarters, written on 16 January 1919 and concerning the division's part in the attack of 1–11 November 1918. (As always, it's tough to be great. Editorial comment.)

9 *Records of the Second Division,* vol. 6.

10 *History Fifth Regiment,* 28

11 *History Sixth Regiment,* 30.

12 The "twin" towns of Landres-et-St.-Georges were located as follows: St. Georges before the 6th Marines in the center of their zone of advance and Landres before the 5th Marines on their right boundary. The land toward the north was extremely steep coming out of both villages and the Germans must have had a "grand time" shooting up the advancing and climbing Marines.

13 In addition to a DSC, Hermle also received a Navy DSM, a couple of SSs and a Croix de Guerre. Like many other officers of the brigade, Hermle would continue his career in the Corps through WWII as would Montague.

14 Harry K. Cochran was described in the final report of Marines killed in the war as having been killed in action on 2 November, but Hamilton's message was on the spot and he was Cochran's CO; therefore 1 November makes more sense. First Lieutenant Aaron J. Ferch is listed as being killed in action on 1 November. I'm not sure who the other three officers, mentioned as casualties, were. I believe that Frank Whitehead replaced Cochran, as Cochran had replaced him at Blanc Mont when he was wounded.

15 Akers, MacRitchie and Hurlbut, *History of the Third Battalion Sixty Regiment, U.S. Marines* (Hillsdale, Michigan: Brass Hat, Pike, NH 1990.), 100.

16 Simons would die of his wounds on 11 December 1918.

17 In addition to the DSC and NC he would receive for his fortitude and resourcefulness this day, he was also awarded a Cluster for what he did at Soissons nearly five months before.

18 They were all recipients of the DSC, NC and Silver Star plus the Croix de Guerre.

19 Fortunately he survived this battle and went on to invent the finest rifle and automatic rifle the world had ever seen. But though the U.S. Marines desired his Johnson rifle and automatic rifle, possibly even more than women, they

weren't to receive but a smattering of them during WWII. Not enough to satisfy anyone.

20 *Records of the Second Division,* vol. 4.

21 Akers, *History of the 3rd Battalion,* 101.

22 The Bois lay centered directly before both regiments about one-half kilometer north of the third objective line.

23 Lubers was awarded three Silver Stars and a Croix de Guerre for his part.

24 During the Christmas season of 1917, Schneider had gone home to St. Joseph, Missouri, and had the bad luck to catch the measles which sidelined him for many months. Even worse luck, he eventually returned to the brigade.

25 *Records of the Second Division,* vol. 5. This verbal chastisement of Hamilton was highly unusual. He was, without a doubt, a real hustler and the fair-haired boy of the regiment. But Feland was correct because there were very few messages from Hamilton to anyone that day. Lieutenant Colonel Julius Turrill was assistant regimental commander. Winans, who had once commanded the 17th Company, had been wounded at Belleau Wood and was at this time the skipper of Headquarters Company, 5th Marines.

26 All received at least one Silver Star citation, some two, plus a Croix de Guerre. In none of the material describing the event does it mention the capture of people, just guns.

27 I can find no mention of any awards to either Sergeant Ellison or Sergeant Fogle for their responsibilities and actions at the Meuse-Argonne. Obviously both should have been cited at this battle.

28 Fagan had recently been promoted to major, while still in command of the 81st Machine Gun Company, 6th Machine Company Battalion. He had subsequently been transferred to the 6th Marines on 24 October.

29 The *2d Division Summary of Operations in the World War* isn't very clear as to why the 3d Brigade was so delayed in making the relief, which was scheduled to be complete by 1330 hours.

30 Slyke's name is listed in a directory of Marines killed during the war as dying that same day, 4 November, of disease but I cannot find it listed in any other source.

31 *Records of the Second Division,* vol. 5.

32 After the war ended the 89th was considered by AEF leadership to be up there with the 1st, 2d, 32d, and 42d as the premier U.S. divisions in the war. They were purposely paired with the 2d for this major thrust toward the Meuse. Even though they were a little late on the night of 10–11 November, they fulfilled their promise in most every other fashion.

33 Sedan was highly important to the French, as it had always been in the line of fire for enemies coming from the east. As late as 1871, upon the defeat of France by Germany, Sedan was removed from France as part of the Alsace-Lorraine subjugation.

34 This material came from many sources but the best was the article by Donald Smythe that appeared in *Prologue* (Fall 1973) as "AEF Snafu at Sedan." Also see Anne Cipriano Venzon, *The United States in the First World War, an Encyclopedia* (New York: Garland Publishing, 1995), 534–536. Interesting point: When FDR was about to select a new chief of staff in 1939, he passed over Drum and selected Marshall. Marshall has an interesting version of these events in his own book.

35 Because a battalion from the 89th Division, which was designated to cross the river, did not arrive on time, 1/5 was its replacement.

36 Metcalf later became famous for writing one of the best volumes of history about the Marine Corps.

37 His reward was the same as Dan Daly's back at Belleau Wood when he performed the same humanitarian act. When Feigle was a private at Belleau Wood, he was a runner and cited for his courage then with another SS.

38 In 1997, I was on both sides of the river and on the east, one could look directly down on the position the 6th Marines occupied, where they were to cross. It would have been murder if they had crossed the river at that point, even in the dark.

39 *Records of the Second Division,* vol. 5.

40 See statement at the end of this chapter regarding the location of the 5th Marines and the footbridges they crossed.

41 Mackin, *Suddenly We Didn't Want to Die,* 252.

42 Kane was also awarded a DSC and SS back at Belleau Wood and another SS at Soissons.

43 Major Hanna, USA (DSC for this action) was only able to gather together 300 men of his battalion. He was killed during his third trip over the river, according to an article by Col. Rolfe L. Hillman, USA (ret), in the November 1988 issue of the *Marine Corps Gazette.* It wasn't only Marines that were taking it on the chin that night.

44 *Records of the Second Division,* vol. 5.

45 Up until the night of 10–11 November, the losses sustained by the 4th Brigade were relatively light, compared to many others of their battles. In total the losses for the Meuse-Argonne campaign were officially listed as 1233 wounded and 185 Marines killed in action. Whereas, on the night of 10–11 November, their losses amounted to thirty one killed and 148 wounded. The 6th Marines came out on the light side as compared to the 5th Marines and the 6th Machine Gun Battalion.

46 Cumming in his memoir makes several claims that are obviously incorrect. First he tells us that his company crossed the river and then turned south, the "correct direction," even though the balance of 2/5 had gone north. His statement that 2/5 was supposed to assist the 6th Marines north of Mouzon was correct BUT according to him he was headed away from that town. He also mentions a German officer with a white flag telling him the armistice has been signed and that firing should have ceased at 1100 hours. The Germans in this version have Cumming surrounded but the officer, not wishing to cause any more casualties, requested Cumming please to stop killing Germans. Following that, the Germans came forward and shared brandy while receiving cigarettes in return. Most likely a good time was had by all.

10: The Occupation of Germany

The race is not always to the swift nor the battle to the strong,
but that's the way to bet.
—Anonymous

According to the agreement reached between the combatants, the Allied forces remained in their positions and the Germans started withdrawal of their armies, even as soon as the guns fell silent. The protocol was for all contact to be broken and that a neutral zone should be created between them. In anticipation of the armistice, plans had already been drawn up and the 3d American Army under Maj. Gen. Joseph T. Dickman's command would be constituted as the American Army of Occupation. It was composed of six divisions in two corps. Later, another corps with three divisions would be added. The 2d Division was assigned to the III Corps, commanded by Maj. Gen. John L. Hines.[1]

The advance into Germany was to begin on 17 November 1918. Meanwhile, the troops were allowed to restock depleted or damaged weapons and ammunition plus anything else, including replacements, that might be required in case a state of war should continue. That was a constant threat, so everyone was on his guard during this entire period.

On the 17th the division moved out with the 4th Brigade in the lead. The scarcity of roads forced the division to march in a single column through Belgium and Luxembourg. A Marine corporal in the division adjutant generals' office wrote a very descriptive letter in which the Americans seemed to be the main heroes to the occupants of that long occupied land.[2] According to Thomas, the streets of every village and town they marched through were lined with natives holding Belgian and American flags. There were French and British flags, too, but the American flag seemed to have the place of honor. There were many former prisoners of the Germans, a great number being civilians who had been forced to work in Germany during the war. Their major complaint was "not enough to eat, but plenty of work." Ever thoughtful, Thomas described his attempts to make friends with a "pretty Italian girl" upon whom he tried some of his high-school Spanish. It didn't work anyway, according to him. Remember his letters home were to members of his immediate family, such as to his mother. I haven't found an original letter from any Marine or doughboy in which he ever scored. Perhaps they were unlucky. Or perhaps prudent.

The occupiers marched sixty miles through Belgium and Luxembourg, cheered in every town and village and forced (reluctantly I presume) to eat and drink the best the occupants had to offer. The first American men reached the German frontier on 25 November and crossed the border on 1 December.[3] The Rhine River was reached on 10 December and crossed three days later. The division created a headquarters in Heddesdorf, a suburb of Neuwied. This would be as far as the American forces would penetrate according to the proviso of the armistice. A bridgehead only. The 4th Brigade was assigned territory around and about Coblenz, a major city in that portion of Germany. Brigade headquarters was frequently moved about but was mainly located in Nieder Bieber. The American zone was in the middle with the French forces of occupation located to the south of the Americans and the British to the north. Most of the troops were quartered within German residences, with or without permission or agreement. That has always been the law of war. You lose, you pay. But the whole effort was made as difficult as possible—for the occupied, of course, but even more so for the occupiers.

The immediate orders were for no fraternization between the occupiers and the native Germans. That lasted a few minutes, or even less. It was nearly impossible for men who generally didn't hate the Germans, as say the French and Belgians would, not to make some friendly gestures to those among whom many were living. As Thomas mentioned in several of his letters, "They looked so much like us, how could we continue to be enemies and not speak to those who tried to be friendly?" It was an order and some attempts were made to enforce it, but it didn't work and soon enough was ignored for the most part.

Early in January the 3d Army had made its plans for the defense of the bridgehead, if that should prove necessary. There was always the possibility that the reluctant Germans would make a fight of it if the terms presented weren't acceptable. The 4th Brigade, supported by the 15th Artillery Regiment, was assigned the duty of defense of the division outpost zone. Third Brigade was assigned the second line in support. Fortunately, nothing ever came of the reluctance of the Germans to accept the proposed treaty, so no one ever had to fight anyone else.

The occupation for all Americans was boring, a seven-month period of uneventful and monotonous duty. We have few memoirs that cover the period beyond brief descriptions. One of the most interesting is the series of letters home by Cpl. Eugene Reynold Thomas, quoted previously. Sometime following the attack upon the Blanc Mont Massif in October 1918 he and a few friends from the 4th Marine Brigade were transferred to the Marine Detachment at 2d Division Headquarters as clerks in the adjutant general's office. Major Keyser was, I believe, their immediate supervisor. Those Marines missed the Meuse-Argonne battles but were in all others from Belleau Wood through Blanc Mont. His description of the division's advance through Belgium as mentioned previously is the best description I've found anywhere. He was a well-educated man who under normal conditions would have been selected for a commission; consequently, his letters are valuable from his perspective as a junior noncom.

In the first few weeks it was "drill, drill, drill." The morale had sunk to a very low point when Pershing and his staff finally got their act together and decided that the war was over. The men needed to get as far away from military life as they could, the life they had been leading for so many months. It wasn't all duty; there was some recreation, mainly sports, as well as amateur theatrical productions and professional entertainers. The 4th Brigade maintained its reputation in most sports and certainly in the interarmy shooting contests. Bellamy tells us that in February the 2d Division whipped the 1st Division at football in the town of Neuwied, 6 to 0. Corporal Thomas had the good fortune to have contact with a firm in Paris, M. du Boisc's, with which his father's company had been doing business for a number of years. They were able to provide him with some spending money when he most desperately needed it. They also hosted him several times while he was in Europe, particularly when in Paris. He described his travels by the Paris Express, along with a number of other American servicemen, in the overly crowded and not terribly comfortable train. The French workers on the train, in particular those in the dining car, were quite different in their attitude toward Americans than they had been only a year before, after Belleau Wood. A good deed is not long remembered, nor easily forgiven.

On 14 March, John J. Pershing came to inspect and review the 2d Division. Nearly 20,000 officers and men had to get out of their reasonably warm racks to start in trucks at 0350 to go to the inspection site. There was great joy along the Rhine that day. "Pershing inspected each platoon, decorated several men and then reviewed the Division. It passed by him to the music of a band of 300 [men], in lines of battalions in platoons columns." The general then mounted a straw pile and addressed the troops. Bellamy worried that some wiseacre might yell out "When are we going home?" but it didn't happen. Pershing told them they were in the AEF and so long as they were needed they would stay. Not the most satisfactory response to what they most earnestly wanted to hear, but "what can not be cured, must be endured" as the Irish would say. So, they endured.

Marines had concentrated on marksmanship for many years. As early as 1918 the Corps officially had announced that no enlisted Marines would be sent overseas if they hadn't qualified as marksman or better. The total percentage of qualified rifleman in 1918 was sixty-seven percent and in 1919 it was up to eighty-three percent. Consequently, when the rifle and pistol competitions occurred during the occupation, the Marines came out with most of the trophies. In May 1919, at a competition held at Le Mans, France, the first three places of individual rifle firing went to Marines. A Marine won the individual pistol competition. The 5th Marines won the regimental trophy; while the 13th, 6th, and 11th Regiments, USMC, were seventh, eighth, and eleventh, in the entire AEF. Finally, a Marine won first place in the individual automatic rifle competition, firing a BAR.

In July, at the same range, the American Expeditionary Force team, on which there were four Marines, defeated all nations, while a Marine took second place in the individual rifle match. In Germany, during the 3d Army shoot, the Marines and the 2d Division won most of the matches. Lastly, a five-man team, which included two Marines on the American team, placed second to the French on a three-hundred-meter range outside Paris.

Life for most of the officers was a step or two above the existence for all enlisted men. Bellamy seemed to be on the move every few days or weeks. Always traveling here and there and always finding good "digs" and pleasant company wherever he went. Being the scion of a wealthy family didn't hurt his social life too badly. On 24 March he mentions that "Daly [Dan] and 600 marines left for home, the best representatives of our regiments that may ever go back together. A sad leaving. The Colonel [Lee?] made a speech and the band played at Neuwied Station. Generals and Colonels to see them off." He also adds that on 29 March

"Nineteen original line officers who came over with the 6th regiment dined together at Coblenz. A rare evening." I guess it would be. Nineteen who survived all that hell.

On 15 April 1919 there appeared a publication produced by and for the 2d Division. It was the now famous *Indian,* a weekly published by the 2d Division under the auspices of the division association, interestingly, an organization already up and running that early. In that first issue there was a leadoff article by the division commander, Maj. Gen. John Archer Lejeune. It was entitled "An Immortal Division: the Remarkable Record of a War Division." On the following page is a cartoon that shows two elderly gentlemen, both attired in World War I uniforms and with long beards and canes. The one man sez, *"We are going home on the 17th of July."* The other responds with *"1959?"* The cover, a fanciful Indian girl in a very brief costume, was designed by 1st Lt. Clagett Wilson, USMC. Hopefully, arthritis never curtailed his hands. The additional issues, fourteen in all, included articles and photos of many different units within the division, but usually with some Marines represented. One issue had a photo of the winning football team of the division, the 73d Machine Gun Company, 6th Marines, which won six and tied two. The 3 June issue was heavily Marine, with a special cartoon showing a Marine looking in a mirror and saying what has been often accredited to a 2d Lt. Louis Cukela; "Next time I send a damn fool, I'll go myself." The 24 June issue had a cover depicting a Marine hurling a grenade with blurb alongside topped by the emblem. The blurb stated, *"And they couldn't lick the Leathernecks in a hundred thousand years, 1917–1919."* The final issue, titled *On-the-high-seas* and with a cover in color showing a Spanish galleon in full sail, had the first article headed "Peace and Home." The balance of it was mostly photos with a full-page cartoon depicting a well-used veteran of the division hugging the Statue of Liberty and saying, *"I always was crazy about you, kid!"*

Serious friction concerning the peace terms flared up into a confrontation between the occupiers and the Germans in June 1919. The AEF was ready to fight if necessary, with the 2d Division leading. The plan developed was to move out in two columns, the 3d Brigade with the 15th Artillery on the right and the 4th Brigade with the 12th Artillery on the left. A few engineers and military police were to accompany each column, with the balance of the division in reserve. The Marines and some units of the division actually marched two days into Germany before they stopped. The 5th Marines went as far as Hatenfels, in which they occupied their easternmost position in Germany when the peace treaty was finally accepted and signed.

In the meantime, some changes in the brigade included the relief of Lt. Col. Earl Ellis by Maj. Charles D. Barrett as adjutant in April 1919. Ellis was assigned as second-in-command to Col. Harold C. Snyder. Synder had relieved Feland in command of the 5th Marines when he was promoted to brigadier general on 17 March 1919. Logan Feland wound up as aide to Secretary of the Navy Daniels, returning to the United States on board the *Von Steuben* on 13 May 1919.

On 3 July orders were received, effective 5 July, transferring the division from the 3d Army to the Services of Supply for transportation home. All other duties were stopped so that everyone could make preparations to return to the United States. Beginning on 15 July, trains were loaded and dispatched with the last units reaching Camp Pontanezan at Brest on 23 July. That same day embarkation began with the 3d Brigade the first to go. Headquarters of the 4th Brigade, the 5th Regiment, and the 2d Battalion of the 6th arrived in New York aboard the *George Washington* on 3 August 1919. The remainder of the 6th Marines arrived a few days later aboard two ships leased from the Dutch, the *Rijndam* and the *Wilhelmina*. The last to arrive, the 6th Machine Gun Battalion, arrived on 5 August, aboard the *Santa Paula*. The 5th Brigade also came home at about the same time. Headquarters, the 13th Regiment, and the Brigade Machine Gun Battalion arrived aboard the *Siboney* on 8 August while the 11th Regiment, aboard the *Orizaba,* arrived on 9 August. The Marines of the Composite Regiment returned with that regiment on 8 September aboard the *Leviathan*, after parading in Paris and London. All USMC units were to return to the naval service soon after arrival, but not until after most of them had paraded in New York and Washington.

The parade in New York took place on 8 August 1919, with Lejeune leading on horseback. The bloom was off the rose, so to speak. There had been so many parades with so many soldiers since late 1918, the American public was rather tired of them, so the spectacle was put on more to please the troops than the watchers.

Back at Quantico the Marine units were transferred back to naval service upon their arrival. Four days later, on 12 August they marched in Washington and were reviewed by President Woodrow Wilson and other dignitaries. Brigadier General Wendell Neville was in command at that parade. Company E, the Marine company of the composite regiment, along with the rest of that unit, paraded in New York and Washington, D.C., as escort for General Pershing.

The only lads left were those who had volunteered for service with the Schleswig-Holstein Battalion.[4]

Demobilization of the Marines

All that was left to do now was to release those Marines, officers and enlisted, who wished to return to civil life. The Corps, efficient in its organization and plans, would now prove itself worthy of the highest commendations by nearly everyone involved.

Realizing that the early release of so many men in a short period of time might cripple the Corps's effectiveness, a decision was made to release first those who were required at home or wished to complete their education. Orders were issued on 20 November 1918, just after the armistice was declared. Many enlisted and officers had managed to effect their releases beginning shortly after the occupation began. Others left periodically during the months following, even until the decision was made for the division to return home. In a tape recording I possess, Elton Mackin described the successful efforts his mother went through to obtain his early release. He arrived home in the late spring of 1919 and was discharged soon afterward.

Following an act approved on 11 July 1919, which provided enough funds to sustain a Corps at a level of 27,400 enlisted men, and with an appropriate number of officers, the Marine Corps established demobilization centers. A number of detailed instructions were promulgated to help carry out an efficient demobilization. Those Marines who had been serving for the duration in the tropics were returned to the United States. An orderly process of discharging those who were enlisted for the duration began. Those who had been in the 4th and 5th Brigades who were returned to either Quantico or Hampton Roads, Virginia, began receiving their discharges soon after they arrival. By 13 August, 6,677 4th Brigade enlisted men had been discharged as well as 6,671 5th Brigade Marines. During this same period about two hundred Marine officers were either discharged or transferred to the inactive reserve.[5] By now the 4th Brigade was just a memory for those who had suffered so during their membership in it. Other than the survivors and families, there wasn't much attention paid to them during their lifetime. All but a handful of them are now gone. Perhaps a half dozen, as I write, are still with us. A very few reupped when Pearl Harbor was gutted but most survivors had the same philosophy as Col. Alphonse De Carre, who in 1942 told Major Merrill B. Twining, "It's a young man's war. . . . I've had enough."[6]

Notes

1 James McB. Sellers relates a story in his memoir about making a one-night stop at the town of Ettelbruck in Luxembourg, while on the march to Germany. The usual guard was established and the officers and men settled down for a short, comfortable stay. The officers were eating in the dining room of the hotel when in walked a general. Everyone leapt to his feet and saluted. The general looked at Lt. Col. Williams and demanded to know why the battalion office hadn't been established. Bull replied, "We don't break out our offices on these one night stands, general." The reply: "Don't you realize that we're still in the state of war?" Williams answered, "Yes, sir." "Don't you think you should have your typewriters and your office staff here, all ready to handle business?" Finally Bull got all red in the neck and said, "Sir, I can tell by your uniform and the insignia that you are a general, but who are you?" The answer: "Young man, I'm your corps commander." The following day Williams was relieved. He happily got to go back home.

2 Unpublished letters of Cpl. Eugene Reynold Thomas, formerly of the 55th Co., 2/5, graciously offered for my use by his daughter, Margaret Thomas Bucholz.

3 Thanksgiving Day, 28 November, was suitably observed.

4 See more details under that heading.

5 Several who took themselves out of the reserve returned sometime later. George W. Hamilton was a slightly different example. His temporary majority was revoked on 21 July 1919 and he reverted to the rank of captain. He resigned his commission on 20 March 1920 but returned on 22 March 1921. In July 1921 he was designated a student naval aviator. Sometime shortly after he died in a crash 26 June 1922.

Gilder Jackson left for an undetermined amount of time but was on active duty in WWII as a colonel.

Bill Eddy, the intelligence officer of the 6th Marines, left the Corps, went to graduate school, and had many academic experiences before throwing the whole thing (presidency of a college) into the can. He returned in 1940 and was looking for a job when Donovan of the OSS learned that he was available and hired him on for the North African campaign. Eddy planned most of the interaction with the Arabs, a great success.

There were more, but this is a sampling which shows that the leaf doesn't fall far from the tree.

6 That was a conversation related to me by General M. B. Twining a number of years ago when I inquired about some of those who, by name, did big things in France but who sort of sat out WWII. Twining wasn't critical; he understood. So do I.

11: Other Marine Activities in France

They also serve who only stand and wait.
—John Milton

The 5th Marine Brigade

Beyond those whose interest lies in the activities of Marines during the Great War, little is known about the 5th Marine Brigade, a lack of knowledge that extends to most Marines as well. The 5th Brigade was established to combine with the 4th Brigade and make a Marine division for service in France, one of Commandant Barnett's grand ideas. His theory, and that of other senior Marine officers, was that a division of Marines would (read "should") be commanded by a Marine. Perhaps several Marine divisions could be foisted upon the AEF. In fact he even had a general picked out for the first such division, John Archer Lejeune. It was not to be. After accepting the 4th Brigade, Pershing was willing to accept additional forces for the AEF, those that could be utilized in various noncombat missions, but no more combat Marines.

The authorized increase in manpower allowed to the Corps in July 1918 enabled it to accept up to 3,000 officers and 75,500 enlisted men. Barnett and his associates, anticipating the major increase from the then current level of 30,000, began recruiting in April 1918. The concept was to provide two brigades to the AEF plus another fifty percent for casualty replacements, a total of about 30,000 Marines. The desired total of enlisted was nearly reached on 11 December 1918 with 75,101 officers and men, including 269 female reservists. This was an all-time maximum number of Marines, until a later war.

When Lejeune arrived in France in June 1918, he brought with him a proposal from Barnett for the authority to provide one or more divisions and a recommendation that Lejeune be given a Marine unit to command.[1] Rumor had it that Lejeune would soon be promoted to major general, precluding anything less than a division for him to command. Pershing simply replied: *No!* In a letter to Newton Baker, secretary of war, he clearly and firmly stated his opposition.

Referring to my conversation with the Secretary . . . on this subject, I am still of the opinion that the formation of such a unit [a
Marine division] is not desirable from a military standpoint. While
the Marines are splendid troops, their use as a separate division is
inadvisable.[2]

Pershing's idea for a pliant Marine force was to use them as provost
guards, base detachments, service troops; anything as long as it was rear-
area.

The 5th Brigade arrived in France in September 1918 and was immediately spread out between Brest and Tours. Brigadier General Eli
K. Cole, the commanding officer of the brigade, was rapidly detached
and placed in command of the 41st (1st Depot Division) based at St.
Aignan, France. He was detached a week or so later as an observer with
the 2d Division, a duty that lasted for approximately twenty days. On 28
October he was back at St. Aignan.[3] Brigadier General Smedley D. Butler, recently in command of Camp Pontanezan, assumed command of
the brigade on 9 April 1919.[4] He retained command until the unit was
demobilized in August 1919.

The 5th Brigade was composed of the 11th and 13th Regiments of
Marines (Infantry). The 5th Machine Gun Battalion was their supporting arm.[5] Colonel George Van Orden commanded the 11th for the entire period the brigade was in France; Col. Smedley D. Butler commanded the 13th. On 19 November 1918, Lt. Col. Douglas C. McDougal
assumed command of that regiment when Butler was assigned to Camp
Pontanezen. Major William C. Wise was brigade adjutant from the date
the brigade organized until 25 September 1918. He was relieved by
Maj. Charles D. Barrett, who was acting adjutant until he relieved Lt.
Col. Earl Ellis as adjutant of the 4th Brigade. Major Calvin B. Matthews
was 5th Brigade adjutant from 11 July until the date the brigade was demobilized.

The 5th Machine Gun Battalion was initially commanded by Maj.
Ernest A. Perkins from its date of organization until 4 November 1918,
whereupon Maj. Allen H. Turnage assumed command on 12 November. Captain Franklin A. Hart served in command during the interim
period of about one week. The battalion served entirely at Camp Pontanezan during its sojourn in France.

Back home, Barnett was making every effort to provide the 10th
Marines, an artillery regiment commanded by Col. Robert H. Dunlap,

with a mixed force of guns. His concept, even as late as August 1918, was to get a balanced military force of Marines in France.[6] The navy was planning upon sending fourteen-inch railway guns to France with seven-inchers on field mounts. The 10th was designated as the unit to take over the seven-inchers, which were removed from old battleships at the Indian Head Proving Ground. For the time, Dunlap and his crew retained their three-inch field guns, waiting for an opportunity to support the 4th or 5th Brigades in action. In April 1918, General Barnett offered their services to the War Department. The response was not positive. "No Marine artillery could be accepted." There was one alternative offered, however; Pershing responded that he would be glad to take Marine artillery officers as replacements instead. In late summer Barnett advised that the Marines could now provide a seven-inch gun regiment. The army chief of staff, Maj. Gen. Peyton C. March, replied that the army didn't need any more artillery units but they would be pleased to take the guns. Barnett and, I suppose, every Marine artilleryman who learned of this was angry. But there was no stopping the super-aggressive Barnett. He tried to make a deal to rearm the regiment with the French 75mm field piece. Regardless, the army leadership was determined not to accept any more Marines in France. Dunlap did get to France. He assumed command of the 17th Field Artillery Regiment of the 2d Division and earned a Navy Cross at the Meuse-Argonne. See the entry and citation following.

The 13th Regiment, already titled the "Hoodoo Regiment" by Butler, was the first force to begin organizing at Quantico in July 1918. In his memoirs Butler tells about buying thirteen black kittens as regimental mascots. I can find no mention of whatever happened to them. Probably they all remained stateside without ever receiving any overseas hashmarks. Bryan Becker, whom we have met in boot camp at Parris Island and later at Galveston, Texas, was reassigned to Company D, of the 13th. While waiting for his transfer to Quantico, Becker wrote telling his mother that

[I leave for] the overseas depot of the Marines it [is] called an overseas depot there but it is not made up of men who are fit to good [sic] over so I think it is a guard detail and so does everybody else . . .[7]

In another letter, in his superlative style he tells us about his company's first meeting with

The Cornel [sic] of our regiment [whose] name is Butler is called the daredevil of the Marines and I guess he believes in working his men alright. The first battalion was over to the Gym that night for singing school and there was about 2000 of us and we sure could make the noise the Cornel said that if we could fight as well as we could sing we could lick all hell you should have heard them sing the Marine Hymn and Sweet Angler [Adeline, I presume] they say there [sic] never heard anything like it here before.

There was a slight delay in the actual training period, since training personnel didn't become available until August. During this period some of the men were victims of "scuttlebutt" (from a sailor, who else?) that they might go to Russia. After a short period, the 13th was transferred to France in dribs and drabs. One of the junior officers of the regiment, 1st Lt. Josephus Daniels Jr., son of the secretary of the navy, probably had much to do with the transfer of the regiment to France.[8] Butler, well aware of the benefits of political support, took young Daniels on as his aide. Had Butler been allowed to be Butler, that might have been a very dangerous job. But he wasn't and consequently young Daniels's life was greatly extended. Finally, the last of the regiment reached Brest by the end of September. Smedley hit the ground running and was ready to take on the entire German army immediately. That was not to be, but it would have been a perfect example of an "irresistible force meeting an immovable object." Later he reminisced,

The Army antagonism toward Marines contributed, naturally, to my failure to reach the front. Although ninety-seven percent of my men were expert riflemen and sharpshooters, troops that hardly knew which end of the gun to shoot were sent to the trenches. My crack regiment was broken up and distributed to do manual labor and guard duty.[9]

Barnett also complained about the poorly trained army troops sent into combat, leaving Marines behind the lines to do lesser tasks.

A Marine could not hope to go abroad and go into the firing line unless he was a qualified "marksman" or better. . . . I crossed on a transport [to France] with 11,000 army troops and I do not think I am exaggerating in saying that almost all of these so-called soldiers had never fired an army rifle.[10]

This sort of thing added to the already bad feelings between the Marines and the army. Meanwhile the men of the Hoodoo regiment would spend nearly a year gathering in the sea breezes along the western coastline of France until they were shipped back to the United States. The 11th Regiment had the same sort of history.

Both regiments were assigned, basically, to the Services of Supply, an organization commanded by Maj. Gen. James A. Harbord, of Belleau Wood "fame." Harbord was extremely pleased to get Marines to guard his supply lines. He knew they would keep the supplies where they belonged. Throughout his later writings about his wartime experiences Harbord continued to laud the Marines.

The 13th Marines were split up. The 1st Battalion was stationed in and around Bordeaux, guarding docks, camps, and supply facilities. The regimental companies plus 2/13 and 3/13 guarded supply facilities in the St. Nazaire area. The 11th Marines were in the general area of Tours, where the SOS was located.

Although the two regiments and the machine-gun battalion were designated for guard duty, they had myriad responsibilities. Those Marines also performed the following duties: provost guard, hospital center guard, camp guard, transportation officers, dock guard, stevedore, military police, warehouse guard, railroad-train guard, prison guard, traffic police, motor transportation convoy guard, railway patrol, and just about anything else that one can imagine. The best description I've found of the duty is that described by James H. Draucker of the 11th Regiment, who spent seven years in the Corps.

> There was a lot of hi-jacking of surplus goods from the storage warehouses at Brest. . . . One of the most famous gangs of hi-jackers was the Murphy gang. . . . They would appear late at night, hold up a guard, ransack a warehouse, load up their trucks, and shove off. The most nerve-wracking job of guard duty was walking post in the eight warehouses loaded with food, clothing and supplies. They were about 500 feet long with an aisle through the center, plus numerous cross aisles. We would walk up and down the center aisle with just enough light for us to see the wharf rats . . . running back and forth across the boxes, up the columns and across the girders over head. . . . After several hours [of this] it was a welcome sight to see your relief coming.[11]

Still, there weren't enough good troops in the 5th Brigade to guard all the SOS facilities. Since most of the wounded Marines of the 4th

Brigade were unable to return to full duty upon release from hospitals, they, too, were added to the SOS for various light duty. They were formed into guard companies, some permanent, others temporary. The latter were sometimes able to provide more strenuous services as their strength grew. The first companies were formed on 23 July 1918 and they served as prisoner-of-war escorts. Twelve guard companies composed of two officers and 100 Marines each were formed from Marines discharged from hospitals between October and November 1918. The designated numbers of the companies ranged between sixty-two and seventy-two. These were formed in the first three months of 1919, and continued in service until July 1919 when they returned to the United States with the 5th Brigade.

Women Marines in World War I

On 8 August 1918, in response to a request by the Commandant George Barnett, Secretary of the Navy Josephus Daniels issued an authority to "enroll women in the Marine Corps Reserve for clerical duty at Headquarters Marine Corps." On 13 August 1918 Mrs. Opha Mae Johnson became the first woman to officially join the Marines. She was immediately assigned to duty as a clerk in the quartermaster's office. By war's end she had attained the rank of sergeant. Mrs. Johnson was indeed the senior woman Marine.

Records indicate that although the inclusive ages at which women could enlist were eighteen to forty, slightly younger women, if judged "very desirable," could enlist with their parents' consent. By "very desirable" was meant females who could perform at a high level rather than those of particular appeal to the opposite sex. The newcomers had to attain certain standards required of male recruits such as meeting physical requirements during a conventional exam.

The Corps was overwhelmed with excited applicants. At least 2,000 women lined the streets waiting for admission to a recruiting office in New York. Those who were recruited on the first day went through a well-developed routine to satisfy the requirements for intelligence and training in the clerical art. After it was ascertained that the women would meet the requirements of what a Marine should be, they were invited back for the physical. This happened before it was decided what kind of clothes should be worn.

The Corps was "unwavering in its determination to accept nothing but the best, most highly trained women possible." To better explain what that meant, of the 2,000 applicants, only five were found to be qualified. One young woman, who wasn't eighteen years at that time, failed her first exam. Because she wanted to be a Marine, she dyed her hair and reappeared the following day to try again. The amazed colonel recognizing her, asked, "Weren't you here yesterday?" "When I said, 'Yes, I was,' he got up and leaned over the desk and shook my hand and said, 'That's the spirit that will lick the Germans, I will allow you to take the test again,'" which she passed with flying colors.

Some of these newly acquired Marines joined so that they could support, ever so indirectly, husbands and other male kinfolk or sweethearts already in the ranks. Others joined because the Marines had made such a name for themselves that these women wanted to be a part of them. There were many who joined because they felt that it was their duty, and that being Marines was going the whole route. Of course, the main reason that women were being enlisted was because there were many qualified male Marines performing tasks that women could do as well or better. No more than 305 women became Marines, but those who did went all the way. Their uniforms were of the same material and with some modifications were cut in the same basic fashion, but with a skirt. Some of the new Marines remembered years after the fact what machinations some of the civilian females would go through trying to get the loan of a "real" uniform, so as to impress male admirers. It was green wool in winter and tan khaki in summer.

Because of the housing shortage, especially in Washington, it was not easy to place the new recruits in any government, or even civilian, housing. Some found ways and means of staying together in apartments scattered all over the city, thereby maintaining their "Marineness" regardless of whatever other problems they had.

Those 300-plus Marines were as proud of their designation as any male Marine ever was, and many years later the veterans maintained a collegiality much as male Marines have. When the war terminated, they were discharged as conditions permitted. By 11 August 1919 all female Marine reservists had reverted to inactive status. Some managed to continue their service with the Corps as civilians, taking on various clerical positions upon release from active duty. A few managed to continue for many years, even through World War II.

The 3d Army Composite Regiment

The Composite Regiment was formed to serve as a ceremonial guard of honor for General of the Armies, John J. Pershing. Each of the first six divisions provided two companies each. The 2d Division elected to provide an army company and a Marine company. The Marine company was designated as Company E.

On 2 May 1919, in Honnigen, Germany, Company E of the proposed regiment was formed. It was composed of Marines selected from both the 5th and 6th Regiments. Major Frederick Barker, who formerly commanded the 1st Battalion, 6th Marines, and Capt. Charley Dunbeck of the 1st Battalion, 5th Marines, were assigned the task of selecting the men to be included. They would have to have military bearing and experience (which included decorations as well as proficiency) and above all, combat experience.

Brigadier General Wendell Neville, commanding the 4th Marine Brigade, headed a panel of officers to select the platoons' leaders. Those considered prospects had personal interviews with the panel and were observed in how well they managed troops on the drill field.

Captain Clifton B. Cates of the 96th Company was selected to be the skipper of Company E. His second-in-command was 1st Lt. Merwin H. Silverthorn, the intelligence officer of 3/5. Other officers included: 1st Lts. Curtis T. Beecher, of 74th Company, 1/6, and George Draine, 83d Company, and 2d Lts. John L. McSweeny of 75th Company, 1/6, and Hugh M. Todd, affiliation unknown. Major Barker was made battalion commander and 1st Lt. Walter S. Gaspar, 76th Company, 1/6, was chosen as the battalion adjutant. An additional 250 enlisted Marines were selected from both regiments to complete the formation.

The enlisted men were issued new Army olive drab service dress to insure a smart, unified appearance. Though the Marines wore their emblem, the 2d Division shoulder patch, with its distinctive indian-head pattern, was with the equally distinctive coloration that signified the unit. All men, throughout the entire 2d Division complement, wore the division pattern, since the company was to represent the division rather than their parent units. Helmets were also issued. They were rough, had been painted with a fresh coat of olive drab, but with the star-and-indian painted on the front. Officers wore leather leggings while the enlisted men had to settle for the standard cloth wraparound puttees.

The many combat veterans of the company had long since forgotten close-order drill, so that was the first order of business. They were really put through their paces because they were to be on public display for the entire time they would be in existence. By mid-May the company was able to join the balance of the regiment at Coblenz, Germany. There they became "brigaded" with the other lads of the 2d Division. As expected, the Marines became fast friends with those soldiers of their division and all others were the "enemy," so to speak.

The regiment left Coblenz on 15 June 1919 to arrive in Paris on the 17th. Their first parade was for Pershing at the Pershing Stadium on 22

June. The Fourth of July was marked by various activities, including a parade viewed by General Pershing, Marshal Foch, President Poincaré of France, Clemenceau, the premier of France, and the American ambassador to France. The regiment then put on an exhibition of their dexterity in the manual of arms. This was followed by ceremonies at the tomb of Lafayette.

Next came one of the highlights for the regiment during their relatively short existence: 14 July 1919, always the most important date in all of France, the regiment participated in the Victory Fête on Bastille Day. Crowds were estimated at seven million people. Two Marine platoons were participants in the 1,500-man group that led the parade of Allied troops marching under the Arc de Triomphe, the first non-French soldiers ever to be so honored. Naturally, Cates, McSweeny, Silverthorn, and Todd were leading the Marine contingent.

David Bellamy, while not a member of the 3d Composite Regiment, was in the parade in Paris and later in London. He well described his experiences. In Paris,

> the marching of the battalion [3/6] evidently made a deep impression and our flags brought everyone to their feet. The expressive French people! *"Vive l'Amérique!"* Five miles of it. Then we came to the arch [de Triomphe]. I'd seen it in its new aspect with the chains away and the great pylon to the dead removed to the left for the march. I've had few thrills since I came over, but passing under the arch was one, a great real one. Then past the President [Poincaré] and down the Champs-Elysées to the Concord where we made a great circuit and then struck the boulevards. At the hadelaine the men began to pick up flowers thrown to us, stuck them in their guns and kept on marching straight.[12]

The regiment's next big time was on 19 July when they marched in an inter-Allied parade in London. The notables viewing that parade were the king and queen of England, Marshals Haig and Foch, General Pershing, and many other notables, before an estimated eleven million cheering Britons. During their short stay in London, the regiment was treated as guests of the city and was entertained with receptions, dinners, and other "big times."

Bellamy's entries in his diary also described, in greater detail, how well the troops were treated when in England in mid-July.

London at 11 P.M. and taken at once to Queen Mary's Club. . . .
Troops of Composite Regiment came . . . saw "Uncle Sam" in p.m.,
then dinner at the Carlton for us, then "Going Up." At both of
which we were guests of British Government . . . shopping. Races
at Sandown in P.M. King and Queen there and it cost me 5 shillings
on a bum horse. . . . July 19th . . . The Victory Peace Day Parade.
I was adjutant of the colors and again marched. This time it was 6
1/2 miles of deep cheering. It drowned out even the drums which
we had been able to hear through the shrillness of the Paris cheers.
Down the Mall to the Royal Pavilion. Another thrill at saluting the
King.[13]

The regiment returned to France on 5 August and at the end of the
month prepared to head for home. They boarded the *Leviathan,* the
largest ship of that time, at Brest on 1 September and were soon on their
way. The trip was unlike any that the troops had so far experienced. Only
the regiment and General Headquarters of the AEF were aboard. Since
there were many officers and a relatively limited number of enlisted
men, the troops had up to three bunks each. It was more like a luxury
cruise than a troop transport.

The ship docked at Hoboken, New Jersey, on 8 September and on
10 September was the big Victory Parade in New York City. With Pershing at its head the regiment marched in advance of the 1st Army Division, Pershing's favorite. The same thing happened in Washington,
D.C., on 17 September, and following this last parade the regiment was
disbanded. The Marines of Company E returned for duty with the
Corps. The Marine commandant, George Barnett, concluded his commendation of those Marines with the following statement:

I appreciate the loyal service of these officers and men and the "always faithful" spirit in which they maintained the traditions and
perpetuated the motto of the Marine Corps.

The Schlesweig-Holstein Battalion

Another unit of Marines, even less well known than the 3d Composite Regiment, comprised the men of the Schleswig-Holstein Battalion.
This organization was formed to insure that a plebiscite in that state
would be as honest as a battalion of Marines could make it.[14]

The battalion would be composed of eighteen officers and 737 enlisted Marines, all under the command of Maj. Charles F. B. Price. It was

formed on 21 July 1919 at Brest of Marines selected from both the 4th and 5th Brigades and the recently arrived 12th Separate Battalion of Marines (replacement battalion).

A member of the Schleswig-Holstein Battalion, Pvt. James H. Draucker, in a later memoir, briefly describes what happened to them. Nothing much in actual fact. As he tells us,

> It was there [Camp Pontanezen] that I heard about the battalion of Marines that was to be formed from men of the 5th, 6th, 11th and 13th Regiments who would volunteer for unlimited service. They would be joined by a battalion of British and French Marines to go to Schleswig-Holstein immediately after the peace treaty was signed [by Germany] to supervise an election as to whether Schleswig-Holstein would attach themselves to Denmark or Germany. I volunteered for the duty, and we did get the 750 men and officers needed. By the end of August, the only combat unit left in France was the Fifteenth Separate Battalion under command of . . . Price. All of us who had volunteered . . . took a lot of kidding as we watched our buddies depart for home. Many wisecracks were made. . . . "Well, boys, maybe we'll see you in say ten, twenty, or forty years from now" and a "ha ha."[15]

What happened to him was just a series of guard posts and some military police duties. The last was mainly to search for lads who had gone over the hill. Some had married, or had just associated with French women and hadn't bothered to come back to duty again. He tells about meeting one who was just coming out of the Métro. He was all dressed up and with a knockout on his arm and told Draucker and his buddy to beat it. "I'm not coming back." So there. Draucker and his buddies eventually returned home, and not in "forty years."

Marines Serving Directly in the U.S. Army While in France
Butler at Camp Pontanezan
Sometime after his arrival at Brest, France, Col. Smedley Darlington Butler received a telegram telling him that Pershing had assigned him to the command of Camp Pontanezan. As he tells it, "I was promoted to brigadier general and at the same time was handed this wretched job at Brest. . . ." As noted previously, Butler wasn't very happy with the development. He was always antagonistic toward the navy during his career and now the army was also creating difficulties for him. But he ac-

cepted his fate and became as famous in the entire European theater as nearly everyone of consequence, and more than most.[16]

He noted that when he took command there were 65,000 troops at the camp and 12,000 had the Spanish flu. Many of the units had no doctors. He assumed command at 1400 and two hours later the great ship *Leviathan* had docked just down the hill at Brest. Four thousand of the troops aboard had the flu and it was his job to put them in the camp "hospital." The collection of buildings humorously labeled "hospital" had a capacity of 250 men. There were another 12,000 sick lying in the mud.

He had his own regiment, the 13th, released from quarantine and sent them down to the docks. For five hours, between 1700 and 2200, making two round trips, the regiment carried the four thousand men on improvised stretchers up the hill to the camp. The navy supplied blankets and tents. The obsolete French kitchen equipment was put back into service and within hours the sick men were being fed. For two days the regiment fed the thousands of desperately sick soldiers coffee and soup and covered them with the warm navy blankets. They made bonfires from wood Butler bought at seventy-five dollars a cord from the locals.

The regiment had a band composed, as Butler described it, of Italians "musical to the fingertips." Sixty players were led by Felix Fernando, son of a famous leader of the Royal Band of Italy. Butler had them and dozens of other bands play for the sick and for those caring for them. The music was popular, jazz and marches, played in shifts throughout the enormous camp. Butler tells us in his memoir,

> The day I took command we had two hundred and fifty deaths. I selected the medical officer of my regiment, Captain Chambers of the Navy Medical Corps, to take control of the situation. Hardly stopping to eat or sleep, he threw himself heart and soul into the fight against the epidemic. In two weeks his skill and energetic drive proved so effective that the deaths were negligible.[17]

Butler wanted to make drastic changes in the camp, which had been constructed for Napoleon's army to accommodate 1,500 soldiers. The U.S. Army never had less than 60,000 doughboys at Camp Pontanezan at any given time. Even for Butler, that was a major challenge. But, he took it and changed forever that camp designed for 1,500 Frenchmen.

He learned that there were "vast storehouses filled with all sorts of supplies that we needed," but Butler also knew he had to get support from some of the top brass to get at them. He went to work on his, by now, buddy James A. Harbord, CO of the Services of Supply. With his subordinates cooperating, whatever Butler wanted, Butler got.

Work on revamping the entire camp began with a vengeance. The first item of transfer was eighty thousand sections of duckboard that he wanted to use as sidewalks through the mud. Down the hill went every able-, and some not so able-bodied, men. He ran across a slacker or two, but soon, as illustrated by the following, put them in their place. He tells of finding a "soldier leaning against a wall with his duckboard beside him . . . 'What's the matter?' I asked, 'Can't you carry your duckboard?' He didn't 'recognize me as an officer. I'm no damned pack mule, I enlisted to fight. . . .'" Within minutes the soldier, twenty-one, six foot one, and 190 pounds from Michigan, learned that the scrawny forty-year-old who weighed in at 140 pounds was a general. The other soldiers were giving him a bad time about his reluctance and soon he was begging Butler to let him take his load. "I should say not, you're not strong enough." This brought more laughter and cheers from the crowd.

The soldiers carrying the duckboards weren't all that anxious to make it back to the camp. Some stayed at various booze joints along the path, from which Butler had to chase them. He wore no insignia and was harassed a number of times by MPs who hadn't the faintest idea who he was. One MP was even going to jail him for blocking the MP's car on the road.

As he said later, some enterprising soldiers of the 8th Infantry came out with a newspaper and called it *The Duckboard*. He was called General Duckboard, much to his delight. Butler always knew how to handle men and this occasion was no exception. The men just ate up the work he designated. In a relatively short time the camp was improved and expanded to such a degree that it was by far the best organized and largest camp in the AEF. On one occasion when Pershing visited the camp they fed 11,250 men and 450 officers from one kitchen in forty-nine minutes, in order to impress him. But apparently Pershing never said anything to Butler about what a great job he had done, after so many soldiers before him had failed miserably. At any rate, for his efforts, Butler received an army and navy Distinguished Service Medal to add to his many other senior decorations.[18]

"Hiking Hiram" Bearss with the 102d Infantry in France[19]

There have been a large number of U.S. Marines who can be selected and named "Fighting Marine"—Butler, Dan Daly, and other greats of the Corps—but Bearss, though perhaps not so well known, is right up in the top three or four. Already an outstanding fighting man, Bearss was as anxious to get to the front as most of the other Marines of his time. He managed to get to France with a replacement unit and later joined the 5th Marines in the autumn of 1917. Upon arrival he was, initially, placed in command of the 5th Marines from 30 October to 31 December 1917, but with the arrival of Col. Wendell C. Neville, Bearss reverted to second-in-command of the regiment. Unfortunately there were a few other, more senior, Marine lieutenant colonels floating around in the 4th Marine Brigade, so he was shunted about a bit before a position was finally located for a man of his high attainments and qualifications.

On 26 February 1918 he assumed command of the 3d Battalion, 9th Infantry, another regiment of the 2d Division, serving with that organization through several months of action in the Verdun Sector. The first of May came and Bearss was transferred to Headquarters, 2d Division, acting in the capacity of assistant provost marshal and commander of Headquarters Troop.

On 6 June, in the very beginning of the Belleau Wood campaign, Colonel Catlin, commanding the 6th Marines, was badly wounded and out of action. Lieutenant Colonel Harry "Lighthorse" Lee, the second-in-command, assumed command of the regiment, a post he was to hold throughout the balance of the war. Lieutenant Colonel Hiram I. Bearss was transferred to the 6th Marines as Lee's second-in-command. On 1 July 1918 Bearss was finally promoted to full colonel. Now he was in real trouble. Colonels only command regiments and there wasn't another regiment left to command in the 4th Brigade or in the 2d Division. But there was a regiment in the 26th "YD" Division. It was the 102d Infantry, which had a long lineage of its own. That regiment needed a "doctor" and "Hiking Hiram" was it.

On the 26th of August he finally received an appointment that would be permanent, at least until the end of the war. He took his orderly with him and it was quite an experience for those two Marines. His first engagement, the St. Mihiel Campaign, proved once again that you can't keep a good man down.

The 26th Division was located on the western side of the St. Mihiel Salient and the 1st U.S. Division (Regulars) was on the eastern side. The orders each had were to make directly, at all speed, for the important town of Vigneulles so as to shut off further retreat for the German divisions trapped at the southern portion of the salient.

And then Colonel "Hiking Hiram" Bearss, with his staff, including his personal messenger, orderly, bodyguard, and all-around handy man, Frank Cummings, with the inevitable box of cigars, swung down to march on foot with the advance guard. . . . He informed the men that it was to be a race between [the 1st Division and] the 102d Infantry to see which would reach Vigneulles first.[20]

That was all those Yankees needed to hear. The relationship between regulars and members of the National Guard divisions was almost as "close" as those between soldiers and Marines. Actually, I believe it is fair to state, almost everyone hated the "Big Red One" mainly because it was the all out favorite of Pershing, just as "teacher's pet" is so regarded today. Anyway, the regiment stepped out and on they went. The following is a large extract from the *Marine's Bulletin,* which the 102d author quoted in full:

Which was to win? This was the question in the mind of Colonel Hiram I Bearss, USMC . . . but [Bearss] decided to take no chances. . . . Whether his men reached the goal first or not, he himself would be there. For shear audacity this course of action would be hard to equal, except in the previous record [when he] once ruined Juan Calcano's revolution in Santo Domingo, single-handed, when he left the Marines behind, penetrated Calcano's stronghold in the mountains and returned, holding the chief by the scruff of the neck. And Colonel Bearss was planning to do the same thing to the Kaiser if the war hadn't stopped and ruined everything. . . . [Bearss and Capt. A. F. Oberlin] turned a corner into the main street of Vigneulles when they were confronted by a large body of German soldiers. [Bearss] shouted to them to surrender in a voice calculated to wake the dead. The Germans came to a full halt.

[Bearss] noticed that one of the Germans in the front line had something in his hand. Proceeding on the rule of act first and then investigate, [Bearss] stepped forward, swung on the suspicious character and landed full upon his boche jaw. [Oberlin, meanwhile, opened fire with his automatic upon an approaching wagon train. The Germans, not knowing how many Americans there were, willingly surrendered.][21]

Bearss, being an old campaigner, knew he didn't know where the troops' next meal was coming from, so he had the Germans prepare coffee for his men, who were expected to appear in the town very shortly. When they arrived they found, instead of Germans and their machine guns, steaming pots of coffee. Just the thing for a morning pick-me-up. The 102d collected 280 German prisoners from that town and another 700 from nearby towns at the incredible loss rate of only four wounded Yankees. Oh! yes. A few hours later the 1st Division showed up on the scene, and were they angry to find that the Damn Yankees had beaten them in.

The audaciously executed maneuver, by the advance party of two officers and an enlisted man and the regiment that followed, could have been the scene for a military disaster. The flanks were uncovered and unprotected the entire night. The regiment had marched through enemy-held country with not even a by-your-leave. Bearss had only given them this brief order before they left: "Empty your magazines, fix bayonets, and if you meet a Hun, stick him! Don't make a sound!" There is more to this exercise but we will now go on to his next fight, which was just that, a bang-up, knock-down, and drag-'em-out brawl.

On 26 September 1918, the 26th Division launched another large-scale offensive. It became known as the Riaville-Marchéville Raid. Colonel Bearss led the raid, with Group I composed of the 1st Battalion, 102d Infantry; two machine-gun companies, A and B of the 102d Machine Gun Battalion; plus a Stokes mortar platoon and a 37mm (one-pounder) platoon, and engineers, of course. Group II consisted of one battalion of infantry from the 103d Regiment plus a platoon from its machine-gun company. In addition there were Stokeses and one-pounders plus assorted service troops. The artillery preparation had begun at 2300 on the previous night. Plans called for the capture of the two towns: Group I on Marchéville and Group II to take Riaville.

Bearss led a small patrol toward Marchéville, cleaned out a machine-gun nest near the town, and gained an entrance on the western side near a château. Soon after that 1/102 also entered and took up positions on the far edge of Marchéville after cleaning out snipers and machine guns. As the official history states so eloquently,

> It was at this point of the fight that it became necessary, for the sake of being humane, to call upon the remaining Germans to surrender. Our men from behind the ruins and walls were simply picking them off like rats.

By 1100 the affair seemed to be over, since the "cleaning-up" process was going on full blast. Up till then, artillery hadn't bothered them that much. But now a German aviator flew over and gave sightings to their artillery. It began with a vengeance and continued for several hours. At 1300 the Germans launched a serious counterattack against Bearss and company. In fact, his PC was in the middle of the town and was getting more than its share of attention from the Boche guns.

Within minutes the Germans had in fact nearly surrounded the PC and Bearss, as he later related, began thinking that he might have over-reached himself somewhat. That was when he turned to his faithful Frank Cummings and said, "Give me a box of cigars, Frank; I'll be damned if I'm going into Germany without some smokes."

However, with the men available and some walking wounded they fired and grenaded their way out of the trap, finally making their way back to their troops now assembled behind stone walls. The situation was very bad. Messages had been relayed back to division that "Colonel Bearss and party had been captured." Captain Oberlin, who was on a scouting expedition, was captured with an engineering officer, but Hiram and his group made it back to relative safety. He and a large group from his party were awarded numerous medals. His was a Distinguished Service Cross, a Croix de Guerre with Palm, and the Légion d'Honneur. The citation reads as follows:

Colonel Hiram I. Bearss, 102nd Infantry. . . . For extraordinary heroism in action at Marcheville and Raiville, France, 26 September 1918, is awarded the DSC. . . . His indomitable courage and leadership led to the complete success of the attack by two battalions of his regiment [sic] on Marcheville and Raiville. During the attack, these two towns changed hands four times, finally remaining in our possession until the troops were ordered to withdraw. Under terrific machine gun and artillery fire, Colonel Bearss was the first to enter Marcheville where he directed operations. Later upon finding his party completely surrounded, he personally assisted in fighting the enemy off with pistols and hand grenades. [For the CdG it partly reads]. . . with his staff he remained there [Marcheville] throughout the day in close contact with the enemy under shell and machine gun fire. Exhibited coolness and confidence [see cigar story previously] throughout the battle; *to him belongs the merit of directing the battle and the withdrawal in order during the night.* [Emphasis added.]

Bearss continued to serve the regiment but later took command, several times during the balance of the war, of the 51st Infantry Brigade. In October he was badly wounded when an exploding shell caused injuries to his spine. He recovered and returned to duty but his soldiering days would soon be over. Sometime during this period he was awarded the coveted Italian Cross of War (Croce di Guerra), which was not known to have ever been awarded to anyone not fighting on Italian soil. On 8 November 1918 he was officially ordered to take command of the brigade under General Order No. 98. Just a few days before the acting brigade commander, Brig. Gen. George H. Sheldon, had refuted a telephone statement made by the colonel commanding the 101st Infantry "that the morale of this brigade is low." Just two days later Sheldon was transferred to the other brigade and Bearss assumed command of the 51st.

Sometime following the armistice, Hiram Bearss gave up his brigade and headed back to the States. In December 1918, he was stationed at the Marine Barracks, Philadelphia. On 22 November 1919, he was declared permanently incapacitated as a result of the spinal wound and released from active service. It was a long time in coming but he eventually, on 16 January 1936, was promoted to brigadier general on the retired list. He died in an auto crash in Indiana on 27 August 1938 at sixty-three years of age. A fighting man still.

Other Marines in U.S. Army Formations During the War

There were a number of Marine officers in army units. There was an abundance of field grade officers, and because the two Marine brigades had little room to accept them, and many Marines wanted to get into the fight, they went to France and the army scooped them up. Many distinguished themselves, others performed at their usual high level. All in all, they were gladly received and well used.

Brigadier General John A. Lejeune is probably the most famous of those Marines. Upon arrival in France he had first joined the 64th U.S. Army Brigade of the 32d Division in July 1918. Within a few weeks he was reassigned to command of the 4th Brigade when Harbord was pushed up to division. He lasted three full days with the Marines and then went up to division command when Harbord was "promoted up" to Services of Supply in late July. Lejeune remained with the 2d Division through the battles of St. Mihiel, Blanc Mont, and the Meuse-Argonne. Lejeune did not earn many medals during his career in the U.S.

Marine Corps, but he did receive both the army and navy Distinguished Service Medal for his handling of the 2d Division.

Brigadier General Eli K. Cole was a most unfortunate man. As you have read, he was relieved of command of the 5th Marine Brigade upon arrival in France and from that point on it was all downhill until he was shipped home. But later, he did receive a Navy Cross for his pains while in command of the 1st Provisional Brigade in Haiti.

Colonel Robert H. Dunlap was placed in command of the 17th Field Artillery Regiment, 2d Division, shortly after his arrival in France. He had been an artilleryman almost from the beginning of his service in the Marine Corps. He was awarded a Navy Cross for his "exceptionally meritorious and distinguished service. . . . He displayed great ability as a leader and commander of men, and the success of his regiment was in no small measure due to his untiring energy and push, and to the offensive spirit which he displayed on many occasions."

Colonel Frederick M. Wise assumed command of the 59th Infantry of the 8th Brigade, 4th Infantry Division, in late August 1918. He was awarded both an army and navy Distinguished Service Medal for

exceptionally meritorious and conspicuous service. He commanded with skill, ability, and gallantry the 59th Infantry, from September 4, 1918, to January 23, 1919. During the St. Mihiel offensive, he personally directed the attack of his regiment against Manheulles and Fresnes-en-Woevre, which resulted in the capture of the enemy's line in this area. On September 28, 1918, his personal courage and aggressive attitude was an important factor in the successful operations of the 8th Infantry Brigade against Bois-de-Brieulles, Bois-de-Fays, Bois-de-Malaumont, Bois-de-Peut, and Bois-de-Fôret. He has rendered services of signal worthy to the American Expeditionary Forces.[22]

Major Robert E. Adams formerly commanded the 1st Battalion, 6th Marines, until 25 April 1918, whereupon he assumed command of the 3d Battalion, 38th Infantry, of the 3d Infantry Division. I have no record of his career with that unit or later.

Major Harry G. Bartlett commanded the 84th Company, 3d Battalion, 6th Marines, until April 1918. He thereupon assumed command of the 3d Battalion, 7th Infantry, of the 3d Infantry Division. I have no record of his career with that unit or later.

Major Edwin H. Brainard commanded the 1st Battalion of the 15th Field Artillery Regiment, 2d Division, with great skill and bravery. He was awarded a Navy Cross, a Silver Star citation, and a Croix de Guerre at Blanc Mont. His citation reads,

> For exceptionally meritorious and distinguished service. As Battalion Commander, 1st Battalion, 15th Regiment, Field Artillery, during the Champagne Offensive, from 2nd to the 12th of October 1918, he commanded his group in perfect manner, not hesitating to move forward through a violent artillery fire, and executing under all circumstances accurate and effective fire on the enemy position.[23]

Major Robert L. Denig commanded the 3d Battalion, 9th Infantry, and distinguished himself at the fight for Médéah Farm on 3 October 1918 during the bloody campaign to conquer Blanc Mont. For his efforts he was awarded a DSC and later a Navy Cross. His citation reads,

> For extraordinary heroism in action near Médéah Farm, France, October 3, 1918. While directing his battalion in cleaning out woods filled with enemy machine guns and snipers, himself severely wounded, he remained on duty until his mission had been accomplished.[24]

Major Edward W. Sturdevant who formerly commanded the 3d Battalion, 5th Marines, until 1 May 1918, when he was relieved by Benjamin Berry, assumed command of the 3d Battalion, 30th Infantry, 3d Division. I have no record of his career with that unit or later.

Major Charles T. Westcott formerly commanded the 3d Battalion, 5th Marines, until relieved by Sturdevant. He was the original commanding officer of the battalion; he formed it and brought the battalion over from the United States. Sometime during the summer of 1918 he was assigned to the command of the 1st Battalion, 104th Infantry, 26th Division, serving in that capacity for a month. Nothing further is known except that his son has conjectured that he probably was sent to school. It is known that he was promoted to lieutenant colonel during his tour in France.

Captain John A. Minnis was attached to the 38th Infantry, 3d Division. During an enemy drive he fearlessly reorganized a unit that had lost its officers and held his position against the enemy assault. A short time later he gallantly led fifteen men in a counterattack under heavy enemy machine-gun fire, then repulsed the enemy and captured twenty four prisoners. He was awarded a DSC and a Navy Cross.[25]

Notes

1 Lejeune was treated like he had cholera. He was just another Marine who arrived looking for a job, even though he was a brigadier general and had been assistant to the commandant.

2 A cable to Baker from Pershing on 19 June 1918.

3 Cole was evidently some kind of a threat to the command at AEF. His tenure in France was unpleasant. He had the following changes in locales: 27 December 1918 to 10 January 1919 he commanded the Replacement Depot; from 12 January to 3 February he commanded the American Embarkation Center at Le Mans; from 23 February to 4 March the forwarding camp at Le Mans; 5 March to 21 March he was busy inspecting units of the 5th Brigade. He left France on 31 March 1919.

4 See in this chapter "Marines in U.S. Army Units" for more on Butler.

5 The 2d Division already had a 5th Machine Gun Battalion.

6 Remember, almost everyone involved, the Allies and the Americans in the AEF, believed that the war would certainly continue into at least 1919. Apparently only Foch thought otherwise.

7 Somebody was working overtime at putting this group down. Or was he trying to smooth-talk his mother so she wouldn't be too frightened?

8 See Anne Cipriano Venzon, ed., *Smedley Darlington Butler: The Letters of a Leatherneck, 1898–1931* (New York: Praeger, 1992) 203–204, and Lowell Thomas, ed., *Old Gimlet Eye* (New York, Farrar & Rinehart, 1933) 243. Daniels wanted his son to serve overseas and Butler claims senior made sure the regiment got overseas.

9 Thomas, op. cit., 246.

10 Barnett, *Soldier and Sailor Too,* Chapter XXV, 2.

11 James H. Draucker, *Telling It Like It Was* (unpublished memoir). I'll bet Murphy managed to get in on the "wholesaling of booze" a few years later.

12 Bellamy, *Personal Diary.*

13 Ibid.

14 Schleswig-Holstein is actually two small states south of Denmark, in northern Germany. Both had been taken from the Danes in 1864 by a powerful Austro-Prussian army. The problem was should a defeated Germany be made to disgorge a previous conquest? On 20 February 1920, Schleswig elected to go back with Denmark while Holstein decided to stay with Germany.

15 Draucker, *Telling It Like It Was.*

16 Years later, when the Bonus Army was encamped in the outskirts of Washington, D.C., Butler came to speak to the men who were there. Many, if not all, remembered him and his care of the troops at Camp Pontanezan. They listened to him and obeyed his dictate to continue acting like soldiers. Essentially, he told them not to lose their discipline so as to give the government a reason to close them down. They didn't but the army did, led by Douglas MacArthur.

17 Thomas, op. cit., 248.

18 Much more on this significant period in Butler's life has been captured in his letters home to his family. See Venzon, op. cit. In addition more information in another, highly significant biography by Hans Schmidt, *Maverick Ma-*

rine: General Smedley D. Butler and the Contradictions of American History (Lexington, KY: University Press of Kentucky, 1987).

19 The author of the article "'Hiking Hiram Bearss' Burnished Corps Wartime Image," Vern McLean, which appeared in *Fortitudine* XXIII, No. 1 (Summer 1993), graciously allowed me to use some of his careful research for this section. I am also indebted to the unit history of the 102d Infantry for a description of Bearss as the soldiers of that regiment saw him.

20 Daniel W. Strickland, *Connecticut Fights: The Story of the 102nd Regiment* (New Haven: prvt prt., 1933), 222 passim.

21 Ibid, 224.

22 G. B. Clark, ed., *Major Awards to U.S. Marines in World War One* (Pike, NH: The Brass Hat, 1992)

23 Ibid.

24 Ibid.

25 I'm not sure what his role with the 38th Infantry was, but possibly he was an "extra" Marine officer who had been assigned to the regiment as liaison? After the war he transferred to Marine air, probably because he believed it was safer, and was killed in a "power dive" at or near Gettysburg in the 1920s.

Conclusion

*That was a hard-fought battle from which no man
returned to tell the tale.*

—Irish proverb

The United States entered this war totally unprepared for what their military forces would face. Reasons given for the death and maiming of so many thousands of American youth were and are so inadequate that they would seem, were they not so absurd, treasonous. Study of the inane activities of the president, the majority of the Congress, and his cabinet is beyond the scope of this volume. Therefore we will concentrate our venom only upon the leadership of the officers to whom the Marines were directly subjected, from division downward, with emphasis upon brigade and regiment.

The following critique will be isolated by events. The massacre at Belleau Wood will come first and be the longest diatribe, with the other engagements following in chronological order. Only the four most important and bloody battles will be considered.

Belleau Wood

This portion will consider the entire action taken by the 4th Marine Brigade in the Château-Thierry Sector. It has been collectively labeled "The Battle for Belleau Wood." As we know, the action took place in a much wider area than just in and around the woods themselves. It was directed by a man who had minimal experience in modern war, as did his followers. Harbord had been a soldier for many years, having enlisted in the army in 1889. He was commissioned three years later as a 2d lieutenant of cavalry and in 1917, when the war began, he was a major. Most of his service, ten years, had been in the insular service constabulary in the Philippines. He was an excellent administrator, as evidenced by his stint as Pershing's chief of staff and later as director of the unmanageable Services of Supply. As every military man of any intellect realized, to improve one's stature (read rank) one had to command a fighting force in the war. This war was the only one Harbord would ever have, so he requested command of an appropriate unit. He was a colonel but was soon to be promoted to brigadier; consequently he required a brigade. Pershing, always true and loyal to his friends, soon found Harbord a brigade and a good one at that.

Brigadier General Charles A. Doyen, USMC, who had brought the 5th Marines to France and in turn commanded both the division for a short period and the 4th Brigade, was found to be physically unfit and therefore was relieved. How the brigade would have fared under his tutelage can only be a matter of conjecture. But, contrary to many popular reports, Harbord came in under a cloud and it took some great effort on his part to shed that disability.[1] He, by careful maneuvering and dispensing of "good will," soon had the support of most every senior officer in the brigade. He was a fine officer, a decent man, and later proved his abilities—as a noncombatant administrator.

Harbord's first engagement with the enemy, as leader of the 4th Brigade, came in June 1918, at the sector assigned to the brigade by division staff. For the first few days he, like most everyone else, was finding his way. He received several orders from the French, through General Bundy's headquarters, directing him to have his brigade move forward with a planned French advance on the morning of 6 June. The first target was Hill 142. That was a badly organized battle. Turrill's battalion had been in a reserve position with two of its companies assigned to aid Wise's 2/5, which was having a rough time at Les Mares Farm. The two companies weren't released in time and Turrill had to go in with two companies and a few machine guns, though more than one company of guns had been assigned to the attack.

What could Harbord have done about that? He could have insured that four companies, no matter where he took them from, plus an adequate number of machine guns, were assigned on time. Lacking that, he failed to provide his men with a modicum of protection and chance to succeed. In any event they did succeed, but not through any assistance from him or his staff. Turrill's unit was badly handled by the enemy, but through their inordinate courage they managed to take the ground and hold it.

Meanwhile Harbord was directing battalions and companies individually, bypassing his middle commanders in almost every instance. He would continue this breach of appropriate conduct for the entire month of June. Why Neville and Catlin/Lee tolerated this, I cannot find written anywhere. It must have been an uncomfortable experience for them. I also fault them for allowing it to continue. Perhaps they were unaware of their rights and also their obligations to their units.

A battalion was badly beaten up in the morning hours, yet Harbord planned another very extensive operation for the afternoon. He wanted the woods taken and assigned two battalions to that attack for 1700 hours that afternoon. Belleau Wood had been evacuated by the French several days before, and Harbord was told by them that there were no Germans there then. He accepted this without further confirmation, but at least three days had elapsed since that information was provided. Consequently, no reconnaissance of the target area was performed. Harbord later remarked that it was probably a mistake and blamed it upon "lack of experience." Further, he planned no artillery bombardment so as "not to warn the enemy that the Marines were coming." The Germans had to have been blind if they couldn't see the various maneuvers going on before them, since it was mostly in the open. He not only had no idea of what he was letting the Marines in for, he also planned further advances for that day when "Belleau Wood was taken." Taking it was a long time coming and most likely wouldn't have taken so long if the early efforts hadn't been so badly bungled. The third plan was never brought into fruition. By the end of that day, 6 June 1918, Harbord had managed to send three full battalions of Marines into a firestorm. Another battalion, 2/6, was split up and half also was sent into the cauldron. The remnants of the latter were successful in taking the most important feature on the entire field, Bouresches. They were all so badly chopped up, however, that it would be many replacements later before any of them would be able to fully perform their duties. On that one day he had managed to literally destroy four battalions of the six he had. In addition, those attacks that day cost the U.S. Marine Corps more losses than in its entire previous 143 years of existence.

It appears, now, that Harbord had no idea how badly his Marines had fared that day because he was ready, willing, and able to send more Marines into that hellhole in his third plan. It would be several days before another attack was launched, that by Hughes and 1/6, but it would go nowhere, certainly nowhere near what Harbord's orders proclaimed it should. It took him days to finally figure out that Hughes was stalled, and not far from where he began his attack. In the meantime Harbord ordered 2/5 to attack the woods several days after the Hughes fiasco.

The next two attacks were noteworthy because neither battalion commander seemed to know what he was supposed to be doing or where he was located. Harbord didn't realize this, because neither he nor his aides went anywhere near the fighting front and he seemed to have believed everything he heard.

Harbord did manage to have the Marines relieved for at least a few days, but when they came back they were forced to retake ground that they'd taken in the first fifteen days. I'm not faulting the 7th Infantry. They were complete babes in the woods. Yet Harbord demanded from them what blooded Marines had failed to produce. Fortunately, the officers and men of the 7th had enough sense not to press their luck too hard. As a result, many survived and went on to bigger things.

It was a long period before Harbord made efforts to have his brigade relieved. They were in combat for almost the entire fifteen days it took before he actually obtained their relief. In that war three or four days in action was the accepted norm. When they were finally relieved, they received their first real meal since 1 June. How those men managed to continue their exertions in that hot weather for that long without regular feeding or sleeping is beyond me. They truly were iron men.

It is apparent that Harbord was out of his league. That was the minors, and this was a major war and the big kids were always at bat. Because of his "great success," he was soon promoted to the command of the 2d Division. The former division commander, Omar Bundy, was apparently as incompetent as Harbord. He was "promoted" to command a paper corps, making way for Harbord to command the division.

The charges against Harbord do not automatically excuse the senior Marine officers. I believe that Neville, the most senior Marine present, was guilty of malfeasance for allowing the continued destruction of his Marines. Neville should have demanded that Harbord stop using the brigade as a battering ram. Catlin wasn't around long enough and Lee was easy to "dispose" of, but Neville had the rank and position to have done something to alter the program of daily slaughter.

In addition to this, although Neville was at least nominally in command of his regiment, he was not to be seen by the troops during the battle. His command post was far behind the lines (I've been there), and according to divisional records he appears to have remained there the entire month. Fortunately, for the brigade and regiment, his assistant, Lt. Col. Logan Feland, was everywhere and generally directed the regiment by being where they were when he was needed. Feland proved his excellence when he commanded the 5th Marines. Recently one Marine historian has charged Neville with being a "ticket puncher." My sentiments entirely.

By virtue of being there, Lee was Catlin's replacement. His record in the Corps, prior to 6 June 1918, was completely undistinguished. Lee had been in command of the Marine Barracks, Philadelphia Navy Yard, in 1916 and in 1920 was back in the same post. He was the author of an article that appeared in the *Gazette* in December 1916, describing how to command small detachments of Marines in the field. "Keep 'em close to you so they can hear your commands on a noisy battlefield," or words to that effect. This in the days when reports of artillery and machine-gun successes were filtering back to the United States from the battlefields in Europe. But one word in his favor: He tried. Appropriately, he was awarded both an army and navy Distinguished Service Medal for assuming command of the regiment on that fateful day, but then, so was Neville.

I can find fault with three of the battalion commanders. Ben Berry formed up his battalion in full view of the enemy, then led his men across a wide-open expanse of wheat fields. Down from one hill across a road and into the maws of a veritable jungle. And he did it according to rules and a formation that were outdated seventy-five years before. I'm not sure why he did that except that it was based upon outdated concepts and, I guess, seemed like the thing to do. He certainly paid, personally, for that performance, but so did many other Marines with him.

Wise duplicated Berry's mistake and then made all kinds of excuses to prove that it never happened. His major fault was in refusing to follow Harbord's directives, which in this case were much better than what he and his company commanders came up with. He seemed to be far beyond his capacity at Belleau Wood but somehow learned enough to later lead an army regiment and then a brigade successfully.

Did Wise try to follow Harbord's directive in Field Order No. 4, or perhaps even the elusive message that he said he received about midnight?[2] Unluckily, when his battalion moved out, they went in the wrong direction—or were they even trying to follow Harbord's "revised order"? Most likely, neither Dunbeck nor Williams could see their objective and consequently lost their direction, probably because of the mist then prevailing. All four company commanders were longtime professionals, so when Wise approached the remaining three at the eastern end of the woods, they all indicated that they believed they were looking out at the north end rather than the east end, and each attested to that fact. They said that they thought that they were looking at the town of Torcy to their left and Belleau to their right. Wise, not having any better idea, was happy with that answer. If he believed it, he therefore accepted it without question. It is quite obvious, after the fact, that all of them, in-

cluding Wise, were confused, or were confusing the story. As we now
know, it was Belleau on the left and Bouresches on the right. When
Mathews reported his conversation with De Carre, no one, especially
Wise, took it seriously. That leaves one with the impression that Wise
surmised the truth but didn't want to be wrong. Years afterward Wise
provided readers with many conflicting statements, none of which
cleared up the many questions still extant today. It seems that he was
engaged in a not very successful "cover-up." Perhaps he was attempting,
as well, to cover for the three younger officers who were also culpable,
but not totally responsible, for those blunders.

Hughes was the enigma of the lot. While Wise did strike, continually,
at the enemy in the woods, Hughes just sat. He was nicknamed "Johnny
the Hard." That would lead one to assume that he, above all, would be
a hard driver. In his one attack, for which his battalion was well rested,
he failed utterly to do any more than attain his predecessor's old positions while being faced with minimal opposition. He failed to attain his
objective by a great degree but notified his brigade command that he
had. That blunder left another battalion at the mercy of its enemies. As
a longtime combatant one would assume that he could easily tell that
he was nowhere near his target, yet he failed completely to realize that.
He miscarried to such an extent that he was greatly responsible for the
massive casualties to Wise's battalion.

Thomason wrote, "The action of 1/6 during 11 June is obscure . . .
[and] the burden of maintaining liaison was laid on 2/5." Hughes either thought he was on the "X-line"[3] or had so much trouble to his front,
he decided to just stay where he was. It would seem that he should have
realized that he had not advanced very far into the woods. Certainly not
to the required "X-line," which was more than a half mile from the
southern edge. This was one of two really serious problems. Had 1/6
been on the X-line, 2/5 would have hit the woods at their position rather
than at the enemy's. Consequently there would only have been the eternal problem of throwing the Boche out of the northern part of the
woods. Wise could have launched an attack northward with support and
possibly some degree of success. Hughes's orders were to support Wise
"when he reached his objective." That, according to Field Order No. 4,
would have been when 2/5 had reached the northeastern tip of Belleau
Wood. Hughes was nowhere near the entry position in Wise's orders but,
through Sergeant Thomas, he had ordered Overton to support Wise as
soon as possible. [When he entered the woods,] Hughes must have seen

Wise's mistakes as they unfolded. Why didn't he notify him or attempt to provide serious support?

Hughes seems to have escaped censure in this affair.[4] There was no doubt, according to various research sources, that Hughes and Wise were not exactly on the best of terms, and during the period and later, Macon Overton was extremely critical of Wise. Thomason came to the conclusion that, when comparing the losses for 1/6 against 2/5, the numbers "do not indicate heavy action." Hughes's loss was one officer and forty-six men, of whom twenty-four were from Overton's company. There should be no question as to which battalion was more heavily engaged that day and later.

I believe that Hughes was well aware of his failure. So much so that when he was literally ordered to fall back out of his gas-doused area he refused, saying something like "I'm here and here I'll stay." I believe he was trying to make up for his gross errors and in so doing he paid for it, by being forced to an early retirement because of gas-related lung disease. It seems to me that the men and junior officers saved the day by their fortitude and endurance.

Soissons

The attack at Soissons has been long held up as the beginning of the end of the war. That may be so, but I'm not exactly sure why. The major attack on 18 July was performed by three divisions: the 1st U.S. Division, the French Moroccan Division, and the 2d U.S. Division, north to south in that order. On the first day the Germans were caught somewhat unprepared and all three divisions, but especially the 2d, were quite successful in taking ground, but all the while taking heavy casualties. On the 2d Division front, three regiments launched the assault: the 5th Marines on the left, the 9th Infantry in the center, and the 23d Infantry on the division right boundary. The 6th Marines were in division reserve. The losses of all three regiments were hideous but they gained about six miles in their advance that day. The following day the division's front was composed entirely of the 6th Marines—one regiment to continue the advance where three were required on the day before when the enemy was nearly completely surprised. But on 19 July the Boche were well prepared. The 6th Marines were cut in half and stopped within a few hundred yards from where they had started. Because of the losses on the 18th and 19th of July, the division's infantry regiments were exhausted and had to be pulled out of the line the following day. Both the other two divisions remained and continued the attack for several more days. Neither had kept up with the 2d and it would be another two days before either attained the same distance forward. Obviously, while their losses were also heavy, they weren't as badly hurt as was the 2d Division.

Why was the 2d Division in such bad shape? Why had all four infantry regiments suffered such extensive casualties to the degree that the division was unable to continue for another day? I'm not quite sure what experiences either the 1st Division or the French colonials had before the attack. I do know that the 1st Division was moved to the area about a week prior to the starting date. Therefore, they started out fresher than did the harried 2d Division. The 2d Division had barely been out of the lines two weeks when they were rushed northward in a manner that left most of the men exhausted before they even got to their bivouac. So poorly handled was the transfer that the division machine guns didn't appear until late on 18 July, too late to help the attack that day. Like the 6th Marines, they, too, were overwhelmed on the following day.

Any plans necessary for the attack were prepared by people other than those in the division. Harbord who had recently been placed in command, had been on special leave and barely returned in time to make the trip to Soissons. When he arrived, the division was not really under his control. He later complained about how junior French officers were ordering around senior officers of the 2d with little if any explanation of what was happening. Harbord allowed his division to be thrust into a major assault when they were ill prepared for anything other than complete rest. Then the 5th Marines were forced to move from their bivouac to their jump-off point under the most distressful conditions any man could be expected to tolerate. They were made to double-time in order to make their entry on time, and had a long day's work before them before they could catch their breath. Many never did.

Why three regiments made the attack on one day and then one regiment was expected to be successful the following day is the real question. Harbord admitted that he questioned that point himself but did nothing to correct it. Actually, there was no way it could be corrected because he didn't seem to be in command. Additionally, the three regiments were badly battered, especially the 9th Infantry, and would not under any normal circumstances have been able to support anyone. That, I see, is the main trouble with Harbord in command. He allowed the Marine Brigade to be destroyed at Belleau Wood and then did the same thing to the division at Soissons. If following Soissons he had been promoted to a corps he might have done the same with it. He was promoted, by his pal Pershing, to command the errant Services of Supply, shortly after Soissons.

Feland and Lee did as well as could be expected under the circumstances, but they had little, if any, control. The battalion commanders performed reasonably well but some of the company commanders went astray. Neither orders nor maps had been dispensed downward, resulting in many units going wide of their assigned objectives. A major reason for the dispersal was the "dog-leg" change in the division's boundaries, just as it came out of the woods. This was especially true of the 55th and 17th Companies and 1/9, all of which were wide of their mark on 18 July. This caused some confusion and consternation, as did the actions of Maj. Ralph Keyser that night in his leadership of 2/5. How he managed to avoid instant relief or prosecution or both for leaving his position on the 9th Infantry's left flank, I'll never know.

The following day was just plain murder. One regiment, late in arriving not through any fault of its members, started out in full daylight against a now well-prepared enemy. The barrage was long gone and had only served to warn the Boche that someone was coming. And they came. Nearly complete destruction was to be their reward. Barely making a half mile or so, the regiment just died. They continued taking a pounding all day and into the night. Harbord sent them a hearty "well done."

Blanc Mont

I became especially interested in this operation while perusing General Order No. 88, AEF, which gave brief citations, many of which seemed to be for one day, 4 October 1918. And each entry told pretty much the same story: "——— distinguished himself for preventing a retreat of certain elements . . . disorganized and demoralized by severe losses, etc." There were a number of awards and the citations weren't always exactly the same but enough were to pique my interest. My next motivation was the question of why, in a 1922 issue of the *Marine Corps Gazette*, the articles on Blanc Mont stopped, abruptly, within the article, never to be continued by the *Gazette* or, apparently, by McClellan the author. The published articles covered the first and second days of October, when not much of substance happened, but just had one paragraph about the third day. Then the articles ceased, never more to appear, although cited "to be continued." The balance of 3 October, the bloody part of that day, and the 4th day of October, the worst day of the war for

the 5th Marines, were avoided entirely. So were the following four or
five days that the 6th Marines continued bleeding around St. Étienne.
For what appear to be similar reasons, the entire Meuse-Argonne portion of that war was never published either. McClellan did a fine job with
all the rest of the events relating to the 4th Brigade and to a certain extent all other Marine activities during the war, until Blanc Mont. That
was the end of the McClellan war series in the *Gazette.*

What happened? I'm sure that no one is alive today privy to the facts
of the case, but one can put two and two together. McClellan was the
historian of the Corps. He had been appointed by the commandant,
Maj. Gen. John A. Lejeune. Lejeune commanded the division at Blanc
Mont and during the Meuse River campaign. He made a rousing speech
at some later date, one which has been constantly referred to, about the
honor that befell any man who had served with the 2d Division at Blanc
Mont. (See following.)

My theory is that "the less said the better." Lejeune's protestations
about the glory of being at Blanc Mont aside, the battle found him far
behind the lines, as a division commander should be, though he should
perhaps not be quite that far. In fact Pershing's staff criticized several
division commanders for being too far behind the lines during the
Meuse-Argonne campaign. It was Lejeune's battle, the first that he
helped plan and one in which the 4th Brigade and the entire division
took tremendous losses. Although he didn't mind basking in the glory
of the push over at St. Mihiel, which had been the work of AEF Headquarters staff officers, he didn't want to take the heat about the Blanc
Mont debacle. Therefore, ignore it and make sure all Marines, then and
later, ignore it. There weren't many Marines left that had been on the
ridge anyway. I wonder what those who were thought about the "glory"
of being shot to pieces with no flank support or protection? Elton E.
Mackin gave the "Box," as he called it, plenty of attention.[5] He didn't
like it much, and neither did his buddies. The enlisted men weren't
alone in their grievances.

What could Lejeune have done to have prevented the stupefying casualties? Possibly not much after he allowed himself to be hoaxed by the
French commander of the 4th Army. But he should at least have demanded that the French forces keep liaison with the flanks of both his
infantry brigades or have threatened to cancel the advance as soon as
they didn't. That was, in my opinion, his greatest crime. In his memoir,

published more than ten years later, he clearly enunciates that he was satisfied with the performance of the French forces, even though he supposedly sent Pershing's Headquarters an "angry telegram . . . he would resign his commission rather than fight with French liaison again."[6] But in his official records he did praise the French forces to a certain degree and that earned him a coveted Commander of the Legion of Honor award from the French government.[7]

The semiofficial history of the 5th Marines, produced by the regiment and dated 15 February 1919, gives the following description of the day:

> October 4th was the bitterest single day of fighting that the 5th Regiment experienced during the whole war. The advance that day was over difficult terrain in the face of the densest barrage of shell and machine gun fire that the Marines ever had to face. The left flank was continually exposed and the advancing waves were exposed to a merciless enfilading fire. Our division commander [Lejeune] was right when he said that "to be able to say when the war is finished, 'I belonged to the 2nd Division, I fought with it at the Battle of Blanc Mont Ridge, will be the highest honor that can come to any man.'"

And that was it. June 6, 1918, the bloodiest day at Belleau Wood, was given three full, closely typed pages; Soissons got three-and-a-half pages even though the 5th Marines casualties on the 18th were, compared to those of the 6th on the 19th, minimal. St. Mihiel, a cakewalk for the 5th Marines, received a half page, and the admission that the regiment had a virtual rest period, with a rather modest loss of twenty-three enlisted men and no officers, while following the gallant 9th Infantry into battle. Why only one paragraph for Blanc Mont?

Major General Omar Bundy was relieved of command of the 2d Division right after the debacle at Belleau Wood by being "promoted" upstairs to a paper corps. Harbord was his replacement, but he, too, was "elevated" after the catastrophe at Soissons. He was basically a fine administrative officer who didn't do very well as a commander of field troops. Why didn't that happen to Lejeune? Who now knows why? Perhaps it was because Pershing didn't want any more pressure from George Barnett, the Marine Corps commandant. There was no other senior Marine in France to take over command of the "Marine Division," and to replace a Marine with an army officer would have caused more trouble than Pershing was willing to absorb. At least that is my impression.

Neville was in command of the 4th Brigade and was way back, but not nearly as far back as Lejeune. The official reports from the more junior levels indicate, in messages, a rather cool attitude toward the brigade and division leadership. Even so steady an officer as Logan Feland had to be told by an equally steady George Hamilton that his 5th Marines were finished. The strong suit was that Feland knew when to quit. Neville never seemed to realize that his brigade was in bad shape. Neither did Lejeune. Staying in shelters doesn't give one a clear picture of the happenings outside, or the suffering of the exposed. Lejeune even had the gall to question the reliability of his officers' reports of casualty numbers. To me, this was another example of the crass behavior of men who send other men into battle and never seem to know what is happening to them. Nor did they seem to care.

Meuse-Argonne

In a way this was the best carried out of all the battles of the 4th Brigade, perhaps because it was the final battle. Planning was at a minimum, as was direction from the top. Most everything was delegated to regimental and battalion level, down where, by this stage of the war, command was a somewhat stronger suit. For the entire division, the first few days were almost another St. Mihiel. It wasn't until the division got close to the Meuse River that unpleasant people made unpleasant resolutions. That was the time when those people who were in total control knew for sure, or at least could guess, that the war was nearly over. Yet, that was when the decision was made to plunge forward in the last day or so to gain as much ground as possible, for a stronger negotiating position, they said. Division command wasn't even a player in this decision. It came from on high. Therefore no blame should be laid upon anyone in the division.

As we have already seen, the 5th Marines, especially 1/5, were, to use the tasteless Haig idiom, "wasted." I know that the same thing happened to the Canadians and most likely to others as well. The same would have happened to the 6th Marines if Shuler had not made the humane decision to "stand pat" when it was obvious that trying to cross that river in full view of the enemy was tantamount to a slaughter. The final consequences, the acceptance by the Germans of the armistice terms, made the crossing of the Meuse River immaterial in the short or long run. Only the casualties and their loved ones really cared. So do I.

Opinion

The usual American reduction in military and naval services after every war would, after the end of WWI, severely trim the sails of all the services. All but the dullest professional military man realized that the sails would never again be unfurled as before. Every professional worth his salt now knew that war was no longer the business of amateurs. The old days would soon be gone forever. No longer would a man be able to get by on his courage alone. From now on higher rank would be for the educated and trained. Fortunately, each branch had a sufficient stock of intelligent individuals who could start planning for the future.

Fortunately for the Marine Corps, it had its intellectuals as well. It was also helped in having, at the right time, a commandant who believed explicitly in education for all Marines. John Lejeune would become the best commandant the Marine Corps ever had. Some of his first administrative actions would be to initiate various educational programs. Even before the United States went to war, some Marines had been busily engaged in "postwar" planning. The concept of an "Advanced Base Force" was just moved a bit further ahead. As the professional navy thinkers planned for a future war with another sea power, Marines were right with them. Where the navy went, the Marines wouldn't be far behind. Plainly ahead was war with Japan. Members of the American naval service were just waiting for *"Der Tag,"* just as German naval officers had toasted a future war with Britain.[8]

Japan had come out of the World War with a maximum of territorial gain and minimal expense. She now controlled the many islands that had formerly belonged to Imperial Germany. The possession of these islands placed a vibrant Japan astride much of the northern Pacific approaches to the continent of Asia and especially of the Philippines. Although, nominally, Japan agreed to curtail building big ships, it was her plan to make everything nice and even by reneging on various treaties. And she did. By the late 1930s, Japan's navy was a serious threat to the U.S. Navy Pacific fleet.

But meanwhile the planners in the Corps knew that the navy would have to cross the Pacific and that bases would have to be taken. To take some bases—many, in fact—would require assaults from the sea. That would force Marine and navy leaders to learn how to successfully make amphibious landings and develop the appropriate equipment for the purpose. During the 1920s the navy/Marine team, not always in harmony, tried and failed in many exercises to determine "how to." Sometimes the mistakes were easy to discern and some were corrected the next time around. Often the same problems continued. Equipment development was an expensive and frequently discouraging business. But eventually, by the time the 1930s came along, they were starting to get on the right track. A former 4th Brigade major of Marines, Holland McT. Smith, was the man, more than many other, who persevered. By 1939–40, with help from some brilliant younger officers, the basic, still unproven plans had coalesced. Modifications were required but eventually proved correct. The ideas just went together until they finally got it right. Even those that appeared correct were occasionally modified during the war when it became evident that changes were required.

When we went to war with Japan, the Marine Corps was able to provide more than half a million well-trained men, many commanded by veterans of the First World War. Then, with the men and ships of the U.S. Navy to propel them across the largest ocean in the world, they overcame a fierce opponent in every engagement, no matter how stubborn the defense. That not only took courage and discipline, of which there was plenty, but superb training, planning, and leadership. The experience of the surviving officers and men of the 4th and 5th Marine Brigades provided the base upon which to expand from two brigades to six combat divisions. Because of its four war experiences, the Corps today is a powerful organization ready to fully support the army and navy in any international confrontation.

Notes

1 There was even a minor effort toward creating a mutiny. Several of the officers, a couple of majors and some captains, were involved and several were selected for courts-martial. Nothing ever came of it and eventually most members of the brigade came to accept the intrusion. Several went so far as to "play up" to Harbord, possibly to further their careers or. . . ?

2 Remember, he is backed up by Mathews and Cooke in having received that message, which presumably "changed" the direction of Field Order No. 4. But it seems as though Wise, many years later, was making attempts to escape the obvious. Even his battalion report reflected Field Order No. 4 as the orders he followed, though most assuredly not as they were spelled out. Somebody screwed up.

3 The line Hughes was on, according to Thomason from "official records," has been reckoned as 261.3 instead of 261.7.

4 Hughes was awarded a Navy Cross long after the war but it wasn't based upon the usual DSC, because there wasn't one.

5 Mackin, *Suddenly We Didn't Want to Die*, 187–188.

6 Stallings, *The Doughboys*, 285. I have never seen another reference to this statement, looking in vain in Pershing's own memoir, Lejeune's, and in Bartlett's recent biography of Lejeune.

7 Merrill L. Bartlett, *Lejeune: A Marine's Life 1867–1942* (Columbia, SC: University of South Carolina Press, 1991), 89.

8 I remember a situation in 1933 that lends support to my theory. My family was visiting Los Angeles that summer. My father knew a chief boatswain serving aboard the USS *Arizona*, which was then, as I remember, in port at Long Beach. Dad and I were invited aboard the ship and had dinner in the chief's mess. They all seemed very anxious for the "war to begin." With Japan, of course. That shocked my civilian father no end. He never forgot it, in fact. Neither have I.

Appendices

APPENDIX A

The Second Division (Regular)
Structure of the 2d Division and officers commanding the
division, brigade, regiments, and battalions

Brig. Gen. Charles A. Doyen, USMC
Maj. Gen. Omar Bundy, USA
Maj. Gen. James A. Harbord, USA
Maj. Gen. John A. Lejeune, USMC
Maj. Gen. Wendell C. Neville, USMC

The 2d Division when complete consisted of 979 officers and 27,080
men. It included:

Two infantry brigades and one brigade of artillery.

One regiment of engineers of two battalions.

One battery of trench mortars; one machine-gun battalion; one field
signal battalion; and a certain number of supply and train services.

The infantry was larger, numerically, than any other allied or German
unit of similar composition but the division was limited in artillery; i.e.,
caliber sizes, numbers of guns, etc.

The 4th Marine Brigade
(formed 23 October 1917, in France)

Brig. Gen. Charles A. Doyen, USMC
Brig. Gen. James A. Harbord, USA
Brig. Gen. Wendell C. Neville, USMC
Brig. Gen. John A. Lejeune, USMC
Brig. Gen. Wendell C. Neville, USMC

The 4th Brigade was composed of two regiments of infantry, the 5th
and 6th, and one battalion, the 6th, of machine guns. An infantry
brigade was composed of 246 officers and 8,169 men. That figure included a staff of four officers and twenty men, a machine-gun battalion

of four companies, and two infantry regiments. The actual numbers were closer to 9,000 effectives, if at full complement, which was not very frequently the case.

The infantry regiment was usually commanded by a colonel assisted by a lieutenant colonel and was composed of three battalions of infantry, one company of machine guns, and one company each of headquarters and supply. Total of 112 officers and 3,720 men.

An infantry battalion consisted of four companies with twenty-six officers and 1,058 men. It was usually commanded by a major with another major or captain assisting. Occasionally a lieutenant colonel would command, until a regiment was found for him.

Finally, the infantry company was composed of six officers and 250 men each. In addition, each company had a headquarters detachment of eighteen men. A captain was in command assisted by another captain, a first lieutenant, or even a second lieutenant, after a battle. The company commander was most always called "Skipper." This was, and may still be, a term used solely in the U.S. Marine Corps. During the war, in several instances, U.S. Army officers assumed command of Marine companies when they were the senior officer present. They were also addressed as "Skipper." Lieutenants were addressed as "Mister."

An infantry headquarters company usually consisted of eight officers and 336 men distributed among five platoons: i.e., one regimental and battalion headquarters platoon, which included the band; one platoon of telephonists and signalers (they were occasionally U.S. Army enlisted men); one platoon of sappers-bombardiers; one platoon of pioneers, and one platoon with three 3.7mm guns, frequently identified as "one-pounders."

The regimental machine-gun company was composed of 6 officers and 172 men, in three platoons of four guns, with four replacement guns.

In the beginning, the American units were issued French automatic rifles, the Chauchat, which were later replaced, but not until near or after the end of the war, with Browning automatic rifles. The first machine guns used were primarily the French Hotchkiss, an essentially good gun, but heavier than the Browning water-cooled gun by fifteen pounds, and, except that the latter required water for a coolant, the Browning was a better all-around weapon. No 2d Division machine-gun units had that weapon, at least while the war was being fought. Many American units at first used the British Enfield rifle, modified for American cartridges, but Marines, and probably the 9th and 23d Infantry, used the Springfield '03 from the beginning. The Marines gave up their Lewis guns, expecting to receive American machine guns in France, but the Chauchat was their primary issue for many months after arrival. The Lewis was a much better weapon than the Chauchat but utilized American ammunition, the same as used with the Springfield and Enfield rifles, and that would have made the supplying of ammunition to the brigade somewhat easier. Later the Chauchat was rechambered for 30.06 ammunition, which conversion, at first, was real bad news. It was soon upgraded and performed reasonably well afterward.

The 5th Marines (Regiment)
(formed at Philadelphia, 7 June 1917)

Col. Charles A. Doyen.[1]
Maj. Frederick M. Wise Jr.[2]
Lt. Col. Hiram Bearss[3]
Col. Wendell C. Neville[4]
Lt. Col. Logan Feland[5]

Doyen, the first officer to command the newly formed regiment, was later to command the Marine brigade and subsequently the newly formed 2d Division, until he was relieved by Maj. Gen. Omar Bundy, USA. Doyen then reverted to command the 4th Marine Brigade until relieved by Brig. Gen. James A. Harbord, USA, in May 1918.

1st Battalion, 5th Marines
(formed at Quantico, VA, 15 May 1917)

Maj. Julius S. Turrill, May 1917–23 September 1917[6]
Lt. Col. Logan Feland, 24 September 1917–24 October 1917
Capt. George W. Hamilton, 25 October 1917–18 January 1918[7]
Maj. Edward A. Green, 19 January 1918–12 March 1918
Maj. Julius S. Turrill, 13 March 1918–19 August 1918
Capt. Raymond S. Dirksen, 20 August 1918–28 August 1918
Lt. Col. James O'Leary, 29 August 1918–19 September 1918
Maj. George W. Hamilton, 20 September 1918–14 December 1918
Capt. LerRoy P. Hunt, 15 December 1918–15 January 1919[8]
Maj. George W. Hamilton, 16 January 1919–20 March 1919
Maj. LeRoy P. Hunt, 21 March 1919–13 August 1919

2d Battalion, 5th Marines
(formed at Philadelphia, 30 May 1917)

Maj. Frederick M. Wise Jr., 1 June 1917–23 June 1918
Maj. Ralph S. Keyser, 24 June 1918–25 July 1918[9]
Lt. Col. Frederick M. Wise Jr., 26 July 1918–29 August 1918
Maj. Robert E. Messersmith, 30 August 1918–October 1918[10]
Capt. Charley Dunbeck, October, 1918–sometime postwar.[11]

3d Battalion, 5th Marines
(formed at Philadelphia, 30 May 1917)

Maj. Charles T. Westcott, 30 May 1917–25 March 1918
Maj. Edward Sturdevant, 26 March 1918–30 April 1918
Maj. Benjamin S. Berry, 1 May 1918–8 June 1918[12]
Capt. Henry Larsen, 8/9 June
Maj. Maurice Shearer, 9 June 1918–September, 1918
Maj. Henry Larsen, September, 1918–sometime postwar

The 6th Marines (Regiment)
(formed at Quantico, VA, 1 August 1917)

Col. Albertus W. Catlin, 26 July 1917–6 June 1918[13]
Lt. Col. Harry Lee, 7 June 1918–August 1919[14]

1st Battalion
(formed at Quantico, 1 August 1917)

Maj. John A. Hughes, 1 August 1917–14 October 1917
Capt. Robert E. Adams, 15 October 1917–25 April 1918
Maj. Maurice Shearer, 26 April 1918–8 June 1918[15]
Maj. John A. Hughes, 9 June 1918–14 June 1918[16]
Maj. Franklin B. Garrett, 15 June 1918–end of June
Maj. John A. Hughes, 16 July 1918–
Maj. Frederick A. Barker, August 1918–sometime postwar[17]

2d Battalion
(formed at Quantico, 1 August 1917)

Maj. Thomas Holcomb, 1 August 1917–16 August 1918[18]
Majs. Robert Denig and Pere Wilmer, during 19 July 1918?[19]
Maj. Robert E. Messersmith, 17 August 1918–29 August 1918
Maj. Ernest C. Williams 30 August 1918–sometime postwar[20]

3d Battalion
(formed at Quantico, 1 August 1917)

Maj. Berton W. Sibley, 1 August 1917–18 September 1918[21]
Maj. George K. Shuler, 19 September 1918–sometime postwar[22]

6th Machine-Gun Battalion
(formed at Quantico, 17 August 1917)

Capt. Edward B. Cole, 17 August 1917–10 June 1918[23]
Capt. Harlan E. Major, 10 June 1918–11 June 1918[24]
Capt. George H. Osterhout, 11 June 1918–20 June 1918[25]
Maj. Littleton W. T. Waller Jr., 20 June 1918–24 October 1918[26]
Maj. Matthew H. Kingman, 25 October 1918–(?)[27]

APPENDIX B

The 2d Division fought in six major, and several minor, battles during the Great War. The technical titles of each are sometimes debated, even at this late date. The titles used by Major Edwin McClellan, USMC, in his reference work *United States Marine Corps in the World War* describes their services very well.

Toulon Sector, Verdun: 15 March–13 May 1918.
Aisne Defensive, Château-Thierry Sector: 31 May–5 June 1918
Château-Thierry Sector: 6 June–9 July 1918. (The capture of Hill 142, Bouresches, and Belleau Wood. McClellan points out that the above-listed operations "were held to be local engagements rather than a major operation. He adds, "The 2d Division suffered about 9,000 casualties in the Chateau-Thierry sector." (More than half of which were from the 4th Brigade, I might add.) Local engagement, hell! In reality the brigade suffered nearly 5,000 casualties during the period 31 May till 9

July, and that comes from his own history, *The United States Marine Corps in the World War.* Washington, D.C.: U.S. Government Printing Office, 1920.

Aisne-Marne Offensive: 18 July–19 July 1918. (Soissons)

Marbache Sector: 9 August–16 August 1918. (Near Pont-à-Mousson on the Moselle River).

St. Mihiel Offensive: 12 September–16 September 1918. (The St. Mihiel sector included, for the 4th Brigade, Thiaucourt, Xammes, and Jaulny).

Meuse-Argonne: Champagne (Blanc Mont): 1 October–10 October 1918. (The Blanc Mont operations, in the Champagne area, 1 October to 10 October, the division fought as part of the French 4th Army, which was located "far to the west" of the western limit of the Meuse-Argonne Sector, rather than with American forces).

Meuse River Campaign: 1 November–11 November 1918. (The 2d Division fought in the Meuse-Argonne area, which was actually just west of the Meuse River and east of the Argonne Forest. Other than those in the 4th Brigade, some individual Marines participated in the Champagne-Marne Defensive, the Oise-Aisne Offensive, and the Ypres-Lys Offensive.)

APPENDIX C

The Marine Brigade suffered approximately 150 percent casualties during the period from spring 1918 until November 1918. I do not have access to the numbers during the Toulon-Verdun period. Following that, the first totals I've come across are:

	Killed in Action	Wounded	Total
Belleau Wood	665	3,633	4,298
Soissons	200	1,632	1,832
Blanc Mont	292	1,893	2,185
Meuse-Argonne	185	1,134	1,319
Totals	**1,342**	**8,292**	**9,634**[28]

APPENDIX D

There has been much speculation, among Marine historians, about several minor points of contention. The issuance of army uniforms to Marines in France has been one of those. Several versions are prevalent one being:

> The green uniforms confused German and French, and in some cases American, soldiers. Most wondered if Marines in green were in fact German soldiers, who wore a gray-green uniform. Consequently some Marines were shot because of that.

And another:

> When Marine uniforms wore out, the Services of Supply did not have replacement Marine-issue uniforms in stock, so Marines were forced to wear the only uniforms they had available: olive-drab khaki.

As could be expected, there was an element of fact in each position. There was consternation about the green uniform among doughboys and the French who were always nearby. The story is that some Marines were shot at and possibly some hit by riflemen of various organizations. The second reason is, or was, invoked as soon as a Marine wore his Marine uniform out, which happened to some at Verdun, many others at Belleau, and most all by Soissons. The only Marine "greens" seen after that were those worn by replacements.

In reality here is what really happened:

The following memorandum was issued by Brigadier Charles A. Doyen on 30 January 1918.

> 1. The anticipated time has come when due to unforseen conditions it is becoming necessary to abandon our distinctive uniform and become a part of the vast army assembling to defend and protect the rights and freedom of individuals. But we must not abandon the other characteristics which have, from the beginning of the history of our country, distinguished our famous organization. Now that the time is here when it will no longer be possible to retain our characteristic uniform, let us be more easily distin-

guished by an increased efficiency, cheerful attitude, military bearing, and esprit-de-corps.

2. In an organization like ours, serving in the present great cause, the necessary abandonment of part of our own uniform should be a matter of small import and its only effect should be to cause even greater efforts on the part of the officers and men to live up to the high standard of military efficiency and appearance which has for so many years been the keynote to the Corps.

3. This memorandum will be published to each separate organization and will be posted on company bulletin boards and report made to these Headquarters when such action has been taken.

In compliance with the order, "the Army uniform was worn by all Marines serving as part of the A.E.F." That from McClellan's history of the war, "In the Marbache Sector."

Another point of contention was the removal of the Marine emblem from their uniforms. As the story goes, following an inspection, Neville was asked by the assistant secretary of the navy, Franklin Delano Roosevelt, what he could do for "his Marines." Neville is quoted as replying that wearing of emblems was the most important thing that could happen to the men. He requested that Roosevelt do something about having them returned. Roosevelt gave the order, which was transmitted to the source of all wealth, the paymaster in Paris. A recent conversation described the outcome. The only type of emblem allowed for Marines would be the same flat disc style being worn by the rest of the AEF. Thousands were manufactured but the time delay between ordering and delivery was, according to my informant, not until the period of occupation in Germany. Shoulder patches, with color variations, were also not available until that same period. As a result only those Marines who had emblems on their "Kelly's" could easily be identified by friend and foe. As usual, there were always more of the latter than the former.

A different version of the "Marine Hymn" based upon the circumstances and experiences during the Great War.

MARINE HYMN

LET'S GO
From Verdun to Château-Thierry,
Through the wheat fields of Soissons;

O'er St. Mihiel's plain and Hell's Champagne,
   Then a wild night in Chalons.
We know we're good, we can't be beat,
   We're the finest of the fine;
In the final race we set the pace
   From the Argonne to the Rhine.
The admiration of the nation,
   We're the best you've ever seen;
And we're damned proud of the title
   of UNITED STATES MARINES.
If the Army or the Navy
   Ever gaze on Heaven's scenes,
They will find the streets are guarded by
   The United States Marines.

That appeared on the "First Annual Reunion of the Third Battalion, Sixth Regiment" program, which reunion met at the Auditorium Hotel in Chicago, Illinois, on 2 June 1923. Some of the speakers debated "Is one war enough?" and another spoke about "How to raise your own Marines" while another spoke of "Why I've never married." I wonder how many more annual reunions that unit had?

Notes

1 Colonel, later Brigadier General, Doyen, was awarded the Distinguished Service Medal because of his personal efforts in bringing the 4th Brigade into a state of high efficiency before he was invalided home. For a short period of time, during October 1917, he commanded the 2d Division, being in actual fact the first Marine to ever command a division. He died of the flu shortly after his return to the United States from France.

2 Frederick "Fritz" Wise was one of the outstanding field commanders of the brigade. He was outspoken and argumentive, hence he found himself relieved of command of the 2d Battalion, 5th Marines, just before the Belleau Wood campaign terminated. He eventually was given command of an army regiment and later the brigade it was a part of. In addition to many lesser awards he was the recipient of the navy and army Distinguished Service Medals for his efforts during the war.

3 "Hiking Hiram" Bearss, already a character of much note in the Corps, also became almost as well known in the army. He was assigned to command the 102d Infantry, 26th "Yankee" Division, which regiment he led with great distinction, capturing a German-held town almost by himself. He was awarded both the army and navy Distinguished Service Medals. He had been awarded the Medal of Honor for actions during the Philippine Insurrection, many years before.

4 Wendell C. "Silent Buck" Neville, later commandant of the Corps, was a recipient of the navy and army Distinguished Service Medals for his high state of efficiency while in command of the 5th Marines and later the 4th Brigade. Neville was awarded the Congressional Medal of Honor for his part in the landing at Vera Cruz in 1914. Neville was also brevetted during the Spanish-American War, receiving the Marine Brevet Medal many years later. He was called "silent" because many claimed that when he spoke in a normal tone he could be heard all up and down the Allies front lines.

5 Logan Feland was awarded the Distinguished Service Cross for his actions at Belleau Wood and both the army and navy Distinguished Service Medals for his ability while in command of the 5th Marines. He was one of the few senior Marines to have graduated from the Massachussets Institute of Technology. Later in his career, along with Smedley Butler, he was a serious candidate for commandant, but both were bypassed by a junior man, Ben Fuller.

6 Julius S. Turrill was awarded both the Navy Cross and the Distinguished Service Cross for his fearless actions while leading the 1st Battalion, 5th Marines at Belleau Wood, 6 June 1918. He was later promoted to lieutenant colonel, and eventually became Feland's assistant regimental commander.

7 George Hamilton was a recipient of the Distinguished Service Cross and later the Navy Cross, among many other lesser awards for his actions at Hill 142, on 6 June 1918 while leading his company. Hamilton became the commanding officer of the 1st Battalion, 5th Marines and led it during the bloodiest Marine battle, at Blanc Mont on 4 October 1918. He was highly respected by everyone, officers and men alike, handsome (often referred to by his command as "our Hollywood actor") and the bravest of the brave. He would survive the war, re-

sign his commission, and later, during the early 1920s return to the Corps, where he would die in an airplane crash.

8 Hunt was awarded both the Navy Cross and the Distinguished Service Cross for his actions at Blanc Mont. He would survive the war and become a regimental commander during the Second World War, when he would command the 5th Marines on Guadalcanal and would later earn a Silver Star for his actions at Saipan.

9 Major Keyser was awarded a Navy Cross for his efforts as a member of the General Staff of the division and for his participation in all the major battles of the regiment.

10 Messersmith got into trouble when his battalion retired in disorder on 4 October 1918 at Blanc Mont. He was accused of leading his men backward. He was highly regarded by officers and men of the 78th Company, which he had commanded previously.

11 Charley Dunbeck received the Distinguished Service Cross and later the Navy Cross for his actions at Blanc Mont. A former enlisted Marine, he was one of the few originals to survive the entire war through the crossing of the Meuse River on 10–11 November 1918. Dunbeck relieved Messersmith of 2/5 and was in command until after the armistice, at least.

12 Ben Berry was badly wounded in the battalion assault on Belleau Wood, 6 June 1918, a portion of his arm being paralyzed. He received both the Distinguished Service Cross and later the Navy Cross for his actions that day. Berry survived and retained his commission in the Corps during the postwar period, but I'm not sure for how long.

13 Catlin was badly wounded leading his regiment on 6 June 1918, far in front of where any colonel of Marines had any right to be. He returned to the United States and survived the war. Catlin was best known, later, for writing a great book entitled *With the Help of God and a Few Marines*.

14 Harry Lee took over the 6th Marines after Catlin was wounded and led the regiment with skill for the balance of the war. He was awarded both the navy and the army Distinguished Service Medal.

15 Shearer was transferred to the 5th Marines and took command of 3/5 just after Berry was wounded. He was awarded the Navy Cross for accomplishing what no other Marine had done before him: He and 3/5 took Belleau Wood on 26 June 1918.

16 Johnny "The Hard" Hughes was another of the old Corps characters. He was as hard upon himself as he was on everyone near him. He was awarded the Navy Cross for his actions at Belleau Wood, exhausting himself during the process. He was hospitalized for gas poisoning for several weeks but later returned to his battalion just in time for Soissons. Health reasons forced him from the Corps in 1920.

17 Barker was awarded a Navy Cross for holding his battalion together when they were being torn to pieces on 1 November 1918 at Sommerance and for keeping his men moving forward, preserving the integrity of the regimental formation.

18 Holcomb was awarded a Navy Cross for "his cool, fearless conduct under fire and acts beyond those required in the ordinary course of duty."

19 Both Wilmer and Denig were awarded Navy Crosses; the former at Sois-

sons and the latter when he commanded the 1st Battalion, 9th Infantry at Blanc Mont.

20 Williams received a Navy Cross for his handling of his battalion at Blanc Mont.

21 Sibley received the Navy Cross for his actions during both attacks in which he led his battalion into Belleau Wood on the 6th and 8th of June.

22 Shuler received both the Navy and the Army Distinguished Service Medals for his actions while in command of the 3d Battalion, 6th Marines at Blanc Mont.

23 Major Cole was awarded the Navy Cross and Distinguished Service Cross for his action at Belleau Wood. He commanded the 6th Machine Gun Battalion until he fell mortally wounded on 8 June 1918. He died on 18 June.

24 Major took command of the battalion after Cole was wounded on 10 June. He was killed in action on 15 June 1918. He was awarded the Silver Star and the Croix de Guerre.

25 Osterhout had been with the supply train but relieved Harlan Major on 12 June and remained in command of the battalion until Maj. Littleton W. T. Waller Jr., who had just been transferred in from the 8th Machine Gun Battalion, 3d Division, assumed command and retained command until he was detached to become division machine-gun officer.

26 Major Waller, the son of one of the most famous of Marine officers, Maj. Gen. Littleton W. T. Waller, received the Navy Cross for his handling of the 6th Machine Gun Battalion during his command.

27 Kingman made an impression during the first week at Belleau Wood. He was awarded two Silver Star citations and two Croix de Guerre for his handling of his company, the 15th, between 1 and 6 June 1918.

28 Totals of each category taken from *2d Division Summary of Operations in the World War* (Washington D.C.: American Battle Monuments Commission, U.S. Government Printing Office, 1944). These do not take into account the losses at Verdun or Marbache, both of which were minimal in comparison.

Selected Bibliography

U.S. Government publications

Annual Reports of the Navy Department for the fiscal year 1920. Washington, D.C.: U.S. Government Printing Office, 1921.

Annual Report of the Secretary of War, 1919. Washington, D.C.: U.S. Government Printing Office, 1919.

Blanc Mont (Meuse-Argonne-Champagne). Monograph No. 9. Reprint, Pike, NH: The Brass Hat, 1994.

Navy Yearbook 1920 and 1921. Washington, D.C.: U.S. Government Printing Office, 1922.

Order of Battle of The United States Land Forces in the World War. Reprint, vols. 1 and 2 of 5 vols. Washington, D.C.: U.S. Government Printing Office, 1988.

Pershing, John J. *Final Report of Gen. John J. Pershing.* Washington, D.C.: U.S. Government Printing Office, 1920.

Report of the First Army, American Expeditionary Force, Organization and Operations. Fort Leavenworth, KS: 1923.

The Genesis of the American First Army. Washington, D.C.: Historical Section, 1938.

U.S. Army, Records of the Second Division (Regular), 9 volumes. Washington, D.C.: The Army War College, 1927.

United States Army in the World War 1917–1919. vols. 1, 3, 4 and various other volumes. Washington, D.C.: Historical Division, 1948.

U.S. Navy, Annual Report of the Secretary of the Navy for the Fiscal Year 1918. Washington, D.C.: 1918. [Corrected to 18 October 1919.]

Personal papers and unpublished memoirs

Barnett, George. *"Soldier and Sailor Too."* N.p. [1923?]

Bellamy, David. *"Personal diary, 23 October 1917–22 August 1919. "* N.p., n.d.

Draucker, James H. *"Telling It Like It Was."* Np., n.d.

Jackson, Warren. *Experiences of a Texas Soldier.* 1930.

Moore, William E. *Personal letters to his mother, 31 March–15 February, 1919.* N.p., n.d.

Paris, Gus. *Hold Every Inch of Ground.* Owensboro, KY: [Unpublished biography of Logan Feland.] N.d.

Publications written and edited by George B. Clark

A List of officers of the 4th Marine Brigade. Pike, NH: The Brass Hat, 1993.
Citations and awards to members of the 4th Marine Brigade. Pike, NH: The Brass Hat, 1992.
Retreat, Hell! We just got here! Pike, NH: The Brass Hat, 1992
The History of the Third Battalion 5th Marines 1917–1918. Pike, NH: The Brass Hat, 1995.
The Marine Brigade at Blanc Mont. Pike, NH: The Brass Hat, 1994.
Their Time In Hell. The 4th Marine Brigade at Belleau Wood. Pike, NH: The Brass Hat, 1996.
ed. *History of the Fifth Regiment Marines (May 1917–December 31, 1918)* Reprint, Pike, NH: The Brass Hat, 1995.
ed. *A Brief History of the Sixth Regiment U.S. Marine Corps July, 1917–December, 1918.* Reprint, Pike, NH: The Brass Hat, 1992.
ed. *Major Awards to U.S. Marines in World War One.* Reprint, Pike, NH: The Brass Hat, 1992.
Clark, George B. see Macgillivray, George C.
Clark, George B. see Collins, Harry and David Fisher.

Published reminiscences and biographies

Asprey, Robert B. see Vandegrift, Alexander A.
Brannen, Carl Andrew. *Over There, A Marine in the Great War.* Edited by Rolfe L. Hillman, Jr. and Peter F. Owen, with an afterword by J. P. Brannen. College Station: Texas A & M University Press, 1996.
Carter, William A. *The Tale of a Devil Dog.* Washington, D.C.: Canteen Press, 1920.
Cates, General Clifton B., see Morrey, Willard.
Collins, Harry with David Fisher & George B. Clark. *The War Diary of Corporal Harry Collins.* Reprint, Pike, NH: The Brass Hat, 1996.
Cooke, Colonel Elliot D.. *"We Can Take It, We Attack": Americans vs. Germans.* 1936, Reprint, 2 volumes in one, Pike, NH: The Brass Hat, 1992.
Daniels, Josephus. *The Cabinet Diaries of Josephus Daniels, 1913–1921.* Lincoln, NE: University of Nebraska Press, 1963.

Derby, Richard. *"Wade in, Sanitary!" The Story of a Division Surgeon in France.* New York: G.P. Putnam and Sons, 1919.

Gordon, George V. *Leathernecks and Doughboys.* 1927. Reprint, Pike, NH: The Brass Hat, 1996.

Gulberg, Martin G. *A War Diary.* 1927. Reprint, Pike, NH: The Brass Hat,1989.

Hemrick, Levi. *Once a Marine.* New York: Carlton Press, 1968.

Kean, Robert W. *Dear Marraine, 1917–1919.* N.p., prvt. prt., 1976.

Lejeune, John A. *Reminiscences of a Marine.* Philadelphia: Dorrance and Co., 1930.

Liggett, Hunter. *AEF Ten Years Ago in France.* New York: Dodd, Mead and Co., 1928.

Ludendorff, Erich von. *Ludendorff's Own Story,* Vol. 2. New York: Harper Bros., 1919.

Mackin, Elton E. *Suddenly We Didn't Want to Die.* Novato, CA: Presidio Press, 1993.

Millett, Allan R. *In Many a Strife: General Gerald C. Thomas and the U.S. Marine Corps, 1917–1956.* Annapolis, Naval Institute Press, 1993.

Morgan, Daniel E. *When the World Went Mad.* 1931. Reprint, Pike, NH: The Brass Hat, 1992.

Pershing, John J. *My Experiences in the World War.* 2 vols. New York: F. A. Stokes and Co., 1931.

Ranlett, Louis Felix. *Let's Go!: The Story of A.S. No. 2448602.* Boston: Houghton Mifflin, 1927.

Rendinell, Joseph E., and George Pattullo. *One Man's War: The Diary of a Leatherneck.* New York: Sears and Co., 1928.

Robillard, Fred S. *As Robie Remembers.* Bridgeport: Wright Investors Service, 1969.

Schmidt, Hans. *Maverick Marine: General Smedley D. Butler and the Contradictions of American Military History.* Lexington: The University Press of Kentucky, 1987.

Sellers, James McB. *World War I Memoirs of Lieutenant Colonel James McBrayer Sellers, USMC.* Pike, NH: The Brass Hat, 1997.

Smythe, Donald. *Pershing, General of the Armies.* Bloomington: Indiana University Press, 1986.

Vandegrift, Alexander A. and Robert B. Asprey. *Once a Marine.* New York: W. W. Norton, 1964.

Vandiver, Frank E. *Black Jack:: The Life and Times of John J. Pershing, vol.* 2. College Station: Texas A & M University Press, 1977.

Official and semi-official unit histories

Akers, Herbert H. *History of the Third Battalion, Sixth Regiment, U.S. Marines.* Hillsdale, Michigan: Akers, MacRitchie and Hurlburt, 1919.

American Battle Monument Commission. *2d Division Summary of Operations in the World War.* Washington: D.C.: U.S. Government Printing Office, 1944.

Burton, Allan. *A History of the Second Regiment of Engineers, United States Army from Its Organization in Mexico, 1916, to Its Watch on the Rhine, 1919.* Engers on the Rhine 1919.

Curtis, Thomas J. and Lothar R. Long. *History of the Sixth Machine Gun Battalion..* Reprint, Pike, NH: The Brass Hat, 1992.

Donaldson, G.H. & W. Jenkins, *Seventy-eighth Company, Sixth Marines, Second Division Army of Occupation.* Reprint, Pike, NH: The Brass Hat, 1994.

Field, Harry B., and Henry G. James. *Over the Top with the 18th Company, 5th Regiment, U.S. Marines, a History.* Rodenbach, Germany, [1919?].

James, Henry G., see Field, Harry B.

Jones, William K. *A Brief History of the 6th Marines.* Washington, D.C.: Headquarters, U.S.M.C., 1987.

Long, Lothar R. see Curtis, Thomas J.

Macgillivray, George C. and George B. Clark, eds. *A History of the 80th Company, Sixth Marines,* Reprint, Pike, NH: The Brass Hat, 1991.

Mitchell, William A. *The Official History of the Second Engineers in the World War, 1916–1919.* Regimental Headquarters, San Antonio, 1920.

Morrey, Willard I. *History of the 96th Company, 2d Battalion, Sixth Regiment, United States Marine Corps.* Washington, D.C.: Headquarters, U.S. Marine Corps, 1967.

———. *Second Division Memorial Day, June 2nd, 1919, 75th Company, 6th Regiment U.S. Marines.* Reprint, Pike, NH: The Brass Hat,1995.

———. *The Ninth U.S. Infantry in the World War.* N.p. [Germany], [1919?]

———. *U.S.M.C. 74th Company, 6th Regiment, Second Division, A.E.F.* Reprint, Pike, NH: The Brass Hat, 1994.

Spaulding, Oliver L. and John W. Wright, *The Second Division; American Expeditionary Force in France 1917–1919.* New York: Hillman Press 1937.

Second Division Association, *Commendations of Second Division, American Expeditionary Forces, 1917–1919.* Cologne, Germany, 1919.

Strott, George G. *History of Medical Personnel of the United States Navy, Sixth Regiment Marine Corps, American Expeditionary Forces in World War 1917–1918.* Reprint, Pike, NH: The Brass Hat, 1995.

Thomason, John W., Jr. *The Second Division Northwest of Chateau Thierry.*

1 June–10 July, 1918. Washington, D.C.: National War College, 1928. [Unpublished manuscript.]

U.S. Army. *The 3rd Battalion 17th F.A. in 1918.* Coblenz, Germany, N.d.

———. *Diary, Machine Gun Co. Twenty Third Inf. Second Division Army of Occupation 1917–1919.* N.p., [1919?]

U.S. Marine Corps, *History of the First Battalion, 5th Regiment, U.S. Marines.* 1919. Reprint, Foster, R.I.: The Brass Hat, 1980.

———. *History of the Second Battalion, 5th Regiment, U.S. Marines.* Reprint, Foster, R.I.: The Brass Hat, 1980.

———. *History of the Second Battalion, Fifth Marines.* Quantico: Marine Barracks, 1938.

———. *History of the Sixth Regiment, U.S. Marines.* Tientsin, China, 1928.

———. *History Third Battalion, Sixth Marines.* N.p., n.d.

Vandoren, Lucien H. *A Brief History of the Second Battalion, Sixth Regiment, U.S. Marine Corps, during the period June 1st to August 10th, 1918.* Reprint, Pike, NH: The Brass Hat, 1995.

Wright, John W. see Spaulding, Oliver L.

Selected books

American Battle Monuments Commission. *American Armies and Battlefields in Europe.* Washington, D.C.: U.S. Government Printing Office, 1938.

Americans Defending Democracy: Our Soldiers Own Stories. New York: World's War Stories, Inc., 1919.

Andriot, Captain R. *Belleau Wood and the American Army.* Trans. by W. B. Fitts. Washington, D.C.: Belleau Wood Memorial Association, N.d.

Asprey, Robert B. *At Belleau Wood.* New York: G. P. Putnam and Sons, 1965.

Blakeney, Jane. *Heroes, U.S. Marine Corps, 1861–1955.* Washington, 1957.

Boyd, Thomas. *Through the Wheat.* New York: Scribner's, 1923. Fiction by a Marine participant.

———. *Points of Honor.* New York: Scribner's, 1925. Short stories by a Marine participant.

Catlin, Albertus W. *With the Help of God and a Few Marines.* New York: Doubleday, 1919.

Chitty, Fred F., see Leonard, John W.

Cooper, Courtney R. see Cowing, Kemper F.

Corbin, Louise, see Hamilton, Craig.

Cowing, Kemper F. and Courtney R. Cooper, *"Dear Folks at Home ———." The glorious story of the United States Marines in France as told by their Letters from the Battlefield.* Boston: Houghton Mifflin, 1919.

De Chambrun, Jacques Aldebert de Pinton, Comte de, and Captain De-Marenches. *The American Army in the European Conflict.* New York: Macmillan, 1919.

Fleming, Charles A. *Quantico: Crossroads of the Corps.* Washington, D.C.: Headquarters, U.S. Marine Corps, 1978.

Frost, Meigs O., see Wise, Frederick M.

Gibbons, Floyd. *And They Thought We Wouldn't Fight.* New York: George H. Doran and Co., 1918.

Hamilton, Craig, and Louise Corbin. *Echoes From Over There.* New York: Soldier's Publishing Co., 1919.

Harbord, James G. *Leaves From a War Diary.* New York: Dodd, Mead and Co., 1925.

———. *The American Army in France 1917–1918.* Boston: Little, Brown and Co., 1936.

Heinl, Robert D., Jr. *Soldiers of the Sea.* Annapolis: U.S. Naval Institute Press, 1962.

Hewitt, Linda L. *Women Marines in World War I.* Washington, D.C.: Headquarters, U.S. Marine Corps, 1974.

Kennedy, David M. *Over Here: The First World War and American Society.* New York: Oxford University Press, 1980.

Leonard, John W. and Fred F. Chitty. *The Story of the United States Marines, "1740–1919."* N.p., [1919?]

March, William, [pseud.] *Company K.* New York: Harrison Smith and Robert Haas, 1933. High level of accuracy in fiction by a former Marine participant.

McCahill, William P. *The Marine Corps Reserve, 1916–1966.* Washington, D.C.: U.S. Government Printing Office, 1966.

McClellan, Edwin N. *The United States Marine Corps in the World War.* Washington, D.C.: U.S. Government Printing Office, 1920.

Metcalf, Clyde H. *A History of the United States Marine Corps.* New York: G. P. Putnam and Sons, 1939.

Michelin. *The Americans in the Great War: Illustrated Guides to the Battlefields, 3 volumes.* France, 1920.

Millett, Allan R. *Semper Fidelis: The History of the United States Marine Corps.* New York: Macmillan, 1980.

NYLIC. *War Stories: Being a Brief Record of the Service in the Great War of Soldiers-Sailors-Marines Who Went from the Home Office of the New York Life Insurance Company.* New York, 1920.

Otto, Ernst. *The Battle at Blanc Mont.* Annapolis: U.S. Naval Institute Press, 1930.

Pattullo, George. *Hellwood.* Philadelphia: Curtis Publishing Co., 1918. [Belleau Wood.]

———. *Horrors of Moonlight.* New York: prvt. prt., 1939. [Belleau Wood.]

———. see Rendinell, Joseph E.

Russell, James C., and William E. Moore. *The United States Navy in the World War.* Washington, D.C.: The Pictorial Bureau, 1921.

Scanlon, William T. *God Have Mercy on Us!* Boston: Houghton Mifflin, 1929. High level of accuracy in fiction by a former Marine participant.

Stallings, Laurence. *The Doughboys.* New York: Harper, 1963.

Stringer, Harry R., ed. *Heroes All!* Washington, D.C.: Fassett, 1919.

Thomason, John W., Jr. *Fix Bayonets!* New York, Scribner's 1925.

Tucker, Spencer C. *The European Powers in the First World War: An Encyclopedia.* New York: Garland, 1996.

U.S. Navy, *Medal of Honor 1861–1949,* Washington, D.C.: [1950?]

———. *The Navy Book of Distinguished Service.* Washington, D.C.: 1921.

———. *The Medical Department of the United States Navy with the Army and Marine Corps in France in World War I.* Washington, D.C.: U.S. Navy, 1947.

Venzon, Anne Cipriano, ed. *The United States in the First World War, An Encyclopedia.* New York: Garland, 1995.

Westover, Wendell. *Suicide Battalions.* New York: G. P. Putnam and Sons, 1929.

———. *Where the Marines Fought in France.* Chicago: Park and Antrim, N.d. [1919?]

Wise, Frederic M., and Meigs O. Frost. *A Marine Tells It to You.* New York: J. H. Sears and Co., 1929.

Articles

Ausland, Jack. "The Last Kilometer." Illustrated by Major John W. Thomason Jr., USMC., *Saturday Evening Post:* 13 November 1937.

Esau, Richard H., Jr. "Belleau Wood Revisited." *Marine Corps Gazette,* November 1981.

Evans, Frank E. "Demobilizing the Brigades." *Marine Corps Gazette* December 1919.

Feland, Logan, "Retreat, Hell." *Marine Corps Gazette,* September 1921.

McClellan, Edwin N. "A Brief History of the Fourth Brigade." *Marine Corps Gazette* December 1919.

———. "The Fourth Brigade of Marines in the Training Areas and the Operations in the Verdun Sector." *Marine Corps Gazette* March 1920.

———. "Operations of the 4th Brigade of Marines in the Aisne Defensive." *Marine Corps Gazette,* June 1920.

———. "Capture of Hill 142, Battle of Belleau Wood, and Capture of Bouresches. *Marine Corps Gazette,* September–December 1920.

———. "The Aisne-Marne Offensive." *Marine Corps Gazette,* March–June 1921.

———. "In the Marbache Sector." *Marine Corps Gazette,* September 1921.

———. "The St. Mihiel Offensive." *Marine Corps Gazette,* December 1921.

———. "The Battle of Blanc Mont Ridge." *Marine Corps Gazette,* March–June–September 1922.

———. "American Marines in the British Grand Fleet." *Leatherneck,* June 1922.

Moore, William E. "The 'Bloody Angle' of the A.E.F." *The American Legion Weekly,* 24 February 1922.

Nelson, Havelock D. "Paris-Metz Road." *Leatherneck,* January 1940.

———. "Lucy-le-Bocage." *Leatherneck,* February 1940.

———. "First Contact: Belleau Woods." *Leatherneck,* March 1940.

———. "Soissons." *Leatherneck,* April 1940.

———. "We Go In." *Leatherneck,* May 1940.

———. "In Action." *Leatherneck,* June 1940.

———. "Under Fire." *Leatherneck,* July 1940.

———. "St. Mihiel." *Leatherneck,* August 1940.

———. "Strafed." *Leatherneck,* September 1940.

———. "Barrage." *Leatherneck,* October 1940.

———. "Advance on Sedan." *Leatherneck,* November, 1940.

———. "Armistice." *Leatherneck,* January 1941.

———. "On German Soil." *Leatherneck,* February 1941.

———. "Watch on the Rhine." *Leatherneck,* April 1941.

Otto, Ernst. "The Battles of Belleau Woods." *Leatherneck,* January 1929.

Owen, Peter. "Courage amid the Chaos. The 79th Company of Marines at Belleau Wood." *Over There!* Spring 1993.

Parker, Laurie. "Lloyd Williams, The Story of Clarke's (County) World War I Hero." *Winchester Evening Star,* 3 January 1980.

Rentfrow, Frank H. "Cease Firing at Eleven." *Leatherneck,* November 1929.

———. "Beyond the Call." *Leatherneck,* 1939. [Soissons.]

Second Division Association, *"The Indian."* Weekly, 14 issues complete, 15 April 1919–15 July 1919[various articles].

Shulimson, Jack. "The First to Fight: Marine Corps Expansion, 1914–1918." *Prologue,* Spring 1976.

Silverthorn, Merwin. "Johnny Came Marching Home." *Military Images,* May–June, 1982.

Thomason, John W. Jr. "The Marine Brigade." *U.S. Naval Institute Proceedings,* November 1928.

Waller, Littleton W. T. Jr. "Machine Guns of the Fourth Brigade." *Marine Corps Gazette,* March 1920.

This is just a selection. Many other books and other printed material have been read or perused, but only those considered of importance have been included. Several works of fiction were included because of the seriousness of the material and accuracy of the situations described. Various articles that have appeared in either the *Marine Corps Gazette* or *Leatherneck* magazine were of assistance.

There has been a dearth of substantial writing about the A. E. F. since immediately after the war, but that is rapidly being rectified by some new and exciting material now coming off the presses. An entirely new generation has "found" the Great War and is taking a serious interest in the A. E. F. I hope this will at least partially fill the, until now, blank space inhabited by the 4th Marine Brigade.

Over the years there have been several publications that have covered the Belleau Wood period. The most comprehensive coverage of that specific engagement, up until now, has been Robert Asprey's *At Belleau Wood,* which has recently been reissued, albeit unamended. There have been several other journalistic versions, most of which have been perused and tossed aside by the author since they are not worth further mention. Ernst Otto's book, *The Battle at Blanc Mont,* though heavily oriented toward the German defenders (a German officer, he was a veteran of the battle) is also a scholarly report on the 2d Division's participation in that bloody mess, through the other end of the telescope. The 2d Division unit history, finally published in 1937, is rather general and somewhat of a disappointment but it is a good place to start. That, too, has been reprinted in recent years. Many years ago, Maj. Elliott D. Cooke, U.S. Army (Infantry), produced several superbly written articles for the *Infantry Journal* about his participation in the 18th Company and as commander of the 55th Company, 2d Battalion, 5th Marines, at Belleau Wood and at Soissons. Unfortunately some, though not all, were self-serving. Carefully used, it is much better than most of the genre.

Captain John W. Thomason, sometimes called the Rudyard Kipling of the Corps, wrote an estimable firsthand account of what he, as a junior officer in the 49th Company, 1st Battalion, 5th Marines, saw, in *Fix Bayonets!* He wrote it to read like fiction, even though most of it isn't. It could be of prime importance for anyone familiar with the people in that company. It is still one of the finest firsthand accounts of what battle in the First World War was all about.

A recent publication, *Suddenly We Didn't Want to Die*, by a private of the 67th Company, 1st Battalion, 5th Regiment, Elton Mackin, is a superb personal account of each of the battles from a private's perspective. There are other personal memoirs, some published, some not.

As mentioned previously, McClellan did write a series for the *Marine Corps Gazette* between 1919 and 1922, of accounts of the various battles Marines were in, but it was never put together as a whole. Worse, it reflects many of the mistakes that were inherent in the sanitized 2d Division's nine-volume set. He furnished a brief recounting of the first two days at Blanc Mont, not completing it or even getting to the heart of that dreadful slaughter. Nor did he write about the Meuse Argonne campaign, including the night crossing of the Meuse River. His own publication entitled *The United States Marine Corps in the World War,* which was produced by the U.S. Government Printing Office in 1920, was really a compilation of data and not a serious historical interpretation because, as he stated in the Explanatory Note,

> the statistics and other information contained herein are as accurate as it is possible to obtain at the present date. Every effort has been made to avoid expressions of opinions and criticisms, or the drawing of conclusions of an important nature; [it] is preliminary to the final and detailed history [of the Corps] which is in course of preparation.

To the best of my knowledge, that "detailed history" has never been completed or published. The only work that might have been considered an "official" history of the U.S. Marine Corps during the period, that I am aware of, is the one that, the then Capt. John W. Thomason Jr., USMC, worked on during his assignment at the Army War College, 1927–1928. His role during the assignment was to prepare the material relative to the 4th Marine Brigade in the 2d Division during the war. A move to prepare and issue a history of that division was the intent. But that history did not come off officially; ever. There has been a load of conjecture about why it died but no one alive today, who I know of, seems to be sure of the facts. In 1937 a division history was published by the 2d Division Association as a private effort, but Thomason's effort does not appear to have been a part of it. His work, at least that portion entitled *Second Division Northwest of Château-Thierry: 1 June–10 July 1918,* was partially used in the seventeen-volume *History of the United States Army in the World War* published by the U.S. Government Printing Office in 1947–1948.

Therefore, this is one of the first serious attempts, if not the only one, to put the entire effort made by the U.S. Marine Corps during the period together for consideration. I have heavily and carefully utilized the multivolume *Records of the Second Division Regular* as often as possible, as well as the *Translations: War Diaries of German Units Opposed to the Second Division (Regular)*. A major part of my research has been into the personal observations and recollections of participants themselves, to try to get that feeling of "being there." Unfortunately, some of the recollections are colored by faded memory or the minimizing of truly important details. A few seemed to be a journalistic exercise by someone who had never been anywhere near the 4th Brigade. Several official histories have been consulted. The *Blanc Mont: Monograph No. 9* published by the U.S. Government Printing Office in 1922, though not always accurate, has been helpful in understanding that bloody engagement, as has the opposite viewpoint of Lt. Col. Ernst Otto, which seems more scholarly and accurate.

The 6th Regiment seems to be the most widely written about. In addition to the semiofficial *A Brief History of the Sixth Regiment U.S. Marine Corps,* which was completed by various officers of the regiment just after the war terminated, there are many individual memoirs in existence which were published after the war. Gulberg's *War Diary* is an especially good one, as is the excellent *History of the Third Battalion, Sixth Regiment, U.S. Marines* produced by former members of that unit in 1919. The semiofficial 5th Regiment history, while not bad, is not as complete as that of the 6th. Other than that, the field is limited to two general battalion reports, the 1st and 2d, 5th Marines, both of which are limited in scope.

Most discouraging has been the reluctant conclusion that most of the personal diaries, memoirs, and so on, are nothing but vaguely worded generalizations with few if any real details. Occasionally there will be mention of people by name, and locations, but basically, most material is a rehash of another rehash, none being useful except the items listed previously. Several seem to have been "put together" by someone other than a participant. They are vague and noncommittal on important periods and issues. The best for original text has been the Mackin memoir. Another very good memoir is that by Martin G. Gulberg, entitled *A War Diary.* Gulberg was a member of the 75th Company, 6th Marine Regiment. The only action he missed was Saint-Mihiel, having been wounded on 19 July 1918 at Soissons. But he was back for Blanc Mont and part of the Meuse Argonne, where he was gassed. His work is either by an unidentified professional or he also was a fine writer. One other memoir, but near psychotic in tone, is that by Daniel Morgan, a former member of the 77th Company, 6th Machine Gun Battalion, entitled *When the World Went Mad.* Mostly, other than those few listed previously, the best personal material has come from occasionally valuable vignettes produced during or shortly after the war terminated, plus an assortment of letters written by participants.

Index